READINGS IN
AMERICAN LEGAL HISTORY

READINGS IN AMERICAN LEGAL HISTORY

COMPILED AND EDITED BY

MARK DeWOLFE HOWE

Professor of Law in Harvard University

"*Reduce things to the first institution, and observe wherein and how they have degenerate; but yet ask counsel of both times; of the ancient time, what is best; and of later time, what is fittest.*"

FRANCIS BACON

HARVARD UNIVERSITY PRESS

Cambridge · Massachusetts

1952

Second Printing

PRINTED IN THE UNITED STATES OF AMERICA

PREFACE

The faculty of the Harvard Law School recently approved a plan for the reorganization of its curriculum. One element in the plan calls for the offering of a two hour elective course in American Legal History in the first semester of the second year. The materials collected in this volume have been brought together with the immediate purpose of meeting the needs of that course.

Whether the volume is read systematically or is referred to casually, certain of its characteristics - or, perhaps I should say many of its limitations - will become quickly apparent. It will be seen that its materials are concerned with a selected group of problems and a limited number of periods in American legal history. The decision thus to limit the volume's scope was partly dictated by circumstances. As a practical matter it seemed impossible within the few months available for the collection of materials to do more than select readings which, as samples, would be suggestive. To a considerable extent, however, the decision was based on a conviction that such concentration of concern has distinct advantages. The study of American legal history is only in its infancy, and any attempt to deal with the subject as a whole seems, for the present, inadvisable.

Some readers of the collection will doubtless feel that the relatively large proportion of the collection which is devoted to the law of Colonial Massachusetts and to the period from 1790 to 1830 bespeaks the arid enthusiasm of an antiquarian. Should I reply in the words of John Winthrop that it is "a fruit of much pride and folly ... to despise the day of small things" the suspicion of such a reader would only be reinforced. It seems wiser, therefore, to meet this criticism with the suggestion that the relevance of history is largely independent of time. This is not to say that the omission of materials reflecting more recent aspects of legal history can be justified on any other ground than that of immediate pressure. It is only to emphasize the fact that early problems may be persistent and possess a significance which outlives the first generations which sought to solve them.

Other readers will feel that there has been insufficient cutting of the original materials. In some instances I fear that that judgment may have justification. Yet I am persuaded that an imaginative understanding of the spirit and quality of periods and persons is best acquired through a largely unedited reproduction of their expression. The collection seeks less to familiarize the reader with the details of American legal history than to give him not only some understanding of what the important questions and suggestive answers have been, but an appreciation of the manner in which questions and answers have been stated.

From these few indications of purpose it will readily be seen that this collection is brought together in the hope that out of it something larger and more inclusive may grow. I like to think that it will hereafter be altered and expanded so that in its pages may ultimately be found the outlines, at least, of a totality which is here merely intimated. That totality - the story of the growth of American law - has so many chapters, so many themes, and so many settings and characters that a collection of materials in which each would be presented with suggestive justice would require many volumes. Its preparation, furthermore, will only be possible if a generation of scholars is at long last born which finds productive fascination in the history of American law. It is my hope that the publication of this volume will do something to encourage that fascination.

M.DeW.H.

Cambridge, Massachusetts
June, 1949

TABLE OF CONTENTS

READINGS IN AMERICAN LEGAL HISTORY

CHAPTER ONE

THE GENERAL PROBLEM OF THE RECEPTION AND REJECTION OF ENGLISH LAW

1. Methods of Reception and Rejection

TITLE 18, SECTION 201, CODE OF THE DISTRICT OF COLUMBIA, 1940 EDITION: "A widow, after the death of her husband, incontinent, and without any difficulty, shall have her marriage and her inheritance and shall give nothing for her dower, her marriage, or her inheritance, which her husband and she held the day of the death of her husband, and she shall tarry in the chief house of her husband by forty days after the death of her husband, within which days her dower shall be assigned her (if it were not assigned before) or that the house be a castle; and if she depart from the castle, then a competent house shall be forthwith provided for her, in the which she may honestly dwell, until her dower be to her assigned, as it is aforesaid; and she shall have in the meantime her reasonable estovers of the common; and for her dower shall be assigned unto her the third part of all the lands of her husband, which were his during coverture, except she were endowed of less at the church door."[1]

<u>Seeley</u> v. <u>Peters</u>
Supreme Court of Illinois, 1848, 10 Illinois 130

TRUMBULL, J. This was an action of trespass to personal property, originally commenced by Peters against Seeley before a justice of the peace, and taken by appeal to the Circuit Court.

---

1. A note to this section of the Code reads as follows: "This section sets forth a British statute continued in force by virtue of the Act of March 3, 1901 (31 Stat. 1189, ch. 854, Sec.1). It was obviously impossible to modernize the language of this statute." The explanation of Congressional adoption of the statute is to be found in the legal history of Maryland. Relevant aspects of that history can be found in Kilty, <u>A Report of English Statutes</u>, etc. (1811), 205; Alexander, <u>British Statutes in Force in Maryland</u> (1870), Preface, and p. 1-11.

Upon the trial in the Circuit Court before a jury, Peters "proved that Seeley's hogs had damaged certain wheat in shock in a field belonging to him and closed." "The defendant (Seeley) then proved that the north side of said field, where the hogs got in, was so badly fenced that hogs which were not breachy could go in and out at pleasure, and that said fence was entirely insufficient to turn hogs. Further, that the north side of said field, where said defective fence was, was bounded by unoccupied and unenclosed prairie, and that a public road passed along said fence at least part of the way on the north side." At the instance of the plaintiff below, the Court instructed the jury: "That if they believe from the evidence, that the defendant's hogs went into the plaintiff's inclosure and did damage to his crops, they will find a verdict for the plaintiff, and assess his damages to amount of the injury actually done, and it matters not what was the condition of the plaintiff's fence, so far as his right to recover some damages is concerned, inasmuch as the owner of a field is not obliged to keep up a fence around his enclosure to keep out his neighbor's cattle or hogs, but the owners of cattle permit them to run at large at their peril." To the giving of which instructions the defendant excepted. The jury found a verdict for the plaintiff below, upon which judgment was entered in his favor.

The errors assigned question the correctness of the instructions of the Circuit Court, which are admitted to have been proper, if the Common Law upon the subject of inclosures prevails in this State; and to determine whether it does, involves a construction of a part of the 51st chapter of the Revised Statutes, concerning "Inclosures and Fences". [The Court here discusses statutory provisions which tended to indicate that legislation in Illinois had altered the rule of the English Common Law.]

It is insisted on the part of the defendant in error, that the foregoing statutes create no obligation upon the owner of land to inclose it with a fence, if he would protect it against the depredations of cattle or hogs, and to support this view of the case, numerous authorities have been cited to show:

<u>First</u>: That by the Common Law, one need not inclose his fields with a fence and that inasmuch as the Common Law has been adopted in this State, "so far as the same is applicable and of a general nature",[1] that therefore this rule of the Common Law prevails in Illinois; and

---

1. The Illinois <u>Revised Statutes of 1845</u>, Chapter 65, Sec. 1 provided that "the Common Law of England, so far as the same is applicable, and of a general nature, and all statutes and

Secondly: That similar statutes to those of Illinois have uniformly been held in other States not to change the rule of the Common Law.

Admitting that at the Common Law, the owner of a close was not bound to fence against the adjoining close, except by force of prescription, yet in adopting the Common Law, as was said in the case of Boyer v. Sweet, 3 Scam. 121, it must be understood only in cases where that law is applicable to the habits and conditions of our society, and in harmony with the genius, spirit and objects of our institutions." See also Penny v. Little, 3 Scam. 301. However well adapted the rule of the Common Law may be to a densely populated country like England, it is surely but ill adapted to a new country like ours. If this common law rule prevails now, it must have prevailed from the time of the earliest settlements in the State, and it cannot be supposed that when the early settlers of this country located upon the borders of our extensive prairies, that they brought with them and adopted as applicable to their condition a rule of law, requiring each one to fence up his cattle; that they designed the millions of fertile acres stretched out before them to go ungrazed, except as each purchaser from Government was able to inclose his part with a fence? This State is unlike any other of the Eastern States in their early settlement, because, from the scarcity of timber, it must be many years yet before our extensive prairies can be fenced, and their luxuriant growth sufficient for thousands of cattle must be suffered to rot and decay where it grows, unless the settlers upon their borders are permitted to turn their cattle upon them.

---

acts of the British Parliament made in aid of, and to supply the defects of the Common Law, prior to the fourth year of James the First ... and which are of a general nature and not local to that Kingdom, shall be the rule of decision, and shall be considered as of full force, until repealed by the legislative authority." The statute had its origin in Virginia where it was enacted in 1776. That portion of the act which referred to English statutes had been repealed by the Virginia legislature in 1792. The Act, however, was "adopted" by the judges of the Northwest Territory in 1795 and had passed as part of the legal inheritance into the statutory law of the Territories of Indiana and Illinois and subsequently of the State of Illinois. For a detailed account of the transmission of this statute from Virginia to the Northwest Territory and to the states created therefrom, see Philbrick's Introduction to The Laws of Indiana Territory, 1801-1809 (1930), pp. c-cii and Blume's Introduction to Vol.I of Transactions of the Supreme Court of Michigan, 1805-1814, (1935), pp. xxxi et seq.

Perhaps there is no principle of the Common Law so inapplicable to the condition of our country and people as the one which is sought to be enforced now for the first time since the settlement of the State. It has been the custom in Illinois so long, that the memory of man runneth not to the contrary,[2] for the owners of stock to suffer them to run at large. Settlers have located themselves contiguous to prairies for the very purpose of getting the benefit of the range. The right of all to pasture their cattle upon uninclosed ground is universally conceded. No man has questioned this right, although hundreds of cases must have occurred where the owners of cattle have escaped the payment of damages on account of the insufficiency of the fences through which their stock have broken, and never till now has the Common Law rule, that the owner of cattle is bound to fence them up been suffered to prevail or to be applicable to our condition. The universal understanding of all classes of the community, upon which they have acted by inclosing their crops and letting their cattle run at large, is entitled to no little consideration in determining what the law is, and we should feel inclined to hold, independent of any statutes upon the subject, on account of the inapplicability of the Common Law rule to the condition and circumstances of our people, that it does not and never has prevailed in Illinois. ... Being, therefore, of opinion, that the rule of the Common Law requiring the owner of cattle, hogs, &c., to keep them upon his own ground does not prevail in Illinois, and that the tenant of land in this State is bound to fence against cattle, it follows that the instruction of the Circuit Court was erroneous, and its judgment is therefore reversed, and the cause remanded for further proceedings.

---

2. Blackstone, summarizing the English doctrines with respect to custom as a source of law, said: "When a custom is actually proved to exist, the next inquiry is into the legality of it. ... To make a particular custom good the following are necessary requisites. 1. That it have been used so long, that the memory of man runneth not to the contrary." I Commentaries 76. In his "republican" edition of Blackstone (1803), St. George Tucker, of Virginia, added the following comment to the quoted passage: "It may be therefore doubted whether any custom can be established in the United States of America. For, Time of memory hath been ascertained by the Law to commence from the reign of Richard I and any custom in England, may be destroyed by evidence of its non-existence, at any subsequent period. Now the settlement of North America by the English did not take place till the reign of Queen Elizabeth, near four hundred years afterwards." This suggestion has had occasional

The following dissenting Opinion was delivered by

CATON, J. Differing, as I do, from the opinion of the majority of the Court, propriety and justice to myself, as one of its members, require that I should assign the reasons which have forced me to the opinion which I entertain. If the influence of this decision might not be felt beyond the case, or even this question, I might let it pass in silence; but the rules of construction which are adopted, not only in construing our statute by which the Common Law of England is adopted here, but the statutes relating to this particular subject, are such that I can give them no sanction by my silence, for I think if they become the settled doctrine of the Court, they will lead to alarming consequences. It is admitted, on all hands, that by the Common Law of England, every man was bound to keep his breasts within his own close, under the penalty of answering in damages for all injury arising for their being abroad, and that the owner of land was not bound to protect his premises from the intrusion of a stranger or his animals. By the first section of the sixty first chapter of the Revised Statutes, it is provided that, "the Common Law of England, so far as the same is applicable, and of a general nature, and all statutes and acts of the British Parliament made in aid of, and to supply the defects of the Common Law, prior to the fourth year of James the First," (excepting three specified statutes) "and which are of a general nature and not local to that Kingdom, shall be the rule of decision, and shall be considered as of full force, until repealed by legislative authority." Let us first inquire whether this admitted principle of the Common Law was adopted by this statute, for this is questioned by those who disagree with me. That it is "of a general nature," is too clear to require argument, and its exclusion, if sustained at all, must be upon the ground that it is not applicable. What did the legislature mean by the use of the word "applicable"? Applicable to the nature of our political institutions, and to the genius of our republican forms of government, and to our Constitution, or to our domestic habits, our wants, and our necessities? I think I must ever be of opinion,

---

acceptance in American cases. See Harris v. Carson, 7 Leigh (Va.) 632 (1836), Delaflane v. Crenshaw, 15 Gratt. 457 (1860), Ocean Beach Assoc. v. Brinley, 34 N. J. Eq. 438, 448 (1881). Its most frequent application has been with respect to the acquisition of title by prescription, Ackerman v. Shelp, 3 Hals. (N. J. Law) 125 (1825). Cf. Coolidge v. Learned, 8 Pick. 504 (1829).

that nothing but the former was meant, and that to adopt the latter is a clear usurpation of legislative power by the Courts. If we adopt the former, but little difficulty will ever be experienced in applying the rule, and the question propounded will always be of a legal character, for legal rules will always determine whether any given portion of the Common Law is consistent with, or hostile to, the genius of a republic or the principles of our Constitution. By this principle, the rule by which any portion of the Common Law is excluded, or adopted, will apply with equal force all over the State. If we adopt the latter, then we are driven to examine, not a question of law and principle, but of convenience and policy. By this latter rule, we might have to hold a principle of the Common Law in force in some portions of the State and not in others; for in some places in it might well be adopted to the genius, and customs, the wants and expectations of the people, while it would be the very reverse in others. We should have to investigate, and decide upon facts, without any legal mode of trying them, and not law. If we say that we will not enforce a principle of the Common Law, because, in our judgment, a different rule would be better for the general good, or more just in principle, or more comformable to the habits and ways of the people, then it seems to me that we are legislating, and I know not where we should stop in this course of judicial legislation. If the Courts may say that this rule, or that, of the Common Law, is not law, because a different rule would be more just, or would suit the people better, then they must assume that their judgments are infallible, and there is no longer any occasion for a Legislature to alter the Common Law, for the Courts will happily make all needful alterations. The very statement of such a proposition, in plain terms, is too startling to find an advocate, and too dangerous to admit of defence and yet, it seems to me, that we are rapidly verging to that alarming position, if we are not already there.

For the purpose of proving that this principle of the Common Law is but ill adapted to a country like ours, and hence not applicable, several assumptions are made, some of which are mere matters of opinion, about which men may well differ, while others originate in a misapprehension of facts. Whether it would be better for each one to take care of his own stock, and allow these "extended prairies" capable of producing grain, sufficient to feed a nation, to be reduced to a state of cultivation, without the owner's expense and great delay of fencing them, where timber is scarce, would be but matter of opinion, which the people's representatives are much more capable of forming than we are. I think it quite as probable that the settlers located on the borders of the prairies, that they might cultivate farms, without the expense and delay of clearing off a heavy growth of timber, as that their moving object was to obtain a range for their cattle. Notwithstanding the privilege which it is said they have always enjoyed, not one part in a thousand of this luxuriant growth of grass, but has rotted and decayed where it grew, or more generally been consumed by fire. So it will ever be, for the want of these thousands of cattle to crop it, until brought into cultivation by the husbandman's plow. One acre in tillage is of more value than many acres of wild grass, which would seem to show, that as a question of political economy, it were better to allow the land to be cultivated without the expense of inclosing it, to keep off strangers' animals, than to impose so onerous a tax upon the tillage of the soil, for the sake of the small value of grass consumed by cattle. Again, it is said by intelligent men, to be capable of demonstration, that one fourth the expense required to inclose the cultivated lands, and meadows in the State, would suffice to make pastures for all our stock. If so, it would show that this principle of the Common Law is not so inapplicable to the condition of our country and people. At least, so long as the Court might be mistaken in its notions of convenience, it demonstrates the propriety of leaving that question to the Legislature, where it properly belongs.

This principle of the Common Law is most unquestionably the law of natural justice, whence it originated, for it secures to each one the quiet enjoyment of his own, without intrusion or molestation from another. There is another principle of the Common Law which, in fact, expresses this in more general terms, and it is this: You shall so use your own as not to injure another. Is this maxim to be repudiated because it is not applicable to the genius of our people, and their customs and habits? The decision of this case would seem to say so. It is not for the benefit of the tiller of the soil that the fence is made, for his crops will grow as well without it; but it is for the benefit of the owner of the animals, that he may be relieved from restraining their natural propensities. I have no more natural right to compel my neighbor to protect his crops against my swine, than I have his orchard against my children or myself. It cannot be successfully denied that this alteration of the Common Law, is imposing a burthen upon one for the benefit of another, which should never be done, at least without his consent, by himself or his representative. Again, it is assumed, that it has ever been the custom in this State, for the settlers to allow their stock to run at large. If this were so, it would not change the Common Law, for that can only be done by legislative authority. But the proposition is by no means universally true, in point of fact. It is within my personal knowledge, that in many portions of the State, and I think it is almost universally so in the prairie settlements, it has never been the custom to allow swine and sheep to go at large, or to fence against them, and now, under this decision, all their crops may be destroyed with impunity. ...

But ours is not the only State where the Common Law seems to be undergoing radical changes in some of its fundamental principles, not by legislative authority, but by the will of the Courts. Nay, we find ourselves quite outstripped in this work of improvement, by some of our more enterprising or more venturesome neighbors. But lately we were informed that it had been discovered in one State, that a testator could not impose as a condition to a devise to his widow, that it should be void upon her second marriage, and that the Common Law on that subject is all wrong, and should be altered, and so the Court alters it and holds the condition void. Again, we learn that, in another case, has been made a great improvement upon the Common Law by holding that an attorney in a cause is an incompetent witness, although a few years ago hardly any enlightened Court would have allowed counsel to argue either proposition. That a condition to a grant or devise prohibiting marriage is void, as a general rule, may not be denied; but the cases are as uniform that by the Common Law (though not by the Civil Law) a devise to the testator's widow is an exception to the general rule; (see 1 Story's Eq. Jur., sec. 285,) and cases cited in note 4) yet all the cases establishing this exception are quite overlooked by that Court in its glowing admiration of the general rule. If startling at first, these innovations upon the Common Law will soon cease to surprise us. Although both may be real improvements, (and I have no doubt but that the exclusion of an attorney in the cause as a witness would be) I think it would be much safer and better that they should be made in a constitutional way by the Legislature.

I will allude to one or two cases for the purpose of seeing what progress we are making in this work of improvement. In the case of Boyer v. Sweet, 3 Scam. 120, the Court professedly decide against the principles of the Common Law, upon the ground that the new rule adopted will be more convenient and just under our business habits, and the alleged pliability of the Common Law is asserted for its overthrow. Now I complain more of the principle avowed than of the decision itself, for authorities may be found sustaining that decision upon Common Law principles. Is the Common Law only clay in the hands of the Courts, to be moulded and shaped by them to suit their wills? In the case of Penny v. Little, 4 Scam. 301, the doctrine avowed in the former case is practically out. The question there involved the right of a landlord to distrain for rent where no such right was reserved in the lease. It is admitted that by the Common Law he had no such right, and that we have no statute conferring the right. In England there is a late statute giving the authority. And here without any such statute, and against the Common Law, it was held that the landlord possesses this despotic power over his tenant. If this is more conformable to the genius of a republic or our people, it remains to be shown. But the people had so understood the law, for they had submitted to its practice for twenty years. This territory once belonged to Virginia, and although it is not shown that her laws authorized such distress, the Court says: "The legislation of the Territory and of our State was adopted in reference to the law as it then existed in the country. Upon this principle and none other, can we account for the numerous cases in which the Common Law has been changed by statute in England since the fourth of James I., and those changes adopted by the Courts in this country without having been first re-enacted by our legislatures." How is it that the Courts in this country possess so much more power to change the law than in Great Britain? There, this very change could only be effected by an Act of Parliament; here, it is done by the Court alone, not only without legislative sanction, but in defiance of the positive mandate of our statute adopting the Common Law, and the principle clearly and deliberately proclaimed that they have the right to do so. This power is not given by the Constitution or laws, but is usurped by the Court, probably in deference to a public opinion of twenty years' standing. But this supposed public opinion has not the merit of having originated in a sense of justice, for the landlord has no more abstract right to distrain for his rent, than the merchant for his goods. By what rule of right or reason should the landlord and none others be allowed to seize and sell his debtor's goods without a judgment and without a trial? Is that in harmony with the equality or genius of a republic? But a mistaken notion of the law by the public cannot make the law, and yet, had this public opinion for these twenty years been the other way, I am inclined to think the decision would have been the other way too. There is a place where public opinion may be legitimately exercised and properly represented, and to the Legislature alone should we look for changes in the law. If we are careful to keep within our own constitutional sphere, I think we shall do the best. Of all others, we should be the last to transcend our powers.

By the construction given to the word applicable, we assume the right to disregard any other provision of the Common Law, which in our judgment would be inconvenient, and no one can safely advise his client relying upon the Common Law. After this assumption no step remains to be taken to unite in our own hands the powers delegated by the Constitution to two separate departments of the government. Should the Legislature as manifestly assume judicial powers, I think we should not hesitate to declare the Act unconstitutional. And yet this principle which is so broadly claimed in the case of Penny v. Little, is now again asserted in unqualified terms, and those cases both referred to with approbation. This has led me to a somewhat extended examination of this doctrine, which, it seems to me, is fraught with so much danger, and to which I cannot consistently subscribe. And I hope the fact that this case is at last decided professedly on other grounds, will prevent it from being used as authority for the extension of this principle. With how much more propriety might the Court have held that the Common Law, as applied to navigable rivers in England, was not applicable here. If physical causes could justify us in holding any portion of the Common Law inapplicable, we might with truth have said, that a rule founded upon and applied to the diminutive streams of Great Britain, where its theory is generally supported by a coincidence of facts, was not applicable to the great rivers of this continent, which are, in fact, navigable for thousands of miles above tide-water, and yet this Court, with a manly firmness which has challenged the admiration of some of the ablest jurists of other States, asserted and administered the Common Law as it found it, without attempting to fritter it away because it was not applicable. See Middleton v. Pritchard, 3 Scam. 510, and note of Chancellor Kent on that case, 3 Kent's Com. (6 ed.) 432.

But this is not the first time that the inapplicability of this portion of the Common Law has been urged. In most of the cases to which reference will hereafter be made was the same argument used, and particularly in the cases in 5 Greenl. 356, and 6 Mass. 90, was it contended by eminent counsel, that this principle of the Common Law should not be enforced because it is not adapted to a new country. But the argument was repudiated by the Courts, and a very strict and limited construction given to their statutes in order to uphold the Common Law, which could only be repealed by the clearly expressed will of the Legislature in a positive enactment for that purpose. Those Courts were content to administer the law as they found it, leaving it to the Legislature to make the change, if desired by the people. How different here! ...

Although this case by itself may be insignificant, yet the principles involved are important, and I have felt that I could not say less than I have, in assigning the reasons which have led me to the conclusion at which I have arrived. I am of opinion that the judgment should be affirmed.

Judgment reversed

Grigsby v. Reib
Supreme Court of Texas, 1913, 105 Tex. 597

MR. CHIEF JUSTICE BROWN delivered the opinion of the court.

Jessie Stallcup Grigsby, hereafter styled plaintiff, instituted this suit in a District Court of Dallas County against Eliza J. Reib, hereafter designated defendant. The husband of

Mrs. Reib was joined, but they having been divorced, he was dismissed from the case.

G. M. D. Grigsby, a childless widower, and brother of Mrs. Reib, died in 1906 leaving a valuable estate, much of which was claimed and held by Mrs. Reib under her brother's will. There is no question of defendants' title to the property except as the claim of plaintiff may be superior thereto. We will therefore omit all description of the property and state the plaintiff's claim.

Plaintiff was keeping what she terms a rooming house in Dallas, in fact, an assignation house, in which girls roomed and received their visitors, and to which men with women resorted for illicit purposes. Adopting the statements of plaintiff and her witness as true, the facts were, in substance, that Grigsby's wife having died, he visited plaintiff in her place and they agreed to be husband and wife and then began sexual intercourse, he coming to that house at different times and frequently. They occupied the same room and the same bed and indulged their sexual desires. Grigsby called plaintiff his wife and introduced her to some persons as such. Plaintiff continued her business, and sold beer to the girls and their visitors and to such others as visited her house. Her business was conducted in the name of Jessie Stallcup; she had her bank account in that name; she did not assume the name of Grigsby until after his death. Grigsby died at Jefferson in 1906, and defendants, under lawful claim, took possession of his property, at least of that part in suit which plaintiff claims to have been acquired by Grigsby after her alleged marriage to him, wherefore she claims one-half of it as community property.

The foregoing statement presents the plaintiff's case. We deem it unnecessary to state the facts relied upon by the defendant because the law which must control can be more clearly stated under this plain condensed statement of plaintiff's claim.

The court gave to the jury this charge: "The court instructs you that a common law marriage is legal and valid under the law of Texas, and neither the issuance of license or ministerial or official marriage ceremony is necessary to constitute a lawful and binding common law marriage. All that is necessary to constitute such a marriage is, that if the parties mutually agree and consent together to become husband and wife and thereafter carry out that agreement and live and cohabit together as husband and wife, the marriage would be valid under our law. If you find and believe from the evidence that the plaintiff and the deceased, G. M. D. Grigsby, on or about the 10th day of April, 1905, mutually consented and agreed together with each other to become husband and wife with the intention at that time of living and cohabiting with each other as husband and wife, and that in pursuance of such agreement, if any, they did professedly live and cohabit together as husband and wife, you will find for the plaintiff that she was the common law wife of the deceased, G. M. D. Grigsby. If however, on the other hand, you fail to find that plaintiff and deceased, G. M. D. Grigsby, mutually consented and agreed together with each other to become husband and wife on or about April 10, 1903, or if you find that plaintiff and deceased, Grigsby, did not professedly live and cohabit with each other as husband and wife in pursuance of such agreement, if any, you will find for the defendant, Eliza J. Reib."

The plaintiff in error challenges the correctness of the charge by this proposition of law: "In order to constitute a valid common law marriage where the parties have mutually agreed and consented together to become husband and wife, it is immaterial as to whether the husband and wife either carried out the agreement or whether they either lived or cohabited together as husband and wife." The proposition clearly defines the issue which must be decided by this court in disposing of the case. If the proposition correctly states the law, the court erred in the charge and the judgment must be reversed.

The marriage asserted in this case, if sustained at all, must find its support and sanction in the common law in force in this State; therefore, the first question to be settled is, what rule of the common law must govern in arriving at our conclusion?

In the year 1840 the Congress of the Republic enacted a law which embraced Article 3258 of our Revised Civil Statutes of 1895, which reads:

"The common law of England (so far as it is not inconsistent with the Constitution and laws of this State) shall, together with such Constitution and laws, be the rule of decision and shall continue in force until altered or repealed by the Legislature."

In 1823, by Act of Parliament, all marriages in England were required to be performed according to the requirements of the statute, the common law on that subject being thereby abrogated. (Laws of England, Vol. 16, pp. 278-286.)

We must first ascertain what the Congress of the Republic intended to designate by the language: "The common law of England." If it was intended to adopt the common law as it was in force in England in 1840, then we have no common law on the subject of marriage, for none such was in force in that Kingdom at that date. Our courts have uniformly recognized the existence in this State of the common law which permitted marriage without compliance with the statute upon that subject; therefore, we conclude that "the common law of England" adopted by the Congress of the Republic was that which was declared by the courts of the different States of the United States. This conclusion is supported by the fact that the lawyer members of that Congress who framed and enacted that statute had been reared and educated in the United States and would naturally have in mind the common law with which they were familiar. If we adopt that as our guide and source of authority, the decisions of the courts of those States determine what rule of the common law of England to apply to this case.

The effect of the Act of 1840, supra, was not to introduce and put into effect the body of the common law, but to make effective the provisions of the common law so far as they are not inconsistent with the conditions and circumstances of our people. Clarendon Land I. A. Co. v. McClelland Bros., 86 Texas, 185.

In the courts of the different States of the United States there are two lines of cases between which we must choose, which Mr. Freeman on his notes to cases in 124 Am. St. Rep., 111, 112, states, in substance, as follows: Both lines of authority rest upon the doctrine that marriage is a civil contract, and that no marriage can be binding which does not rest upon the consent of the parties. One rule is "that a marriage is complete when the parties agree, in words of the present tense, to take each other as husband and wife." That statement of the law is endorsed by Mr. Freeman, in support of which he cites a number of cases. The other rule is stated thus: "An assumption of the marriage status is essential to a common law marriage, that an agreement presently to be husband and wife is not sufficient to constitute marriage until it is acted upon by the parties." ...

The writer has examined every case that he could discover in the Supreme Court library which had a bearing upon the question before the court, and has found but two cases in which a common law marriage has been sustained in the absence of any cohabitation or other acts of consummation. In Jackson v. Winne, 7 Wend., 47, 22 Am. Dec., 563, the facts stated were: "It appeared that Enoch was arrested in the year 1800, on the complaint of the overseers of the poor of the town of Blenheim, under the bastardy act, on a charge of having gotten Joanna with child. He was taken to the house of Joanna's father, and thence with the father and the mother of Joanna, in company of the constable, to a justice of the peace to be married. The justice asked Enoch and Joanna if they consented to be married and told them to join hands; Enoch dropped his hand and turned from Joanna; she took it and held it until they were pronounced man and wife. The justice hesitated when Enoch refused to take Joanna's hand, but proceeded in a minute or two and concluded the ceremony. It was customary for the justice to offer a prayer, but he did not do so on this occasion, and Joanna's father did so instead. During the whole time Enoch said nothing. After the ceremony, Joanna returned to her father's house but Enoch did not go with her, nor did they ever afterwards cohabit." Under that state of facts the court held that the marriage was valid. There was neither cohabitation nor contract; but that court held that it was a contract on the part of the man, who, being a prisoner, stood mute, refusing his hand to the woman who seized it and made the declarations. If it be conceded that Enoch by silence gave consent and thereby made a contract then to become and thereafter to be her husband, it stands as one of two cases within my reach that sustain the proposition that a marriage by contract alone establishes the status of husband and wife. ...

In Dumarseley v. Fishly, 10 Ky., 368, the question was squarely before the court, and a divided court held that a marriage by contract, without any subsequent recognition by the parties, constituted a valid marriage. Chief Justice Boyle delivered the opinion concurred in by Justice Owsley. The parties had gone from Kentucky to Indiana for marriage, which was the home of the bride's father. A license was procured and a ceremony performed, but the bride refused to cohabit. We infer these facts, which are not fully stated. The majority said: "Marriage is nothing but a contract; and to render it valid it is only necessary, upon the principles of natural law, that the parties should be able to contract, willing to contract, and should actually contract. A marriage thus made, without further ceremony, was, according to the simplicity of the ancient common law, deemed valid to all purposes, and such continued to be the law of England until the time of Pope Innocent the Third." Judge Mills dissented in a very able opinion and contended for the rule that cohabitation was necessary to complete a marriage by agreement. Besides, the marriage was entered into in the State of Indiana and should have been determined by the law of that State. I can find no decision by the Supreme Court of Indiana that promulgates the "contract only" doctrine. ...

We are confident that there is no state court - except in the two cases cited - which holds such marriage without cohabitation to be valid. There are a number of cases in which the "stock phrase," "Marriage is a civil contract and to constitute such marriage requires only the agreement of the man and the woman to become then and thenceforth husband and wife," is used, but in each case, which sustained the marriage, except the two, there was cohabitation. ...

Marriage was not originated by human law. When God created Eve, she was a wife to Adam; they then and there occupied the status of husband to wife and wife to husband. When God created the first pair, He gave the command: "Multiply and replenish (people) the earth," which was enjoined upon their expulsion from the garden. When Noah was selected for salvation from the flood, he and his wife and his three sons and their wives were placed in the Ark, and when the flood waters had subsided and the families came forth, it was Noah and his wife and each son and his wife, and God repeated to them the command: "Multiply." All of the duties and obligations that have existed at any time between husband and wife existed between those husbands and wives before civil government was formed. The truth is that civil government has grown out of marriage; marriage by cohabitation, not by contract, which created homes, and population, and society, from which government became necessary to settle differences in matters of private interest, to protect the weak and to conserve the moral forces of society, to the support of religion and free government. In what respect does the contract of marriage of B and C contribute to their happiness? How does that marriage benefit society? It will contribute nothing to sustaining the dignity of the State, nor add to its citizenship. Such a contract if it be regarded as such, is worse than a nudum pactum, for it is without consideration or obligation to or from either party. Such life is in defiance of the commands of God, and in disregard of every obligation to society and State. Such a transaction has but one element of a contract, mutual consent to do nothing for themselves, their country, or their God. The abstract theory has had little influence in the determination of causes except to confuse the judicial mind. Contract marriages exist when the parties, for some pecuniary or social advantages have desecrated the sacred status by their union, and such marriages often furnish business to the divorce courts and scandals to society.

If the rule of law claimed in this case is not given effect it should be repudiated, because it is unsound and inapplicable to present conditions, serving only to confuse courts and juries. If it were put into effect, as is sought to be done in this case, it would open a wide door with a strong invitation to perjury and fraud. It would be a menace to the heirs of men like Mr. Grigsby and make their estates the prey of the bawd and the adventuress, with no possible safeguard, one party being dead and no witnesses to the contract nor publicity of the marriage. One of the parties to such a contract might marry and raise a family and, dying without disclosing the former marriage, the "common-law widow" could come forward, claim to be the surviving wife, and thus displace the woman who had borne the hardships of wife and mother, brand the children as bastards and take the position as survivor with her rights in the estate. A rule for the regulation of the sacred rights of marriage and the rights of families that make such wrongs possible should not be recognized in civilized governments.

The term, "civil contract," as applied to marriage, means nothing now, for there does not exist the church's claim that it is a religious right; there is nothing to be differentiated by the language; it is obsolete. Marriage is not a contract, but a status created by mutual consent of one man and one woman. The method by which it is solemnized, or entered into, may be by proceedings prescribed by statute, or by mutual agreement with cohabitation, but, however contracted, having the same elements and producing the status of husband and wife. The sole difference which can legally exist is in the method of expressing consent, and the only particular in which a marriage as at common law can differ from the statutory method is the absence of license and the ceremony. The cohabitation must be professedly as husband and wife, and public, so that by their conduct towards each other they may be known as husband and wife. Such marriages may be equally the consummation of a mutual affection which will produce a home and family that will contribute to good society, to free and just government and to the support of christianity - to the common weal. It would be sacrilegious to apply the designation "a civil contract" to such a marriage. It is that and more; a status ordained by God, the foundation and support of good government, and absolutely necessary to the purity and preservation of good society. When the "wedding day" of the parent ceases to be revered by the offspring there will be a weakening of the family ties and a lowering of the standard of marriage and home.

The court instructed the jury correctly, and the jury seem to have found correctly on the facts. The judgments of the courts are affirmed.

Affirmed.[1]

Jesse Root, <u>The Origin of Government and Laws in Connecticut</u>
Preface to Volume I, Root's Reports (1798)

OUR ancestors, who emigrated from England to America, were possessed of the knowledge of the laws and jurisprudence of that country; but were free from any obligations of subjection to them: The laws of England had no authority over them, to bind their persons; nor were they in any measure applicable to their condition and circumstances here: Nor was it possible they should be; for the principle of their government, as it respected the prerogatives of the crown, the estates, rights and power of the lords, and the tenure of their lands, were derived from the feudal system: The privilege of sending members to parliament, from the towns, cities, and bor-

---

1. There is a useful summary of the American reception, rejection and modification of the English law of common law marriages in LRA, 1915 E, 8.

oughs, to compose one branch of the legislature, called the house of commons, and an exemption from taxation, only by their consent, was extorted from the kings by the barons, and is confirmed by the great charter of liberties as of his gift and grant. Their other laws were calculated for a great commercial nation. As to their criminal code, it was adapted to a people grown old in the habits of vice, where the grossest enormities and crimes were practised. In every respect therefore their laws were inapplicable to an infant country or state; where the government was in the peoples; and which had virtue for its principle, and the public good for its object and end; where the tenure of their lands was free and absolute, the objects of trade few, and the commission of crimes rare.

OUR ancestors therefore as a free, sovereign, and independent people, very early established a constitution of government by their own authority; which was adapted to their situation and circumstances; and enacted laws for the due and regular administration of justice; for the propagation of knowledge and virtue; for the preservation of the public peace, and for the security and defense of the state against their savage enemies. New Haven did the same with little variation in point of form.

Their common law was derived from the law of nature and of revelation; those rules and maxims of immutable truth and justice, which arise from the eternal fitness of things, which need only to be understood, to be submitted to; as they are themselves the highest authority; together with certain customs and usages, which had been universally assented to and adopted in practice, as reasonable and beneficial. ...

This constitution of our government, framed by the wisdom of our ancestors about 160 years ago, adapted to their condition and circumstances, was so constructed as to enable the legislature to accommodate laws to the exigencies of the state, through all the changes it hath undergone; and is nearly coeval with our existence as a community; and analogous to the spirit of which all our laws have been made, from time to time, as cases occurred and the good of the public requires. And can it be said with the least color of truth, that the laws of the state are not adequate to all the purposes of government and of justice.

We need only compare the laws of England with the laws of Connecticut, to be at once convinced of the difference which pervades their whole system. This is manifest in the spirit and principles of the laws, the objects, and in the rules themselves; with respect to the tenure of lands, descents, and who are heirs, and the settlement of insolvent estates, and of other estates testate and intestate, the probate of wills, registering of deeds; the arrangement and jurisdiction of our courts, the forms of civil processes, and the mode of trial, the appointing and returning jurors; and with respect to the settlement and support of the poor, the appointment and regulation of sheriffs, gaols and gaolers, the orderly celebration of marriages and granting of divorces; the means of propagating knowledge, and with respect to the punishments annexed to crimes; and in innumerable other instances too tedious to mention; which every lawyer is acquainted with. May the citizens of Connecticut, glory in this system of government and jurisprudence; which, at first, was the produce of wisdom, is perfected and matured by long experience; which has carried us safe through many a storm, withstood every attack, for more than a century and a half, is grown venerable by age and the wisdom of its regulations, and the rich profusion of blessings which it confers, as the noblest birthright of themselves and their children; and the highest interest and honor of the state as an independent member of a great nation; the rising empire of America.

These rights and liberties are our own; not holden by the gift of a despot; our government and our rulers are from amongst ourselves; chosen by the free uninfluenced suffrages of enlightened freemen; not to oppress and devour, but to protect, feed, and bless the people, with the benign and energetic influence of their power, (as ministers of God for good to them). This shows the ignorance of those who are clamorous for a new constitution, and the mistake of those who suppose that the rules of the common law of England are the common law of Connecticut, until altered by a statute.[1]

---

1. Cf. Fitch v. Brainerd, 2 Day (Conn.) 163, (1805). In holding that a married woman cannot dispose of real estate by will the court, at p. 189, said: "For though the common law of England hath not, as such, nor ever had, any force here; yet, in the progress of our affairs, whatever was imagined at the beginning, it long since became necessary, in order to avoid arbitrary decisions, and for the sake of rules, which habit had rendered familiar, as well as the wisdom of ages matured, to make that law our own, by practical adoption - with such exceptions as a diversity of circumstances, and the incipient customs of our own country, required." In 1823, Chief Justice Hosmer of the Supreme Court of Errors of Connecticut, said: "Undoubtedly, by an assumption of legislative power, this court can promulgate as law, any provision which will meet a particular mischief; but with a very eminent judge [Lord Kenyon] I take pleasure in declaring, 'It is my wish and my comfort to stand super anitquas vias: I cannot legislate; but by my industry, I can discover what our predecessors have done, and I will servilely tread in their footstep.' Bauerman et al.

On The Common Law of Connecticut

THESE questions are frequently asked, What is the common law of America? Have we any common law in Connecticut? I know not how I can better resolve these questions than by answering another, (viz.) What is common law? And first,

Common law is the perfection of reason, arising from the nature of God, of man, and of things, and from their relations, dependencies, and connections: It is universal and extends to all men, and to all combinations of men, in every possible situation; and embraces all cases and questions that can possibly arise; it is in inself perfect, clear and certain; it is immutable, and cannot be changed or altered, without altering the nature and relation of things; it is superior to all other laws and regulations, by it they are corrected and controlled; all positive laws are to be construed by it, and wherein they are opposed to it, they are void. It is immemorial, no memory runneth to the contrary of it; it is co-existent with the nature of man, and commensurate with his being; it is most energetic and coercive; for every one who violates its maxims and precepts are sure of feeling the weight of its sanctions.[2]

Nor may we say, who will ascend into heaven to bring it down, or descend into the depths to bring it up, or traverse the Atlantic to import it; it is near us, it is within us, written upon the table of our hearts, in lively and indelible characters; by it we are constantly admonished and reproved, and by it we shall finally be judged. It is visible in the volume of nature, in all the works and ways of God; its sound is gone forth into all the earth, and there is no people or nation so barbarous, where its language is not understood.

---

v. Radenius, 7 Term Rep. 664. The English common law, so far as it was not unadapted to the legal circumstances of this country, our ancestors, on their emigration hither, brought with them; and until it is abrogated, by statute, I must, with the exception mentioned, consider it as the common law of this state." Card v. Grisiman, 5 Conn. 164, 168 (1823).

2. Coke, who stated that common law "is the perfection of reason" saw other elements in that perfection than those which Mr. Justice Root admired. "Reason is the life of the law, - nay, the common law is nothing else but reason; which is to be understood of an artificial perfection of reason gotten by long study, observation and experience, and not of every man's natural reason." Co. Litt. 97b. Finch, Law (1636) 74-75 traces this identification of common law and reason to Plato.

The dignity of its original, the sublimity of its principles, the purity, excellency and perpetuity of its precepts, are most clearly made known and delineated in the book of divine revelations; heaven and earth may pass away and all the systems and works of man sink into oblivion; but not a jot or title of this law shall ever fail.

By this we are taught the dignity, the character, the rights and duties of man, his rank and station here and his relation to futurity; that he hath a property in himself, his powers and faculties; in whatever is produced by the application of them; that he is a free agent subject to the control of none, in his opinions and actions but to his God and the laws, to which he is amenable. This teaches us, so to use our own as not to injure the rights of others: This enables us, to explain the laws, construe contracts and agreements, to distinguish injuries, to determine their degree and the reparation in damages which justice requires. This designates crimes, discovers their aggravations and ill-tendency; and measures out the punishments proper and necessary for restraint and example: This defines the obligations and duties between husbands and wives, parents and children, brothers and sisters, between the rulers and the people, and the people or citizens towards each other: This is the Magna Charta of all our natural and religious rights and liberties - and the only solid basis of our civil constitution and privileges - in short, it supports, pervades and enlightens all the ways of man, to the noblest ends by the happiest means, when and wherever its precepts and instructions are observed and followed - the usages and customs of men and the decisions of the courts of justice serve to declare and illustrate the principles of this law; but the law exists the same, - nor is this a matter of speculative reasoning merely; but of knowledge and feeling; we know that we have a property in our persons, in our powers and faculties, and in the fruits and effects of our industry, we know that we have a right to think and believe as we choose, to plan and pursue our own affairs and concerns; whatever judge to be for our advantage, our interest or happiness, provided we do not interfere with any principle of truth or of reason and justice. We know the value of a good name, and the interest we have in it, we know that every man's peace and happiness in his own; nay, more when our persons are assaulted, our lives attacked, our liberties infringed, our reputation scandalized, or our property ravaged from us or spoiled; we feel the injury that is done to us, and by an irrepressible impulse of nature, resent the violation of our rights, and call upon the powerful arm of justice to administer redress. We also know that other men have the same rights, the same sensibility of injuries, when their rights are violated this law is therefore evidenced both by the knowledge and the feelings of men. These ought to be the governing principles with all legislators in making of laws, with all judges in construing and executing the laws, and with all citizens in observing and obeying them.

Secondly, another branch of common law is derived from certain usages and customs, universally assented to and adopted in practice by the citizens at large, or by particular classes of men, as the farmers, the merchants, etc. as applicable to their particular business, and to all others of the same description, which are reasonable and beneficial.

These customs or regulations, when thus assented to and adopted in practice, have an influence upon the course of trade and business, and are necessary to be understood and applied in the construction of transactions had and contracts entered into with reference to them: To this end the courts of justice take notice of them as rules of right, and as having the force of laws formed and adopted under the authority of the people.

That these customs and usages must have existed immemorially, and have been compulsory, in order to their being recognized to be law; seems to involve some degree of absurdity - that is, they must have the compulsory force of laws, before they can be recognized to be laws, when they can have no compulsory force till the powers of government have communicated it to them by declaring them to be laws: That so long as any one living can remember when they began to exist they can be of no force or validity whatever, however universally they may be assented to and adopted in practice; but as soon as this is forgotten and no one remembers their beginning, then and not until then they become a law; this may be necessary in arbitrary governments, but in a free government like ours, I suppose, the better reason to be this:

That as statutes are positive laws enacted by the authority of the legislature, which consists of the representatives of the people, being duly promulgated, are binding upon all, as all are considered as consenting to them by their representatives: So these unwritten customs and regulations which are reasonable and beneficial, and which have the sanction of universal consent and adoption in practice, amongst the citizens at large or particular classes of them, have the force of laws under the authority of the people, and the courts of justice will recognize and declare them to be such, and to be obligatory upon the citizens as necessary rules of construction and of justice. The reasonableness and utility of their operation, and the universality of their adoption, are the better evidences of their existence and of their having the general consent and approbation, than the circumstance of its being forgotten when they began to exist.

Thirdly, another important source of common law is, the adjudications of the courts of justice and the rules of practice adopted in them. These have been learned by practice only, as we have no treatises upon the subject, and but one small volume of reports containing a period of about two years only, and a treatise lately wrote by Mr. Swift, containing a commentary on the government and laws of this state. We learn from history, the constitutions of government and the laws of foreign countries, the adjudications and rules of practice adopted in their courts of justice; but this will not give us the knowledge of our own, and although we may seem to have borrowed from them, yet ours is essentially different from all; in that, it is highly improved and ameliorated in its principles and regulations, and simplified in its forms, is adapted to the state of our country, and to the genius of the people, and calculated in an eminent manner to improve the mind by the diffusion of knowledge, and to give effectual security and protection to the persons, rights, liberties and properties of the citizens; and is clothed with an energy, derived from a source, and rendered efficacious by a power, unknown in foreign governments, (viz.) the attachment of the citizens who rejoice in being ruled and governed by its laws, for the blessings it confers. Let us, Americans then, duly appreciate our own government, laws and manners, and be what we profess, an independent nation; and not plume ourselves upon being humble imitators of foreigners, at home and in our own country; but let our manners in all respects be characteristic of the spirit and principles of our independence.

I trust by this time the reader has anticipated in his own mind the answer to the questions, what is the common law of America? and have we any common law in the State of Connecticut? These principles, as applied to the situation and genius of the people, the spirit of our government and laws, the tenure of our lands, and the vast variety of objects, civil and military, ecclesiastical and commercial, in our own state have been exemplified in practice, defined, explained and established by the decisions of the courts in innumerable instances, although reports of but few of them have been published. To these I think we ought to resort, and not to foreign systems, to lay a foundation, to establish a character upon, and to rear a system of jurisprudence purely American, without any marks of servility to foreign powers or states; at the same time leave ourselves open to derive instruction and improvement from the observations, discoveries, and experience of the literate, in all countries and nations, respecting jurisprudence and other useful arts and sciences.[3] And indeed, a great part of our

---

3. Cf. James Sullivan in the preface to his History of Land Titles in Massachusetts (1801), p. iv - v: "The idea of our

legal ideas were originally derived from the laws of England and the civil law, which being duly arranged, have been incorporated into our own system, and adapted to our own situation and circumstances.

It is of great importance to a country or state that the laws which regulate the intercourse among the citizens determine property, construe and enforce contracts, define crimes and their punishments, and provide remedies for the recovery of rights, and for the redress of wrongs, should be just in principle; clear, concise, and unequivocal in expression; uniform, permanent, and consistent in their meaning and application; and energetic and coercive in their operation; extending to and embracing every possible case. This would enable the courts of law to do justice in all cases, and would supersede the necessity of the courts of chancery; and indeed are not the courts of chancery in this state borrowed from a foreign jurisdiction, which grew out of the ignorance and barbarism of the law judges at a certain period in that country, from whence borrowed: - And would it not be as safe for the people, to invest the courts of law with the power of deciding all questions and of giving relief in all cases according to the rules established in chancery, as it is to trust those same judges as chancellors to do it; those rules might be considered as a part of the law, and the remedy be made much more concise and effectual.

Further, would not this remedy great inconveniences and save much expense to suitors, who are frequently turned round at law, to seek a remedy in chancery; and as often turned round in chancery, because they have an adequate remedy at law; these are serious evils and ought not to be permitted to exist in the jurisprudence of a country, famed for liberty and justice; and which can be remedied, only by the interposition of the legislature.

Statutes are positive laws framed by the wisdom, and enacted by the authority of the legislature, and like the most perfect system of human composition, however well intended and wisely devised, would often, if literally pursued, fail of the

---

having adopted legal maxims and principles from that nation, of which we have lately been a part, is a very honorable one to our country.

"But having imported the seed, and sown it in our own soil, it would, in some measure, be relinquishing our independence, to be under a necessity for new importations. ... It is not becoming an independent nation to repair ordinarily to the seashore, to listen for opinions recently given in a foreign realm."

good ends proposed, through some ambiguity in the expressions, or some defect in the remedy provided, unless construed and corrected by reason and equity, agreeably to the intent of the legislature, according to the following rules: 1st. By considering what the mischief was which the statute designed to remedy. 2d. The remedy the statute hath or mean to have provided. 3d. The true reason of the remedy. And it is the province of the courts of law to explain and declare what both the written and unwritten laws are, and from their decisions we are to learn the law and its determinate meaning.

Thomas Jefferson, _Inquiry Whether Christianity is a Part of the Common Law_ [1764?]
1 Jefferson's Reports 137 (1829)

In Quare impedit, in C. B. 34 H. 6. fo. 38, the defendant, Bishop of Lincoln, pleads that the church of the plaintiff became void by the death of the incumbent; that the plaintiff and I. S. each pretending a right, presented two several clerks that the church being thus rendered litigious, he was not obliged, by the ecclesiastical law, to admit either until an inquisition _de jure patronatus_ in the ecclesiastical court; that, by the same law, this inquisition was to be at the suit of either claimant, and was not _ex officio_ to be instituted by the Bishop, and at his proper costs; that neither party had desired such an inquisition; that six months passed; whereon it belonged to him of right to present as on a lapse, which he had done. The plaintiff demurred. A question was, How far the ecclesiastical law was to be respected in this matter by the Common law court? And Prisot c. 5. [sic] in the course of his argument uses this expression, "á tels leis que ils de seint eglise ont en _ancien scripture_, covient á nous á donner credence; car ceo common ley sur quel touts manners leis sont fondus. Et auxy, Sir, nous sumus obligés de conustre lour ley de saint eglise; et semblablement ils sont obligés de conustre nostre ley, et, Sir, si poiteapperer or a nous que l'evesque ad fait come un Ordinary fera en tiel cas adonq nous devons ceo adjuger bon, our autrement nemy," &c. It does not appear what judgment was given. Y. B. ubi supra, 3 c. Fitzh. Abr. Qu. imp. 89. Bro. Abr. Qu. imp. 12. Finch mis-states this in the following manner: "to such laws of the church as have warrant in _holy scripture_, our law giveth credence;" and cites the above case, and the words of Prisot in the margin. Finch's law, B. 1. c. 3. published in 1613. Here we find "ancien scripture" converted into "holy scripture"; whereas it can only mean the antient written laws of the church. It cannot mean the scriptures, 1st., Because the term _antient_ scripture must then be understood as meaning the _Old_ Testament in contradistinction to the New, and to the exclusion of that; which would be absurd; and contrary to the wish of those who cite this passage to prove that the scriptures, or Christianity, is a part of the common law. 2nd. Because Prisot says, "ceo (est) Common ley sur quel touts manners leis sont fondés." Now it is true that the ecclesiastical law, so far as admitted in England, derives its authority from the common law. But it would not be true that the scriptures so derive their authority. 3rd. The whole case and arguments shew, that the question was, How far the ecclesiastical law in general should be respected in a common law court? And in Bro's Abr. of this case, Littleton says "les juges del Common ley prendra conusans quid est lex ecclesiae vel admiralitatis et hujus modi." 4th. Because the particular part of the ecclesiastical law then in question, viz. the right of the patron to present to his advowson, was not founded on the law of God, but subject to the modification of the law-giver; and so could not introduce any such general position as Finch pretends. Yet Wingate (in 1658) thinks proper to erect this false quotation into a maxim of the common law, expressing it in the very words of Finch, but citing Prisot, Wing. Max. 3. Next comes Sheppard (in 1675) who states it in the same words of Finch, and quotes the Y. B. Finch and Wingate. 3 Shep. Abr. tit. "Religion". In the case of the King and Taylor, Sir Matthew Hale lays it down in these words; "Christianity is parcel of the laws of England." 1 Ventr. 293. 3 Keb. 607. But he quotes no authority. It was from this part of the supposed common law, that he derived his authority for burning witches. So strong was this doctrine become in 1728, by additions and repetitions from one another, that in the case of the King v. Woolston, the court would not suffer it to be debated, Whether to write against Christianity was punishable in the temporal courts, at common law? saying it had been so settled in Taylor's case, ante, 2 Stra, 834. Therefore Wood, in his Institute, lays it down, that all blasphemy and profaneness are offences by the common law, and cites Strange, ubi supra. Wood, 409. And Blackstone (about 1763) repeats, in the words of Sir Matthew Hale, that "Christianity is part of the laws of England", citing Ventr. and Stra, ubi supra. 4 Bl. 59. Lord Mansfield qualified it a little, by saying, in the case of the Chamberlain of London v. Evans, 1767, that "the essential principles of revealed religion are part of the common law". But he cites no authority, and leaves us at our peril to find out what, in the opinion of the judge, and according to the measure of his foot or his faith, are those essential principles of revealed religion, obligatory on us as a part of the common law. Thus we find this string of authorities when, examined to the beginning, all hanging on the same hook; a perverted expression of Prisot's; or on nothing. For they all quote Prisot, or one another, or nobody. Thus, Finch quotes Prisot; Wingate also; Sheppard quotes Prisot, Finch and Wingate; Hale cites nobody; the court, in Woolston's case, cite Hale; Wood cites Woolston's case; Blackstone that and Hale; and Lord Mansfield, like Hale, ventures it on his own authority. In the earlier ages of the law, as in the Year Books for instance, we do not expect much recurrence to authorities by the judges; because, in those days, there were few or none such made public. But in later times we take no judge's word for what the law is, further than he is warranted by the authorities he appeals to. His decision may bind the unfortunate individual who happens to be the particular subject of it; but it cannot alter the law. Although the common law be termed Lex non scripta, yet the same Hale tells us, "when I call those parts of our laws Leges non Scriptae, I do not mean as if all those laws were only oral, or communicated from the former ages to the latter merely, by word. For all these laws have their several monuments in writing, whereby they are transferred from one age to another, and without which they would soon lose all kind of certainty. They are for the most part extant in records of pleas, proceedings and judgments, in books of reports, and judicial decisions, in tractates of learned men's arguments and opinions, preserved from antient times, and still extant in writing." Hale's Com. Law, 22. Authorities for what is common law, may, therefore, be as well cited as for any part of the lex scripta. And there is no better instance of the necessity of holding the judges and writers to a declaration of their authorities, than the present, where we detect them endeavoring to make law where they found none, and to submit us, at one stroke to a whole system, no particle of which, has its foundation in the common law, or has received the "esto" of the legislator. For we know that the common law is that system of law which was introduced by the Saxons, on their settlement in England, and altered, from time to time, by proper legislative authority, from that, to the date of the Magna Charta, which terminates the period of the common law, or lex non scripta, and commences that of the statute law, or lex scripta. This settlement took place about the middle of the fifth century; but Christianity was not introduced till the seventh century; the conversion of the first Christian King of the Heptarchy, having taken place about the year 598, and that of the last about 686. Here, then, was a space of two hundred years, during which the common law was in existence, and Christianity no part of it. If it ever, therefore, was adopted into the common law, it must have been between the introduction of Christianity and the date of the Magna Charta. But of the laws of this period, we have a tolerable collection, by Lambard and Wilkins; probably not perfect, but neither very defective; and if any one chooses to build a doctrine on any law of that period, supposed to have been lost, it is incumbent on him to prove it to have existed, and what were its contents. These were so far alterations of the common law, and became themselves a part of it; but none of these adopt Christianity as a part of the common law. If, therefore, from the settlement of the Saxons, to the introduction of Christianity among them, that system of religion could not be a part of the common law, because they were not yet Christians; and if, having their laws from that period to the close of the common law, we are able to find among them no such act of adoption; we may safely affirm (though contradicted by all the judges and writers on earth) that Christianity neither is, nor ever was, a part of the common law. Another cogent proof of this truth is drawn from the silence of certain writers on the common law. Bracton gives us a very complete and scientific treatise of the whole body of the common law. He wrote this about the close of the reign of Henry III, a very few years after the date of the Magna Charta. We consider this book as the more valuable, as it was written about the time which divides the common and statute law; and therefore gives us the former in its ultimate state. Bracton, too, was an ecclesiastic, and would certainly not have failed to inform us of the adoption of Christianity as a part of the common law, had any such adoption ever taken place. But no word of his, which intimates any thing like it, has ever been cited. Fleta and Britton, who wrote in the succeeding reign of E. I., are equally silent. So also is Glanvil, an earlier writer than any of them, to wit, temp. H. 2; but his subject, perhaps, might not have led him to mention it. It was reserved then for Finch, five hundred years after, in the time of Charles II., by a falsification of a phrase in the Year book, to open this new doctrine, and for his successors to join full-mouthed in the cry, and give to the fiction the sound of fact. Justice Fortescue Aland, who possessed more Saxon learning than all the judges and writers before mentioned put together, places this subject on more limited ground. Speaking of the laws of the Saxon Kings, he says, "the ten commandments were made part of their law, and consequently were once part of the law of England; so that to break any of the ten commandments, was then esteemed a breach of the common law of England; and why it is not so now, perhaps, it may be difficult to give a good reason." Pref. to Fortescue's Rep. xvii. The good reason is found in the denial of the fact.

Houared, in his Coutumes Anglo-Normandes, I. 87, notices the falsification of the laws of Alfred, by prefixing to them four chapters of the Jewish law, to wit, the 20th, 21st, 22nd and 23rd chapters of Exodus; to which he might have added the 15th of the Acts of the Apostles, v. 23 to 29, and precepts from other parts of the scripture. These he calls Hors d' oeuvre of some pious copyist. This awkward monkish fabrication, makes the preface to Alfred's genuine laws stand in the body of the work. And the very words of Alfred himself prove the fraud; for he declares in that preface, that he has collected these laws from those of Ina, of Offa, Aethelbert and his ancestors, saying nothing of any of them being taken from the scripture. It is still more certainly proved by the inconsistencies it occasions. For example, the Jewish legislator, Exodus, xxi. 12, 13, 14 (copies by the Pseudo Alfred sec. 13) makes murder, with the Jews, death. But Alfred himself, Ll. xxvi. punishes it by a fine only, called a weregild, proportioned to the condition of the person killed. It is remarkable that Hume (Append. I. to his History) examining this article of the laws of Alfred, without perceiving the fraud, puzzles himself with accounting for the inconsistency it had introduced.[1] To strike a pregnant woman, so that she die, is death by Exod. xxi. 22, 23, and Pseudo Alfred sec. 19, 20, if of a servant by his mater, is freedom to the servant; in every other case, retaliation. But by Alfred Ll. xi. a fixed indemnification is paid. Theft of an ox or a sheep, by the Jewish law xxii. Exod. 1, was repaid five fold for the ox, and four fold

---

1. Jefferson's effort to explain away the Biblical portions of the Code of Alfred seems to have resulted in some distortion of history. See, Turk, The Legal Code of Alfred the Great (1893), p. 30-38. (An interesting summary of the influence of Biblicism on the law of England is in Goebel, "King's Law and Local Custom in Seventeenth Century New England" (1931) 31 Col. L. Rev. 416, 423-424, footnote.) On the other hand, Jefferson seems to have taken a position on the basic question of whether Christianity is part of the common law of England with which later English judges have agreed. See, e.g., Bowman v. Secular Society, Ltd. [1917] A. C. 406. The accuracy and perception of Jefferson's scholarship is commended by Professor Kenny in "The Evolution of the Law of Blasphemy", (1922) 1 Camb. L. J. 127, 130. Cf. 8 Holdsworth, History of English Law (1926) 403. See also Kent, C. J. in People v. Ruggles, 8 Johns, 290 (1811).

The most striking example of Jefferson's desire to model the law of Virginia upon that of the Anglo-Saxons is in his proposed Bill for proportioning Crimes and Punishments. His learned annotation of that Bill indicates how thoroughly he was soaked in the antiquities of the common law and how thoroughly he was persuaded that primitivism in law offered hope for Virginia. See Writings of Jefferson (Ford, ed.) 203 et seq.

for the sheep; by the Pseudograph sec. 24, double for the ox, and four fold for the sheep. But by Alfred Ll. xvi he who stole a cow and calf, was to repay the worth of the cow and 40s. for the calf. Goring by an ox, was the death of the ox, and the flesh not to be eaten; Exod. xxi. 28. Pseud. Alfr. sec. 21. By Ll. Alfr. xxiv. the wounded person had the ox. This Pseudograph makes municipal laws of the ten commandments: sec. 1 - 10, regulate concubinage; sec. 12, makes it death to strike, or to curse father or mother; sec. 14, 15, gives an eye for an eye, tooth for tooth, hand for hand, foot for foot, burning for burning, wound for wound, stripe for stripe; sec. 19, sells the thief to repay his theft; sec. 24, obliges the fornicator to marry the woman he has lain with; sec. 29, forbids interest on money; sec. 28, 35, makes the laws of bailment and very different from what Lord Holt delivers in Coggs v. Bernard, and what Sir William Jones tells us they were; and punished witchcraft with death, sec. 30, which Sir Matthew Hale 1. P. C. ch. 33, declares was not a felony before the statl. 1. Jac. c. 12. It was under that statute, that he hung Rose Cullender, and Amy Duny, 16 Car. 2 (1662) on whose trial he declared, "that there were such creatures as witches, he made no doubt at all; for 1st. The scriptures had affirmed so much. 2nd. The wisdom of all nations had provided laws against such persons - and such hath been the judgment of this kingdom, as appears by that act of parliament which hath provided punishments proportionable to the quality of the offence." And we must certainly allow greater weight to this position "that it was no felony till James's statutes," deliberately laid down in his H. P. C., a work which he wrote to be printed and transcribed for the press in his lifetime, than to the hasty scriptum, that "at common law, witchcraft was punished with death as heresy by writ de heretico comburendo," in his methodical summary of the P. C. pa. 6; a work "not intended for the press, nor fitted for it and which he declared himself he had never read over since it was written." Preface. Unless we understand his meaning in that to be, that witchcraft could not be punished at common law as witchcraft, but as a heresy. In either sense, however, it is a denial of this pretended law of Alfred! Now all men of reading know that these pretended laws of homicide, concubinage, theft, retaliation, compulsory marriage, usury, bailment, and others which might have been cited from this Pseudograph, were never the laws of England, not even in Alfred's time; and of course, that it is a forgery. Yet, palpable as it must be to a lawyer, our judges have piously avoided lifting the veil under which it was shrouded. In truth, the alliance between church and state in England, has ever made their judges accomplices in the frauds of the clergy; and even bolder than they are; for instead of being contented with the surreptitious introduction of these four chapters of

Exodus, they have taken the whole leap, and declared at once that the whole Bible and Testament, in a lump, make a part of the common law of the land; the first judicial declaration of which was by this Sir Matthew Hale, And thus they incorporate into the English code, laws made for the Jews alone, and the precepts of the gospel, intended by their benevolent author as obligatory only in foro conscientiae; and they arm the whole with the coercions of municipal law. They do this, too, in a case where the question was, not at all, whether Christianity was a part of the law of England, but simply how far the ecclesiastical law was to be respected by the common law courts of England, in the special case of a right of presentment. Thus identifying Christianity with the ecclesiastical law of England.

Th: Jefferson[2]

Sampson, Discourse Upon The History Of The Law (1823) p. 6-13, 36-38

It is perhaps to be regretted, that the youth who dedicate themselves to the study of our legal constitutions, should be greeted on the threshold with phrases strange to the ears of freedom: that they cannot enter the vestibule without paying constrained devotion to idols which their fathers have levelled in the dust. The Commentaries of Sir William Blackstone are still the only clue whereby to tread the mazy labyrinth through which they have to pass; and the fascinating eloquence of that author, conceals a thousand sophistries, dangerous to the principles which every citizen of our free republic ought, and every professor of our laws is sworn, to maintain. Impressions thus stamped in young minds, are not quickly eradicated; and if once taught to believe that excellence is only to be found abroad, they will not care to seek for it at home. The Commentaries it is true, deserve our admiration, and we owe some gratitude to the author, who has rendered the complicated and perplexed code upon which our wiser, though yet imperfect system,

---

2. Compare the observation of James Wilson in his lectures delivered in 1790: "The common law, as now revised in America, bears, in its principles, and in many of its more minute particulars, a stronger and a fairer resemblance to the common law as it was improved under the Saxon, than to that law, as it was disfigured under the Norman government." 1 Works of James Wilson (Andrews, ed., 1896). p. 445. Cf. 4 Blackstone, Commentaries 420. Coke, like Blackstone, had accepted much if not all of the false learning on the antiquities of the English law. See Preface to 2 Rep. xiv et seq.

has been engrafted, accessible and tangible. What it was before he wrote, may be gathered from this, that the benefactor and founder whose intentions he was appointed to carry into effect, spent half a century in compiling, in the most condensed form, four and twenty elephantine folios, to serve as a brief index to the books which even when composed the lawyers' libraries, but are tenfold increased with us, and continue to increase in the like accumulated ratio. Various amendments, also, first suggested by Blackstone, have been carried into execution with us, and from the able manner in which he has laid bare many defects and anomalies of the English law, though its professed apologist, we may imagine how he would have written and taught, had it been his fortune to witness, as we do, the wonderful effects of true liberty upon human prosperity and happiness: how a people, without hierarchy, nobility, monarchy, distinction of condition, rank, or privilege, can govern themselves, and flourish beyond what hope or fancy could predict. Had he experienced this, and been endowed and appointed to eulogize our laws and constitutions, how ingeniously, how impressively, would he have contrasted them with the decayed and vicious institutions which he has so extolled. ...

The vices of the Norman jurisprudence, he exposes with no tender hand. The trial by battle, the forest laws, the curfew, the dependence of the nobles on the crown, and their tyranny over the commons: the feudal exactions and forfeitures; the 60,000 knights, bound, upon pain of confiscation, to quell all resistance; the enslaving of men's consciences, by sour ecclesiastics, who were themselves exempt from the secular power, and who had imported the whole farrago of superstitious novelties, engendered in the blindness and superstition of the times between the first mission of St. Augustine, the monk, and the Norman conquest. The administration of both the prayers of the church and the law of the land, in a foreign and unknown language; the frittering both law and divinity, into logical distinctions and metaphysical subtleties, till what ought to be a plain rule of action, became a science of the greatest intricacy; the interweaving, by the scholastic reformers, as he calls them, of their dialect and finesses into the body of the judicial polity, so that they could not be taken out without injury to the substance; and that, through statute after statute was made, to pare off the excrescences and restore the common law to (what he calls) its pristine vigor, the scars remained still deep and visible; how the liberality of modern courts was frequently obliged to have recourse to unaccountable fictions and circuities, to recover that equitable and substantial justice, which was long totally buried under the narrow rules and fanciful niceties of the metaphysical Norman jurisprudence. This picture, truly, is not seducing; and, had the author dealt the same measure to the jurisprudence that preceded that of the Normans, instead of the rhapsodies which he has uttered upon its antiquity, its purity and its pristine vigor, it would have been easy to conclude, that the further we were from the one or the other, the better for ourselves. The enthusiasm, however, which grave writers indulge upon this subject, makes it important for us to determine for ourselves, whether there be such a long lost treasure, or whether it be but a fabulous tradition, or fond dream. ...

Let us keep in mind, that we too must become ancestors and be judged by posterity. We cannot altogether foresee what may be said of us, but part we may imagine. These people, (it may be said,) long after they had set the great example of self-government upon principles of perfect equality, had reduced the practice of religion to its purest principles, executed mighty works, and acquired renown in arts and arms, had still one pagan idol to which they daily offered up much smoky incense. They called it by the mystical and cabilistic name of Common Law. A mysterious essence. Like the Dalai Lama, not to be seen or visited in open day; of most indefinite antiquity; sometimes in the decrepitude of age, and sometimes in the bloom of infancy, yet still the same that was, and was to be, and evermore to sit cross-legged and motionless upon its antique altar, for no use or purpose but to be praised and worshipped by ignorant and superstitious votaries. Its attributes were all negative, its properties all enigmatical and its name a metaphor. Taken in many senses, it had truly none. It was oral tradition opposed to written law; it was written law, but presuming the writing lost; it was that of whose origin there was no record or memory, but of which the evidence was both in books and records. It was opposed to statute law, to civil law, to ecclesiastical law, to military law, to maritime and mercantile law, to the law of nations; but most frequently contrasted with equity itself. It was common sense, but of an artificial kind, such as is not the sense of any common man; it was the perfection of reason, but that meant artificial reason. And as to its growth and progress, there is as little agreement among its panegyrists at this hour. Some tell us it was perfect in its inception, and became corrupt through time; others, that it had a barbarous origin, but gradually grew to perfection. Some, that it was anciently wise, and then grew foolish, and from thence has been in a state of convalescence. One speaks of it, in his day, as being the perfection of human reason; another shows it to have been, at that very period, under a dark and fearful inumbration. With false theories it must ever be so; for there is but one thing uniform, and that is, truth; one thing wise, and that is, simplicity.

We have seen the historical plan with which Sir William Blackstone sets out in his first volume; let us now see how he winds up in his fourth and last.

"I have endeavored", says he, "to delineate some rude outlines of a plan for the history of our laws and liberties, from their first rise and gradual progress among our British and Saxon ancestors, till their total eclipse at the Norman conquest from which they have gradually emerged. Our religious liberties were not established till the Reformation; our civil and political liberties were not thoroughly regained till the restoration of King Charles, nor fully and explicitly acknowledged till the era of the happy Revolution."

Here, then, we find the laws and liberties of our sky-blue British ancestors, of our ancestors the Picts and Scots, which being interpreted, means robbers and rovers, of Jutes and Angles, and Saxon princes, and Scandinavian sea kings, and such other barbarians as successively invaded, plundered, exterminated, or enslaved each other, in the long ages of night and darkness, eclipsed by a body still more opaque-the Norman jurisprudence; - a fearful and ominous occulation! Five centuries our civil and religious liberties remained in total darkness; in another half century a few digits of our political liberties had emerged, but the eclipse was not fairly ever for more than six hundred years! Who that had a choice, would remain in a planet or a sphere where such phenomena might be repeated? And, considering that the reformation was not owing to any virtue of the common law, but to the passions of a murderous king, seeking to destroy his wife, gratify his lust, and bastardize his lawful issue; that the restoration of King Charles was preceded by the decapitation of his father, and by long and bloody civil wars; and that the happy Revolution was the dethroning of a father by his son-in-law, and a bloody civil war, it must be allowed that the going off of this eclipse was little less portentous than its coming on. Yet mark how the eloquent commentator, after bringing us through six centuries of bondage and darkness, concludes: "Of this constitution, so wisely contrived, so strongly raised, and so highly finished, it is impossible to speak with that praise which is so justly and severely its due; but to sustain, to repair, to beautify this noble pile, is a charge entrusted principally to the nobility and such gentlemen as are delegated by their country to Parliament!" Now, let the pile be as beautiful and noble as it may, as we have no nobility, and our Legislative Representatives are to obey, and not to judge of our constitution, this may serve as one, among many reasons, why we should cease to deal in maxims that have no application to our affairs: why, being of full growth and stature, we should no longer go in leading strings but manfully take upon us the burthen of our own concerns; and why we should not do as the foolish fowls, who, after the period of incumbation is complete, and the law of their nature protrudes them from the egg, still carry the shell upon their backs. ...

Our law is justly dear to us - and why? because it is the law of a free people, and has freedom for its end; and under it we live both free and happy. When we go forth, it walks silent and unobtrusive by our side, covering us with its invisible shield from violence and wrong. Beneath our own roof, or by our own fireside, it makes home our castle. All ages, sexes, and conditions, share its protecting influence. It shadows with its wing the infant's cradle, and with its arm upholds the tottering steps of age. Do the smiles of the babe give gladness to the mother's heart, her joy is perfect in the consciousness that no tyrant's power dare snatch it from her arms; that when she consigns it to repose, its innocent slumbers are guarded by a nation's strength, and that it sleeps more free from danger than kings amidst their armed myrmidons. And when life's close draws near, we feel the cheering certitude, that those we love and leave shall possess the goods that we possessed, and enjoy the same security in which we lived and died. But that we are indebted for this, to Saxon, Scandinavian, Gaul, Greek, or Trojan, is what unsophisticated reason will not endure. We owe it to the growth of knowledge, and to the struggles of virtuous patriots, many of whom have bled and died for it: we owe it to fortunate occasion and favoring Providence. But even this part of our law, which thus secures our rights and liberties, is not untainted with pedantry, nor free from all absurdity. A sister State has already set on foot the experiment of a penal code, and committed its execution to the hands of one of its most capable citizens. Let us hail the happy augury, and prepare for a still nobler effort, which imperious necessity will force upon us, and which cannot and ought not to be long delayed.

If the experiment had never before been made of a judicial code, substituted in the place of antiquated legends, usages, and customs, we might fear to engage in an untried and hazardous undertaking. If no attempt had ever yet been made, to reduce to a body of written reason, the scattered fragments of a nation's laws or usages, or if, when such attempts were made, disorder and mischief had constantly ensued, we might take warning from such examples. If no wise jurists had ever recommended the digesting and new ordering of the law, there might be temerity in the proposal; but Hale and Bacon have not only approved, but offered their views and plans. And are not our own written statutes periodically revised; why not that part of our laws that rests upon less solid evidence? It has been the first glory of the greatest sovereigns, and the best policy of the wisest people. The most celebrated lawgivers have travelled into all regions, where early civilization had left its luminous traces, to gather the chosen flowers and fruits of every clime. If the fathers of our Revolution, at the peril of much more than life, of all the vengeance that offended power can visit on the unsuccessful patriot, dared to uproot the three great pillars of the Common Law, the monarchy, the hierarchy, and privileged orders, shall we stand in superstitious awe of unlaid spectres; shall we still be amused by nursery tales, and tremble at the thoughts of innovations upon institutions, which their admirers themselves assimilate to the practices of the Genie the Mexicans, and the children of the Sun; which have not half the imposing dignity of those of our ancestors, the red men of the five nations, as may be seen by any one, who will read the account of them by Mr. Colden, and compare it with the uncouth manners of the Saxon Heptarchists? It is true, at the same time, that the English reports contain, amidst a world of rubbish, rich treasures of experience, and that those of our own courts, contain materials of inestimable worth, and require little more than regulation and systematic order. This, with fixing and determining the principles on which they ought to depend, and settling, by positive exactments, all doubts that hang upon them, abolishing, forever, all forms that impede the march of justice, and firmly establishing those which are needful to its ends, and translating into plain and intelligible language, those borrowed, ill-penned statutes, of which every word gives rise to endless commentaries will complete the wished for object. Particular cases will not then be resorted to, instead of general law. The law will govern the decisions of judges, and not the decisions the law. Judgments will be legibus non exemplis. And it will not be necessary that, at least, one victim should be sacrificed to the making of every new rule, which, without such immolation, would have no existence.

Our jurisprudence then will be no longer intricate and thorny; nor will it need those fictions, which give it the air of occult magic, or those queer and awkward contrivances, which, by rendering it ridiculous, greatly diminish its dignity and efficacy. We shall be delivered from those odious volumes of special pleading, which cannot be used without degrading and lowering the tone of moral sentiments which destroy, by their verbose jargon, the very end of logical precision at which they profess to aim; where the suitor's story is told in twenty different ways, and answered in as many, and must be hunted for with fear and trembling, in printed books, (but, oh! such books!) and made conformable to precedents, composed before the party was in being, and which, in no one single instance, conform to the truth: insomuch, that he who dares to tell his case, according to the simple and honest truth, will, for that very reason, if for no other, fail in his suit. We shall be delivered too from those ever increasing swarms of foreign reports and treatises, which darken the very atmosphere, by their multitude, and generate their kind amongst us, and against which, we must either rise in arms, as certain oriental nations are said to do against the flight of locusts, or else abandon our own fair fields, and the fruits of our own genial soil, to their pernicious action.

Du Ponceau, Dissertation On The Jurisdiction Of The Courts Of The United States (1824)
p. 106-29.

The common law may be viewed under different aspects. Hence the variety of opinions that have been and are still maintained respecting it. There is an ancient and a modern, an English and an American common law, making in some respects a whole system, in some others distinct codes. Viewed altogether it presents a rude and mis-shapen mass, rudis indigestaque moles. Like certain works of art, its separate parts must be dwelt upon for some time before its beauties or its defects can be justly appreciated. It is not to be wondered at, therefore, if it has warm enthusiasts and violent enemies. It would require a consummate artist to delineate it as it ought to be; as I do not possess the requisite talent, I shall content myself with a plain statement of my ideas upon the subject.

I admire and I venerate the common law; not, indeed, the common law of the Saxons, Danes, and Normans, nor yet that which prevailed in England during the reigns of the Plantagenets, the Tudors, and the first Stuarts, but that which took its rise at the time of the great English revolution in the middle of the 17th century, to which the second revolution in 1688 gave shape and figure, which was greatly improved in England in the reigns of William, Anne, and the two first Georges, but which, during that last period and since, has received its greatest improvement and perfection in this country, where it shines with greater lustre than has ever illumined the island of Great Britain. In former times, its present defects excepted, it bore no resemblance to what it is now.

If the common law had remained in England as it was in the reigns of Elizabeth and James, it would not have deserved the high encomiums that have been justly bestowed upon it, nor would it have been worth being claimed by Americans as their birth right. England, it is true, had a kind of representative government, but so had almost every other country in Europe. As England had her parliament, other nations had their States, their Cortes, and their Diets, but all weighed down by the supreme authority of the sovereign, by virtue of the dispensing power, borrowed from the example of the emperors and popes, and strengthened by the famous maxim of the imperial law, Quod principi placuit, legis habet vigorem. The celebrated writ of habeas corpus was a part of the English code, but the civil law had also its title, De liberis exhibendis, and neither of them was adequate to the protection of the subject against the attempts of arbitrary power. Even trial by jury was no safeguard to the innocent, when powerful men thirsted for his life; the history of those ages offers no example of those independent juries who distinguished themselves in later times by the noble stand which they made against tyranny and oppression. All the firmness and eloquence of William Penn would have availed him but little in former reigns, and, indeed, when we consider the power which the Courts had and exercised even at this time, we cannot withhold our astonishment from the result of this prosecution. The trial of William Penn is one of the brightest examples of successful virtue and courage which History affords.

The civil jurisprudence was a complex system in which the Judges lost themselves in refinements and distinctions without end. The method of reasoning by induction, which Bacon recommended and exemplified, and which the celebrated Stewart and the philosophers of the Scotch school have so elegantly elucidated, was then unknown, or not understood; the logic of the schools prevailed, and every thing was discussed by syllogisms in _Barbara_ and _Baralipton_. A highly complicated system of _litis contestatio_, or, as we call it, _pleading_, overdriven to excess, excluded plain reason and common sense from the bar and from the bench, and a great majority of the cases brought before Courts of justice were decided upon some nice point of form. This artificial logic produced the same effects in England, which the Aristotelian Dialectics had produced in Greece and at Rome; sophistry became in vogue, and Seneca, if he had lived in those times, might have applied to the English lawyers and Judges what he says of the Roman sophists in his eighty-second letter to Lucilius. The plain rules of right and wrong were lost sight of in the midst of a sea of metaphysical subleties. The greatest talents were misapplied in endeavouring to find reason beyond the bounds of common sense. As theology had had her Thomas Aquinas, so jurisprudence had her Coke; both men of great mental powers, superior to most of their contemporaries, but not to their age. One man alone arose, whom no country and no age ever surpassed, who held up the torch of truth to a generation whose eyes were too weak to bear its resplendence. This was the great BACON:

> Qui genus humanum ingenio superavit & omneis
> Praestinxit; stellas exortus uti aethereus Sol.

I invite you, my dear fellow students, to read with the utmost attention and to compare with the writings of the other jurists of those times, his admirable treatise "_De justitia universali, seu de fontibus juris_". It is at the end of the eighth book of his celebrated work "_De dignitate & augmentis_ scientiarum". It is divided into ninety-seven aphorisms, every one of which ought to be studied and meditated on by every lawyer and statesman, and by every student who aspires to become either.

If we wish to have an idea of what the civil jurisprudence of England was towards the end of the wars of the two Roses (and if we except the bankrupt system, the acts of Elizabeth against fraudulent conveyances, and perhaps, a few more statutes, it was not much improved from that time to the period of the revolution) we have only to turn to the book of Chancellor Fortescue De laudibus legum Angliae, a work professedly written to prove the superiority of the law of England over all others, and particularly the civil law. Setting aside what he says of the representative form of government and of trial by jury, he adduces no instance of that superiority, but the illegitimacy of ante-nuptial children, the maxim, quod partus non sequitur ventrem, and the doctrine of feudal wardships, none of which would be considered at this day as giving an advantage to one system of law over another. Yet Chancellor Fortescue was a very learned man, and appears to have been equally skilled in the civil and in the common law.

The true era of the common law is the period which followed the great revolution of 1648, to the time of our own emancipation. It was then that it assumed that bold and majestic shape, those commanding features which have made it the pride of the nations who possess it, and the envy of those that do not. During that period the rights of man have been acknowledged and defined, and limits have been set to the sovereign authority. The prerogatives of the crown (I am speaking here of England) have been ascertained and restricted within proper bounds, the legislative, executive and judicial authorities have taken their respective stations and known the extent of their several powers; Judges have been rendered independent, and juries have been freed from ignoble shackles. The writ of habeas corpus has been made effectual, a fair and unexceptionable mode of trial has been provided for cases of high treason. The press has been freed from the unhallowed touch of State licensers, religious toleration has been established. The hand of arbitrary power has been paralysed, and man has been taught to walk erect and to feel the dignity of his nature. Civil jurisprudence has also been considerably improved, and is in a progressive state of further amendment.[1]

---

1. Sampson wrote a review of DuPonceau's volume in which he sought to meet the contention that the United States should gladly accept its inheritance of the English common law of the 18th century. See Sampson's Discourse (Pishey Thompson ed.

2. The Relationships of Historical Fact and of Current Policy

Williams v. Williams
New York Court of Appeals 1853, 8 N.Y. 525

The plaintiffs, residuary legatees under the will of Nathaniel Potter, late of Huntington, in Suffolk county, filed their bill in the late court of chancery to obtain the judgment of the court against the validity of two legacies; one in favor of the Presbyterian church and congregation of the village of Huntington, and the other in favor of trustees of a fund for the gratuitous education of certain poor children. ...

The [second] gift was in the following language: "With a desire to raise the standard of intellectual and moral improvement among the poor, I constitute and appoint Zophar B. Oakley, John Wood and Charles Sturges, of the village of Huntington, and their successors, to be appointed in the manner hereinafter authorized, a board of trustees of a fund, which I hereby constitute for the exclusive education of the children of the poor; and in order to maintain the number of the said trustees in perpetuity, I hereby authorize the surviving or remaining trustees, to fill up any vacancy as often as it shall occur by death, resignation or removal from the village, of any one of the said trustees by the choice of another, to be entered upon the minutes of their proceedings. I give and bequeath to the above named trustees and their successors, appointed as aforesaid, the sum of six thousand dollars, in trust, for a perpetual fund for the education of the children of the poor, who shall be educated in the academy in the village of Huntington; or in case of the destruction of the academy by fire or otherwise, then in the school house next west of the academy, until it shall be rebuilt. No part of this fund ever to be appropriated to the erection or repair of buildings. It is my will

---

1826).41 Judge Waties of South Carolina in State v. Lehre, as reported in 4 Hall's Amer. Law. J. 48, 51 (1816) expressed a distrust of the primitive law of England in terms to which DuPonceau would surely have agreed: "It is a great error, to look to the first sources of the common law, for the purity of its principles. The best and purest of these are of later accession. The sources of the common law (except such parts as were derived from the laws of Rome) were shallow and muddy. In its downward course, it has been continually filtered and enlarged, by passing through courts of increased wisdom and science; and it is owing to these continued filterings and accessions, that we see it as it now is, a clear, wholesome, deep and majestic stream."

that this fund shall be managed in manner following, to wit: the principal to be loaned on bond, secured by mortgage of lands of twice the value of the sum loaned, and one half of the interest annually accruing to be added to the principal, until the whole fund amounts to the sum of ten thousand dollars, then it is my will that the whole interest of the said fund shall be annually appropriated and expended in the education of the children of the poor, in the academy of the village of Huntington. ...

Denio, J., delivered the opinion of the court. ...

The bequest in favor of Zophar B. Oakley and others, by the general rules of law, would be defective and void as a conveyance in trust, for the want of a cestui que trust, in whom the equitable title could vest. The terms, "the children of the poor", refer to a class of persons to come into existence from time to time, not by inheritance, or any order of succession defined by law, but who are ascertained only by their answering the description mentioned. Such a line of succession not being known or recognized by the ordinary rules of law, cannot be made the channel for the perpetual transmission of the legal or beneficial ownership of property, unless by force of that peculiar system of law known in England under the name of the law of charitable uses. The direct donees of the fund, not being a corporation, cannot take and transmit the money in perpetual succession, according to the plan provided in the will; though, if the trust were valid, courts possessing the powers of the late court of chancery, would supply this defect, by appointments from time to time, as the exigencies of the case might require; and by directing conveyances when necessary; the rule being that the trust shall not fail for the want of a trustee (Lewin on Trusts, 574, et seq; and McGirr v. Aaron, 1 Penn. R. 49.) The objection that the bequest in its nature calls for, and that the provisions of the will assume to create a perpetuity, is urged against this as well as the other bequest; and it cannot now be met, as in the other case, by the answer that the legatee is a corporation authorized to hold in perpetuity. If the Revised Statutes apply to gifts for charitable purposes, this objection is fatal to the bequest.

According to the law of England, as understood at the time of the American Revolution, and as it exists at this day, conveyances, devises and bequests, for the support of charity or religion, though defective for the want of such a grantee or donee as the rules of law require in other cases, would (when not within the purview of the mortmain act) be supported and established in the court of chancery. This I understand to be entirely undisputed. (Case of Christ's College, Cambridge, 1 Wm. Blackstone's Rep. 90; Moggridge v. Thackwell, 7 Ves. 36.) In the numerous discussions upon charitable gifts which have taken place in the courts in the United States, it has been uniformly assumed that the English doctrine, to the effect above stated, was well settled in that country, and was constantly acted upon there, while this state was an English colony. ... So far as my researches have gone, I have found no case or dictum which would cast a doubt upon the validity of this bequest in the courts in England, at any time during the century preceding the nineteenth day of April, 1775. Having adopted the common law of England, so far as it was applicable to our circumstances, and conformable to our institutions, the law of charitable uses is in force here, unless, first, it was established by an English statute which has been abrogated; or, secondly, unless there is something in the system repugnant to our form of government; or, thirdly, unless it can be shown by the history of our colonial jurisprudence, that it was not in force here prior to the revolution;[1] or, lastly, unless it has been abolished by the Revised Statutes.[2] ...

In this class of cases it has always been strenuously

---

1. Article 35 of the New York Constitution of 1777 provided as follows: "such parts of the common law of England, and of the statute law of England and Great Britain, and of the acts of the legislature of the colony of New York, as together did form the law of the said colony on the nineteenth of April in the year of our Lord one thousand, seven hundred and seventy-five, shall be and continue the law of this State, subject to such alterations and provisions as the legislature of this State shall, from time to time, make concerning the same". In 1787 and 1788 Samuel Jones and Richard Varick submitted to the New York legislature a series of British and Colonial statutes which were considered suitable for continued operation in the state, and these statutes were enacted by the Legislature. In 1789 this group of statutes was published as the Jones and Varick Revision. In 1788 the Legislature adopted a statute providing that after the first of May, 1789, "none of the statutes of England or of Great Britain shall operate or be considered as laws of the State". N. Y. Laws 1788, c. 46, Sec. 37. Section 13 of Article Seven of the Constitution of 1821 provided that "such parts of the common law and of the acts of the legislature of the colony of New York as together did form the law of the said colony" on April 19, 1775, should continue as the law of the state. Concerning certain aspects of the Jones and Varick Revision, see Howe, "The Process of Outlawry in New York", (1938) 23 Cornell L. Q. 558.

2. By Title 2, Chapter 1, of Part II of the Revised Statutes of 1828 it was provided that express trusts might be created for four purposes only. Those did not explicitly include charitable purposes.

maintained by those who have resisted an alleged charitable donation, that the law of charitable uses originated in, and was created by, the statute of 43d Elizabeth, chapter 4; and that statute having been repealed in 1788, among the mass of English statutes which were not revised or re-enacted, it is plausibly if not conclusively argued from these premises, that the doctrine referred to has no existence in this state. (Stat. 1788, ch. 46, §37.) This argument is usually answered by a reference to cases adjudged in the English courts prior to the 43d of Elizabeth, showing that the peculiar law of charities was known and recognized before the statute, and to the opinion of distinguished judges in equity, who have affirmed that trusts and devises to charities, which would be void but for this doctrine, were sustained in England as well before as since the statute. These adjudications and dicta, have been so often cited and commented upon, that it is unnecessary to do more than, to refer to the books where they may be found collected. (McCarty v. The Orphan Asylum, 9 Cow. 437, per Jones, Chancellor; Executors of Burr v. Smith, 7 Vermont, 241; Vidal v. Girard's Executors, 2 Howard, 127; Story's Commentaries on Eq., ch. 31, §1136 et seq.) From a careful examination of these authorities, I have come to the conclusion that the law of charities was at an indefinite but early period in English judicial history, engrafted upon the common law: that its general maxims were derived from the civil law, as modified in the later periods of the Empire by the ecclesiastical element introduced with Christianity; and that the statute of charitable uses was not introductory of any new principles, but was only a new and less dilatory and expensive method of establishing charitable donations, which were understood to be valid by the laws antecedently in force. The provisions of the statute itself afford irresistible evidence to my mind, that such was its design and effect. ...

The research of another member of the court has brought to light an authentic piece of evidence to prove that the English doctrine of charities was considered in force in this colony prior to the revolution. In a manuscript volume of the orders of the court of chancery, under the colonial government, which is preserved in the office of the clerk of the court of appeals there is found a record of the proceedings in a case determined in that court, held before the governor and council, in the year 1708, which bears directly upon the question. The attorney general filed an information against William Cullin, to compel the payment of seventy five pounds, bequeathed by one Nicholas Cullin for the benefit of the poor of New York and Albany, which was directed to be distributed by certain trustees named in the will, - fifty pounds among the poor people in New York, and twenty-five pounds to those in Albany. The bill of complaint alleged that the defendant, under a power of attorney from the executor in England, had possessed himself of the testator's estate in the colony, "out of which, according to equity, he ought to have paid the legacies aforesaid, forasmuch as the said legacies were given to pious and charitable uses." "And as the preservation of charitable uses is of great public benefit, and great concern to our Lady the Queen, and the poor aforesaid, in consideration whereof," &c., the attorney general prayed that the defendant might answer, and be decreed to pay the amount, &c. The defendant answered, and the cause being heard upon the pleadings, a decree was made that he should pay to the trustees the amount of the legacies to be distributed to the poor according to the will of the testator. ...

The result of my examination of the case is, that the law of charitable uses as it existed in England at the time of the revolution, and the jurisdiction of the court of chancery over these subjects, became the law of this state on the adoption of the constitution of 1777; that the law has not been repealed, and that the existing courts of this state having equity jurisdiction are bound to administer that law. It follows that the respondents are not entitled to the relief asked for by their bill; that the decree of the supreme court should be reversed, and the respondent's bill be dismissed. No costs are to be allowed to either party as against the other.

Ruggles, Ch. J., Mason, Morse and Willard, JJ., concurred.

Gardiner, Johnson and Taggart, JJ., dissented

Judgment reversed, and complainant's bill dismissed.[3]

<u>Gallego's</u> <u>Executors</u> v. <u>Attorney</u> <u>General</u>
Court of Appeals of Virginia 1832, 3 Leigh 450

Carr, J. This case involves several very important questions, which I shall consider in the order they were discussed at the bar.

First, then, as to the charities. The attorney general filed an information and bill, to have them applied to the objects for which they were bequeathed, and to enforce the execution of the trusts in respect to them; and the chancellor considering them good and valid, decreed them. It was contended

---

3. The elaborate learning with which counsel dealt with the issue of this case in the middle years of the 19th century is well exemplified in the arguments of Horace Binney in <u>Vidal</u> v. <u>Girard's</u> <u>Executors</u>, <u>infra</u>, and which was published in 1844 as a pamphlet of 144 pages, and in the argument of William Curtis Noyes in <u>Beekman</u> v. <u>Bonson</u>, 23 NY, app. at p. 575 (1861).

in the argument that this decree was erroneous, because the devise and bequests were vague and indefinite, and therefore void. Let us examine this. The pecuniary legacies of 4000 dollars are, in effect, given to the roman catholic congregation, but for the building and support of a chapel; and the ground is given to trustees to permit the roman catholics to build a church on, for the use of themselves, and all persons of that religion, residing in Richmond. The bare statement seems sufficient to shew, that under the general rule, as applicable to ordinary legacies, these would be void. Who are the beneficiaries? the roman catholic congregation residing in Richmond. And who are they? Suppose you name them to-day: are those the same persons who constituted the congregation yesterday? or who will constitute it tomorrow? Will none remove from, or come to Richmond, to reside? Will none be converted to or from the roman catholic religion? For it is to the roman catholic congregation for the time being, that the legacies are given. This however is a point which need not be pressed; for it was not pretended, that they could be supported, as legacies to individual persons. But it was strongly insisted, that as charitable legacies they were entitled to the aid and protection of a court of equity; and the practice of the english courts, in similar cases, was referred to in proof of the position. The course of decisions in England was admitted on the other side, but it was contended, that they rested entirely on the statute of charitable uses, 43 _Eliz_. and did not at all belong to the ordinary powers of a court of equity. This was the only serious question. I certainly shall not discuss it; for I find this completely done to my hand, by chief justice Marshall, in the case of _The Baptist Association_ v. _Hart's ex'ors_. [4 Wheat. 1 (1819)]. The cases cited and examined, and the reasons given by him, prove, conclusively to my mind, that in England, charitable bequests, where no legal interest is vested, and which are too vague to be claimed by those for whom the beneficial interest was intended, cannot be established by a court of equity, either exercising its ordinary jurisdiction, or enforcing the prerogative of the king as _parens patriae_, independently of the statute 43 _Elizabeth_; and as that statute, if ever in force here, was repealed in 1792, I conclude that charitable bequests stand on the same footing with us, as all others, and will alike be sustained, or rejected, by courts of equity. I think the bill of the attorney general must be dismissed. ...

Tucker, P. It cannot be denied, that the principal question in this case, is one of the deepest interest and importance. It is worthy of the diligent research and great ability which have been devoted to the discussion of it, and will justify the enlarged view which may be found necessary in the decision: I mean the question as to the charities.

It is contended, on the one hand, that these several bequests are void and ineffectual, for uncertainty as to the beneficiaries who are to take under them: and, on the other, that they are good as bequests to charitable purposes, which the law will support, and which the court of chancery, upon the general principles of its equitable jurisdiction, will enforce at the instance of the attorney general.

There is no principle supposed to be more perfectly settled in reference to conveyances, than that every deed must have sufficient certainty as to the grantee who is to take under it. If there be such uncertainty as to the grantee, that it cannot be known distinctly who is to take by the grant, it is ipso facto void, for that uncertainty. This, it would seem to me, was not merely a principle of common law, but the dictate of common sense; and hence this defect is equally fatal, whoever may be the grantor; for it is a defect, not of power in him, but growing out of the utter impossibility of effectuating the grant, by reason of the undefined character of the grantee. The absurdity of such a grant cannot be better exposed, than by an attention to its operation in this very case, if it could be supposed to be valid. It is obvious that the bequest here, though for building a church, is a bequest to the roman catholic congregation in Richmond; and it is equally obvious that the testator designed no individual benefit to the members of that congregation: yet, as the society or congregation is not incorporated, it may well be asked, who are to be regarded as the beneficiaries entitled to the advantage of this bequest? Who can present himself as a claimant of this aid designed for the roman catholic religion? If membership of the congregation is to be the test of right, then the title will be in a continual state of flux. What belongs to A. today will by his removal from Richmond, or apostacy from the church, cease to be his tomorrow; whereas B. by removal to the city, or conversion to the church, might, by the converse of the principle, acquire tomorrow, a right which he has not today. Moreover, who would be the legally constituted triers of the fact of conversion or apostacy, whereby one man is to gain, or another is to lose, the interest in the property? Who, indeed, constitute the society? Whom does the law recognize, or the testator designate, as having the power to decide this essential question? Are all who have been baptised in the church, within the operation of the will? or those only who are received as partakers of its most solemn ordinances? These, and a multitude of like difficulties, present themselves to the notion of any grant or conveyance to a religious society, or to trustees for their use. For, in the eye of the law, the intervention of a trustee does not remove a single difficulty. There is not more necessity for a properly defined grantee, in a deed, than for a <u>cestui que trust</u> capable of taking, and so defined and pointed out, that the trust will not be void for uncertainty. In short, there cannot be a trust without a *cestui que trust*; and if it cannot be ascertained who the *cestui que trust* is, it is the same thing as if there were none.

These principles, it is confidently believed, are the general principles of the common law upon this subject. If there are exceptions to these principles, those exceptions may without doubt be shewn. A diligent search has led me to the conviction, that there was no case at common law, in which a bequest or a trust of this indefinite character, could be supported; and the learned counsel on both sides, have acknowledged, that they have been unable to discover any case anteriour to the statute 43 *Elizabeth*, in which the validity of such bequests or trusts has been distinctly recognized by the courts. It ought, therefore, perhaps, to suffice to rest the argument here; since if under the general principle the bequest would be void, it is incumbent upon those who claim to be protected by an exception, to establish that exception. Accordingly, it is contended, that gifts for charitable uses, furnish an exception: and when it is answered, that indefinite charities received their whole force and efficacy from the statute 43 *Elizabeth*, it is confidently replied that charities existed, and were recognized by law, anteriour to that statute; that the statute itself affords evidence of the fact; that it ought not to be regarded as an enabling statute, or as creative of an original power not before existing, but as affording new and additional facilities for the administration of charities of a particular description. It is indeed further contended, that, by the common law, the king, as *parens patriae*, had the general superintendence of all charities, which he exercised by the keeper of his conscience the lord chancellor; that, whenever it was necessary, the attorney general, at the relation of some informant, filed an information in the court of chancery, to have the charity established; that the exercise of this jurisdiction by that court, was by virtue of its general judicial functions, and of its extraordinary equitable jurisdiction, which has been transferred to the courts of equity in Virginia; that this authority, of the king, as *parens patriae*, is inherent in all governments, and therefore vested in this; that it embraces the protection of infants, lunatics and idiots, and the execution of charities, and that this inherent authority is devolved upon the courts of chancery in Virginia, the nature of whose jurisdiction and powers are peculiarly adapted to its judicious and faithful exercise. In this general, and, I own, very imperfect view of the outlines of the argument for the charities, it is sufficiently obvious that there are many grave and important questions involved. A hasty review of some of them, however, must suffice here. ...

Upon the whole, I am well satisfied, that the whole of the

doctrine of the english courts in reference to indefinite charities, springs from the statute of 43 Elizabeth, which is not in force in Virginia. Whether that statute ever was in force here, has been made a question in the cause. I incline to think it may have been, at least according to the construction which was given to it, and which considered it not as merely constituting a commission for inquiring into breaches of charitable trusts, but as greatly enlarging, if not as opening an entirely new filed for the exercise of benevolence. Though local in its provisions in some respects, it was general in its operation in others. If it ever was in force, however, it was repealed in the year 1792, in the general repeal of english statutes. That repeal was no rash or unadvised act. By an act of the session of 1789, ch. 9, followed by the act of 1790, ch. 20, a commission, consisting of six gentelmen of the most distinguished acquirements, was appointed, whose duty was, among other things, "to prepare bills upon the subject of such english statutes, if any there were, which were suited to this commonwealth, and had not been enacted in the form of Virginia laws." The committee of revisors proceeded to the discharge of the duty confided to it, and the result was the act of 1792, by which all english statutes then in force, were declared to be repealed; the legislature reciting that, at that session, it had specially enacted such of them as appeared worthy of adoption. The repeal of this statute must, therefore, be looked upon as an advised act of legislation, and in the same light as if it had been specially repealed by its title.

I have already taken occasion to remark, that, if there were any recognized charities of an indefinite character at common law, the broad language of the statute of Elizabeth comprehended them. In so far as it did comprehend them, it reduced only to the form of a statute, what was law before the statute; and our legislature, in repealing it, must be regarded as having repealed not its mere naked words, but the principle which they involved. Although, therefore, it should be admitted that certain indefinite charities were recognized at common law yet as the statute also comprehended them, and was itself repealed, the common law was repealed eodem flatu with the statute. In this aspect of the case, it is unnecessary to decide whether, if an english statute prior to the 4 James I. which repealed the common law, be itself repealed, the common law is thereby revived; notwithstanding the provision 1 Rev. Code, ch. 41 §2.[1] and notwithstanding the common law principle so repealed, was not at the settlement of the colony, nor ever since the law of Virginia.

---

1. "Whensoever one law which shall have repealed another shall

If I have been correct in this course of argument, there can be no pretense for the enforcing of the charities under this will of Mr. Gallego, as they were void at common law, and are not entitled to the protection of the statute of the 43 Elizabeth. Be this as it may, I must have argued to little purpose, and chief justice Marshall must for once have been also singularly unfortunate, if what has been said has not at least shewn, that it is a matter of very serious doubt, whether the power to enforce charities ever did exist independent of the statute. If it be a matter even of doubt, to what conclusion must we come? I am deliberately of opinion, that in that case, a just respect to the policy of the legislature, in relation to religious charities especially; a prudent caution on our part, in assuming doubtful powers; a due sense of the infinite difficulty and embarrassment, which must attend the search after the common law doctrines anteriour to the statute of Elizabeth; and a just view of the danger of reviving those obsolete doctrines; - must determine us to leave the subject to the wisdom of the legislature itself. A few remarks on these topics, will close this part of my opinion.

No man at all acquainted with the course of legislation in Virginia, can doubt, for a moment, the decided hostility of the legislative power to religious incorporations. Its jealousy of the possible interference of religious establishments in matters of government, if they were permitted to accumulate large possessions, as the church has been prone to do elsewhere, is doubtless at the bottom of this feeling. The legislature knows, as was remarked by the counsel, that wealth is power. Hence, the provision in the bill of rights; hence, the solemn protest of the act on the subject of religious freedom; hence, the repeal of the act incorporating the episcopal church and of that other act which invested the trustees appointed by religious societies with power to manage their property;[2] hence

---

itself be repealed, the former law shall not be revived without words to that effect."

2. The preamble of the Act of January 24, 1709 (Chap. IX of Dec. 1798 Session) provided as follows: "Whereas the constitution of the state of Virginia, hath pronounced the government of the King of England to have been totally dissolved by the revolution: hath substituted in place of the civil government so dissolved, a new civil government; and hath in the bill of rights, excepted from the powers given to the substituted government, the power of reviving any species of ecclesiastical or church government, in lieu of that so dissolved, by referring the subject of religion to conscience: And whereas

too, in part, the law for the sale of the glebe lands:[3] hence the tenacity with which applications for permission to take property in a corporate character (even the necessary ground for churches and graveyards) have been refused.[4] The legislature seems to have been fearful, that the grant of any privilege, however trivial, might serve but as an entering wedge to greater demands. Nor did this apprehension of the dangers of ecclesiastical establishments, spring up for the first time with our republican institutions. The history of ages had attested the proneness of such establishments to vast accumulations of property, and the statute book of England is loaded with statutes of mortmain, which were rendered necessary by the rapacity of the clergy, at least in the early periods of the church. So long as there have been church establishments, with power to receive and accumulate property, so long has the tendency to such accumulation been manifested distinctly. The history of the papal see, and of the religious houses under its

---

the several acts presently recited, do admit the church established under the regal government, to have continued so, subsequently to the constitution: have bestowed property on that church: have asserted a legislative right to establish any religious sect; and have incorporated religious sects, all of which is inconsistent with the principles of the constitution, and of religious freedom, and manifestly tends to the reestablishment of a national church:" The statute then proceeds to repeal a number of earlier acts of the legislature including an act concerning compulsory contributions to the maintenance of the ministry, and a statute incorporating the Protestant Episcopal Church. See Terrett v. Taylor, 9 Cranch 43 (1815).

3. Collection of Acts, 1802, Ch. cclxxix. This act was held to be invalid and in violation of natural law and the spirit and letter of the Federal Constitution in Terrett v. Taylor, supra, Note 2.

4. Important aspects of the early history of the Protestant Episcopal Church in Virginia were dealt with by the Court of Appeals in Turpin v. Locket, 6 Call 113 (1804) and in Selden v. Overseers, 11 Leigh 127 (1840). Henry St. George Tucker as Chancellor had written a long opinion in the second of these cases. That opinion is printed as an appendix to the second volume of his Commentaries on the Law of Virginia (1837). The two cases concerned the status of the Church of England after the American revolution, and touched incidentally upon the question of the effect of English ecclesiastical law on the canon law of the Protestant Episcopal Church. See Hoffman, The

dominion, is but a history of the cupidity of monks and devotees, veiled under the sacred garb of our holy religion. The vast domains of the clergy acquired by the catholic establishment of France, are known to us all. From this fatal source, among others, sprung a revolution, which deluged the fairest country in Europe in blood, and, in its horrible progress, spread desolation over adjoining states, and shook the civilized world to its centre. And in protestant England, fenced around as it has been with mortmain acts, we see a church establishment possessed of overgrown wealth and power, less devoted to the cause of genuine religion, than to pamper the luxury and indolence of the high dignitaries of the church. With these examples before our eyes, it is not wonderful that our statesmen have been cautious. They have been wise in their caution. The evil has not sprung from particular creeds, or the peculiarities of a confession of faith. It grows out of the very nature of the thing. The church, if made capable to take, while it is continually acquiring, from the liberality of the pious, or the fears of the timid, or the credulity of the ignorant, never can part with any thing; and thus, like those sustaining powers in mechanics, which retain whatever they once have gained, it advances with a step that never retrogrades. The natural cupidity of the human heart, is watched by the devotee himself, with the less jealousy in his pursuit after acquisitions for the church, since he believes it to be purified from the dress of selfishness, and sanctified by the holy object of his ambition. Thus it is, that however humble in its beginning, accumulation is the natural result of the power vested in any religious society to acquire property. The same influence which enables it to gain from the state its first insignificant privileges, will secure to it, from time to time, new though apparently inconsiderable accessions; until at last the power will be acquired which legislative jealousy has apprehended. Property, indeed, it need not ask of the legislature. The power to take and accumulate, alone, is necessary: all time has shewn, that the influence of feelings of devotion will do the rest. I speak of those feelings which exist without any undue influence from the pastor of the society. But, if we go farther, and suppose it possible, that those abuses which once have existed, may exist again, the progress will be more rapid, though not more certain. "What (says the accomplished sir Samuel Romilly) is the authority of a guardian, or even of a parent, compared with the power of religious impressions under the ascendancy of a spiritual adviser, with such an engine to work upon the passions; to inspire (as the

---

Law of the Church (1850) and White, American Church Law (1911).

object may be best promoted) despair or confidence; to alarm the conscience by the horrors of eternal misery, or support the drooping spirits, by unfolding the prospect of happiness which is never to end."

Such, I conceive, are the general grounds, upon which rests the legislative policy, in relation to the power of acquiring and holding property by religious societies. We have seen, too, a similar policy evinced as to charities generally, in striking at the root of them all, by the repeal of the statute of Elizabeth. It is not (to use the language of one of the counsel) that charity is banished from Virginia. Its benign and salutary influence may warm and animate every heart, and lead to a generous munificence, as the daily habit of our lives, without exposing the state to the evils which have always flowed from what are called conveyances in mortmain. It is not necessary here to detail those evils. But it is relevant to observe, that conveyances in mortmain to corporations, were not more calculated to produce a pernicious locking up of property, than charitable bequests of this indefinite character. A corporation may be dissolved, and the property may be again taken up into the general circulation, by reverting to the donor. But these charities never die. There is no means of putting an end to them in the lapse of ages; for according to this celebrated doctrine of cy pres, if the original object should fail, the attorney general and the master in chancery go to work to digest another scheme, cy pres the original intention of the donor. Such was the case with the charity to William & Mary college. Experience has justified these complaints, and accordingly about one hundred years ago, the parliament of G. Britain found itself compelled to pass the statute of 9 George 2. ... It is at this moment when the country whose laws we have adopted, has partly receded from the wretched policy of permitting the whole property of society to be swallowed up in the insatiable gulph of public charities, that we are called upon to reanimate the pernicious principle, which they now deprecate, and which with us has been sleeping in inaction, for nearly two centuries and an half. And this too, when we have put off the panoply of the mortmain acts, by the general repeal of them in 1792. It is said, indeed, that the

---

5. This statute (9 Geo. II, c. 36) forbade devises of land either to natural persons or to corporations for charitable uses. The statute remained in force until 1891 (54 & 55 Vict. c. 72). See 3 Scott, Trusts (1939) Sec. 362.3. Professor Scott emphasizes the fact that one of the important purposes of the statute was to prevent the taking of land out of commerce. Cf. Wright, J. in Levy v. Levy, infra, at p. 58.

legislature may pass the necessary laws for regulating these charitable gifts, and thus prevent the evils that might flow from the unlimited permission of them. But I think, under the existing doubts which hang around the subject, and after the lapse of centuries, during which the law respecting charities, if it ever existed here, has been silent and quiescent, it behoves the judiciary to leave to the legislature, the duty of waking it into life.

This leads me to remark, lastly, that the occasion calls for a prudent caution on the part of the judiciary in the assumption of this jurisdiction. We have already seen, that no cases are to be found, no guide is afforded, as to the course pursued by courts of equity in respect to charities anteriour to the statute of Elizabeth, if they ever took cognizance of them. But it is said that the king as parens patriae, from the earliest times had the power to superintend and enforce charities: that this power was exercised by him through the lord chancellor, the keeper of his conscience: that it was so exercised, not under a specially delegated authority, but by virtue of his general judicial functions or extraordinary jurisdiction in matters of equity: that this authority of the parens patriae is inherent in all governments, and therefore is this; and is devolved upon the court of chancery here, whose jurisdiction is general over all matters in chancery, and is peculiarly adapted to the judicious administration of the law of charities. I shall content myself with referring to the conclusive argument of the chief justice, 4 Wheat. 47. for the position, that the jurisdiction of the chancellor of England over charities, is a branch of the prerogative, and not a part of the ordinary powers of the chancery court, in the exercise of its equitable jurisdiction. The authorities to which he refers are entirely satisfactory upon the point. If this be so, it is sufficiently obvious, that the act which established the court of chancery in Virginia, cannot have transferred to that court this branch of the prerogative. The powers conferred by that act are judicial in their character, and not such as belonged to the chancellor of England, as the keeper of the conscience of the king, as representing his person, and administering, as his agent, his prerogatives and duties. Admitting then, as we well may, the superintending power of the crown, as parens patriae, over charities, and admitting that this power is inherent in the sovereignty, I will ask upon what ground shall we arrogate it to the judicial branch of the government? That there inheres in every sovereign power, a right and a duty to protect those who have no other protector, as infants and lunatics, cannot be denied: and that there is an inherent power also in the sovereign, to declare that vague and indefinite charities shall be administered, if, in its wisdom, it shall so decree, is equally undeniable. But it remains to be proved, that this power is judicial, and not legislative: it remains to be proved, that the flowers of royal prerogative, which have fallen from the crown of England, have devolved upon the chancellors here. In this government of prescribed and limited powers, no public functionary, no organ of the sovereign power, no department, can assume a power which is not to be found in the law or the constitution. They constitute the commission under which alone authority can be duly exercised. It was in this view, very truly said, that this branch of the royal prerogative, if it had not been withered by the repeal of the statute, would have devolved upon the legislature. That body is the parens patriae, under our system, and it would have remained for it to point out the organ which should administer its important function. My own opinion is, decidedly, that it does not now belong to the judiciary, even if it has existence any where in relation to charities. They must first be established, to call this guardian power into existence; and I have endeavored to shew, that there is nothing, now recognized by law in relation to charities, upon which it can operate; for definite charities are but trusts which equity will execute by virtue of its ordinary jurisdiction, and with which, even in England, the attorney general cannot interfere; and indefinite charities are not recognized by law, and cannot therefore be enforced, either with or without his aid.

The result of this view of the subject is, that the interlocutory order of the chancellor must be reversed, and the bill of the attorney general dismissed. ...

Vidal v. Girard's Executors

Supreme Court of the United States, 1844 - 2 How. 127

This case came up by appeal from the Circuit Court of the United States, sitting as a court of equity, for the eastern district of Pennsylvania.

The object of the bill filed in the court below was to set aside a part of the will of the late Stephen Girard, under the following circumstances:

Girard, a native of France, was born about the middle of the last century. Shortly before the declaration of independence he came to the United States, and before the peace of 1783 was a resident of the city of Philadelphia, where he died, in December, 1831, a widower and without issue. Besides some real estate of small value near Bordeaux, he was, at his death, the owner of real estate in this country which had cost him upwards of $1,700,000, and of personal property worth not less than $5,000,000. His nearest collateral relations were, a brother, one of the original complainants, a niece, the other complainant, who was the only issue of a deceased sister, and three nieces who were defendants, the daughters of a deceased brother.

The will of Mr. Girard, with two codicils, was proved at Philadelphia on 31st of December, 1831.

After sundry legacies and devises of real property to various persons and corporations, the will proceeds thus: -

"XX. And, whereas, I have been for a long time impressed with the importance of educating the poor, and of placing them, by the early cultivation of their minds and the development of their moral principles, above the many temptations, to which, through poverty and ignorance they are exposed; and I am particularly desirous to provide for such a number of poor male white orphan children, as can be trained in one institution, a better education, as well as a more comfortable maintenance, then they usually receive from the application of the public funds: ... Now, I do give, devise and bequeath all the residue and remainder of my real and personal estate of every sort and kind wheresoever situate, (the real estate in Pennsylvania charged aforesaid) unto 'the Mayor, Aldermen, and Citizens of Philadelphia,' their successors and assigns, in trust, to and for the several uses, intents, and purposes hereinafter mentioned and declared of and concerning the same. ...

"XXI. And so far as regards the residue of my personal estate, in trust, as to two millions of dollars, part thereof, to apply and expend so much of that sum as may be necessary, in erecting, as soon as practicably may be, in the centre of my square of ground between High and Chestnut streets, and Eleventh and Twelfth streets, in the city of Philadelphia, (which square of ground I hereby devote for the purposes hereinafter stated, and for no other, for ever), a permanent college, with suitable out-buildings, sufficiently spacious for the residence and accommodation of at least three hundred scholars, and the requisite teachers and other persons necessary in such an institution as I direct to be established, and in supplying the said college and out-buildings with decent and suitable furniture, as well as books and all things needful to carry into effect my general design. ...

"When the college and appurtenances shall have been constructed, and supplied with plain and suitable furniture and books, philosophical and experimental instruments and apparatus, and all other matters needful to carry my general design into execution, the income, issues, and profits of so much of the said sum of two millions of dollars as shall remain unexpended, shall be applied to maintain the said college according to my directions. ...

"As many poor white male orphans, between the ages of six and ten years, as the said income shall be adequate to maintain, shall be introduced into the college as soon as possible;

and from time to time as there may be vacancies, or as increased ability from income may warrant, others shall be introduced. ...

"I enjoin and require that no ecclesiastic, missionary, or minister of any sect whatsoever, shall ever hold or exercise any station or duty whatever in the said college; nor shall any such person ever be admitted for any purpose, or as a visitor, within the premises appropriated to the purposes of the said college.

"In making this restriction, I do not mean to cast any reflection upon any sect or person whatsoever; but, as there is such a multitude of sects, and such a diversity of opinion amongst them, I desire to keep the tender minds of the orphans, who are to derive advantage from this bequest, free from the excitement which clashing doctrines and sectarian controversy are so apt to produce; my desire is, that all the instructors and teachers in the college shall take pains to instil into the minds of the scholars the purest principles of morality, so that, on their entrance into active life, they may, from inclination and habit, evince benevolence towards their fellow-creatures, and a love of truth, sobriety, and industry, adopting at the same time such religious tenets as their matured reason may enable them to prefer. ..."

By an act, passed on the 4th of April, 1832, entitled "A supplement to the act entitled 'An act to enable the Mayor, Aldermen, and Citizens of Philadelphia, to carry into effect certain improvements, and to execute certain trusts,'" the Select and Common Council of the city of Philadelphia, are authorized to provide by ordinance, or otherwise, for the election or appointment of such officers or agents as they may deem essential to the due execution of the duties and trusts enjoined and created by the will of the late Stephen Girard. ...

Under the act of 1832, the corporation of Philadelphia passed an ordinance providing for the building of the college, and the board of trustees created thereby was organized in March, 1833. The building was commenced and carried on from year to year under the direction of the authorities appointed in this ordinance.

On the 28th April, 1841, the cause came on for hearing in the Circuit Court upon the bill, amended bill, and bill of revivor, answers, replications, depositions, and exhibits, when after argument of counsel, it was ordered, adjudged, and decreed, that the complainants' bill be dismissed with costs.

The complainants appealed to this court.

Story, J. ... We are, then, led directly to the consideration of the question which has been so elaborately argued at the bar, as to the validity of the trusts for the erection of the college, according to the requirements and regulations of the will of the testator. That the trusts are of an eleemosynary nature and charitable uses in a judicial sense, we entertain no doubt. Not only are charities for the maintenance and relief of the poor, sick, and impotent, charities in the sense of the common law, but also donations given for the establishment of colleges, schools and seminaries of learning, and especially such as are for the education of orphans and poor scholars.

The statute of the 43 of Elizabeth, ch. 4, has been adjudged by the Supreme Court of Pennsylvania not to be in force in that state. But then it has been solemnly and recently adjudged by the same court, in the case of Zimmerman v. Andres, 6 W. & S. 218, that "it is so considered rather on account of the inapplicability of its regulations as to the modes of proceeding, than in reference to its conservative provisions." "These have been in force here by common usage and constitutional recognition; and not only these, but the more extensive range of charitable uses which chancery supported before that statute and beyond it." Nor is this any new doctrine in that court; for it was formally promulgated in the case of Witman v. Lex, 17 Serg. & Rawle, 88, at a much earlier period (1827).

Several objections have been taken to the present bequest to extract it from the reach of these decisions. In the first place, that the corporation of the city is incapable by law of taking the donation for such trusts. This objection has been already sufficiently considered. In the next place, it is said that the beneficiaries who are to receive the benefit of the charity are too uncertain and indefinite to allow the bequest to have any legal effect, and hence the donation is void, and the property results to the heirs. And in support of this argument we are pressed by the argument that charities of such an indefinite nature are not good at the common law, (which is admitted on all sides to be the law of Pennsylvania, so far as it is applicable to its institutions and constitutional organization and civil rights and privileges) and hence the charity fails; and the decision of this court in the case of the trustees of the Philadelphia Baptist Association v. Hart's Executors, 4 Wheat. 1, is strongly relied on as fully in point. There are two circumstances which materially distinguish that case from the one now before the court. The first is, that that case arose under the law of Virginia, in which state the statute of 43 Elizabeth, ch. 4, had been expressly and entirely abolished by the legislature, so that no aid whatsoever could be derived from its provisions to sustain the bequest. The second is, that the donees (the trustees) were an unincorporated association, which had no legal capacity to take and hold the donation in succession for the purposes of the trust, and the beneficiaries also were uncertain and indefinite. Both circumstances, therefore, concurred; a donation to trustees incapable of taking, and beneficiaries uncertain and indefinite. The court upon that occasion, went into an elaborate examination of the doctrine of the common law on the subject of charities, antecedent to and independent of the statute of 43 Elizabeth, ch. 4, for that was still the common law of Virginia. Upon a thorough examination of all the authorities and all the lights, (certainly in no small degree shadowy, obscure, and flickering) the court came to the conclusion that, at the common law, no donation to charity could be enforced in chancery, where both of these circumstances, or rather, where both of these defects occurred. ...

But very strong additional light has been thrown upon this subject by the recent publications of the Commissioners on the public Records in England, which contain a very curious and interesting collection of the chancery records in the reign of Queen Elizabeth, and in the earlier reigns. Among these are found many cases in which the Court of Chancery entertained jurisdiction over charities long before the statute of 43 Elizabeth; and some fifty of these cases, extracted from the printed calendars, have been laid before us. They establish in the most satisfactory and conclusive manner that cases of charities, where there were trustees appointed for general and indefinite charities, as well as for specific charities, were familiarly known to, and acted upon, and enforced in the Court of Chancery. In some of these cases the charities were not only of an uncertain and indefinite nature, but, as far as we can gather from the imperfect statement in the printed records, they were also cases where there were either no trustees appointed, or the trustees were not competent to take. These records, therefore, do in a remarkable manner, confirm the opinions of Sir Joseph Jekyll, Lord Northington, Lord Chief Justice Wilmot, Lord Redesdale, and Lord Chancellor Sugden. Whatever doubts, therefore, might properly be entertained upon the subject when the case of the Trustees of the Philadelphia Baptist Association v. Hart's Executors, 4 Wheat. 1, was before this court (1819), those doubts are entirely removed by the late and more satisfactory sources of information to which we have alluded.

If, then, this be the true state of the common law on the subject of charities, it would, upon the general principle already suggested, be a part of the common law of Pennsylvania. It would be no answer to say, that if so it was dormant, and that no court possessing equity powers now exists, or has existed in Pennsylvania, capable of enforcing such trusts. The trusts would nevertheless be valid in point of law; and remedies may from time to time be applied by the legislature to supply the defects. It is no proof of the non-existence of equitable rights, that there exists no adequate legal remedy to enforce them. They may during the time slumber, but they are not dead.

But the very point of the positive existence of the law of charities in Pennsylvania, has been (as already stated) fully recognized and enforced in the state courts of Pennsylvania, as far as their remedial process would enable these courts to act. This is abundantly established in the cases cited at the bar, and especially by the case of Witman v. Lex, 17 Serg. & Rawle, 88, and that of Sarah Zane's will, before Mr. Justice Baldwin and Judge Hopkinson. In the former case, the court said "that it is immaterial whether the person to take be in esse or not, or whether the legatee were at the time of the bequest a corporation capable of taking or not, or how uncertain the objects may be, provided there be a discretionary power vested anywhere over the application of the testator's bounty to those objects; or whether their corporate designation be mistaken. If the intention sufficiently appears in the bequest, it would be valid". In the latter case certain bequests given by the will of Mrs. Zane to the Yearly Meeting of Friends in Philadelphia, an unincorporated association, for purposes of general and indefinite charity, were, as well as other bequests of a kindred nature, held to be good and valid; and were enforced accordingly. The case, then, according to our judgment, is completely closed in by the principles and authorities already mentioned, and is that of a valid charity in Pennsylvania, unless it is rendered void by the remaining objection which has been taken to it. ...

Upon the whole, it is the unanimous opinion of the court, that the decree of the Circuit Court of Pennsylvania dismissing the bill, ought to be affirmed, and it is accordingly affirmed with costs.

Levy et al. v. Levy et al.
New York Court of Appeals, 1865, 33 N.Y. 97

Wright, J. By his will, the bulk of the testator's estate is appropriated to the foundation and endowment of a school in the State of Virginia for educating, as practical farmers, children between the ages of twelve and sixteen years, of warrant officers of the United States navy; and contingently for educating the children between those ages of certain Hebrew congregations in the cities of New York, Philadelphia and Richmond, and children of like ages of all other Hebrew and Christian denominations. It is, in terms, provided that the institution must be kept within the revenue derived from the endowment, and under no circumstances should any part of the real or personal estate devised or bequeathed for the establishment and maintenance of the school be disposed of, but the rent and income of all such estate shall be held forever inviolate for the purpose of sustaining the institution. To effectuate the intent of the testator, his real property at Monticello, in the State of Virginia, together with the residue of his estate, real and personal, not by his will otherwise disposed of, is given in trust "to the people of the United States or such persons as congress shall appoint to receive it". Apprehensive, however, that the primary devisee and legatee might decline to receive the title and take the necessary steps to execute the trust, in such contingency the estate is given "to the people of the State of Virginia instead of the people of the United States," provided they, by act of their legislature, accept and carry out the trust as directed; and should the people of Virginia, by neglect of their legislature, decline to accept the bequest, then and, in that event, it is given "to the Portuguese Hebrew Congregation of the city of New York, whose synagogue is in Crosby street, New York, and the old Portuguese Hebrew Congregation, whose synagogue is in Cherry street, Philadelphia, and the Portuguese Hebrew Congregation of Richmond, Virginia," provided they procure the necessary legislation to entitle them to hold the estate, and to establish an agricultural school at Monticello for the fatherless children between certain ages, of those, and any other religious societies, Hebrew or Christian. The executors named in the will were directed to invest the funds arising from the estate thus set apart for the agricultural school in some safe paying stocks as fast as they accumulated, and hold "the whole of the property and estate devised and bequeathed for said school, and in their hands, until the proper steps have been taken by congress, or the legislature of Virginia, or the said Hebrew benevolent congregations, to receive the same and discharge the said executors". And the testator also gave, for the purposes of fuel and fencing for "said Monticello farm school," two hundred acres of wood land from his Washington farm in Virginia.

The validity of this disposition is the subject to be considered. If valid in law it is to be so declared, and effect given to the will of the testator. On the other hand, if it cannot be legally upheld, the property goes to his heirs and next of kin; the law giving the ownership to them, in case of an ineffectual devise or bequest.

It is insisted that the disposition is invalid, whether tested by common law rules, or by our statutes in respect to trusts of lands, or the alienability of real, and the absolute ownership of personal estate. It will be my object to inquire whether the ground be well or illy taken. ...

An attentive study of the legislative history of the State, will lead to the conclusion, that if the legislative power has not succeeded in extirpating the law of charitable uses as it prevailed in England in 1775, and establishing a State policy and system of her own in respect to indefinite uses, either for charity or religion, or any other purpose, the intention has plainly existed to do so. It is difficult, not to say impossible, to satisfactorily account for State legislation, beginning soon after the formation of the government, and continued down to the present time, upon any other theory. It may be conceded that the Record Commission of 1827 shows that prior to the statute of 43 Elizabeth, the English chancery, by bill and information in the name of the attorney-general, and it may be by intervention of an amicus curiae, exercised a loose and imperfect jurisdiction in enforcing trusts for certain "charitable purposes". Be it so, and let it be conceded that prior to the statute, what were afterwards denominated in the law of the British realm "charities" and "charitable uses" were sometimes enforced in chancery, independently of the royal prerogative, still it remains true, as matter of fact, that when the first State Constitution was adopted, and in the infancy of the State government, it was the universal opinion in England and this country, among lawyers and jurists, that all charitable trusts depended for their validity, and had their origin in the statute of Elizabeth. (Collinson's Case, Hob., 136; 2 Black. Com., 374; Attorney-General v. Bowyer, 3 Vesey, 713; Baptist Association v. Hart's Ex'rs. 4 Wheaton, 1, and cases cited; Yates v. Yates, 9 Barb., 324; Owens v. The Missionary Society, 4 Kern., 380; Dashiel v. The Attorney-General, 6 Har. and John., 292; Story's Eq. Jur., §§ 1142, 1143, 1144.) Although the Record Commission may be said to have thrown a doubt over the question, it is easy to see how this understanding arose. Take Collinson's Case, decided 17 years after the statute of Elizabeth was enacted. It was an indefinite trust, viz., to repair highways. The report says: "We resolved clearly that it was within the relief of the statute of 43d Elizabeth, for though the devise was utterly void, yet it was within the words [of the statute] "limited and appointed to charitable uses;" and in that case it was held that the proceeding to maintain a charitable use, under the statute, might be by bill in equity, although the statute itself speaks only of a commission. And so it has been held ever since. The case of the Baptist Association v. Hart's Ex'rs. (4 Wheaton, 1), was among the first, if not the first one of charitable use ever decided in this country; and in that it was expressly determined that charitable uses had their origin only in the statute of Elizabeth. In this Judge Story concurred with Chief Justice Marshall, though the former, after the Record Commission, inclined to a different opinion. It is to be supposed that the legislature, in 1788, had the same understanding of the law on this subject as the judges and lawyers of that time. In 1788 the legislature, by a general enactment, repealed the statute of Elizabeth, the statute against superstitious uses, and the mortmain acts, including that of 9

Geo. II (2 Greenleaf's Laws, 136, 137), thus sweeping away all the great and distinctive land-marks of the British system. Why this repeal of a statute defining what in English law and jurisprudence were charities, unless the legislature intended by the act, and supposed that would be the effect of the repeal, to abrogate the entire system of indefinite trusts which were understood to be supported by that statute alone. It will hardly do to say that the form was gone through of repealing the statute, because it had become practically obsolete in England as a mode of proceeding, and was unfitted to our political and social condition. As a mode of proceeding it may not then have been often resorted to, but as a legislative definition of charities, within the authority of chancery, and capable of being established and regulated thereby, it was then, and always had been appealed to. And then, the repeal of the statute of mortmain still more significantly evidenced an intention to abrogate the system. The mortmain act of 9th Geo. II, was enacted to restrain the sweeping influence of the statute of Elizabeth. This latter statute had been, for many ages, construed with the most surprising liberality, and under it charities, so called before the statute so termed them, grew up until the system in some of its aspects had come to be considered an enormous public evil. It is not to be assumed that the sagacious men, who shaped the legislation of the State in the early periods of the government, would designedly leave in force a system of indefinite trusts, without any restraint whatever, when the experience of the mother country had dhown that a system of public or charitable uses, without legislative definition and restraint, was not to be tolerated. It cannot be reasonably inferred, from a repeal of the great mortmain act, so called, an intention, in a State without an established religion, to give full scope to the founding and endowing of all sorts of religious establishments, and putting in mortmain, for their benefit, the property of the State. From the beginning, the founders of the government clearly indicated a different policy from that which prevailed in England, in respect to trusts for charitable and religious purposes. That policy was not to introduce any system of public charities, except through the medium of corporate bodies. Accordingly, before and cotemporaneously with the repeal of the statute of Elizabeth and the mortmain acts, in addition to the general law enacted in 1784,[1] for the incorporation of religious societies,

---

1. Chancellor Kent considered that religious societies incorporated under this statute were "ecclesiastical" rather than "lay" corporations. 2 Commentaries 274. The New York Court of Appeals, however, in Robertson v. Bullions, 11 N. Y. 243

special acts for incorporating such societies were passed. There were likewise other acts passed, creating or authorizing corporations for various religious and charitable purposes; in all of which are to be found limitations upon the amount of revenue to be held by such societies, and the purposes to which it was to be applied, and requirements for furnishing inventories, and reporting any excess of property to the legislature. This legislation indicates that the policy, from the foundation of the government, was to confine within certain and narrow limits the accumulation of property perpetually appropriated, even to charitable and religious objects. The absolute repeal of the mortmain act, and of the statute of Elizabeth, was wholly inconsistent with the policy thus indicated, except only upon the ground of the understanding and conviction of the early legislators of the State, that charitable uses, if they had ever existed in the colony or State, were not founded upon or sustained, except by force of the latter statute; for the effect of that repeal, with other British statutes, was to remove (it being true that indefinite charities were maintainable in chancery without its aid) every restraint upon individual action, and put it in the power of any man to appropriate his whole property in perpetuity to the purposes of charity or religion, making the Court of Chancery his trustee. How idle was it for the legislature to limit so carefully the powers they bestowed upon religious and charitable corporations. How useless for benevolent individuals to seek acts of incorporation, or to trust private trustees, when the Court of Chancery, upon the mere will of the founder of the charitable gift, would insure its perpetuity and superintend its administration. To my mind, the evidence is irresistible that the legislature of 1788 intended to abrogate (and that that was the effect of their action) the whole law of charitable uses, as understood and enforced in England. If the law of charity, as it existed at the time of the revolution, was based upon the statute of Elizabeth, then the repeal of that statute directly worked its abrogation. If the system of indefinite charities could be enforced in equity, prior to the statute, it was, nevertheless, the intention by such repeal to abrogate the system; and the effect of the repeal, and the cotemporaneous initiation of a different policy, and one better suited to our social and political condition, was to effectually displace it.

(1854) held that incorporated religious societies are not ecclesiastical corporations in the sense of the English law but belong to the class of civil corporations. Do any significant consequences result from the acceptance of one or the other of these classifications?

It is unnecessary, however, to rely exclusively upon the early legislative action referred to in determining whether the State has not, by her laws and policy, rejected the British system, and substituted and established a different one, resting upon legal principles and enactments. Throughout our whole existence, learning, piety and benevolence - every truly charitable object - has been amply encouraged; the result being attained through the medium of corporate bodies created by the legislative power; their charters specifying the precise nature of the charity intended to be sanctioned and encouraged, and in all cases limiting the amount of property to be enjoyed, and otherwise, such as the public welfare was supposed to require. This policy, as has been suggested, was inaugurated contemporaneously with the repeal of the British statutes, and, it may be now added, has been followed up to the present time. An allusion to the course of legislation will show it. In 1784, a general law was passed for the incorporation of religious societies, with limitations upon the amount of estate they could acquire and enjoy, and requiring the trustees to render stated accounts to the chancellor. (1 Greenl. Laws, 71.) The statute was substantially reenacted in 1813, and is now in force. In April, 1796, a general act was passed for the incorporation of public libraries, with capacity to take and hold real and personal estate, but limiting the amount; and in 1853 the policy of this act was revived upon a broader basis (Laws of 1852 ch. 395). As early as 1790, the legislature began incorporating, by special charters, societies for a great variety of religious, literary, scientific, benevolent and charitable objects, and this policy has been continued and enlarged by chartering, from time to time, hundreds of such societies, but in all cases with limitations and restrictions upon the amount of property to be enjoyed. (See Index to Laws of New York, by Gillett, 1859, pp. 171-178, 373-397). At more recent periods general laws were enacted affording a still broader field for charities, and at the same time keeping the subject under legislative control and supervision. In 1840, an act was passed authorizing gifts of real and personal estate to any incorporated college or other literary incorporated institution in trust, to found observatories, professorships and scholarships, and for any other specific purposes comprehended in the general objects authorized by their respective charters; also, providing for gifts to the corporation of any city or village in the State, to be held in trust for any purpose of education, or the diffusion of knowledge, or for the relief of distress, or for parks, gardens and other means of recreation and health; and, also, providing for like gifts to commissioners of common schools and trustees of school districts for educational objects. (Laws of 1840, ch. 318) In 1846, this act was amended so as to allow income to be accumulated, in certain cases, to a specified extent. (Laws of 1846, ch. 74) In 1848 a general act was passed, entitled "An act for the incorporation of benevolent, charitable, scientific and missionary societies. By this act corporations might be formed by filing a certificate for any of the purposes comprehended in the title; but a majority of the signers must be citizens, and the certificate must be approved, in writing, by a justice of the Supreme Court. Corporations thus formed might take, by purchase, devise or bequest, gifts of real estate to the value of $50,000 and of personal, to the value of $75,000. It was provided that no person leaving a wife, child or parent, could, by will, give more than one-fourth of his estate to these institutions and no gift by will should be valid unless the will be executed at least two months before the death of the testator. Such corporations were made subject to visitation by the justices of the Supreme Court or persons appointed by that court and the trustees were required to make annually a public statement of their affairs. (Laws of 1848, ch. 319) In 1849, the statute was amended so as to provide that all existing benevolent, charitable, scientific and missionary societies might reincorporate themselves under the act (Laws of 1849, ch. 273) and in 1862, the benefits of the act were extended so as to authorize the incorporation of historical and literary societies. (Laws 1862, ch. 273) In 1860 another statute was passed restricting bequests to corporations and associations, in certain cases, to one-half of the testator's estate after payment of his debts. (Laws of 1860, ch.360)

Thus, it is seen, that a policy and system, in its essential characteristics, differing from the British system, and absolutely inconsistent with the supposition that uses for public or indefinite objects could be created and sustained without legislative sanction or restraint, began with the formation of the State government, and has been persistently continued throughout all its existence. The British statutes which supported, regulated and restrained indefinite uses, deemed religious and charitable, were abrogated, and at a time when the opinion was universal that they depended wholly upon those statutes. The intention was to abolish the system, and not, as has been suggested elsewhere, to free it from all restrictions and control. We cannot suppose for a moment, that by the repeal it was intended (and that would have been the consequence unless the system itself fell to the ground) that indefinite trusts of every kind and description, however irrational or absurd, superstitious, fanatical or idolatrous, should become valid in equity; and that the property of the donors, without limit or restraint, might, at their own will, and for the promotion of such objects, be withdrawn and put in mortmain, away from the general uses of society. It was important, at that early time, that the property of the State should not be largely withdrawn from general and devoted to special uses, even though the latter was the founding and endowment of institutions of useful learning and true piety, or setting on foot truly benevolent schemes for ameliorating social evils; but it was of the last importance then, and ever will be to the public interests and welfare, that such property should not be withdrawn from circulation, and the general uses of society, for promoting objects, public in their nature, unsanctioned by the legislative power, and which may be in themselves the offspring of the grossest ignorance, caprice and folly. In all civilized societies, the dissemination of learning and the encouragement of religion and charity, are objects to justly engage the attention of the law making power; but it is a necessity of the subject that trusts or uses of property for the promotion of those objects, which affect the public interests and well being, should be created under legislative sanction and control. Who shall say what is useful learning, what is benevolence, and what is charity, unless it be the legislature? The judiciary can apply no tests. Who, also, shall determine the amount of property that may, consistently with the public interests and welfare, be withdrawn from circulation and the general uses of society, and put in mortmain for the special use, but the legislature? It is obvious that with us no object can be charitable, in a legal sense, that has not the legislative sanction. We have no general statute defining what is charity in law. The gift, in the present case, is said to be to a charitable use, and so it is in a general sense and within the statute of Elizabeth. But we have no statute declaring what is legal charity. Here, necessarily, in respect to trusts or uses, public in their nature, where the legislature has not defined or sanctioned the particular object to be promoted, it can only be dealt with by the courts as a question of uses without a beneficiary - uncertain trusts without any equitable donees known to the law. ...

In my judgment, then, that peculiar system of English jurisprudence for supporting, regulating and enforcing public or charitable uses, void by the rules of law, is not the law of the State. If it ever was the law here, it has been abrogated or displaced by a system and policy of our own in respect to such uses. A system which allows the purpose of the charitable donation to be declared by the donor, and who, at his own will, may appropriate his property to any extent to promote such purpose, making the Court of Chancery his trustee and superintendent in administering the gift, has now no existence among us. I am aware that the question has been heretofore incidentally examined in this court, with great power and ability, and an opposite conclusion reached by a majority of its members. I should be as reluctant as any one to reexamine a question and disturb a decision deliberately made here; but when a decision is so far-reaching in its consequences, and the court itself has not since adhered to the principle decided, it is not unbecoming or improper to reexamine the subject at large. Indeed we should do so, if there is a probability that we erred, and when a particular class of trusts are to be sustained, if at all, by violating the rules of the common law, and the express statutes of the State. That there has not been an adherence by the court to the original decision, and the case of Williams v. Williams (4 Seld., 525) followed, is easily shown. In Williams v. Williams, it was held that the Englist law of charitable uses was the law of the State; and, consequently, a bequest to three persons (naming them), and to their successors, to be appointed by themselves, in trust, "for the education of the children of the poor, who shall be educated in the academy in the village of Huntington," was upheld. Neither the trustees or beneficiaries were legally ascertainable, nor had the trustees legal capacity to take and administer the gifts; but that made no difference if the Englist doctrine of charitable uses was to be applied to the bequest. Three years afterwards, in Owens v. The Missionary Society of the M. E. Church (4 Kern., 380), the question again arose. The bequest there was of all the residue of the testator's estate "to the Methodist General Missionary Society, appointed to preach the gospel to the poor. L. C." This was treated as a bequest in trust for charitable purposes; one in general void, as well in equity as in law, and only to be sustained by the doctrine of the English courts of equity in regard to charitable trusts. Judge Selden again examined the question of the introduction of the law of charity, as understood and enforced in England, into the law of the State, and reached directly the opposite conclusion to that enunciated in Williams v. Williams, holding that the law was not in force here, and as a consequence, the bequest could not be sustained. In this opinion a majority of the court concurred. Of course, there could be no pretense, that where there was uncertainty both in the trustee or administrator of the fund, and in the beneficiaries, there was a valid trust, or one ever sustained without the aid of the peculiar jurisdiction exercised by the English courts of equity over "charities". The judge, in his opinion, undertook to distinguish the case from Williams v. Williams on the ground that in the latter there were competent trustees to take the fund in the first instance, whereas in the former there were none. This was, as matter of fact, a misapprehension. There was not, in either case, any ascertained or competent trustee. In one, the bequest was in trust to a voluntary association of persons; in the other, to three persons named by the donor, and both equally unknown to the law. It was this misapprehended distinction, together with an erroneous dictum to be noticed, that probably induced the remark in Beekman v. Bonsor (23 N. Y. 298), that the diversity of views of the judges delivering opinions in the two cases on the question of the introduction of the law of charitable uses into the law of the State, led to no practical difference in conclusion or result. So, also, the judge appeared to think, that independent of the peculiar system of jurisprudence in regard to indefinite charitable gifts, if, in a devise or bequest, a trustee was named for a definite purpose, a legal and valid trust would be created, although there was no ascertained beneficiary. This was a mere dictum, not countenanced by his associates, and running counter to all authority prior to the case, although approved since by a former judge of this court. The proposition is false in both its branches. A trustee is not necessary to the validity of a trust, for a use being well declared, the law will find a trustee wherever it finds the legal estate; and the definiteness of the purpose of the trust does not make a good use if there is no definite object or beneficiary. The value of the decision consists in a deliberate protest, at the earliest time, against the conclusion so ably enunciated in Williams v. Williams, that the law of charitable uses, existing in England at the period of the American revolution, is now the law of the State. In Marshall v. Downing (23 N. Y. 366), a gift to the American Home Missionary Society, an unincorporated association, was held void. It was admitted that the society was a charitable organization and the gift for charitable or pious purposes. It is true, that there was no competent trustee, or any ascertained beneficiary to take the gift, and in whom theequitable interest could vest, and hence, a valid common law trust was not created; but if the "law of charity" prevailed here, there would have been no difficulty in upholding and effectuating the bequest. Indeed, in Vermont, a gift to the same religious association was sustained as a charitable use. (Burr's Ex'rs. v. Smith, 7 Vermont, 247) It was immaterial under the peculiar system, whether the donor had designated the trustee or administrator of the fund or not; or whether such trustee, if pointed out, was legally competent to take. Chancery would be the donor's trustee, and execute his will. So that, in at least two cases in this court, since that of Williams v. Williams, has the principle that decided one of the bequests in the latter case to be valid, been disaffirmed.

It being true, then, that trusts for "charity" have no peculiar privilege in the courts of this State over other trusts of property, it follows that the one attempted to be created by the testator, in the present case, is invalid for want of a cestui que trust in whom the equitable title to the estate, devised and bequeathed, could vest. There is no ascertained beneficiary in whose favor performance may be enforced. The gift is for the use and benefit of an indefinite object. ...

Seaburn's Executor v. Seaburn
Court of Appeals of Virginia, 1859 - 15 Gratt. 423

Moncure, J. delivered the opinion of the court. After stating the case, he proceeded as follows:

In the case of Gallego's Ex'ors. v. The Attorney General, 3 Leigh 450, it was held, that the English doctrine in regard to indefinite charities does not prevail in this state; that it was founded, mainly if not entirely, upon the statute 43 Elizabeth, called the statute of charitable uses, which, if it ever was in force here, was repealed by the general repealing act of 1792; that charitable bequests stand on the same footing with us as all other bequests, and will alike be sustained or rejected by courts of equity; and that a bequest of money to be applied to the erection and support of a Roman Catholic chapel in Richmond, and a devise of a lot in said city to trustees in fee, upon trust to permit all and every person belonging to the Roman Catholic church, as members thereof, or professing that religion, and residing in Richmond at the time of the testator's death, to build a church on the lot for the use of themselves and all others of that religion who may hereafter reside in said city; were uncertain as to the beneficiaries and therefore void.

The authority of that case, although some of the positions therein held have been impugned elsewhere, and although the case of The Baptist Association v. Hart's ex'ors, 4 Wheat. 1, therein much relied on, has been supposed to have been founded on a misconception of the English law (Vidal, &c. v. Girard's ex'ors, 2 How. U. S. R. 127), is still firm and stable in this state, except so far as it may have been since modified by statute; having been repeatedly recognized by this court, and expressly affirmed in the recent case of Brooke, &c. v. Shacklett, 13 Gratt. 301.

The devises and bequests contained in the will and codicil of Nathaniel Seaburn, now under consideration, would undoubtedly be void for uncertainty, according to the principles of the case of Gallego's ex'ors v. The Attorney General, before cited. Indeed, this seems not to have been controverted in the argument.

But the counsel for the appellant contended that they are valid devises and bequests, under the Code, ch. 77, §8, p. 362, which is as follows:

"Every conveyance, devise or dedication shall be valid, which since the first day of January 1777 has been made, and every conveyance shall be valid which hereafter shall be made, of land for the use or benefit of any religious congregation as a place for public worship or as a burial place or a residence for a minister; and the land shall be held for such use or benefit and for such purpose and not otherwise."

On the other hand, the counsel for the appellees contended that the said devises and bequests are not valid, under the Code: First, because it does not authorize a devise, but only a conveyance, as contradistinguished from a devise; and, if it does, secondly, because it only authorizes land to be given for the purposes therein mentioned, and not money, though it be directed to be applied to the erection of a church on land held for such purposes; and much less, if it be directed to be applied to other purposes, as for instance, the support of a minister; and thirdly, because the devises and bequests in question are void for uncertainty, even though they might otherwise be valid under the Code. ... [The court then gave its reasons for accepting as valid the argument of counsel for the appellees.]

It was argued by the counsel for the appellant, that the jealousy of church encroachments which existed at the time of the revolution, and for a period thereafter, has long since ceased, that the policy of the state on this subject has undergone a material change, and that we ought now to apply a liberal, and not a strict, rule of construction to a statute authorizing the acquisition of property for religious uses.

It is not perceived that there has been any such material change of the policy of the state as the counsel supposed. No trace of any such change is to be found in the first amended constitution of 1830, nor in the case of Gallego's ex'ors. v. The Attorney General, decided so late as 1832. The opinion of President Tucker in that case, in which the policy of the state is so ably vindicated, has since met with general, if not universal approbation; which seems to be still unabated. In the amended constitution of 1851 it was, for the first time, provided, as a part of our organic law, that "the general assembly shall not grant a charter of incorporation to any church or religious denomination; but (it is added) may secure the title to church property to an extent to be limited by law." Art.iv, §32. The object of this section was to prevent the accumulation of church property, and to authorize the title only to so much as might be deemed necessary, and consisted with the welfare of the state, to be secured by law to religious uses. The latter part of the section seems to have been designed to sanction and authorize such legislation as had already been adopted to secure the title to church property to a limited extent, and which had been introduced by the act of February 3, 1842, entitled "an act concerning conveyances or devises of places of public worship". Sess. Acts, p. 60, ch. 102. The revisors recommended, in their report to the legislature, a more liberal provision on this subject than had been made by that act. They proposed not only that conveyances and devises (as provided by that act) but parol dedications of land should be authorized for the use or benefit of any religious congregation as a place for public worship, or for religious or other instruction, or as a burial place or a residence for a minister. And also that books, furniture or other things, "given or acquired for the benefit of such congregation, to be used on the said land in the ceremonies of public worship, or in religious or other instruction, or at the residence of their minister", should "stand vested in the trustees having the legal title to the land, to be held by them as the land is held, for the benefit of the congregation." Rep. Rev. p. 412 §§ 8 and 10. And they suggested, that if the legislature should prefer it, the 10th section could readily be made more extensive in its operation, by substituting therefor the following: "When any money or other thing shall be given by will or otherwise acquired by or for, any congregation having for its use or benefit such land as before mentioned, the same shall stand vested", &c. Id. note. The legislature not only did not adopt this suggestion, but amended the 8th and 10th sections proposed by the revisors, not only by limiting the mode of future acquisition of land to a conveyance as before stated, but by striking out the words in italics above written, to wit, the words "or for religious or other instruction", in the 8th, and the words "or other things", and the words "or in religious or other instruction", in the 10th section: Thus embodying in the Code a more limited scheme of church endowment than had been provided by the act of 1842.

Under these circumstances, we think we ought not to apply a very liberal rule of construction to the statute, but to construe it according to the general rule. And so construing it, we think the conveyance by which it authorizes a transfer of land to be made for the use of a religious congregation, does not embrace a devise. We think the legislature plainly intended to alter the pre-existing law, by not authorizing such a transfer of land by devise in future. Whether the reason for the alteration was good or not, is a question which it belongs not to this court to decide. We may readily conceive what that reason was. And we must admit that the danger of an excessive and inordinate alienation of property to religious uses, so jealously guarded against by the policy of our law and the provision of our constitution before referred to, would be greatly increased by authorizing such alienation to be made by will, as well as by deed. And especially so, if the argument of the appellant's counsel be correct, that a religious congregation may take and hold (by its trustees) not only land, but money, and that without limit, provided it be to be laid out in land of the quantity and for the purposes prescribed by the statute, or in the erection of a church or a residence for a minister thereon, or in repairing the same, or in the purchase of books or furniture to be used on said land in the ceremonies of public worship, or at the residence of the minister. The legislature may well have supposed that there was no necessity for encountering this increased danger; and that authority in future to convey land for the purposes aforesaid by deed only, would fully answer the object in view.

If a devise of land for the purposes aforesaid would be void, a fortiori a bequest of money, though to be laid out in building a church on land held for such purposes, and much more, to be invested in stock for the support of a minister to preach in said church, would be void. The statute says nothing about money; and the only argument used to sustain the validity of the bequest in this case, is that the money is equivalent to land, according to the doctrine of equitable conversion.

It may be proper to state that nothing in this opinion is intended to be in conflict with the opinion delivered in the case of Brooke, &c. v. Shacklett. The conveyance in that case was by deed, executed before the adoption of the present Code; and it was not intended to express any opinion upon the question, whether a devise for the use of a religious congregation is authorized by the Code, which did not arise in the case.

For the foregoing reasons, and without expressing any opinion upon the other objections taken to the validity of the devises and bequests in question by the counsel for the appellees, the court is of opinion that the said devises and bequests are void and that the decree of the Circuit court be therefore affirmed.

Allen, P. concurred in the results of the opinion of the court, but not in the reasons given for it. He thought that the term "conveyance" was sufficient to embrace devises. But he was of opinion that according to Gallego's ex'ors. v. The Attorney General, 3 Leigh 450, affirmed as that case was by The Literary Fund v. Dawson, 10 Leigh 147, and Brooke v. Shacklett, 13 Gratt. 301, the bequest was void: and that this case was not embraced in the statute. Decree Affirmed.[1]

---

1. The ultimate rejection of the holding in the Gallego case occurred in Fitzgerald v. Doggett's Executors, 155 Va. 112 (1930), in which the legislation and judicial decisions of the intervening years were fully reviewed. See, 17 Va. L. Rev. 302 (1931).

CHAPTER TWO

THE CONDITION OF THE ENGLISH LAW, 1550 - 1650

1. The Competing Jurisdictions in English Law, 1550-1650

a. Ecclesiastical Courts

Prior to the Reformation the Ecclesiastical Courts in England, responsible to the Pope, had administered the canon law through forms substantially similar to those used throughout Catholic Europe. The substantive rules of law administered by those courts were also largely the same as those established by Rome. The existence of these tribunals and this body of law within the realm, yet not responsible to the King, inevitably led to friction and hostility.

With the Reformation it would in theory have been possible to confer upon the courts of common law the jurisdiction which had perviously been exercised by the Ecclesiastical Courts, and thus to secularize the whole of the law of England. That solution, however, seems not to have been seriously considered, and instead the system of ecclesiastical law, both in matters of substance and procedure, was retained, with the King claiming and effectively exercising that supreme authority in spiritual matters which had previously been the Pope's.

The passages from Coke's report of Caudrey's Case which follow show the lawyer's explanation of the consequences of the Reformation and indicate something of the nature of the problem of divided jurisdiction between ecclesiastical and temporal courts. Needless to say these problems were lively realities at the time of the settlement of the American colonies.

<u>Caudrey's Case</u>, King's Bench, 1591. 5 Rep. 1a

"And therefore by the ancient laws of this realm, this kingdom of England is an absolute empire and monarchy consisting of one head, which is the King, and of a body politic, compact and compounded of many, and almost infinite several, and yet well agreeing members: all which the law divideth into two several parts, that is to say, 'the clergy and the laity', both of them, next and immediately under God, subject and obedient to the head: also the kingly head of this politic body is instituted and furnished with plenary and entire power, prerogative and jurisdiction to render justice and right to every part and member of this body, of what estate, degree, or calling soever in all causes ecclesiastical or temporal, otherwise he should not be a head of the whole body. And as in temporal causes, the King, by the mouth of the Judges in his courts of Justice doth judge and determine the same by the temporal laws of England: so in causes ecclesiastical and spiritual, as namely, blasphemy, apostasy from Christianity, heresies, schisms, ordering admissions, institutions of clerks, celebration of divine service, rights of matrimony, divorces, general bastardy, subtraction and right of tithes, oblations, obventious, dilapidations, reparation of churches, probates of testaments, administrations and accounts upon the same, simony, incests, fornications, adulteries, solicitation of chastity, pensions, procurations, appeals in ecclesiastical causes, commutation of penance, and others (the conusance whereof belongs not to the common laws of England) the same are to be determined and decided by ecclesiastical Judges, according to the King's ecclesiastical laws of this realm: for as the Romans fetching divers laws from Athens, yet being approved and allowed by the estate there, called them notwithstanding Jus civile Romanoraum: and as the Normans borrowing all or most of their laws from England, yet baptized them by the name of the laws or customs of Normandy: so albeit the Kings of England derived their ecclesiastical laws from others, yet so many as were proved, approved and allowed here, by and with a general consent, are aptly and rightly called, the King's Ecclesiastical Laws of England, which whosoever shall deny, he denieth that the King hath full and plenary power to deliver justice in all causes to all his subjects, or to punish all crimes and offences within his kingdom: for that as before it appeareth the deciding of matters so many, and of so great importance, are not within the conusance of the common laws, and consequently that the King is no complete monarch, nor head, of the whole and entire body of the realm. ...

"If it be demanded what canons, constitutions, ordinances and synodals provincial, are still in force within this realm; I answer that it is resolved and enacted by authority of Parliament, that such as have been allowed by general consent and custom within the realm, and are not contrariant or repugnant to the laws, statutes, and customs of the realm, nor to the damage or hurt of the King's prerogative royal, are still in force within this realm, as the King's ecclesiastical laws of the same.[1] Now, as consent and custom hath allowed these canons,

---

1. The problem of the status in the English ecclesiastical courts of the Papal codes and decretals presented problems strikingly analagous to that of the status in the courts of the American colonies of English statutes and English common law. On the problem of the canon law in English ecclesiastical courts, see Maitland, Roman Canon Law in the Church of England

so no doubt by general consent of the whole realm, any of the same may be corrected, enlarged, explained or abrogated. For example, there is a decree that all clerks that have received any manner of orders, greater or smaller, should be exempt, pro causis criminalibus before the temporal judges. This decree never had any force within England: first, for that it was never approved and allowed of by general consent within the realm: secondly, it was against the laws of the realm, as it doth appear by infinite precedents; thirdly, it was against the prerogative and sovereignty of the King that any subject within this realm should not be subject to the laws of this realm.

"Now albeit the proceedings and process in the ecclesiastical courts be in the name of the Bishops, &c. it followeth not therefore, that either the court is not the King's, or the law whereby they proceed is not the King's law: for taking one example for many, every leet or view of frank-pledge holden by a subject, is kept in the lord's name, and yet it is the King's court, and all the proceedings therein are directed by the King's laws, and many subjects in England have and hold courts of record, and other courts, and yet all their proceedings be according to the King's laws and customs of the realm. ..."

If Coke in Caudrey's Case went far to justify the royal supremacy over spiritual matters, he did not hesitate on other

---

(1898), 81-87. See also, The Canon Law of the Church of England (1947), 35-38. Similarly, the problem of the continuing force of the accepted principles of the canon law after the Reformation suggests problems very much like those which the American courts dealt with after the American revolution. The Act for the Submission of the Clergy (25 H. viii, c. 19), which is the statute to which Coke referred, provided for the continued force, pending codification of the canon law, of such canons, constitutions, and ordinances of the earlier canon law as were "not contrarient or repugnant to the law, statutes and customs of this realm". Concerning the interpretation of this statute, see The Canon Law of the Church of England, supra, Chap. 4.

The charter of incorporation issued to the Governor and Company of the Massachusetts Bay in New England in 1629 contained a provision characteristic of those inserted in the charters of other colonizing organizations by which the power to enact laws for colonial government was qualified by the limitation that such laws and statutes as the Colonists might enact should not be "contrary or repugnant to the Laws and statutes of our Realm of England". Is there any likelihood that the provision in the Act for the Submission of the Clergy was remembered by the Crown lawyers when they inserted the analalater occasions to assert that that supremacy like other royal prerogatives was itself subject to the control of the common law. He thus brought to the surface an issue of enormous importance - whether the life of men in society was ultimately to be subjected to the control of one body of law and one set of courts or whether the mediaeval inheritance of competing laws and competing tribunals was to be preserved.

Nicholas Fuller's Case
12 Rep. 41 (1607)

"In the great case of Nicholas Fuller of Gray's Inn, these points were resolved upon conference had with all the Justices and Barons of the Exchequer.

"1. That no consultation can be granted out of the term, for this, that it is an award of the court, and is final, and cannot be granted by all the Judges out of the term, nor by any of them within the term out of court; and the name of the writ, viz, a writ of consultation, imports this, that the court upon consultation amongst them ought to award it.

"2. That the construction of the statute I Eliz. cap. I[1] and of the letters patent of high commission in ecclesiastical causes founded upon the said act, belongs to the Judges of the common law; for although that the causes, the cognizance of which belongs to them, are merely spiritual, and the law by which they proceed is merely spiritual, yet their authority and power is given to them by act of Parliament, and letters patent the construction of which belongs to temporal Judges; and for the this, the consultation which was granted is with this restraint. _Quatenus non agat de authoritate et validitate literarum patentium pro causis ecclesiasticis vobis vel aliquibus vestrum direct' aut de expositione_ & _interpretatione statuti de anno primo nuper Reginae_, &c. In the same manner as if the King hath a _benefice donative_ by letters patent, although that the function and office of the incumbent be spiritual; yet inasmuch as he comes to it merely by letters patent of the King, he shall not be visitable, nor deprivable by any ecclesiastical authority but by the Chancellor of the King, or by Commissioners under the great seal.

"3. It was resolved when there is any question concerning

---

gous provision in the colonial charters of incorporation?

1. In this statute is found one of the principal sources of the authority of the High Commission. See, Usher, _The Rise and Fall of the High Commission_ (1913), Chapter 1.

what power or jurisdiction belongs to ecclesiastical Judges, in any particular case, the determination of this belongs to the Judges of the common law, in what cases they have cognizance, and in what not; for if the ecclesiastical Judges shall have the determination of what things they shall have cognizance; and that all that appertains to their jurisdiction, which they shall allow to themselves, they will make no difficulty ampliare jurisdictionem suam: ... And so, the determination of a thing, whether it belongs to Court-Christian, doth appertain to the Judges of the common law, and the Judges of the common law have power to grant a prohibition. And all this appears in our books, that the Judges of the common law shall determine in what cases the ecclesiastical Judges have power to punish any pro laesione fidei, 2 H 4. fol. 10 II H. 4.88 22 Ed. 4 20. So of the bounds of parishes in 5 H 5.10 39 Ed. 3.23. So it belongs to the Judges of the common law, to decide who ought to certify excommunication, and to reject the certificate, when the Ordinary of Commissary is party, 5 Ed. 3.8.8 Ed. 3. 69, 70 18 Ed. 3. 58. 12 Ed. 4.9H 7.I 10 H 7.9. For this it was resolved clearly, that if any person slander the authority or power of the High Commissioners, this is to be punished before the Judges of the common law, for that the determination of their authority and power which is given to them by the statute, and the letters patent of the King belongs to them, and not to Court-Christian: and for this, that the many articles objected against Fuller concerning the slander of their authority and power, was solely determinable and punishable before the Judges of the common law. One other restraint was added in the consultation: et quatenus non agat de aliquibus scandalis, contemptibus, seu alis rebus, quae ad communem legem aut per statuta regni nostri Angl'sunt punienda & determinanda.

"4. It was resolved, that if a Counsellor at law, in his argument shall scandal the King or his government, temporal or ecclesiastical, this is a misdemeanor and contempt to the court; for this he is to be indicted, fined, and imprisoned, and not in Court-Christian: but if he publish any heresy, schism, or erroneous opinion in religion, he may be for this convened before the ecclesiastical Judges, and there corrected according to the ecclesiastical law; for the rule is, quod non est juri consonum quod quis pro aliis quae in curiis nostris acta sunt, quorum cognitio ad nos pertinet, trabatur in placitum in Curia Christianitatis, as it appears in the Book of Entries, fol. 448. So that the intent is, there heresy, schism, or such enormous opinions in religion, do not appertain to the cognizance of temporal courts; ...

"5. It was resolved, that when any libel in Ecclesiastical Court contains many articles, if any of them do not belong to the cognizance of Court-Christian, a prohibition may be generally granted; and upon motion made, consultation may be made as to things which do belong to the spiritual jurisdiction; for the writ of consultation with a quoad, is frequent and usual, but a prohibition with a quoad, is rara avis in terra nigroque simillima cygno. And for these reasons it was resolved by all, that the prohibition in the case at bar was well granted, which in truth was granted by Fenner and Croke Justices, in the time of the vacation."[2]

b. Other Tribunals Competing with the Courts of Common Law

A glance at the Table of Contents of Coke's Fourth Institute is sufficient to indicate the complexities of the English judicial system at the opening of the 17th century. Though Coke found "admirable benefit, beauty, and delectable variety"[3] in these complexities, others considered them less entrancing. The details of the complication need not concern us for they probably had a relatively small effect on the legal institutions of the American colonies. The general fact of the complication, however, was of great importance in the Colonies for it meant that the tradition of "the common law" was only one of the legal traditions of the Colonists, and that the first settlers, except as they were conscious allies either of Coke, the predominant champion of common law, or of the King, its chief antagonist, were largely unaware that one portion of their legal inheritance had greater significance than other portions. In Coke on Littleton, 11b, it is stated that "There be divers lawes within the realme of England. As first Lex coronae, the law of the crowne. 2. Lex et consueto parliamenti. Ista lex est ab omnibus quaerenda, a multis ignorata, a paucis cognita. 3. Lex naturae, the law of nature. 4. Communis Lex Angliae, the common law of England, sometimes called lex terrae .... 5. Statute law. Lawes established by authority of parliament. 6. Consuetudines, Customes reasonable. 7. Jus belli the law of armes, war, and chivalrie .... 8. Ecclesiastical or canon law in courts in certain cases. 9. Civil law in certaine cases not onely in courts ecclesiastical, but in the

---

2. Among the most dramatic of constitutional legends is that concerning Coke's conversation with the King after the decision in Nicholas Fuller's Case. That the account of the meeting in 12 Rep. 63b may make Coke's conduct somewhat more heroic than it was in fact is suggested in a learned article by Usher in 18 English Historical Review 664.

3. Proeme to Fourth Institute

courts of the constable and marshall, and of the admiraltie, in which court of the admiraltie is observed _la ley Olyron_ ... 10. _Lex forestae_, forest law. 11. The law of marque or reprisal. 12. _Lex mercatoria_, merchant, etc. 13. The lawes and customes of the isle of Jersey, Guernsey and Man. 14. The law and privilege of the Stannaries. 15. The lawes of the east west, and middle Marches, which are now abrogated."

A persuasive if somewhat overstated case in favor of the proposition that the legal inheritance which was important to the New England Colonists was not that of the common law but of the law administered in the English local courts has been made by Professor Goebel in his article _King's Law and Local Custom in Seventeenth Century New England_ (1931) 31 Columbia Law Rev. 416. See also the introduction to Goebel and Naughton, _Law Enforcement in Colonial New York_ (1944).

No writing more brilliantly suggests the critical condition of the English law in the middle of the 16th century than Maitland's "English Law and the Renaissance", 1 _Select Essays in Anglo-American Legal History_ 168. No student of legal history should long postpone its reading.

2. The English Movement for Law Reform

The desire for fundamental changes in the law of England found many different forms of expression in the century from 1550 - 1650. Maitland's essay (_supra_) deals with one phase of that desire. By the beginning of the 17th century, when the triumph of civil law was no longer a substantial danger, proposals for reform took on a more precise form. Some of those proposals were made by lawyers of the very highest distinction, others, and the more frequent, were made by radical Puritan reformers. The essay of Francis Bacon indicates the extent to which even one who was close to the King recognized the necessity of drastic change; the recommendations of Matthew Hale were made in the same spirit but in very different circumstances. The proposals in _Examen Legem Angliae_ are far more radical but are perhaps more representative of the Puritanism which played such an important part in the contemporaneous establishment of government in the New England Colonies.

The best description of the movements for law reform in the Commonwealth period are in Inderwick, _The Interregnum_ (1891) p. 180-284, and in Robinson, _Anticipations under the Commonwealth of Changes in the Law_, 1 Select Essays 467.

Francis Bacon: A Proposition for Compiling and Amendment of our Laws (1616)
13 Bacon's Works (Spedding ed.) 61-71

1. Sir, I shall not fall into either of those two extremes, concerning the laws of England; they commend themselves best to them that understand them; and your Majesty's chief Justice of your bench hath in his writings magnified them not without cause: certainly they are wise, they are just, and moderate laws; they give to God, they give to Caesar, they give to the subjects that which appertaineth. It is true, they are as mixt as our language, compounded of British, Roman, Saxon, Danish, Norman customs. And as our language is so much the richer, so the laws are the more complete: neither does this attribute less to them, than those that would have them to have stood out the same in all mutations; for no tree is so good first set, as by transplanting.

2. As for the second extreme, I have nothing to do with it, by way of taxing the laws. I speak only by way of perfecting them, which is easiest in the best things; so that which is far amiss, hardly receiveth amendment; but that which hath already, to that more may be given. Besides, what I shall propound is not to the matter of the laws, but to the manner of their registry, expression and tradition; so that it giveth them rather light than any new nature. This being so, for the dignity of the work I know scarcely where to find the like; for surely that scale, and those degrees of sovereign honour, are true and rightly marshalled. First, the founders of estates; then the law-givers; then the deliverers and saviours after long calamities; then the fathers of their countries, which are just and prudent princes; and lastly, conquerors, which honour is not to be received amongst the rest, except it be, where there is an addition of more country and territory to a better government, than that was of the conquered. Of these, in my judgment, your Majesty may with more truth than flattery be intitled to the first, because of your uniting of Britain and planting Ireland, both which savour of the founder. That which I now propound to you, may adopt you also into the second: law-givers have been called _principes perpetui_; because, as bishop Gardiner said in a bad sense, that he would be bishop an hundred years after his death, in respect of the long leases he made: so law-givers are still Kings and Rulers after their decease, in their laws. But this work, shining so in itself, needs no taper. For the safety and convenience thereof, it is good to consider, and to answer those objections or scruples which may arise, or be made against this work.[1]

---

1. With this willingness of Bacon to improve the condition of

Obj. 1 That it is a thing needless; and that the law, as it now is, is in good estate, comparable to any foreign law; and that it is not possible for the wit of man, in respect of the frailty thereof, to provide against the incertainties and evasions, or omissions of law.

Resp. For the comparison with foreign laws, it is in vain to speak of it; for men will never agree about it. Our lawyers will maintain for our municipal laws; civilians, scholars, travellers, will be of the other opinion.

But certain it is, that our laws, as they now stand, are subject to great incertainties, and variety of opinion, delays and evasions: whereof ensueth,

1. That the multiplicity and length of suits is great.
2. That the contentious person is armed, and the honest subject wearied and oppressed.
3. That the judge is more absolute; who, in doubtful cases, hath a greater stroke and liberty.
4. That the chancery courts are more filled, the remedy of law being often obscure and doubtful.
5. That the ignorant lawyer shroudeth his ignorance of law, in that, doubts are so frequent and many.
6. That mens assurances of their lands and estates by patents, deeds, wills are often subject to question, and hollow; and many the like inconveniences.

It is a good rule and direction (for that all laws, secundum magis & minus, do participate of incertainties) that followeth: Mark, whether the doubts that arise are only in cases of ordinary experience, or which happen not every day: If in the first only, impute it to frailty of man's foresight, that cannot reach by law to all cases; but if in the latter, be assured there is a fault in the law. Of this I say no more, but that (to give every man his due) had it not been for Sir Edward Coke's reports (which, though they may have errors, and some peremptory and extrajudicial resolutions, more than are warranted; yet they contain infinite good decisions, and rulings over of cases,) the law by this time had been almost like a ship without ballast; that the cases of modern experience, are fled from those that are adjudged and ruled in former time. But the necessity of this Work is yet greater in the statute law. For the first, there are a number of ensnaring penal laws which lie upon the subject; and if in bad times they should be awaked, and put in execution, would grind them to powder.[2]

English law should be compared the reluctance of Coke to admit the desirability of change. See 4 <u>Rep</u>., Preface.

2. Even Coke recognized that there was need for the reform of

There is a learned civilian that expoundeth the curse of the prophet; Pluet super eos laqueos, of multitude of penal laws; which are worse than showers of hail or tempest upon cattle, for they fall upon men.

There are some penal laws fit to be retained, but their penalty is too great; and it is ever a rule, that any over-great penalty (besides the acerbity of it) deads the execution of the law.

There is a farther inconvenience of penal laws, obsolete, and out of use; for that it brings a gangrene, neglect, and habit of disobedience upon other wholesome laws, that are fit to be continued in practice and execution; so that our laws endure the torment of Mezentius:

The living die in the arms of the dead.

Lastly, there is such an accumulation of statutes concerning one matter, and they so cross and intricate, as the certainty of law is lost in the heap; as your Majesty had experience last day upon the point, Whether the incendiary of Newmarket should have the benefit of his clergy.[3]

Obj. 1. That it is a great innovation; and innovations are dangerous beyond foresight.

Resp. All purgings and medicines, either in the civil or natural body, are innovations: so as that argument is a common place against all noble reformations. But the truth is, that this work ought not to be termed or held for any innovation in the suspected sense. For those are the innovations which are quarrelled and spoken against, that concern the consciences, estates, and fortunes of particular persons: but this of general ordinance pricketh not particulars, but passeth sine strepitu. Besides, it is on the favourable part; for it easeth, it presseth not: and lastly, it is rather matter of order and explanation, than of alteration. Neither is this without president in former governments. ...

Obj. 3. In this purging of the course of the common laws

---

criminal law, particularly for that portion of the criminal law which was based on statutes. See 4 Rep., Preface. In 1614 Bacon had introduced a bill in Parliament providing for the appointment of commissioners "to review the state of penal laws, to the end that such as are obsolete and snaring may be repealed, and such as are fit to continue and concern one matter may be reduced respectively into one clear form of law. See 13 Spedding, supra, p. 60.

3. Probably Powlter's Case, 11 Rep. 29a (1611).

and statutes, much good may be taken away.

Resp. In all purging, some good humours may pass away; but that is largely recompensed, by lightening the body of much bad.

Obj. 4. Labour were better bestowed, in bringing the common laws of England to a text law, or customs well registered, with received and approved grounds and maxims, and acts and resolutions judicial from time to time duly entered and reported, be the better form of declaring and authorizing laws. It was the principal reason or oracle of Lycurgus, that none of his laws should be written; customs are laws written in living tables; and some traditions the church doth not disauthorize. In all sciences they are the soundest, that keep close to particulars; and sure I am, there are more doubts that rise upon our statutes, which are a text law, than upon the common law, which is no text law. But, howsoever that question be determined, I dare not advise to call the law into a new mould. The work which I propound tendeth to pruning and grafting the law, and not to plow up and planting it again; for such a remove I should hold indeed for a perilous innovation.

Obj. 5. It will turn the judges, counsellors of law, and students of law to school again, and make them to seek what they shall hold and advise for law; and it will impose a new charge upon all lawyers, to furnish themselves with new books of law.

Resp. For the former of those, touching the new labour, it is true it would follow, if the law were new moulded into a text law; for then men must be new to begin, and that is one of the reasons for which I disallow that course.

But in the way that I shall now propound, the entire body and substance of law shall remain, only discharged of idle and unprofitable, or hurtful matter; and illustrated by order and other helps, towards the better understanding of it, and judgment thereupon.

For the latter, touching the new charge, it is not worth the speaking of, in a matter of so high importance; it might have been used of the new translation of the Bible, and such like works. Books must follow sciences, and not sciences books.

The Work Itself: and the way to reduce and recompile the Laws of England

This work is to be done (to use some few words which is the language of action and effect) in this manner.

It consisteth of two parts; the digest or recompiling of the common laws; and that of the statutes.

In the first of these three things are to be done:

1. The compiling of a book, de antiquitatibus juris

2. The reducing or perfecting of the course or corps of the common laws.

3. The composing of certain introductive and auxiliary books touching the study of the laws.

For the first of these, all antient records in your Tower, or elsewhere, containing acts of parliament, lords patents, commissions, and judgments, and the like are to be searched, perused, and weighed: and out of these are to be selected those that are of most worth and weight, and in order of time not of titles, (for the more conformity with the year-books,) to be set down and register'd, rarely, in _haec verba_; but summered with judgment, not omitting any material part; these are to be used for reverend precedents, but not for binding authorities.

For the second, which is the main, there is to be made a perfect course of the law in _serie temporis_, or year-books (as we call them) from Edward the First to this day: in the compiling of this course of law, or year-books, the points following are to be observed.

First, all cases which are at this day clearly no law, but constantly ruled to the contrary, are to be left out; they do but fill the volumes, and season the wits of students in a contrary sense of law. And so likewise all cases, wherein that is solemnly and long debated, whereof there is no question at all, are to be entered as judgments only, and resolutions, but without the arguments which are now become but frivolous, yet for the observation of the deeper sort of lawyers, that they may see how the law hath altered, out of which they may pick sometimes good use, I do advise, that upon the first in time of those obsolete cases, there were a memorandum set, that at that time the law was thus taken, until such a time, &c.

Secondly, Homonymiae, (as Justinian calleth them) that is, cases merely of iteration and repetition, are to be purged away; and the cases of identity, which are best reported and argued, to be retained instead of the rest; the judgments nevertheless to be set down, every one in time as they are, but with a quotation or to the case where the point is argued at large; but if the case consist part of repetition, part of new matter, the repetition is only to be omitted.

Thirdly, as to the Antinomiae, cases judged to the contrary, it were too great a trust to refer to the judgment of the composers of this work, to decide the law either way, except there be a current stream of judgments of later times; and then I reckon the contrary cases amongst cases obsolete, of which I have spoken before; nevertheless this diligence would be used, that such cases of contradiction be specially noted and collected, to the end those doubts, that have been so long militant, may either by assembling all the judges in the exchequer chamber, or by parliament, be put into certainty. For to do it by bringing them in question under feigned parties, is to be disliked. _Nil habeat forum ex scena_.

Fourthly, all idle queries, which are but seminaries of doubts and incertainties are to be left out and omitted, and no queries set down, but of great doubts well debated and left undecided for difficulty; but no doubting or upstarting queries which though they be touched in argument for explanation, yet were better to die than to be put into the books.

Lastly, cases reported with too great prolixity, would be drawn into a more compendious report; not in the nature of an abridgement, but tautologies and imperitences to be cut off: as for misprinting, and insensible reporting, which many times confound the students, that will be obiter amended; but more principally, if there be any thing in the report which is not well warranted by the record, that is also to be rectified: the course being thus compiled, then it resteth but for your Majesty to appoint some grave and sound lawyers, with some honourable stipend, to be reporters for the time to come, and then this is settled for all times.

For the auxiliary books that conduce to the study and science of the law, they are three; Institutions; a treatise _De regulis juris_; and a better book _De verborum significationibus_, or terms of the law. For the Institutions, I know well there be books of introductions (wherewith students begin) of good worth, especially Littleton and Fitzherbert's Natura brevium; but they are no ways of the nature of an institution; the office whereof is to be a key and general preparation to the reading of the course. And principally it ought to have two properties; the one a perspicuous and clear order or method; and the other, an universal latitude or comprehension, that the students may have a little pre-notion of every thing, like a model towards a great building. For the treatise _De regulis juris_, I hold it, of all other things, the most important to the health (as I may term it) and good institutions of any laws; it is indeed like the ballast of a ship, to keep all upright and stable; but I have seen little in this kind, either in our law, or other laws, that satisfieth me. The naked rule or maxim doth not the effect: It must be made useful by good differences, ampliations, and limitations, warranted by good authorities; and this not by raising up of quotations and references, but by discourse and deducement in a just _tractate_. In this I have travelled myself, at the first more cursorily, since with more diligence, and will go on with it, if God and your Majesty will give me leave. And I do assure your Majesty, I am in good hope, that when Sir Edward Coke's reports, and my rules and decisions shall come to posterity, there will be no (whatsoever is now thought) question, who was the greater lawyer? For the books of the terms of the law there is a poor one, but I wish a diligent one, wherein should be comprised not only the exposition of the terms of law, but of the words of all antient records and precedents.

For the abridgments I could wish, if it were possible, that none might use them, but such as had read the course first, that they might serve for repertories to learned lawyers, and not to make a lawyer in haste, but since that cannot be I wish there were a good abridgment composed of the two that are extant, and in better order. So much for the common law.

Statute Law

For the reforming and recompiling of the statute law, it consisteth of four parts.

1. The first, to discharge the books of those statutes, whereas the cause by alteration of time, is vanished: as Lombards, Jews, Gauls half-pence, &c. Those may nevertheless remain in the libraries for antiquities, but no reprinting of them. The like of statutes long since expired and clearly repealed; for if the repeal be doubtful, it must be so propounded to the parliament.

2. The next is, to repeal all statutes which are sleeping and not of use, but yet snaring and in force; in some of those it will perhaps be requisite to substitute some more reasonable law instead of them agreeable to the time; in others a simple repeal may suffice.

3. The third, that the grievousness of the penalty in many statutes be mitigated, though the ordinances stand.

4. The last is, the reducing of concurrent statutes heaped one upon another to one clear and uniform law. Towards this there hath been already, upon my motion, and your Majesty's direction, a great deal of good pains taken; my Lord Hobart, myself, Serjeant Finch, Mr. Heneage Finch, Mr. Noye, Mr. Hackwell and others, whose labours being of a great bulk, it is not fit now to trouble your Majesty with any further particularity therein: only by this you may perceive the work is already advanced: but because this part of the work, which concerneth the statute laws, must of necessity come to parliament, and the houses will best like that which themselves guide, and the persons that themselves employ, the way were to imitate the precedent of the commissioners for the canon laws in 27 Hen. VIII and 4 Edw. VI and the commissioners for the union of the two realms, primo of your Majesty, and so to have the commissioners named by both houses; yet not with a precedent power to conclude, but only to prepare and propound to parliament: this is the best way, I conceive, to accomplish this excellent work, of honour to your Majesty's times, and of good to all times; which I submit to your Majesty's better judgment.

Examen Legum Angliae: Or The Laws of England Examined by Scripture, Antiquity, and Reason (1656)[1]

Chapter I - Of the Supposed Excellency and Antiquity of the Common Laws of England; and what is to be thought thereof in general.

It may well be accounted a matter of Admiration to the Vulgar and more Unlearned of the People of this Nation; and the wiser sort may well stagger in their Judgements, to consider what high Encomiums, or rather Hyperbolical Elogies, are given to the Laws of the Land, generally by all the Practicers and Professors thereof; and yet what abundance of Pains and Labour hath been taken, in order to the Amendment and Reformation of the same without any considerable benefit or satisfaction to the People.

It is hyperbolically, yet confidently, affirmed by one of the Chief Champions of the Law, (whose Reports go for Law generally without control) that there is no Humane Law within the Circuit of the whole World, by Infinite Degrees, so apt and profitable, for the honourable, peaceable, and prosperous Government of this Nation, as the Common Law is: which he endeavors to prove to be most just and ancient; and saith, That the same is contained in the old Statutes, Magna Charta, Charta Foresta, Merton, Marlebridge, Westminster, De Bigamis, Glocester, Westminster 2, Articuli Super Chartas, Articuli Cleri, Statu Ebor, and Praerogativa Regis, 25 Edw. 3. and in the Original Writs in the Register, and the Indictments of Judgments thereupon, as the very Text itself; and that all the subsequent Year-books and Records for four hundred years, are but Commentaries and Expositions thereof. And in another place the same Author speaking of Littleton's Book, saith, That Littleton is not only the name of a Lawyer, but of the Law itself; Which Book he affirms to be the most absolute and perfect Work, that ever was written in any Human Science. And afterwards reckons up Fifteen sorts of Laws, which, he saith, are in force in England: Concerning many of which, it doth not appear, that Littleton wrote anything. I will not say, That these Testimonies are repugnant: But this may well be said, That if the Assertions be true (considering also the huge multitude of Statutes now in force) then is the Law such an Individuum vagum, as no man living knows what it is, in respect of the variance and alteration thereof, from what it was in former times, both before and since Edw. the 4th in his Reign when Littleton wrote.

---

1. In the copy of this book in the Harvard Law School Library the author is identified as A. Booth.

And hence it is, that the Judges themselves (who are said to be the speaking Law) in many cases are divided, and Truth it self is oft-times set upon the Tenters, for want of a standing Rule, and because the Law lies merely in Opinion, without other Foundation: which appears sufficiently every Term, by the Arguments of the Judges; and may be gathered by view of the many Quare's affixed to the Reports of former and latter times. And these Differences are not about Niceties or Trivial things, but about that which is called, The Foundation of Law, and, The Propriety or Liberty of the Subject. ...

<u>Chapter II</u> - That the Law of God contained in the Holy Scriptures ought to be the Foundation of all Laws used or practiced amongst Christians.

That the Holy Scriptures are the Foundation of all just Laws, is a Truth undeniable, and evident to every one who hath any competent knowledge therein; comprehending in them as well the Dictates of the Law of Nature and right Reason, as all other things necessary for the Ruling, Guiding, and Ordering all the affairs of this life, whether Political, Economical, or Personal: which appears by this, That the Law of God is perfect; That the Holy Scriptures are able to make a man of God (not only the Minister, but every other man) perfect, thoroughly furnished to every good work. And upon this ground is that Maxime founded, That no Act of Parliament or Law, repugnant to the law of God, is of any force. This is agreed amongst the Lawyers, and it's cited out of <u>Augustine</u>, by one of the most Learned for Arts and Tongues of that Profession, That <u>Omnium Legum est inanis Censura, nisi Divine Legis Imaginem gerat</u>. That Renowned King Alfred, who reigned <u>Anno Christi</u> 872, began his Laws thus: <u>Locutus est Dominus ad Mosem hos sermones, Ego sum Dominus Deus tuus</u>; and so recites the Decalogue, and then proceeds to mention the most material Laws set down in the 20, 21, 22, and 23 Chapters of <u>Exodus</u>, which he affirms to be the most apt and compatible for the Government of his Kingdome: and according to his Laws, his Government was blessed with universal Peace and Quiet, above other Kings of this Nation: There being neither Thieves nor Robbers to molest the People.

Now not only the Decalogue, but also the Judicial Laws of <u>Moses</u>, are an eminent Foundation of Politick Laws, holding forth plainly the Reason of Commanding and Prohibiting. Of these Judicial Laws, some belonged to the Jews properly, as being appendent to the Ceremonial Law, as the punishment of him that touched a dead body; Others concerned the Jews Commonwealth in their own Land, as that concerning the year of Jubilee, &c. The rest are Laws of Common Justice and Equity, belonging to the Moral Law, as Expositions thereof, as the punishment of Murther, and Adultery, &c. with death. These, as many others, (which shall be touched in their proper places) were given to the Jews as men, and did not only bind the Conscience of the Jews, but also of the Gentiles: and as the Morall Law is principally grounded upon the Law of Nature; so these Judicial Laws (called by Moses Judgements) flowed from the same Fountain, and necessarily declared the punishments for the breach of the Moral Law, which are not therein expressed. And this use our Lord Jesus makes of the Judicial Laws. ...

Chapter III - That the Law of England, as now it is in use, is a departing from the Law of God, and a taking of a Law from Heathens and Idolators.

It is not to be doubted, but as these Judicial Laws were the Foundation of the Imperial or Civil Law; so were they of the Saxons, Danes, and Normans Laws; amongst which, many particulars of those Judicial Laws are found extant, as amongst the Laws of this Nation, which herein in their fit places shall be made appear. But the Roman Clergie, or rather Idolatrous Priests, being Chancellors, Judges, Reporters, Scribes and Compilers of our Laws; to these Laws of Common Equity, added many Heathenish, Impious, Superstitious, and wicked Customes, and imposed the same upon the poor conquered and enslaved People, for Laws: Which things when we consider, and what is reported by Sir Edward Coke, that in the time of William the Conqueror, and long after his time, the Chancellor, Treasurer, and Judges, were for the most part Bishops, Monks, & men of the Church, (as he calls them) of whom he names very many expert in the Common Laws, and such as wrote the same; We may easily judge what Laws we were like to have from such men; surely such as their Religion then was, in the very darkest night of Popery, which must needs produce nothing so much as Idolatry, and the Oppression and Persecution of the Saints; like the Statutes of Omri and Ahab, according to that of the Psalmist, The dark places of the earth are full of the habitations of cruelty.

Upon these grounds it may be clared, That we are much departed from the Law of God, and have received a Law from Antichrist: and it will further appear in the particulars following, That many wicked and profane Incroachments are made by our Laws upon the honour of God, in abuse of his holy Name and Worship and thereby also great Iniquities, Injustice, Wrongs, Oppressions, Deceits, and Falsehoods, practised, maintained and acted continually towards all sorts of men, as well by colour of divers Statutes, as the Common Law now in use and practice.

But for the present, let it be observed, That the whole Body of Popery is (in a manner) comprehended, in Littleton's Book (which is so much commended by Sir Edward Coke) and that the old Statutes made in affirmance of the Common Law, and the

Books and Entries whereof he makes mention, are stuffed with all manner of Superstitions, and Idolatrous Rights and Customs.

And if any man shall be offended, that I do not lick the sores of Justice Littleton and Sir Edward Coke, the two great Idols of the Law: It sufficeth me to know, That the first did according to the Religion then in use, and it may be according to the Dictates of his own Conscience; and in many things hath judiciously taught the succeeding Ages: but therefore hath not deserved to be accounted an Oracle. And for the other, I think of him according to the Character given him by the Incomparable Learned Sir Francis Bacon, in a Letter to him after his disgrace.

And something more I could say, That he was a man of a bitter spirit against the dear Servants of God: and if he should be judged according to the Judgement he gave of the most sincere Professors of Christs Gospel, the followers of John Wickliff, abusively called Lollards; and his judgement of Queen Elizabeth and King James, whom he blasphemously calls, The Fountain of all Piety and Justice, and the life of the Law: A rational man, indued with any knowledge of God, would think such a man too ignorant of the wayes of God, to be accounted an Oracle, or termed, The speaking Law (as every Judge is), or A Promulgator thereof. ...

<u>Chapter IX</u> - That there ought not to be a Court of Law or Justice, and another of Equity (Such as now are in England) maintained or suffered in any Nation professing the Gospel.

This Position is so clear, that the contrary hath no manner of Foundation of Truth, either in the Law of Nature, Right Reason, or the Word of God: For that Justice is but one, as Truth is but one, and simply one; and Justice and Injustice are opposites. I speak of distributive Justice, not of Essential Justice in God; from whom some Arguments might be brought, to confirm the point in hand; but that appertains to another Confederation: nor have I here to do with Commutative Justice, concerning the various management of Affairs in Commerce between man and man, for rectifying the Abuses, Frauds, Oppressions, Wrongs, and other Enormities therein: It pleaseth Almighty God to set up this Light, and to Ordain Powers and Authorities to distribute Justice and Equity amongst men, for the upholding of Society, Political and Economical, and the preserving of Sobriety and Temperance, and for encouragement of men in well-doing. Nature holds forth but one Light to men, and God gives but one Law to Christians. This is the end of Magistracy, The Execution of Justice: which in their hands, whether Supreme or Subordinate, is that Virtue which is commonly called, Distributive Justice, and comprehends in it Equity;

and the same likewise is called Righteousness. Now that Justice and Equity are the same thing, there is nothing more clear: as _Aequum_ & _Justum_, are _Termini convertibiles_; so are Justice and Equity. ...

These two Courts can no more consist with Justice, than two Weights or Measures of different bigness or length. I use this familiar Comparison, because it pleaseth the Holy Ghost to make use thereof to this very purpose, Prov. 20. 10. Diverse weights and diverse measures, word for word out of the Original, are a stone and a stone, that is, different Weights and Measures, of several sizes, one bigger, another less: and this is expounded by that in Deut. 25. 13, 14. _Thou shalt not have in thy bagge diverse Weights, a great and a small: Thou shalt not have in thy house diverse Measures, a great and a small_. These words by a Synecdoche speciei, forbid all unjust and unequal dealing and commerce amongst men, and all Injustice and Iniquity, and the instruments, tools, and means thereof; and implicitely, the same Law commands, all Justice and Equity; and directly forbids two Courts, having contrary Powers and Jurisdictions, and executing things Repugnant and contrary one to another: If the one proceed justly, the other must needs be unjust. Neither do the Scriptures anywhere mention Justice and Equity as two several things, to be distributed in one Case; as if that might be done by the one, which might not be done by the other; nor that ever any good Judges gave any such Judgments: but rather, when they are said to do Justice, it's intended, That they did justly and equally. It's true, that the Judicial Laws are called Judgements, and the execution of the Moral Law, is called Justice. And so David is said, to execute Judgement and Justice; that is, to judge justly and righteously both in respect of the Moral and Judicial Laws. As for the Ceremonial Law, that was not properly belonging to distributive Justice, but concerned every particular man, as the immediate service of God. To conclude this point: If the Law were just and equal, as it ought to be, there were no need of any Court of Equity; and the Law, as now it is, having need of such Courts of Equity as there are, is an Oppression of the People, and so clearly against the Law of God. ...

Chapter X -

... Object 6. The last and main thing for upholding these Courts of Equity, is That commonly Frauds and Deceipts can never be discovered, nor Private Contracts proved, but by the Defendants Oaths; which are not elsewhere to be taken in such cases: and this enforceth so many Bills of Discovery to be exhibited into those Courts every Term.

Answ. This Objection doth in it self, in _foro Conscientiae_ clearly overthrow the practice of these Courts. For the very exacting this Oath is against the Law of Nature, whose dictates are the same with those of the Law of God written; from which are derived undenyable Maximes and Principles, whereof this is one: Nemo tenetur accusare seipsum: This Maxime is agreed by all men; and the Lawyers allow it. The reason if it is, (although it need none to confirm it; for it is also a Maxime, Contra Negantem Principia non est disputandum) because every man is nearest to himself; and it's against Nature, for him to be a means of his own punishment; a man ought to preserve himself, although to the hurt of another: it were better to kill another, than to kill himself, or to suffer himself to be killed; if of necessity the one must needs be. Therefore, to exact this Inquisitory Oath against a man own self, is against the Law of Nature, and so against the Law of God. This is the very same Oath which was brought into England by Pope Martin the fifth, for extirpation of the followers of John Wickliff, called Lollards, about the Reign of King Hen. 4. and was taken up by the Ecclesiastical Courts (as they were called) I suppose, long before it was used in any English Court; and afterwards, it was most famously used in the Star-Chamber, and in the High Commission, called The Oath Ex Officio; the Defendants being, besides their answer, examined upon Interrogatories as sometimes they are in other Courts. And it's reported, (which I had from good hands) that one Mr. Fuller of Grays Inn having this Oath tendered to him (as all Non-conformists had, who came into the High Commission) refused to take it, saying, he was not bounden to accuse himself; but said, he would swear, and answer upon his Oath to what they should ask him, so far as he was bounden by Law. He was answered, There was no more desired of him. Thereupon, the honest Gentleman (although a Lawyer) was deluded and cozened with this word Law; which was equivocal, either referring to the Common Law, or to their Popish Tyrannical Canon or Ecclesiastical Law: and taking his Oath, had Questions demended of him, of things which intrenched upon his Estate and Liberty (for which he might be fined and imprisoned) if not his life. To these he answered, That he was not bounden by Law to answer to them, being against himself; according to that Rule of Right Reason above mentioned: No man is bound to accuse himself. This they declared Perjury; and for that they fined him 300 l. What difference is there between these proceedings, and the proceedings in Courts of Equity, especially when Answers are made to Exceptions, or when the party is examined upon Interrogatories against himself? The best that can be made of it is, that it is a profaning the holy Name of God, and the abuse of an Oath, as being here, not the end, but the beginning, or rather occasion of strife; and if this Oath were taken away, men would be sure to have Witnesses present to all their Contracts and Agreements. And it may be observed, that there is no manner of credit given to the Defendants Answer: for the Practicers in Chancery use to say, It's no matter if the defendant swear the Crow is white, if the Plaintiff can prove she is black. And upon this ground all wise men proceed, in reference to Suits in courts of Equity; not to prefer their Bill, unless they can prove it, or at least the material points thereof. I have observed, That in almost thirty years practice, I never found one Defendant, who wanted conscience to pay a just Debt, (where it could not be proved by Witnesses) that would ever confess in it an Answer upon his Oath; but rather use the help of some skilful man, to draw his Answer to equivocal, or caurelously, that it might not prejudice in his Cause. This hath been, and is a heavie temptation and provocation to Perjury, and so a breach of the Law of God: which causeth the Land to mourn, and therefore ought to be abolished.

Object 7. And where it is alleadged, that although in Criminal Cuases, which are popular, men are not bounden to accuse themselves; yet for discovery of Fraud and Deceit in Cases Personal, they are bounden by Law to declare the truth upon their oaths in their Answers:

Answ. It may be answered, first, That all Frauds and Deceipts are things criminal in <u>foro Conscientiae</u>, and for which in most Cases a man may be indicted at Common Law; and, in some Cases, by virtue of several Statutes; as for fraudulent Conveyances, and for some deceipts in Bargaining, and for cozenage in selling of Wares, and in many other Cases. And if a man in any case were to be enforced to confess the truth against himself, there is most reason it should be done in Criminal Causes most capital; as, when Treason, Adultery, Murder, or some great Felony is committed, and several men accused, Were it not a fair pretence, that every man, to clear himself, and to the end to find out the Truth, should be examined upon his Oath? And yet this is not allowed in the Law, nor ought to be done, for the reason aforesaid; unless the Defendant will voluntarily offer his Oath: which may be admitted by the Law of God, otherwise Joshua would not have done it in the case of Achan: although he exhorted him to confess the truth, and give glory to God; yet he did not enforce him to swear, but searched his tent for the wedge of gold and the Babylonish garment: neither did our Lord Jese Christ urge the woman taken in adultery to accuse her self, but asked where her accusers were; and when he saw that no witnesses accused her, he said, No more do I; and bid her go her ways, and sin no more.

Now in those Cases which are not criminal, as about Trusts, and Estates in Land in Extent, and such like, which may usually be proved by Witnesses, where men are forced to answer upon Oath; these do many times intrench more upon mens Liberty and Estates, in respect of the consequence, than an hundred trivial Frauds or Thefts: and therefore this will not warrant their answering upon Oath. All the arguments which have been brought against the Oath Ex Officio, (if I mistake not) make directly against this Oath (with Compurgators) which was used to be administered in the Spiritual, or rather Baudy Courts, to purge men of Incontinencie or Fornication. And this is all which I shall say in this place, of these Courts of Equity.[2]

<u>A Post-Script</u>

Containing sundry Positions, founded upon the holy Scriptures, serving for principal grounds of Laws amongst Christians

... 12. Many thing are to be judged according to the discretion of the judges with reference to the Law of God, and such Judgments not to be accounted Arbitrary, much less to favour of tyrannical Government, Exod. 21. 22, 30, 35. Numb. 27.8 I Kings 2.44. and 3.16, 25, 27. ...

24. That for felonies of Goods, or Cattle stollen, the Thief not to suffer death, but to make restitution, according to Gods Law, as the case shall be, and be bounden to serve in case he cannot satisfie. Prov. 6.30.31. Exo. 22. 1.7.4.7. Job 20.15.18. 2 Sam. 12.6. Luk. 19.8. ...

26. That no man to be convicted in any case Capital, but by the Testimony of two witnesses at least. Deut. 17.6. 2 Cor. 13.1. Heb. 10.28. Numb. 35.30.

27. That a single witnesse shall convict no man, in any case without other proof, or evincing circumstances, Deut. 19. 15. 18. John 8.17. and 5.31. Math. 18.16. I Cor. 13.1.

28. That a perjured, or malitious false witnesse shall suffer the same punishment, or losse, which his false Testimony regularly should cause another to suffer, and the suborner of Perjury in like manner, Dan. 6.24 Deut. 19.18. 19.21. Prov.19. 5. ...

37. All estates of inheritance, are to be Estates in Fee simple, and no Intails upon the Heirs Males, Numb. 27. 7.8. I Tim. 5.8. Gen. 23. 11, 17.20.

38. All estates with the Owners Pedegree, are to be Inrolled in some convenient known place, for avoiding strife and contention, Jer. 32.11.12. Josh. 14.14.15. Josh. 15.89. 19. 20. Ezra 2.62. ...

40. The eldest Son not being guilty of any Notorious of-

---

2. Excluding the postscript, the balance of the volume is devoted to a detailed examination of particular rules of law, both substantive and procedural, which are considered to violate the law of God. There are also specific suggestions as to needed additions to the law of England.

fence, ought to have a double portion, Deut. 21. 17. I Kings 2.15. Gen. 25.33. and 48.22.

41. All younger children to have parts of their Parents Estates, according to their deserts, and as the Estate will bear, Gen. 25. 6. Luke 15.12. Josh. 14.15. and 16.17. ...

43. Schooles of learning are to be maintained, and godly learned men to be countenanced and encouraged, Acts 19.9. I Kings 18.4. I Sam. 19.20. ...

45. That such as run in Debt, shall have their estates sold, to pay their Debts, he that hath nothing to pay, not to be imprisoned for Debt, 2 Kings 4.7. Exo. 22.26, 27. Luke 6. 35. and 7.42. Math. 18. 25, 27, 33, 34. ...

50. That no Counsel be retained for any Suters, but that the Pleaders be rewarded by the State, and be sworn as assistants to the Judges, as indifferent men to endeavour to finde out the truth, and not to obscure, or overthrow it, Exo. 23.2 Lam. 3.35, 36. Judges 19.30 and Judges 20.7, 8 Numb. 22.7, 17. 2 Pet. 2.15. Acts 24.5. ...

54. That the circumstances and equity of every Cause be weighed together with the Justice, and matter of fact, and Judgement to be given accordingly, Isa.59.13,14,15. 2 Sam. 8, 15. Josh. 7. 11,25. ...

57. That the Oaths of two, or more witnesses may be a sufficient conviction in Law, without any Indictment, Deut. 17. 6. and 19.15. Math. 18.16. 2 Cor. 13.1. ...

59. That all Suits and controversies, although popular, or Criminal, be determined, upon hearing witnesses sworn, and giving evidence on both parts as well as for the party accused, as the Commonwealth, and in cases where there are no witnesses, that the accused's own voluntary Oath be taken for his discharge, Exod.22.9.10,11. I Kings 8.31. Job 29.16. Acts 26.5. Isa. 43. 9,10.

60. That there be Judicatories, and Courts established in every Citie and County, where the Judges may sit constantly in open places to hear, and determine all controversies, Exod. 18.13,25,26. Deut. 21.19. Prov. 31,23. and 25.7. Ruth. 4, 1, 2, 9. ...

72. That the Process in all Cases of Suite, be onely a Summons, which being duely served, if the Defendant refuse to appear, or shew not sufficient cause to the contrary, the Plaintiffe may proceed to his proof, and so to hearing, or trial, as if the Defendant had appeared, Numb. 16.11.14.28.32. Deut. 25.8. Hest. I. 10.11.19.21.

73. That no man have final Judgement against him by default without proof in any Case, be it never so small, unless the party accused do at the time of the Judgement openly confess the fact, Numb. 35.30. Deut.17.6. I Kings 8.31. ...

76. That the body of the Law may be collected into a volume, that it may be known to the Supream Magistrate, and to

the Judges, and the people, I Sam. 10.25. Deut. 17.18.19. Exod. 20. from verse 3 to the 9. verse of Chap.23. Hester I.19.

Sir Matthew Hale - Considerations Touching The Amendment or Alteration of Lawes

(Date unknown - before 1690), Hargrave Tracts, 249, 258-260, 268-271

And now possibly some may say, that since all human laws are imperfect, and only the counsells and determinations of Almighty God are perfect, why then may we not take a short compendious course, and take in the judicials given by God by the hand of Moses, and so avoid that inconvenience of the imperfections of human lawes, the positive judicial law of Almighty God being substituted in the place of all other human lawes, and all human lawes abrogated and exterminated?

To this I say, that most certainly the judicial law given by Moses was the law of God, and consequently a most perfect law, according to the use and end for which it was designed; a law of perfect wisdom, as being the production of an infinite wisdom. But yet this must be observed in relation to the perfection of things of this kind. That is in truth perfect that is perfect in relation to its use and end, cui nihil deest that may be useful and apposite to that end. And if a man be to fit any thing to the use of any other particular thing, and for a certain determinate time, that is said to be perfect, that is perfectly fitted to that use and duration, though it be not fitted to another thing or a longer duration for that were a kind of imperfection, because it would be redundant and superfluous.

This being premised, I say,

1. Although the moral law, or the law of the two tables, were materially universal both in respect of extent and duration, and therefore, the use being that of amplitude, the divine wisdom fitted it according to the use and extent thereof, both in respect of all people and ages; yet the judicial lawes, as likewise the ritual or ceremonial, were never in the design of Almighty God intended farther than that people to whom they were given, and no longer possibly to that people than the state of that republic continued. It was indeed exactly accommodate to the state of that people to which it was given; and therein the wisdom of God is not only justified, but manifested and exalted; for it was exactly suitable to the end it was designed. But we cannot say it was fitted, or that there was any need it should be fitted for another people; for that was not within the design of Almighty God; and this indeed is a circumstance that ought to be an ingredient in the due constitution of all laws, that they should be accommodate to the condition

constitution and exigence of the people to whom they are given. Consequently, inasmuch as there be things peculiar and proper to the state and condition of one people, that are not common to the state of another, nay not of the same people at another time; hence it is scarce possible to frame one judicial law for all people; or if it were possible, yet it were not prudent, because inconvenient. Let any man but consider the judicials given to the Hebrews, he will find them in a special manner accommodated and attempered to the state of that people, which would not be apposite to the state of another people; as some of their judicials, that referred to the distributions of their possessions, to their discrimination from the rest of mankind, to the redemption of their possessions and keeping them within their tribes, to their late state of captivity amongst the Egyptians, and the extermination of their practices used in Egypt. And divers other particular reasons, purely concerning that state and unapplicable to another, were the most wise and just foundations of divers of their laws. But these judicials, that were given to them that were not upon an appropriate reason delivered to them, and that are consistent with the frame of the constitutions of other nations, have been as far as may be transcribed into, as it were, the judicials of other people, at least since the Christian religion obtained, as the laws touching the degrees of marriage, touching murder, and other things.

2. But yet farther it is to be observed, that even in that very people, although the text of the judicial law was that which was the basis and rule of their government and policy, yet the wisdom of Almighty God, even in the very giving of that law, and divers times after upon variety of emergencies, instituted a clause for the accommodation of things in the same state according to the exigence of things and emergencies, viz. the great council of that people their Sanhedrim, and the governors of that people their kings, which were authorized by Almighty God as the exigence of things required in the civil or political administration, though not to change the judicials given by God by the hand of Moses, yet to discriminate, supply, and provide for new cases and emergencies. So that Almighty God in his infinite wisdom did find, that there was a necessity of supplementals even in his own state, according as succession of time and various emergencies might occur, and even during the consistency of that policy or republick.

Upon the whole therefore, I conclude, that that law was contrived with most perfect wisdom for that people, and during that state; and therein consisted in a great measure the wisdom of it in that accommodation. But to translate that law to another people, to whom it was not accommodate, were a wrong to the divine wisdom. It is most certain, the specifical natural law that is given to birds is most wisely accommodate to them by the divine wisdom. But for any man to say, because it is a most wise law, therefore it were fit to be used by beasts or fishes, were to distort and wrong the divine wisdom, by misapplying it to such a use and such animals, for whom it was never intended to be a rule or law. And though the specifical nature of Jews and Gentiles and all nations be the same, yet it is certain, that there were, and ever will be, great variety in the states of dispositions and concernes of several people; so that that law, which would be a most wise apt and suitable constitution to one people, would be utterly improper and inconvenient for another. ...

As all sublunary things are subject to corruption and putrefaction, to diseases and rust, so even lawes themselves by long tract of time gather certain diseases and excrescences; certain abuses and corruptions grow into the law, as close as the ivy unto the tree or the rust to the iron, and in a little tract of time gain the reputation of being part of the law. So that a great and considerable part of that reformation, that is pleaded for, is not so much of the law, as of abuses and corruptions, and wens and excrescences, and delays and formalities and exactions, that do adhere to the law, and will in time strangle and stifle it with its close adherence to it. And when these dear and profitable exuberances and ulcers are looked after, presently those, that are concerned in the profit thereof, or do not duly distinguish between the law and its abuses and diseases, cry out upon destroying the law and altering of the law, when in truth it is the rescuing of the law from those encroachments or abuses that are made upon it or brought into it. ...

But yet farther, I do not think, that the only things fit to be reformed in the law are the abuses and corruptions of it; but there are some things, that are really and truly parts of the law, as necessary to be reformed as the errors of abuses of it.

And we must remember, that lawes were not made for their own sakes, but for the sake of those who were to be guided by them; and though it is true they are and ought to be sacred, yet, if they be or are become unusefull for their end, they must either be amended if it may be, or new lawes be substituted and the old repealed, so it be done regularly, deliberately, and so far forth only as the exigence or convenience justly demands it. And in this respect the saying is true, _salus populi suprema lex esto_. Now lawes become or are unusefull to their end upon two accounts. 1. When in their very constitution and fabrick they are rotten and faulty, and unjust, and impossible to be born without remarkable and common inconvenience. I shall not apply this part to the thing in question - But 2dly, when a law, tho' never so good in its first institution, yet by reason of some accidental emergencies that do most usually happen in tract of time, either becomes obsolete and out of use, or weak and unprofitable to its end, or inconsistent with some new superinduction that time and variety of occasions have introduced. And as this is most clear in all lawes, so in our English lawes we shall find, what was in use, and possibly very effectual in its time, is now deserted and antiquated, and utterly unapplicable to the present state of administration in England. Glanville wrote a system of our English lawes in the time of H. 2. Bracton in the time of H.3. Britton in the time of E. 1. Let any man read them, and see, whether he can by any means accommodate that administration to the present state of things, or the present regiment or order of things to that. Nay, if we come to the year-books of the time of E. 3. any man, that knowes any thing in this kind, will most certainly find, that it cannot fit us; for where is there now one assise or real action brought, unless where they have no other remedy? So that the stream of things have as it were left that channell, and taken a new one; and he, that thinks a state can be exactly steered by the same lawes in every kind, as it was two or three hundred years since, may as well imagine that the cloaths that fitted him when he was a child should serve him when he is grown a man. The matter changeth the custom; the contracts the commerce; the dispositions educations and tempers of men and societies change in a long tract of time and so must their lawes in some measure be changed, or they will not be usefull for their state and condition. And besides all this, as I before said, time is the wisest thing under heaven. These very lawes, which at first seemed the wisest constitution under heaven, have some flawes and defects discovered in them by time. As manufactures, mechanical arts, architecture and building, and philosophy itself, receive new advantages and discoveries by time and experience; so much more do lawes, which concern the manners and customs of men.

All that, which I contend for in the first and second chapter, is, not to render lawes of men like lawes of nature fixed and unalterable, but that it be done with great prudence, advice, care, and upon a full and clear prospect of the whole business.

4. But yet further, by length of time and continuance lawes are so multiplied and grown to that excessive variety, that there is a necessity of reduction of them, or otherwise it is not manageable; as we have before observed touching the Roman lawes, which in a tract of 1300 years grew to 2000 great volumes. And the reason is, because this age for the purpose received from the last a body of lawes, and they add more and transmit the whole to the next age, and they add to what they had received and transmit the whole stock to the next age. Thus as the rolling of a snow-ball, it increaseth in bulk in every age, till it become utterly unmanageable. And hence it

is, that even in the lawes of England we have so many varieties of forms of conveyances, feoffment, fines, release, confirmation, grant, attornment, common recovery, deeds, enrolled &c. because the use coming in at several times, every age did retain somewhat of what was past, and added somewhat of it's own, and so carried over the whole product to the quotient. And this produceth mistakes. A man perchance useth one sort of conveyance, where he should have used another. It breeds uncertainty and contradiction of opinion, and that begets suits and expence. It must necessarily cause ignorance in the professors and profession itself; because the volumes of the law are not easily to be mastered.

5. There be in the law to this day some things continuing, which, though possibly of ordinary use or occurrence, yet are mischievous when they come to be used, and would not at all be missed if taken away, and which I shall in the pursuit of particulars evidence to the satisfaction I believe of every knowing considering and unprejudiced mind.

6. I shall add but this one thing more, that it may justly be feared, that if something considerable for the reformation of this amiss in the law be not done by knowing and judicious persons, too much may some time or other be done by some, either out of envy at the professors, or mistaken apprehensions or popular humours. The amendment of things amiss timely, by knowing able and judicious men that understand their business, may do very much good, and prevent very much evil that may otherwise ensue; and when the business is begun by such hands, it may possibly be too late to allay it. And although it be true, that as the legislative power is established there be many reserves to prevent or stop such an inundation, yet we know not how high the publick necessities of supplies may arise, considering our many great undertakings in the kingdom; and it is no new thing to observe very hard and unreasonable terms granted as the price and purchase of supplies, when they cannot be had upon easier terms. And it will have this plausible pretence, that the judges and lawyers will do nothing to the lawes, and therefore it shall be done by other hands. Such a humour would be more easily prevented by a wise and seasonable undertaking in this kind, which would not be so easily diverted or allayed, if once it should be flying. And thus much shall serve for this chapter.

CHAPTER THREE

THE LAW IN THE MASSACHUSETTS BAY COLONY

1. The Charter of Incorporation and the First Processes of Law-Making

Many purposes inspired the first settlers of the American colonies. However intense the religious and the commercial motives of colonization may have been, colonial enterprise could never entirely escape the limitations which the legal structure prescribed by the home authorities imposed upon overseas government and administration. Since the legal history of the colonies as dealt with in this volume centers around the government of Massachusetts Bay, where the corporate rather than the proprietary organization was established, it is with the provisions of the Bay Colony's charter of incorporation that we shall first be concerned. That charter was drawn by lawyers who were familiar with corporate affairs; being lawyers the draftsmen used phrases and formulas which were already known to them in other contexts. The lawyers also knew much of the developing problems of empire, and as statesmen they sought with more or less success to anticipate the problems of government with which any agency of overseas administration, whether corporate or proprietary, was likely to be confronted. The lawyers were also living in a society in which the institutions of feudalism had persistent though diminishing vitality. In examining significant provisions of the charter issued on March 4, 1629, to "The Governor and Company of the Massachusetts Bay in Newe-England", consideration should be given to the extent to which the familiar language of charters of incorporation, the problems of imperial government, and the institutions of feudalism served to mold the structure of government.

The charter opened with the confirmation of a prior grant of a defined area of lands in New England to named individuals, "their heirs and assigns for ever, to their only proper and absolute use and behoof for ever more". The *tenendum* clause of the grant was as follows: "To be holden of us, our heirs and successors, as of our manor of East Greenwich in the County of Kent, in free and common socage,[1] and not in capite nor by

---

1. See, Haskins, "Gavelkind and the Charter of Massachusetts Bay", 34 *Transactions of Colonial Society of Mass*. 483 (1941). Though this tenure as of the manor of East Greenwich was fre-

knight's service, and also yielding and paying therefor to us, our heirs and successors, the fifth part only of all ore and gold and silver, which from time to time ... shall be there gotten, had or obtained."

Following the clauses by which the Massachusetts lands were granted to the named individuals came the provisions by which these persons were constituted a corporation. Those provisions took the following form: "To the end that the affairs and business which, from time to time, shall happen and arise concerning the said lands and the plantation of the same, may be the better managed and ordered, we ... further ... will and ordain that [the individuals named] and all such others as shall hereafter be admitted and made free of the Company and Society hereafter mentioned, shall ... be, by virtue of these presents, one body corporate and politic in deed, fact and name ... and that by that name they shall have perpetual succession, and that by the same name they ... shall ... be capable and enabled, as well to implead and to be impleaded ... in all and singular suits, causes, quarrels, and actions of what kind and nature soever; and also to have, take, possess, acquire, and purchase any lands, tenements, or hereditaments, or any goods or chattels, and the same to ... dispose of as other our liege people of this our realm of England or any other corporation or body politic of the same may lawfully do; and further that the said Governor and Company and their successors may have for ever one common seal. ..."

With respect to the management of the corporation thus established the following provisions were of predominant importance: "And we do hereby ... ordain and grant that ... there shall be one Governor, one Deputy Governor, and eighteen Assistants of the same Company, to be from time to time constituted, elected, and chosen out of the freemen of the said Company, for the time being ..., which said officers shall apply themselves to take care for the best disposing and ordering of the general business and affairs of ... the said lands and premises hereby mentioned to be granted, and the plantation thereof, and the government of the people there. ... And [we order and ordain] that the said Governor, Deputy Governor, and Assistants of the said Company ... shall or may once every

---

quently found in Colonial charters the tenure of Maryland lands granted to Lord Baltimore was "To Hold of us ... as of our Estate of Windsor, in our County of Berks" MacDonald, Select Charters (1899) 53, 55. The tenure of Georgia lands, under the charter of 1732, was described in the following terms: "to be holden of us ... as of our honour of Hampton - court, in our county of Middlesex." MacDonald, id. p. 235, 242.

month, or oftener at their pleasure, assemble, and hold, and keep a Court or Assembly of themselves, for the better ordering and directing of their affairs ... and that there shall or may be held and kept by the Governor or Deputy Governor ... and seven or more of the said Assistants ... upon every last Wednesday in Hilary, Easter, Trinity, and Michelmas terms respectively ... one great, general, and solemn Assembly, which four General Assemblies shall be styled and called the Four Great and General Courts of the said Company. In all ... of which said Great and General Courts so assembled we do ... give and grant to the said Governor and Company ... that the Governor, or, in his absence, the Deputy Governor ... and such of the Assistants and Freemen of the said Company as shall be present, or the greater number of them so assembled, whereof the Governor or Deputy Governor and six of the Assistants, at the least to be seven, shall have full power and authority to choose, nominate, and appoint such and so many others as they shall think fit ... to be free of the said Company and body, and them into the same to admit, and to elect and constitute such officers as they shall think fit ... for the ordering, managing and dispatching of the affairs of the said ... Company. ..."

The Charter of incorporation went on to provide that the Great and General Court was empowered from time to time "to make, ordain, and establish all manner of wholesome orders, laws, statutes, and ordinances, directions, and instructions not contrary to the laws of this our realm of England,[2] as well

---

2. In another passage in the Charter this limitation was worded slightly differently: "so such laws and ordinances be not contrary or repugnant to the laws and statutes of our realm of England". With these provisions should be compared the equivalents in the Charter of Maryland: "So nevertheless, that the laws aforesaid be consonant to reason and be not repugnant or contrary, but (so far as conveniently may be) agreeable to the Laws, Statutes, Customs and Rights of this Our Kingdom of England". MacDonald, supra, 53, 57.

Is it significant that in charters of incorporation issued to trading companies the activities of which were to be carried on only within the realm similar limitations on the "legislative" power of the governing bodies were customarily included? For examples of such limitations in the charters of domestic trading companies see, Select Charters of Trading Companies, (Vol. 28, Selden Society), p. 113, 127, 139.

Attention has frequently been called to the fact that the commissions issued to colonial and provincial judges under Royal authority contained, in one form or another, explicit pro-for settling of the forms and ceremonies of government and magistracy fit and necessary for the said plantation and the inhabitants there, and for naming and styling of all sorts of officers ... which they shall find needful for that government and plantation ... and the forms of such oaths warrantable by the laws and statutes of this our realm of England as shall be respectively ministered unto them ... and for impositions of lawful fines, mulcts, imprisonment, or other lawful correction, according to the course of other corporations in this our realm of England. ..."

One other provision, not related specifically to limitations on the legislative power, but nonetheless suggesting that certain basic standards of the English law must be observed, deserves special reference. That provision was as follows: "And further our will and pleasure is, and we do hereby ... ordain, declare, and grant to the said Governor and Company ... that all and every the subjects of us ... which shall go to and inhabit within the said lands and premises hereby mentioned to be granted, and every of their children which shall happen to be born there, or on the seas in going thither or returning from thence, shall have and enjoy all liberties and immunities of free and natural subjects within any of the dominions of us, our heirs or successors, to all intents, constructions, and purposes whatsoever, as if they and every of them were born within the realm of England."

It has often been pointed out that in at least one important respect the charter issued to the Massachusetts Bay Company differed from others issued to other groups of overseas settlers. That difference was in the omission of clauses indicating that the governing authority of the corporation was to remain in England. Both the first and the second charters issued to the Virginia settlers contained, for instance, specific provisions to the effect that the governing Council of the body should be "established here in England".[3] The omission of an equivalent of that clause made an unusually high

---

visions empowering the judges to hear and try cases "according to the laws, statutes, and customs of England". See, e.g., Goebel and Naughton, Law Enforcement in Colonial New York (1944) 48. It should not be overlooked that the commission of a judge in England contained similar clauses. See, Prothero, Select Statutes (1913) 362, 363.

3. The charters issued to the East India Company in 1601 and 1609 explicitly empowered the governing bodies of the corporation to convene "within our dominions or elsewhere, and there to hold Court for the said Company". This suggests that the

degree of independence of home authority possible in Massachusetts Bay. It is probable that the omission was intentional, and that if the usual provision had been retained in the Massachusetts charter a number of the leaders of the venture would not have joined the enterprise. See 1 Osgood, The American Colonies in the 17th Century (1904) 141 et seq. The view of Mr. Justice Story that the transfer of the government from England to Massachusetts was in violation of the express or implied provisions of the Charter seems to have little support. See Parker, "The First Charter and the Early Religious Legislation of Massachusetts", Massachusetts and Its Early History (Lowell Institute Lectures, 1869) 357, 365.

Following the election of John Winthrop as Governor of the Corporation and of a Deputy Governor and of Assistants from among those members who had undertaken to cross over into New England, these elected officers with other emigrants set sail for Massachusetts Bay, with the charter in their possession. Upon their arrival in August, 1630, the Court of Assistants assumed the powers of government. At the first Court of Assistants to be held in America, a number of significant votes were adopted, among which were the following.

"It was ordered that in all civil actions, the first process or summons by the beadle or his deputy shall be directed by the Governor or Deputy Governor, or some other of the Assistants, being a Justice of the Peace; the next process to be a capias or distringas, at the discretion of the Court. ...

"It was ordered that /Thomas/ Morton, of Mount Woolison, should presently be sent for by process. ...

"It was ordered that the Governor and Deputy Governor, for the time being, shall always be Justices of the Peace, and that Sir Richard Saltonstall, Mr. Johnson, Mr. Endicott, and Mr. Ludlow shall be Justices of the Peace for the present time, in all things to have like power that Justices of Peace hath in England for reformation of abuses and punishing of offenders; and that any Justice of the Peace may imprison an offender, but not inflict any corporal punishment without the presence and consent of some one of the Assistants." 1 Records of Massachusetts Bay 74.

At the next sitting of the Assistants, two weeks later, the following proceedings, among others, are recorded:

"It is ordered by this present Court, that Thomas Morton, of Mount Wolliston, shall presently be set into the bilbowes,

---

omission from the Massachusetts charter of clauses localizing the corporate government to England was not as unprecedented as it is generally assumed to have been. See, Charters Granted to The East India Company (undated), 13, 41.

and after sent prisoner into England, by the ship called The Gift, now returning thither;[4] that all his goods shall be seized upon to defray the charge of his transportation, payment of his debts, and to give satisfaction to the Indians for a canoe he unjustly took away from them; and that his house, after the goods are taken out, shall be burned down to the ground in the sight of the Indians, for their satisfaction for many wrongs he hath done them from time to time.[5]

"It is ordered that Mr. Clarke shall pay unto John Baker the sum of 38 shillings, in recompense for the damage he received by a bargain of cloth, wherein Mr. Clarke dealt fraudulently with the said John Baker, as hath been proved upon oath." 1 Records 75.

At a sitting of the Court of Assistants on September 28, 1630, a jury of fifteen was empanelled "to inquire concerning the death of Austen Bratcher". The jury's "verdict" was that "we find that the strokes given by Walter Palmer were occasionally the means of the death of Austen Bratcher, and so to be manslaughter". Thereupon Palmer bound himself, with sureties, to appear personally at the next sitting of the Court. (1 Records 77-78)

The next sitting was of the General Court, on October 19. At that time Palmer made his appearance, but was bound over for the sitting of the Court of Assistants on November 9. The one important vote of the General Court on October 19 was that "the

---

4. Perhaps the justification for this removal of Morton was to be found in the clause of the Charter authorizing the officers of the corporation "to encounter, expulse, repel ... all such person and persons as shall ... attempt or enterprise the destruction, invasion, detriment, or annoyance to the said plantation or inhabitants". Governor Winthrop stated, however, that Morton was sent prisoner to England "upon the Lord Chief Justice's warrant". 1 Winthrop, Journal *57. Concerning Morton's career in the colonies see Morison, Builders of the Bay Colony (1930) 14-19.

5. Concerning the archaic punishment of house destruction, familiar in English and Scottish boroughs, see 2 Bateson, Borough Customs (21 Selden Society) xxxv, 38. In the Scottish Leges Burgorum (ca. 1270) appears the following provision: "If any burgess be a rebel against the community of the town or should defraud (the community) and be convicted of this, his house shall be razed to the ground and he himself shall be put out of the town." Bateson, supra, p. 39. Cf. the King's right of year, day, and waste as described in 4 Blackstone Commentaries 385-386.

freemen should have the power of choosing Assistants ... and the Assistants from amongst themselves to choose a Governor and Deputy Governor, who with the Assistants should have the power of making laws and choosing officers to execute the same." 1 Records 79.

On November 9, Walter Palmer appeared before the Court of Assistants, a jury of twelve was empanelled and found "Walter Palmer not guilty of manslaughter whereof he stood indicted, and so the Court acquits him". 1 Records 81.

During the period from 1630 to 1632 the Court of Assistants continued to function as the principal legislative and judicial body of the Colony. Evidently the officers and individuals named Justices of the Peace at the first meeting of the Assistants in August, 1630, exercised their judicial power from time to time, for at a Court of Assistants which met in Boston on November 30, 1630, Sir Richard Saltonstall, who was sitting as a member of the Court, was fined 5 pounds "for whipping 2 several persons without the presence of another Assistant" contrary to the earlier act. (1 Records 82)

It was not long before objections to the exercise of legislative powers by the Assistants began to be voiced. In Winthrop's Journal for February, 1632, the following account of that first expression of discontent appears:

"The Governor and Assistants called before them ... divers of Watertown; the pastor and elder by letter, and the others by warrant.[6] The occasion was, for that a warrant being sent to Watertown for levying of £8, part of a rate of £60, ordered for the fortifying of the new town, the pastor and elder, etc., assembled the people and delivered their opinion, that it was not safe to pay moneys after that sort, for fear of bringing themselves and posterity into bondage. Being come before the Governor and Council, after much debate, they acknowledged their fault, confessing freely, that they were in an error, and made a retraction and submission under their hands, and were enjoined to read it in the assembly the next Lord's day. The ground of their error was, for that they took this government to be no other but as of a mayor and aldermen, who have not power to make laws or raise taxations without the people; but understanding that this government was rather in the nature of a parliament, and that no assistant could be chosen but by the freemen, who had power likewise to remove the assistants and put in others, and therefore at every General Court (which was

---

6. It seems likely that the difference between the forms of summons was based upon the belief that it would be impolitic, if not illegal to issue compulsory process to ecclesiastical officials. Cf. 2 Winthrop, Journal 264-265.

to be held once every year) they had free liberty to consider and propound anything concerning the same, and to declare their grievances, without being subject to question or, etc., they were fully satisfied; and so their submission was accepted, and their offense pardoned." 1 Journal 70.

Although this submission of the Watertown remonstrants seemed to leave the Assistants in control of the legislative power, at the meeting of the General Court on May 9, 1632, the earlier delegation of authority to the Assistants to elect the Governor was repealed, and it was voted that henceforth "the Governor, Deputy Governor, and Assistants, should be chosen by the whole Court of Governor, Deputy Governor, Assistants, and Freemen". Until 1634, however, legislative and judicial power continued to be concentrated in the Court of Assistants.

The constitutional revolution which occurred at the May sitting of the General Court in 1634 evidently had its origin in grievances which Winthrop describes in a Journal entry for April 1 of that year.

"Notice being sent out of the General Court to be held the 14th day of the third month, called May, the Freemen deputed two of each town to meet and consider of such matters as they were to take order in at the same General Court; who, having met, desired a sight of the patent, and conceiving thereby that all their laws should be made at the General Court, repaired to the Governor to advise with him about it. ... He told them that when the Patent was granted, the number of Freemen was supposed to be (as in like corporations) so few, as they might well join in making laws; but now they were grown to so great a body, as it was not possible for them to make or execute laws, but they must choose others for that purpose. ... Yet this they might do at present, viz., they might, at the General Court, make an order that, once in the year, a certain number should be appointed ... to revise all laws, etc., and to reform what they found amiss therein; but not to make any new laws, but prefer their grievances to the Court of Assistants. ..." 1 Journal 128-129.

As matters turned out, however, Winthrop was unable to control the constitutional impulses of the Deputies of the Towns when they appeared at the meeting of the General Court on May 14. At that meeting Thomas Dudley was elected Governor, in place of Winthrop, and the following votes were passed:

"That none but the General Court hath power to make and establish laws, nor to elect and appoint officers. ...

"That none but the General Court hath power to raise monies and taxes. ...

"It is likewise ordered that there shall be four General Courts held yearly, to be summoned by the Governor, for the time being, and not to be dissolved without the consent of the major part of the Court." 1 Records 117, 118.

As a result of these votes the legislative powers were reinvested in the General Court, where the Charter had placed them. One other vote, however, was adopted which served to alter the system of government as it had been outlined in the Charter. That vote made provision for the election of Deputies from each town. These Deputies, at all meetings of the General Court, should represent the Freemen "to deal in their behalf, in the public affairs of the Commonwealth" and should "have the full power and voices of all the said Freemen, derived to them for the making and establishing of laws". It was provided, however, that the officers of the corporation should continue to be elected by the Freemen themselves, rather than by their deputies. 1 Records 118-119.

2. The Judicial System

In 1636 and 1638 the fundamentals of the judicial system were established by legislation of the General Court. At the base of that system there were so-called Commissioners' Courts. In every town where an Assistant resided he was to be the single judge of this Court. In each of the other towns the General Court from time to time named three men, two of whom together had the powers of a single Assistant. These courts had a jurisdiction, both civil and criminal, over "small causes" (1 Records 239). From time to time the General Court increased the jurisdiction of these Commissioners' Courts, but so far as we know they never handled cases of appreciable importance. Much the more important of the tribunals established by the General Court were the so-called County, or Quarterly Courts. By March of 1636, when they were created, experience had evidently shown that even though the Assistants had ceased, except in association with the Deputies, to function as legislators, the Court of Assistants alone could not adequately meet the needs of the community for judicial tribunals. Accordingly four County Courts were established in 1636 at Boston, Newtown (Cambridge), Ipswich, and Salem. Each of these four courts exercised a general civil jurisdiction (subject to variable limitations), and a jurisdiction in criminal cases in which the penalty was less than banishment, loss of member or of life. The Assistants (frequently known as Magistrates) were the judges of these County Courts, though on nomination of the towns the General Court appointed other persons than the annually elected Assistants to sit on the County Court when a particular county did not have an Assistant among its residents. It was provided in the basic statute, however, that at least one Assistant must always be included among the quorum of five judges. (1 Records 169).[1] Trial by jury was customary in these courts.

Above the County Courts there was, of course, the Court of Assistants. This Court, which normally sat in Boston, had an appellate jurisdiction over the County Courts and an original jurisdiction of somewhat indeterminate scope. Normally a criminal case in which the penalty was banishment or loss of member or life was tried there in the first instance. Questions of fact heard in the Court of Assistants, whether on appeal or otherwise, were normally tried to a jury. Its records have been published by the state in three somewhat unsatisfactory volumes.

A notable feature of this judicial system was the fact that the Assistants were of controlling importance at each of its levels. Any person elected Assistant might find himself called upon to exercise the judicial office as a Commissioner, of Small Causes, as a Judge of the County Court, as a member of the Court of Assistants, and as we shall see shortly, as a member of the General Court. This concentration of judicial power in the hands of a relatively small group of men inevitably was a persistent source of difficulty and irritation. The fact that the Assistants were elected annually must have somewhat alleviated the disadvantages of the system. Those who possessed the judicial power, however, seem to have sought to find means of preventing the elective process from weakening it. At the same sitting of the General Court in which the County Courts were established, an office, nowhere mentioned in the Charter, was created. The order creating the new office provided that at each annual election "a certain number of magistrates" should be named who should hold office "for terms of their natural lives [and] not to be removed but upon due conviction of crime, insufficiency, or for some other weighty cause". (1 Records 167). Although it is not entirely clear what function these magistrates were intended to fulfill, it appears that for some three years they claimed the right to act as judges. The claim, however, was resisted and in 1639 the General Court passed an order "interpreting" the earlier legislation. That interpretive act was as follows: "Whereas [the order of 1636] has been taken by some as if the Court had cre-

---

1. The most important of the published records of the County Courts are the eight volumes of the Records of the Quarterly Courts of Essex County, 1636-1683, published by The Essex Institute between 1911 and 1921, and the Records of the Suffolk County Court, 1671-1680, published in two volumes by The Colonial Society in 1933, and containing a learned introduction by Professor Chafee.

ated a new order of magistrates contrary to the sense and intent of his majesty's grant, this Court doth now declare that the intent of the said order was not to make any such order of magistrates not warranted by our patent ... and accordingly we do now order that no such counsellor so chosen, or hereafter to be chosen, shall be accounted a magistrate, nor that any acts of power to be done by any such shall be of force and warrantable except he or they shall be chosen to some place of magistracy ... by annual election, according to the tenure of the patent. ..." (1 Records 264) With the passage of this order the threat to the principle of an elective judiciary seems finally to have been destroyed.

3. The General Court as a Judicial Tribunal

It is a notable fact that the Colony's records indicate that until May of 1634 it was only on the rarest occasions that the General Court exercised judicial power. Thereafter, however, the Records show that the General Court at each sitting devoted a very substantial portion of its time to judicial business, that is, to the hearing of civil and criminal cases. Some of these cases seem to have been brought before the General Court in the first instance; the majority, however, came there from the lower courts - chiefly from the Court of Assistants. One of the most important, and certainly one of the most famous cases to come to the General Court on original petition and not on appeal was the case of Sherman v. Keayne. No complete record of the proceedings has survived, but from the following account of the case, which was evidently made by John Winthrop, then Governor of Colony, one can see something of the course which the proceedings followed in the General Court.

John Winthrop's Summary of The Case Between Richard Sherman and Robert Keayne
General Court of Massachusetts Bay, 1642
4 Winthrop Papers 349

Att the generall Courtt (3) 18-1642

A breaviate of the Case betwene Richard Sheareman plaintiff by petition and Capt. Robert Keaine defendantt aboute the title to A straye Sowe supposed to be broughtt from Deare Iland about (9)ber 1636.

The poynts in the Case agreed

1. The plaintiff had a Sowe all white, Saue a black Spott vnder the eye of the biggnesse of a Shilling and a ragged Eare.

2. This Sowe was Carryed to deare Iland.

3. Noe profe thatt it was brought back. onelye probablie itt might be though neare 40 Swine miscaryed there thatt yeare.

4. The defendant had a straye Sowe soposed to be brought from Deare Iland that yeare.

5. This Sowe was Cryed divers tymes, and many came and sawe her, in the tyme the defendant keept her, which was betwene one and 3 yeares.

6. The defendant had before this tyme, a faire white Sowe of his owne which he keept in his yarde with the straye Sowe aboue a yeare.

7. The defendant killed one of these Sowes about (8ber) 1637.

8. The plaintiffs wife soone after, charged the defendant to haue killed her Sowe.

9. The defendant shewing the plaintiffs wife the Sowe which remained aliue she disclaimed itt.

10. Upon Complaint of the plaintiffs wife, the cause was brought to the Elders (as matter of offence) and vpon hearing all Allegations, and the most materiall wittnesses on booth parts, the defendant was Cleared.

11. The cause thus rested till (2) - 1640 and then the plaintiffs wife brought itt to the Inferyer Courte att Boston where (vpon a full hearinge) the Jurye founde for the defendant and awarded him about 3li costs.

12. Now (about 2 yeares after) the plaintiff brings the cause (by petition) into the generall Courte declyning the Court of Assistants to which itt properlye belonged, and declares againe for the Sowe which was killed (8ber-37).

The Evidence

pro plaintiff Two or three wittnesses that the Sowe killed (8ber 37) had sume such black spott vnder the Eye and some cutts or ragges on the eare.

pro defendant I This contradickted by more wittnesses (which yet may be reaconsiled by other wittnesses of thee plaintiffs (viz.) that the defendants owne Sowe had sume such spott there aboute in the skinne butt not in the haire and soe might not be easy to discerne when the haire was thick, but apparent when the heire was off.

2 proued by 6 or 7 wittnesses whoe then lived in the defendants famelye, but are all gone since (but one or two) that this Sowe was the defendants owne and bought of one Houghton.

For the other Sowe which was aliue a year after

pro plaintiff diuers wittnesses that this Sowe had such markes as the plaintiffs.

pro defendantt 11 more wittnesses (and of as good credytt) that this Sowe (which was the straye) had other markes and not such as the plaintiff Claimed itt by.

2 Itt was clearelye proued that this was the onelye straye Sowe the defendant had, that this was offered to be shewed to the plaintiffs wife before the first Sowe was killed though att another tyme denyed her, for some reasons then alledged by the defendantt and that she was shewed itt after, in thee defendants yeard and confidently disclamed itt as none of hers. And now againe, vpon her Oath in the Courtt did claime A Sowe by other markes, and not such as this Sowe had.

For A 3 Sowe never spoaken off before this Courte

pro plaintiff A wittnesse or 2 that they sawe a 3d Sowe in the defendants yarde.

pro defendant 1 This can be of noe waight against soe manye wittnesses to the contrarye.

2 This 3d Sowe is not proued to have such markes as the plaintiffs.

3 This might be one of the breede of the other sowes, or some Neighbors swine taken in the defendantts garden and keept vp with his owne, till the owner fetched it awaye.

4 the plaintiffs claime and the scope of his Euidence being for the Sowe killed about (8)ber - 37 if he faile of that, the Courte is not to seeke out a Sowe for him.

The whole Eauidence is thus Ballanced

pro plaintiff The testimony considered apart amount to a probable eauidence, that the defendantt had and converted to his owne vse the plaintiffs Sowe.

Ballance The testimonyes reaching noe further, maye albe true, and yett the defendantt not guiltye, nor anye of these Sowes the plaintiffs.

pro defendantt The testimonyes (whither considered apartt or with the other) afforde Euidence of Certaintye, raised vpon certaine grownds, as occasion, oppertunitye, familiaritye, freaquencye, etc.

Ballance If this testimonye be true, Itt is not possible the defendantt should be guiltye or anye of these Sowes the plaintiffs.

For Instance

Joseph wanders alone in the wildernesse his Coate is found torne and bloudie, he is never heard off for manye yeares: vpon this probable euidence, Jacob concludes that Joseph was deuowred of a wilde beast: But when evidence of certaintye comes out of Aegipt that he was ther aliue, and Lord of Egipt the former aeuidence was invailed and the Spirit of Jacob reviued, and now he concludes he was liuing: though he knewe not how he should come thither, or how he should be soe aduansed there. Now lett anye impartiall hande hold the Scales while Religion and sounde reason give Judgment in the case.

Yett (if neede weare) this might be added, that whereas the plaintiffs wife was allowed to take her Oath for the markes of her Sowe, the defendant and his wife (being denyed the like libertye) came voluntarelye into the Court and solomelye in the preasence of god declared 1 that the Sowe which was first killed was there owne. 2. that the Sowe which remained and was shewed the plaintiffs wife and which she disclaimed was the Straye Sowe. 3. that they never had anye other straye Sowe.

This cause (after the best part of 7 dayes spent in Examination and agitation) is by the breakeing vp of the Courte dismissed, not by occasion of A negatiue voate in the Magistrats (as is misreported) but by A fundamentall and Just Lawe agreable to sounde reason as shall appeare (the Lord willinge) in due season: The Lawe was made vpon searious consideration and Aduise with all the Elders (i) 1635 to this effect.

Noe Law Sentence, etc. shall passe as an act of the Courte without the consent of the greater part of the magistrates of the one parte and the greater number of the deaputies on the other parte.

There were present in the courte, when the voate was to be taken 9 Magistrates and 30 deaputies whoe had all heard the Cuase examined and argued, soe as noe centance could be legally passed without Consent of 5 magistrates and 16 deaputies which neither plaintiff nor defendantt had, for there were but 2 magistrates and 15 deputies for the plaintiff and 7 magistrates and 8 deputies for the defendant the other 7 stood doubtfull. yett was there noe necessitye, that the cause might not haue bene brought to an issue, for eyther the Court might haue Argued the Case againe by which meanes some who were doubtfull might haue come to a reasolucion or others might haue changed there Judgments and soe haue proceeded to a new voate, or else Committyes might haue bene Chosen, to order the Cause according to Lawe.

That this is the true state of the Case for the substance of itt, as it hath bene considered and allowed, by other of my breethren and Assotiates booth Magistrats and deaputies with our proseedings therein and which we shall not be ashamed (by the Lords helpe) to avouch and maintaine, before all the world, I doe heare affirme vnder my hand: dated att Boston this 5 - 15 - 1642. John Winthop governor

Certain constitutional consequences of Sherman v. Keayne are dealt with in the following paper.

Howe and Eaton, "The Supreme Judicial Power in the Colony of Massachusetts Bay"
20 New England Quarterly 1-13 (1947)

Much has been written of our constitutional indebtedness to Goody Sherman's sow.[1] A learned son of Massachusetts has suggested that a monument to her memory as mother of Senates might appropriately be erected on Beacon Hill.[2] It is in any case clear that when the white sow with "a black spott under the eye of the bignesse of a shilling and a ragged ear" disappeared in 1636, she mothered solid constitutional doctrine which is still our inheritance. Of course, the litigious Goody Sherman, wife and attorney of the sow's master, may claim our gratitude as well, for had she not pursued the alleged converter through all but one of the principal courts of the Colony of Massachusetts Bay, the particular pig who wandered would have remained as obscure in history as her brothers and sisters who stayed at home.

The claim of Goody Sherman was that Captain Richard Keayne had taken and killed her husband's stray sow.[3] Unsuccessful before the church officials in her efforts to prove Keayne's misconduct, she turned to secular justice but failed to establish her case in the County Court at Boston. For two years she let the matter lie, preferring apparently not to take her case on appeal to the Court of Assistants. In 1642, however, she presented a petition to the General Court in which once more she sought to hold the Captain liable for his alleged conversion of the sow. The General Court to which she came was constituted of two elected groups of representatives of the Freemen - the smaller group of Assistants, or Magistrates, chosen by the Deputies, and the larger body, the Deputies, represent-

---

1. Arthur P. Rugg, "A Famous Colonial Litigation", Proceedings of the American Antiquarian Society, New Series (Worcester 1921), xxx, 217. John G. Palfrey, History of New England (Boston, 1858), I, 618-623; Charles McLean Andrews, The Colonial Period of American History (New Haven, 1934), I, 450-454; Herbert L. Osgood, The American Colonies in the Seventeenth Century (New York, 1904), I, 165-166.

2. Samuel E. Morison, Builders of The Bay Colony (Boston, 1930), 93.

3. The most detailed contemporary account of the proceedings is John Winthrop's. See Winthrop Papers (Boston, 1944), IV, 349; John Winthrop, The History of New England (Boston, 1853) II, *69-72; *115-119; *160.

ing the towns. The Records of the General Court contain the following entry concerning the disposition of her petition: "It was voted by 2 magistrates & 15 deputies for the plaintiffe, & by 7 magistrates & 8 deputies for the defendant, & 7 deputies were newters."[4] Thus a majority of the Assistants found for the defendant, whereas a majority both of the Deputies and of the whole court, excluding the "newter" deputies, found for the plaintiff. A statute of the Colony enacted in 1636 after consultation with the Elders and in resolution of a dispute between Magistrates and Deputies concerning the emigration of Thomas Hooker to Connecticut, contained the following provision: "And whereas it may fall out that in some of theis General Courts, to be helden by the magistrates & deputies, there may arise some difference of judgment in doubtfull cases, it is therefore ordered, that noe law, order, or sentence shall passe as an act of the Court, without the consent of the greater parte of the magistrates on the one parte, & the greater number of the deputyes on the other parte; & for want of such accorde, the cause or order shalbe suspended, & if either partie thinke it soe materiall, there shall be forthwith a committee chosen, the one halfe by the magistrates, & the other halfe by the deputyes, & the committee soe chosen to elect an umpire, whoe together shall have power to heare & determine the cause in question."[5] The dissolution of the General Court in June, 1643, apparently prevented the naming of a committee under the statute, and Goody Sherman, being unable to secure the votes of a majority of the Assistants, was frustrated by their negative vote, and got nothing more tangible than the gratitude of historians for all her pains.[6] Interest in the rights of the par-

---

4. N. B. Shurtleff, editor, Records of the Governor and Company of The Massachusetts Bay (Boston, 1853), II, 12 (henceforth referred to as Records).

5. Records, I, 170. The Records of the General Court indicate that the order was enacted at the March session, 1635-1636. Why Winthrop spoke of the statute as an enactment of 1634 is not known. See Winthrop Papers, IV, 380-383. The details of the controversy between Magistrates and Deputies concerning Hooker's emigration are found in Winthrop, History of New England, I, *141-142, *155, *159-160. On at least one occasion the Committee procedure seems to have been utilized. See Winthrop, History of New England, II, *227.

6. It has been stated, how accurately we do not know, that the matter later was referred by the parties to arbitration. See Oliver Ayer Roberts, History of The Ancient and Honorable Artillery (Boston, 1895), I, 14.

ticular parties was quickly forgotten in the fervent disputation of the constitutional question whether the Assistants properly had, as the statute of 1636 indicated, a negative voice in matters coming before the General Court or whether a majority vote of the whole body was essential for effective decision.[7]

We shall have occasion later to touch upon some of the principal arguments advanced at the time when the constitutional issue presented by Sherman v. Keayne was under discussion. For an introductory moment it will be helpful to examine the resolution adopted by the General Court in the following year by which it was sought to put the issue at rest.[8] It has been suggested that the act of March, 1644, in continuing the negative voice of Magistrates, was merely confirmatory of the 1636 order under which Goody Sherman had been denied relief, and that no appreciable change in significant procedures of the General Court resulted from the legislation of 1644.[9] Both suggestions are misleading. It seems quite clear that between 1636 and 1644 the General Court had deliberated as a single body, conducting all its business in unicameral sittings. The Magistrates sat separately only when they met as the Court of Assistants for the despatch of judicial business. When the General Court convened, whether for the consideration of legislative, judicial, or administrative matters, though a majority of the Magistrates possessed a negative voice and thus could effectively block action, they sat together with the Deputies. The Act of 1644 terminated this practise and provided that in the future the two bodies should sit separately and that both must concur in all legislation. The order concluded with the explicit proviso that "all matters of iudicature which this Court shall take cognizance of shalbe issued in like manner." Under this act it seems that two significant changes in prac-

---

7. The only surviving documents of the period in which the conflicting arguments are set forth are Winthrop's "Reply to the Answer to the Discourse about the Negative Vote," Winthrop Papers, IV, 380, a "small treatise", perhaps by John Norton, Proceedings of the Massachusetts Historical Society (Boston, 1913), XLVI, 279, and the advice of the Elders, Records, II, 90-96. The Discourse of the Deputies to which Winthrop replied apparently has not been preserved.

8. Records, II, 58-59.

9. Rugg, "A Famous Colonial Litigation", Proceedings of the American Antiquarian Society, New Series, XXX, 217, 227, (1920).

tice were effected: bicameral sittings were substituted for unicameral sittings, and the procedure prescribed in 1636 for resolution of disagreements between the two houses by committee action was abandoned. Furthermore, and for our purposes perhaps most significantly, the act of 1644 made an explicit reference to the distinction between the legislative and the judicial business of the General Court.

It is as the mother of Senates that Goody Sherman's sow has achieved immortality. For what was settled as a result of the disputation of 1643-1644 was that the Colonial legislature, like Parliament, was to be bicameral. This meant that the government of Massachusetts Bay was not to be "a meere democratie"[10] which "in effect puts out one of the eyes (if not the right one) of the common wealth,"[11] but "A forme mixt of an Aristocracy and Democracy."[12] Power was to be shared by, yet appropriately divided between persons of superior quality and those of inferior condition. Though equality is a desirable objective, "Tis not an Arithmeticall equality but a Geometricall that is to be attended to; that is, not equality of number, but of vertue."[13] The act of 1644 embodied those principles in law and in doing so settled upon Massachusetts the inheritance of a bicameral legislature. So significant is that inheritance that only the most casual attention has been paid to the issue which was really central in the crisis of the sow but which to us, since it does not appear to be a living part of our inheritance, seems unreal - the issue, that is, of the appropriate allocation of judicial power between the upper and the lower houses of the General Court. Lawyers and historians, anxious to fit yesterday's institutions into today's categories, have been quite willing to treat the jurisdiction of the General Court in matters of judicature as of negligible significance. The casual feeling that the General Court must have been modelling itself on Parliament in which legislative and judicial powers were merged has, perhaps, discouraged inquiry into the nature and scope of the General Court's jurisdiction in judicial matters. Historians have paid no attention to the significant

---

10. The phrase is Winthrop's: See, Winthrop Papers, IV, 383.

11. Proceedings of the Massachusetts Historical Society, XLVI, 282.

12. Proceedings of the Massachusetts Historical Society, XLVI, 280.

13. Proceedings of the Massachusetts Historical Society, XLVI, 283.

difference that the House of Commons, if it possessed a theoretical authority to share responsibility with the Lords in matters of judicature, at no time demanded that theory should become practice;[14] whereas the Deputies persistently asserted that it should. Though lawyers have known that supreme judicial power was exercised by the General Court, they have nonetheless looked upon the Court of Assistants as "for practical purposes, the head of the judicial system."[15] Such deceptive simplifications as this and such inaccurate statements as that "in 1644 the question [of the negative voice] was forever laid to rest by the legal separation of the legislature into two coequal houses"[16] have resulted in the virtually complete disregard of significant materials. The story of the lively struggle between Magistrates and Deputies throws considerable light not only on the gradual separation, during the seventeenth century, of the legislative and judicial powers, but on the conflicting conceptions of that period as to the proper allocation of supreme judicial authority in a modern commonwealth. Until all the archives of the Colonial period have been systematically examined and the wealth of information which they contain concerning the General Court's role in matters of judicature has been sifted, it will be impossible entirely to correct traditional misconceptions. An examination of a few of those papers will, however, do something to show the necessity for further research, and will, perhaps, add something to our understanding of persistent tendencies in American legal history.

I

The statute of 1636, in which the negative voice was first sanctioned, as we have seen, made no distinction between the

---

14. There has, of course, been some disagreement among modern scholars both as to the reality and as to the legitimacy of the claim of the Commons to a share in the judicial power of Parliament. See Sir William Holdsworth, History of English Law (Boston, 1922), I, 362-365; Charles Howard McIlwain, The High Court of Parliament (New Haven, 1910), 190-216; Albert Frederich Pollard, The Evolution of Parliament (London, 1926), 331, 445-446. It is evident that the Massachusetts Deputies contended that the Commons in England shared in Parliament's judicial power. See Winthrop Papers, IV, 387.

15. Frank Washburn Grinnell, The Two Hundred Fiftieth Birthday of the Supreme Judicial Court, 1692-1942 (Boston, 1942), 9.

16. Osgood, American Colonies in the Seventeenth Century, I, 166.

judicial and the legislative problems which might come before the General Court. It spoke of the possibility of differences of judgment in doubtful cases, laws, orders, and sentences, and, finally, in "the cause in question". When it is remembered that the act was adopted as a result of a dispute between Magistrates and Deputies concerning Hooker's emigration, a question which it is difficult to classify either as legislative or as judicial in character, one can see a good reason why no all-inc. ·ive dichotomy between legislative matters and matters of judicature was considered appropriate. It is, in any case, unlikely that the distinction so real to us (if still so elusive) was clear to the General Court in 1636. John Norton, who in 1643 spoke of an "act judiciall in either making or executing Lawes,"[17] was quite surely not alone among his contemporaries in failing to draw our line between enactment and judgment.

Unfortunately, no statement of the Deputies' argument as formulated in 1643-1644 has been preserved. Its scope, however, is quite clearly indicated in Winthrop's memorandum on the negative vote[18] and in Norton's argument on behalf of the Magistrates. It seems evident that the Deputies denied the negative voice to Magistrates in all types of cases, and did so partly on the basis of the text of the Patent and partly on broader grounds. They evidently contended that any argument in favor of magisterial power which was based on the analogy of General Court to Parliament was unsound because "of the disproportion betweene that Court and ours [and] because our magistrates are not of the nobility, as the upper House there is."[19]

---

17. Proceedings of the Massachusetts Historical Society, XLVI, 279. I ascribe the "small treatise" to Norton, though its authorship is not certain.

18. Winthrop Papers, IV, 380.

19. Winthrop Papers, IV, 386. Evidently the Deputies, who argued that there was an analogy between their claim to a dominant share in the supreme judicial power and the claim of the Commons (supra note 14), were unwilling to admit that the breeding and talents of Magistrates were so nearly equal to those of the Lords that they could exercise a negative voice in legislation. Winthrop answers the Deputies by saying that if the Deputies would yield the English Lords a negative vote "in respecte of their Nobilitye: the reason is stronger for our magistrates: for those Nobles onely represent their owne familyes, but our magistrates doe represent the Authoritye of all the people as well as the deputyes do." (Winthrop Papers, IV, 387.) The ex-

Becoming more lawyer-like, the Deputies had evidently argued that the spirit if not the letter of an act of Parliament of 33 Henry VIII forbade the concentration of corporate powers in the hands of a few of its officers,[20] and thus significantly, conceded the applicability of Parliamentary legislation to the Colony - a concession to which Winthrop characteristically replied that "the statutes of England doe not binde in any other parts out of that kingdome."[21]

One cannot, from the existing documents, find any clear evidence of an appreciation by Deputies or Magistrates of an analytical distinction between legislative and judicial powers. Differences which theory had not yet discovered were, however, being made apparent by experience. The Deputies in 1642-1643 formulated one objection to the negative voice of Magistrates which they were to reiterate throughout the century. In considering that objection, it must be remembered that the Magistrates sat as judges both in the County Courts and in the Court of Assistants. The normal route of appeals was from County Court, through the Court of Assistants to the General Court."[22] The original jurisdiction of the General

---

tent to which current English controversy influenced the argument in Massachusetts Bay is uncertain, but it is significant that Winthrop referred to Prynne's Soveraigne Power of Parliaments (London, 1643), in which there was considerable discussion of the "negative voyce" of the King over acts of Parliament. (Part 2, 73 et seq.) There is a striking similarity between Winthrop's thesis and views later enunciated by Prynne in his Plea For the Lords (London, 1658). The suggestion that discussion of the negative voice was not affected by analogous English political issues but was carried on primarily in terms of corporate management does not seem to be entirely accurate. Andrew C. McLaughlin, Foundations of American Constitutionalism (New York,1932), 46.

20. 33 H. VIII, c.27. The act applied to hospitals, colleges, deaneries, and "other corporations". Winthrop contended that the act did not apply to the Company of Massachusetts Bay.

21. Winthrop Papers, IV, 382. Winthrop also argued that the statute "extends not to Acts of Courts in Corporations."

22. Constant efforts were made to regularize appellate procedures and to confine the jurisdiction of the General Court to appellate matters. The basic statute on the matter was enacted in 1642 (Records, II, 16), and with slight variations, was embodied in the Codes of 1648, 1660, and 1672. A signifi-

Court in judicial matters seems after 1642 to have been of diminishing importance.[23] Not unnaturally it was objectionable to the Deputies that Magistrates sitting in the General Court should be empowered through the negative vote to prevent reversal of cases which they themselves had decided in the Court of Assistants, and this objection they pressed vigorously.[24] If the Colonists were unable to appreciate the analytical difference between legislative and judicial powers, they were sufficiently sensitive to political realities to see a difference between the Magistrates' claim of a veto power in matters on which they were not already committed and their claim of authority to render the appellate jurisdiction of the General Court illusory. It was in replying to this argument of the Deputies that Winthrop, unlike his ally Norton, made an explicit difference between "the power legislative" and "the chiefe power Juditiall" of the General Court.[25]

Although, as we have seen, the solution of the issue in the Act of 1644, was a victory for the Magistrates in that it left their negative voice in all matters unmodulated, the pro-

---

cant attempt to narrow the appellate jurisdiction of the General Court was made in 1659. Records, IV (Part I), 281-282.

23. This generalization is based upon the provision in the statute of 1642 that "all causes between parties should first be tried in some inferior Court". Records, II, 16. A detailed examination of the Records might, however, show that matters of judicature continued with some regularity to come before the General Court as a court of first instance.

24. Winthrop summarized this argument of the Deputies as follows: "If the Court of Assistants should give an unjust sentence in any Cause, the partye iniured can have no remedye in the General Court, if the magistrates (as they are like to doe) shall persist in their former Judgment." Winthrop Papers, IV, 390. An Act of 1653 denying a vote to those appellate judges who heard the case in the court below (Records, IV [Part 1], 152) must have substantially weakened this argument of the Deputies. One may presume, however, that even after 1653 the Deputies feared that the corporate interest of the Assistants would lead them to sustain the action of their brothers. A related objection of the Deputies, not very consistent with their own claim to supreme legislative and judicial power, was that "the Judges in Engld. have no hand in makinge those Lawes, by which they are to Judge". Winthrop Papers, IV, 390.

25. Winthrop Papers, IV, 383.

viso in the statute making the bicameral rule explicitly applicable to matters of judicature, brought into the open the distinction on which the Deputies had insisted. The distinction, politically substantial and analytically fruitful, having secured statutory recognition, became a factor of considerable significance in later discussion of the negative voice.

II

There is every reason to suppose that Winthrop and the Magistrates were well pleased with the settlement of 1644.[26] The negative voice in all matters coming before the General Court had been preserved and no loss of power, and perhaps some increase, in autonomous dignity might be expected to result from bicameral sittings. The Deputies, however, showed early signs of dissatisfaction with the settlement.[27] The records of their deliberations show that in May, 1645, a com-

---

26. It is hard to understand why Professor Andrews considered the settlement of 1644 a victory for the Deputies, in which "the superior power of the magistrates was measurably reduced." Andrews, The Colonial Period of American History, I, 452. From the standpoint of the Deputies the geometrical equality resulting from the bicameral organization of the General Court was certainly less desirable than the previous mathematical equality of the unicameral body. The only indication that the solution satisfied the Deputies is the fact that it was upon their motion that the Act of 1644 was adopted. Winthrop, History of New England, II, *160.

27. In November, 1644, six months after the settlement of the issue, the problem appears to have arisen in connection with a suit of Robert Saltonstall against the town of Watertown. The Records indicate that after the General Court heard the case an order was entered for Saltonstall. The Watertown Deputies thereupon "tooke exception against it, alleadging that the maior part of the magistrates did not vote for the complainant". The question was then put to a vote of the whole court "whether the said order should not be judged good & effectuall, notwithstanding the allegation; and the vote was, that it should stand good." Records, II, 89-90. Though it is possible that the only question here involved was whether there was a quorum of magistrates present, it seems more probable that the Watertown Deputies were urging that the terms of the statute of the preceding May should be followed. This seems to be the only instance in which the Deputies insisted that the negative voice of magistrates should control the decision of cases.

mittee was appointed "to consider some way whereby the negative vote may be tempered, that justice may have free passage."[28] Though the Report of the Committee has not been preserved, it may fairly be assumed, from the language of the order appointing the Committee, that the Deputies were more concerned to abolish the negative vote of Magistrates in matters of judicature than in legislative matters. The direction which the dispute took in later years indicates that they were not satisfied with Norton's geometrical equality in exercising the supreme judicial power. So far as the archives and published records indicate, the issue between Magistrates and Deputies lay dormant between 1645 and 1649. Evidently the view of the Assistants was dominant in 1648, for the Laws and Liberties published in that year included the provision of 1644 preserving the negative vote in the Magistrates and modifying it only to the extent of adding the explicit proviso that in matters of judicature the court "upon some particular occasion or business" might agree to proceed otherwise.[29] The principal significance of this addition is its suggestion that the Court saw itself as constitutionally free to deny the negative voice to the Magistrates, in other words, as not being bound by the charter to follow an invariable procedure.[30]

One might have supposed that the reiteration in 1648 of the agreed formula of 1644 promised some tranquillity. In 1649 however the whole issue was re-opened. An indication of how drastic were the demands of the Deputies appears from an entry in their Journal, dated 19 October 1649: "For the prevention [of] suspitions and jealousies and that aequall justice may be donne to all men, ... it is ordered, that all such cases as shall be brought before this Courte by petition, for review of any case tryed in any other Courte, or by order of this Courte, as in the case of judges and juryes disagreement, shallbe determined by the major vote of the Courte mett together, and all cases that shallbe brought before this Courte by way of complainte of vnjust or vnaequal proceedings in any other Courte,

---

28. Records, III, 11.

29. The Laws and Liberties of Massachusetts (Cambridge, 1929), 16. The Records of the General Court do not indicate when the proviso was added and it may be presumed, therefore, that it was inserted in the process of codifying the laws in 1647-1648.

30. The Court's disposition of the issue in Saltonstall v. Watertown, Records, II, 89 - 90, would indicate that a similar view prevailed in 1644.

shall be determined by the major parte of the Deputies only."[31] This vote not only sought, by the initiation of a majority rule in matters of judicature, to make the equality of justice mathematical by subordinating the Magistrates, but it appears also to have attempted to confer on the Deputies alone appellate jurisdiction in a large proportion of the cases coming to the General Court. Had the will of the Deputies prevailed in this matter, it seems clear that all persons defeated in the Court of Assistants would have based their appeal to the General Court, in part at least, on the ground that the proceedings in the Court of Assistants had been "unjust or unequal", thus entirely excluding the Magistrates from participation in the review. In making this proposal the Deputies were pressing political logic farther than they had in the course of the 1642-1643 dispute, for there is no indication that on the earlier occasion they had urged that Assistants should be excluded from a mathematically equal share in the appellate jurisdiction of the General Court.

Though the Records of the Deputies, as quoted above, indicate that this amendment, drastic in the extreme and largely excluding the Magistrates from an effective share in the judicial power of the General Court, was proposed in 1649, the authoritative records of Secretary Rawson indicate that no such change was agreed upon by the two houses. His official records show that the amendment enacted in 1649 was considerably less radical. It did, nonetheless, involve a drastic modification, if not complete reversal of the 1644 settlement. It appears from Rawson's official, but in this instance excessively succinct record, that in 1649 the General Court voted "in cases wherein there hath bein difference the Generall Court should heare the case together, & determine the case by the major vote."[32] On its face this statute would seem to be applicable both to legislative and to judicial matters, and so interpreted, would effect a substantial reversal of the 1644 settlement. Giving it its broadest possible interpretation, it would mean that though the two houses should sit and deliberate separately, as provided in the statute of 1644, if their respective majorities were in disagreement, the whole membership should assemble and dispose of the matter in hand by a majority vote of the whole. Evidently the suggestion that the new act was applicable both to legislative and judicial matters was seriously advanced in 1652, for in that year an order was entered stating, in effect, that it was intended to cover matters of judicature

---

31. Records, III, 179-180.

32. Records, II, 285.

only.[33] Even this modification of the 1644 settlement, however, constituted a very substantial victory for the Deputies. Though the statute of 1649 gave them less than their own Journal indicates they were seeking, its enactment marked the establishment of a right for which they had unsuccessfully fought in Goody Sherman's case. In legislative matters the Magistrates retained the negative voice without qualification, but in judicial matters that voice ceased to be of controlling importance in 1649. ...

Note on Appeals and Actions of Review

The statutes and judicial practices in colonial Massachusetts to an extraordinary extent permitted the re-examination of questions of fact and law. The Code of 1648 in its section on Appeals provided that it should be "the liberty of every man cast, condemned, or sentenced in any Inferior Court," to appeal to the next higher court. The one surprising exception was that an appeal was to be allowed in a capital case, only if a designated proportion of the magistrates sitting in the Court of Assistants dissented. When a case was taken to a higher court it was provided that if the issue was of law it should be determined by the bench, but if it was of law and fact it should be decided by the bench and the jury. Under this statute it is clear that appellants customarily sought and obtained a second jury trial in the appellate court. It is to be noted, however,

---

33. Records, IV (Part I), 82. The act opens with a recital of the fact that there was a manifest mistake in "the penning" of the order of 1649 when it was reprinted in the first supplement of the Laws and Liberties of 1648, and that the error "leaves all or most of the cases formerly issued in the Generall Court doubtfull & uncertaine, and takes away the negative vote, both of Magistrates and Deputies, in making lawes as well as in case of judicature, which was not intended ..." It then goes on to order that "for time to come, if there fall out any difference betwixt the Magistrates and Deputies, in any case of judicature, either civill or criminall, it shall be determined by the major part of the whole Court, and the forementioned lawe is hereby repealed." It seems clear that all that this enactment was intended to do was to remove any justification for the contention that the act of 1649 had eliminated the negative voice of the Magistrates in legislation. The suggestion of Mr. Chief Justice Rugg that this order of 1652 shows that no effective change in the practice of the Court was intended in 1649 is obviously misleading.(Rugg, "A Famous Colonial Litigation", Proceedings of the American Antiquarian Society,New Series,xxx,217 229.)

that a jury was not used in the General Court. An act of 1649 (2 Records 279) evidently caused difficulties in its provision that "all appeals ... are to be accounted in the nature of a writ of error", for in 1654 a new act was adopted reciting that this indication that an appeal was to operate as a writ of error had been interpreted to require reversal for trivial or technical error. It was therefore enacted that "in all cases of appeals the Court appealed to shall judge the case according to former evidence and no other, rectifying what is amiss therein; and where matter of fact is found to agree with the former Court, and the judgment according to law, not to revoke the decree or judgment, but to abate or increase damages as is apprehended to be just, any law, custom, or usage to the contrary notwithstanding." 4 Records, Part 1, 184.

A fruitful source of appellate jurisdiction were the statutes providing for an appeal when there was disagreement on the verdict between bench and jury. For a short time it seems that whenever there was such disagreement in a County Court the appeal would be to the General Court, but in 1659 a statute was adopted by which such appeals should be from the County Court to the Court of Assistants. 4 Records, Part 1, 381-382. Even this change, however, left the General Court with such an extensive appellate jurisdiction that it was unreasonably burdened. Experience had also evidently shown that disagreements between bench and jury were so common that appeals were excessively frequent. Accordingly in 1672, a statute, extraordinary in its reversion to and modification of antiquated and abandoned procedures of the English law, was adopted. In its substance it provided the judges of the County Courts in civil cases were bound to accept the jury's verdict and enter judgment thereon, even if they disagreed with the jury's finding, but that if there were disagreement in such cases in the Court of Assistants and the source of the disagreement was "apparent corruption or error of the jury in giving in their verdict contrary to law or evidence, the party cast shall in open court attaint the jury". Thereupon, it was provided, the "court shall summon a jury of twenty-four able and discreet men ... to attend the service of the court ... and if on trial of the case there shall be found manifest error or mistake, the party complaining shall be repaired his full damage from the other party to the original suit; and if by the said jury of twenty-four there shall be found bribery, conspiracy, or other corruption in the jury attainted, they shall be punished by fine or imprisonment, proportionable to the degree of their offense... ."[1]

---

1. Thomas Sheppard, English author of legal texts, and Puritan law reformer, in his England's Balme (1657) 50-52 proposed

The statute concluded with the repeal of the earlier acts allowing the judges to "not concur with or refuse the verdict of the jury". 4 Records, Part 2, 508-509. The statute was substantially modified in 1684 (5 Records 449). The amendment gave to the jurors who had been "reproached" by the proceedings in attaint a right to sue the attainting party for slander. Perhaps that was a factor which contributed to the discontinuance of the procedure.

In the Code of 1648, title Trials, there was included a provision first adopted in 1642 (2 Records 16), stating that "if the party against whom the Judgment shall pass shall have any new evidence, or other new matter to plead, he may desire a new trial in the same court upon a Bill of Review". This statute, which evidently applied only to civil cases, was in force during the whole of the Colonial period, and judging by the published records of the County Courts and of the Court of Assistants a vast number of cases, by virtue of its provisions, were re-tried on "review" and then taken to a third jury for reconsideration on appeal to a higher court. Evidently review was granted without regard to whether the applicant in fact had newly discovered evidence to introduce or new matter to plead. This peculiar system, with slight alterations, continued to be followed throughout the 18th century, giving the people a feeling that every man has a right to have his case heard by three juries (See, 6 Dane's Abridgment (1824) 453 et seq.) The procedure of review was at length abolished in 1818 (Ch. 85, Stats of 1818) as a result, it is said, of the unselfish (and unpopular) conviction of the bar that three jury trials of any issue of fact were too many. (See 6 American Jurist 338, ft. 1.)

4. Civil and Ecclesiastical Discipline

The division of disciplinary power between the church and the state was, of course, familiar to the Puritan immigrants, for in England the authority of the Church to impose ecclesiastical penalties upon those who committed offenses against morality was still a living reality. "Penalties for breaking any of the multitudinous rules laid down in the statutes for guidance of civil affairs, were inflicted by justices of the peace in their sessions. Offenses against the rules prescribed for the regulation of religious life and moral conduct were visited by punishment in the ecclesiastical court."[1] There

---

the introduction of similar procedure into the English law.

1. S.A. Peyton, Introduction to The Churchwarden's Presentments in the Oxfordshire Peculiars, Vol. 10, Oxfordshire Record

was frequent emphasis in the literature of New England Puritanism upon the difference between the civil peace and the church peace[2] and this emphasis indicates that the dualism, familiar in England, was continued here, though with many variations in its details. In any case it is clear that the Reformation had by no means terminated the power of the Church to exercise disciplinary authority over the moral life of the community.[3] In England where the vast majority of the population were members of the Church of England this meant that nearly all men were as much within the reach of ecclesiastical authority as they were within the control of civil authority. The concern of the Church was most frequently shown in connection with matters directly related to Church affairs. Such concern is indicated in the following proceedings in the Church of the Archdeaconry of Essex in 1615 (Hale, Precedents and Proceedings in Criminal Cases (1847), p. 238):

Eastham. Contra Thomas Milborne. - Presentatur, for spreadinge mowle hills with a shovell in the churchyard upon the Sundaye nexte Septuagesima last being the xiiith daye of Februarie 1613 and that betweene morninge and eveninge prayer; and was then taken at worke by the minister and other of the parishioners, and for that he doth not kneele on his knees in tyme of devine service when as it is fittinge he should and the rather in that he is the parishe clerke who ought to give good example thereby unto others that are negligent therein, and he hath often tymes bene admonished for to kneele by the minister but he doth altogether refuse it. And for that he singeth the psalmes in the church with such a jesticulus tone and altitonant voyce, viz. squeakinge like a gelded pigg which doth not onlie interrupt the other voyces, but is altogether dissonant and disagreeing unto any musicall harmonie and he hath been requested by the minister to leave it, but he doth obstinatlie persist and contynue therein. Prox. - f. 294b.

The Ecclesiastical Courts in England dealt with many immoralities not directly affecting church services. Typical of such proceedings were those which came before the Court of the Archdeaconry of Essex in 1599 (Hale, supra, p. 220.)

Nicolaum Marden, de Curringham - Detêcted, that he & one John Smith of the parishe of Curringham & one Richard Cottes

---

Society (1928), p. vii.

2. See, e.g. Roger Williams, The Bloody Tenent of Persecution, reprinted in Miller and Johnson, The Puritans (1938), 216,220.

3. See, Hale, Precedents and Proceedings in Criminal Causes, 1475-1640 (1847) p. v - vi.

of Orsett & George Landishe of Barkinge, after greate abuse in drinkinge, did at theire parting, take with them into the fielde at the townes ende where they ment to parte, foure or sixe potts of beere; & there setting them downe, did themselves upon theire bare knees humbly kneele downe, & kissinge the potts & drinking one to the other, & prayed for the health of all true & faythfull drunckards; & especiallie for Mr. Andrew Browghton, as they said the mainteiner & upholder of all true & faythful drunckards; and having done they kissed ech other & for a memorye of their worthy acte did every man make his marke or name, upon an ashen tree, that stood there by them. (Ad agnoscendam culpam) - f. 212.

Although the Puritan immigrants came to New England with a deep hostility to the ways of the Church of England they did not abandon all of the institutions with which they were familiar. To them, as to the majority of Englishmen, it seemed entirely appropriate for ecclesiastical agencies to enforce a moral discipline upon church members. Since, however, church membership was reserved for the elect there were many persons in the Puritan community over whom ecclesiastical discipline could not be applied. The morals of this group, however, were of profound concern to the civil state, and therefore one finds the courts of Massachusetts Bay dealing persistently with matters of morality and dealing with them in much the same way as Ecclesiastical Courts in England dealt with the moral offenses of church members. One must not, however, overlook the fact that the churches of Massachusetts Bay constantly exercised a disciplinary jurisdiction over their members and that the exercise of this jurisdiction was an essential part of the legal process.

A characteristic example of the effort of the General Court to secure the enforcement of church discipline upon church members before the civil authorities should be called upon to take action is shown in an elaborate order adopted in September, 1638. After reciting that there had been many complaints concerning the "excessive wearing of lace and other superfluities tending to little use or benefit", and after making it a criminal offense to manufacture garments with short sleeves "whereby the nakedness of the arme may be discovered in the wearing thereof" the order proceeded as follows: "And whereas some have been grieved that such excesses were presented to the Court, which concerned members of Churches, before the parties had been dealt with at home, intimating thereby that the churches would ... have taken such course as would have reformed their members, and so have prevented the trouble of the Court; - This Court hath therefore thought fit (in the great confidence it hath of the care and faithfulness of the churches) to stay all proceedings upon the said presentments, in expectation that the officers and members of all the churches ... will speedily and effectually proceed against offenders in this kind, and that they will also ... keep the more strict watch over all sorts for time to come; and this Court doth hereby intimate to all whom it may concern (of what quality or estate soever they may be) that all such persons as ... shall obstinately persist in their excesses inthis kind, shall be looked at as contemners of authority, and regardless of the public weale, and must expect to be proceeded against by the strictest course of justice, as their offenses shall deserve." 1 Records 274-275.

Of all the striking differences between the processes of ecclesiastical discipline in England and in Massachusetts Bay none is more notable than the fact that in the Congregational system there were no Ecclesiastical Courts. Each congregation, i.e. all the church members in a particular parish, participated as judges and jurors in the decision of cases. Was this practice, perhaps, one of the factors encouraging the development of democratic institutions?

The following examples of the way in which the Massachusetts churches exercised their disciplinary authority and of the wide scope of their jurisdiction are taken from Charles Francis Adams's account of the records of the First Church in Quincy (Some Phases of Sexual Morality and Church Discipline in Colonial New England, II Mass. Hist. Soc. Proc., Vol. 6, p. 477):

"Temperance, the daughter of Brother F__, now the wife of John B__ , having been guilty of the sin of Fornication with him that is now her husband, was called forth in the open Congregation, and presented a paper containing a full acknowledgment of her great sin and wickedness, - publickly bewayled her disobedience to parents, pride, unprofitableness under the means of grace, as the cause that might provoke God to punish her with sin, and warning all to take heed of such sins, begging the church's prayers, that God would humble her, and give a sound repentence,&c. Which confession being read, after some debate, the brethren did generally if not unanimously judge that she ought to be admonished; and accordingly she was solemnly admonished of her great sin, which was spread before her in divers particulars, and charged to search her own heart wayes and to make thorough work in her Repentance,&c. from which she was released by the church vote unanimously on April 11th 1698."

"(Sept. 8, 1735) At a meeting of the First Church of Christ in Braintree at the house of the Pastor, September the 8th 1735, after prayer - Voted, That it is the duty of this Church to examine the proofs of an unhappy quarrel between Benjamin Owen and Joseph Owen, members in full communion with this Church on May 30th 1735, whereby God has been dishonored and religion reproached.

"After some examination thereof it was unanimously voted by the brethren - That the Pastor should ask Benjamin Owen whether he would make satisfaction to the Church for his late offensive behaviour, which he refused to do in a public manner, unless the charge could be more fully proved upon him. Whereupon there arose several debates upon the sufficiency of the proof to demand a publick confession of him; and there appearing different apprehensions among the brethren about it, it was moved by several that the meeting should be adjourned for further consideration of the whole affair. ...

"Then the meeting was adjourned to the 29th Inst. at 2 o'clock P.M.

"The brethren met upon the adjournment, and after humble supplication to God for direction, examined more fully the proofs of the late quarrel between Benj. Owen and Joseph Owen but passed no vote upon them.

"[Oct. 22, 1735] At a meeting of the 1st Church in Braintree at the house of the Pastor, Oct. 22, 1735 - after prayer, Benj. Owen offered to the brethren a confession of his late offensive behavior which was not accepted.

"Then it was voted by the brethren that he should make confession of his offence in the following words, viz: Whereas I have been left to fall into a sinful strife and quarrel with my brother Joseph Owen, I acknowledge I am greatly to blame that I met my brother in anger and strove with him, to the dishonor of God, and thereby also have offended my Christian brethren. I desire to be humbled before God, and to ask God's forgiveness: I desire to be at peace with my brother, and to be restored to the charity of this Church, and your prayers to God for me.

"To which he consented, as also to make it in public.

"At the desire of the brethren the meeting was adjourned to Friday the 24th Inst. at 4 o'clock P.M. that they might satisfy themselves concerning the conduct of Joseph Owen in the late sinful strife between him and his brother. And the Pastor was desired to send to him to be present at the adjournment.

"The brethren met accordingly, and after a long consideration of the proof had against Joseph Owen, it was proposed to the brethren whether they would defer the further consideration of Joseph Owen's affair to another opportunity. It was voted in the negative.

"Whereupon a vote was proposed in the following words viz: Whether it appears to the brethren of this Church that the proofs they have had against Joseph Owen in the late unhappy strife between him and his brother be sufficient for them to demand satisfaction from him. Voted in the affirmative.

"And the satisfaction the brethren voted he should make for his offence was in the following words: - I am sensible that in the late unhappy and sinful strife between me and my brother Benj. Owen, I am blameworthy, and I ask forgiveness of God and this Church, and I desire to be at peace with my brother and ask your prayers to God for me.

"Then it was proposed to the brethren whether they would accept this confession, if Joseph Owen would make it before them at the present meeting - Voted in the negative.

"Whereupon it was voted that he should make this satisfaction for his offense before the Church upon the Lord's day immediately before the administration of the Lord's supper. With which he refusing to comply though he consented to make it before the Church at the present meeting, the meeting was dissolved.

"October 26, 1735. Benj'n Owen made a public confession of his offence, and was restored to the charity of the Church.

"[Nov. 10, 1735] ... Upon a motion made by some of the brethren to reconsider the vote of the church Oct. 24 relating to Joseph Owen, it was voted to reconsider the same. Voted also that his confession be accepted before the brethren at the present meeting, which was accordingly done, and he was restored to their charity."

The uncertain boundary which separated the jurisdiction of churches from that of the state, when the conduct of a church member was in issue, necessitated close cooperation between the two agencies of law enforcement. That cooperation was frequent and effective, as can be seen in the following matter which arose in 1692 in the inter-charter period. The civil proceedings are reported in Volume 1 of the _Records of the Court of Assistants_ (1901), p. 361; the record of the supplementary church proceedings is in Adams, _supra_, p. 484.

"Hannah Owen of Braintree comitted to the Prison in Boston for that by indirect meanes Josiah Owen & s^d^ Hannah Owen procured a marriage they being within the line of kindred or affinity forbidden Marriage by the Word of God & Statutes of England,[1] Appeared, and owned she was s^d^ Josiah Owen's Brothers Relect. The Court do order, That the s^d^ Hannah do for the future no more cohabit wth s^d^ Josiah Owen, or have fellowship with him as with an husband, and that she make a publick acknowledgment of her sin & evil before the Congregation at Braintree on their Lecture day, or on the Lords day.

---

1. The colonial statutes contained no specific prohibition of such a marriage. The Code of 1672, however, included a resolution of the general court of 1670 answering in the negative the quest in "whether it be lawful for a man that hath buried his first wife to marry with her that was his first wife's natural sister". Whitmore, _Colonial Laws_, 1672, p. 102; IV _Records_, Part II, 454.

"Josiah Owen, the son of William Owen (whose parents have been long in full communion), a child of the covenant, who obtained by fraud and wicked contrivance by some marriage with his brother Ebenezer Owen's widdow, as the Pastor of the church had information by letters from the Court of Assistance touching the sentence there passed upon her (he making his escape). And living with her as an husband, being, by the Providence of God, surprised at his cottage by the Pastor of the Church with Major Quinsey and D. Thompson (of whom reports were that he was gone, we intending to discourse with her and acquaint [her] with the message received from the said Court informing her their appointment of an open confession of their sin in the congregation), he was affectionately treated by them, and after much discourse, finding him obstinate and reflecting, he was desired and charged to be present the next Sabbath before the Church, to hear what should be spoken to him, but he boldly replied he should not come. And being after treated by D. Thompson and his father to come, and taking his opportunity to carry her away the last weeke, after a solemn sermon preached on 1 Cor. 5. 3, 4 and 5, and prayers added, an account was given to the church and congregation of him, the Brethren voting him to be an impenitent, scandalous, wicked, incestuous sinner, and giving their consent that the sentence of excommunication should be passed upon and declared against him, which was solemnly performed by the Pastor of the Church according to the direction of the Apostle in the above mentioned text: this 17 of January, 169½."

When cooperation was called for it was not always forthcoming, and there are a number of instances in which conflicts developed between the ecclesiastical and the civil authorities. Such conflict was clearly involved, and was evidently piously stubborn in the litigation involving Andrew Mansfield and William Longley on the one hand, and John Hathorne on the other which occurred in Essex County in 1663.

Mansfield v. Hathorne
Longley v. Hathorne

County Court, Essex County, 1663. 3 Essex Quarterly Court Records 24, 30.

[The background of these two actions can be reconstructed from the published records of the Essex County courts. In 1662 William Longley (or Langley) brought suit against Henry Collins and John Hathorne, residents of Lynn, charging that though the plaintiff had been a resident of Lynn since 1638 no lands had been allotted to him by the town, as they should have been. At the commencement of the suit the town common in Lynn had been attached (2 Essex Records 351). Collins and Hathorne were named defendants in this action "in behalf of the town of Lynn". In that suit the plaintiff prevailed, and the verdict was that he should either recover £ 40 or have 40 acres of land allotted to him. (2 id. 268) Evidently no allottment was made, for in October a writ of execution issued against Collins and Hathorne, once more "in behalf of the town of Lynn" (2 id. 351). The marshall went to Hathorne, attached his horse, which was appraised at £ 15, and delivered the horse to the successful plaintiff, Longley. Thereafter the marshall went to Collins's house to obtain execution for the balance of the judgment. Evidently Collins was reluctant to have any of his property taken to satisfy an obligation of the town, and he accordingly refused to produce any goods in satisfaction of the writ of execution. Thereupon the marshall announced that he took execution on the body of Collins. Hathorne, the co-defendant, who was on hand refused the marshall's request that he assist him in effecting the arrest of Collins. In the next stage of the controversy, Hathorne and Collins brought actions against the marshall for his allegedly illegal conduct in levying execution against their property and person. In those proceedings Longley and Andrew Mansfield by deposition testified concerning Hathorne's conduct at the time when the marshall sought to arrest Collins. Thereafter Hathorne had appeared before the church in Lynn, charging that this testimony which Longley and Mansfield had given in the County Court was false. Out of that charge came the suits for slander herein reported.7

Slander. Writ: Andrew Mansfield v. John Hathorne; slander; charging him before the church at Linn the last summer that he had broken the ninth commandment in bearing false witness against his neighbor in the testimony he had given at Ipswich court, and at another church meeting, also charging him with the same; dated Mar. 18, 1662-3; signed by Tho. Fiske, for the court; and served by Allen Bread, constable of Linn by attachment of defendant's dwelling house.

John Longlye, aged about twenty-three years, deposed that he heard John Hathorne charge Andrew Mansfield before the church at Lynn in the meeting house, saying "I charge you with beareing false wittnesse against mee & others conserned in the testimonye you swore unto at Ipswich Court," and that he would prove it by the papers he had given to the church. Mansfield said he never understood that to be his charge and said Hathorne asked him where he had been all this while. Mansfield replied, "Just where I am now." This matter was in hand before the church a considerable part of the last summer. Sworn, 25: 1:116, before Wm. Hathorne. ...

Robert Lord, marshal, and William Longlye, aged about forty-eight years, deposed. The latter said that he heard marshal Robert Lord tell Andrew Mansfield that he had taken John Hathorne's horse by execution, and would have said Mansfield appraise it, which he did and the marshal delivered the horse to deponent, etc. Mary Longley testified to the same.

Verdict for plaintiff. The defendant was to make a public acknowledgment in the meeting house at Linn within thirty days. Not consented to by the court.

Slander. William Longly v. John Hathorne - ... John Mansfield, aged about forty-four years, deposed that at a church meeting at Mr. Whitting's house, John Hathorne, charged William Longley with the breach of the ninth commandment in bearing false witness against his neighbor. Said Longley asked said Hathorne who that neighbor was, and he replied against him and Henry Collins. Sworn, 27: 1: 1663, before Wm. Hathorne. ...

Jonathan Wallkett testified that "being at the house of Henry Collins when the Marshall (as they called him) of Ipswich was there to leuie an execution (as he said) after the execution was read & goods demanded by the sd Marshall: Henry Collinges said after he had made an excuse: it not being his proper debt, the sd Collins said to mee & to the rest that were by: take notis what I saye to the Marshall, and said you are best take the land that was attached to the action which is by or buerieing place or els sd he here is the Towne Common: before my gate take that for your satisfaction, the Marshall said he would not or that he was not bound to goe out of the yard but I must sd he have some of yor own goods then said Henry Collins here is twenty acres of my owne land behind my house you shall haue that for to satisfie yor excecution many words the sd Collins used for to perswade the sd Marshall sd seuerall times he would medle with noe lands but still did demaund of the sd: Collins to shew him some cattell for to leuie his excecution upon then when we were in the yard, after other discourse the Marshall read the Excecution & sd I leuie this excecution upon yor body and charged assistance, there being some space of time between the seasing of the excecution ther goeing into the house all which time John Hathorne was some distance from Henry Collins till the sd marshall sd to Henry Collins gett yor hatt & then we all torned & went into the house and that when we were in the yard asone as the Marshalls word was out of his mouth in saying I leuie it upon yor body says william longly here be horses or meares in the yard that he owned except a colt of his sonns the Marshall said he would not leuie an excecution twice." John Collins and Edward Ireson testified to a portion of the same. Sworn, 25: 1: 1663, before Wm. Hathorne. ...

John Witt and Thomas Newall deposed that they heard William Longlye acknowledge in the church that he was troubled because the marshal levied the execution upon the body of Henry Collins, and said he should have thought he would have taken his cattle. Sworn in court. ...

Verdict for plaintiff. The defendant was to make a public

acknowledgment in Linn meeting house within thirty days. The court did not consent to this verdict.

[The Court files also contain the following letters addressed, evidently, to the church at Lynn.]

"Reverend & loveing Friends & brethren, wee understand that Jo. Haythorne hath accused And. Maynsfeild & Langley in the Ch: of Lyn for giveing a false test. agst himselfe & Z. Collins att the Court of Ipswich in Marsh was 12 month & for wch the s^d^ M & Longly stand convicted in y^r^ Church & finding himself greived thereat hath brought this complt. agst the s^d^ Haythorne in seurall acconts of scland^r^ wch hath had a full & imptiall heareing & due examinacon & by the virdict of the Jury the s^d^ H found guilty now because it is much to be desired that contrary iudgement in one & the same case may be prevented if possibly it may be attained & one power not to clash agst the other wee thought it expedient before wee giue judgement in the case to commend the same to the serious consideration & further examinacon thereof of the church wee doubt not but there hath bene err^rs^ more then a few both in the words & carriage of all the pties (though not the crime alleadged) wch if it may please god to putt into their hearts to see & owner soe as may giue the Church optunty & cause to change their mynd & reverse sensures soe farr as concernes the pticular case in question wee hope it willbe acceptable to god satisfactory to orselues & others & the beginging of yr owne peace & quyet, the disterbance whereof hitherto wee are very senceable of & shall att all tymes be ready to afford yu o^r^ best releife as wee may haue optunity or cognisance thereof & had you beene pleased before y^r^ final conclusion to haue giuen us the grounds of your offence wee should kinly have resented such a request, and, probably much of your trouble might have beene prevented wee haue deferrd giuing iudgment in this case till the next Sessions of this Court to see w^t^ effect this o^r^ mocon may haue the god of peace & widedome giue you understanding in all things & guide you to such conclusions in this & all other causes of consequence as may be agreable to his will & conduceing to y^r^ peace & welfaire. soe prayes

Y^r^ lo: Friends & brethren
"Apr. 4. 63 "Robt Lord Clerk
"by order of the County Clerk
"at Ipswich."

[The reply from the church at Lynn has not been preserved. Its contents are suggested however by this second letter from the Ipswich Court.]

"Reverend & beloved

"Wee are very sorry our endeauours haue not produced that effect wee hoped and desired but seems to haue beene interpreted contrary to our intentions (& wee conceiue our words) as an incroachment upon and destruction to the right or power of the chhs, wee haue beene taught & doe verily beleeue the ciuil and ecclesiastical power may very wel consist, and that no cause is so purely ecclesiastical but the ciuil power may in its way deale therein, wee are farr from thinking the chhs haue no power but what is deriuved fro the chtian magistrate or that the ciuil magistrate hath ecclesiastical power, yet may and ought this matter so requiring take cognizance and giue judgment in ecclesiastical cause not in a chh but ciuil way wee suppose wee haue kept much within these bounds in the case that hath beene before us and that our opinnions & practice heerein hath beene as cleare from ecclesiasticisme as some mens assertions haue beene from the opposite error the declared judgments of our congregational divines in that point wee owne & desire to regulate our proceedings accordingly The God of order guide all o^r^ administration to his glory and the peace & edification of his people.

"By order and unanimous consent
"of the county court sitting at Ipswich
"May 5th 1663
"p me Robert Lord cleric."

[Judgment in the two cases was evidently entered at some stage of the findings in favor of the plaintiffs. In September, 1663, the Court of Assistants affirmed the decision. See 3 Records of the Court of Assistants, p. 137. Cf. Farnsworth v. Storrs, S Cush. 412 (1850); Fitzgerald v. Robinson, 112 Mass. 371 (1823)]

At a somewhat higher level similar difficulties between civil and church authorities are indicated in John Winthrop's account of the proceedings which were brought in 1639 against Nathaniel Eaton of the Harvard College faculty.

Extract from Winthrop's Journal - Vol. I, P. *308-*313
[September, 1639]

"A church was gathered at the Mount. At the general court at Boston, one Mr. Nathaniel Eaton, brother to the merchant at Quilipiack, was convented and censured. The occasion was this: He was a schoolmaster, and had many scholars, the sons of gentlemen and others of best note in the country, and had entertained one Nathaniel Briscoe, a gentleman born, to be his usher, and to do some other things for him, which might not be unfit for a scholar. He had not been with him above three days but he fell out with him for a very small occasion, and, with reproachful terms, discharged him, and turned him out of his doors; but, it being then about eight of the clock after the

Sabbath, he told him he should stay till next morning, and, some words growing between them, he struck him and pulled him into his house. Briscoe defended himself, and closed with him and, being parted, he came in and went up to his chamber to lodge there. Mr. Eaton sent for the constable, who advised him first to admonish him, etc., and if he could not, by the power of a master, reform him, then he should complain to the magistrate. But he caused his man to fetch him a cudgel, which was a walnut tree plant, big enough to have killed a horse, and a yard in length, and, taking his two men with him, he went up to Briscoe, and caused his men to hold him till he had given him two hundred stripes about the head and shoulders etc. and so kept him under blows (with some two or three short intermissions) about the space of two hours, about which time Mr. Shepherd and some others of the town came in at the outcry and so he gave over. In this distress Briscoe gate out his knife, and struck at the man that held him, but hurt him not. He also fell to prayer (supposing he should have been murdered) and then Mr. Eaton beat him for taking the name of God in vain. After this Mr. Eaton and Mr. Shepherd (who knew not then of these passages) came to the governor and some other of the magistrates, complaining of Briscoe for his insolent speeches, and for crying out murder and drawing his knife, and desired that he might be enjoined to a public acknowledgment, etc. The magistrates answered, that they must first hear him speak, and then they would do as they should see cause. Mr. Eaton was displeased at this, and went away discontented, etc., and, being after called into the court to make answer to the information, which had been given by some who knew the truth of the case, and also to answer for his neglect and cruelty, and other ill usage towards his scholars, one of the elders (not suspecting such miscarriages by him) came to the governor, and showed himself much grieved, that he should be publicly produced, alleging, that it would derogate from his authority and reverence among his scholars, etc. But the cause went on notwithstanding, and he was called, and these things laid to his charge in the open court. His answers were full of pride and disdain, telling the magistrates that they should not need to do anything herein, for he was intended to leave his employment. And being asked, why he used such cruelty to Briscoe his usher, and to other of his scholars (for it was testified by another of his ushers and divers of his scholars, that he would give them between twenty and thirty stripes at a time, and would not leave till they had confessed what he required) his answer was, that he had this rule, that he would not give over correcting till he had subdued the party to his will. Being also questioned about the ill and scant diet of his boarders (for, though their friends gave large allowance, yet their diet was ordinarily nothing but porridge and pudding, and that very homely) he put it off to his wife. So the court dismissed him at present, and commanded him to attend again the next day, when being called, he was commanded to the lower end of the table (where all offenders do usually stand) and, being openly convicted of all the former offences, by the oaths of four or five witnesses, he yet continued to justify himself; so, it being near night, he was committed to the marshall till the next day. When the court was set in the morning, many of the elders came into the court (it being then private for matter of consultation) and declared how, the evening before, they had taken pains with him, to convince him of his faults; yet, for divers hours, he had still stood to his justification; but, in the end, he was convinced, and had freely and fully acknowledged his sin, and that with tears; so as they did hope he had truly repented, and therefore desired of the court that he might be pardoned, and continued in his employment, alleging such further reasons as they thought fit. After the elders were departed, the court consulted about it, and sent for him, and there, in the open court, before a great assembly, he made a very solid, wise, eloquent, and serious (seeming) confession, condemning himself in all the particulars, etc. Whereupon, being put aside, the court consulted privately about his sentence and, though many were taken with his confession, and none but had a charitable opinion of it; yet, because of the scandal of religion, and offence which would be given to such as might intend to send their children hither, they all agreed to censure him, and put him from that employment. So, being called in, the governor, after a short preface, etc., declared the sentence of the court to this effect, viz: that he should give Briscoe £ 30, fined 100 marks, and debarred teaching of children within our jurisdiction. A pause being made, and expectation that (according to his former confession) he would have given glory to God, and acknowledged the justice and clemency of the court, the governor giving him occasion, by asking him if he had ought to say, he turned away with a discontented look, saying, "If sentence be passed, then it is to no end to speak." Yet the court remitted his fine to £ 20, and willed Briscoe to take but £ 20.[1]

"The church at Cambridge, taking notice of these proceedings, intended to deal with him. The pastor moved the governor, if they might, without offence to the court, examine other witnesses. His answer was, that the court would leave them to their own liberty; but he saw not to what end they should do it, seeing there had been five already upon oath, and

---

1. The official report of the proceedings - which apparently were before the General Court - is in 1 Records 275.

those whom they should examine should speak without oath, and it was an ordinance of God, that by the mouths of two or three witnesses every matter should be established. But he soon discovered himself; for, ere the church could come to deal with him, he fled to Pascataquack, and, being pursued and apprehended by the governor there, he again acknowledged his great sin in flying, etc., and promised (as he was a Christian man) he would return with the messengers. But, because his things he carried with him were aboard a bark there, bound to Virginia, he desired leave to go fetch them, which they assented unto, and went with him (three of them) aboard with him. So he took his truss and came away with them in the boat; but, being come to the shore, and two of them going out of the boat, he caused the boatsmen to put off the boat, and because the third man would not go out, he turned him into the water, where he had been drowned, if he had not saved himself by swimming. So he returned to the bark, and presently they set sail and went out of the harbor. Being thus gone, his creditors began to complain; and thereupon it was found, that he was run in debt about £ 1000, and had taken up most of this money upon bills he had charged into England upon his brother's agents, and others whom he had no such relation to. So his estate was seized, and put into commissioners' hands, to be divided among his creditors, allowing somewhat for the present maintenance of his wife and children. And, being thus gone, the church proceeded and cast him out. He had been sometimes initiated among the Jesuits, and, coming into England, his friends drew him from them, but, it was very probably, he now intended to return to them again, being at this time about thirty years of age, and upwards."

If much of the Puritan practise with respect to the coordination of ecclesiastical and civil authorities had its English counterpart and precedent, there was one very significant addition to traditional habits made by the Bay Puritans. This concerned the role of the Ministers and Elders of the churches as advisers to the civil authorities in "matters of conscience" in other words in matters on which the relevant rule of law was uncertain. As usually was the case when radical departures from familiar practices occurred, justification for this reference of questions of law to the churchmen was found in the Bible: "For the priest's lips should keep knowledge, and they should seek the law at his mouth: for he is the messenger of the Lord of Hosts". (Malachi, II, 7) Although the opinions of churchmen on matters of state seem to have been taken as merely advisory by the civil authorities they were nonetheless of great weight and importance. In a period when judges did not customarily prepare written opinions on constitutional and other issues coming before them for decision the advisory opinions of Elders and Ministers are a suggestive guide to Puritan conceptions of the nature of law and the meaning and scope of particular rules of law. When, in 1642, Governor Bellingham of the Bay Colony sought the advice and counsel of the authorities at Plymouth on perplexing questions of law which were causing difficulties in both colonies, Governor Bradford of Plymouth referred the questions to the Elders of the Plymouth Church for their consideration. He then forwarded those opinions to Bellingham. The views of Charles Chauncey, one of the Plymouth Elders, and later President of Harvard College, are expressed in a characteristic form in the following communication (Vol. 2, Bradford, History of Plymouth Plantation, 1620 - 1647 (Mass. Hist. Soc., 1922), p. 326):

"Question the second, upon the pointe of examination, how farr a magistrate may extracte a confession from a delinquente to accuse him selfe in a capitall crime, seeing Nemo tenetur prodere seipsum.

"Ans: The words of the question may be understood of extracting a confession from a delinquente either by oath or bodily tormente. If it be mente of extracting by requiring an oath, (ex officio, as some call it,) and that in capitall crimes I fear it is not safe, nor warented by Gods word, to extracte a confession from a delinquente by an oath in matters of life and death. (1) Because the practise in the Scriptures is other wise, as in the case of Achan, Jos: 7.9 (19). Give, I pray you, glorie to the Lord God of Israll, and make a confession to him, and tell me how thou hast done. He did not compell him to sweare. So when as Johnathans life was indangered, 1 Sam. 14, 43. Saule said unto Johnathan, Tell me what thou hast done; he did not require an oath. And notable is that, Jer: 38.14. Jeremiah was charged by Zedechias, who said, I will aske thee a thing, hide it not from me; and Jeremiah said, If I declare it unto ye, wilt thou not surely put me to death? impling that, in case of death, he would have refused to answer him. (2) Reason shews it, and experience; Job. 2.4. Skin for skin, etc. It is to be feared that those words (what soever a man hath) will comprehend also the conscience of an oath, and the fear of God, and all care of religion; therefore for laying a snare before the guiltie, I think it ought not to be donn. But now, if the question be mente of inflicting bodyly torments to extracte a confession from a mallefactor, I conceive that in matters of highest consequence, such as doe conceirne the saftie or ruine of states or countries, magistrates may proceede so farr to bodily torments, as racks, hote-irons, etc. to extracte a confession, espetially wher presumptions are strounge; but otherwise by no means. God sometimes hides a sinner till his wickedness is filled up.

"Question 3. In what cases of capitall crimes, one witness with other circumstances shall be sufficente to convicte, or is ther no conviction without .2. witnesses?[2]

"Ans: Deut. 19.25 (15). God hath given an express rule that in no case one witness shall arise in judgmente, espetially not in capitall cases God would not put our lives into the power of any one tounge. Besides, by the examination of more wittneses agreeing or disagreeing, any falsehood ordenarilly may be discovered; but this is to be understood of one witness of another; but if a man witnes against him selfe, his owne testimony is sufficente, as in the case of the Amalakite, 2. Sam: 1.16. Againe, when ther are sure and certaine signes and evidences by circumstances, ther needs no witnes in this case, as in the bussines of Adoniah desiring Abishage the Shunamite to wife, that thereby he might make way for him selfe unto the kingdome, I. King: 2. 23, 24. Againe, probably by many concurring circumstances, if probability may have the strength of a witnes, something may be this way gathered, me

---

2. The Code of 1648, in the title Witnesses, provided as follows: "It is ordered, decreed, and by this Court declared, that no man shall be put to death without the testimony of two or three witnesses, or that which is equivalent thereunto." John Cotton in his draft of a code of laws, generally known as Moses His Judicials, had a provision of much broader scope. "In trial of all causes, no judgment shall pass but either upon the confession of the party, or upon testimony of two witnesses." 1 Mass. Hist. Soc. Coll. Vol. 5, 185. It is evident that the Colonial courts were generally under the impression that two witnesses, at least, were required in every type of case, whether civil or criminal. This problem was constantly considered by the Colonial courts and by the elders. In a case tried in the Court of Assistants in 1672, in which the defendant, an Indian, was charged with rape, the jury dealt with the matter by special verdict: "The Jurys verdict concerning the Indian called Twenty Rod: The Jury finds that if all the circumstances of this case doth amount to one evidence, then the girl's testimony makes it two, and so we find Twenty Rod guilty according to indictment. The circumstances that we mean are as followeth, viz., first, his being in the place or near it. 2 his not denying the fact when accused before Major Hathorne, but excusing himself that if he did it he was in drink. 3 no other person being found near the place by the Indian before specified. And he alleging no other person to clear himself." The record concludes with the following entry: "The bench judges the evidence good and so he is found guilty." 3 Records of Assistants 216. The English ecclesiastical courts following the rules of evidence of the civil law, seem also to have accepted substitutes for the testimony of a second eyewitness. See Usher, High Commission 117-118, and 12 Rep. 65.

thinks, from Sallomons judging betweexte the true mother, and the harlote, I. King. 3. 25. Lastly, I see no cause why in waighty matters, in defecte of witneses and other proofes, we may not have recourse to a lott, as in the case of Achan, Josu: 7. 16. which is a clearer way in shuch doubtfull cases (it being solemnely and religiously performed) then any other that I know, if it be made the last refuge. But all this under correction.

"The Lord in mercie directe and prosper the desires of his servants that desire to walk before him in truth and righteousnes in the administration of justice, and give them wisdome and largnes of harte."

The present generation of lawyers finds it difficult to consider such facile utilization of scriptural authority as Chauncey's the serious expression of a cultivated philosophy of law. They might have considerable sympathy for Anne Hutchinson's comment on absorption of the New England ministry in the text of the Old Testament: "A company of legall professors lie poring on the law which Christ hath abolished."[3] Yet the seriousness of the Puritan conviction that particular cases and general problems of law were to be decided by reference to Biblical precedents and analogies is beyond question. That conviction was supported by a body of learning with which the Puritan churchmen were thoroughly familiar. Chauncey's opinions quoted above were prefaced by the following passage in which he briefly justified his use of the Bible as the text in which the answer to the problem presented to him might be found:

"That the judicials of Moyses, that are appendances to the morall law, and grounded on the law of nature, or the decalogue, are immutable, and perpetuall, which all orthodox devines acknowledge; see the authors following. Luther, Tom. I, Whitenberge: fol. 435. and fol. 7. Melancthon, in loc: com loco deconjugio. Calvin, l. 4. Institu. c.4. sect. 15. Junious de politia Moyses, thes. 29. and 30. Hen: Bulin: Decad. 3 sermo. 8 Wolf: Muscu. loc: com: in .6. precepti explicaci: Bucer de regno Christi, l. .2. c. .17. Theo: Beza, vol: I. de hereti: puniendis, fol. 154. Zanch: in 3. precept: Ursin: Pt. 4. explicat. contra John. Piscat: in Aphorismi loc. de lege dei aphorism. 17. And more might be added. I forbear, for brevities sake, to set downe their very words; this being the constante and generall oppinion of the best devines, I will rest in this as undoubtedly true, though much more might be said to confirme it."

---

3. Quoted in Johnson's Wonder Working Providence (1867 ed) p. 102. cf. Parker, C. J. in Pearce v. Atwood, 13 Mass. 324, 345-46 (1816).

Had Chauncey considered such citations relevant he could easily have found in such a learned champion of the common law as Coke references to Scripture as the foundation of the law of England. See, e.g., Ratcliffe's Case, 3 Rep. 37a, 40a-b (1592).

5. The Trials of John Wheelwright and Anne Hutchinson

The most complete contemporary account of the proceedings of the General Court against Wheelwright and Anne Hutchinson was in the Short Story of the Rise, Reign, and Ruine of the Antinomians, Familists & Libertines that Infected The Churches of New England (London, 1644). Its authorship is not entirely free from doubt, but it seems reasonably clear that John Winthrop, rather than Thomas Welde, wrote the bulk of the narrative. See, Adams, Antinomianism in the Colony of Massachusetts Bay (1894). It must be remembered, however, that The Short Story is not an official account of the proceedings and that it is told by a partisan.

Of the first stage of the proceedings recounted in The Short Story the only official record is the following entry in the Records of the General Court for March, 1637: "It was concluded by the Court that Mr. Wheelwright was guilty of contempt & sedition." (1 Records 189) The first excerpt from The Short Story is an account of the proceedings of the General Court out of which that judgment arose. The second excerpt describes the proceedings at the session of the General Court in November, 1637, when sentence was entered against Wheelwright. (1 Records 207) During the first stage of the proceedings Henry Vane was Governor and John Winthrop Deputy Governor.

A briefe Apologie in defence of the generall proceedings of the Court, holden at Boston the ninth day of the first moneth, 1636 [March, 1637] against Mr. J. Wheelwright a member there, by occasion of a Sermon delivered there in the same Congregation.

Forasmuch as some of the Members of the Court (both of the Magistrates and Deputies) did dissent from the major part, in the judgement of the cause of Mr. Wheelwright, and divers others have since censured the proceedings against him as unjust, or (at best) over hasty, for maintaining of which censures, many untruths are like to be spread abroad, whereby the most equall Judges may be in danger of prejudice; and so the honour not of the Court onely, but also of the tryall and justice it selfe may be blemished: It is thought needful to make this publike Declaration of all the proceedings, with the reasons and grounds thereof, so farre as concerneth the clearing of the justice of the Court. ...

In the beginning of the Court, the Deputies upon the fame of a Sermon delivered by Mr. Wheelwright (upon the first day) which was supposed to tend to sedition, and disturbance of the publike peace, desired that he might be sent for, which the Court assenting unto, one of the Magistrates (his speciall friend) undertooke to give him notice thereof, and accordingly at the next meeting he was in the Towne, ready to appeare, when he should be called for, which was not till two or three dayes after, and then he was sent for (not by the Marshall, as the usuall manner is; but) by one of the Deputies his intimate friend upon his appearance he was made acquainted with the cause why he was sent for, viz. To satisfie the Court about some passages in his Sermon, which seemed to be offensive, and therewith a copy of it was produced, and he was demanded whether he would owne it: whereupon he drew forth another copy which he delivered into the Court, as a true copy, (for the substance of it) so he was dismissed very gently, and desired to be ready when he should be called for againe.

The next day he was againe sent for by the former messenger: About this time a Petition was delivered into the Court, under the hands of above forty persons, being most of the Church of Boston (being none of the Petitions before mentioned, which were delivered after) to this effect, that as free-men they might be admitted to be present in the Court in causes of judicature, and that the Court would declare whether they might proceed in cases of conscience, without referring them first to the Church. To this the Court answered on the backside of the Petition, that they did conceive the Petition was without just ground, for the first part of it, the Court had never used privacie in Judiciall proceedings, but in preparation thereto by way of examination of the party, &c. they might and would use their liberty, as they should see cause; and for the other part of the Petition, when any matter of conscience should come before them, they would advise what were fit to be done in it.

When Mr. Wheelwright came in, the Court was private, and then they told him they had considered of his Sermon, and were desirous to aske him some questions which might tend to cleare his meaning, about such passages therein as seemed offensive; he demanded whether he were sent for as an innocent person, or as guilty? It was answered neither, but as suspected onely; Then he demanded, who were his accusers? It was answered, his Sermon; (which was there in Court) being acknowledged by himselfe they might thereupon proceed, ex officio: at this word great exception was taken, as if the Court intended the course of the High Commission, &c.[1] It was answered that the word ex

---

1. In the same year in which these proceedings against Wheel-

officio was very safe and proper, signifying no more but the authority or duty of the Court, and that there was no cause of offence, seeing the Court did not examine him by any compulsory means, as by oath, imprisonment, or the like, but only

---

wright occurred in Massachusetts the Star Chamber proceedings against John Lilburn took place in England. See 3 How. *State Trials* 1315. In the course of a preliminary examination Lilburn, after denying the charge of importing or printing certain heretical or seditious books on which he had been held prisoner, refused to answer supplementary questions of fact, even though, at that stage of the proceedings he was not under oath. In refusing to answer he made the following statement: "I am not willing to answer you to any more of these questions, because I see you go about by this examination to ensnare me ... . If you will not ask me about the thing laid to my charge, I shall answer no more; ... and of any other matter that you have to accuse me of, I know it is warrantable by the law of God, and I think by the law of the land, that I may stand upon my just defence, and not answer to your interrogatories." At a later stage of the proceedings, when he was directed to take the oath to answer truthfully the questions which the judges might put to him, and that before the bill of charges against him was prepared, he refused to take the oath saying: "I perceived the oath to be an oath of inquiry; and for the lawfulness of which oath, I have no warrant." When, later, one of the judges said that Lilburn was "one of the notoriousest dispersers of libellous books that is in the kingdom", Lilburn replied as follows: "Sir, I know you are not able to prove and to make that good which you have said." "I have testimony of it", said he. "Then", said I, "Produce them in the face of the open court that we may see what they have to accuse me of; and I am ready here to answer for myself and to make my just defence." At a later stage of the proceedings, after he had, "on the word of a Christian", denied specific charges made against him by a named individual, Lilburn described the oath on which the Star Chamber was insisting as "an oath of inquiry, and of the same nature as the High-Commission oath". When asked by the Court whether he would take an oath to the truth of his denial of the specific allegations against him he replied: "By God's appointment I know an oath ought to be an end of all controversy and strife, Heb. 6, 16, and if it might be so in this my present cause, I would safely take my oath, that what I have said is true." On Lilburn's continued refusal to take the proferred oath he was "censured" to be whipped and to stand upon the pillory.

In *Twining* v. *New Jersey*, 211 U. S. 78, 102-103 (1908)

desired him for better satisfaction to answer some questions, but he still refused, yet at last through perswasion of some of his friends, he seemed content; The question then put to him was, whether before his Sermon he did not know, that most of the Ministers in this jurisdiction did teach that doctrine which he in his Sermon called a Covenant of works; to this he said, he did not desire to answer, and hereupon some cried out that the Court went about to ensnare him, and to make him to accuse himselfe, and that this question was not about the matter of his Sermon, &c. Upon this he refused to answer any further, so he was dismissed till the afternoone; The reason why the Court demanded that question of him, was not to draw matter from himselfe whereupon to proceed against him, neither was there any need, for upon a conference of the Ministers not long before there had beene large dispute betweene some of them and himselfe about that point of evidencing Justification by Sanctification, so as the court might soone have convinced him by witnesses, if they had intended to proceed against him upon that ground.

In the afternoone he was sent for againe in the same manner as before, and the Ministers also being in the Towne, and come thither to confere together for further discovery of the ground of the differences which were in the Countrey about the Covenant of Grace, &c. they were desired to be present also in the Court, to beare witnesse of the proceedings in the case, and to give their advice as the Court (upon occasion) should require: so the doores being set open for all that would to come in (and there was a great Assembly) and Mr. Wheelwright being willed to sit downe by the Ministers, his Sermon was produced, and many passages thereof was read to him, which for the better understanding we have digested into this order following. [The account of Wheelwright's sermon in which the distinction between a covenant of grace and a covenant of works was developed is omitted.]

The Court proceeded also to examine some witnesses about another Sermon of his, whereat much offence had also beene taken, and not without cause, (as appeared to the Court) for in that he seemed to scare men not onely from legall righteousnesse, but even from faith and repentance, as if that also were

---

Mr. Justice Moody says that an examination of the report of the trial of Anne Hutchinson shows that Governor Winthrop "was not aware of any privilege against self-incrimination or conscious of any duty to respect it". Cf., 8 Wigmore, Evidence (3rd ed.) p. 301. Does the report of the Wheelright trial indicate that Mr. Justice Moody was in error in suggesting that Winthrop knew nothing of the privilege against self-incrimination.

a way of the Covenant of workes; but this being matter of Doctrine, the Court passed it by for the present, onely they (and the Ministers present, divers of them) declared their griefe to see such opinions risen in the Country of so dangerous consequence, and so directly crossing the scope of the Gospell, (as was conceived) and it was retorted upon him which he in his Sermon chargeth his adverse party with, (though uncharitably and untruly) when he saith they would take away the true Christ, that to make good such a doctrine as he held forth (to common intendment) must needes call for a new Christ and a new Gospell for sure the old would not owne or justifie it.

Then the Court propounded a question to the Ministers, which (because they desired time of consideration to make answer unto) was given them in writing upon the outside of Master Wheelrights Sermon, in these words: Whether by that which you have heard concerning Master Wheelrights Sermon, and that which was witnessed concerning him, yee doe conceive that the Ministers in this Country doe walke in and teach such a way of Salvation and evidencing thereof, as he describeth, and accounteth to be a Covenant of workes? To this question (being againe called for into the Court the next morning) they returned an affirmative answer, in the very words of the question, adding withall, that they would not be understood, that their doctrine and Master Wheelwrights about Justification, and Salvation, and evidencing thereof, did differ in all things, but onely in the point presented, and debated now in Court, and that of this their answer they were ready to give reasons when the Court should demand them, and that to this they all consented, except their brother the teacher of Boston [John Cotton]: After this (by leave of the Court) the Ministers all spake one by one in order, some more largely, laying open by solid arguments and notorious examples, the great dangers that the Churches and Civill State were falne into, by the differences which were growne amongst us in matters of Religion, offering themselves withall to employ all their studies to effect a reconciliation, showing also their desires that Mr. Wheelwright would be with them, when they should meete for this purpose, and blaming his former strangenesse as a possible occasion of these differences of judgement. Others spake more briefely, but consented with the former; and all of them (as they had occasion to speake to Mr. Wheelwright, or to make mention of him) used him with all humanity and respect; what his carriage was towards them againe, those who were present may judge, as they say cause.

The matters objected against Mr. Wheel. being recollected, and put to the vote, the opinion of the Court was, that he had run into sedition and contempt of the Civill authority, which accordingly was recorded to the same effect, and he was enjoyned to appeare at the next generall Court to abide their further sentence herein. And whereas motion was made of enjoyning him silence in the meane time, the Ministers were desired to deliver their advice what the Court might doe in such a case: Their answer was, that they could not give a cleare resolution of the question at the present, but for Mr. Wheel. they desired that the Court would rather referre him to the Church of B. to deale with him for that matter; which accordingly was done, and so he was dismissed: such of the Magistrates and Deputies, as had not concurred with the major part in the vote (some of them) moved that the dissent might be recorded, (but it was denyed) as a course never used in this or any such Court. Afterward they tendered a Protestation, which was also refused, because therein they had justified Mr. Wheel. as a faithfull Minister of the Lord Jesus, and condemned the Court for undue proceeding; but this was offered them, that if they would write downe the words of the record, and subscribe their dissent without laying such aspersion upon the Court, it should be received.[2]

Although the simple narration of these proceedings might be sufficient to justifie the Court in what they have done especially with these of this jurisdiction, who have taken notice of the passages in the generall Court in Decem. last, yet for satisfaction of others to whom this case may be otherwise presented by some or mis-report, we will set downe some grounds and reasons thereof, some whereof were expressed in the Court, and others (though not publickly insisted upon, yet) well conceived by some, as further motives to leade their judgments to doe as they did. ...

Sedition and contempt are laid to his charge.

Sedition doth properly signifie a going aside to make a party, and is rightly described by the Poet, (for it is lawfull to fetch the meaning of words from humane authority). In _magno populo cum saepe coorta est seditio saevitique animis_, &c.[3]

---

2. Some of those persons who objected to the decision of the majority evidently urged that the failure to secure unanimity among the judges rendered the determination of the majority void. Dealing with that thesis as published in a pamphlet circulated after the trial, Thomas Shepard, the minister in Cambridge, wrote to John Winthrop as follows: "His maxime that a sentence given by the major part of the Court when another do dissent is a nullity [is] as monstrous, devilish, hellish a birth as ever wickedness could bring forth...". 3 _Winthrop Papers_ 416.

3. In _Lord Cromwell's Case_, 4 Rep. 12b, 13a, Coke had relied on Virgil's description of sedition:

"Ac veluti magno in populo cum saepe coorta est

whence it doth appeare that when the minds of the people being assembled are kindled or made fierce upon some suddaine occasion, so as they fall to take part one against another, this is sedition; for when that furor, which doth arma ministrare, is once kindled, the sedition is begun, though it come not to its perfection, till faces et saxa volant: Tully saith, Seditionem, esse dissensionem omnium inter se, cum eunt alii in aliud, when the people dissent in opinion and goe severall wayes.

Isidore saith, Seditiosus est, qui dissentionem animorum facit discordias gignit. He that sets mens minds at difference, and begets strife: And if we look into the Scripture we shall find examples of sedition agreeing to these descriptions. The uproare moved by Demetrius, Acts. 19. was sedition, yet he neither took up armes, nor perswaded others so to doe, but onely induced the minds of the people, and made them fierce against the Apostles, by telling them they were enemies to Diana of the Ephesians. Korah and his company moved a most dangerous sedition, yet they did not stirre up the people to fight, onely they went apart and drew others to them against Moses and Aaron; here was nothing but words, and that by a Levite, who might speake by his place, but it cost more then words before it was pacified. Now in our present case, did not Mr. Wheel. make sides when he proclaimed all to be under a Covenant of works, who did not follow him (step by step) in his description of the Covenant of Grace? did he not make himselfe a party on the other side, by often using these and the like words, We, us? Did he not labour to heat the minds of the people, and to make them fierce against those of that side, which he opposed (and whereof he knew that most of the Magistrates and Ministers had declared themselves) when with the greatest fervency of spirit and voyce, he proclaimes them Antichrists, enemies, Philistims, Herod, Pilate, persecuting Jewes, and stirred up them on his part to fight with them, to lay load on them, to burne them, to thresh them, to bind them in chaines and fetters, to kill them and vexe their hearts, and that under the paine of the curse of Meroz? Tantoene animis coelestibus irae? would one think that any heavenly spirit could have breathed so much anger, when an Angel would have given milder language to the Devill himselfe? and all this without vouchsafing one argument to convince these enemies of their evil way, or one word of admonition or advice to themselves, to draw them out of danger. But it is objected,

---

Seditio, saevitque animis ignobile vulgus,
Jamque faces et saxa volant, furor arma ministrat."

For elaborate contemporary discussions of the meaning of "sedition" in the English law, see Stroud's Case, 3 How. State Trials 235 (1629).

that he expressed his meaning to be of a spirituall fighting and killing, &c. with the sword of the spirit onely. It is granted he did so, yet his instances of illustration, or rather enforcement, were of another nature, as of Moses killing the Egyptian in defence of his brother, Sampson losing his life with the Philistims, the fight of Jonathan and his armour-bearer, and of Davids worthies, Baruc and Jael, &c. these obtained their victories with swords and hammers, &c. And such are no spirituall weapons, so that if his intent were not to stirre up to open force and armes (neither doe we suspect him of any such purpose, otherwise then by consequent) yet his reading and experience might have told him, how dangerous it is to heat peoples affections against their opposites, a mind inflamed with indignation (among some people) would have beene more apt to have drawne their swords by the authority of the examples he held forth for the encouragement, then to have beene kept to spirituall weapons, by the restraining without cautions, such as cannot dispute for Christ with Steven, will be ready to draw their swords for him, like Peter; for _furor arma ministrat_, like him who when he could not by any sentence in the Bible confute an Heretick, could make use of the whole booke to break his head; we might hold forth instances more then enough. The warres in Germany for these hundred yeeres arose from dissentions in Religion, and though in the beginning of the contention, they drew out onely the sword of the Spirit, yet it was soone changed into a sword of steele; so was it among the confederate Cantons of Helvetia, which were so many Townes as neerely combined together, as our here; so was it also in the Netherlands betweene the Orthodox and the Arminians; so hath it beene between the Calvinists and Lutherans: In every place we find that the contentions began first by disputations and Sermons, and when the minds of the people were once set on fire by reproachfull termes of incendiary spirits, they soone set to blowes, and had alwayes a tragicall and bloudy issue; and to cleare this objection, Mr. Wheel, professed before hand, what he looked for, _viz_. that his doctrine would cause combustions even in the Commonwealth, as well as in the Churches, which he could not have feared if he had supposed (as in charity he well might) that those who were set over the people here in both States were indeed true Christians; yea he not onely confesseth his expectation, but his earnest desire also of such combustions and disturbances, when he saith that it is the Saints desire to have the fire kindled, as if hee were come among Turks or Papists, and not among the Churches of Christ, amongst whom Paul laboured to quench all fire of contention, but with the Corinthians, Romans, and Galatians, and wished that those were cut off who troubled them, setting a mark upon such as made division, and a note of carnall mind: therefore this objection will not save him, his offence is yet without excuse, hee did intend to trouble our peace, and hee hath effected it; therefore it was a contempt of that authority which required every man to study Peace and Truth, and therefore it was a seditious contempt, in that hee stirred up others, to joyn in the disturbance of that peace, which hee was bound by solemn Oath to preserve.

It is objected, that the Magistrates may not appoint a messenger of God, what hee should teach: admit so much, yet hee may limit him what hee may not teach, if hee forbid him to teach heresy or sedition, &c. hee incurres as well a contempt in teaching that which hee was forbidden, as sins in teaching that which is evill. Besides, every truth is not seasonable at all times. Christ tels his Disciples that hee had many things to teach them, but they could not beare them then, Joh. 16. 12. and God giveth his Prophets the tongue of the learned, that they may know how to speak a word in season, Isa. 50, 40. and if for every thing there bee a season, then for every Doctrine, Eccles. 3. 1. ...

A further objection hath been made against the proceedings of the Court, as if Mr. Wheelwright had not a lawfull tryall, as not being put upon a Jury of freemen. But the answer to this is easie, it being wel known to all such as have understanding of matters of this nature, that such Courts as have power to make and abrogate Laws, are tyed to no other Orders, but their own, and to no other rule but Truth and Justice, and why thrice twelve men sitting as Judges in a Court, should bee more subject to partiality than twelve such called as a Jury to the barre, let others judge.

...But wee meet yet with another objection, viz. that disturbance of unity is not sedition, except it also lead to the hurt of utility.

To this wee answer, first, that if it tend immediately to such hurt, wee deny the truth of the proposition; for it in the time of famine, a man should stir up the people to fetch corn out of the houses of such as had it to spare, this were to an immediate publick good, yet it were sedition. ...

That this course of Mr. Wheel. did tend directly to the great hinderance of publike utility, for when brethren shall looke one at another as enemies and persecutors, &c. and when people shall looke at their Rulers and Ministers as such, and as those who goe about to take Christ and salvation from them, how shall they joyne together in any publike service? how shall they cohabite and trade together? how hardly will they submit to such Over-seers? how will it hinder all affaires in Courts, in Townes, in Families, in Vessels at Sea, &c. and what can more threaten the dissolution and ruine of Church and Commonwealth? Lastly, if it be alleadged that such warlike termes are used by Christ and his Apostles in a spirituall sense, we deny it not, but we desire that the usuall manner of their applying them may be also considered, for Paul saith, 1 Cor. 9. So fight I, &c. I beate downe my body, &c. 1 Tim. 6.12. Fight the good fight of faith, lay hold on eternall life, and 1 Pet. 2. 11. and Sam. 4. 1. there is speech of the fight of our lusts, and Ephes. 6. 11. he bids them put on armour, but it is to resist the Devill, not flesh and bloud, not to fight against their brethren, towards who he forbids all bitternesse and clamour, &c. Eph. 4. And when he speaks of spirituall weapons, 2 Cor. 10. he doth not draw them out against the persons of brethren, but against high thoughts and imaginations, &c. And if Mr. Wheel. had found out any such among us, and planted his battery against them by sound arguments, he had followed our Apostolike rule; Christ indeed threatneth to fight against the Nicholaitans with the sword of his mouth, and if Mr. Wheel. had knowne any such here, as certainly as Christ knew those, he might have beene justified by the example, otherwise not. ...

[The next scheduled sitting of the General Court following this interlocutory decree was to occur in two months, and was to be the Court of Elections at which the freemen would be in attendance to elect the Governor, Deputy Governor, and Assistants. Sentiment in Boston was largely in favor of Wheelwright and his supporter, Governor Vane. Apparently with the intention of escaping the influences of the Boston atmosphere the General Court, after the completion of this first phase of the Wheelwright proceedings, voted that the next Court of Elections should meet in Cambridge. Charles Francis Adams's account of that meeting at which Winthrop was elected Governor in place of Vane gives a helpful sidelight on the final stages of the Wheelwright trial as reported in the Second excerpt from The Short Story.]

C. F. Adams, Three Episodes in Massachusetts History (1892), Vol. 1, p. 451-455

As the election day drew near, Winthrop and Vane were put forward as opposing candidates, and the adherents of neither neglected any precaution likely to influence the result; while the deep interest felt in that result of itself insured not only a full vote, but a large personal attendance. Though recorded as of May 17, 1637, it is to be borne in mind that the events now to be described really took place on what is with us the 27th of the month, so that, as spring was merging into early summer, the verdure was far advanced. The day was clear and warm, when at one o'clock the freemen gathered in groups about a large oak-tree which stood on the north side of what is now Cambridge Common, where Governor Vane, in English fashion and beneath the open sky, announced the purpose of the meeting - the annual charter-election. Most of the notabilities of the province, whether magistrates or clergy, were among the large number present. As soon as the meeting was declared ready for business, a parliamentary contest was opened over a petition offered on behalf of many inhabitants of Boston. It was in effect an appeal, in the case of Wheelwright, taken from the deputies to the body of freemen themselves, in General Court assembled. As such, its presentation at that time was clearly not in order; for, as the day was specially set apart for the choice of magistrates, the choice of magistrates took precedence over everything. If other business could be thrust on the meeting first, it was obvious an election might in this way be defeated, and the colony left without a government. Vane took advantage of his place as presiding officer to insist upon having the paper read. To this Winthrop objected, contending very properly that the special business of the day should first of all be disposed of. As Vane stood firm, an angry debate ensued, and the significance of the change in locality became at once apparent. Had the Court met in Boston, there can be little doubt that Vane, who had forgotten the magistrate in the party leader, would have been sustained in his arbitrary rulings by the voices of those actually present. The position assumed by the youthful governor was striking and dramatic enough; but it was also suggestive of memories connected with that greater and more turbulent forum, in which Gracchus and Sulpicius appealed directly from the senate to the people of Rome. That, under the strain to which the eager and too zealous patrician now subjected it, the meeting did not break into riot, was due only to the self-control and respect for law and form - the inherited political habit - of those who composed it.

Separated as the two places were by a broad arm of the sea, and the adjoining flats and marshes, Boston was then a long way from Cambridge. ... Accordingly, as had doubtless been intended when the place was chosen, it had proved much easier for the freemen of Roxbury, Watertown, Charlestown and the northern towns to assemble on Cambridge Common than for those of Boston; and it speedily became manifest that the larger number of those present sided with Winthrop. This fact held in check the friends of Vane. None the less, threatening speeches drew forth angry words, and a few of the more hot-headed were on the verge of coming to blows; some, indeed, did lay hands upon each other. In the midst of the tumult the pastor Wilson - his gravity of calling, the stoutness of his person and his fifty years of age notwithstanding - clambered up against the trunk of the spreading oak, and, clinging to one of its branches, began vehemently to harangue the meeting, exhorting the freemen there present to look to their charter, and to consider of the present work of the day, which was therein set apart for the choosing their magistrates. In reply to this sudden appeal, a loud cry was raised of "Election! Election!!" in response to which Winthrop as deputy-governor, cut the knot by declaring that the greater number should decide on the course to be pursued. He then put the question himself. The response did not admit of doubt. The majority were clearly in favor of proceeding to an immediate election.

Vane still refused to comply. Then, at last, Winthrop flatly told him that, if he would not go on, they would go on without him. Remembering how Endicott had dealt with him under very similar circumstances only two months before, Vane now gave way to the inevitable, and the election was allowed to proceed. It resulted in the complete defeat of his party. He was himself left out of the magistracy, as also were Wheelwright's two parishioners at the Mount, Coddington and Hough. The conservative party resumed complete political control under Winthrop as governor, with the stern and intolerant Dudley as his deputy. As if also to indicate in a special way their approval of Endicott's decided course throughout these proceedings, the deputies, among their first acts when they met, chose him a member of the standing council for the term of his life - an honor which a year before, in plain defiance of the charter, had been conferred upon Winthrop and Dudley, the governor and deputy now elected, and which never was conferred on any except these three. The reaction was complete. ...

The Proceedings of the Generall Court holden at New Towne ... November, 1637, against Mr. Wheelwright and Other Erroneous and Seditious Persons for Their Disturbances of the Publick Peace [continued from The Short Story]

Although the Assembly of Churches had confuted and condemned most of those new opinions which were sprung up amongst us, and Mr. Cotton had in publique view consented with the rest, yet the leaders in those erroneous wayes would not give in, but stood still to maintain their new light, which they had boasted of, and that the difference was still as wide as before, viz. as great as between heaven and hell: Mr. Wheelwright also continued his preaching after his former manner, and Mistris Hutchinson her wonted meetings and exercises, and much offence was still given by her, and others in going out of the ordinary assemblies, when Mr. Wilson began any exercise; and some of the messengers of the Church of Boston, had contemptuously withdrawn themselves from the generall Assembly, with professed dislike of their proceedings, and many evidences brake forth of their discontented and turbulent spirits; it was conceived by the Magistrates, and others of the Country, that the means which had been used, proving uneffectuall, the case was now desperate, and the last remedy was to bee applyed, and that without further delay, lest it should bee attempted too late, when fitter opportunity might bee offered for their advantage, as they had boasted, and did certainly expect upon the returne of some of their chiefe supporters, who by a speciall providence were now absent from them: And for this end the generall Court being assembled in the ordinary course, it was determined to begin with these troublers of our peace, and to suppresse them by the civill authority, whereunto there was a faire occasion offered upon a seditious writing, which had been delivered into the Court in March, when Mr. Wheel. was convict of sedition, &c. under the hands of more than threescore of them, and intitled A Remonstrance or Petition, the Contents whereof were as followeth:

"Wee whose names are under written (have diligently observed this honoured Courts proceedings against our deare and reverend brother in Christ, Mr. Wheel. now under censure of the Court, for the truth of Christ) wee do humbly beseech this honourable Court to accept this Remonstrance and Petition of ours, in all due submission rendred to your Worships.

"For first, whereas our beloved Brother Mr. Wheel. is censured for contempt, by the greater part of this honoured Court, wee desire your Worships to consider the sincere intention of our Brother to promote your end in the day of Fast, for whereas wee do perceive your principal intention the day of Fast looked chiefely at the publick peace of the Churches, our Reverend Brother did to his best strength, and as the Lord assisted him, labour to promote your end, and therefore indevoured to draw us neerer unto Christ, the head of our union, that so wee might bee established in peace, which wee conceive to bee the true way, sanctified of God, to obtaine your end, and therefore deserves no such censure as wee conceive.

"Secondly, Whereas our deare Brother is censured of sedition; wee beseech your Worships to consider, that either the person condemned must bee culpable of some seditious fact, or his doctrine must bee seditious, or must breed sedition in the hearts of his hearers or else wee know not upon what grounds hee should bee censured. Now to the first, wee have not heard any that have witnessed against our brother for any seditious fact. Secondly, neither was the doctrine it selfe, being no other but the very expressions of the Holy Ghost himselfe, and therefore cannot justly be branded with sedition. Thirdly, if you look at the effects of his Doctrine upon the hearers, it hath not stirred up sedition in us, not so much as by accident; wee have not drawn the sword, as sometimes Peter did, rashly, neither have wee rescued our innocent Brother, as sometimes the Israelites did Jonathan, and yet they did not seditiously. The Covenant of free Grace held forth by our Brother, hath taught us rather to become humble suppliants to your Worships, and if wee should not prevaile, wee would rather with patience give our cheekes to the smiters. Since therefore the Teacher, the Doctrine, and the hearers bee most free from sedition (as wee conceive) wee humbly beseech you in the name of Jesus Christ, your Judge and ours, and for the honour of this Court, and the proceedings thereof, that you will bee pleased either to make it appeare to us, and to all the world, to whom the knowledge of all these things will come, wherein the sedition lies, or else acquit our Brother of such a censure.

"Further, wee beseech you remember the old method of Satan, the ancient enemy of Free Grace, in all ages of the Churches, who hath raised up such calumnies against the faithfull Prophets of God, Eliah was called the troubler of Israel, 1 King. 18.17,18. Amos was charged for conspiracy, Amos 7.10. Paul was counted a pestilent fellow, or moover of sedition, and a ring-leader of a Sect, Acts 24.5. and Christ himselfe, as well as Paul, was charged to bee a Teacher of New Doctrine, Mark 1. 27. Acts 17.19. Now wee beseech you consider, whether that old serpent work not after his old method, even in our daies. ..."

[The account of the Court's action against the remonstrants is omitted. One was banished, others were disenfranchised and fined.]

When Mr. Wheelwright appeared, it was declared to him, that whereas hee was long since convict of sedition and contempt of authority, and time had been given him from Court to Court, to come to the knowledge of his offence, the Court thought it now time to know how his mind stood, whether he would acknowledge his offence, or abide the sentence of the Court? His Answer was to this effect, that hee had committed no sedition nor contempt, hee had delivered nothing but the truth of Christ, and for the application of his doctrin it was by others, and not by him, &c.

To which it was answered by the Court, that they had not censured his doctrine, but left it as it was; but his application, by which hee laid the Magistrates, and the Ministers, and most of the people of God in these Churches, under a Covenant of works, and thereupon declared them to bee enemies to Christ, and Antichrists, and such enemies as Herod and Pilate, and the Scribes and Pharisees, &c. perswading the people to look at them, and deale with them as such, and that hee described them so, as all men might know who hee meant, as well as if hee had named the parties; for he was present in the Court a little before, when both Magistrates and Ministers did openly professe their judgment in that point, and that they did walk in such a way of evidencing justification by sanctification, &c. as hee held forth to bee a Covenant of works.

Secondly, the fruits of that Sermon of Mr. Wheelwright, together with the Declaration of his judgment in that point both before and since, have declared it to tend to sedition: for whereas before hee broached his opinions, there was apeaceable and comely order in all affaires in the Churches, and civill state, &c. now the difference which hee hath raised amongst men, by a false distinction of a Covenant of grace and a Covenant of works; whereby one party is looked at as friends to Christ, and the other as his enemies, &c. all things are turned upside down among us: As first, in the Church, hee that will not renounce his sanctification, and waite for an immediate revelation of the Spirit, cannot bee admitted, bee hee never so godly; hee that is already in the Church, that will not do the same, and acknowledge this new light, and say as they say, is presently noted, and under-esteemed, as favouring of a Covenant of works; thence it spreads into the families, and sets divisions between husband and wife, and other relations there, till the weaker give place to the stronger, otherwise it turnes to open contention: it is come also into Civill and publick affaires, and hath bred great disturbance there, as appeared in the late expedition against the Pequods; for whereas in former expeditions the Towne of Boston was as forward as any others to send of their choyce members, and a greater number then other Townes in the time of the former Governour; now in this last service they sent not a member, but one or two whom they cared not to be rid of, and but a few others, and those of the most refuse sort, and that in such a carelesse manner, as gave great discouragement to the service, not one man of that side accompanying their Pastour, when he was sent by the joynt consent of the Court, and all the Elders upon that expedition, nor so much as bidding him farewell. ...

Further the Court declared what meanes had beene used, to convince him and to reduce him into the right way, as first at the Court, when he was convict of his offence, the Ministers being called together did labour by many sound arguments, both in publick and private to convince him of his errour and sinne, but he contemptuously slighted whatsoever they or the Magistrates said to him in that behalfe; and since that much paines had beene taken with him, both by conference and writing, not onely privately, but also by the late Assembly of the Churches, wherein his erroneous opinions, which were the groundworke of his seditious Sermon, were clearely confuted, and himselfe put to silence, yet he obstinately persisted in justification of his erroneous opinions; and besides there was an Apologie written in defence of the proceedings of the Court against him which though it were kept in for a time in expectation of a Remonstrance, which some of his party were in hand with, for justification of his Sermon, yet it was long since published, and without question he hath seene it: besides the Court hath used much patience towards him from time to time, admonishing him of his danger, and waiting for his repentance, in stead whereof he hath threatned us with an appeale, and urged us to proceed: To this Mr. Wheelwright replyed, that he would, by the helpe of God, make good his doctrines, and free them from all the arguments which had beene brought against them in the late Assembly, and denyed that he had seene the Apology, but confessed that he might have seene it if he would. This was observed as an argument of the pride of his spirit, and wilfull neglect of all the meanes of light in that he would not vouchsafe to read a very briefe writing, and such as so much concerned him.

Although the cause was now ready for sentence, yet night being come, the Court arose, and enjoyned him to appeare the next morning.

The next morning he appeared, but long after the houre appointed; the Court demanded what he had to alleadge, why sentence should not proceed against him; he answered, that there was no sedition or contempt proved against him, and whereas he was charged to have set forth the Magistrates and Ministers, as enemies to Christ, &c. he desired it might be shewed him in what page or leafe of his Sermon he had so said of them; The Court answered, that he who designes a man by such circumstances, as doe note him out to common intendments, doth as much as if he named the party: when Paul spake of those of the circumcision, it was as certaine whom he meant as if he named the Jewes; when in Bohemia they spake of differences betweene men, sub una & sub utraque, it was all one as to have said Papists and Protestantsl so of the Monstrants and Remonstrants: for by the meanes of him and his followers, all the people of God in this Countrey were under the distinction of men under the Covenant of the grace, and men under a Covenant of workes. Mr. Wheelwright alleadged a place in Matth. 21 where Christ speaking against the Scribes and Pharisees, no advantage could they take against him because he did not name them, but it was answered they did not spare him for that cause for then they would have taken their advantage at other times, when he did name them. One or two of the Deputies spake in his defence, but it was to so little purpose (being onely more out of affection to the party, then true judgement of the state of the cause) that the Court had little regard of it. Mr. Wheelwright being demanded if he had ought else to speake, said that there was a double Pharisee in the charge laid upon them. 1. In that the troubles of the Civil State were imputed to him, but as it was by accident, as it is usuall in preaching of the Gospel. 2. That it was not his Sermon that was the cause of them but the Lord Jesus Christ. To which the Court answered, that it was apparent he was the instrument of our troubles, he must prove them to be by such accident, and till then the blame must rest upon himselfe, for we know Christ would not owne them, being out of his way. After these and many other speeches had passed, the Court declaring him guilty for troubling the civill peace, both for his seditious Sermon, and for his corrupt and dangerous opinions, and for his contemptuous behaviour in divers Courts formerly, and now obstinately maintaining and justifying his said errours and offences, and for that he refused to depart voluntarily from us, which the Court had now offered him, and in a manner perswaded him unto; Seeing it was apparent unto him, from that of our Saviour, Matth. that we could not continue together without the ruine of the whole, he was sentenced to be disfranchised, and banished our jurisdiction, and to be put in safe custody, except he should give sufficient security to depart before the end of March: Upon this he appealed to the Kings Majesty, but the Court told him an appeale did not lie in this case, for the King having given us an authority by his graunt under his great Seale of England to heare and determine all causes without and reservation, we were not to admit of any such appeales for any such subordinate state, either in Ireland, or Scotland, or other places; and if an appeale should lie in one case, it might be challenged in all, and then there would be no use of government amongst us: neither did an appeale lie from any Court in any County or Corporation in England, but if a party will remove his cause to any of the Kings higher Courts he must bring the Kings Writ for it; neither did he tender any appeale, nor call any witnesses, nor desired any Act to be entered of it: then he was demanded if he would give security for his quiet departure, which he refusing to doe, he was committed to the custody of the Marshall. The next morning he bethought himselfe better, and offered to give security, alleadging that he did not conceive the day before that a sentence of banishment was pronounced against him, he also suffered to relinquish his appeale, and said he would accept of a simple banishment; The Court answered him, that for his appeale he might doe as he pleased, and for his departure, he should have the liberty the Court had offered him, provided he should not preach in the meane time; but that he would not yeeld unto; so in the end the Court gave him leave to goe home, upon his promise, that if he wer not departed out of his jurisdiction within foureteene dayes, he would render himselfe at the house of Mr. Stanton, one of the Magistrates, there to abide as a prisoner, till the Court should dispose of him.

At the same time that the General Court was by decision establishing a rule of law with respect to sedition it formulated in legislation a rule with respect to aliens. After the close of the first stage of the proceedings against Wheelwright the following statute was enacted:

"It is ordered that no town or person shall receive any stranger, resorting hither with intent to reside in this jurisdiction, nor shall allow any lot or habitation to any, or entertain any such above three weeks, except such person shall have allowance under the hands of some one of the council, or of two other of the magistrates, upon pain that every town that shall give or sell any lot or habitation to any such not so allowed, shall forfeit £ 100 for every offence... ." (1 Records 196)

Immediately the friends of Wheelwright and Mrs. Hutchinson made strenuous protests against this order. In reply to those protests John Winthrop published the following paper.

John Winthrop, "A Declaration in Defense of an Order of Court Made in May, 1637", 3 Winthrop Papers 422

For clearing of such scruples as have arisen about this order, it is to be considered, first, what is the essentiall forme of a common weale or body politic such as this is, which I conceive to be this - The consent of a certaine companie of people, to cohabite together, under one government for their mutual safety and welfare.

In this description all these things doe concurre to the well being of such a body, 1 Persons, 2 Place, 3 Consent, 4 Government or Order, 5 Wellfare.

It is clearely agreed, by all, that the care of safety and wellfare was the original cause or occasion of common weales and of many familyes subjecting themselves to rulers and laws; for no man hath lawfull power over another, but by birth or consent, so likewise, by the law of proprietye, no man can have just interest in that which belongeth to another, without his consent.

From the premises will arise these conclusions.

1. No common weale can be founded but by free consent.

2. The persons so incorporating have a public and relative interest each in other, and in the place of their co-habitation and goods, and laws etc. and in all the means of their wellfare so as none other can claime priviledge with them but by free consent.

3. The nature of such an incorporation tyes every member thereof to seeke out and entertaine all means that may conduce to the wellfare of the bodye, and to keepe off whatsoever doth appeare to tend to theire damage.

4. The wellfare of the whole is to be put to apparent hazard for the advantage of any particular members.

From these conclusions I thus reason.

1. If we heere be a corporation established by free consent, if the place of our cohabitation be our owne, then no man hath right to come into us etc. without our consent.

2. If no man hath right to our lands, our government priviledges etc., but by our consent, then it is reason we should take notice of before we conferre any such upon them.

3. If we are bound to keepe off whatsoever appears to tend to our ruine or damage, then we may lawfully refuse to receive such whose dispositions suite not with our and whose society (we know) will be hurtfull to us, and therefore it is lawfull to take knowledge of all men before we receive them.

4. The churches take liberty (as lawfully they may) to re-

ceive or reject at their discretion; yea particular towns make orders to the like effect; why then should the common weale be denied the like liberty, and the whole more restrained than any parte?

5. If it be sinne in us to deny some men place etc. amongst us, then it is because of some right they have to this place etc. for to deny a man that which he hath no right unto, is neither sinne nor injury.

6. If strangers have right to our houses or lands etc. then it is either of justice or of mercye; if of justice let them plead it, and we shall know what to answer: but if it be only in way of mercye, or by the rule of hospitality etc.,then I answer 1st a man is not a fit object of mercye except he be in miserye. 2d. We are not bound to exercise mercye to others to the ruine of ourselves. 3d. There are few that stand in neede of mercye at their first coming hither. As for hospitality, that rule doth not bind further than for some present occasion, not for continual residence.

7. A family is a little common wealth, and a common wealth is a greate family. Now as a family is not bound to entertaine all comers, no not every good man (otherwise than by way of hospitality) no more is a common wealth.

8. It is a generall received rule, turpius ejicitur quam non admittitur hospes, it is worse to receive a man whom we must cast out againe, than to denye him admittance.

9. The rule of the Apostle, John 2. 10, is that such as come and bring not the true doctrine with them should not be received to house, and by the same reason not into the common weale.

10. Seeing it must be granted that there may come such persons (suppose Jesuits etc.) which by consent of all ought to be rejected, it will follow that by this law (being only for notice to be taken of all that come to us, without which we cannot avoyd such as indeed are to be kept out) is no other but just and needfull, and if any should be rejected that ought to be received, that is not to be imputed to the law, but to those who are betrusted with the execution of it. And herein is to be considered, what the intent of the law is, and by consequence by what rule they are to walke, who are betrusted with the keeping of it. The intent of the law is to preserve the wellfare of the body: and for this ende to have none received into any fellowship with it who are likely to disturbe the same, and this intent (I am sure) is lawful and good. Now then, if such to whom the keeping of this law is committed, be persuaded in theire judgments that such a man is likely to disturbe and hinder the publick weale, but some others who are not in the same trust, judge otherwise, yet they are to follow their owne judgments, rather than the judgments of others who are not alike interested: As in tryall of an offender by jury; the twelve men

are satisfied in their consciences, upon the evidence given, that the party deserves death: but there are 20 or 40 standers by, who conceive otherwise, yet is the jury bound to condemn him according to their owne consciences, and not to acquit him upon the different opinion of other men, except theire reasons can convince them of the errour of their consciences, and this is according to the rule of the Apostle. Rom. 14. 5. Let every man be fully persuaded in his own mynde.

If it be objected, that some prophane are received and others who are religious are rejected, I answer 1st, It is not knowne that any such thinge has as yet fallen out. 2. Such a practice may be justifiable as the case may be, for younger persons (even prophane ones) may be of lesse danger to the commonweale (and to the churches also) than some older persons, though professors of religion: for our Saviour Christ when he conversed with publicans etc. sayeth that such were nearer the Kingdom of heaven than the religious pharisees, and one that is of large parts and confirmed in some erroneous way, is likely to doe more harme to church and common weale, and is of lesse hope to be reclaymed, than 10 prophane persons, who have not yet become hardened, in the contempt of the meanes of grace.

Lastly, Whereas it is objected that by this law, we reject good christians and so consequently Christ himselfe: I answer 1st. It is not knowne that any christian man hath been rejected. 2. a man that is a true christian, may be denyed residence among us, in some cases, without rejecting Christ, as admitt a true christian should come over, and should maintain community of goods, or that magistrates ought not to punish the breakers of the first table, or the members of churches for criminal offences: or that no man were bound to be subject to those lawes or magistrates to which they should not give an explicite consent, etc. I hope no man will say, that not to receive such an one were to reject Christ; for such opinions (though being maintained in simple ignorance, they might stand with a state of grace yet) they may be so dangerous to the publick weale in many respects, as it would be our sinne and unfaithfullness to receive such among us, except it were for tryall of theire reformation. I would demand then in the case in question (for it is bootlesse curiosity to refrayne openesse in things publick) whereas it is sayd that this law was made of purpose to keepe away such as are of Mr. Wheelwright his judgment (admitt it were so which yet I cannot confesse) where is the evill of it? If we conceive and finde by sadd experience that his opinions are such, as by his own profession cannot stand with externall peace, may we not provide for our peace, by keeping of such as would strengthen him and infect others with such dangerous tenets? and if we finde his opinions such as will cause divisions, and make people looke at their magistrates, ministers and brethren as enemies to Christ and Antichrists etc., were it not sinne and unfaithfullness in us, to receive more of those opinions, which we already finde the evill fruite of: Nay, why doe not those who now complayne joyne with us in keeping out of such, as well as formerly they did in expelling Mr. Williams for the like, though lesse dangerous? Where this change of theire judgments should arise I leave them to themselves to examine, and I earnestly entreat them so to doe, and for this law let the equally mynded judge, what evill they finde in it, or in the practice of those who are betrusted with the execution of it.*

Trial of Ann Hutchinson
General Court, November, 1637
2 Hutchinson's History of Massachusetts Bay
(Mayo edition) 366 et seq.

The Examination of Mrs. Ann Hutchinson at
the court at Newtown

Mr. Winthrop Governor	Mrs. Hutchinson, you are called here as one of those that have troubled the peace of the commonwealth and the churches here;[1] you are known to be a woman that hath had a great share in the promoting and divulging of those opinions that are causes of this trouble, and to be nearly joined not only in affinity and affection with some of those the court had taken notice of and passed censure upon, but you have spoken divers things as we have been informed very prejudicial to the honour of the churches and ministers thereof, and you have maintained a meeting and an assembly in your house that hath been condemned by the general assembly as a thing not tolerable nor comely in the sight of God nor fitting for your sex, and notwithstanding that was cried down you have continued the same, therefore we have thought good to send for you to understand how things are, that if you be in an erroneous way we may reduce you that so you may

* An answer to this Declaration of Winthrop's, which has been attributed to Vane, is in 1 Hutchinson Papers 84, and Winthrop's replication thereto is in 3 Winthrop Papers 463.

1. The proceedings against Mrs. Hutchinson opened immediately after the decree banishing Wheelwright was issued. Sec. 1 Records 207.

become a profitable member here among us, otherwise if you be obstinate in your course that then the court may take such course that you may trouble us no further, therefore I would intreat you to express whether you do not assent and hold in practice to those opinions and factions that have been handled in court already, that is to say, whether you do not justify Mr. Wheelwright's sermon and the petition.

Mrs. Hutchinson I am called here to answer before you but I hear no things laid to my charge.

Gov. I have told you some already and more I can tell you.
Mrs. H. Name one Sir.
Gov. Have I not named some already?
Mrs. H. What have I said or done?
Gov. Why for your doings, this you did harbour and countenance those that are parties in this faction that you heard of.
Mrs. H. That's matter of conscience, Sir.
Gov. Your conscience you must keep or it must be kept for you.
Mrs. H. Must not I then entertain the saints because I must keep my conscience.
Gov. Say that one brother should commit felony or treason and come to his brother's house, if he knows him guilty and conceals him he is guilty of the same. It is his conscience to entertain him, but if his conscience comes into act in giving countenance and entertainment to him that hath broken the law he is guilty too. So if you do countenance those that are transgressors of the law you are in the same fact.
Mrs. H. What law do they transgress?
Gov. The law of God and of the state.[2]
Mrs. H. In what particular?
Gov. Why in this among the rest, whereas the Lord doth say honour thy father and thy mother.
Mrs. H. Ey Sir in the Lord.
Gov. This honour you have broke in giving countenance to them.
Mrs. H. In entertaining those did I entertain them against any act (for there is the thing) or what God hath appointed?

---

2. A statute adopted in May, 1636, had been stated that pending the adoption of fundamental laws in a code "the magistrates

Gov.	You knew that Mr. Wheelwright did preach this sermon and those that countenance him in this do break a law.
Mrs. H.	What law have I broken?
Gov.	Why the fifth commandment.
Mrs. H.	I deny that for he saith in the Lord.
Gov.	You have joined with them in the faction.
Mrs. H.	In what faction have I joined with them?
Gov.	In presenting the petition.
Mrs. H.	Suppose I had set my hand to the petition what then?
Gov.	You saw that case tried before.
Mrs. H.	But I had not my hand to the petition.
Gov.	You have councelled them.
Mrs. H.	Wherein?
Gov.	Why in entertaining them.
Mrs. H.	What breach of law is that Sir?
Gov.	Why dishonouring of parents.
Mrs. H.	But put the case Sir that I do fear the Lord and my parents, may not I entertain them that fear the Lord because my parents will not give me leave?
Gov.	If they be the fathers of the commonwealth, and they of another religion, if you entertain them then you dishonour your parents and are justly punishable.
Mrs. H.	If I entertain them, as they have dishonoured their parents I do.
Gov.	No but you by countenancing them above others put honor upon them.
Mrs. H.	I may put honor upon them as the children of God and as they do honor the Lord.
Gov.	We do not mean to discourse with those of your sex but only this; you do adhere unto them and do endeavor to set forward this faction and so you do dishonour us.
Mrs. H.	I do acknowledge no such thing neither do I think that I ever put any dishonour upon you.

[The examination then turned to the question of what had transpired and what views Mrs. Hutchinson had expressed at the meetings which she had held in Boston. Mrs. Hutchinson justified the holding of the meetings by the command or "rule", as she considered it, of the Bible (Titus). Governor Winthrop and Mr. Endicott, one of the Assistants, denied the applicability of

---

and their associates shall proceed in the courts to hear and determine all causes according to the laws now established, and where there is no law, then as near the law of God as they can". 1 Records 174-75.

the alleged command. The examination then continued.

Mr. Dudley [Dep. Gov.] Here hath been much spoken concerning Mrs. Hutchinson's meetings and among others answers she saith that men come not there, I would ask you this one question then, whether never any man was at your meeting?

Gov. There are two meetings kept at their house.

Dep. Gov. How; is there two meetings?

Mrs. H. Ey Sir, I shall not equivocate, there is a meeting of men and women and there is a meeting only for women.

Dep. Gov. Are they both constant?

Mrs. H. No, but upon occasions they are deferred.

Mr. Endicot [an assistant] Who teaches in the men's meetings none but men, do not women sometimes?

Mrs. H. Never as I heard, not one.

Dep. Gov. I would go a little higher with Mrs. Hutchinson. About three years ago we were all in peace. Mrs. Hutchinson from that time she came hath made a disturbance, and some that came over with her in the ship did inform me what she was as soon as she was landed. I being then in place dealt with the pastor and teacher of Boston Wilson and Cotton and desired them to enquire of her, and then I was satisfied that she held nothing different from us, but within half a year after, she have vented divers of her strange opinions and had made parties in the country, and at length it comes that Mr. Cotton and Mr. Vane were of her judgment, but Mr. Cotton hath cleared himself that he was not of that mind, but now it appears by this woman's meeting that Mrs. Hutchinson hath so forestalled the minds of many by their resort to her meeting that now she hath a potent party in the country. Now if all these things have endangered us as from that foundation and if she in particular hath disparaged all our ministers in the land that they have preached a covenant of works, and only Mr. Cotton a covenant of grace, why this is not to be suffered, and therefore being driven to the foundation and it being found that Mrs. Hutchinson is she that hath depraved all the ministers and hath been the cause of what is fallen out, why we must take away the foundation and the building will fall.

Mrs. H. I pray Sir prove it that I said they preached nothing but a covenant of works.

Dep. Gov. Nothing but a covenant of works, why a Jesuit may

	preach truth sometimes.
Mrs. H.	Did I ever say they preached a covenant of works then?
Dep.Gov.	If they do not preach a covenant of grace clearly, then they preach a covenant of works.
Mrs. H.	No Sir, one may preach a covenant of grace more clearly than another, so I said.
Dep.Gov.	We are not upon that now but upon position.
Mrs. H.	Prove this then Sir that you say I said.
Dep.Gov.	When they do preach a covenant of works do they preach truth?
Mrs. H.	Yes Sir, but when they preach a covenant of works for salvation, that is not truth.
Dep.Gov.	I do but ask you this, when the ministers do preach a covenant of works do they preach a way of salvation?
Mrs. H.	I did not come hither to answer to questions of that sort.
Dep.Gov.	Because you will deny the thing.
Mrs. H.	Ey, but that is to be proved first.
Dep.Gov.	I will make it plain that you did say that the ministers did preach a covenant of works.
Mrs. H.	I deny that.
Dep.Gov.	And that you said they were not able ministers of the new testament, but Mr. Cotton only.
Mrs. H.	If ever I spake that I proved it by God's word.
Court	Very well, very well.
Mrs. H.	If one shall come unto me in private, and desire me seriously to tell them what I thought of such an one. I must either speak false or true in my answer.
Dep.Gov.	Likewise I will prove this that you said the gospel in the letter and words holds forth nothing but a covenant of works and that all that do not hold as you do are in a covenant of works.
Mrs. H.	I deny this for if I should so say I should speak against my own judgment.
Mr.Endicot	I desire to speak seeing Mrs. Hutchinson seems to lay something against them that are to witness against her.
Gov.	Only I would add this. It is well discerned to the court that Mrs. Hutchinson can tell when to speak and when to hold her tongue. Upon the answering of a question which we desire her to tell her thoughts of she desired to be pardoned.
Mrs. H.	It is one thing for me to come before a public magistracy and there to speak what they would have me to speak and another when a man comes to me in a way of friendship privately there is difference in that.

Gov.	What if the matter be all one.
Mr. Hugh Peters /Minister of Salem/	That which concerns us to speak unto as yet we are sparing in unless the court command us to speak, then we shall answer to Mrs. Hutchinson notwithstanding our brethren are very unwilling to answer.[3]
Gov.	This speech was not spoken in a corner but in a public assembly, and though things were spoken in private yet now coming to us, we are to deal with them as public.

/Seven ministers of neighboring churches, including Hugh Peters, then each testified, but not under oath, that on behalf of the Churches they had examined Mrs. Hutchinson as to the criticisms which she had allegedly made of the Massachusetts ministry. They agreed in substance that she told them that John Cotton was the one minister who preached the covenant of grace and that the others preached a covenant of works. After hearing this testimony the Court adjourned, directing that the proceedings should continue on the next morning./

Gov.	We proceeded the last night as far as we could in hearing of this cause of Mrs. Hutchinson. There were divers things laid to her charge, her ordinary meetings about religious exercises, her speeches in derogation of the ministers among us, and the weakening of the hands and hearts of the people towards them. Here was sufficient proof made of that which she was accused of in that point concerning the ministers and their ministry, as that they did preach a covenant of works when others did preach a covenant of grace, and that they were not able ministers of the new testament, and that they had not the seal of the spirit, and this was spoken not as was pretended out of private conference, but out of conscience and warrant from scripture alledged the fear of man is a snare and seeing God had given her a calling to it she would freely speak. Some other speeches she used, as that the letter of the scripture held forth a covenant of works, and this is offered to be proved by probable grounds. If

3. Concerning the problem of whether the canon law and the common law treated private communications to priests and ministers as privileged see Badelay, Religious Confessions (1865) and 8 Wigmore, Evidence (3rd ed.) Sec. 2394 et seq.

there be any thing else that the court hath to say they may speak.

Mrs. H. The ministers come in their own cause. Now the Lord hath said that an oath is the end of all controversy; though there be a sufficient number of witnesses yet they are not according to the word, therefore I desire they may speak upon oath.

Gov. Well, it is in the liberty of the court whether they will have an oath or no, and it is not in this case as in case of a jury. If they be satisfied they have sufficient matter to proceed. ... For that which you alledge as an exception against the elders it is vain and untrue, for they are no prosecutors in this cause but are called to witness in the cause.

Mrs. H. But they are witnesses of their own cause.

Gov. It is not their cause but the cause of the whole country and they were unwilling that it should come forth, but that it was the glory and honour of God.

Mrs. H. But it being the Lord's ordinance that an oath should be the end of all strife, therefore they are to deliver what they do upon oath.

Mr. Bradstreet [an assistant] Mrs. Hutchinson, these are but circumstances and adjuncts to the cause, admit they should mistake you in your speeches you would make them to sin if you urge them to swear.

Mrs. H. That is not the thing. If they accuse me I desire it may be upon oath.

Gov. If the court be not satisfied they may have an oath.

Mr. Nowel [an assistand] I should think it convenient that the country also should be satisfied because that I do hear it affirmed, that things which were spoken in private are carried abroad to the publick and thereupon they do undervalue the ministers of congregations.

Mr. Brown [a Deputy] I desire to speak. If I mistake not an oath is of a high nature, and it is not to be taken but in a controversy, and for my part I am afraid of an oath and fear that we shall take God's name in vain, for we may take the witness of these men without an oath.

Mr. Endicot I think the ministers are so well known unto us, that we need not take an oath of them, but indeed an oath is the end of all strife.

Mrs. H. There are some that will take their oaths to the contrary.

Mr. Endicot Then it shall go under the name of a controversy, therefore we desire to see the notes and those also that will swear.

Gov. Let those that are not satisfied in the court speak.

Many say ...... We are not satisfied.

Gov. I would speak this to Mrs. Hutchinson. If the ministers shall take an oath will you sit down satisfied?

Mrs. H. I can't be notwithstanding oaths satisfied against my own conscience.

Mr. Stoughton [an assistant] I am fully satisfied with this that the ministers do speak the truth but now in regard of censure. I dare not hold up my hand to that, because it is a course of justice, and I cannot satisfy myself to proceed so far in a way of justice, and therefore I should desire an oath in this as in all other things. I do but speak to prevent offence if I should not hold up my hand at the censure unless there be an oath given.

Mr. Peters We are ready to swear if we see a way of God in it.

Here was a parley between the deputy governor and Mr. Stoughton about the oath.

[Further discussion followed as to the taking of the testimony of the ministers under oath. Some of the ministers indicated an unwillingness to take the oath; others, including Peters, said that they would do so since its purpose would be to satisfy the Court, not Mrs. Hutchinson. Before that issue was finally disposed of two witnesses, Mr. Coggeshall and Mr. Leverett unsworn, testified that they were present when Mrs. Hutchinson was examined by the ministers and that she had not answered the questions of the ministers as they had testified that she had. Mr. John Cotton then gave testimony tending to controvert the evidence of the other ministers. After he had stated that he did not recall Mrs. Hutchinson having said that the other ministers were not able ministers of the New Testament, Mrs. Hutchinson intervened as follows:]

Mrs. H. If you please to give me leave I shall give you the ground of what I know to be true. Being much troubled to see the falseness of the constitution of the church of England, I had like to have turned separatist; whereupon I kept a day of solemn humiliation and pondering of the thing; this scripture was brought unto me - he that denies Jesus Christ to be come in the flesh is antichrist - This I considered of and in considering found that the papists did not deny him to be come in the flesh, nor we did not deny him - who then was antichrist? Was the Turk antichrist only? The Lord knows that I could not open scripture; he must by his prophetical office open it unto me. So after that being unsatisfied in the thing, the Lord was pleased to bring this scripture out of the Hebrews. He that denies the testament denies the testator, and in this did open unto me and give me to see that those which did not teach the new covenant had the spirit of antichrist, and upon this he did discover the ministry unto me and ever since, I bless the Lord, he hath let me see which was the clear ministry and which the wrong. Since that time I confess I have been more choice and he hath left me to distinguish between the voice of my beloved and the voice of Moses, the voice of John Baptist and the voice of antichrist, for all those voices are spoken of in scripture. Now if you do condemn me for speaking what in my conscience I know to be truth I must commit myself unto the Lord.

Mr. Nowel: How do you know that that was the spirit?

Mrs. H.: How did Abraham know that it was God that bid him offer his son, being a breach of the sixth commandment?

Dep.Gov.: By an immediate voice.

Mrs. H.: So to me by an immediate revelation.

Dep.Gov.: How! an immediate revelation.

Mrs. H.: By the voice of his own spirit to my soul. ... Therefore I desire you to look to it, for you see this scripture fulfilled this day and therefore I desire you that as you tender the Lord and the church and commonwealth to consider and look what you do. You have power over my body but the Lord Jesus hath power over my body and soul, and assure yourselves thus much, you do as much as in you lies to put the Lord Jesus Christ from you, and if you go on in this course you begin you will bring a curse upon you and your posterity, and the mouth of the Lord hath spoken it.

Dep.Gov.: What is the scripture she brings?

Mr.Stoughton: Behold I turn away from you.

Mrs. H.: But now having seen him which is invisible I fear not what man can do unto me.

Gov.: Daniel was delivered by miracle do you think to be deliver'd so too?

Mrs. H.: I do here speak it before the court. I look that the Lord should deliver me by his providence. ...

Mr.Endicot: I would have a word or two with leave of that which hath thus far been revealed to the court. I have heard of many revelations of Mr. Hutchinson's, but they were reports, but Mrs. Hutchinson I see doth maintain some by this discourse, and I think it is a special providence of God to hear what she hath said. Now there is a revelation you see which she doth expect as a miracle. She saith she now suffers and let us do what we will she shall be delivered by a miracle. I hope the court takes notice of the vanity of it and heat of her spirit. Now because her reverend teacher is here I should desire that he would please to speak freely whether he doth condescend to such speeches or revelations as have been here spoken of, and he will give a great deal of content. ...

Mr.Cotton I know not whether I do understand her, but this I say, if she doth expect a deliverance in a way of providence - then I cannot deny it.

Dep.Gov. No Sir we did not speak of that.

Mr.Cotton I know not whether I do understand her, but this I say, if she doth expect a deliverance in a way of providence - then I cannot deny it.

Dep.Gov. No Sir we did not speak of that.

Mr.Cotton If it be by way of miracle then I would suspect it.

Dep.Gov. Do you believe that her revelations are true?

Mr.Cotton That she may have some special providence of God to help her is a thing that I cannot bear witness against.

Dep.Gov. Good Sir I do ask whether this revelation be of God or no?

Mr.Cotton I should desire to know whether the sentence of the court will bring her to any calamity, and then I would know of her whether she expects to be delivered from that calamity by a miracle or a providence of God.

Mrs. H. By a providence of God I say I expect to be delivered from some calamity that shall come to me.

Gov. The case is altered and will not stand with us now, but I see a marvellous providence of God to bring things to this pass that they are. We have been hearkening about the trial of this thing and now the mercy of God by a providence hath answered our desires and made her to lay open her self and the ground of all these disturbances to be by revelations. ... The ground work of her revelations is the immediate revelation of the spirit and not by the ministry of the word, and that is the means by which she hath very much abused the country that they shall look for revelations and are not bound to the ministry of the word, but God will teach them by immediate revelations and this hath been the ground of all these tumults and troubles, and I would that these were all cut off from us that trouble us, for this is the thing that hath been the root of all the mischief.

Court	We all consent with you.
Gov.	Ey it is the most desperate enthusiasm in the world, for nothing but a word comes to her mind and then an application is made which is nothing to the purpose, and this is her revelations when it is impossible but that the word and spirit should speak the same thing.
Mr.Endicot	I speak in reference to Mr. Cotton. I am tender of you Sir and there lies much upon you in this particular, for the answer of Mr. Cotton doth not free him from that way which his last answer did bring upon him, therefore I beseech you that you'd be pleased to speak a word to that which Mrs. Hutchinson hath spoken of her revelations as you have heard the manner of it. Whether do you witness for her or against her.
Mr. Cotton	This is that I said, Sir, and my answer is plain that if she doth look for deliverance from the hand of God by his providence, and the revelation be in a word or according to a word, that I cannot deny.
Mr.Endicot	You give me satisfaction.
Dep. Gov.	No, no, he gives me none at all.
Mr. Cotton	But if it be in a way of miracle or a revelation without the word that I do not assent to, but look at it as a delusion, and I think so doth she too as I understand her.
Dep. Gov.	Sir, you weary me and do not satisfy me.
Mr. Cotton	I pray Sir give me leave to express my self. In that sense that she speaks I dare not bear witness against it.
Mr. Nowell	I think it is a devilish delusion.
Gov.	Of all the revelations that ever I read of I never read the like ground laid as is for this. The Enthusiasts and Anabaptists had never the like.
Mr. Cotton	You know, Sir, that their revelations breach new matters of faith and doctrine.
Gov.	So do these and what may they breed more if they be let alone. I do acknowledge that there are such revelations as do concur with the word but there hath not been any of this nature. ... I am persuaded that the revelation she brings forth is delusion. All the court but some two or three ministers cry out we all believe it - we all believe it.

Mr.Endicot I suppose all the world may see where the foundation of all these troubles among us lies. ...

Mr. Brown Inasmuch as I am called to speak, I would therefore speak the mind of our brethren. Though we had sufficient ground for the censure before, yet now she having vented herself and I find such flat contradiction to the scripture in what she saith, as to that in the first to the Hebrews - God at sundry times spake to our fathers - For my part I understand that scripture and other scriptures of the Lord Jesus Christ, and the apostle writing to Timothy saith that the scripture is able to make one perfect - therefore I say the mind of the brethren - I think she deserves no less a censure than hath been already past but rather something more, for this is the foundation of all mischief and of all those bastardly things which have been overthrowing by that great meeting. They have all come out from this cursed fountain.

Gov. Seeing the court hath thus declared itself and hearing what hath been laid to the charge of Mrs. Hutchinson and especially what she by the providence of God hath declared freely without being asked, if therefore it be the mind of the court, looking at her as the principal cause of all our trouble, that they would now consider what is to be done to her.

Mr. Coddington [a Deputy] I do think that you are going to censure therefore I desire to speak a word.

Gov. I pray you speak.

Mr. Coddington Where is one thing objected against the meetings. What if she designed to edify her own family in her own meetings may none else be present?

Gov. If you have nothing else to say but that, it is pity Mr. Coddington that you should interrupt us in proceeding to censure.

Mr. Coddington I would say more Sir, another thing you lay to her Charge is her speech to the elders. Now I do not see any clear witness against her, and you know it is a rule of the court that no man may be a judge and an accuser too. I do not speak to disparage our elders and their callings, but I do not see any thing that they accuse her of witnessed against her and therefore I do not see how she should be censured for that. And for the other thing which hath fallen from her occasionally by the spirit of God, you know the spirit of God witnesses with our spirits, and there is no truth in scripture but God bears witness to it by his spirit, therefore I would entreat you to consider whether these things you have alledged against her deserve such censure as you are about to pass, be it to banishment or imprisonment. And again here is nothing proved about the elders, only that she said they did not teach a covenant of grace so clearly as Mr. Cotton did, and that they were in the state of the apostles before the ascension. Why I hope this may not be offensive nor any wrong to them.

Gov. Pass by all that hath been said formerly and her own speeches have been gound enough for us to proceed upon.

Mr. Coddington I beseech you do not speak so to force things along for I do not for my own part see any equity in the court in all your proceedings. Here is no law of God that she hath broken nor any law of the country that she hath broke, and therefore deserves no censure, and if she say that the elders preach as the apostles did, why they preached a covenant of grace and what wrong is that to them, for it is without question that the apostles did preach a covenant of grace, though not with that power, till they received the manifestation of the spirit, therefore I pray consider what you do, for here is no law of God or man broken.

Mr. Harlakenden [an assistant] Things thus spoken will stick. I would therefore that the assembly take notice that here is none that condemns the meeting of christian women; but in such a way and for such an end that it is to be detested. And then tho' the matter of the elders be taken away yet there is enow besides to condemn her, but I shall speak no further.

Dep. Gov. We shall be all sick with fasting.

Mr. Colburn [a Deputy] I dissent from censure of banishment.

Mr. Stoughton The censure which the court is about to pass in my conscience is as much as she deserves, but because she desires witness and there is none in way of witness therefore I shall desire that no offence be taken if I do not formally condemn her because she hath not been formally convicted as others are by witnesses upon oath.

Mr. Coddington That is a scruple to me also, because Solomon saith every man is partial in his own cause, and here is none that accuses her but the elders, and she spake nothing to them but in private, and I do not know what rule they had to make the thing publick, secret things ought to be spoken in secret and publick

	things in publick, therefore I think they have broken the rules of God's word.
Gov.	What was spoken in the presence of many is not to be made secret.
Mr. Coddington	But that was spoken but to a few and in private.
Gov.	In regard Mr. Stoughton is not satisfied to the end all scruples may be removed we shall desire the elders to take their oaths.

Here now was a great whispering among the ministers, some drew back others were animated on.

Mr. Eliot	[Minister of Roxbury] If the court calls us out to swear we will swear.
Gov.	Any two of you will serve.
Mr. Stoughton	There are two things that I would look to discharge my conscience of, 1st to hear what they testify upon and 2dly to ---
Gov.	It is required of you Mr. Weld and Mr. Eliot
Mr. Weld) Mr. Eliot)	[Minister of Roxbury] We shall be willing
Gov.	We'll give them their oaths. You shall swear to the truth and nothing but the truth as far as you know. So help you God. What do you remember of her speak, pray speak.

Mr. Peters held up his hand also.

Mr. Eliot	I do remember and I have it written, that which she spake first was, the fear of man is a snare, why should she be afraid but would speak freely. The question being asked whether there was a difference between Mr. Cotton and us, she said there was a broad difference. I would not stick upon words - the thing she said - and that Mr. Cotton did preach a covenant of grace and we of works and she gave this reason - to put a work in point of evidence is a revealing upon a work. We did labour then to convince her that our doctrine was the same with Mr. Cotton's: She said no, for we were not sealed. This is all I shall say.
Gov.	What say you Mr. Weld?
Mr. Weld	I will speak to the things themselves - these two things I am fully clear in - she did make a difference in three things, the first I was not so clear in, but that she said this I am fully sure of that we were not able ministers of the new testament and that we were not clear in our experience

because we were not sealed.

Mr. Eliot: I do further remember this also, that she said we were not able ministers of the gospel because we were but like the apostles before the ascension.

Mr. Coddington: This was I hope no disparagement to you.

Gov.: Well, we see in the court that she doth continually say and unsay things.

Mr. Peters: I was much grieved that she should say that our ministry was legal. Upon which we had a meeting as you know and this was the same she told us that there was a broad difference between Mr. Cotton and us. Now if Mr. Cotton do hold forth things more clearly than we, it was our grief we did not hold it so clearly as he did, and upon those grounds that you have heard.

Mr. Coddington: What wrong was that to say that you were not able ministers of the new testament or that you were like the apostles - me thinks the comparison is very good.

Gov.: Well, you remember that she said but now that she should be delivered from this calamity.

Mr. Cotton: I remember she said she should be delivered by God's providence, whether now or at another time she knew not.

Mr. Peters: I profess I thought Mr. Cotton would never have took her part.

Mr. Stoughton: I say now this testimony doth convince me in the thing, and I am fully satisfied the words were pernicious, and the frame of her spirit doth hold forth the same.

Gov.: The court hath already declared themselves satisfied concerning the things you hear, and concerning the troublesomness of her spirit and the danger of her course amongst us, which is not to be suffered. Therefore if it be the mind of the court that Mrs. Hutchinson for these things that appear before us is unfit for our society, and if it be the mind of the court that she shall be banished out of our liberties and imprisoned till she be sent away, let them hold up their hands.

(All but three.)

Those that are contrary minded hold up yours.

(Mr. Coddington and Mr. Colborn, only.)

Mr. Jennison [a Deputy]: I cannot hold up my hand one way or the other, and I shall give my reason if the court require it.

Gov.	Mrs. Hutchinson, the sentence of the court you hear is that you are banished from out of our jurisdiction as being a woman not fit for our society, and are to be imprisoned till the court shall send you away.
Mrs. H.	I desire to know wherefore I am banished?
Gov.	Say no more, the court knows wherefore and is satisfied.[4]

* * *

After the imposition of this civil sentence of banishment, but before her departure from Massachusetts Bay, the Church in Boston initiated disciplinary proceedings against Mrs. Hutchinson. After lengthy and strenuous proceedings she was excommunicated. The record of those church proceedings is reprinted in Adams, Antinomianism.

Governor Winthrop was evidently not held blameless for the Court's proceedings in the Wheelwright and Hutchinson matters. The following account of the difficulties which he had with the Church immediately after those trials throws some light on the relationship between church and state as conceived by Winthrop.

Excerpt from Winthrop's Journal, Vol. 1, p. *249

After this, many of the church of Boston, being highly offended with the governor for this proceeding, were earnest with the elders to have him called to account for it; but they were not forward in it, and himself, understanding their intent, thought fit to prevent such a public disorder, and so took occasion to speak to the congregation to this effect: -

1. That if he had been called, etc., he would have desired, first, to have advised with the elders, whether the church had power to call in question the proceedings of the civil court.

2. He would have consulted with the rest of the court, whether he might discover the counsels of the court to this assembly.

---

4. The report of the proceedings against Mrs. Hutchinson in the records of the General Court is as follows: "Mrs. Hutchinson ... being convented for traducing the ministers and their ministry in this country, she declared voluntarily her revelations for her ground, and that she should be delivered and the Court ruined, with their posterity, and thereupon was banished ... ." 1 Records 207.

3. Though he knew, that the elders and some others did know, that the church could not inquire into the justice and proceedings of the court, etc.; yet, for the satisfaction of such as did not, and were willing to be satisfied, he would declare his mind herein.

4. He showed, that, if the church had such power, they must have it from Christ, but Christ had disclaimed it in his practice and by rule, as Luke   Matt.   and the scripture holds not out any rule or example for it; and though Christ's kingly power be in his church, yet that is not that kingly power whereby he is King of kings and Lord of lords, for by that kings reign and princes, etc. It is true, indeed, that magistrates, as they are church members, are accountable to the church for their failings, but that is when they are out of their calling; for we have examples of the highest magistrates in the same kind, as Uzzia, when he would go offer incense in the temple, the officers of the church called him to account, and withstood him. ... If a magistrate shall, in a private way, take away a man's goods or his servants, etc., the church may call him to account for it; but if he doth thus in pursuing a course of justice, (though the thing be unjust) yet he is not accountable, etc.

5. For himself, he did nothing in the cases of the brethren, but by the advice and direction of our teacher and other of the elders. For in the oath, which was administered to him and the rest, etc., there was inserted, by his advice, this clause, - In all causes wherein you are to give your vote, etc. you are to give your vote as in your judgment and conscience you shall see to be most for the public good, etc.; and so for his part he was persuaded, that it would be most for the glory of God, and the public good, to pass sentence as they did.

6. He would give them one reason, which was a ground for his judgment, and that was, for that he saw, that those brethren, etc., were so divided from the rest of the country in their judgment and practice, as it could not stand with the public peace, that they should continue amongst us. So, by the example of Lot in Abraham's family, and after Hagar and Ishmael, he saw they must be sent away.

* * *

That the orthodox churchmen did not agree with Winthrop's thesis that the judges could not be subjected to church discipline for their official action is indicated in the following passage from A Model of Church and Civil Power (1634), which though ascribed by Roger Williams to John Cotton seems to have been written by Richard Mather.

Magistrates may be censured for apparent and manifest

sinne against any Morall Law of God, in their judiciall proceedings, or in the execution of their office. Courts are not Sanctuaries for sin; and if for no sin, then not for such especially.

First, because sinnes of Magistrates in Court are as hatefull to God. 2. And as much spoken against, Isa. 10. 1. Mic. 3. 1. Thirdly, God hath no where granted such immunity to them. Fourthly, what a brother may doe privately in case of private offence, that the Church may doe publikely in case of publike scandall. But a private brother may admonish and reprove privately in case of any private offence, Mat. 18. 15. Luc. 19.16. Psal. 141.5. ...

We like it well, the Churches be slower in proceeding to excommunication, as of all other, so of Civill Magistrates especially in point of their Judiciall proceedings, unlesse it be in scandalous breach of a manifest Law of God, and that after notorious evidence of the fact, and that after due seeking and waiting for satisfaction in a previous Advertisement.

6. The Movement for Codification

a. The Body of Liberties

After the constitutional revolution of 1634 when the General Court recaptured the legislative power, the Deputies came to see that the Assistants were still engaged, through the independent exercise of their judicial powers, in the process of making law for the Colony. Winthrop in his Journal for May, 1635, described the effort the Deputies made to limit the discretion of the magistrates: "The deputies having conceived great danger to our state in regard that our magistrates, for want of positive laws, in many cases might proceed according to their discretions, it was agreed that some men should be appointed to frame a body of grounds of laws, in resemblance to a Magna Charta, which being allowed by some of the ministers, and the general court, should be received for fundamental laws." (1 Winthrop, Journal *160) The Commissioners then appointed by the General Court were slow to fulfill their duties and in May, 1636, the General Court, increasing the personnel of the Commission by adding three ministers (John Cotton, Hugh Peter, and Thomas Shepard) again directed the commissioners "to make a draught of laws agreeable to the word of God, which may be the fundamentals of this Commonwealth, and to present the same to the next General Court". It was further provided that, pending the compilation of these fundamental laws, the magistrates should "proceed in the courts to hear and determine all causes, according to the laws now established, and where there is no law, then as near the laws of God as they can". (1 Records 176.)

The Records of the General Court nowhere indicate that the men appointed to effect the compilation performed any part of their duty during the period specified by the General Court. From Winthrop's Journal it appears, however, that in October, 1636, John Cotton introduced in the General Court "a copy of Moses his judicials, compiled in an exact method". (1 Winthrop, Journal *202) Cotton's draft of a code of laws, though never adopted by the General Court,[1] was published in England in 1641 under a deceptive title indicating that it had been adopted in New England. That misleading title page led many to accept the Code as something more than a draft, and it was not until 1842 that it was conclusively established that Moses his Judicials was never a part of the law of Massachusetts.[2] Its influence in that colony seems merely to have been that of a thoughtful draft of a Code which was taken into account as such by those who did frame the first code to be adopted - The Body of Liberties of 1641.

Although never enacted in Massachusetts the Cotton Code has interest as an effort by a leading churchman of the colony to put the law of God into a statutory form. Had the author of Examen Legum Angliae (supra, p. 86) attempted to carry out his objectives he might well have been forced to make an attempt like Cotton's. His effort might have been more successful in its details, but it is doubtful if it would in its substance have been substantially different. A few excerpts from Cotton's draft, as published in England in 1641, will give an impression of the whole. They are taken from the reprint in Mass. Hist. Soc. Coll., 1st series, Vol. 5, p. 173.[3]

Chapter I - Of Magistrates

1. All magistrates are to be chosen. Deut. I. 13,17,15.
   First, By the free burgesses.
   Secondly, Out of the free burgesses

---

1. It is not known to what extent there were significant changes in Cotton's draft between the session of October, 1636, and that of the fall of 1639, when evidently another examination of Cotton's proposal occurred. See 1 Winthrop Journal *321-22. Certain portions of Cotton's first draft seem to have been used by the first settlers of New Haven in 1639. See, Calder, "John Cotton and the New Haven Colony", 3 New England Qu. 82 (1930).

2. Francis C. Gray, "Remarks on the Early Laws of Massachusetts Bay", Mass. Hist. Soc. Coll. 3rd Series,Vol.8, p.191.

3. The text of the 1655 edition is reprinted in 1 Hutchinson

Thirdly, Out of the ablest men and most approved amonst them. Ex. 18, 21.

Fourthly, Out of the rank of noblemen or gentlemen among them, the best that God shall send into the country, if they be qualified with gifts fit for government, either eminent above others, or not inferior to others. Eccle. 10. 17. Jer. 30. 21. ...

Chapter IV - Of the right of Inheritance

...5. Inheritances are to descend naturally to the next of kin according to the law of nature, delivered by God.

6. Observe, if a man have more sons than one, then a double portion to be assigned and bequeated to the eldest son, according to the law of nature; unless his own demerit to deprive him of the dignity of his birth-right. ...

Chapter VI - Of Trespasses

...4. If a man's ox, or other beast, gore or bite, and kill a man or woman ... the beast shall be killed, and no benefit of the dead beast reserved to the owner. But if the ox, or beast, were wont to push or bite in time past, and the owner hath been told of it, and hath not kept him in, then both the ox, or beast, shall be forfeited and killed, and the owner also put to death, or fined to pay what the judges and persons damnified shall lay upon him.

5. If a man deliver goods to his neighbor to keep, and they be said to be lost or stolen from him, the keeper of the goods shall be put to his oath touching his own innocency; which if he take, and no evidence appear to the contrary, he shall be quit: but if he be found false or unfaithful, he shall pay double unto his neighbour. ...

Chapter VII - Of Crimes. And first, of such as deserve capital punishment, or cutting off from a man's people, whether by death or banishment.[4]

1. First, blasphemy, which is a cursing of God by atheism or the like, to be punished with death. ...

Papers (Prince Society) 183.

4. On banishment as a capital penalty, see Godolphin, A View of the Admiral Jurisdiction (1661) p. 57-58.

6. To worship God in a molten or graven image, to be punished with death. ...

17. Murder, which is wilful man-slaughter, not in a man's just defense, nor casually committed, but out of hatred or cruelty, to be punished with death. Ex. 21, 12, 13, Num. 35.16, 17, 18, to 33. Gen. 9. 6. ...

[The total number of "capital" offenses was 24.]

Chapter VIII - Of other Crimes less heinous, such as are to be punished with some corporal punishment or fine.

...2. Drunkenness, as transforming God's image into a beast, is to be punished with the punishment of beasts: a whip for the horse, a rod for the fool's back. ...

6. If any man steal a beast, if it be found in his hand he shall make restitution two for one; if it be killed and sold, restitution is to be made of five oxen for one; if the thief be not able to make restitution, then he is to be sold by the magistrate for a slave, till by his labour he may make due restitution. Ex. 22. 1, 4.

Chapter IX - Of the trial of causes, whether civil or criminal and the execution of sentence.

1. In the trial of all causes, no judgment shall pass but either upon confession of the party, or upon the testimony of two witnesses.

2. Trial by judges shall not be denied, where either the delinquent requireth it in causes criminal, or the plaintiff or defendant in civil causes, partly to prevent suspicion of partiality of any magistrates in the court. ...

5. No freeman, whether free burgess or free inhabitant, to be imprisoned, but either upon conviction, or at least probable suspicion, or [of?] some crime formerly mentioned; and the cause of his imprisonment, be declared and tried at the next court following, at the furthest. ...

We do not know the reasons which led the General Court to reject Cotton's draft of a code; it seems certain, however, that the Deputies would have been opposed to the section in which provision was made for permanent tenure of the judicial office of the Assistants: "And because these great affairs of state cannot be attended or administered, if they be after changed; therefore the counsellors are to be chosen for life, unless they give just cause of removal, which if they do, then they are to be removed by the general court. Kings. 2. 6." (Chapter I, Sec. 3) If there were special grounds for the

Deputies' hostility to the Cotton draft there were considerations no less significant explaining the desire of the Assistants to postpone the adoption of any code. In December, 1639, when the drafting of a code was still in leisurely process, Governor Winthrop told something of the reason for the delay.

1 Winthrop's Journal, *322-23

"The people had long desired a body of laws, and thought their condition very unsafe, while so much power rested in the discretion of magistrates. Divers attempts had been made at former courts, and the matter referred to some of the magistrates and some of the elders; but still it came to no effect; for, being committed to the care of many, whatsoever was done by some, was still disliked or neglected by others. At last it was referred to Mr. Cotton and Mr. Nathaniel Warde, etc., and each of them framed a model, which were presented to this general court, and by them committed to the governor and deputy and some others to consider of, and so prepare it for the court in the 3d month next. Two great reasons there were, which caused most of the magistrates and some of the elders not to be very forward in this matter. One was, want of sufficient experience of the nature and disposition of the people, considered with the condition of the country and other circumstances, which made them conceive, that such laws would be fittest for us, which should arise *pro re nata* upon occasions, etc., and so the laws of England and other states grew, and therefore the fundamental laws of England are called customs, *consuetudines*. 2. For that it would professedly transgress the limits of our charter, which provide, we shall make no laws repugnant to the laws of England, and that we were assured we must do. But to raise up laws by practice and custom had been no transgression; as in our church discipline, and in matters of marriage, to make a law, that marriages should not be solemnized by ministers, is repugnant to the laws of England; but to bring it to a custom by practice for the magistrates to perform it, is no law made repugnant, etc. At length (to satisfy the people) it proceeded, and the two models were digested with divers alterations and additions, and abbreviated and sent to every town, to be considered of first by the magistrates and elders, and then to be published by the constables to all the people, that if any man should think fit, that any thing therein ought to be altered, he might acquaint some of the deputies therewith against the next court."

In the long run the opposition of the Assistants was overridden by the wishes of the people. In 1641 the General Court gave its approval to The Body of Liberties,[5] a compilation prepared by Nathaniel Ward, "pastor of the church of Ipswich: [who] had been a minister in England and formerly a student and practiser in the course of the common law" (2 Winthrop, Journal *55). This work was fundamentally different from Cotton's "Moses his Judicials"; though it was colored by the same Biblicism, it was a far more hard-headed piece of work, and broader in its scope. Ward did not, for the most part, seek to assemble in one document the previous legislation of the General Court, but attempted instead to lay down the sort of fundamental propositions which today might be embodied in a written constitution. Though one section of the work bore the subtitle "Capital Laws", for the most part there was a studied effort to avoid describing the "liberties" as "laws". In one of the concluding paragraphs this effort is explicitly mentioned:

"96. Howsoever these above specified rites, freedoms, immunities, authorities and privileges ... are expressed only under the name and title of Liberties, and not in the exact form of laws or statutes, yet we do with one consent fully authorize, and earnestly entreat all that are and shall be in authority to consider them as laws, and not to fail to inflict condign and proportionable punishments upon every man impartially, that shall infringe or violate any of them."

One reason for not labelling the "liberties" "laws" may have been the fear that if they were so described their repugnancy to the laws of England would have brought the charter in jeopardy.[6] A less practical reason may have been the Puritan's belief that no rule of conduct prescribed by human authority could properly be classed as law.[7] This belief was expressed by William Aspinwall in his introduction to an edition of Cotton's Code which was published in England in 1655.

---

5. The Body of Liberties is included in Whitmore, Colonial Laws, 1660-1672 (1889).

6. See Letchford, Plain-Dealing (Trumbull, ed.) p. 62, ft.

7. That this notion may have been important in the Body of Liberties is suggested by the fact that it is only the capital offenses which are described as "laws", and that it is only with respect to those offenses that Biblical citations supporting the statutory rules are included.

William Aspinwall's Preface to the 1655 edition of John Cotton's Abstract of the Laws of New England (Massachusetts Historical Society Collections Series I, Vol. 5, p. 47)

... And if thou possibly meetest with some rules, to which no scriptures are annexed for proof (as in the 2d and 3d chapters, and some sections in the 4th, 5th, and 9th chapters) consider, that those are not properly laws, but prudential rules, which he commended to that colony, to be ratified with the common assent of the freemen in each town, or by their representatives in the general court, as public contracts. Which being once made and assented to for their own convenience, do bind as covenants do, until by like public consent they be abrogated and made void. For though the author attribute the word [law] unto some of them; yet, that it was not his meaning they should be enacted as laws (if you take the word law in a proper sense) appears by his conclusion, taken out of Isaiah 33.22. The Lord is our Judge, the Lord is our Law giver, the Lord is our King; he will save us. He knew full well that it would be an intrenchment upon the royal power of Jesus Christ, for them or any other of the sons of Adam to ordain laws: And indeed laws of righteousness, such as Christ's laws be, have these three incommunicable properties.

1. They are unvariable, and bind all persons in all ages and in all nations.

2. They are undispensable by any created powers.

3. They bind not only the outward man to obedience, but also the spirit and conscience. None of which can be spoken of any human laws or constitutions whatsoever - Wherefore, when thou meetest with such an expression (calling such prudential rules and contracts by the name law) interpret it candidly. Because such agreements being once made by mutual consent, the covenantees are obliged by the law of righteousness, to make good their agreements, until they be reversed by the like common consent, for a public good, which in all prudential contracts and covenants may lawfully be done. For cujus est instituere, ejus est destituere. ...

Probably the most striking paragraph in the Body of Liberties is the first. Though its sources are obviously to be found in English constitutional history, the rule of law which it established was a rule different from that which England knew.

"1. No mans life shall be taken away, no mans honour or good name shall be stained, no mans person shall be arrested, restrained, banished, dismembered, nor any ways punished, no man shall be deprived of his wife and children, no mans goods or estate shall be taken away from him, nor any way endamaged under colour of law or countenance of authority, unless it be by virtue or equity of some express law of the country warranting the same, established by a General Court and sufficiently published, or in case of the defect of a law in any particular case by the word of God. ..."

The 18th Liberty, reminiscent of the Petition of Right, indicates that Nathaniel Ward and the colonists were not unaware of recent constitutional struggles in England, and that they saw a need in the Bay Colony for the security which their English contemporaries had struggled so vigorously to secure.

"18. No man's person shall be restrained or imprisoned by any authority whatsoever, before the law hath sentenced him thereto, if he can put in sufficient security, bail or mainprise, for his appearance and good behavior in the meantime, unless it be in crimes capital and contempts in open court, and in such cases where some express act of Court doth allow it."

Other characteristic provisions dealing with the rights of individuals were the following:

"42. No man shall be twice sentenced by Civil Justice for one and the same crime, offense, or trespass.

"43. No man shall be beaten with about 40 stripes, nor shall any true gentleman, nor any man equal to a gentleman be punished with whipping, unless his crime be very shameful, and his course of life vicious and profligate.

"45. No man shall be forced by torture to confess any crime against himself nor any other unless it be in some capital case, where he is first fully convicted by clear and sufficient evidence to be guilty, after which if the cause be of that nature, that it is very apparent there be other conspirators, or confederates with him, then he may be tortured, yet not with such tortures as be barbarous and inhumane."

The 97th Liberty indicates that the "rights, freedoms, immunities, authorities, and privileges" defined in the code were conceived to possess a substantive and not merely a theoretical validity, and that the judiciary was responsible for their enforcement.

"97. We likewise give full power and Liberty to any person that shall at any time be denied or deprived of any of them to commence and prosecute their suit, complaint or action against any man that shall so do in any court that hath proper cognizance of judicature thereof."

The only striking difference between Cotton's list of the Capital Laws and that which was included in the Body of Liberties is that Cotton's seventeen capital crimes were reduced to twelve. This reduction does not seem to signify any fundamentally different point of view; partly it was the inevitable result of the fact that Ward did not classify the offenses for which banishment was the penalty as "capital", and partly it was the result of the entire exclusion of some substantive offenses, such as incest, from Ward's list.

b. The Hingham Affair and the Child Remonstrance

Although Winthrop and the magistrates must have hoped that the adoption of the Body of Liberties would give the people and the Deputies a sufficient sense of legal and constitutional security to alleviate their distrust of the judiciary, it was not long before new difficulties arose. In Hingham the office of Captain of Militia had fallen vacant in 1645. The townsmen at first nominated Anthony Eames to fill the facancy. While the nomination was pending before the council in Boston the voters of Hingham, encouraged by their minister, Peter Hobart, sought to have the earlier nomination cancelled and the name of Bozoun Allen substituted for that of Eames. While the whole problem was under consideration by the council, Allen was called before the church in Hingham and charged with spreading false reports of the standing of the matter before the council. Peter Hobart, far from supporting these charges against Allen, urged that Eames should be excommunicated. Before the church disposed of these charges and counter-charges Eames's supporters secured a warrant from the Judges ordering a number of Allen's friends, including the brothers of the minister, to appear before the court in Boston to answer for the disturbances which they had brought about. Peter Hobart, however, before the return day, appeared before the magistrates to protest the issuance of the warrant, "taking it very disdainfully that his brethren should be sent for by a constable, [and protesting] with other high speeches, which were so provoking, as some of the magistrates told him, that, if it were not for respect to his ministry they would commit him". (2 Winthrop, Journal *223). Upon the subsequent appearance of the defendants they were bound over to the next sitting of the Court of Assistants. Winthrop's account of the further proceedings in which he, as Deputy Governor, played such a central part, throws considerable light on the issues of law and politics which had not been solved by the adoption of the Body of Liberties, but for the solution of which further efforts were later to be made.

Winthrop *Journal*, Vol. II, p. *223-26; *227-30

... After this five others were sent for by summons (these were only for speaking untruths of the magistrates in the church). They came before the deputy governour, when he was alone, and demanded the cause of their sending for, and to know their accusers. The deputy told them so much of the cause as he could remember, and referred them to the secretary for a copy, and for their accusers he told them they knew both the men and the matter, neither was a judge bound to let a criminal offender know his accusers before the day of trial, but only in his own discretion, least the accuser might be taken off or perverted, etc.[1] Being required to give bond for their appearance, etc., they refused. The deputy labored to let them see their error, and gave them time to consider of it. About fourteen days after, seeing two of them in the court, (which was kept by those four magistrates for smaller causes,) the deputy required them again to enter bond for their appearance, etc., and upon their second refusal committed them in that open court.

The general court falling out before the court of assistants, the Hubberts and the two which were committed, and others of Hingham, about ninety, (whereof Mr. Hubbert their minister was the first,) presented a petition to the general court, to this effect, that whereas some of them had been bound over, and others committed by some of the magistrates for words spoken concerning the power of the general court, and their liberties, and the liberties of the church, etc., they craved that the court would hear the cause, etc. This was first presented to the deputies, who sent it to the magistrates, desiring their concurrence with them, that the cause might be heard, etc. The magistrates, marvelling that they would grant such a petition, without desiring conference first with themselves, whom it so much concerned, returned answer, that they were willing the cause should be heard, so as the petitioners would name the magistrates whom they intended, and the matters they would lay to their charge, etc. Upon this the deputies demanded of the petitioners' agents (who were then deputies of the court) to

---

1. When the propriety of this ruling of Winthrop's was subsequently considered by the General Court the Deputies found that "the Deputy Governor did offend in saying that it was contrary to the law of God and man to know their accusers before the time of trial". The Assistants, commenting on this vote of the Deputies, answered that "if the words 'did offend' be meant criminally we dissent; but if the meaning be he did err and

have satisfaction in those points, thereupon they singled out the deputy governour, and two of the petitioners undertook the prosecution. Then the petition was returned again to the magistrates for their consent, etc., who being desirous that the deputies might take notice, how prejudicial to authority and the honor of the court it would be to call a magistrate to answer criminally in a cause, wherein nothing of that nature could be laid to his charge, and that without any private examination preceding, did intimate so much to the deputies, (though not directly, yet plainly enough,) showing them that nothing criminal, etc. was laid to his charge, and that the things objected were the act of the court, etc., yet if they would needs have a hearing, they would join in it. And indeed it was the desire of the deputy, (knowing well how much himself and the other magistrates did suffer in the cause, through the slanderous reports wherewith the deputies and the country about had been possessed,) that the cause might receive a public hearing.

The day appointed being come, the court assembled in the meeting house at Boston. Divers of the elders were present, and a great assembly of people. The deputy governour, coming in with the rest of the magistrates, placed himself beneath within the bar, and so sate uncovered. Some question was in the court about his being in that place (for many both of the court and the assembly were grieved at it). But the deputy telling them, that, being criminally accused, he might not sit as a judge in that cause, and if he were upon the bench, it would be a great disadvantage to him, for he could not take that liberty to plead the cause, which he ought to be allowed at the bar, upon this the court was satisfied.

The petitioners having declared their grievances, etc., the deputy craved leave to make answer, which was to this effect, viz., that he accounted it no disgrace, but rather an honor put upon him, to be singled out from his brethren in the defense of a cause so just (as he hoped to make that appear) and of so public concernment. And although he might have pleaded to the petition, and so have demurred in law, upon three points, 1, In that there is nothing laid to his charge, that is either criminal or unjust; 2, if he had been mistaken either in the law or in the state of the case, yet whether it were such as a judge is to be called in question for as a delinquent, where it doth not appear to be wickedness or wilful-

---

speak amiss in so saying, we assent...". 3 Records 22, 23. For descriptions of the contemporaneous English rule on this matter see 1 Stephen, History of Criminal Law 398 et seq.; 9 Holdsworth, History of English Law 223 et seq.

ness; for in England many erroneous judgments are reversed, and errors in proceedings rectified, and yet the judges not called in question about them; 3, in that being thus singled out from three other of the magistrates, and to answer by himself for some things, which were the act of a court, he is deprived of the just means of his defence, for many things may be justified as done by four, which are not warrantable if done by one alone and the records of a court are a full justification of any act, while such record stands in force. But he was willing to waive this plea, and to make answer to the particular charges, to the end that the truth of the case, and of all proceedings thereupon might appear to all men.

Hereupon the court proceeded to examine the whole cause. The deputy justified all the particulars laid to his charge, as that upon credible information of such a mutinous practice, and open disturbance of the peace, and slighting of authority, the offenders were sent for, the principal by warrant to the constable to bring them, and others by summons, and that some were bound over to the next court of assistants, and others that refused to be bound were committed; and all this according to the equity of laws here established, and the custom and laws of England, and our constant practice here these fifteen years. And for some speeches he was charged with as spoken to the delinquents, when they came before him at his house, when none were present with him but themselves, first, he appealed to the judgment of the court, whether delinquents may be received as competent witnesses against a magistrate in such a case; then, for the words themselves, some he justified, some he explained so as no advantage could be taken of them, as that he should say, that the magistrates could try some criminal causes without a jury, that he knew no law of God or man, which required a judge to make known to the party his accusers (or rather witnesses) before the cause came to hearing. But two of them charged him to have said, that it was against the law of God so to do, which had been absurd, for the deputy professed he knew no law against it, only a judge may sometimes, in discretion, conceal their names, etc., least they should be tampered with, or conveyed out of the way, etc.

Two of the magistrates and many of the deputies were of opinion that the magistrates exercised too much power, and that the people's liberty was thereby in danger; and other of the deputies (being about half) and all the rest of the magistrates were of a different judgment, and that authority was overmuch slighted, which, if not timely remedied, would endanger the commonwealth, and bring us to a mere democracy. By occasion of this difference, there was not so orderly carriage at the hearing, as was meet, each side striving unseasonably to enforce the evidence, and declaring their judgments thereupon, which should have been reserved to a more private debate, (as after it was,) so as the best part of two days was spent in this public agitation and examination of witnesses, etc. This being ended, a committee was chosen of magistrates and deputies, who stated the case, as it appeared upon the whole pleading and evidence, though it cost much time, and with great difficulty did the committee come to accord upon it.

The case being stated and agreed, the magistrates and deputies considered it apart, first the deputies, having spent a whole day, and not attaining to any issue, sent up to the magistrates to have their thoughts about it, who taking it into consideration, (the deputy always withdrawing when that matter came into debate,) agreed upon these four points chiefly; 1. That the petition was false and scandalous, 2. That those who were bound over, etc., and others that were parties to the disturbance at Hingham, were all offenders, though in different degrees, 3. That they and the petitioners were to be censured, 4. That the deputy governour ought to be acquit and righted, etc. This being sent down to the deputies, they spent divers days about it, and made two or three returns to the magistrates, and though they found the petition false and scandalous, and so voted it, yet they would not agree to any censure. The magistrates, on the other side, were resolved for censure, and for the deputy's full acquittal. ... The deputies finding themselves now at the wall, and not daring to trust the elders with the cause, they sent to desire that six of themselves might come and confer with the magistrates, which being granted, they came, and at last came to this agreement, viz., the chief petitioners and the rest of the offenders were severally fined, (all their fines not amounting to 50 pounds,) the rest of the petitioners to bear equal share to 50 pounds more towards the charges of the court, (two of the principal offenders were the deputies of the town, Joshua Hubbert and Bozone Allen, the first was fined 20 pounds, and the other 5 pounds) lieutenant Emes to be under admonition, the deputy governour to be legally and publicly acquit of all that was laid to his charge.

According to this agreement, (5) 3, presently after the lecture the magistrates and deputies took their places in the meeting house, and the people being come together, and the deputy governour placing himself within the bar, as at the time of the hearing, etc., the governour read the sentence of the court, without speaking any more, for the deputies had (by importunity) obtained a promise of silence from the magistrates. Then was the deputy governour desired by the court to go up and take his place again upon the bench, which he did accordingly, and the court being about to arise, he desired leave for a little speech, which was to this effect.

I suppose something may be expected from me, upon this charge that is befallen me, which moves me to speak now to you; yet I intend not to intermeddle in the proceedings of the court, or with any of the persons concerned therein. Only I bless God, that I see an issue of this troublesome business. I also acknowledge the justice of the court, and, for mine own part, I am well satisfied, I was publicly charged, and I am publicly and legally acquitted, which is all I did expect or desire. And though this be sufficient for my justification before men, yet not so before the God, who hath seen so much amiss in my dispensations (and even in this affair) as calls me to be humble. For to be publicly and criminally charged in this court, is matter of humiliation, (and I desire to make a right use of it,) notwithstanding I be thus acquitted. If her father had spit in her face, (saith the Lord concerning Miriam,) should she not have been ashamed seven days? Shame had lien upon her, whatever the occasion had been. I am unwilling to stay you from your urgent affairs, yet give me leave (upon this special occasion) to speak a little more to this assembly. It may be of some good use, to inform and rectify the judgments of some of the people, and may prevent such distempers as have arisen amongst us. The great questions that have troubled the country, are about the authority of the magistrates and the liberty of the people. It is yourselves who have called us to this office, and being called by you, we have our authority from God, in way of an ordinance, such as hath the image of God eminently stamped upon it, the contempt and violation whereof hath been vindicated with examples of divine vengeance. I entreat you to consider, that when you choose magistrates, you take them from among yourselves, men subject to like passions as you are. Therefore when you see infirmities in us, you should reflect upon your own, and that would make you bear the more with us, and not be severe censurers of the failings of your magistrates, when you have continual experience of the like infirmities in yourselves and others. We account him a good servant, who breaks not his covenant. The covenant between you and us is the oath you have taken of us, which is to this purpose, that we shall govern you and judge your causes by the rules of God's laws and our own, according to our best skill. When you agree with a workman to build you a ship or house, etc., he undertakes as well for his skill as for his faithfulness, for it is his profession, and you pay him for both. But when you call one to be a magistrate, he doth not profess nor undertake to have sufficient skill for that office, nor can you furnish him with gifts, etc., therefore you must run the hazard of his skill and ability. But if he fail in faithfulness, which by his oath he is bound unto, that he must answer for. If it fall out that the case be clear to common apprehension, and the rule clear also, if he transgress here, the error is not in the skill, but in the evil of the will: it must be required of him. But if the case be doubtful, or the rule doubtful, to men of such understanding and parts as your magistrates are, if your magistrates should err here, yourselves must bear it.

For the other point concerning liberty, I observe a great mistake in the country about that. There is a twofold liberty, natural (I mean as our nature is now corrupt) and civil or federal. The first is common to man with beasts and other creatures. By this, man, as he stands in relation to man simply, hath liberty to do what he lists; it is a liberty to evil as well as to good. This liberty is incompatible and inconsistent with authority, and cannot endure the least restraint of the most just authority. The exercise and maintaining of this liberty makes men grow more evil, and in time to be worse than brute beasts: omnes sumus licentia deteriores. This is that great enemy of truth and peace, that wild beast, which all the ordinances of God are bent against, to restrain and subdue it. The other kind of liberty I call civil or federal, it may also be termed moral, in reference to the covenant between God and man, in the moral law, and the politic covenants and constitutions, amongst men themselves. This liberty is the proper end and object of authority, and cannot subsist without it; and it is a liberty to that only which is good, just, and honest. This liberty you are to stand for, with the hazard (not only of your goods, but) of your lives, if need be. Whatsoever crosseth this, is not authority, but a distemper thereof. This liberty is maintained and exercised in a way of subjection to authority; it is of the same kind of liberty wherewith Christ hath made us free. The woman's own choice makes such a man her husband; yet being so chosen, he is her lord, and she is to be subject to him, yet in a way of liberty, not of bondage; and a true wife accounts her subjection her honor and freedom, and would not think her condition safe and free, but in her subjection to her husband's authority. Such is the liberty of the church under the authority of Christ, her king and husband; his yoke is so easy and sweet to her as a bride's ornaments; and if through frowardness or wantonness, etc. she shake it off at any time she is at no rest in her spirit, until she take it up again; and whether her lord smiles upon her, and embraceth her in his arms, or whether he frowns, or rebukes, or smites her, she apprehends the sweetness of his love in all, and is refreshed, supported, and instructed by every such dispensation of his authority over her. On the other side, ye know who they are that complain of this yoke and say, let us break their bands, etc., we will not have this man to rule over us. Even so, brethren, it will be between you and your magistrates. If you stand for your natural corrupt liberties, and will do what is good in your own eyes, you will not endure the least weight of authority, but will murmur, and oppose, and be always striving to shake off that yoke; but if you will be satisfied to enjoy such civil and lawful liberties, such as Christ allows you, then will you quietly and cheerfully submit unto that authority which is set over you, in all the administrations of it, for your good. Wherein, if we fail at any time, we hope we shall be willing (by God's assistance) to hearken to good advice from any of you, or in any other way of God; so shall your liberties be preserved, in upholding the honor and power of authority amongst you.

The deputy governour having ended his speech, the court arose, and the magistrates and deputies retired to attend their other affairs. Many things were observable in the agitation and proceedings about this case. It may be of use to leave a memorial of some of the most material, that our posterity and others may behold the workings of satan to ruin the colonies and churches of Christ in New England, and into what distempers a wise and godly people may fall in times of temptation; and when such have entertained some false and plausible principles, what deformed superstructures they will raise thereupon, and with what unreasonable obstinacy they will maintain them. ...

[The Hingham affair did not end with Winthrop's acquittal. When the marshall sought to levy the fines which the General Court had imposed upon the offenders - including Peter Hobart - a "rescue" of the offenders took place. Thereupon the Governor and his associates on the council once more summoned the parties to appear before them. On the return day the stubborn minister failed to appear. Winthrop's account of the subsequent proceedings follows.]

Winthrop, Journal, Vol. II, *255-56

... Whereupon he was sent for by attachment directed to the constable, who brought him at the day of the return. And being then charged with joining in the said rescue by animating the offenders, and discouraging the officer, questioning the authority of his warrant because it was not in the king's name, and standing upon his allegiance to the crown of England, and exemption from such laws as were not agreeable to the laws of England, saying to the marshal that he could never know wherefore he was fined, except it were for petitioning, and if they were so waspish that they might not be petitioned, he knew not what to say to it, etc. All the answer he would give was, that if he had broken any wholesome law not repugnant to the laws of England, he was ready to submit to censure. So he was bound over to the next court of assistants.

The court being at Boston, Mr. Hubberd appeared, and the marshal's information and other concurrent testimony being read to him, and his answer demanded, he desired to know in what state he stood, and what offence he should be charged with, or what wholesome law of the land, not repugnant to the law of England, he had broken. The court told him, that the matters he was charged with amounted to a seditious practice and derogation and contempt of authority. He still pressed to know what law, etc. He was told that the oath which he had taken was a law to him;[2] and beside the law of God which we were to judge by in case of a defect of an express law. He said that the law of God admitted various interpretations, etc. Then he desired to see his accusers. Upon that the marshal was called, who justified his information. Then he desired to be tried by a jury, and to have the witnesses produced viva voce. The secretary told him that two were present, and the third was sworn to his examination, (but in that he was mistaken, for he had not been sworn,) but to satisfy him, he was sent for and sworn in court. The matters testified against him were his speeches to the marshal before thirty persons, against our authority and government, etc. 1. That we were but as a corporation in England; 2. That by our patent (as he understood it) we could not put any man to death, nor do divers other things which we did; 3. That he knew not wherefore the general court had fined them, except it were for petitioning, and if they were so wapish (or captious) as they might not be petitioned, etc., and other speeches tending to disparage our authority and proceedings. Accordingly a bill was drawn up, etc., and the jury found that he seemed to be ill affected to this government, and that his speeches tended to sedition and contempt of authority. Whereupon the whole court (except Mr. Bellingham, who judged him to deserve no censure, and desired in open court to have his dissent recorded) adjudged him to pay 20 pounds fine, and to be bound to his good behaviour, till the next court of assistants, and then farther if the court should see cause. At this sentence his spirit rose, and he would know what the good behaviour was, and desired the names of the jury, and a copy of all the proceedings, which was granted him, and so he was dismissed at present. ...

[Hobart's insistence on his rights under English law marked the opening of a new chapter in the legal history of the Colony. It should be kept in mind that during the next phase in the controversy one of the issues of predominant importance concerned the validity of the statute of 1631 prescribing that only persons admitted to membership in one of

---

2. The reference is presumably to the oath by which each inhabitant submitted himself to the laws and constitutions of the Colony. 1 Records 115 On other occasions men were considered to be criminally punishable for violation of their oath. See Waverick's case, 3 Records 113.

the churches could enjoy the rights of freemen.[3] To those of Presbyterian leanings (and Peter Hobart was evidently one of them) the contemporary successes of Presbyterianism in England gave some hope that if the injustices of the Massachusetts government were brought to the attention of Parliament action on their behalf would be taken by the home authorities. In 1646 William Vassal, of Scituate, caused considerable consternation both in the Plymouth Colony and in the Bay Colony when he transmitted to Parliament a petition praying that the colonists "might be wholly governed by the laws of England" (2 Winthrop, Journal *261), and protested that the freeborn subjects of England were being denied the liberties of Englishmen. It was not however the Vassal petition but the Remonstrance of Robert Child and others which created the great turmoil in 1646.[4] Child and the majority of his associates spoke as Presbyterians but they also complained as friends, neighbors, and associates of Peter Hobart and the men of Hingham who a year before had been in such serious difficulties with the authorities. Disregarding the lesson which might have been learned from the experience of those who had petitioned the General Court in behalf of John Wheelwright, Child and his six associates filed their Remonstrance with the General Court in May, 1646. Not only did they file the Remonstrance with the General Court but they made successful efforts to circulate copies throughout the American colonies generally.[5] Significant passages from the Remonstrance follow.7

---

3. 1 Records 87. Though this statute appears to have remained in force until 1664, it is, perhaps, significant that it was contained neither in the Body of Liberties of 1641 nor in the Codes of 1648 and 1660. The omission may well have been intentional. Certainly its inclusion in the Code of 1648, following the Child Remonstrance, would have created special hazards. The grant of substantial privileges to non-freemen in matters of local government, which occurred in 1647, was probably not unrelated to the Child Remonstrance. See 2 Records 197.

4. Concerning the Child Remonstrance, see Kittredge, "Dr. Robert Child the Remonstrant", 21 Publications, Colonial Society, 1919, 1; Morris, "Massachusetts and the Common Law: The Declaration of 1646", 31 American Hist. Rev. 443 (1926); Miller, Orthodoxy in Massachusetts (1933) 298 et seq.

5. See Winslow, New England's Salamander Discovered (1647) reprinted 3 Mass. Hist. Soc. Coll., Vol. 2, 110, 116-17.

The Remonstrance of Robert Child and Others
1 <u>Hutchinson Papers</u> 214

... Whereas this place hath been planted by the incouragment, next under God, of letters patents given and granted by his Majesty of England to the inhabitants thereof, with many privileges and immunities, viz. Incorporation into a company, liberty of choosing governors, settling government, making lawes not repugnant to the lawes of England, power of administering the oath of allegiance to all, &c. as by the said letters patents more largely appeareth. Notwithstanding, we cannot, according to our judgments, discerne a setled forme of government according to the lawes of England, which may seem strange to our countrymen, yea to the whole world, especially considering we are all English. Neither do we so understand and perceyve our owne lawes or libertyes, or any body of lawes here so established, as that thereby there may be a sure and comfortable enjoyment of our lives, libertyes, and estates, according to our due and naturall rights, as freeborne subjects of the English nation. By which, many inconveniences flow into plantations, viz. jealousies of introducing arbitrary government, which many are prone to believe, construing the procrastination of such setled lawes to proceed from an overgreedy spirit of arbitrary power (which it may be is their weaknes) such proceedings being detestable to our English nation, and to all good men, and at present a cheife cause of the intestine warre in our deare country: Further it gives cause to many to thinke themselves hardly dealt with, others too much favored, and the scale of justice too much bowed and unequally balanced: From whence also proceedeth feares and jealousies of illegal committments, unjust imprisonments, taxes, rates, customes, levyes of ungrounded and undoing assessments, unjustifiable presses, undue synes, unmeasurable expenses and charges, of unconceyvable dangers through a negative or destructive vote unduly placed, and not well regulated, in a word, of a non certainty of all things we enjoy, whether lives, liberties, or estates; and also of undue oaths, being subject to exposition, according to the will of him or them that gives them, and not according to a due and unbowed rule of law, which is the true interpreter of all oathes to all men, whether judge or judged.

Wherefore our humble desire and request is, that you would be pleased to consider of our present condition and upon what foundation we stand, and unanimously concurr to establish the fundamentall and wholesome lawes of our natire country, and such others as are no wayes repugnant to them, unto which all of us are most accustomed; and we suppose them best agreeable to our English tempers and yourselves obliged thereunto by the generall charter and your oathes of allegiance. Neither can we tell, whether the Lord hath blest many in these parts with such eminent politicall gifts, so as to contrive better lawes and customes than the wisest of our nation have with great consideration composed, and by many hundred yeares experience have found most equall and just; which have procured to the nation most honour and renowme amongst strangers, and long peace and tranquillity amongst themselves. And for the more strict and due observation and execution of the said lawes by all the ministers of justice, That there may be a settled rule for them to walke by in all cases of judicature, from which if they swerve there may be some power setled, according to the lawes of England, that may call them to account for their delinquences, which may be a good means to prevent divers unnecessary appeales into England. ...

We therefore desire that civil liberty and freedom be forthwith granted to all truely English, equall to the rest of their countrymen, as in all plantations is accustomed to be done, and as all freeborne enjoy in our native country; (we hoping here in some things to enjoy greater liberties than elsewhere, counting it no small losse of liberty to be as it were banished from our native home, and enforced to lay our bones in a strange wildernes) without imposing any oathes or covenant on them, which we suppose cannot be warranted by the letters patent, and seeme not to concur with the oath of allegiance formerly enforced on all, and later covenants lately imposed on many here present by the honorable houses of parliament, or at least to detract from our native country and lawes, which by some are stiled foreign, and this place termed rather a free state, than a colonie or corporation of England; all of us being very willing to take such oathes and covenants as are expressions of our desires of advanceing the glory of God and good of this place, and of our dutyes to the state of England, and love to our nation, being composed according to the lawes and customes of other corporations of England; but all of us are exceeding unwilling by any pollicies whatsoever to be rent from our native country, though far distant from it, valuing our free derivations, the immunities and privileges which we and our posterity doe and we hope shall alwayes enjoy above the greatest honors of this country, not cemented to the state of England, and glory to be accounted though but as rushes of that land, yet that we may continue to write that we and ours are English; or least we entreat that the bodyes of us and ours (English subjects possessing here no privileges) may not be impressed, nor goods forcibly taken away, least we, not knowing the justice of this warre, may be ignorantly and unwillingly enforced upon our own destruction, and that all assessment, taxes, impositions, which are many and grievous (if civill liberty be not granted) may be taken of, that in all things we may be strangers, otherwise we suppose ourselves in a worse case here and lesse free than the natives amongst whom we live, or any aliens. Further, that none of the English nation, who at this time are too forward to be gone, and very backward to come hither, be banished, unles they break the known lawes of England in so high a measure, as to deserve so high a punishment; and that those few that come over may settle here without having two magistrates hands, which sometimes not being possible to obtain, hath procured a kind of banishment to some, who might have been serviceable to this place, as they have been to the state of England, &c. And we likewise desire that no greater punishments be inflicted upon offenders than are allowed and sett by the laws of our native country.

The General Court did not deal with the Remonstrance immediately. Instead, its consideration was postponed until the fall session, though careful attention was given to it during the summer months (2 Winthrop, <u>Journal</u> *284). At the October sitting of the Court it was learned that two of the remonstrants Fowle and Smith were about to leave the Colony, and they were accordingly sent for. "Being asked by the Governor [Winthrop] whether they owned it, or saw any evil in it which they would retract, ... they answered they stood to justify the same. Being demanded to give in £ 100 security to be responsible to the judgment of the court ... Mr. Smith spake, and said he would not give in security, but did appeal to the gentlemen Commissioners for Plantations,[6] and would engage himself to prosecute it; and so did Mr. Fowle, in the same expressions. Being asked by the Governor whether they did appeal, with deliberation they answered, Yea. Being called in and demanded again to give in security to answer that matter of the petition, they refused to answer, Mr. Fowle saying, if the Court shall draw up any charge against them as doing wrong to the Court, the Court were parties, and not competent judges; therefore they stood to their appeal for competent justice. The Court committed them to the custody of the marshall till they gave security to be responsible to the judgment of the Court". (3 <u>Records</u> 88-89) When, shortly after this, Dr. Child and other remonstrants were summoned and required, like Smith and Fowle, to give security for satisfaction of such judgment as the Court might enter against them, Child took the same position which Smith and Fowle had taken - he demanded that he be informed of the charges which were made against him, and concluded with the announcement that he appealed to the Commis-

---

6. This body appointed by the long Parliament in 1643 was responsible for the supervision of Colonial affairs.

sioners in England. Winthrop records the response of the Court: "The Governor told them he would admit no appeal, nor was it allowed by our charter, but by this it appeared what their aim was in their petition; they complained of fear of perpetual slavery, etc., but their intent was to make us slaves to them and such as themselves were .... For ourselves it was well known we did ever honour the parliament, and were ready to perform all due obedience, etc. to them according to our charter." (2 Winthrop, Journal *285)

At length, after these preliminary stages of the proceedings were concluded, the fundamental question came on for hearing by the General Court. It will be remembered that Smith, Fowle and Child had all insisted, as John Wheelwright and Anne Hutchinson before them had insisted, that the General Court could only proceed on the basis of specific charges. The insistence this time brought results, for after the Remonstrance was publicly read in the General Court a specific charge, prepared in advance by a committee of the Court, was made against the remonstrants. They were charged with "diverse false and scandalous passages in a certain paper, entitled A Remonstrance ... against the Churches of Christ and the civil government here established, derogating from the honour and authority of the same and tending to sedition...". (3 Records 90) Going beyond that general charge the Court specified in twelve numbered paragraphs the particulars in which the Remonstrance was objectionable. Among those particular specifications were the following:

"4. They closely insinuate into the minds of the people that those now in authority do intend to exercise an unwarranted dominion and an arbitrary government, such as is abominable to the Parliament and that party in England, thereby to make them slaves....

"5. They go about to weaken the authority of our laws and the reverent esteem of them, and consequently their obedience to them by persuading the people, through want of the body of English laws and partly through the insufficiency or ill fame of those we have, they can expect no sure enjoyment of their lives and liberties under them."

The final specification - not, to be sure, concerning the Remonstrance itself - was that Child and his associates had denied the jurisdiction of the General Court before the Court had given any sentence against them.

The relatively formal procedure which was followed by the Court in hearing the charge is described by Winthrop: "Their petition being read, and this charge laid upon them in open court before a great assembly, they desired time to make answer to it, which was granted. And giving the court notice that their answer was ready, they assembled again, and before all people caused their answer to be read, which was large and to little purpose, and the court replied to the particulars ex tempore as they were read."[7] (2 Winthrop, Journal *287)

The answer which the remonstrants made to the 4th specification consisted of an assertion that their fear of arbitrary government was based upon the fact that neither the body of English law nor another law not repugnant to English law had been established. Winthrop describes the reply which the Court made to this answer. "To this it was replied, 1. that the constant care and pains the court hath taken for establishing a body of laws, and that which hath been effected herein beyond any other plantation will sufficiently clear our government from being arbitrary, and our intentions from any such disposition, 2. for the laws of England (though by our charter we are not bound to them, as will appear by our declaration, which is to be published upon this occasion)[8] and the government of England itself is more arbitrary in their chancery and other courts than ours is, 3. because they could make men believe, that the want of the laws of England was such a grievance to them, they were pressed to show what laws of England they wanted, and it was offered them (before all the assembly who were desired to bear witness of it) that if they would produce any one law of England, the want whereof was a just griev-

---

7. There is some reason to doubt whether the proceedings were exactly as Winthrop described them. One of the defendants Samuel Maverick, later asserted that the proceedings depended upon the refusal of the remonstrants to answer interrogatories under oath. See his petition to the General Court, reprinted in Kittredge, loc. cit. supra, note 4, at 58-59. Kittredge, I believe, was in error in treating the Maverick petition as descriptive throughout of a later phase of the proceedings. Unfortunately the Records of the General Court on the whole matter are incomplete.

8. This declaration was prepared by the General Court and sought, somewhat disingenuously, to show that the law of Massachusetts was entirely consistent with the common law of England. It set out in parallel columns rules of English law and rules of Massachusetts law considered to be in conformity with each other. Characteristic of the deceptive similarity was the statement that by English law "the eldest son is preferred before the younger in the ancestor's inheritance" and that by Liberty 81 of the Colony that preference also existed. The Declaration is published in I Hutchinson Papers 223. Although the parallels are not persuasive the essay on the whole makes quite a convincing case for the proposition that English law contains much more than the common law, and that Massachusetts

ance to them, the court would quit the cause, whereupon one of them instances in a law used in London, (where he had been a citizen,) but that was easily taken away by showing that that was only a bye-law, or peculiar custom of the city, and none of the common or general laws of England." (2 Winthrop, Journal *288)

To the 5th specification the remonstrants answered that the charter of the colony required conformity to English law and that if that law were not observed they saw no security for their liberties as freeborn Englishmen. Winthrop summarizes the reply which the court made to this answer: "To this it was replied, that they charge us with breach of our charter and of our oaths of allegiance, whereas our allegiance binds us not to the laws of England any longer than while we live in England, for the laws of the parliament of England reach no further, nor dothe the king's writs under the great seal go any further; what the orders of state may, belong not in us to determine.[9] And whereas they seem to admit of laws not repug-

---

is empowered to supplement the common law with doctrines of its own. On the significance of the Declaration as a whole, see Morris, loc. cit. supra, note 4.

9. Edward Winslow in his pamphlet New England's Salamander Discovered (1647), defending the proceedings of the General Court in this matter, made the following observations concerning the applicability of English law in the Colonies: "As for the law of England, I honour it and ever did, and yet know well that it was never intended for New-England. ... And however we follow the custom and practice of England so near as our condition will give way: yet as the garments of a grown man would rather oppress and stifle a child if put upon him, than any way comfort or refresh him, being too heavy for him, so I have often said the laws of England, to take the body of them, are too unwieldy for our weak condition. Besides which there are some things supported by them which we came from thence to avoid, as the heirarchy, the holy days, the book of Common Prayer, etc. ... But I have been so far from slighting the law of England as I have brought my own book of the statutes of England into our court that so when we have wanted a law or ordinance we might see what the statutes provided in that kind, and found a great readiness in our General Court to take all help and benefit thereby. ... Indeed this I have said ... that if the Parliaments of England should impose laws upon us having no Burgesses in their house of Commons, nor capable of a summons by reason of the vast distance of the ocean, being three thousand miles from London, then we should lose the

nant they mean, as the word truly imports, and as by the charter must needs be intended, they have no cause to complain, for we have no laws diametrically opposite to those of England, for then they must be contrary to the laws of God and of right reason, which the learned in those laws have anciently and still do hold forth as the fundamental basis of their laws, and that if any thing hath been otherwise established it was an error, and not a law, being against the intent of the law-makers, however it may bear the form of a law (in regard of the stamp of authority set upon it) until it be revoked.[10] ... I should also have noted the Doctor's logic who undertook to prove, that we were subject to the laws of England. His argument was this, every corporation of England is subject to the laws of England; but this was a corporation of England, ergo, etc. To which it was answered, 1. that there is a difference between subjection to the laws in general, as all that dwell in England are, and subjection to some laws of state, proper to foreign plantations, 2. we must distinguish between corporation within England and corporations of but not within England; the first are subject to the laws of England in general, yet not to every general law, as the city of London and other corporations have divers customs and by-laws differing from the common and statute laws of England. Again, though plantations be bodies corporate, (and so is every city and commonwealth,) yet they are also above the rank of an ordinary corporation. If one of London should say before the mayor and aldermen, or before the common council, you are but a corporation, this would be taken as a contempt. And among the Romans, Grecians, and other nations, colonies have been esteemed other than towns, yea than many cities, for they have been the foundations of great commonwealths. And it was a fruit of much pride and folly in these petitioners to despise the day of small things." (2 Winthrop, Journal 288-89, 290-91)

After the Court had heard answers and replies it proceeded to impose fines upon the defendants varying between £ 10

---

liberty and freedom I conceived of English indeed, where every shire and corporation by their Knights and Burgesses make and consent to their law, whatsoever they conceive may be hurtful to them...." 3 Mass. Hist. Soc. Coll. Vol. 2, p. 137-39.

10. It seems probable that Winthrop had in mind the observations of Thomas Aquinas on this matter. At the conclusion of his essay on Arbitrary Government (infra, p. 208) Winthrop copied out a passage from Aquinas in which the preeminence of the law of nature over acts of legislation was emphasized. See 4 Winthrop Papers 482.

and £ 50 - those who had threatened to appeal to the Commissioners for Plantations having to pay the larger sums, but all being offered the opportunity to escape the fines by making public acknowledgment of their misdemeanors (3 Records 94). The defendants refused to make acknowledgment and instead tendered their appeal in writing which was rejected by the Court (2 Winthrop, Journal *292). Surprisingly the defendants were neither imprisoned nor otherwise compelled to give security for the payment of the fines. Perhaps, as has been suggested,[11] this leniency was designed to tempt the defendants into fresh indiscretions. In any case, it was soon discovered that Dr. Child and another of the defendants, John Dand, were about to set sail for England with a file of protestations and appeals in their possession. Winthrop again reports the events in his Journal (2 Winthrop, Journal *294-95):

"Dr. Child, being upon this apprehended and brought before the governour and council, fell into a great passion, and gave big words, but being told, that they considered he was a person of quality, and therefore he should be used with such respect as was meet to be showed to a gentleman and a scholar, but if he would behave himself no better, he should be committed to the common prison and clapped in irons. Upon this he grew more calm; so he was committed to the marshal, with Smith and Dand, for two or three days, till the ships were gone. For he was very much troubled to be hindered from his voyage, and offered to pay his fine; but that would not be accepted for his discharge, seeing we had now new matter and worse against him (for the writings were of his hand). Yet, upon tender of sufficient bail, he was set at liberty, but confined to his house, and to appear at the next court of assistants. His confinement he took grievously, but he could not help it. The other two were committed to prison, yet lodged in the keeper's house, and had what diet they pleased, and none of their friends forbidden to come to them. There was also one Thomas Joy, a young fellow, a carpenter, whom they had employed to get hands to the petition; he began to be very busy, and would know of the marshal, when he went to search Dand's study, if his warrant were in the king's name, etc. He was laid hold on, and kept in irons about four or five days, and then he humbled himself, confessed what he knew, and blamed himself for meddling in matters belonging not to him, and blessed God for these irons upon his legs, hoping they should do him good while he lived. So he was let out upon reasonable bail. But Smith and Dand would not be examined, and therefore were not bailed; but their offence being in nature capital, etc., bail might be refused in that regard.

---

11. See Kittredge, supra, note 4 at p. 38-9.

"For their trial at the general court in (4) 47, and the sentence against them, etc., it is set down at large in the records of that court, with their petitions and queries intended for England, and all proceedings. Mr. Dand not being able to pay his fine of two hundred pounds, nor willing to acknowledge his offence, was kept in prison; but at the general court (3) 48, upon his humble submission, he was freely discharged."

The somewhat anticlimactic ending in Boston, with the remonstrants either paying their fines or escaping payment by acknowledgment of their fault need not concern us. The uneasiness of the government in the Colony continued for many months for it was realized that despite the efforts which had been made to prevent the remonstrance from being heard in England representatives of the discontented faction were making protests to Parliament. Anticipating trouble in England, the General Court had designated Edward Winslow agent of the Colony to represent it before the Commissioners for Plantations. The Court had also transmitted a communication to the Commissioners in which it had vigorously denied that appeals lay to England. Such appeals, the court urged, "cannot stand with the liberty and power granted us by our charter...". Stirring the memory of a Puritan Parliament lest it might forget the Reformation, the Court reminded the Commissioners that the problems of appeal to distant tribunals were not unprecedented. "These considerations are not new to your honours and the high court of parliament, the records whereof bear witness of the wisdom and faithfulness of our ancestors in that great council, who, in those times of darkness, when they acknowledged a supremacy in the bishops of Rome in all causes ecclesiastical, yet would not allow appeals to Rome, etc. to remove causes out of the courts in England."[12] At length, in the late summer of 1647, word reached the Colony that the efforts of the Court and of Winslow had been successful. The Commissioners informed the Colony that it was not their intention "to encourage any appeals from your justice, nor to restrain the bounds of your jurisdiction to a narrower compass than is held forth by your letters patent, but to leave you with all that freedom and latitude that may, in any respect, be duly claimed by you...".[13] This striking confirmation of the Colonial claim to independence in legal matters came but a few months before the enactment of the Laws and Liberties of 1648, a code which went far beyond the Body of Liberties in competeness, and served not only as

---

12. 3 Records 97.

13. 2 Winthrop, Journal *319-20.

the basic code for the life of the Colony under its first charter, but had enormous influence on the legislation of the American colonies generally.

While the Hingham affair and the Child Remonstrance were occupying so much of the attention of the Government in the Bay Colony, the Deputies in the General Court continued their efforts to limit the discretion of magistrates through the codification of law. To a considerable extent the Hingham and the Child matters were a reflection of the controversy between those who wanted the magistrates to have a largely free hand in the making of law through the judicial process and those who wanted the discretion of judges to be controlled by definite rules of law. The adoption of the Laws and Liberties of 1648 was a distinct victory for the latter group - and in one sense was a postponed victory for Dr. Child. Since no colonial advocate of a Code systematically stated the grounds of the case for codification there remains some uncertainty as to the precise nature of the argument by which that case was supported. One can, however, get some understanding of the seriousness of the issue between the judges on the one hand and the people and the Deputies on the other in Winthrop's "treatise" on Arbitrary Government. The essay was written in 1644 while the issue of the "negative voice", arising out of Goody Sherman's case was at its height and while the Deputies were clamoring "for such a body of laws, with prescript penalties in all cases, as nothing might be left to the discretion of the magistrates...".[14] It expressed, furthermore, the views of an orthodox Puritan on problems of law and government more effectively than did any other single writing by any person holding high judicial (and political) office in the Bay Colony.

John Winthrop - Arbitrary Government
(4 Winthrop Papers 468)

> Arbitrary Government described and the Common mistakes about the same (both in the true nature thereof, and in the representation of the Government of the Massachusetts, under such a notion) fully cleared. (5) 1644.

Arbitrary Government is, where a people have men set over them without their choice, or allowance: who have power, to govern them, and judge their causes without a rule.

God only hath this prerogative: whose Sovereignty is absolute, and whose will is a perfect rule, and reason itself:

---

14. 2 Winthrop, Journal * 231.

so as for man, to usurp such authority is tyranny and impiety.

Where the people have liberty to admit, or reject their Governors; and to require the rule, by which they shall be governed and judged, this is not an arbitrary government.

That the government of the Massachusetts is such, will appear 1: by the foundation of it: 2: by the positive lawes thereof: 3: by the constant practice, which proves a custom, than which (when it is for common good) there is no law of man more inviolable.

1: The foundation of this government, is the King's Letters Patents: this gave them their form, and being, in disposing a certain number of persons, into a body politic; whereby they became then (in such a politic respect) as one single person consisting of several members; and appointing to each, its proper place: it regulates their power and motions, as might best conduce to the preservation, and good of the whole body:

The parties or members of this body politic are reduced under 2 kinds, Governor and Company, or Freemen: to the Governor it adds a Deputy, and 18 Assistants: in these is the power of authority placed, under the name of the Governor (not as a person, but as a State) and in the other (which is named the Company) is placed the power of liberty; which is not a bare passive capacity of freedom or immunity, but such a liberty, as hath power to act upon the chief means of its own welfare (yet in a way of liberty, not of authority) and that under 2 general heads, Election and Counsel: 1: they have liberty to elect yearly (or oftener if occasion require) all their Governors, and other their general officers, viz: such as should have influence (either judicial or ministerial) into all parts of the jurisdiction. 2: They have liberty of counsel, in all the general assemblies, so as, without their counsel and consent, no laws, decrees, or orders of any public nature or concernment, nor any taxes, impositions, impresses, or other burdens of what kind soever, can be imposed upon them, their families or estates, by any authority in the Government: which notwithstanding remains still a distinct member, even in those general assemblies: otherwise our state should be a mere Democracy, if all were governors, or magistrates, and none left, to be an object of government which cant fall out in any kind of aristocracy.

To make this clear, we will set down the very words of the Patent. [Here Winthrop paraphrases and summarizes provisions in the Charter by which the powers of government were defined.]

Thus it appears that this government is not arbitrary in the foundation of it, but regulated in all the parts of it.

2: It will be yet further found by the positive laws thereof: And first by that of (3) 14, 1634, where it is declared, that the general court only may make Freemen: make laws; choose General Officers, as Governor, Deputy, Assistants, Treasurer etc: remove such: set out their power and duty: raise money: dispose of lands in propriety: not to be dissolved, but by consent of the major part. The Freemen of the several towns may send their deputy to every general court who may do all that the body of Freemen might do, except in election of magistrates and officers.

And in the 67 Liberty, it is thus described viz. It is the constant liberty of the Freemen, to choose yearly at the Court of Election, out of the Freemen, all the general officers of this jurisdiction. If they please to discharge them, at the Court of Election, by vote, they may do it without showing cause: but if at any other general court, we hold it due justice, that the reasons thereof be alledged and proved. By general officers, we mean our Governor, Deputy Governor, Assistants, Treasurer, General of our Wars, and our Admiral at Sea; and such as are or may be hereafter of like general nature.

3: According to these fundamental rules, and positive laws, the course of government, hath been carried on in the practice of public administrations to this very day, and where any considerable obliquity hath been discerned, it hath been soon brought to the rule and redressed: for it is not possible in the infancy of a plantation, subject to so many and variable occurrents, to hold so exactly to rules, as when a state is once settled.

By what hath been already manifested, this government is freed from any semblance of arbitraryness either in the form of it, or the general officers in it, which is the first branch in the description of arbitrary government.

The other branch (wherein the main question lies) is concerning the rule: so as if it shall appear, also, that the Governor and other officers are prescribed such a rule, as may be required of them in all their administrations, then it must needs be granted, that this government (even in the present state thereof) is in no respect arbitrary.

I might show a clear rule out of the patent itself, but seeing it is more particularly (and as it were membratim) delineated in later laws, I will begin there (3) 25, 1636. It was ordered, that until a body of fundamental laws (agreeable to the word of God) were established, all causes should be heard and determined, according to the laws already in force; and where no law is, there, as near the law of God as may be. To omit many particular laws enacted upon occasion, I will set down only the first authority in the Liberties: which is as here followeth. No mans life shall be taken away: no mans honor or good name shall be stained: No mans person shall be arrested, restrained, banished, dismembered or any ways punished: No man shall be deprived of his wife or children: No mans goods or estate shall be taken away from him: or any way damaged, under colour of law or countenance of authority unless it be by the virtue or equity, of some express law of the country, warranting the same, established by a general court and sufficiently published: or, in case of the defect of a law, in any particular case, by the word of God, and in capital cases, or in cases concerning dismemberment or banishment, according to that word, to be judged by the General Court.

By these it appears, that the officers of this body politic have a rule to walk by, in all their administrations, which rule is the Word of God, and such conclusions and deductions as are or shall be regularly drawn from thence.

All Commonwealths have had some principles, or fundamentals, from which they have framed deductions to particular cases, as occasion hath required. And though no Commonwealth ever had, or can have, a particular positive rule, to dispence power, or justice by in every single case: yet where the fundamentals or general rule hold forth such direction, as no great damage, or injury can befall, either the whole, or any particular part, by any unjust sentence, or disorderly proceeding, without manifest breach of such general rule, there the rule may be required: and so the government is regular and not arbitrary.

The fundamentals which God gave, to the Commonwealth of Israel, were a sufficient rule to them, to guide all their affairs: we having the same, with all the additions, explanations and deductions, which have followed: it is not possible, we should want a rule in any case: if God give wisdom to discern it.

There are some few cases only (besides the capitals) wherein the penalty is prescribed: And the Lord could have done the like in others, if he had so pleased, but having appointed governments upon earth, to be his vicegerents, he hath given them, those few, as precedents, to direct them, and to exercise his gifts in them: Deut. 17: 9: 10: 11) In the most difficult cases, the judges in supreme authority, were to show the sentence of the law: whence 3 things may be observed: 1: this sentence was to be declared out of the law established: though not obvious to common understanding 2: this to be expected in that ordinance: therefore v:19: the King was to have a copy of the law, and to read them all the days of his life: 3: Such a sentence was not ordained to be provided before the case fell out, but pro re nata, when occasion required God promised, to be present in his own ordinance, to improve such gifts as he should please to confer upon such as he should call to place of government. In the Scripture, there are some forms of prayers and of sermons set down: yet no man will infer from thence, that ministers should have sermons and prayers prescribed them for every occasion: for that would destroy the ordinance of the ministry: and a reading priest might serve in that office, without any learning or other gifts of the Spirit: So if all penalties were prescribed the jury should state the case, and the book hold forth the sentence, and any schoolboy might pronounce it: and then what need were there of any special wisdom, learning, courage, zeal or faithfulness in a judge?

This being so great a question now on foot, about prescript penalties it will be of use to search as deep into it, as we may by the light of Scripture, approved patterns and other rational arguments: not tying our discourse to method, but laying down things as they come to hand.

England in the right constitution, is not an arbitrary government: nor is our of the Massachusetts: yet Juries, both there and here, give damages which (in vulgar sense) are arbitrary, in most cases: as in actions of slander, trespass, battery, breach of covenant, etc: all which concern the peoples liberties, no less, than fines and other penalties: And if 12 men, who have no calling to office, may (in expectation of Gods assistance) be trusted with mens estates in a way of distributive justice, without a prescript rule etc: why may not those whose calling and office hath promise of assistance have like trust reposed in them, in vindictive justice?

In the liberties enacted here of purpose to prevent arbitrary government, there are near 40 laws, to the violation whereof no penalty is prescribed: nor was ever moved.

God may pronounce sentence against an offender, before the offence be committed, both by his absolute sovereignty, and also because he foreseeth all facts, with all their circumstances: and besides the least degree of the same offence deserves more then that full punishment before his justice: but man must proceed according to his commission; by which he cannot sentence another, before he hath offended, and the offence examined, proved, laid to the rule, and weighed by all considerable circumstances, and liberty given to the party to answer for himself, nor is there any thing more prejudicial to a subject liberty, then to be sentenced before his cause be heard.

England is a state of long standing, yet we have had more positive and more wholesome laws enacted in our short time than they had in many hundred years. They have indeed some laws with prescribed penalties annexed, but they are for the most part so small, as do under value the least degree of those offences: they have xijd for an oath: 5s for drunkenness etc. but for all great offences and misdemeanors, as perjury, forgery, conspiracy, cosinage, oppressions, riot, batteries, and other breaches of the peace etc.: there is no penalty prescribed how it is in other States in Europe, I cannot relate (because we know not their laws) otherwise than what appears in their histories, where we find some great offenses punished, by the discretion of their judges.

Justice ought to render to every man according to his deserving, eye for eye, hand for hand etc: and Luk: 12:47: the servant, who transgressed against knowledge was to be beaten with more stripes than he who transgressed of ignorance: If we had a law, that every lie should be punished 40s and 2 offenders should be convicted at the same time: the one a youth of honest conversation, never known to lie before: and now suddenly surprised, with fear of some discredit, had told a lie, wherein was no danger of harm to any other: The other, an old notorious lier: and his lie contrived of purpose. for a pernitious end: It were not just, to punish both these alike: as 40s were too little for the one, so it were too much for the other. Besides penalties (we know) coming of poena, should cause pain or grief to the offenders. It must be an affliction yet not a destruction, except in capital, or other heinous crimes: but in prescript penalties authority shoots at adventure: if the same penalty hits a rich man, it pains him not, it is not affliction to him, but if it lights upon a poor man, it breaks his back.

Every law must be just in every part of it, but if the penalty annexed be unjust, how can it be held forth as a just law? To prescribe a penalty, must be by some rule, otherwise, it is an usurpation of Gods prerogative: but where the law makers, or declarers cannot find a rule for prescribing a panalty, if it come before the judges pro re nata, there it is determinable by a certain rule, viz: by an ordinance set up of God for that purpose, which hath a sure promise of divine assistance, Exo: 21: 22, Deut: 16: 18: Judges and officers shalt those make etc. and they shall judge the people with just judgment: Deut: 25: 1: 2: and 17: 9: 10: 11. If a law were made that if any man were found drunken he should be punished by the judges according to the merit of his offence: this is a just law, because it is warranted by a rule: but if a certain penalty were prescribed, this would not be just, because it wants a rule, but when such a case is brought before the judges and the quality of the person and other circumstances considered, they shall find a rule to judge by; as if Naball, and Uriah and one of the strong drunkards of Ephraim were all 3 together accused before the judges for drunkenness, they could so proportion their several sentences, according to the several natures and degrees of their offences, as a just and divine sentence might appear in them all: for a divine sentence is in the lips of the King his mouth transgresseth not in judgment Pro: 16: but no such promise was ever made to a paper sentence of human authority or invention. ...

Prescript penalties take away the use of admonition, which is also a divine sentence and an ordinance of God, warranted by

Scripture: as appears in Solomons Admonition to Adonijah and Nehemiahs to those that brake the Sabbath: Eccl: 12: 11: 12: The Words of the wise are as goads, and as nailes fastened by the masters of Assembly - by these (my son) be admonished, Pro: 29: 1: Isay. 11: 4: Pro. 17: 10: A Reproofe entereth more into a wise man, then 100 stripes into a foole.

Judges are Gods upon earth: therefore, in their administrations, they are to hold forth the wisdom and mercy of God, (which are his attributes) as well as his justice: as occasion shall require, either in respect of the quality of the person or for a more general good; or evident repentance, in some cases of less public consequence, or avoiding imminent danger to the state, and such like prevalent considerations. Exo: 22: 8: 9: for theft and other like trespasses, double restitution was appointed by the law: but Lev: 6: 2: 5: in such cases, if the party confessed his sin, and brought his offering, he should only restore the principal, and add a fifth part thereto. Adultery and incest deserved death, by the law, in Jacobs time (as appears by Juda his sentence, in the case of Thamar): yet Ruben was punished only with loss of his birthright, because he was a Patriot. David his life was not taken away for his adultery and murder, (but he was otherwise punished) in respect of public interest and advantage, he was valued at 10000 common men: Bathsheba was not put to death for her adultery, because the kings desire, had with her, the force of a law. Abiathar was not put to death for his treason, because of his former good service and faithfulness. Shemei was reprived for a time, and had his pardon in his own power, because of his profession of repentence in such a season. Those which brake the Sabbath in Nehemiah his time, were not put to death but first admonished, because the state was not settled etc. Joab was not put to death for his murders, in Davids time, for avoiding imminent public danger, the sons of Zeruiah had the advantage of David, by their interest in the men of War: and the Commonwealth could not spare them. But if judges be tied to a prescript punishment, and no liberty left for dispensation or mitigation in any case, here is no place left for wisdom or mercy: whereas Solomon saith Pro: 20: 28: mercy and truth preserve the King; and his throne is upholden by mercy.

I would know by what rule we may take upon us, to prescribe penalties, where God prescribes none. If it be Answ: from Gods example, I must reply 1: God prescribes none except Capital, but only in such cases as are between party and party, and that is rather in a way of satisfaction to the party wronged, then to justice and intention. 2. Gods examples are not warrants for us, to go against Gods rules; our rule is to give a just sentence, which we cant do (in most cases) before the offence is committed etc. 5s now may be more than 20s hereafter and _e contra_. if examples in scripture be warrant for us to proceed against rule, then we may pass by murders, adulteries, idolatries, etc; without capital punishments; then we might put the children to death for parents offences etc: ...

It may be further demanded, what power we have over the persons and estates of the succeeding generations? If we should now prescribe, where our posterity etc. should dwell, what quantities of land they should till: what places they should tend unto: what diet they should use, what clothes they should wear etc: by what rule could we challenge this power? yet we have example for some of these in Scripture, as of Jonadab the son of Rechab: etc: but no man will take these as warrant for us to lay such injunctions upon those which come after us, because they are to have the same interest, and freedom in their estates and persons that we have in ours.

And for preventing of oppression, etc: is there no way to help that, but by breach of rule? shall we run into manifest injustice, for fear of I know not what future danger of it? is there not a clear way of help in such cases, by appeal, or petition, to the highest authority? If this will not relieve, in a particular case, we shall then be in a very ill case, for all our prescript penalties. Besides, there may be such a general law made (as in magna charta) that may prevent the overthrowing of mens estates, or lands, etc: by fines, etc: (and I think it as needful, as any law or liberty we have) whereby the judges may be restrained, within certain limits, which (if occasion should require to exceed) may be referred to the General Court. And in corporal punishments, a liberty in such and such cases, to redeem them at a certain rate: This would sufficiently assure the proper persons and estates, from any great oppression, if withal, our courts of judicature, were kept but by 3 or 5 magistrates at most, which may well be ordered, without any deviation from our patent. and so the greater number of magistrates should be free from engagement in any case, which might come to a review upon appeal or petition.

It is an error so to conceive of laws, as if they could not be perfect without penalties annexed, for they are as truly distinct as light and darkness: Law was created with and in man, and so is natural to him: but penalty is positive and accidental. Law is bonum simpliciter, but poena is simpliciter malum in subiecto: therefore laws may be declared and given, without any penalties annexed.

Isay. 10: 1: Woe to them that decree unrighteous decrees and write grievousness, which they have prescribed: so that where the penalty proves grievous by the unrighteousness of a prescript decree, it will draw a woe after it, as well as unrighteous sentence: Deut: 25: 15: thou shalt have a perfect and a just weight and measure: If God be so strict in commutative justice, that every act therein must be by a just and perfect rule, what warrant have we, to think that we may dispence distributive or vindictive justice to our brethren by guess, when we prescribe measure to an uncertain merit.

But it will be objected: volenti non fit injuria: the people giving us power to make laws to bind them, they do implicitly give their consent to them. To this it may be answered: that where they put themselves into our power to bind them to laws and penalties, they can intend no other but such as are just and righteous: and although their implicit consent may bind them to outward obedience, yet it neither ties them to satisfaction, nor frees such lawmakers from unrighteousness nor the law itself from injustice; nor will such a law be a sufficient warrant to the conscience of the judge, to pronounce such a sentence, as he knows to be apparently disproportionable to the offence brought before him.

Although my arguments conclude against prescript penalties indefinitely, yet I do not deny but, they may be lawful in some cases: for an universal affirmative proposition may be true, though it comprehend not every particular, as when we say all the country was rated to such a charge, no man will conceive that every person and every woman etc. was rated; and when we say such an one was cast out by the whole church, this is a true speech (to common intendment) though every particular member did not consent. Where any penalty may be prescribed by a rule, so as the judge may pronounce a just sentence, I have formerly, and shall still join in it.

We will now answer such objections, as are made, against the liberty required to be left to judges, in their sentences. [Winthrop here disposes of the objection that since judges are subject to temptation there must be prescribed penalties in the laws.]

3 ob: If the determination of the law were left to the judges, that were arbitrary government: and is it not in reason the same, if the punishment of the transgression of the law, be committed to them?

Answ: The Reason is not alike in both cases.

1. The determination of law belongs properly to God: he is the only lawgiver: but he hath given power and gifts to men to interpret his laws: and this belongs principally to the highest authority in a commonwealth and subordinately to other magistrates and judges according to their several places.

2. The law is always the same, and not changeable by any circumstances of aggravation, or extenuation, as the penalty is: and therefore draws a certain guilt upon every transgressor whether he sins of ignorance, or against knowledge, or presumptuously: and therefore laws or the interpretation of them, may be prescribed, without any danger, because no event can alter the reason, or justice of them: as it may of punishments.

3. The law is more general and lies as a burden, upon all persons and at all times: but the penalty reaches to none, but

transgressors and to such, only when they are brought under sentence, and not before.

4. It is needful that all men should know the laws, and their true meanings, because they are bound to them, and the safety and welfare of the commonwealth consists in the observation of them: therefore it is needful they should be stated and declared, as soon as is possible; but there is not the like necessity or use of declaring their penalties before hand, for they who are godly and virtuous, will observe them, for conscience, and virtues sake: and for such as must be held in by fear of punishment, it is better they should be kept in fear of a greater punishment than to take liberty to transgress through the contempt of a smaller.

4 ob: It is safe for the Commonwealth to have penalties prescribed, because we know not what magistrates or judges we may have hereafter.

Answ: 1: God foresaw, that there would be corrupt judges in Israel, yet he left most penalties, to their determination.

2: There is no wisdome of any state can so provide, but that in many things of greatest concernment, they must confide in some men: and so it is in all humane affairs: the wisest merchants, and the most wary, are forced to repose great trust in the wisdom and faithfulness of their servants, factors, masters of their ships, etc. All states, in their generals of war, admirals, ambassadors, treasurers, etc: and these are causes of more public consequence, then the sentence of a judge in matters of misdemeanor, or other smaller offences.

3: When we have provided against all common, and probable events, we may and ought to trust God for safety from such dangers, as are only possible, but not likely, to come upon us: especially when our striving to prevent such possible dangers, may hazard the deprivation, or weakning of a present good; or may draw those, or other evils, nearer upon us. ...

This discourse is run out to more length than was intended: the conclusion is this: The government of the Massachusetts consists of Magistrates and Freemen: in the one is placed the authority, in the other the liberty of the Commonwealth either hath power to act, both alone, and both together, yet by a distinct power, the one of liberty, the other of authority: the Freemen Act of themselves in electing their magistrates and officers: the magistrates act alone in all occurrences out of court: and both act together in the General Court: yet all limited by certain rules, both in the greater and smaller affairs: so as the government is regular in a mixed aristocracy and no way arbitrary.

After the essay on Arbitrary Government was published, a Committee of the Deputies prepared a memorandum in which specific objections were taken to Winthrop's thesis. After examining those objections, Winthrop evidently re-examined his essay and wrote a brief postscript or "review" of his writing. In this short document he states more clearly than he did in any other place the theoretical grounds for his preference for common law, whether English or Colonial, over statutory law. It might well be considered whether this preference of Winthrop's did not become characteristic of many later generations of American lawyers.

John Winthrop - The Author's Review of His Writing
4 Winthrop Papers 486

That which gave me occasion first to inquire after a rule for prescript penalties, was the inequality I saw in some prescribed sentences upon the breach of diverse moral laws: and proceeding in this inquiry, I kept my intention still upon that subject, without respect to such laws as are merely positive, having their authority only and wholly from human institution: therefore you shall find that all my instances are of that kind, and all my arguments look that way, as in the instances I bring of the laws of England. If I had intended the positive and statute laws, it had been a great mistake, for I know well that most of the later statute laws have their penalties prescribed, and it must needs be so, for such as are merely positive, for a judge can have no rule for his sentence upon the breach of such a law, except he have it from the law itself: as for instance, if the law which forbids any man to kill an hare or partridge with a gun, had not also set down the penalty, the judge could not have found out any, which might have been just because no law of God or nature makes such an act any offence or transgression. But for the common laws of England (which are the ancient laws and of far more esteem for their wisdom and equity, then the statute laws) they had no penalties prescribed, and it may be conceived that for such of them as were grounded upon the word of God, and the light of nature, there must needs be that in the same word and in the same light of nature (especially where the image of God in man is in part renewed by Christ) which may lead us to a just punishment for the transgression of such a law. Nor do I oppose all prescript penalties in moral cases but only such as do cross some clear rules in the word of God as will appear by all my arguments. And for avoiding all danger to the subject for want of prescript penalties in some cases, you may see that I require some such law to be made, as may limit judges within such bounds of moderation, as may prevent such dangers, and it is one of my express conclusions in the first page, that judges ought to be tied to a rule, and such a rule as may be required of them in all their administrations, and therefore upon what grounds I should be charged to assert arbitrary government, and that judges should have liberty to do what they may, I leave to your judgments.

As for laws, you shall find also, that I conclude the necessity of declaring and stating them, so as all the people may know them, for I ever held it unjust, to require of men their obedience to any law, which they may not (be common intendment) take notice of. Answerable hereunto hath been my practice: All the useful laws we have, had my consent, and such poor help as the Lord enabled me, to yield to them: some of which have prescribed penalties, and where I have withheld my consent to any such penalties, I have given my reasons for it, which have been such, as in some cases have satisfied the court, and herein I have taken no more liberty then is allowed to every member of the court. I will not justify every passage in my book: there are 2 or 3 words that offence have been taken at, and although I can give a safe account of them, yet I must confess they do not now please me, but where the matter is good, and the intention of the writer honest, the Lord forbids us to make a man an offender in a word.

Whatsoever is erroneous (I say as I did from the first) I shall leave it to its due censure: but for all that is of God and of the Truth, or the sincerity of my intentions herein to the public will, or the liberty I had by my place to propound such considerations to the court if these be questioned I must stand and fall with them. Jo: Winthrop

c. The Laws and Liberties of 1648

Enough has been said of the background of the Code of 1648 to make superfluous any detailed discussion of the legislative processes by which it was at length prepared and published. Until 1906 no copy of the Code was known to be in existence, and until 1929, when a reprint of the one known copy (at the Huntington Library) was published, its contents could only be surmised. Attention to a few of its important and characteristic provisions will give some sense of its quality as a whole.

The introductory Epistle suggests its general purpose and scope.

To Our Beloved Brethren and Neighbours
the Inhabitants of the Massachusetts, the Governour,
Assistants and Deputies assembled in the General
Court of that Jurisdiction with grace and peace
in our Lord Jesus Christ

So soon as God had set up Politicall Government among his people Israel hee gave them a body of lawes for judgment both in civil and criminal causes. These were brief and fundamental principles, yet withall so full and comprehensive as out of them clear deductions were to be drawne to all particular cases in future times. For a Commonwealth without lawes is like a Ship without rigging and steeradge. Nor is it sufficient to have principles or fundamentalls, but these are to be drawn out into so many of their deductions as the time and condition of that people may have use of. And it is very unsafe & injurious to the body of the people to put them to learn their duty and libertie from generall rules, nor is it enough to have lawes except they be also just. Therefore among other priviledges which the Lord bestowed upon his peculiar people, these he calls them specially to consider of, that God was neerer to them and their lawes were more righteous then other nations. God was sayd to be amongst them or neer to them because of his Ordnances established by himselfe, and their lawes righteous because himselfe was their Law-giver: yet in the comparison are implyed two things, first that other nations had something of Gods presence amongst them. Secondly that there was also somwhat of equitie in their lawes, for it pleased the Father (upon the Covenant of Redemption with his Son) to restore so much of his Image to lost man as whereby all nations are disposed to worship God, and to advance righteousnes: which appears in that of the Apostle Rom. I. 21. They knew God &c: and in the 2. 14. They did by nature the things contained in the law of God. But the nations corrupting his Ordinances (both of Religion, and Justice) God withdrew his presence from them proportionably whereby they were given up to abominable lusts Rom. 2. 21. Whereas if they had walked according to that light & law of nature they might have been preserved from such moral evils and might have injoyed a common blessing in all their natural and civil Ordinances: now, if it might have been so with the nations who were so much strangers to the Covenant of Grace, what advantage have they who have interest in this Covenant, and may injoye the special presence of God in the puritie and native simplicitie of all his Ordinances by which he is so neer to his owne people. This hath been no small priviledge, and advantage to us in New England that our Churches, and civil State have been planted, and growne up (like two twinnes) together like that of Israel in the wildernes by which wee were put in minde (and had opportunitie put into our hands) not only to gather our Churches, and set up the Ordinances of Christ Jesus in them according to the Apostolick patterne by such light as the Lord graciously afforded us: but also withall to frame our civil Politie, and lawes according to the rules of his most holy word whereby each do help and strengthen other (the Churches the civil Authoritie, and the civil Authoritie the Churches) and so both prosper the better without such aemulation, and contention for priviledges or priority as have proved the misery (if not ruine) of both in some other places.

For this end about nine years since wee used the help of some of the Elders of our Churches to compose a modell of the Iudiciall lawes of Moses with such other cases as might be referred to them, with intent to make use of them in composing our lawes, but not to have them published as the lawes of this Jurisdiction: nor were they voted in Court. For that book intitled The Liberties &c: published about seven years since (which containes also many lawes and orders both for civil & criminal causes, and is commonly (though without ground) reported to be our Fundamentalls that wee owne as established by Authoritie of this Court, and that after three years experience & generall approbation: and accordingly we have inserted them into this volume under the severall heads to which they belong yet not as fundamentalls, for divers of them have since been repealed, or altered, and more may justly be (at least) amended heerafter as further experience shall discover defects or inconveniences for Nihil simul natum et perfectum. The same must we say of this present Volume, we have not published it as a perfect body of laws sufficient to carry on the Government established for future times, nor could it be expected that we should promise such a thing. For if it be no disparagement to the wisedome of that High Court of Parliament in England that in four hundred years they could not so compile their lawes, and regulate proceedings in Courts of justice &c: but that they had still new work to do of the same kinde almost every Parliament: there can be no just cause to blame a poor Colonie (being unfurnished of Lawyers and Statesmen) that in eighteen years hath produced no more, nor better rules for a good, and setled Government then this Book holds forth: nor have you (our Bretheren and Neighbours) any cause, whether you look back upon our Native Country, or take your observation by other States, & Commonwealths in Europe) to complaine of such as you have imployed in this service; for the time which hath been spent in making lawes, and repealing and altering them so often, nor of the charge which the Country hath been put to for these occasions, the Civilian gives you a satisfactorie reason of such continuall alterations additions &c: Crescit in Orbe delus.

These Lawes which were made successively in divers former years, we have reduced under severall heads in an alphabetical method, that so they might the more readilye be found, & that the divers lawes concerning one matter being placed together the scope and intent of the whole and of every of them might the more easily be apprehended: we must confesse we have not been so exact in placing every law under its most proper title as we might, and would have been: the reason was our hasty indeavour to satisfie your longing expectation, and frequent complaints for want of such a volume to be published in print: wherein (upon every occasion) you might readily see the rule which you ought to walke by. And in this (we hope) you will finde satisfaction, by the help of the references under the severall heads, and the Table which we have added in the end. For such lawes and orders as are not of generall concernment we have not put them into this booke, but they remain still in force, and are to be seen in the booke of the Records of the Court, but all generall laws not heer inserted nor mentioned to be still of force are to be accounted repealed.

You have called us from amongst the rest of our Bretheren and given us power to make these lawes: we must now call upon you to see them executed: remembering that old & true proverb, The execution of the law is the life of the law. If one sort of you Viz: non-Freemen should object that you had no hand in calling us to this worke, and therfore think yourselves not bound to obedience &c. Wee answer that a subsequent, or implicit consent is of like force in this case, as an expresse precedent power: for in putting your persons and estates into the protection and way of subsistance held forth and exercised within this Jurisdiction, you doe tacitly submit to this Government and to all the wholesome lawes thereof, and so is the common repute in all nations and that upon this Maxim. Qui sentit commodum sentire debet et onus.

If any of you meet with some law that seemes not to tend to your particular benefit, you must consider that lawes are made with respect to the whole people, and not to each particular person: and obedience to them must be yielded with respect to the common welfare, not to thy private advantage, and as thou yieldest obedience to the law for common good, but to thy disadvantage: so another must observe some other law for thy good, though to his own damage; thus must we be content to bear anothers burden and so fullfill the Law of Christ.

That distinction which is put between the lawes of God and the lawes of men, becomes a snare to many as it is misapplyed in the ordering of their obedience to civil Authoritie; for when the Authoritie is of God and that in way of an Ordinance Rom. 13. 1. and when the administration of it is according to deductions, and rules gathered from the word of God, and the clear light of nature in civil nations, surely there is no humane law that tendeth to commõ good (according to these principles) but the same in mediately a law of God, and that in way of an Ordinance which all are to submit unto and that for conscience sake. Rom. 13. 5. By order of the General Court

Jncrease Nowel

Secr.

[Particular titles and sections of the Code follow.]

Arrests

It is ordered and decreed by this Court & Authoritie therof, That no mans person shall be arrested or imprisoned for any debt or fine if the law can finde any competent means of satisfaction otherwise from his estate. And if not his person may be arrested and imprisoned, where he shall be kept at his own charge, not the Plaintiffs, till satisfaction be made; unles the Court that had cognisance of the cause or some superiour Court shall otherwise determine: provided neverthelesse that no mans person shall be kept in prison for debt but when there appears some estate which he will not produce, to which end any Court or Commissioners authorized by the General Court may administer an oath to the partie or any others suspected to be privie in concealing his estate, but shall satisfie by service if the Creditor require it but shall not be solde to any but of the English nation. [1641: 1647] see sect. I. page I.

Attachments

It is ordered by this Court and Authoritie therof that no attachment shall be granted in any civil action to any Forreigner against a setled Inhabitant in this Jurisdiction before he hath given sufficient securitie or caution to prosecute his action and to answer the defendant such costs as the Court shall award him. And further it is ordered that in all attachments of goods and chattels, or of lands, or hereditaments legall notice shall be given unto the partie or left in writing at his house, or place of usuall aboad, otherwise the sute shall not proceed; notwithstanding if he be out of this Jurisdiction the cause shall then proceed to triall, but judgement shall not be entered before the next court. And if the Defendant doe not then appear judgement shall be entered but execution shall not be granted before the Plaintiffe hath given securitie to be responsall to the Defendant if he shall reverse the judgement within one year or such further time as the Court shall limit. [1644] see actions. see El. writts. see Presidents. see Rates. see Recorder.

Bills

It is ordered by the Authority of this Court that any debt, or debts due upon bill, or other specialtie assigned to another; shall be as good a debt & estate to the Assignee as it was to the Assigner at the time of its assignation. And that it shall be lawfull for the sayd Assignee to sue for and recover the said debt, due upon bill, and so assigned, as fully as the originall creditor might have done, provided the said assignement be made upon the backside of the bill or specialtie. [1647] see usurie.

Burglarie and Theft

Forasmuch as many persons of late years have been, and are apt to be injurious to the goods and lives of others, notwithstanding all care and meanes to prevent and punish the same:

It is therefore ordered by this Court and Authoritie therof that if any person shall commit Burglarie by breaking up any dwelling house, or shall rob any person in the field, or high wayes; such a person so offending shall for the first offence be branded on the forehead with the letter (B). If he shall offend in the same kinde the second time, he shall be branded as before and also be severally whipped: and if he shall fall into the like offence the third time he shall be put to death, as being incorrigible. And if any person shal commit such Burglarie, or rob in the fields or house on the Lords day besides the former punishments, he shal for the first offence have one of his ears cut off. And for the second offence in the same kinde he shal loose his other ear in the same manner. And if he fall into the same offence a third time he shal be put to death if it appear to the Court he did it presumptuously. [1642: 1647]

For the prevention of Pilfring and Theft, it is ordered by this Court and Authoritie thereof; that if any person shal be taken or known to rob any orchard or garden, that shall hurt, or steal away any grafts or fruit trees, fruits, linnen, woollen, or any other goods left out in orchards, gardens, backsides, or any other place in house or fields: or shall steal any wood or other goods from the waterside, from mens doors, or yards; he shall forfeit treble damage to the owners thereof. And if they be children, or servants that shall trespasse heerin, if their parents or masters will not pay the penaltie before expressed, they shal be openly whipped. And forasmuch as many times it so falls out that small thefts and other offences of a criminall nature, are committed both by English & Indian, in townes remote from any prison, or other fit place to which such malefactors may be committed till the next Court, it is therfore heerby ordered; that any Magistrate upon complaint made to him may hear, and upon due proof determin any such small offences of the aforesayd nature, according to the laws heer established, and give warrant to the Constable of that town where the offender lives to levie the same: provided the damage or fine exceed not fourty shillings: provided also it shall be lawfull for either partie to appeal to the next Court to be holden in that Jurisdiction, giving sufficient caution to prosecute the same to effect at the said

Court. And everie Magistrate shall make return yearly to the Court of that Jurisdiction wherin he liveth of what cases he hath so ended. And also the Constables of all such fines as they have received. And where the offender hath nothing to satisfie such Magistrate may punish by stocks, or whipping as the cause shall deserve, not exceeding ten stripes. It is also ordered that all servants & workmen imbeazling the goods of their masters, or such as set them on work shal make restitution and be lyable to all lawes & penalties as other men. [1646]

Constables

It is ordered by this Court, that Constables are to whip or punish any to be punished by order of Authoritie (where there is not another officer appointed to doe it) in their own towns; unles they can get another to do it.

It is farther ordered by the Authoritie aforesaid, That any person tendered to any Constable of this Jurisdiction by any Constable or other Officer belonging to any foreign Jurisdiction in this Countrie, or by warrant from any such authoritie, such shall presently be received, and conveyed forthwith from Constable to Constable, till they be brought unto the place to which they are sent or before some Magistrate of this Jurisdiction who shall dispose of them as the justice of the cause shall require. And that all Hue-&-Cries shall be duly received and dilligently pursued to full effect. [1641: 1647]

It is ordered by the authoritie of this Court, That everie Constable within our Jurisdiction shall henceforth have full power to make, signe & put forth Pursutes or Hue-&-Cries after Murtherers, Manslayers, Peace-breakers, Theevs, Robbers, Burglarers and other Capital offenders, where no Magistrate is neer hand, also to apprehend without Warrant, such as are overtaken with drink, swearing, Sabboth-breaking, lying, vagrant persons, night-walkers, or any other that shall offend in any of these. Provided they be taken in the manner, either by sight of the Constable, or by present information from others. As also to make search for all such persons, either on the Sabboth day or other, when there shal be occasion, in all houses licensed to sell either beer or wine, or in any other suspected or disordered places, and those to apprehend and keep in safe custodie, till opportunitie serve to bring them before one of the next Magistrates for farther examination. Provided when any Constable is imployed by any of the Magistrates for apprehending of any person, he shall not doe it without warrant in writing, and if any person shall refuse to assist any Constable in the execution of his office, in any of the things aforementioned being by him required therto, they shal pay for neglect therof ten shillings, to the use of the Country to be levied by warrant from any Magistrate before whom any such offender shal be brought. And if it appear by good testimonie, that any shal wilfully, obstinately or contemptuously refuse or neglect to assist any Constable as is before expressed, he shall pay to the use of the Country fourty shillings. And that no man may plead ignorance for such neglect or refusal, it is ordered that everie Constable shall have a black staffe of five foot long, tipped at the upper end, about fine inches with brasse, as a badge of his office, which he shal take with him when he goeth to discharge any part of his office: which staffe shall be provided at the charge of the town, and if any Magistrate or Constable or any other, upon urgent occasion, shall refuse to doe their best indeavours, in raising & prosecuting Hue-&-cries by foot, & if need be, by horse, after such as have committed Capital crimes, they shall forfeit for everie such offence to the use aforesaid fourty shillings. [1646] See In-keepers, Masters, Oaths, Rates, Untimely death, watching.

Conveyances Fraudulent

It is ordered by this Court and the Authoritie therof, That all covenous or fradulent alienations or conveyances of lands, tenements or any hereditaments shall be of no validitie to defeat any man from due debts or legacyes, or from any just title, claim or possession of that which is so fradulently conveyed.

For avoiding all fradulent conveyances and that every man may know what estate or interest other men may have in any houses, lands or other hereditaments they are to deal in, it is therfore ordered by the authoritie of this Court;

That after the end of October 1640 no morgage, bargain, sale, or graunt made of any houses, lands, rents or other hereditaments where the Grauntor remains in possession, shall be of force against other persons except the Graunter and his Heirs, unles the same be acknowledged before some Magistrate & recorded as is heerafter expressed: and that no such bargain, sale or graunt already made, in way of morgage, where the Graunter remains in possession shall be of force against other but the Graunter or his Heirs, except the same shall be entred as is heerafter expressed within one month after the date aforementioned: if the partie be within this Jurisdiction or else within three months after he shal return. And if any such Grauntor being required by the Grauntee, his Heirs or Assignes to make an acknowledgment of any graunt, sale, bargain or morgage by him made shall refuse so to doe, it shall be in the power of any Magistrate to send for the partie so refusing, & commit him to prison without Bayle or Main-prize, untill he shall acknowledge the same, and the Grauntee is to enter his caution with the Recorder, and this shall save his interest in the mean time. And if it be doubtfull whether it be the deed and graunt of the partie, he shal be bound with Suerties to the next court of Assistants & the caution shal remain good as aforesaid. And for recording of all such graunts sales, bargains or morgages; it is further ordered, that there shall be one appointed in everie Shire chosen by each court of the said Shires for Recorders to enter all such graunts, sales, bargains, morgages of houses, lands, rents and other hereditaments as aforesaid together with the names of Graunter and Grauntee, thing and estate graunted & the date therof. All which entries shall be certified unto the Recorder or Secretarie for the Generall Court within six months from time to time. [1640:1641]

Dowries

Forasmuch as no provision hath yet been made for any certein maintainance for Wives after the death of their Husbands, be it ordered and enacted by this present Court and Authoritie therof;

That every married Woman (living with her Husband in this Jurisdiction or other where absent from him with his consent or through his meer default, or inevitable providence, or in case of divorce where she is the innocent partie) that shal not before marriage be estated by way of joynture in some houses, lands, tenements or other hereditaments for term of her life, shall immediatly after the death of her Husband have right and interest by way of dower, in, and to one third part of all such houses, lands, tenements, rents and hereditaments as her said Husband was seized of, to his own use, either in possession, reversion or remainder in any estate of inheritance (or franctenement not then determined at any time during the marriage) to have and injoy for term of her natural life according to the estate of such Husband free, and freely discharged of and from all titles, debts, rents, charges, judgements, executions and other incumbrances whatsoever had, made, or suffered by her said Husband during the said marriage between them; or by any other person claiming by, from, or under him otherwise then by any act or consent of such Wife, as the laws of this Court shall ratefie and allow: and if the Heir of the Husband or other person interrested, shall not within one month after lawfull demand made, assigne and set out to such widow, her just third part with conveniencie or to her satisfaction according to the intent of this Law, then upon a writt of dower in the Court of that Shire where the said houses, lands, tenements or other hereditaments shall lye; or in the Court of Assistants (if the same lye in several Shires) her dower or third part shal be assigned her to be set forth in severall by mets and bounds, by such persons as the same Court shall appoint for that purpose, with all costs and damages susteined. Provided alwayes that this Law shall not extend to any houses lands, tenements or other hereditaments solde or conveyed away, by any husband bona fide for valuable consideration, before the last of the ninth month now last past. And it is farther inacted that everie such Wife as is before expressed immediatly after the death of her Husband, shal have interest in, and unto one third part of all such monie, goods and chattels, real and personal of what kinde soever as her Husband shall dye possessed of (so much as shall be sufficient for the discharge of his Funerall and just debts being first deducted) to be allowed and set out to her as is heer before appointed for her Dowrie. Provided alwayes that every such widow so endowed as aforesaid shall not commit or suffer any strip of wast, but shal maintain all such houses, fences and inclosures as shal be assigned to her for her Dowrie, and shal leave the same in good and sufficient repairations in all points. [1647]

Ecclesiasticall

All the people of God within this Jurisdiction who are not in a Church way and be orthodox in judgement and not scandalous in life shall have full libertie to gather themselves into a Church estate, provided they doe it in a christian way with due observation of the rules of Christ revealed in his word. Provided also that the General Court doth not, nor will heerafter approve of any such companyes of men as shall joyne in any pretended way of Church fellowship unles they shal acquaint the Magistrates and the Elders of the neighbour Churches where they intend to joyn, & have their approbation therin. ...

Idlenes

It is ordered by this Court and Authoritie therof, that no person, Housholder or other shall spend his time idlely or unproffitably under pain of such punishment as the Court of Assistants or County Court shall think meet to inflict. And for this end it is ordered that the Constable of everie place shall use speciall care and diligence to take knowledge of offenders in this kinde, especially of common coasters, unproffitable fowlers and tobacco takers, and present the same unto the two next Assistants, who shall have power to hear and determin the cause, or transfer it to the next Court. [1633]

Inditements

If any person shall be indicted of any capital crime (who is not then in durance) & shall refuse to render his person to some Magistrate within one month after three Proclaimations publickly made in the town where he usually abides, there being a month betwixt Proclaimation and Proclaimation, his lands and goods shall be seized to the use of the common Treasurie, till he make his lawfull appearance. And such withdrawing of himselfe shall stand in stead of one wittnes to prove his crime unles he can make it appear to the Court that he was necessarily hindred. [1646]

Juries, Jurors

It is ordered by this Court and Authoritie therof, that the Constable of everie town upon Proces from the Recorder of each Court, shall give timely notice to the Freemen of their town, to choos so many able discreet men as the Proces shal direct which men so chosen he shall warn to attend the Court whereto they are appointed, and shall make return of the Proces unto the Recorder aforesaid: which men so chosen shall be impannelled and sworn truly to try betwixt partie and partie, who shall finde the matter of fact with the damages and costs according to their evidence, and the Judges shall declare the Sentence (or direct the Jurie to finde) according to the law. And if there be any matter of apparent equitie as upon the forfeiture of an Obligation, breach of covenant without damage, or the like, the Bench shall determin such matter of equitie.

Nor shall any tryall passe upon any for life or bannishment but by a special Jurie so summoned for that purpose, or by the General Court.

It is also ordered by the Authoritie aforesaid that there shall be Grand-Juries summoned everie year unto the several Courts, in each Jurisdiction; to inform the Court of any misdemeanours that they shall know or hear to be committed by any person or persons whatsoever within this Jurisdiction. And to doe any other service of the Common-wealth that according to law they shall be injoyned to by the said Court; and in all cases wherin evidence is so obscure or defective that the Jurie cannot clearly and safely give a positive verdict, whether it be Grand, or Petty Jurie, it shall have libertie to give a Non liquet or a special verdict, in which last, that is, a special verdict the judgement of the Cuase shall be left unto the Bench. And all Jurors shall have libertie in matters of fact if they cannot finde the main issue yet to finde and present in their verdict so much as they can.

And if the Bench and Jurors shall so differ at any time about their verdict that either of them cannot proceed with peace of conscience, the Case shall be referred to the General Court who shall take the question from both and determin it.

And it is farther ordered that whensoever any Jurie of tryalls, or Jurors are not clear in their judgements or consciences, concerning any Case wherin they are to give their verdict, they shall have libertie, in open Court to advise with any man they shall think fit to resolve or direct them, before they give in their verdict. And no Freeman shall be compalled to serve upon Juries above one ordinary Court in a year: except Grand-jurie men, who shall hold two Courts together at the least, and such others as shall be summoned to serve in case of life and death or bannishment. [1634 1641 1642] See Secresie.

Masters, Servants, Labourers

It is ordered by this Court and the Authoritie therof that no servant, either man or maid shall either give, sell or truck any commoditie whatsoever without licence from their Masters, during the time of their service under pain of Fine, or corporal punishment at the discretion of the Court as the offence shall deserve.

2 And that all workmen shall work the whole day allowing convenient time for food and rest.

3 It is also ordered that when any servants shall run from their masters, or any other Inhabitants shall privily goe away with suspicion of ill intentions, it shall be lawfull for the next Magistrate, or the Constable and two of the chief Inhabitants where no Magistrate is to presse men and boats or pinnaces at the publick charge to pursue such persons by Sea or Land and bring them back by force of Arms.

4 It is also ordered by the Authoritie aforesaid, that the Free-men of everie town may from time to time as occasion shall require agree amongst themselves about the prizes, and rates of all workmens labours and servants wages. And everie person inhabiting in any town, whether workman, labourer or servant shall be bound to the same rates which the said Freemen, or the greater part shall binde themselves unto: and whosoever shall exceed those rates so agreed shall be punished by the discretion of the Court of that Shire, according to the qualitie and measure of the offence. And if any town shall have cause of complaint against the Freemen of any other town for allowing greater rates, or wages then themselves, the Quarter Court of that Shire shall from time to time set order therin.

5 And for servants and workmens wages, it is ordered, that they may be paid in corn, to be valued by two indifferent Freemen, chosen the one by the Master, the other by the servant or workman, who also are to have respect to the value of the work or service, and if they cannot agree then a third man shall be chosen by the next Magistrate, or if no Magistrate be in the town then by the next Constable, unles the parties agree the price themselves. Provided if any servant or workman agree

for any particular payment, then to be payd in specie, or consideration for default therin. And for all other payments in corn, if the parties cannot agree they shall choos two indifferent men, and if they cannot agree then a third as before.

6 It is ordered, and by this Court declared, that if any servant shall flee from the tyrannie and crueltie of his, or her Master to the house of any Freeman of the same town, they shall be there protected and susteined till due order be taken for their releif. Provided due notice thereof be speedily given to their Master from whom they fled, and to the next Magistrate or Constable where the partie so fled is harboured.

7 Also that no servant shall be put off for above a year to any other, neither in the life time of their Master nor after their death by their Executors or Administrators, unles it be by consent of Authoritie assembled in some Court, or two Assistants: otherwise all, and everie such Assignment to be void in Law.

8 And that if any man smite out the eye, or tooth of his man-servant, or maid-servant; or otherwise maim, or much disfigure them (unles it be by meer casualtie) he shall let them goe free from his service, and shall allow such farther recompence as the Court shall adjudge him.

9 And all servants that have served diligently and faithfully to the benefit of their Masters seven years shall not be sent away emptie: and if any have been unfaithfull, negligent, or unprofitable in their service, notwithstanding the good usage of their Masters, they shall not be dismissed till they have made satisfaction according to the judgement of Authoritie. [1630 1633 1635 1636 1641] See Oppression.

Protestation contra Remonstrance

It is ordered, decreed, and by this Court declared; that it is, and shall be the libertie of any member, or members of any Court, Council or civil Assemblie in cases of making or executing any Order or Law that properly concerneth Religion, or any cause Capital, or Wars, or subscription to any publick Articles, or Remonstrance in case they cannot in judgement and conscience consent to that way the major Vote or Suffrage goes to make their contra-Remonstrance or Protestation in speech or writing, and upon their request, to have their dissent recorded in the Rolls of that Court, so it be done christianly and respectively, for the manner, and the dissent only be entred without the reasons therof for avoyding tediousnes. [1641]

Wills intestate

It is ordered, and by this Court declared; that when Parents dye intestate, the eldest son shall have a double portion of his whole estate reall, and personall unles the General Court upon just cause alledged shall judge otherwise. And when Parents dye intestate having no Heirs males of their bodyes, their daughters shall inherit as co-partners, unles the General Court upon just reason shall judge otherwise. [1641]

d. The Code and the Common Law

As a result of the decision of the Commissioners for Plantations that they would not hear appeals from the Colonial courts the Colony seemed to have a largely free hand in the making of its own body of law. Having embodied the law of the Colony in the Code of 1648 the principal problem left for solution concerned the enforcement of that Code by the judicial process. It would probably be an exaggeration to suggest that it was a central purpose of the Massachusetts Puritans to abandon the whole of the common law, but certainly it was their intention to let their own law develop without special regard to the technicalities of the law of England. While lawyers trained in England were few, and while English reports and texts were rare it was, of course, natural that English rules of law should play a negligible part in the growth of Colonial law. It was almost inevitable, however, that as the population grew and as the ardor of the Puritan faith and ambition cooled, the concepts of the common law should become useful as standards of interpretation when statutes were ambiguous and that particular rules of the common law should seem useful to litigants when the Code was silent.

<u>Giddings</u> v. <u>Brown</u>
County Court, Essex County, 1657; 2 <u>Hutchinson Papers</u> 1
[Opinion of Samuel Symonds, Assistant]

In an action of trespass upon the case for entering his house and severing his pewter dishes or platters and marking of them.

I find in this case for the plaintiff,

Damage 0--1--0
Costs 0--5--8

And the case being of very weighty concernment in the countrey (I conceive) I shall expresse the groundes of my judgment.[1]

---

1. In the <u>Laws and Liberties of 1648</u>, under the title "Charges Public" there appeared the following provision, derived from an

I understand this to be about a fundamentall law, and that a fundamentall law properly so called. It is such a law as that God and nature have given to a people. So that it is in the trust of their governors in highest place and others, to preserve, but not in their power to take away from them. Of which sort are these, viz.

1. Election of the supreame governours.

2. That every subject shall and may enjoy what he hath a civell right or title unto, soe as it cannot be taken from him, by way of gift or loan, to the use or to be made the right or property of another man, without his owne free consent.

3. That such lawes (though called libertyes) yet more properly they may be called rights, and in this sense this may be added as a third fundamentall law, viz.

That no custome or precedent ought to prevayle in any morall case, that may appear to be sinfull in respect of the breach of any law of piety against the first table, or of righteousness against the second. ...

A coppy of the vote [of a town meeting at Ipswich] as I have taken it, viz.

"Voted to give 100l towards building or buying a house for Mr. Cobbet."

Whereas when I gave my sentence in the case before me, betweene George Giddings plaintiff, and Edward Browne defendant, in an action of trespas upon the case, &c. I did expresse some grounds of my judgment to be seen in the records. Now I shall add further what doth induce me to that apprehension in the case, viz.

---

act of the General Court of 1638 (1 Records 240): "... every inhabitant shall henceforth contribute to all charges both in Church and Commonwealth whereof he doth or may receive benefit: and every such inhabitant who shall not voluntarily contribute proportionably to his ability with the Freemen of the same town to all common charges both civil and ecclesiastical shall be compelled thereto by assessment and distress to be levied by the Constable or other Officer of the town as in other cases ..." Under the title "Ecclesiastical" appeared a statute of 1647 (2 Records 217): "And to the end there may be a convenient habitation for the use of the ministry in every town ... to remain to posterity ... where the major part of the inhabitants ... shall grant, build, or purchase such habitation, it shall be good in law ... provided always that such grant ... and the deed of gift thereupon to the use of the present preaching Elder and his next successor and so from time to time to his successors be entered in the town book and acknowledged ... and recorded in the Shire Court."

First, This may be given as a reason, that it is against a fundamentall law in nature to be compelled to pay that which others doe give. For then no man hath any certaynty or right to what he hath, if it be in the power of others (by pretence of authority or without) to give it away (when in their prudence they conceive it to be for the benefit of the owner foe to doe) without his owne consent.

Secondly, This to me is some strengthning to induce my apprehension in this case, viz. That notwithstanding in England, it cannot be denied, but that mens estates were sometymes unduly taken from them: Some by force, some by fraud, some by sinister wresting of evidences, yea, and sometimes of lawe itselfe as about knighthood-money, shipmoney, &c. yet I dare say, if search be made into histories, lawyers bookes of reports, records &c. it cannot be made to appeare that in the most exorbitant times any man hath had his estate taken from him as by the guift of others, under colour of lawe, or countenance of authority. Noe, noe, lawyers would have blushed to have given such a construction of lawes; and suddenly their faces would have waxed pale. For the Kinge would have beene too wise to have owned the plea. And what would all wise men have said for such taking away the greatest outward right or liberty from them? For it may be understood, that benevolencies, incouraging gratuities, leaves, or privy seales, were not required by lawe, or by pretence of lawe, but desired as by favour. However they were obtained by illegall and tyranicall meanes, as was apprehended.

This I say further, and I doe argue it from the greater to the lesse. That if noe kings or parliament can justly enact and cause that one mans estate, in whole or in part, may be taken from him and given to another without his owne consent, then surely the major part of a towne or other inferior powers cannot doe it. But shew us any man that can produce any footstep for such a way, either directly or indirectly.

But to the contrary it appeareth unto me. See Dalton page 401, where it is to this effect. That the kinge cannot release a man out of prison (being in at a private mans suit) to his damage, without his owne consent.[2] Also to the same

---

2. At p. 401 of Dalton's <u>Country Justice</u> (1643 ed.) appears the following passage concerning ravishment of wards: "And it is said, that it is at the election of the Justices to award the offender to abjure the realm, or to have perpetual imprisonment: and that if the Justices shall award him to perpetual imprisonment, that the King cannot pardon him that imprisonment, for that it is in lieu of damages to the Plaintiff, and that imprisonment is an execution thereof, the which the King cannot pardon, without the assent of the party plaintiff."

purpose see Sir Henry Finch, recorder of London, in his first booke of lawe, page 74, having ended his rules about native or fundamentall lawes, he saith in the next page, Therefore lawes positive doe lose their force and are noe lawes at all, which are directly contrary to the former viz. native or fundamentall. ...

But now to answer some objections that may be made to the case in hande.

Objection. Suppose it be true what is expressed, and granted that he were a strange man that should deny the same in the generall: Yet, notwithstanding, it hindereth not but that a towne (when and as often as they thinke good, in their prudence) may doe it for good ends, and soe (in speciall cases) it may lawfully be done in the particular, upon the lawe made page the 9th, that every inhabitant shall contribute to all charges in church and commonwealth (whereof he doth or may receive a benefitt) else he shall be strayned.

Answer. I conceive that it is an extreame dishonour cast upon the generall court, to make such a construction of their positive laws as doth infringe the fundamentall law of mine and thine; for it must needs be voyd, if it should indeed be necessarly construed against the right or liberty of the subject. But the law in its true sense is good.

Before this recited law was made, though some churches, or townes rather, did agree how much yearely maintenance the minister should have, yet it was not rated, at least in any compellable way, by the towne, but men did pay their proportion in a way of voluntary contribution. But some (especially non members) some of them did grow slacke; and so the burthen grew too hevy upon church members, &c. And upon consideration it was found lawfull to make a law to compell every one to beare his owne share; forasmuch as by hearing the word and publique prayer, &c. he did or might receive a benefitt and (in a way of God) be received as a member with the rest. And yet the law was framed soe, as such churches as chose rather to goe in a voluntary way of weekly contribution or soe, might soe continue, notwithstanding this law, as some churches in this country doe to this day.

But for the right understanding of the word benefitt in the law, it is worthy the consideration or attendance, that benefit and necessary duty must goe together. The law both of God and the country doth require people to goe to the meeting for publique worship.

But it is not understood that any law doth provide that every towne shall buy or build a house for the minister as often as there is a removall by death or otherwise, I mean to be his in propriety. ...

About a bargain or contract.

Obj. Suppose it should be endeavoured to be made a bargain, &c.

Ans. It is no matter to the case in question: For though it be in the power of a person or of many (each person consenting) to make a bargain never so much to his owne losse, yet he or they must be holden to it: But otherwise it is with a derived power in trust, being a society; for they have not such an unlimited domination over other mens estates or persons; For, setting aside the consideration of the fundamentall law (before sufficiently spoken unto) they are limited by statute law. And such bargains as bind the non consenters must be equalle, rationall, and the termes or conditions also expressed or certayne: If any of these fayle noe law will bind them. This is knowne, that upon motions in towne meetings and other companies, some use one argument or motive, some another. Some are moved with one argument or valuable consideration in his mind, some with another. And is the rule to seeke then (or onely so in this case) what is the way of nations to understand the mind of the company? Must not recourse be had to the record? ...

And certayne such as plead on the now defendants party must say it is either a gift or a bargain. If this be endeavoured to be a bargain or contract, it is a very blind bargain, as they say, which (acting upon oath) I could not allow. If a gift (for there may be motives and high considerations in the minds of the granters to give as well as to conclude a bargain) then it doth not bind such as doe not consent to be forced to pay what doe move other men to give away out of their estates.

So much about the matter of contract or consideration. Now a little about interpretation of lawes and of rules to be attended therein.

Let us not (here in New-England) despise the rules of the learned in the lawes of England, who have both great helps and long experience.

1. First rule is, that where a law is such as that, by wresting, a man may give such an interpretation as will overthrow it, when it might be construed to be good; this is a corrupt interpretation.[3] So holy scripture may be wrested.

If repugnant to fundamentall law, its voyd; as if it gives power to take away an estate from one man and give it to another. [Citing Finch, Law, 75]

It is then consonant, if it be to compell men to pay necessary duties in church and common wealthe, as yearely maintenance.

---

3. Citing, Finch, Law (1636 ed.) 33: "Nothing to be void that by possibility may be good", is one of the fundamental rules of law derived from logic.

2. Another rule is about equality. Hence where a company in trust doth act, if any will imply conditions (noe way exprest) yet, to hold forth any color of binding, they must be knowne to be equall and certaine; though a statute law should provide or expresse mischiefously. See his words at large, justly applyable as is expressed.[4]

3. Another rule appeareth to this effect. That where a person is sued at a private mans suit, and put in prison upon execution, the king cannot pardon that imprisonment without the consent of the party plt. and the reason is there given; for it is in lieu of damage to the party, as hath been touched before.[5]

4. The law construeth things with equity and moderation; and therefore restrayneth a generall act, if there be any mischief or inconveniency in it. [Citing Finch, Law, 55]

So far touching rules for interpretation of laws. ...

Precedents and Judgments in Courts

Although there had been noe precedent in the like case, yet I ought (I conceive) to have judged, in the case in question, according to the rules aforegoing: Notwithstanding, I grant that what I find to have beene judged already and acted both justly and honourably, I ought to be the more confirmed thereby.

1. In Ipswich, some years since, the town greatly wanted a good chirurgeon, &c. and the inhabitants then generally being desirous of such a person to inhabite amongst us; the chiefe sort consulted how to effect it. It must cost above 50l to bring it about.

It was concluded that it could not be justly done by way of rate, but each mans name being drawne out (according to a rate) such as were willing did signify the same, and the rest were left to use their liberty.

2. I am informed and doe partly remember it, that some yeares since there was a six acre lott in Ipswich purchased for Jeffery Snellings; but some of the inhabitants consented not: It came at last to a suite in Ipswich court, and it was found against the towne, because by law they could not give away any mans estate against his owne consent, notwithstanding the considerations and motions inducing.

---

4. Citing Finch, ibid. 20, where the rules of logic as to comparison and equality were said to require that "things are to be construed secundum equalitatern rationis".

5. See Note 2, supra.

And admitt there were not such weighty considerations or benefitt as in some other case there may be, the degree is not the poynt; for majus et minus non variant speciem. Ambrose Leach the seller of the land. Daniell Clarke was sued.

3. There is yet, I conceive, a concluding judgment (in the like case) in the generall court, I referr to the record it-selfe (but till an understanding man, then an inhabitant of Weymouth (as I am informed) mentioned it since the passing of my sentence in the case in question) it was out of my mind.

I remember the substance of it, and I suppose so doe many more. That towne of Weymouth did generally agree to provide an house and meet accommodations for the use of the ministry, to remaine for posterity. The matter came into the generall court. Mrs. Richards stood out, and not many (if any more be-sides) and although the court did soe well like their ayme, or the thing (in itselfe considered) as may by and by appeare, yet it was judged in court that they could not justly impose payment upone one, or more persons, not consenting. One Dyer was then deputy of that towne, and did prosecute in behalf of the towne: Yet herein the court gave a testimony of their good liking in respect of the townes intent, viz. in that way to provide for the ministry. And accordingly the law was framed, and enacted for the future, that very court.[6] This provision was not to give away, but to remaine for posterity, and the like provision was for every towne in the country; and that which a great part, if not the greater part, of Ipswich have desired and do still stand for. ...

Quest. If it be demanded whether there be any difference betweene disposing mens estates by way of guift (under colour of law and countenance of authority) unto other men against or without the consent of the owners and the doctrine of levell-isme.

Ans. It may be answered (I conceive) to this effect, viz. That of the levellers, though wicked and absurd, yet it is as yet but doctrinall (I thinke) but this kinde of transposeing mens estates is both doctrinall and practicall alsoe, and soe leadeth more directly to tiranny as it seemeth.

Secondly, Levellisms (I take it) reacheth but to the es-tate, &c. But this (if accounted legall) men may for a debt soe obtained (as in other cases) upon execution for a debt in-force the person to prison, or expose him to be sould to make payment.

Quest. But what if there be an interpretation put upon the words of the records, and call it a contract, will not this help the matter?

---

6. See Note 1, supra.

Ans. This liberty to interprett acts or records against the playne words thereof (if it be a help) I suppose it is to make the matter worse in this respect (if worse can be) than the doctrine of levellisme, for by their doctrine (I thinke) a man may understand what they meane by their words, and their words are used (its likely) in one sence.

But this kinde of liberty of interpreting seems to countenance and strengthen the opinion of the scepticks, which makes all things true, and soe indeed nothing true or certayne. Hence when an act will serve the turne let the words stand, else take liberty to interpret them for the purpose.

If this kind of liberty be good, either to construe laws (provided for necessary payments) or turning guifts into contracts (as men please) then indeed it is all one whether both parties be present when the busines is in hand or not. And though it was wont to be lawe that a bargain, whether it proveth gaynfull or loosing, yet being made bindeth both parties. But had this vote beene for 20 l. (or soe) instead of 100 l. would it be interpreted good, binding and disanulling of the vote for the 150 l? But this was intended doubtless by some, namely by granting a new sume to change or repeale the act for the former way agreed one, according to the lawe and the townes contentment, though herein alsoe they did mistake, for there appeareth to be noe vote to disanull the former. See that if there were divers more graunts or gifts in this kind, they were all additionall, and would all be gotten by suit and distresse, and if this may, justly be obtained by lawe. ...

To conclude this matter, I thank God, I am for ordinances both in church and commonwealth; and consequently for due meanes for the upholding of them (and doe account it not only a great wickednes to be contraryminded, but extreme folly and madnes) and I thinke it tends to the honour of them, when in referance thereunto, provision is made either in a voluntary or else in a way of compulsion, grounded upon such principles as both here and in other nations will be owned as just and equall.

I doe sometymes remember what is said of Levy. In poynt of right and truth, he tooke noe notice of father or mother. And that is the way to establish love and peace in this our Israel. And the holy scripture doth oblige the doctrine and practice of piety according to the first table, and of distributive justice in the second, both expressly, or by necessary consequence, at the hands of such as are called to dispence the same, though they take not oath soe to doe.

It is supposed that noe man is come to New England to have his goods given and taken from him, unto, or for what good end, or under what pretence soever.

If this should be confirmed for good law; henceforth then

(I conceive) there will be noe more need, or little, to make any more propositions for voluntary contributions.[7]

Patten v. Dyer[1]
1 Records of Suffolk County Court, 1671-1680 373 (1673/4)

Thomas Patten Attourny unto John Patten of Severls in the parish of Crewkern in the County of Somers[t] in the Kingdom of England yeoman who is the Lawfull and proper heire of or to the Estate of Nathaniell Patten late of Dorchester in New-England deceased plaint. ags[t] Gyles Dyer Defend[t] in an accion of the case for that the s[d] Dyer doth refuse to deliver possession & rent for one yeare or thereabout at fifteen pounds per yeare for a certain house & teniment which the s[d] Dyer now occupieth in Boston, which belongeth unto the s[d] John Patten as heire aforesaide, by reason of which refusall of possession & rent the s[d] heire is damnified to the value of the afores[d] Summe or thereabout with other due damages according to Attachment Dat January 20 1673. ... The Jury ... founde for the Defend[t] costs of Court: The plaint. appealed from the judgm[t] to the next Court of Assistants & the s[d] Tho: Patten as principall in ten pounds & Rich[d] Wharton & Anthony Checkly as Sureties in five pounds apeice acknowledged themselves respectively bound to ... prosecute his Appeal. ...

[Plaintiff's Reasons for Appeal]

Thomas Patten Atturny of John Patten of Seueralls in the Parish of Crewkerne in Somersett Sheire in England his Reasons of Appeale from ye Judgment of ye County Court in Boston in January 1673. To the Hono[rd] Court of Asistance Sitting in Boston in March following Jn the Case betwixt the Said The Patten

---

7. The case was later considered by the General Court and it was there resolved that all inhabitants were bound to contribute to the assessment. 4 Records, Part I, 310-311. Cf. Adams v. Howe, 14 Mass. 340 (1817). The Supreme Judicial Court there held, with evident reluctance that the legislature had constitutional power to exempt persons who were affiliated with unincorporated religious societies from the payment of ministerial taxes.

1. There is a detailed account of the issues involved in the Patten litigation in Professor Chafee's article "Professor Beale's Ancestor" in Harvard Legal Essays (1934) p. 39.

plaintiff & Gyles Dyer defendant - Viz -

1. Reason is because all Estates espetially Lands & Heridatements belonging to A Soluent Jntestate person Dieing without Jssue falls to ye next of kin: See: Law Wills fo: 158 Sec. 2. Administration Must bee granted to ye next of Kin or to Some body to preserue for ye next of Kin[2] Againe Law Conueyances - Shews plainely that y^r is An Heire & Estate of Jnheretance here & theirfor directs how Land & Houses in fee Simple Shall bee Conveighed.[3]

2. Reason is because m^rs Justin Patten ye Relict of m^r Nath Patten Deceased (Although Administratorix) yet is not either Heire or Asignee of m^r Nath Patten Deceased but only hath A title of Dowrie fo 1/3 of ye Housing & Land according to ye Law title Dowrie (which is not denied hir) dureing hir life,[4] The deed is to Nath Patten his Heires & Assignes - Jf

---

2. As found in the Code of 1672 Section 2 of the Title "Wills" read as follows: "And because many Merchants, Seamen and other Strangers, resorting hither oftentimes, Dying and leaving their Estates undisposed of, and very difficult to be preserved in the interim from one County Court to another: It is therefore Ordered, that it shall...be Lawfull for any two Magistrates... to allow of any Will of any deceased party, to the Executors or other persons in the Will mentioned, so as the Will be testified on the Oath of two or more Witnesses, and also to grant Administration to the Estate of any person dying intestate within the said County, to the next of Kin, or to such as shall be able to secure the same for the next of Kin...." <u>Laws of 1672</u> (Whitmore, ed.) 258.

3. An act of 1651 which appeared in the Code of 1672 in the Title "Coneyances" carried the following preamble: "Whereas the unskilfullness of some, that make Deeds and Conveyances of Houses and Lands, the word Heire is oftentimes omitted, when as an Estate of Inheritance is intended to be passed...this Court ordereth...." The statute then went on to provide that in all deeds and conveyances in which it was intended that an estate of inheritance should pass the deed should be "in these words, or to the like effect; viz, To Have and to Hold the said House or lands respectively, to the Partie or Grantee, His Heires and Assignes for ever; or if it be an Estate entayled, then to Have and to Hold &c: to the Partie or Grantee, and to the Heires of his body Lawfully begotten, or to the Heires Male of his body Lawfully begotten, between such an one his wife...." Whitmore <u>supra</u>.

4. This statute as it appeared in the Code of 1672 was de-

m^rs^ Justin Patten bee neither of y^m^ how Comes Shee by hir right or title Their is noe Conveighance (appearing) vnd^r^ m^r^ Pattens hand & Seale either Deed or Will to Assigne ye premises to hir - And our Law Saith their Shall bee noe Allienation of Houses & Lands but by deed in Wrighting - or by will - Now y^r^ is noe Will neither Written or Nuncupatiue - as apeares per Administration being granted which is neuer done but vpon Jntestate persons Estates.

Neither is Shee Heire A woman is not Heire to hir husband but only hath A title of Dowry as our law prouides.

3. Reason is Because J Conceiue with all humble Subjeci The County Court hath not power to alienate Houses or Land of an Jntestate from ye Heirs -- allthough as for Mouables they may Asigne ye widow hir part & ye Children & other Heires their portions as per ye Law wills which Shews their is other heirs in law (besides Children) vnto mouables much more to Houses & Lands which are Estates reall, allso the Said Law Shews (in my Aprehension) that ye Courts power is limited in ye Disposall & Setlement of Mouables of an Jntestate they must bee disposed to Widow Children & other Heires, & not from ye Heires And J thinke this law Relates only to mouables or Estates personall - Jf Soe y^n^ ye Court hath noe power at all to dispose of Lands & hereditaments ye Law Dowries saith ye widow Shall haue A third part. See dowries fol: 42 - This Law Dowries is not repealed - but is of force theirfore Jt Canot bee rationall to Assigne ye widow Such A part of as they Shall Judg Just & equall - Can bee men^t^ of houses & Land - but only of Mouables - for then The Law would Contradict it Selfe, ye Law wills would Say A widow may haue either 9/10 or but 1/10 of hir Husband Houses & Land as ye County Court Shall Judg Just & equall - & ye Law Dowries Saith Shee shall haue Just

---

rived from the Laws and Liberties of 1648. In its first form it not only contained provisions consistent with the English law as to the widow's dower interest in her husband's lands, but it contained a provision giving the widow "one third part of all such monie, goods and chattels, real and personal... as her Husband shall dye possessed of...to be allowed and set out to her as is heer before appointed for her Dowrie...". In 1649 this latter portion of the act was repealed, and in place of the widow's absolute right to one third of her husband's personal property she was given "such part of his personal estate" as the judges of the County Court "shall conceive just and equal". 2 Records 281. In the Codes of 1660 and 1672 this latter provision appeared in a somewhat altered form in the third section of the title "Wills": "And it is ordered that when the Husband or Parents dye intestate, the County Court of

1/3 part but J hope y^r is noe Such disagreement or Jncongruitie in ye Law - Theirfore it Seemes plaine to mee y^t ye County Court hath noe power at all by ye Law - Wills to Settle Lands & Heridataments of an Jntestate - but They fall to ye Heire -

Againe J request ye honord Court to Consid^r ye Law Dowries proues plainly The widow of An Jntestate & ye Heire are two Distinct persons - ye widow is not ye Heire - the Heire is to Set out to ye widow of ye Jntestate the Just 3d part ye heire is ye person Seting out & ye person to whom ye 1/3 part is to bee sett out is ye widow - one ye Heire ye other ye Widow.

4. Reason is because Jn° Patten aforesaid is Right Heire to Nath. Patten aforesaid hee is his next Brother theirfore ye next of Kin as appears by ye testimonies Theirfore hath ye Right per Law vnto the premises, and its noe wrong to ye Widow who hath not only hir title of Dowry but A very Considrble estate allso-in-Mouables-as per the Jnuetory may appeare - Jf ye Estate Reall in houses & Lands bee Substracted from ye whole Jmuentory[5] Their is Remaineing in ye Widows hand in Mony goods & good Debts - the vallue of £562-00 money - which with ye 1/3 of ye Estate Reall is A very Comfortable Estate which J hope may bee enough to find hir A Comfortable maintenance during hir Life And allso bee Suficient to Raise A portion for Bonn Beale Sutable either to ye Relation y^r was betwixt him & Nath Patten as A Remoate kinsman Not of ye wholl blod - And allso Sutable to all ye Jngagements y^r was in m^{rs} Patten to doe for him, soe as Shee as ye widow Nor hee as A Kinsman need not Seeke to disinherit ye Right & Lawfull Heire -

Humbly requesting the honoured Court & Jury to Consid^r ye premises which is of Soe great Consequence Not only to Jn° Patten But vnto posterity Crauing pardon for what may seems to reflect vpon ye Honoured Court appealed from herby Solemnly de claring that J Jntende noe reflection vpon y^m but only A Cleare Dem.ration (According to Law) of ye Justness & equitye of my Case Now Comitted vnto yo^w whose J am Acording as in duty bounde.

The Patten-Attorny as aforesaid

---

that Jurisdiction where the party had his last Residence, shall have power to assign to the widdow such part of his estate as they shall judge just and equal...". Those provisions of the Code of 1648, however, in which the widow was given a life estate in one third of the lands of her husband continued in the Code of 1672 under the special Title "Dowries".

5. In the first section of the Title "Wills" the Code of 1672 spoke of the duty of executors and administrators to bring in "a true Inventory of all the known Lands, Goods and Debts of the deceased".

These Reasons of Appeal were received from Thomas Patten Feb^{ry} 25th 1673. per Js^{a} Addington Cler

[Defendant's Answer to Plaintiff's Reasons]

Giles Dyer His Answ^{r} to Thomas Patten Attorney to his Father John Patten Reasons of Appeale:

Jmp^{rs} As to his First p^{r}tended Reason or Assertion that the whole Estate of a p^{r}son Dying Jntestate falls to ye next A kin: Wee Vtterly Deny. And for his proofe he sites ye Law title Wills sect: 2d: Which Law Wholly belongs to Merch^{ts} Seamen And other Straing^{rs} Resorting hither Dying & Leauing there Estates vndisposed of and hauing noe Wife nor Children here but haue there Relations as Wife & Children Jn Other parts of ye Wourld as ye Law Doth absolutely & Clearely Demonstrate and hath noe Ration at All to Nath^{ll} Patten of Dorchester that Dyed here: And before ye Law bee Altered ye Appellantts Case Can haue noe Dependance vpon itt.

2: To his 2d Assertion or p^{r}tended Reson itt hath Litle of Reson or Law in Itt as J Conceaue. For him to say that she is neith^{r} Heire nor Assigne of m^{r} Nath^{ll} Patten deceased, I Answ^{r} Although shee Be neither Heire or Assigne yet she is the Relict of Nath^{ll} Patten And that part of ye Estate that she hath Allowed to her is hers of Right by vertue of Law title Wills Sect the 3d Page 158 wch saith ye County Courtt hath pow^{r} to Allow the Widdow such A part of ye Estate of ye Deceased as they shall Judg Just and Equall And this Estate now sued for they haue allowed And giuen to ye Relict of ye said m^{r} Patten As Appeareth by the Courtt Record. Which Law Form^{r}ly Coated Title Wills Sec^{t}: the 3d Doth Absolutely Say That the County Court Are Jmpowred Soe to Act which J Desire the Honord Court and Jury to Consid^{r} of and peruse the same:

3: And To his 3d Reson whereas he saith the County Courtt hath noe pow^{r} To Allienate Houses and Lands from the Heire: I Answer first the Honord Courtt Hath pow^{r} to Alienate or Giue to ye Widdow what Part of ye Estate ye Deseased Left And If houses and Lands be part of ye Relicts Estate then they haue Pow^{r} to giue to ye Widdow ye houses and Lands - or what part of them they please as by ye Law before Recited Appeares; but from ye heire it is nott Giuen butt A partt As they see good Js giuen to ye Widow and the Rest Js giuen to ye Right Heire in Law According to or Law: 2dly Whereas He saith it is only Ment the Meoueables: All Estates in this Country by o^{r} Law Are Chatles nott Jnheritances soe y^{t} ye Widdow hath A Just and Legall Right to A partt in All & such A part as the Courtt shall Judg meettee: And for him to say shee Must Come to him for her thirds of ye Estate, ye Defend^{t} Humbly Conceaues that the Relict would haue As Little A partt of ye Estate as she had of the mony her husband Left in his Chest when he Dyed and that he was too much betrusted with ye kee of her husbands

Chest, For Jf he had been true & trusty he wold haue made his Words good that it Wold after his vnkells Death Appeare y[t] benjamin Beale was y[e] sole Executor & Heire of her Husbands Estate, and 3dly to y[e] Law, Title Dowries Jtt hath Relation to Estates sold by y[e] Husband without the Consentt of y[e] Wife that she shall haue her thirds of y[e] Same During her life notwithstanding Sold by her husband before his Death which Js to p[r]uentt men from Leauing there Wiues Destitute.

4: To his 4th Reson That John Patten Js Right Heire to M[r] Nath[ll] Patten And the nextt Brother Js yett to proue and that He is y[e] next Akin is nott att all Proued: Butt wee haue Sufficiently proued Benjamin Beale to bee the Next of kin And the Rightt Heire to the Estate by Will and by Gift for he had partt of M[r] Nath[ll] Pattens Estate giuen to him and Jn his possession before his Death as all that att Halseys wharfe and Receiued the Rentt of the same and After y[e] fire was & had burned Downe the Housing M[r] Nath[ll] Paten Wold not build them vp againe because he said he had given them to Benjamin Beale: soe y[t] by Will and by Gift Jtt is sufficiently proued y[t] Benjamin Beale is y[e] Rightfull Heire to y[e] Estate for y[e] Deceased Patten And for him to say that the meoueables were A sufficient Estate for m[rs] Justin Patten and for Benjamin Beales Portion J hope it will nott Come to y[t] that the Widdow and the Heire shal be Att his Disposall, the Estate being already Disposed of By the Hono[rd] County Courtt who had Sufficient pow[r] soe to Doe & haue Done According to Law: And for the Appellantt to say y[t] Benjamin Beale is Nott of Blood I Wond[r] he will Assert such A positiue vntruth, But Jf an own sisters son be nott Blood I Leaue to y[e] Hono[rd] Courtt and Jury to Judg: soe Hauing sufficiently proued the Estate of Right by Law to belong to m[rs] Justin Patten J shall Leaue Jtt to y[e] Hono[rd] Court and Jury Hoping & nott questioning butt the Hono[rd] Courtt and Gentlemen of the Jury Will see Just Cause to Confirme the form[r] Juries Verdict.

Giles X Dyre

[The record of the case on review in the Court of Assistants is in 1 <u>Records of the Court of Assistants</u> 4.]

Thomas Pattyn Atturney to John Pattyn plaintiff ag[t] Giles Dyer Deffend[t] in an Accon of Appeale from the Judgment of the last County Court in Boston. After the Attachment Court Judgment reasons of Appeale & euidences in the case produced were read Comitted ot the Jury & remajne on file wth the Records of this Court the Jury brought in their virdict they found for the Deffendant confirmation of the former Judgment & Costs of Courts fifty one shillings & sixpence - 1st Jur.

<u>Patten</u> v. <u>Winsley</u>
1 <u>Records of Suffolk County Court</u> 377 (1673/4)

Thomas Patten Attourny unto Iohn Patten of Severells in the parish of Crewkern in the County of Sommers^{t} in the Kingdom of England yeoman who is the Lawfull & proper heire of or to the Estate that sometimes was Nathaniell Pattens Late of Dorchest in New England deceased plaint. ags^{t} Iohn Winsley Defend^{t} in an accion of the case for that the s^{d} Iohn Winsley doth refuse to deliver possession of a certain warehouse & Land belonging & adjoining to the same lying & being upon the Land commonly called Halsey's wharge which warehouse & Land is between the brewhouse & Land in the possession of Robert Cox & another Warehouse in the possession & occupation of s^{d} Iohn Winsley which belongeth unto s^{d} Iohn Patten as heire afores^{d} by reason of which refusall of possession the s^{d} heire is damnified to the value of the aboues^{d} Summe or thereabout with other due damages according to Attachm^{t} Dat Ianuary 20 1673. ... The Iury ... founde for the Defend^{t} costs of Court.

The plaint. appealed from this judgm^{t} to the next Court of Assistants & the s^{d} Tho: Patten as principall in ten pounds & Nicholas Page & Anthony Checkly as Sureties in five pounds apeice acknowledged themselves respectively bound to ... prosecute his Appeal. ...

[The following depositions throw light on the issues involved.]

S.F.1281.11

Justin Patten aged about Eighty six Yeares deposed testifieth that Shee was present when her Sister Bale the mother of Benjamin Bale & Sister to her husband Nathaniell Patten deceased lay upon her death bed Long since in England & Shee the sd. mrs Bale at that time expressed much trouble lying upon her concerning her sonn Benjamin how hee might bee provided for after her decease? Whereupon the husband of this Deponant aforesd. applying himselfe to his sd. Sister Bale desired her not to trouble herselfe in that matter for hee would take her Sonn Benjamin to bee as his own Childe whereupon Shee was much gladded and cheered And accordingly the sd. Nathaniell Patten did forthwith take charge of the sd. Benjamin & paide for his Nursing & Education in England for many Yeares together & afterwards hee brought over the sd Benjamin into New-England & here tooke the like care of him & still expressed the same purpose towards him. And further this Deponent saith that her husbands Father when hee dyed gaue all his land to Iohn & Thomas Patten the younger brothers of her husband Nathaniell Patten & further saith not.

Taken upon Oath May 5th 1673 Before us. William Stoughton
Edward Tyng

... true Coppie ... Js^{a} Addington Cler

The Deposicion of Robert Cox aged about 40 yeares testifieth & saith That about three yeares past Nathaniell Patten of Dorchester now deceased did positiuely declare to him at his house at Dorchester & severall times since that hee had appointed & ordered Benjamin Beale to act in & dispose of his concerns in a house scituate or being on the land formerly belonging to George Halsy, in which house the sd. Deponant formerly lived: and that mr Patten Ordered the Keys of the sd. house to bee left by the Deponant in the hands of Benjamin Beale, the sd. Patten Saying that hee had giuen possession & giuen order unto the sd. Benjamin Beale & full power to dispose of & looke after the land neere to the sd. house & further this Deponant saith not.

Taken upon Oath, Novemb^r 1:1672: before Edw: Tyng Assist.
Copia vera per Js^a Addington Cler

The Deposicion of Iohn Carthew aged about 33 yeares testifieth & saith. That about three yeares past hee was tenant in a house hee tooke & rented of Benjamin Beale in a short time after Robert Cox had left it: and the Deponant further testifieth & saith that hee did severall times make a tender & offer of the rent of the sd. house to mr Nathaniell Patten of Dorchester now deceased, the sd Patten affirming that there was noe rent due unto him refused to receive it & further this Deponant saith not.

Taken upon Oath. Novemb^r 1:1672. before Edw. Tyng Assist.
Copia Vera per Js^a Addington Cler

[Plaintiff's Reasons for Appeal]

Thomas Patten Attourny to his Father John Patten of Severalls in the parish of Crewkern in the County of Sommersett in the Kingdom of England, his Reasons of Appeal to this Honoured Court of Assistants from the Iudgment of the Last County Court held in Boston in January. 1673. in the case betwixt himselfe plaintiff & Mr John Wensley Defendant.

1. Reason, the Legall Right & title unto the purmises doth appertain unto the sd. John Patten.

2. Because Benjamin Beale who is the pretended Owner hath noe title unto the same.

For the Explanation of these foregoing Assertions I shall Lay down & prove

1. That all Lands & hereditaments belonging to a solvent person, the sd person dying intestate not having disposed of sd Lands in his lifetime fall to the next of Kinn.

2. That mr Nathaniell Patten dyed intestate.

3. That hee did not by what appeares dispose of this Estate in his lifetime.

4. That John Patten aforesd is that person next of Kinn & the right heire of Nathaniell Patten aforesd deceased.

1. For the first see Law, Wills, 2, Sect. fo: 158. where Administracion must bee granted to the next of Kinn or to such as shall keepe & secure the same for the next of Kinn: here it's plain the next of Kinn haue the title - Again the same Law. Sect. 3rd when the husband or parent dye intestate the County Court of that Iurisdiction shall have power to Settle the Estate per assigning & setting out the Widow & Children or other heires theire severall parts & portions of the sd Estate here the Courts power I humbly conceive is limited - they may Settle the Estate upon the heires but not give it from them, this Law shews plainly there are heires unto whome Estates descend - Moreover the Law Conveyances. Sect. 2. directeth how to convey Jnheritances - Namely to have & to hold the houses or Lands to the Grantee his heires & assignes for ever; well then here is Estates of Inheritances & heires per o^r^ Law, from whome the County Courts have not power to give these Jnheritances - I hope I shall not bee soe mistaken as if I ment o^r^ Lands to bee such Inheritances as cannot bee alienate per will or Deed or taken per Execucion for Debt I doe not argue soe (although per intailes they may bee made soe). Yet this is true that though they may bee sold or give or taken for debt[6] Yet when noe such thing is & the Owner dyeth intestate, then they fall to the heire - Namely to the next of Kinn or most worthy of the whole blood; by o^r^ Charter wee hold o^r^ Land

---

6. An act of the General Court of October 1640, had provided as follows: "Wheras many men in the plantation are in debt, & heare is not money sufficient to discharge the same, though their cattle and goods should bee sould for halfe their worth, as experience hath shewn upon some late executions, whereby a great part of the people in the country may bee undone, & yet their debts not satisfied, though they have sufficient upon an equall valewation to pay all, & live comfortably upon the rest, it is therefore ordered, that upon every execution for debts past, the officer shall take land, houses, corne, cattle, fish or other commodities, & deliver the same in full satisfaction to the creditor at such prices as the same shalbee valewed at by 3 understanding & indifferent men, to bee chosen, the one by the creditor, another by the debtor, & the third by the marshall; and the creditor is at liberty to take his choice of what goods hee will; & if hee hath not sufficient goods to discharge it, then hee is to take his house or land as aforesaid." 1 Records 307. The substance of this statute was incorporated in the Codes of 1648 and 1672 under the titles "Levies" and

in free & common Soccage, now that tenure descends to heires as other Lands doe-being in fee Simple as this house & Land in question is: See the Deed from Halsey to Nathaniell Patten is it not to him his heires & Assignes for ever; which tearmes make it fee simple - This Estate must fall to the heire or to the Assignes - now if it bee not legally Assigned it is Iohn Pattens as heire - Now concerning Assignements such as may Alienate land & houses from the Grantor & his heires they must bee made either per will or by Deed; as for Wills they may bee either Nuncupative or written; but mr Nathaniell Patten dyed intestate; neither making Nuncupative or written Will, the Courts granting Administracion upon the Estate sufftiently proveth that, therefore I shall not insist upon it; Jt being cleare that here is noe Assignement of the pu[r]misses per will Again there is noe Assignement of this Estate per Deed & without it bee done either per will or Testament or per Deed in writing it's not good in Law: - See Conveyances Deeds & writings Sect: 1: 2: - fo: 32 - where it's plaine that alienations of houses & Land shall not bee good in Law except the same bee done per Deed in writing except Land given per a Town or per will - Now all the testimonies which the Defendant hath brought doe not at all prove there was any Deed of gift made to Ben: Bale per mr Nath: Patten some say hee promised to doe it & some say hee saide hee had done it, but none say soe much as that hee declared J doe doe such a thing: But if there had been 20. Witnesses that had Sworn they hear mr Patten Say I doe give Ben[n] Bale this or that house or Land - it's noe title for o[r] Law allowed of noe verball Deeds or alienations, except per will & here is noe will at all: Therefore Ben[n] Bale is not the Assignee of mr Nathaniell Patten in the pu[r]misses, there being noe Deed or Will to make him soe: And as for what is conteined in the testimonies concerning mr Pattens taking Ben[n] Bale as his heire, Some say hee brought him over as his Childe, some others say mr Patten saide hee intended to doe well for him & some say hee saide hee intended it: But where is the act of Adoption proved or any other legall act either per Deed or Will to prove Ben[n] Bale either heire or Assigne to the pu[r]misses: If soe bee that mr Nathaniell Patten had such a kindness for him that hee intended to use him as a Sonn; why did hee not Settle [torn] something considerable at his coming to age, which is long sin[torn] marriage - Soe it's plaine that Ben[n] Bale is neither heire n[torn] to Nathaniell Patten: The Deed is made to Nathaniell Patten [torn] & assignes for ever: Ben: Bale is neither of them: how comes[torn] his title? Jf it's saide it is setled upon him per the County Court - I

"Marshal" respectively.

haue saide & proved per Law that the Court hath noe such power, in the Law title Wills. Sect. 3. (which Estate relates onely to Movables as J shall after demonstrate). There the Courts power is Limited, it cannot bee given from Children or other heires, and there the eldest Sonn must have a double portion and if no Sonns, then the Daughters shall inherit as Copartners - Now if the Courts power bee so Limited, that they cannot dispose of intestate persons Movables, but to widow, Children, or other heires; much more must it bee Limited in disposall of Lands in fee simple - My Arguments to prove the Law before quoted relates onely to Movables & not to houses & Lands & other hereditaments are the Law, title Dowers - fo: 42 expressly sith, a woman shall haue a third of houses & Lands &c. but the Law title Wills gives power to the County Court to give such a part of the Estate as they judge just & equall to the Widow - Now if this bee ment of house & land the Law Dowries & Wills contradict one another; but I hope there is noe such incongruity in o^r Law - J hope it's proved that the Court hath noe power to alienate houses & Lands from the right heires. Again in point of Reason it cannot bee thought they may dispose of intestate persons Estates according to theire own pleasure - Jf soe then might they Settle Estates upon Strangers as well as upon Relations; which would prove of ill consequence to posterity.

Again for the proofe of the last thing - namely that John Patten is next of Kinn to Nathaniell Patten, the severall testimonies relating thereuntil will & do sufficiently prove it.

Therefore the pu^r misses in controversy doe appertain unto him falling unto him per naturall descent, in regard m^r Nathaniell Patten dyed intestate, & also noe other way alienated his Estate from his heire at Law, nor could it bee soe alienated per the Court - Neither was hee soe indebted as to require any of his houses & Lands to goe for Satisfaction - humbly requesting this Honored Court & Iury seriously to consider the pu^r misses; which doe not onely deeply concern the Appealants Father; but also is of publique concernment to the Country; Craving pardon for any thing that may bee taken amiss herein - J subscribe myselfe:

Yo^r humble Servant
Tho:Patten Attoruny as aforesd.

These reasons of appeal were received from Thomas Patten February 25, 1673.

per Js^a Addington Cler.

[Defendant's Answer to Plaintiff's Reasons]

Imp^rs To his First Wee possitiuely Deney And Doe Affirme he hath Rightt nor title to ye p^r mises sued for.

2. To His 2d Wee Waue his Negation and Affirme y^t Benjam

Beal Js ye True and Rightfull Owner of ye prmises sued for:

And As to his Explanation of his forgoing Assertions yt ye Said Patten Dying Jntestate Jtt Doth of Right belong to ye nextt of Kin. 1st J Deny he dyed Jntestate for Wee haue proued he made a verball Nuncupatiue Will For he ye said Mr Nathll Patten vpon his Death bed said before Seuerall Wittnesses thatt ye Pattens should haue Nothing to Doe wth Any part of his Estate nott somuch As a Doit of it therefore ye pattens yt prtend An Jntrest Jn itt are Cutt off by Will wch Wee haue proued & Jf they Will goe to ye next of Kin Benjamin Beale who is ye sisters son is ye nextt of Kin, so yt Jf Right ye nextt of Kin must haue ye Estate then Benjamin Beale must haue it by his Own Argumentt And Also Jtt Doth belong to him being ye Adopted son of ye deceased who took him from his Mothers Breast & promised ye same to his sister vpon her Death bed to Make him his heire & so putt him Outt and paid For his Nurseing & scooling in England and Went Ouer out of New Engld to old England to fetch him & Entertained him Jn ye Cabbin of ye Ship, 2dly By Donation Wee proue by Sufficientt Wittness that said Beale should haue All his Estate After his Decease and this Estate In Controursy the Deceased gaue both befor in his Life time and vpon his Death bed Just befor he Dyed he gaue all he had to Benjamin Beale Before seuerall Wittnesses Therefore hauing proued by Donation and by a Noncupatiue Will the Estate to bee Benjamin Beales, and if it Were only by two Wittnesses, Jtt Were Sufficient by ye Law of God and or Law. For ye Law of God Saith thatt by ye Mouth of Two or:3: Wittnesses Euery thing shall be Confirmed, Especially vpon Wills wch is a sollemn thing to be Obserued And kept by ye Scripture Rules. And Also or Law saith & Confirmeth ye same and Js grounded therevpon and hath ben ye practise of or Courts Jn New England.

3. Jf this Estate belongeth to any prson by vertue of Heireship Then to Benj: Beale And not to Jno Patten, 1st that Jtt Doth belong to Ben. Beale as Heire Js Euidentt for Wee haue Sufficiently proued yt he is ye Adopted Heire of the person Deceased for he Brought him ouer from England from his Friends, and Relations For that Very End And or Lands by or Law being Chatles goe nott by Right of Jnheritance but to whom a Man pleaseth to giue them, And that he Gaue the Estate to ye Said Beale and yt he is his Heire We haue sufficiently proued, 2dly That it Doth nott att all belong to the said John Patten is Euidentt by the Resons Last Giuen Also by his possitiue Will. Vpon his Death bed From time to Time the Said patten declared thatt the Pattens should not haue any partt of his Estate butt had Cheated him of Enough Already But the said Benjamin Beale should be Heire of all he had, & And yt he should be A knaue Jf he Did not Doe soe Well for him ye Said Beale as he had Done Jn giuing him his Estate.

3. As To ye Assertion of ye Appellt Jn Taking vpon him to Jterprit or Laws, J hope ye Honord Courtt will Take notise

of and there plea to ye Law of England Js quite besides or Byases & whatt or Jury are Sworne to, who are to goe According to or Law, & J question nott but they will mind and Attend too, Butt that yt they Assertt Jf there had ben A Will to bee seene of ye Deceaseds there had ben noe Need of Administration (We Doubt nott butt Jf ye Appellantt had ben Honest there had ben A sufficient Will seen before now to haue Cleared vp this Case Fully For he ye [Ap]lt said that after his vnkell was Dead thatt itt should appeare thatt ye said Beale was Heire & executor of all: And yt they should see itt Butt it was quicly Lost:) But Administration many times Js graunted where there is A will made: where pt of ye Estate is Left Outt, And Especially vpon Nuncupatiue Wills where a man hath an Estate graunte & giuen to him, he must haue some thing from Authority to shew by vertue of whatt Rightt he hould ye same And that the Courtt hath Acted According to Law Js plaine and Evidentt as ye Law Title Will Sect: 3d: For ye County Courtt hath Powr by Law to sett outt to the Widdow and other Heires if noe Children the Estate of ye Deceased persons, and yt Benj: Beale Is the Heire Wee haue sufficiantly proued, And as to the Law one which he Grounds his Resons of Appeale vpon, Title Wills sect: 2d: hath only Refferance to Merchts Seamen - other Strainrs Resorting hither Dying and Leauing there Estates vndisposed of Butt this prson mr Nathll Patten Was Noe such prson butt an Jnhabitantt here Att Dorchester & there Dyed and the Estate he Left is Disposed of According to Law as Wee haue before Cited, And Jf ye plt will haue yt to be Law wch he Cites Title Wills sect: 2d: he must stay while the Genrll Courtt hath Altered itt As ye Court and Jury may se by ye prface how it Runs & Whom it hath Relation too One wch the whole Law hangs & Depends & hath Relation too: And thus Hauing Sufficiently Proued Benj. Beale The Rightfull Heire to the Estate Wee Doubt Nott butt ye Honord Courtt and Jury Will see Justt Cause to Confirme the formr Courtts Judgt.

4: To His many Other Large prtences they are nott Worth Answering, Only ye Law Title Conveyances itt hath Only Relation to Lands Sold nott to any gift by Will or otherwise as the Law. Sect: 2d. There Clearely Demonstrates, All Which Wee shall Leaue To ye Honord Courtt and Jury to Judg off

Richard Way

[The record of this case on appeal in the Court of Assistants is in 1 Records of the Court of Assistants 4.]

Thomas Pattyn Atturney to Jno Pattyn plaintiff agt Jno Winsley defendt in an action of Appeale from the Judgment of the last County Court in Boston - After the Attachment Courts Judgment Reasons of Appeale & other euidences in the case produced were read comitted to the Jury & remajne on file wth the Records of this Court the Jury brought in their verdict they found for the deffendant Confirmation of the former Judgment & Costs of Courts twenty /shillings/ pence.

/After his unsuccessful appeal to the Court of Assistants in Patten v. Winsley the plaintiff petitioned the General Court for relief. There it was judged meet "to grant the petitioner a hearing of his case at the next session (5 Records 9). At the October sitting (1674) the following proceedings of the General Court are recorded (5 Records 23):/

In ans[r] to the petition of Thomas Pattyn, sonn and atturney to John Pattyn of the parish of Crookehorne, in the county of Somerset, in England, clayming right as next heire vnto Nathaniell Patten, late of Dorchester, in New England, deceased who died intestate, this Court hauing considered the pleas & euidences of y[e] s[d] Patten, & just allegations & euidences of Benjamin Beale, of Dorchester, in New England, sisters son to the deceased, doe not see reason according to our lawe to admitt John Pattyn, of Crookehorne, aforesaid, to be heire vnto the reall estate of Nathaniel Patten, deceased; but for a fynall issue of this case, doe order and determine as followeth: 1. That the relict & widdow of Nathaniel Patten doe quietly and peaceably enjoy to hir and hir heires, executors, and administrators for euer, that part of the estate set out & ordered vnto her by the County Court of Suffolke. Secondly. Touching all the rest of the estate of Nathaniel Patten, deceased, it is ordered that it be divided into two aequall parts, one pte whereof shall be & is hereby given to Benjamin Beale, aforesaid, his heires, executors, administrators, & assignes for euer; and the other part shall be & is hereby given to Thomas Patten, aturney vnto John Patten, for the vse of the said John Patten, or any other person concerned, to him or them, & to his or their heires, executors, administrators, & assignes for euer; and Thomas Patten (according to his engagement) is ordered to pay forthwith ten pounds in money for the Courts chardges in hearing the case.

In 1684 the charter of The Massachusetts Bay Company was annulled in scire facias proceedings in Chancery. It was not until 1691 that settled forms of government were reestablished under the Provincial Charter then issued. With respect to the problems of law its most important provisions were those under which the General Court was continued as the legislative body, made up of an elected House of Representatives and of an upper chamber, the Council, chosen, subject to the Governor's veto, by the House of Representatives. The Governor, of course, became a non-elective officer, appointed by the King. The home government, having learned by experience that effective controls over the legislative and judicial processes of law-making were essential if conformity to the law of England was to be a reality, included in the Provincial charter provisions for the royal examination of all legislation and for appeals to the King in Council.

The establishment of a new system of government did not, however, eradicate all colonial habits and customs. No general repeal of earlier legislation occurred, nor was any systematic effort made to consolidate or codify the law of the Province. The result of this informality was that much of the earlier legislation of the colonial period continued to have effect as the common law of the Province. The consequence necessarily was confusion. The character of that confusion is shown in the issues presented in the case of Winthrop v. Lechmere, where the Connecticut and Massachusetts courts, and the Privy Council in England dealt with issues which had been of critical importance in the Patten cases, above.

The following statutes of the provincial legislature of Massachusetts sought in a characteristic way to keep alive under provincial administration rules and habits of the Colonial period.

Province Law of November 1, 1692
1 Acts and Resolves of the Province of
Massachusetts Bay, p. 43

Whereas estates in these plantations do consist chiefly of lands which have been subdued and brought into improvement by the industry and labour of the proprietors, with the assistance of their children, the younger children generally having been longest and most serviceable unto their parents in that behalf, who have not personal estates to give unto them in portions or otherwise to recompence their labour,

Be it therefore enacted ...

That every person lawfully seized of any lands, tenements, or hereditaments within this province, in his own proper right in fee simple, shall have power to give and dispose, and devise ... all such lands, tenements and hereditaments to and among his children or others, as he shall think fit at his pleasure; and if no such disposition, gift or devise be made by the owner of such lands, tenements and hereditaments, the same shall be subject to a division, with his personal estate, and be alike distributed, according to the rules hereinafter expressed for intestate estates. And whereas and so often as it shall happen, that any person dyes intestate, administration of such intestate's goods and estate shall be granted unto the widow or next of kin to the intestate, or both, as the judge for probate of wills and granting of administration shall think fit; who thereupon take bond with sureties in manner as is directed by the statute of the twenty-second and twenty-third of Charles the Second,[1] and shall and may proceed to

1. In this Statute of Distributions, dealing with the re-

call such administrators to account for, and touching the goods of the intestate; and, upon due hearing and consideration thereof ... the said judge shall, and hereby is fully impowered to order and make a just distribution of the surplusage or remaining goods and estate as well real as personal, in manner following ... one third part of the personal estate to the wife of the intestate forever, besides her dower or thirds in the houses and lands during life ... and all the residue ... by equal portions, to and among his children ... except the eldest son then surviving ... who shall have a double portion of the whole. ...

Province Law of December 5, 1719
2 Acts and Resolves of the Province of
Massachusetts Bay, p. 151

Be it enacted ... 1. That after the death of any person intestate, letters of administration be taken out within thirty days, or sooner, and an inventory taken of all of the estate of the deceased within three months, or sooner, by three suitable persons, appointed and put upon oath for their due performance of that service ...

2. That when the executor or administrator of any estate shall obtain license from the superior court to make sale of all or any part of the housing and lands of the deceased, for the payment of debts, before sale be made of any such housing and lands, the executor or administrator shall give thirty days publick notice ...

3. That from and after the end of this present session of the general assembly, all such estate, whether real or personal that is not plainly given away or disposed of in and by the last will and testament ... the same accordingly shall be distributed in the same manner as if it were an intestate estate, and the executor or executors shall administer on the same as such.

---

sponsibility of administrators to the ecclesiastical courts, the form of bond to be given by administrators was prescribed. That bond made it the duty of the administrator to make a "true and perfect inventory of all and singular the goods, chattels, and credits" of the decedent.

Winthrop v. Lechmere[1]
Decree of King in Council
7 Conn. Colonial Records 571 (1727)

At the Court at St. James's, the 15th day of February, 1727 ...

Upon reading this day at the Board a Report from the Rt. Honble the Lords of the Committee for hearing Appeals from the Plantations, dated the 20th day of December last, in the words following, viz:

In obedience to an Order in Council of the 13th of May last referring to this committee the humble petition and appeal of John Winthrop, of New London in his Majesty's Colony of Connecticut, Esq., only son and heir at law of Major General Wait Winthrop, of Boston in New England, Esq., his late father, deceased, ... their Lordships this day took the said petition into consideration; which said petition sets forth (amongst other things) the charter of incorporation granted to the said Province by King Charles the second, on the 13 of April, in the 14th year of his reign, by which the lands of the said colony are held of the Crown, as of the manor of East Greenwich in Kent, in free and common soccage, and the laws which they are empowered to make are to be wholesome and reasonable, and not contrary to the law of England; and that the petitioner was possessed of and entitled to a very considerable real estate in the said Province, as heir at law to his said father Wait Winthrop, and his uncle the Honorable Fitz John Winthrop, both deceased: That his said father Waite Winthrop dyed intestate, leaving issue only the petitioner and one daughter, Anne, who was preferred in marriage in her father's life time to Thomas Lechmere, of Boston aforesaid, merchant; and that on his said father's death he became intitled to all his real estate wherof he dyed seized in fee, as his heir at law; and that on the 21 of February, 171 7/8, at the court of probate held for the county of New London in Connecticut, letters of administration were granted to the petitioner of the goods, chattels, rights and credits of his father, and he entered into bond to the judge of the said court of probates in 3000 l. penalty, with condition for his making a true inventory of all and singular the goods, chattels and credits of the said deceased, and exhibit the same into the registry of the said court of probates, and truly to administer

---

1. For a detailed account of this litigation see Andrews, The Influence of Colonial Conditions as illustrated in the Connecticut Intestacy Law, 1 Select Essays 431.

the same according to law.[2] But the petitioner having paid and advanced more to and for and on account of the said Thomas Lechmere than the said Ann his wife's share of the said intestate's personal estate come to the petitioner's hands amounted to, and the said Thomas and Ann Lechmere having possessed most part of the said Waite Winthrop's personal estate, and not having required the petitioner to exhibit any inventory or account of his administration, and the petitioner having discharged all his said father's debts, save only one bond for 300 l. on which he duly discharged all interest, and would have paid off the principal but the obligee declined accepting the same, the petitioner did not, for these reasons, think it necessary to exhibit any inventory or account of his said administration. But in order to ruin and oppress the petitioner, six years after the said letters of administration so granted to the petitioner (viz.) in July, 1724, the said Thomas Lechmere applied to the court of probates, insisting he was, in right of his wife, entituled to a proportion of the said Wait Winthrop's real estate, but that he was kept thereout by the petitioner's not having inventoried and adminstred the same, and caused the petitioner to be summoned by the court of probates, to shew cause why he neglected to inventory the intestate's estate and finish his administration according to his bond; upon which the petitioner exhibited an inventory of the said intestate's personal estate in the said court of probates, and the petitioner at the foot thereof insisted, administrators had nothing to do with lands, they belonging to the heir at law, and that he was in possession thereof as his right of inheritance according to the law of England, and therefore he was not obliged to exhibit any account of the real estate, that not being cognizable by a court of probates and which inventory the petitioner prayed might be accepted and recorded: but the court declared they were satisfyed the same was not a true and perfect inventory of all the said intestate's estate within that county, and that the petitioner's objections were against law, and decreed that the said inventory should not be admitted, and refused to accept it as such an inventory of the intestate's estate as ought to be exhibited; and the said Thomas Lechmere in the same July put the petitioner's said administration bond in suit against

---

2. The Connecticut statute of distributions (4 Conn. Records 306) enacted in 1699 was substantially identical with the Massachusetts statute of November 1, 1692, supra. That statute had been transmitted to England, in accordance with the requirements of the Province Charter, and had not been disallowed. The Connecticut Act, instead of incorporating by reference the bond prescribed in the statute of 22 and 23 Charles II, set forth

him, and at the same time, in his own name and the name of Abel Wally, brought another action against the petitioner, as they had been sureties for him in an administration bond for his duty administring the intestate's estate, in the county of Suffolk in the Massachusetts Bay, alledging such administration bond had been sued and recovered from them, on account of the petitioner's not having exhibited an inventory or brought in his administration accounts; and the said Thomas Lechmere also, at the same time, brought four several writs of partition in his own name and in the name of his wife Ann, stiling her only daughter and coheir of the said Wait Winthrop, to recover from the petitioner one third of the real estate in the said writs mentioned, insisting the said Ann was coheir thereto with the petitioner, and as such, by the law of the Province, she was entitled to one third of the said real estate; and that on full and fair hearings, the final judgments in all said six actions were given for the petitioner.

That it thus appearing the petitioner's inheritance could not be split and tore to pieces by the common ordinary means of justice, as the law was then understood, some more irresistable way was to be found out to oppress the petitioner; and for that purpose, the said Thomas Lechmere preferred a petition to the General Assembly, in 1725, in the name of himself and his wife, setting forth the said several judgments given against him, and that they were never likely to recover of the petitioner one third of the said real estate, tho' the same descended, as they alledged, to the said Ann and the petitioner as coheirs of their father, without the aid and relief of that Assembly, and that, either by reason of the insufficiency of the diction of the law of the Colony already made, or by the court's sense or exposition thereof; for they had no remedy by the court of probates, for that the petitioner refused to inventory the real estates; and, as the law of the Colony had given them a right to one third of the premises, it was not consistent with the honour of the Colony but that the government would afford some indisputable method for their better obtaining their said right; and to that end they prayed the Assembly to set aside the said judgments and to grant a new tryal, wherein they might, notwithstanding the exposition of the superiour court upon the law, well support their said actions of partition: which petition, tho' of so very extraordinary nature, the Assembly received and ordered the petitioner to attend to answer the same. That the petitioner put in his answer, insisting there was nothing contained in the said petition that called for the interposition of the Assem-

---

the provisions of that bond <u>in extenso</u>.

bly, or in which they ought or could give any relief; notwithstanding which, and without any hearing, the Assembly resolved that relief might and ought to be had in the probates in such like cases by a new grant of administration, exhibiting an inventory of the whole estate, and a distribution made according to the rules of law upon the whole; and at the same time, tho' they came to this resolve, they dismissed the said Lechmere's petition.

That the petitioner, by this very extraordinary resolve finding the danger he was in, again exhibited to the court of probates a full and true inventory of his father's personal estate come to his hands, valued and appraised, and again insisted in writing at the foot thereof, that administrators had nothing to do with lands, they belonging to him as heir at law and as his right of inheritance according to the law of England, and that no real estate ought by law to be exhibited not cognizable by a court of probates; and the petitioner moved the court to have the same accepted as a full inventory of all the intestate's estate within that Colony proper for a court of probates by law to demand, and offered his oath that it was the whole personal estate of the deceased: But the court insisting on the petitioner's taking an oath, that it was an inventory of the whole of the intestate's real as well as personal estate, which the petitioner refused to comply with, insisting he ought not to inventory any real estate: Whereupon the said court, by their sentence of the 29th of June, 1725, rejected the said inventory and refused to accept the same; from which sentence of denyal the petitioner appealed to the superior court. That after the said appeal, and before it came on to be determined, the said Lechmere commenced a suit in the court of probates to have administration granted to him of the said intestate's estate; and the petitioner being summoned to show cause, why administration should not be granted to the said Lechmere, for cause insisted on his said appeal being depending and which cause the said court allowed. From which allowance the said Lechmere also appealed to the said superior court.

That on the 28th Sept. 1725, the superior court, on hearing the petitioner's appeal, declared that they were of opinion that real as well as personal estates were ordered to be inventoried by the law of that Colony, and that all courts of probates ought to be guided in their administrations thereby, notwithstanding the laws of England do not ordain that real estates should be inventoried; and that thereupon ordered that the petitioner should not be admitted to evidence to the said inventory by any other oath than that which was agreeable to the laws of the Province; and affirmed the judgment of the court of probates, and condemned the petitioner in costs: from which judgment the petitioner prayed, and was allowed, a review to the next superior court. And the said Lechmere's appeal coming on at the same time, the court also in that suit affirmed the judgment of the court of probates; from which sentence the said Lechmere prayed, and was allowed, a review likewise.

That, on hearing the petitioner's said appeal on the review, on the 22d of March, 172 5/6, the court affirmed their said former judgment and condemned the petitioner in costs; and on the said Lechmere's review, which came on at the same time, the said superior court, forasmuch as the petitioner's said appeal was then determined, adjudged that the said letters of administration formerly granted the petitioner should be vacated, and the same was thereby vacated, and that the said Thomas Lechmere and Ann his wife should have administration on the deceased's estate; and the said superior court thereby granted the power of administration to the said Thomas and Ann Lechmere on the said intestate's estate, and condemned the petitioner in costs; from both which judgments of the superior court the petitioner prayed, but was in a very extraordinary manner denyed, an appeal to his late Majesty in Council; but which appeal he was admitted to, upon his petition to his late Majesty.

That the petitioner, finding his inheritance in this imminent danger of being torn to pieces, all application for relief to his Majesty being denyed him: to prevent, if possible, any thing being done in the premises till he could lay his case before his Majesty, entered and filed his protest, as heir at law to his father, against granting letters of administration to his father's estate to any other person whatever, the court having before lodged that power with the petitioner, and also against any division of any real estate pretended to belong to the petitioner's father, all such real estate being the petitioner's undoubted right of inheritance, who was seized and possessed of the same according to the laws of England, and which he was entituled to under the charter of the said court contrary to the law of England: Notwithstanding which, the judges of the said superior court, the same 22d of March, granted letters of administration to the said intestate's estate to the said Thomas Lechmere and Ann his wife, and took the usual administration bond from the said Thomas Lechmere and his sureties, which letters of administration and bond extend only to the goods, chattels, rights and credits of the deceased, which the petitioner had before duly administered.

That the said Thomas Lechmere under colour hereof, inventoried and appraised all the petitioner's real estate, and exhibited an inventory thereof before a special superior county court held for that purpose on the 29th of April, 1726, which the said court, notwithstanding the said Lechmere, either by his letters of administration or his administration bond, had nothing to do with real estates, took upon them, contrary to law, to sit specially and receive the said inventory, and by their acts of that date approved the same, and ordered it to be received; and the said Lechmere also then exhibited to the court an account of 38 l, 7s. 4d. for charges and time spent in the administration, and of a debt due to Robert Lattimore for 318 l. silver money, which was the bond the petitioner had offered to discharge as aforesaid, and for which he had duly paid interest; which account the said court also allowed and ordered to be kept on fyle; and the 12th of May, 1726, the said Lechmere (being conscious that he had no power over any real estate by virtue of the administration) petitioned the Assembly, setting forth that no personal estate of the intestate had come to his hands, the estate come to his hands being all real, and finding there was due from the said estate 356 l. 7s. 4d., being the two sums in his above account mentioned, and no moveables to pay the same, he prayed the Assembly to enable him to pay the said debts by ordering him to sell and dispose of so much of the said lands, thereby to defray the said debts with other necessary charges.

That the petitioner being informed of this application, that the Assembly might do nothing herein without the fullest notice possible, the petitioner presented a memorial to the Governor and Company, agreeing in substance with the above recited protest, and declaring that he, being aggrieved with the aforementioned proceedings, should lay the whole by appeal before his Majesty: But which remonstrance of the petitioner's the Assembly the same day dismissed, and immediately afterward, on the said Lechmere's petition, granted him a power to sell the said lands, and ordered that a bill should be brought in for that end in form; whereupon the petitioner entered and fyled his protest with the said Governor and Company, to the effect with that before mentioned, and further protesting against their proceeding to grant power to any pretended administrator to sell any part of the petitioner's real estate under colour of debts due from the said deceased, as they would answer the same before his Majesty in Council; which protest, the Assembly declared, had in it a shew of contempt to the Governor and Assembly and the authority there established, and, therefore, on the 25th of the same May, they ordered the sheriff to bring the petitioner to the bar of the said Assembly, to answer for the contempt manifested in the said protest, and immediately afterwards passed an act empowering the said Thomas Lechmere to sell so much of the said lands as might be sufficient to discharge the said debts and the necessary costs, the said Lechmere taking the advice of the superior court in such sale, and enacting such deed or deeds of sale to be good.

That the petitioner humbly lays the whole of these proceedings before his Majesty, by which the many extraordinary and unjustifiable steps may appear that have been taken against him, in order to disinherit him of his inheritance, and to set up his sister as coheir with him, and to make a division of his real estate between him and his sister, contrary to the common law of England and the royal charter of the said Province; and, in consideration thereof, and of the many hardships of the petitioner's case, the petitioner humbly prays his Majesty to reverse the said two sentences of the superior court of the 22d of March, 172 5/6, with costs and damages to the petitioner, and to order the said administration, so illegally and irregularly granted to the said Thomas and Ann Lechmere, to be called in; and also to set aside and discharge all subsequent proceedings grounded thereon; and that his Majesty would repeal the said act passed by the Assembly empowering the said Thomas Lechmere to sell and dispose of the petitioner's real estate; and that his Majesty would be pleased to grant him all such further and other relief as the circumstance and nature of his case should require.

Their Lordships having heard all parties concerned, by their counsel learned in the law, on the said petition and appeal, and there being laid before their lordships an act passed by the Governor and Company of that Colony, entituled An Act for the Settlement of Intestate Estates, by which act (amongst other things) administrators of persons dying intestate are directed to inventory all the estate, whatsoever, of the persons so deceased, as well moveable as not moveable, and to deliver the same upon oath to the court of probates; and by the said act (debts, funeral and just expences of all sorts, and the dower of the wife (if any) being first allowed) the said court of probates is empowered to distribute all the remaining estate of any such intestate, as well real as personal, by equal portions, to and amongst the children and such as legally represent them, except the eldest son who is to have two shares or a double portion of the whole; the division of the estate to be made by three sufficient freeholders, on oath, or any two of them, to be appointed by the court of probates. Their Lordships, upon due consideration of the whole matter, do agree humbly to report as their opinion to your Majesty, that the said act for the settlement of intestate estates should be declared null and void, being contrary to the laws of England, in regard it makes lands of inheritance distributable as personal estates, and is not warranted by the charter of that Colony; and that the said three sentences of the 29th of June, 1725, of the 28th of September, 1725, and of the 22d day of March, 172 5/6, rejecting the inventory of the said intestate's estates exhibited by the petitioner, and refusing to accept the same, because it did not contain the real as well as personal estate of the said intestate, and declaring real as well as personal estates ought to be inventoried, may be all reversed and set aside; and that the petitioner be admitted to exhibit an inventory of the personal estate only of the said intestate; and that the court or probates be directed not to reject such inventory, only, because it does not contain the real estate of the said intestate; and that the said sentence of the 22d March, 172 5/6, vacating the said letters of administration granted to the petitioner, and granting administration to the said Thomas and Ann Lechmere, should be also reversed and set aside; and that the said letters of administration, so granted to the said Thomas Lechmere and Ann his wife, should be called in and vacated; and that the said inventory of the said real estate, exhibited by the said Thomas Lechmere and Ann his wife, should be vacated; and that the order of the 29th of April, 1726, approving of the said inventory and ordering the same to be recorded, should be discharged and set aside; and that the original letters of administration granted to the petitioner should be established and ordered to stand; and that all such costs as the petitioner hath paid unto the said Thomas Lechmere, by direction of the said sentence, may be forthwith repaid him by the said Thomas Lechmere; and that the suit brought by the said Lechmere and his wife, on which the said sentence was made, may be dismissed; and that all acts and proceedings done and had under the said sentences, or any of them, or by virtue or pretence thereof, may be discharged and declared null and void; and also that the said act of Assembly, passed in May, 1726, empowering the said Lechmere to sell the said lands, should be declared null and void. And it appearing to their lordships that the said superior court, by an order bearing date the 27 of September, 1726, and made pursuant to the said act of Assembly, allowed the said Thomas Lechmere to sell of the said real estate to the value of ninety pounds current money there, for his charges, and three hundred and eighteen pounds silver money, to answer the said bond debt due from the intestate, their lordships are of opinion that the said order of the superior court should be declared null and void; and also that the petitioner should be immediately restored and put into the full and quiet possession of all such parts of the said real estate as may have been taken from him, under pretence of, or by virtue or colour of the said sentences, orders, acts and proceedings, or any of them; and that the said Thomas Lechmere do account for and pay to the said petitioner the rents and profits thereof received by him or any one under him, for and during the time of such his unjust detention thereof.

His Majesty, taking the same into his royal consideration, is pleased, with the advice of his Privy Council, to approve of the said report, and confirm the same in every particular part thereof; and pursuant thereunto, to declare, that the aforementioned act, entituled an Act for the settlement of intestate estates, is Null and Void; and the same is hereby accordingly declared to be null and void, and of no force or effect whatsoever. ...

And his Majesty doth hereby likewise further order, that the petitioner be immediately restored and put into the full, peaceable and quiet possession of all such parts of the said real estate as may have been taken from him, under pretence of or by virtue or colour of the said sentence, orders, acts and proceedings, or any of them; and that the said Thomas Lechmere do account for and pay to the said petitioner the rents and profits thereof, and of every part thereof, received by him or any one under him, for and during the time of such his unjust detention thereof.

And the Governour and Company of his Majesty's Colony of Connecticut for the time being, and all other officers and persons whatsoever, whom it may concern, are to take notice of his Majesty's royal pleasure hereby signified, and yield due obedience to every particular part thereof, as they will answer the contrary at their peril.[2]

Henshaw v. Blood & al.

Supreme Judicial Court, Massachusetts, 1804; 1 Mass.35

This was an action of debt, brought in the name of Samuel Henshaw, Esq. judge of probate, &c., for this county, on an administration bond, against Martha Blood and Hezekiah Fiske, administrators of the estate of Isaiah Blood, Jun., and their two sureties, for the benefit of A, B, C, &c., creditors of the intestate.

The defendants prayed oyer of the condition, which was in the form prescribed by the statute, passed March 9th, 1784, (stat. 1783, c. 36, §8,) and pleaded in bar that the administrators from the time of making the writing obligatory aforesaid had well and faithfully observed, performed and kept all and every part of the things in the condition of the writing obligatory aforesaid, on their part to be observed, performed and fulfilled.

---

2. Before many years the Privy Council in reviewing a case on appeal from Massachusetts sustained the Massachusetts statute of distributions (supra, p. 254) as valid. Phillips v. Savage, 3 Acts of Privy Council (Col. Series) 432 (1737) Although no formal reversal of the determination in Winthrop v. Lechmere ever occurred, Connecticut continued to enforce the act invalidated by the Privy Council in that decision. See Andrews, loc. cit., supra, Note 1.

To this plea the plaintiff replied that the intestate, in his lifetime, viz., on ___, at ___ was seised in fee simple of certain real estate (describing it) and that afterwards, *viz.*, on ___ died so seised thereof, whereby the whole of the same real estate, of the value as the plaintiff averred of $2000 was and became the proper estate of the intestate at the time of his death; and when administration of the estate of the intestate was committed to the said *M.* and *H.* (viz. on the 5th day of June, 1798) the same real estate came to the knowledge and into the hands and possession of the said *M.* and *H.* as the estate of the intestate, and at the date of the administration bond was, thenceforth, always hitherto hath been and still is liable by law to be inventoried by them, the said *M.* and *H.* as the estate of the intestate; and, in case the personal estate of the said intestate was insufficient for the payment of the debts of the intestate, to be administered by them, the said *M.*and *H*, for the payment of the debts aforesaid. The plaintiff then averred that the personal estate of the intestate was insufficient to pay and satisfy the debts due and owing from him at the time of his death - that the administrators represented the estate of the intestate to be insolvent - that the commissioners to receive and examine the claims against his estate were duly appointed -that A, B, C, &c., creditors of the intestate, for whose use and benefit this action is brought, duly proved their respective claims and demands under the said commission - that the same were severally allowed by the commissioners, and that their doings and proceedings were duly returned into the Probate Court, and by the same court accepted, ratified and approved. The plaintiff then averred that the estate of the intestate, exclusive of the real estate above described, was in fact insolvent, and insufficient to pay the debts of the intestate - yet that the said *M.* and *H.*, well knowing the premises, did not, and each of them did not, make or cause to be made an inventory of the same real estate, or any part thereof, or exhibit or cause to be exhibited such inventory into the Probate Court for said county of Hampshire at or before the said fifth day of September next ensuing the date of the said writing obligatory, in the condition thereof specified, or at any time since - but that always hitherto had, and each of them had, neglected, and still did unjustly neglect and refuse, to make inventory, and return the same to be administered for the payment of the debts of the intestate, although often thereto requested - and that at a court of probate for said county, holden at ___ on ___, they the said *M.* and *H.*, having been duly cited to appear at the same probate court, and show cause why said real estate should not be inventoried and sold for the payment of the debts of the said intestate, it was duly ordered and decreed that the said *M.* and *H.* should return into the probate office for said county an inventory of said real estate, on receiving bonds from any creditor or creditors of the estate of said intestate, sufficient to indemnify the said M. and H. from all costs and charges which might thereafter arise in consequence of any suit or legal process for the recovery of said real estate for the benefit of the creditors aforesaid, and for inventorying the same; of which order and decree they, the said M. and H., thereafterwards, viz., on the same day, had notice - which decree the plaintiff averred to be in full force, not reversed, annulled, or appealed from. The plaintiff then averred that A, aforesaid was then and there a creditor of the said intestate, and that afterwards, viz., on ___ at ___ he, the said A, being then and there a creditor as aforesaid, tendered and offered to the said M. and H. the bond of C. D. of ___, sufficient for all the purposes in said decree mentioned - but that the said M. and H. had always hitherto refused to accept said bond, or inventory said real estate, or any part thereof, - all which the plaintiff is ready to verify, &c.

The defendants protesting that the intestate did not die seised of the real estate in the replication mentioned, nor of any part thereof, and that the said M. and H. duly inventoried all the estate, both real and personal, whereof the intestate died seised and possessed, which came to the hands, possession or knowledge of the said M. and H., and whereof they had any notice, demurred generally - and the plaintiff joined in demurrer.

Sedgwick, J. (after stating the pleadings) The only question referred by this record to the decision of the Court, is the extent of the obligation of an administrator as to the inventory which he is to make of the estate of his intestate. Is it confined to "goods and chattels, rights and credits" according to the technical meaning of those words, or does it extend to real estate of inheritance? The words are, "make, or cause to be made, a true and perfect inventory of all and singular, the goods, chattels, rights and credits of the said deceased, which have or shall come into the hands, possession or knowledge of the said administrators, or into the hands and possession of any other person or persons for them, and the same so made do exhibit, or cause to be exhibited, into the registry of the Court of Probate, &c." - It is undoubtedly true that in all instances where a contract is reduced to writing, and the reason is strongest in the instance of a deed the meaning of the parties and the extent of their obligations and duties are to be sought for in the writing only, unless there be in it some latent ambiguity; and there is none in this case. When, then, the administrators by this bond became obliged to make an inventory of the goods and chattels, rights and credits of their intestate, were they bound also to make an inventory of the real estate which had descended to his heirs; and of which they had not, in words bound themselves to make an inventory? Certainly the words import no such obligation, and to them only can we resort. That the words do not, of themselves, import such obligation is conceded by the counsel for the plaintiffs, and this I think is decisive of the merits of this case. But the counsel for the plaintiff says, "that we are to resort to the former part of the same section of the act, which prescribes the form of the administration bond, to know the kind of inventory which an administrator is to make; and that from thence it will appear that he is bound to inventory not the goods and chattels, rights and credits only, but also the real estate of inheritance." In the first place, this would compel us to go out of the deed to find its meaning, which, by law, I think, we cannot do; and in the next place, even if we could resort to this means of investigation, I do not think that the meaning of the condition would be found to be such as is contended for. This sect. of the act, after prescribing the power and duty of the judge relative to granting administration, proceeds - "and the administrator shall give bond, upon condition, among other things, to make and return a true inventory of the estate administered on, which bond shall be in the form following:..." ...Here, under the words, "estate administered on" (the expression being indefinite) it is insisted, is included as well the real as the personal estate; and that this ought the rather to be the construction, because the real estate is by law put under the control of the administrator, and made liable to the payment of debts, provided the personal, including the rights and credits, is insufficient. But to this may be answered, that immediately on the death of the intestate, the real estate descends to his heirs, and is not even subject to the control of the administrator but on a contingency, which at that time is unknown - the insufficiency of the personal estate and credits of the intestate; and, but in that event, the administrator has no right to enter upon, or in any manner intermeddle with, such real estate. The real estate is not then, but in any event which is not and cannot be known, in any relation to the administration; and there could result no use nor benefit from making an inventory of it. When therefore the legislature speaks generally of estate, it seems reasonable to believe that such only was intended as was in any event to be "administered on", and that that which is not ordinarily to go into the hands of an administrator is not comprehended. ...

CHAPTER FOUR

CRITICAL PROBLEMS OF AMERICAN LAW, 1790-1820

1. General Character of American Law

Richard Rush[1] - American Jurisprudence (1815)

... If we were inclined to run a parallel between the mind of this country and of Europe, but especially of Britain, we know of no line to which we could so fairly resort as to that of the law. Here it is where we think that a test of the relative intellectual cultivation and force of the two hemispheres may be found with the fewest intrinsic disadvantages to ourselves in the comparison. The theory upon this subject may plainly be resolved into this. That the prodigiously greater incentive which is forever applying itself to mind in Europe rouses it into more keen action, and gives it momentum towards purposes which it does not yet require, and which therefore it cannot be supposed to reach, here. A numerous and condensed population; an infinitely intricate organization of society producing habits and tastes not merely artificial, but in the highest degree fastidious and dainty in a countless variety of ways; every possible avenue in which human genius can exert itself thronged with the most eager competition; the spectres of poverty at hand to reanimate by their powerfully stimulating admonitions flagging industry, with resulting rewards proportioning their enticements to the difficulty and the rarity of success - these, and not royal munificence, have in all countries been the essential promoters of literature and the arts.

In the department of jurisprudence the United States probably approach if not in all of these yet in other great excitements of mind, nearer to a par with the old nations than in any other that could be named. Here the law is every thing. It makes its appeal to the strongest motives of interest and of ambition. In most instances it leads to a comfortable subsistence, and in many to independence and wealth. To public honors, if so they are to be denominated, it unquestionably opens a wider door than any other pursuit. But we do not mean to dwell upon the connexion in this country between politics and the law, which would open a space that it is not our purpose on

---

1. Richard Rush (1780-1859) was a Philadelphia lawyer, ardent Jeffersonian and Jacksonian democrat, negotiator of the Rush-

this occasion to occupy. The unbounded freedom of our institutions begets, throughout every portion of the country, a corresponding latitude of conduct and of discussion which exultingly and fiercely disdains to acknowledge any limit or any regulator but the law. Hence the habit of bringing every thing to its test. The bolts of criticism shot from the most exalted heights of intellect on the one hand, and the shafts of unlettered simplicity upon the other, a Burke or a Jack Cade, may fall in eloquent vengeance or in harmless mirth upon this profession; but in a country of equal rights it has ever been a formidable engine of influence in public affairs, and scarcely less of credit and authority in private life. We can only mean, when it is associated with those strict principles of probity and honor which not only constitute its first ornament, but without which it is impossible that it can ever in any country signally and ultimately prosper. So endowed, it is, after all, in the beautiful words of the first Vinerean lecturer, a profession which employs in its theory the noblest faculties of the soul and exerts in its practice the cardinal virtues of the heart.

As we outstrip England in her freedom, there is a still greater call amongst us for those who are found to be so usefully its ministers. It is like the rule of the political economist in all other cases, where the supply of the commodity adapts itself to the demand. It may be that the English loom makes a demand for ten or for twenty workmen where the American as yet does for one. Hence the comparative extent, variety, and perfection of their manufactures. But it is probable that the habits, the manners, and the contentions, of the universally thriving and self-supported freemen on this side of the Atlantic, call for at least a couple of lawyers, take the two countries throughout, where the English do for one. Considering Burke's assertion in 1775 that nearly as many of Blackstone's Commentaries were sold in the American colonies alone at that period as in all England, we think it may be agreed that we set down the proportion at a safe rate. The noble definition of law, that nothing is so high as to be above its reach or so low as to be beyond its care, is probably true to a greater practical extent in this country than in any other. The cause obviously is, not our liberty alone, but an alliance between an active and restless spirit of freedom and the comfortable condition of all classes of the community, not excepting, relatively considered, even the poor. This encourages and provokes the disposition to go to law by

---

Bagot treaty (1817) and United States Minister to Great Britain and, later, to France. See J.H.Powell, Richard Rush (1942).

supplying it almost universally with the means. We have honest blacksmiths suing banks for false imprisonment, and street cleaners fine gentlemen for assaults and batteries as the common occurrences of our courts. Dear, too, as law is supposed to be in this country, it falls short of the expenses which are generally the concomitants of its benefits in England. The sums which under the various denominations of fees and costs fall upon the suitor by the time he gets into the house of lords, when he carries his claims to that final stage of appellate authority, sometimes become enormous. A member of the house of commons stated in his place in 1810, that a bill of costs had been presented in a court of one of their colonial dominions three fathoms in length, and Sir William Scott himself gives us to understand, that there are "some suits famous in English juridical history for having outlived generations of suitors".

Under the names of Lee, Paul, Ryder, and Murray, and on an occasion so solemn as the answer of the English court to the Prussian memorial, was it formally said, that "in England the crown never interferes with the courts of justice".[2] True. And this is a legitimate boast. The holy sanctury is never safe but when this is uniformly, sacredly, and unconditionally, the case.

But he who has carefully surveyed the spirit of our own in contrast with that of British jurisprudence, deceives himself if he supposes that it mounts no higher in a disdainful exemption from all extraneous impression. Taking the remark in its genuine meaning, we are called upon to invert it before we can arrive at the bold anomaly which sits upon the stern portals of American justice. Here the courts are always in fact interfering with the government. Pass but an embargo law; pass but an act for the enlistment of minors; let the legislature venture to abolish a court, or touch with only the pressure of a hair the supposed rights of the citizen, and you will soon see what a storm will be raised about the ears of their supposed sovereign authority. Sometimes too, in its own way, it will rage terribly. The merchant, or the master, or the judge, or the citizen, declares he is aggrieved. The lawyers meet. They ponder, they deliberate, they analize, they investigate; finally they denounce. Or, it may be, that they denounce first, and do all the rest afterwards. Then approaches a scene of high expectation. We behold crowded lobbies, witness a palpitating array of judges, and barristers, and bystanders. The selected advocate rises, the motive to his duty is momentous,

---

2. See 3 Campbell, Lives of the Chief Justices 376-7; Holliday, Life of Lord Mansfield (1797) 428, 439.

a crises has arrived, posterity may be implicated in the decision; this is the exordium; and then - with a scrutinizing severity of critical examination, tasking the deepest stores of acquired learning and drawing upon the powers of an invention sharpened by patriotic or by unworthy passions, he proceeds to lay open the incompatibility of the exercise of the delegated trust with the limits and injunctions of the constitutional charter. If he be successful, as sometimes happens, away goes the act of congress or the act of assembly with all its virtues or all its blunders upon its head. The representatives of the people complain, but what follows? They submit to the defeat; or, roused by the discomfiture, are invoked anew to review their work, supplying its oversights, filling up its defects, and making it proof in short against the well directed, the bold, the ceaseless, shocks of these terrible legal battering rams. The Constitution with captain Hull in her, did not come down upon the Gurriere in a spirit of more daring and triumphant energy than the Philadelphia or New York lawyers will sometimes do upon a statute that happens to run a little amiss! ...

The law itself in this country, is, moreover, a science of great extent. We have an entire substratum of common law as the broad foundation upon which every thing else is built. It fills its thousand volumes like that of England, whose volumes in this respect are at the same time ours. But the extent of this law, its beginning, its termination; upon what subjects precisely it operates and where it falls short, where the analogy of situation holds and where not, with the shades under which it may do the one or the other, (witness the great argument of Hamilton in Croswel's case at Albany,[3] that in the case of Blight's assignees at Washington so far as prerogative was implicated, with numerous others that might be referred to) these start questions upon which the nicest discriminations of ingenuity and learning have been for a century at work. Often therefore the American lawyer has gone through but half his task when he has informed himself of what the common law is. The remaining and perhaps most difficult branch of inquiry is, whether it does or does not apply to his case. Notwithstanding the determination of the Supreme Court in the case of the _United States_ v. _Hudson and Goodwin_,[4] it is still by no means certain that that tribunal would not sustain another and more full argument at this day on the question in its nature so extensive and fundamental as whether or not the

---

3. _People_ v. _Croswell_, _infra_, p.376, footnote.

4. 7 Cranch 32 (1812).

federal government draws to itself the common law of England in criminal matters. When we speak of the great body of this system of law as a substratum, we mean of course as applied to the individual states.

The statute law of England during our provincial day, or anterior to it, is another great division liable to much the same sort of counter-argument at the hands of those who have been charged with the heavy task, at which they still toil, of rearing up the fabric of American jurisprudence. Next comes the prolific exuberance of our own statute law superinducting its daily modifications upon the English code, and giving birth to original systems to meet the new exigencies of our incessant enterprise, our growing population, and the genius of all our other institutions. The statutes and the lawsuits to which steam boats alone have given rise within the last two or three years would probably occupy several volumes. Those relative to turnpike roads and the contentions they have bred, taking all the states, would probably fill a dozen, and it would be difficult to limit the further illustrations we could give. Patents for new inventions would make an ample not to say curious figure. ...

Lastly in the structure of our judicature we have a multitude of different sorts of courts. We have courts of common law and courts of chancery, admiralty and maritime courts, courts civil and courts criminal, sittings at <u>nisi prius</u> and full terms in bank, register's courts, orphan's courts, escheator's courts, justices' courts, with the many gradations of some of them, and with others that might be made to swell the catalogue. It may be said, that this is nothing more than the judicial polity of other countries, particularly Britain, is liable to; that if you will begin at the piepoudre and go up to the peers in parliament you will run through, under some modification or others, as long an enumeration. This may be true. But the difference is, that the profession here is not subdivided, in any of the states, in the ways that it is [in] England, and the American lawyer is called upon at one period or other of his life to understand the constitution of each of these forums; to be familiar at least with their principles if not with their forms as he passes on through the usual stages to the head of his profession.

It may be supposed that great labor is necessary to master such a range of knowledge. And such, undoubtedly, is the case. The men among us who reach the vantage ground of the science, who become as well the safe counselors as the eloquent advocates, are only those who in their early day explore its ways with repetitions of intense and, through all its dreadful discouragements to the young mind, unwearied assiduity; and who are afterwards content to devote their days to business and their nights to study. Sparing indeed must be their relaxations. If they stop for repose or turn aside for indulgence, like the son of Abensina in the affecting oriental tale they will be reminded when perhaps it is too late of the impossibility of uniting the gratifications of ease with the rewards of diligence. The true enjoyments to be gathered from the rugged path of the profession, and happily they are at once animating and refined, are those reflections which come sweetly over the mind, under the consciousness of duty successfully performed, and of eminence honorably achieved.

While the law with us is so copious, we are still willing to believe, that it has all the essential characteristics of a good code. That its comprehensiveness is the unavoidable result of our wants, and the glorious evidence of our freedom. That its occasional darkness, supposed or real, is nothing more than belongs to all free codes in a greater or less degree, and is generally to be dispelled by the penetrating rays of a comprehensive knowledge. That above all, if in the unravelling and adjustment of complicated concerns, it may sometimes at first sight seem itself complicated, it never fails to throw a broad effulgence upon all the fundamental securities of the liberty and property of the citizen.

The English jurisprudence, with all it has to boast, was our first inheritance. But we hope it will not be thought we are presumptuous in supposing, that we have but secured to ourselves the more signally its advantages by shaking off more freely than is done there the shackles fixed upon it in early and rude periods. In making this remark we think we shall largely carry with us the concurrence of informed and liberal readers when it is applied to the whole criminal branch. When our sober minded and profound names as Hale, Blackstone, Romilly and McIntosh, will agree, at epochs distant from each other, in condemning the deplorable severity of the English penal code, it may surely be permitted to others to join in the grateful opinion. Scarcely indeed does a year now pass over in which modern parliaments are not paying homage to this opinion by lopping off or mitigating some of the harsh and cruel features, a work in which they have long ago been anticipated by the intelligent and humane wisdom of our own legislators. We still think, making all allowances for the exigencies of the two countries, that they have a great deal to do before they get to the point we have reached in this happy race of melioration. It cannot be said of us, as it is truly said of the English, in reference to the numerous and small offences for which they punish capitally, that while for centuries every thing else had become dearer in its price among them, the life of man had been continually allowed to grow cheaper.

The systems of law recently compiled for the French nation, if we will but abstract the political associations that go along with them, will challenge an almost universal judgment in their favor for the lights of ancient and modern wisdom so extensively intermingled in their formation. The imperialist bows to them from the auspices under which they were compiled, and Louis the 18th in his proclamation of January 1814, speaks of them as containing "under other modifications and names the wisdom of all the ancient laws of France". If they do this they also do more. They embody much of the wisdom which the further experience of more recent times has evolved. It is gratifying to think, that the one which passes under the name of the penal code of the French empire is marked by many of the improvements familiar to the American states. To the Pennsylvanian it must be particularly so when he finds, that the law of homicide has been divided into the same degrees, and is couched in nearly the same terms, with the statute of that state upon this subject passed more than twenty years ago.[5]

Leaving the criminal branch, and bringing into view, the entire scope of jurisprudence in the two countries, we are disposed to place ours at a high pitch in the comparison. If the advantage even be with us, we should say, in searching for the cause, that it is owing to our having gotten rid in the greatest number of instances of that feudal turn, and of those perplexed and cumbrous forms of the Norman day which so long disfigured the admirable system upon which, by force or by artifice, they were incorporated. These nothing but a prying eye, coupled with a resolution bold enough to lift up its hand against gray hairs, can ever effectually root out. Time, says Lord Bacon "is the greatest innovator; and if time is always altering things for the worse, and wisdom and counsel do not sometimes alter them for the better, what shall be the end thereof?"

The English are rooting out these abuses; but perhaps from a greater dread of touching the hoar that encircles the old trunk seem more backward than we at tearing away the poisonous shoots which, at the subjugation of the true proprietors of the soil, were suffered to grow up rank around it.

---

5. The credit for this statute of 1794 (15 Pa. Stats. 174) is commonly given to William Bradford. His pamphlet, "An Enquiry how Far the Punishment of Death is Necessary in Pennsylvania" (1793) suggested that there should be different degrees of murder. That proposal, however, was made by others at approximately the same time (see, e.g.Benjamin Rush, "On the Punishment of Murder by Death" (London reprint, 1793) p.13-14), and it appears that the proposal that there should be two degrees of murder was already under consideration in the state legislature when Bradford's pamphlet was published. See Bradford, id. (Glasgow reprint, 1795) p. 71-2. The national influence

In the law of ejectment and entails, in the order of paying debts, in the law of descent independent of the principle of primogeniture, in the liability of real estate to the demands of the creditor, in the law of executors and wills, with other points that might be enumerated did not the nature of this discussion, which aims at nothing but drawing outlines, forbid, we think the liberal and less manacled judgment of several of the American states has outstripped the judicial wisdom of England in wholesome amendments. The luminous mind of Lord Mansfield did wonders towards many and obvious prunings. But much more remains to be accomplished; and perhaps his efforts successful as they may have been, are in theory too bold for precedent even in his own meridian. Left to himself by the sluggishness of parliament, he was forced to substitute a sort of judicial for what would have been performed if not more efficaciously, more appropriately, by parliamentary legislation. ...

We have been indulging in the foregoing train of reflections with a view to clear the way for the remaining and chief question. And that is, how the profession of the law here, does, in point of fact, compare with the profession in England? If the reflections collectively be at all just, they have already more than half afforded the answer and shown how safely we may go into the comparison. For there seem to be good reasons why, in this country, the profession should stand upon high ground.

If mind be the result of external stimuli forcing it into action, our jurisprudence is surrounded by what must provoke and improve its powers. There are reasons why it ought not to be expected of us to produce a Lord Byron, or a Walter Scott, a Dugal Stewart perhaps, or other men of like stamp with those who enrich the British press with such a copious and constant flow of profound or elegant literary and scientific productions. We are yet at some distance, though we trust no very great, from the age that can feed in any extent the merely classic mind into fullness and perfection. But we see no reasons at all why we may not breed Gibbs's, and Garrows, and Saubeys, and Lawrences, and breed them in abundance. If we have not gained that stage of our growth when the luxury of the arts and sciences goes hand in hand with all other luxuries, we enjoy in a proud degree, to use an expression of the Edinburgh review, "the luxury of liberty"; and it is not irrational to suppose that those who officiate so largely at her alters should arrive at a perfection in their duty.

---

of the Pennsylvania statute was very great. See Wharton, Law of Homicide (1855) 354 et seq.

In throwing out a conjectural sentiment, and one not altogether hasty, we presume to think, that the law-mind, if we may so speak, of the United States has, from adequate causes, forerun the general condition of literature, and already been accelerated and matured into as much force and discipline as it is likely to reach in any more distant period of the country's advancement. How it may be in medicine, and in divinity, we do not presume on this occasion to intimate. If there be fit matter for reflection under these heads it must be gone into in some separate disquisition. In painting there might be room to say something, keeping to the walk of native genius at least. We pass to our proper subject. The profession of the law with us, then, seems to be absorbed by duties as numerous and as commanding at this day, as it is probable that it can be at any more remote epoch of fuller population and greater riches. Those scenes of portentous convulsion which in their occasional visitations rouse the mind of a whole community into temporary and preternatural force, and which more frequently belong to a full than a slender population, and to age than to youth, may indeed form exceptions. But we speak of the settled and ordinary course of things. As our lonely territory continues to be overspread with cultivated fields, and to glitter with the spires of villages and cities, we shall, to be sure, witness a corresponding increase in the professors of this science; but it does not appear to follow that their faculties will be tasked to a higher compass of exertion than the faculties of those who now flourish in the walks of full occupation. There are, doubtless, more men in England at the present day who write well, than there were in the time of queen Anne or queen Elizabeth; but it will scarcely be said that they write better than those who were at the head of the list at either of those periods.

As to profound scholarship, as a Wakefield or a Porson might define the term, it is not to be looked for as an adjunct of the profession in any country. But for those classical embellishments which are ancillary, and whose tincture lends its chastening without monopolizing, it is probable that they are as much its concomitants with us at the present as they will be at a more distant era, because as much so we incline to think, taking the profession upon a large scale, as can be made compatible at any time with its unrelaxing and intrinsic toil. The necessity of those preparatory studies which alone can form the taste, and lift up the mind to proper conceptions of eminence, cannot be too anxiously and too constantly impressed upon the youth who is destined for the bar. But when once he has plunged into the profession he will find that, to the precepts of Blackstone's valedictory to his muse, he must submit in the full spirit of obedience.

It may possibly be supposed, that the subdivision of the

profession in England affords a cause for its greater eminence in each particular line than in a country where this system is not known; and that here we are consequently thrown under a disadvantage. We do not simply mean the subdivision into counsellors and attorneys, but that which assigns to counsellors and advocates of high standing a distinct range of business in distinct courts. Upon this opinion we must be permitted to bestow a moment's examination, being, as we own we are, decided and zealous dissentients. We admit also that it constitutes the stress of the argument.

It is certainly true, as a general proposition, that as you subdivide labor you increase its excellence. _Ars longa, vita brevis_, is a remark that every school boy knows. But the proposition has its modifications, and it has its limits. Its truth runs into a greater extreme as to the hand, than it does as to the mind. It may well enough be conceived that a pin will be better made for being divided into eighteen distinct operations. So, that palaces, orreries, optical instruments, or steam frigates, may be made to exhibit a result of greater capability and perfection from the number of artisans employed in their construction. But he who should as a general rule infer from this, that a book will be better written because one man furnishes the ideas and another the words, might be in danger of falling into a strange mistake.

Under what limitations precisely the proposition must be brought, is not easy to say by any previous definition; but there are some general principles by following which we may in all probability be led to sound conclusions. The law is, in itself, one entire science. Its various departments are but so many smaller orbs moving within the one grand outline of a larger one. They all harmonize with each other. They enlarge, they illustrate, they enrich each other. They are social handmaids flourishing and delighting in proximity. That, with the requisite diligence, life is not long enough to arrive at an acquaintance with them all, we can by no means admit. Still less that the knowledge of one will weaken the knowledge of another. Did not Sulpicius, who was so celebrated an orator, also find time to write out more than a hundred volumes of the law? In rendering homage to intellect let us rather wish to see its powers carried to the utmost practical verge, than compressed within the scantiest limits. ...

Open, at random, a volume of Burrow or of East, and then do the same with one of Dallas or Cranch. We declare, that, to us, there seem in the general discussions of the former, a certain stiffness; nearly every thing appears to turn upon the memory; the argument is a statement, accurate if you will, but scarcely any thing in most instances beyond a naked statement, of the cases decided upon the same point, nicely fixed off in chronological order. The work, shall we add, appears to wind up like that of the mechanic, who has been less deeply engaged in thinking than in keeping to the rules of the trade. In those of the latter it strikes us that there is more freedom; more fullness; more learning poured out; more illustration borrowed from the whole science; more trials of the mind's strength in the higher province of reasoning; and, mixed with no dearth of authorities from the books, a more frequent mounting up to principles. ...

There is indeed, at the present day in England a judge, perhaps their first, of the volumes containing whose decisions it has been said in the British house of commons, "that they were no less valuable to the classical reader than to the student of law by perpetuating the style in which the judgments of the court were delivered." A man he is of dazzling mind. Born, we believe, a miller's son, he can talk of giving a _rusticum judicium_. Yet, surely no judge upon the face of the earth was farther from having rendered such a one. His intellect is so polished that it has been called transparent. Some of his pages are as if diamond sparks were on them. When he deals in wit, it is like a sunbeam and gone as quick. But so much the worse; we pity the more the suitor, or the poor vice-admiralty judge, it may happen to hit. Abundant learning is also his. We must say of him, that if he wants qualities necessary to consummate the fame of a great judge, he has others which perhaps no judge ever possessed before, or in the same degree. It was said, "How sweet an Ovid was in Murray lost". But the judge we speak of is an Ariel. He holds a judicial wand. Touching the scales with it they at once look even, no matter what preponderance an instant before. How can such a judge be truly great? One day, in the midst of some of those beautiful little judicial aphorisms the web of which he can weave so fine, he declares "that astutia does not belong to a court." The next "that humanity is but its second virtue, justice being forever the first." The third that it is "monstrous to suppose that because one nation falls into guilt others are let loose from the morality of public law." But a frost comes on the fourth! Certain retaliating orders are laid upon his desk, that shrine which no foreign touch ought ever to pollute. Unlike an illustrious British judge who has just returned from India, the pliant spirit bows obedience.[5] Instead of the dignity of his mind upholding the independence of justice, its subtlety is enlisted to show that on her majestic form no violation was imprinted. In one breath admitting that the rescript of the throne was the rule of his decision, he strives in the

---

5. The complimentary reference is evidently to the decision of Sir James Mackintosh sitting on the Vice Admiralty Court in Bombay in _The Minerva_, 1 _Memoirs of Life of Sir James Mackintosh_ (1835) 318-19.

next to hide the consciousness of judicial obeisance. In an argument where the utmost attenuation of thought is drawn out into corresponding exilities of expression, he labors with abortive yet splendid ingenuity to show, that justice and such rescripts must ever be in harmonious union.[7] So spake not the Holts and the Hales! No doubt it is a keen, and an exquisite, and a suple mind. It can enchain its listeners. Leaving its strength, it can disport in its gambols; it can exhale its sweets. But is it, can it be, great? Where is the lofty port when it can thus bend? Acknowledging its confinement within royal orders, can it hold in true keeping, the divine attribute it was sworn to cherish unsullied? It is impossible.

There graces the first seat of judicial magistracy in this country a man of another stamp, and exhibiting different aspects of excellence. Venerable and dignified, laborious and intuitive, common law chancery law and admiralty law each make their demands upon his profound, his discriminating, and his well stored, mind. Universal in his attainments in legal science, prompt and patient, courteous and firm, he fills up, by a combination of rare endowments, the measure of his difficult, his extensive and his responsible duties; responsible not to the dictates of an executive, but, moving in a sphere of true

---

7. Presumably the reference is to Sir William Scott's opinion in The Fox, Edw. 311 (1811). In considering whether a British Prize Court should enforce the King's Orders in Council if such Orders violated the law of nations, Scott had said: "These two propositions, that the Court is bound to administer the Law of Nations, and that it is bound to enforce the King's Orders in Council, are not at all inconsistent with each other; because these Orders and Instructions are presumed to conform themselves, under the given circumstances, to the principles of its unwritten law. ...this Court will not let itself loose into speculations as to what would be its duty under such an emergency, because it cannot, without extreme indecency, presume that any such emergency will happen." Id. p. 313-14. The war of pamphlets between American and British critics of Sir William Scott (later Lord Stowell) began some years before the outbreak of armed hostilities. The most elaborate defense of Scott was in James Stephen's War in Disguise (1806), and the American argument was well presented in Governor Morris's, Answer to "War in Disguise" (1806). A more journalistic attack on British doctrine was Duane's The Law of Nations Investigated in a Popular Manner (1809). Maitland later said of Sir William Scott that "a public international law that was intensely, if privately, national, was his chief contribution to the jurisprudence of the world." Roman Canon Law in England (1898) 97.

independence, responsible to his conscience, to his country, and to his God. What a grand, and to a mind exalted and virtuous, what an awful sphere? How independent, how responsible! Vain would it be for us to expect to do justice to the full orbed merit with which he moves in it. Bred up in a state rich in great names, counting her Washingtons, her Jeffersons, her Madisons, he long sustained a career of the highest reputation at the bar. Passing to the bench of the supreme court of the United States, he carried to its duties a mind matured by experience, and invigorated by long daily and successful toil. In the voluminous state of our jurisprudence, every portion of which is occasionally brought under his review, and in the novelties of our political state, often does it happen that questions are brought before him where the path is untrodden, where neither the book case nor the record exist to guide, and where the elementary writer himself glimmers dimly. It is upon such occasions that he pierces what is dark, examines what is remote, separates what is entangled, and draws down analogies from the fountain of first principles. Seizing with a large grasp what few other minds at first see, he embodies his comprehensive and distinct conceptions in language not sarcastic, but suited to the gravity and to the solemnity of the temple around him; thus he is found always with masterly ability, and most frequently with conviction, to lay open and elucidate the difficult subject. If there be any applicable learning, to a mind so formed, so furnished, and so trained, it is reasonable to think that it will be at hand. Where there is none, the fertile deductions of its own independent vigor and clearness stand in the place of learning, and will become learning to those who are to live after him. His country alternately a neutral and a belligerent, again and again is he called upon to expound the volume of national law, to explore its intricate passages, to mark its nicest limitations. Upon such occasions, as well as upon the entire body of commercial law so copiously in the last resort intermingled with his adjudications, his recorded opinions will best make known to the world the penetration of his views, the extent of his knowledge, and the solidity of his judgment. They are a national treasure. Posterity will read in them as well the rule of conduct, as the monuments of a genius that would have done honor to any age or to any country. Such is the sketch we would attempt of the judicial character of the chief justice of our country. That country is on a swift wing to greatness and to glory. To the world at large the early day of her jurisprudence may remain unknown until then; but then it will break into light, and his name, like the Fortesques and the Cokes of the early day of England, fill perhaps even a wider region from the less local foundations upon which it will rest. Let the courts of England boast of Sir William Scott. Those of America will boast of John Marshall.

Case of John V. N. Yates
Supreme Court of New York, 1809; 4 Johnson 317

On the second day of the last February term, Emmet moved for a habeas corpus to bring up the body of John V. N. Yates, a prisoner in the custody of the sheriff of Albany. The motion was grounded on sundry affidavits which were read. ...

The writ of habeas corpus having been allowed, on the following day, the prisoner was afterwards, (Thursday, the 9th of February) brought up, and the following return was made by the sheriff: That the prisoner was, on the 7th day of February, arrested by him, and in his custody, by virtue of an order of the court of chancery, made the 5th day of December, 1808, which states, that the court of chancery did, on the 20th day of September last, make another order, as follows, to wit: "Upon reading the order made in this matter on the 5th day of September, and the certificate of the sheriff, stating 'that on the 12th September, he had arrested the defendant, and that by virtue of a writ of habeas corpus, Judge Spencer did, on the same day, discharge him on the ground, that the original cause of the caption was illegal, and that the taking and detaining him, for the same matter,"was illegal and unwarrantable, and subversive of the liberties of the citizens;" that as the commitment for the mal-practice and contempt, before adjudged by the court to have been committed by the defendant, has not been remitted by the court, nor the said contempt purged, and the court deeming the discharge repugnant to the laws of this state, and void, ordered that the sheriff retake the defendant and recommit him, for his contempt and mal-practice, as, in the attachment before issued, was commanded, there to remain, until the further order of the court;' and the sheriff having returned to the said order of the 20th September, that the defendant was not found, it is, therefore, ordered that the sheriff retake the defendant, and recommit him for his contempt and

8. If Rush seems slightly boastful of American talent in the law, it was, perhaps, not unnatural for him to be so; it had not been very many years since an English judge had spoken of the "wildness" in our Revolutionary legislation, a quality "that marks strongly the real character of the Americans; it is perfectly savage, and breathes the spirit of persecution ... it is among the many proofs we find in the history of mankind that conquerors and new settlers in all ages have adopted, in a very great degree, the manners of the ancient inhabitants and taken even the features, colours, and tempers of the climate." Sir James Marriott in The Rebecca, Hay and Marriott Decisions, at 208 (1778).

mal-practice, &c. there to remain until the further order of the court."

The sheriff further certified, and returned to the habeas corpus, that the writ of attachment, referred to in the foregoing order, was dated 17th August, and is as follows: "whereas, in and by a certain order of the court, on the 13th June, in the matter of complaint of Samuel Bacon against the defendant, during the time he was a master of the court, had filed a bill of complaint with Richard S. Treat, one of the clerks, in behalf of Samuel Bacon, complainant, against Henry Garretse and Charles Morris, as defendants, and thereto subscribed the name of Peter W. Yates, one of the solicitors of this court, without the knowledge or consent of the said Peter W. Yates, and had acted as a solicitor in the said cause, in the prosecution thereof, in the name of the said Peter W. Yates contrary to the statute in that case made and provided,[1] in wilful violation of his duty as master, and in contempt of the authority of this court; it was therefore ordered by the court, among other things, that the defendant be committed, for his said mal-practice and contempt, to gaol, there to remain until the further order of the court; therefore the court commanded the sheriff to attach the defendant, and convey him to gaol, there to remain until the further order of the court."

And the sheriff further certified, and returned, that the defendant was discharged, on a habeas corpus, by Mr. Justice Spencer, after being arrested on the said writ of attachment, on the 19th August, and the judge certified in his discharge, that "it having been made satisfactorily to appear to him, that the said commitment was not for any contempt committed by the defendant, towards the said court, but that the same was for an alleged mal-practice, on the part of the defendant, as a master in chancery, in using the name of Peter W. Yates, as a solicitor, in a certain cause, without his consent, and in violation of the 9th section of the act, concerning counsellors, attornies and solicitors, &c. he was of opinion, that the commitment was illegal and unprecedented."

The sheriff further certified, and returned, that the or-

---

1. An act of 20 March 1801 (Chap. 23, 24th Session) provided as follows in its 6th and 9th sections:

"That if any counsellor, attorney or solicitor be guilty of any manner of deceit, or collusion, or consenting thereto, whereby to deceive the court or the party, he shall be punished by fine and imprisonment....

"That no clerk, deputy clerk ... nor any examiner, or master of the court of chancery shall act as counsellor, attorney, or solicitor in any action or matter in the same court...."

der of the 5th September was as follows: to wit, "upon reading and filing the attachment aforesaid, and due deliberation having been had thereon, and the court deeming the said discharge repugnant to the laws of the state, legally inoperative and void, it is ordered that the sheriff retake the defendant, and recommit him for his contempt and mal-practice, as in the said attachment he was commanded, there to remain until the further order of the court."

The sheriff further certified, and returned, that the defendant was taken on the said order, and again discharged by Mr. Justice Spencer, on a habeas corpus, on the 12th September, who certified, in his discharge, as follows, to wit: "it appearing that the defendant has been again taken and imprisoned, for the same matter and cause, whereon he was imprisoned, when discharged on habeas corpus, on the 18th August, I am of opinion, not only that the original cause of the caption of the defendant was illegal, but that the taking and detaining him on the said order was illegal and unwarrantable, and subversive of the liberties of the citizens;" and he therefore discharged him.

The sheriff also certified and returned, that, after the last discharge, by Mr. Justice Spencer, the order first above mentioned, was received by him, by virtue of which order he took the defendant, on the 7th day of February, inst. and still detains him in his custody &c. ...

Kent, Ch. J. The return to the habeas corpus has imposed upon the court, the necessity of discussing and deciding some interesting questions. We are called to examine into the validity of the commitment of the court of chancery, into the authority of a judge of this court, to interfere, in vacation, upon habeas corpus, and to set aside such commitment. It is also made a question, whether the act of the judge be not, at all events, conclusive upon the subject matter of the commitment. This inquiry is, in every view, important, and I shall endeavour to acquit myself of my public duty, by bestowing upon the case, a free, full and diligent investigation. ...

1. The first point raised by the counsel for the prisoner is, whether the discharge of the judge be not conclusive and final, so as to preclude the court of chancery, from examining into the correctness of the discharge, and from recommitting the prisoner for the same cause.

The habeas corpus act, among the exceptions, states those "of persons convict, and in execution by legal process" as being entirely out of the purview of the third section, under the authority of which the habeas corpus was awarded.[2]

---

2. The 3rd section of the Habeas Corpus Act of 24 March 1801 (Chap. 65, 24th Session) was as follows: "... all such writs

And if the prisoner, when he was discharged, was a person answering to either of those descriptions, the judge had no authority to bail or discharge him, and he ought to have been immediately remanded. If such a prisoner should be discharged, the discharge cannot be binding or valid, for this would be placing power without law, upon the same foundation with power exercised according to law. A proceeding without jurisdiction, is void, and a mere nullity. The judge in this case, derived all his authority from the statute, and that does not apply, and of course does not make his discharge binding, if the prisoner came within one of the exceptions stated.

The 5th section of the act which prohibits reimprisonment, for the same offence, of persons discharged upon habeas corpus, most evidently applies only to cases in which the writ and discharge were had, pursuant to the statute.[3] And even this prohibition extends only to magistrates acting individually, in vacation, and does not extend to any court having jurisdiction of the cause of the commitment. Such courts are expressly excepted from the prohibition, and of course retain the same powers as before the passing of the statute. If, then, the attachment had in itself been so defective, as not to have been sufficient to have held the prisoner, the court of chancery might still have awarded a new and competent warrant of commitment, for the same cause, for which the first warrant issued, provided the case was one of which that court had jurisdiction. ...

There are numerous instances, in which the court of K.B.

[of habeas corpus] shall be signed by the person awarding the same ... and if any person be imprisoned as aforesaid in vacation time, it shall be lawful for every such person (other than persons convict, or inexecution by legal process or committed for treason or felony, plainly and specially expressed in the warrant of commitment) to apply in person, or by any one on his behalf to the chancellor, or any judge of the supreme court...."

3. "That no person who shall be set at large, upon any habeas corpus, shall be again imprisoned for the same offence, unless by the legal order or process of the court wherein he is bound by recognizance to appear, or other court having jurisdiction of the cause; and if any person shall knowingly, contrary to this act, recommit or imprison ... for the same offence or pretended offence, any person so set at large, ... he shall forfeit to the party grieved one thousand two hundred and fifty dollars, any colourable pretence or variation in the warrent of commitment notwithstanding."

and some cases, in which the court of C.B. has, upon habeas corpus, undertaken to examine, and decide upon the cause and the authority for the commitment by another court. But in all these cases, the habeas corpus was awarded by the Court, and returnable therein; and except, in a few anomalous cases, in the time of James I. and of which I shall take notice hereafter the examination into the authority of the court to commit, arose upon commitments by some inferior court. [Citations omitted] They were all cases of habeas corpus, at common law; and I apprehend, that there is not an instance in the English law, of a judge in vacation, undertaking to decide upon the legality of a commitment in execution, by the judgment of any court of record, and much less, of a court of the highest degree.

The powers granted by the habeas corpus act, to a judge in vacation, were never intended to apply in any such case, because, cases of that kind appear to be carefully excepted in the statute; and it was not requisite to include them, for the purpose of guarding against arbitrary and groundless imprisonment. The statute seems, with a studied precaution, to have declared that the powers granted to a judge in vacation time, were not to affect cases of imprisonment, under the authority of a competent court. In the first place, "persons convict, and persons in execution by legal process" are not to apply to a judge, for the allowance of a writ of habeas corpus. In the second place, a judge is not to discharge the prisoner brought before him, if it appears that he is detained "upon any legal process, out of a court having jurisdiction of criminal matters". And lastly, if the prisoner be set at large, the prohibition to reimprison him, for the same offence, does not extend to any "court having jurisdiction of the cause". It appears to me, to be unfit, and dangerous to the orderly administration of the law, for a single judge, in vacation, to be charged with a summary and plenary power of review of the judgments and executions of a regular court of justice. The abuse of the powers of the established courts, was never, in any period of our law, so grievous, as to require such a prompt control. And, perhaps, as much, and more danger was to be apprehended from the abuse of such a remedy, than from the abuse of the original power.

The uniform practice, under the statute of Charles II, appears to have coincided with the construction which I adopt: and which strikes my mind, as founded on the strongest principles. This settled practice ought to govern and conclude us; for our habeas corpus act is almost a literal transcript of the statute of Charles. The act of 1787 followed the English statute, _verbatim_, and the revised act of 1807, made only some slight abbreviations in the mode of expression, which cannot, without violence, be construed to alter, in the least degree, the sense and settled construction of the former act. That the "mere change of phraseology" in the revised laws, was not to work a change in the established interpretation, was the unanimous decision of the court for the correction of errors, in 1805, in the case of Taylor v. Delancy. (2 Caines' cases in error, 150, 151.)

There seems to be a degree of propriety and consistency in a superior court of appellate jurisdiction taking cognisance, upon the return of a writ of habeas corpus, of the legality of a judgment and commitment, in an inferior court. But for a single judge to possess such a power, to be exercised in vacation, in a summary manner, without argument of counsel, and upon the judgment and commitment of any and of every court in the state, would be an alarming innovation upon our judicial system.

If, therefore, upon the return of a writ of habeas corpus, awarded in vacation, it appears, that the prisoner stands committed, by the judgment of a court of record, or other court of competent authority, the judge is bound, immediately, to remand the prisoner; and he has no power to examine and decide, touching the legality of the judgment, or the jurisdiction of the court. These questions belong to the cognisance of this court, as possessing general appellate powers, and as having the supreme control of all inferior courts. ...

My opinion, on the first point raised in this case, accordingly is, that the discharge which took place in the vacation, was in no respect conclusive, either upon the court of chancery, or upon this court, and I am also of opinion that, if the first commitment was good, the recommitment was equally lawful, for that the discharge was unauthorized and void, inasmuch as it was not in a case within the provision of the habeas corpus act, and because a judge in vacation, has no authority, either under the act, or without it, to review, and set aside, as illegal and void, a formal commitment and conviction, by a court of chancery.

I shall next proceed to examine the merits of the present application, as appearing upon that part of the return, which sets forth the original warrant of commitment, and as unconnected with any thing which took place subsequent to the first execution of the attachment. The case is now to be considered, as if this was the first writ of habeas corpus, which had been sued out by the prisoner.

The counsel for the prisoner, submitted to the court three objections to the legality of the original warrant of commitment, and they contended, that upon either of the grounds, the commitment was illegal, and that the prisoner ought to be discharged. I shall examine these several objections in their order.

1. It is said, that the matter laid to the charge of the defendant, was a misdemeanor prohibited by the statute, and

not cognisable in chancery, and that the conviction and imprisonment were for that offence, and not for a contempt of the court.

The attachment recites a previous order of the court, in which it was declared, that the defendant, during the time that he was a master, filed a bill in the name of one of the solicitors, and had acted as solicitor in the prosecution of the bill, in the name of the person, "contrary to the statute in that case made and provided, in wilful violation of his duty as master, and in contempt of the authority of the court". Here is a plain and specific statement of the cause of the commitment, and I feel no difficulty in saying, that it was a palpable case of contempt, of which the court had jurisdiction. That the court meant to proceed on the ground of the contempt, appears from the charge in the order, which amounts to a conviction for a contempt, and from the subsequent part of the order, directing the prisoner to be committed, "for his said mal-practice and contempt." I cannot perceive, in this order, any colour for the inference, that the court of chancery assumed a criminal jurisdiction, distinct from the jurisdiction which the court has over contempts. Why should the court have done it? The offence was, in itself, a contempt of that court. This point cannot well be controverted. For an officer in chancery to practice as a solicitor, in the name of another solicitor, was mal-practice and contempt; and to do it without the knowledge or consent of such other solicitor, was a more aggravated mal-practice and contempt, for it was a gross fraud. The order does, indeed, go on to say, that such conduct was "contrary to the statute in that case made and provided, and in wilful violation of his duty as master". And are those words to warrant the inference, that the court intended to depart from the exercise of its undoubted jurisdiction in the case of contempts, when it had a contempt fully before it, and to usurp the criminal jurisdiction of a court of law? Is such a conclusion necessary, or even tolerable, when resting on such grounds, and applied to such a court? The inference would be very severe, and one which I could never indulge, even if the order stopped there. But when we connect this paragraph with the words which follow, "and in contempt of the authority of this court", and when we add the order thereon, that the party be committed, "for such mal-practice and contempt" the intention of the court appears to me to be manifest.

The statute, which the court is supposed to have alluded to, is the act entitled "an act concerning counsellors, attorneys, and solicitors", which declares, that no master in chancery, shall act as solicitor in any action or matter in that court. A violation of this prohibition, by a master, may possibly be indictable, on the ground that every contempt of a statute is indictable, if no other punishment be prescribed.

But an offence against this statute, may also be a contempt of the court, though indictable; and the court may punish the contempt. A great part of the contempts which may be committed against a court of justice are indictable offences; such, for instance, as assaults committed in the presence of the court, resistance to its process, and libels upon the court or its suitors, in respect to matters pending before it. Because the offence is indictable, that circumstance does not, in any case, destroy the right of the court to proceed against the party for the contempt, provided the act complained of amounts to a contempt. ...

Every illegal and unauthorized interference with the process or proceedings of a court, is clearly a contempt of such court, whether that illegality be created by statute, or be declared by the rules and practice of the court. This is a principle so well settled, as to become elementary. The court of chancery was therefore bound, in respect to its own character, and the rights of its suitors, to animadvert, as for a contempt, upon a master, or practising as solicitor, contrary to the statute; because, as far as relates to the punishment for contempts, a court of chancery is as much a court of criminal jurisdiction, as any court of law.

The case stated in the return, was not an ordinary violation of a statute, of which the courts of common law have exclusive cognisance. It was a violation of a law relative to proceedings and practice in chancery, and committed, upon the records, and in the very heart of the court, by one of its officers. This gave the court cognisance of the case, as a contempt. The conduct of the prisoner, as set forth in the order, was a fraud, practised upon a suitor of this court, and it was an abuse by practice, which tended to injustice, deceit and oppression.

"The law", says serjeant Hawkins, (b.2.c.22.s.2.and 12.) gives all courts of record a kind of discretionary power over all abuses, by their own officers, in the administration, or execution of justice, which bring a disgrace on the courts themselves, as not taking sufficient care to prevent them" and he says, that the court may proceed by attachment not only against attorneys, sheriffs, &c. but against any other officer of the court, for any act of disobedience or injustice, that concerns the practice of the court. Lord Ch. Baron Comyns lays it down generally, that "an attorney, being an officer of the court, if he attempts any thing which he cannot, or ought not to do, it will be a contempt of the court, for which an attachment shall go". (Tit. Attorney, B. 13.)

The mal-practice of officers, if frequent or unpunished, reflects dishonour on the administration of justice, and creates among the people a disgust against the courts themselves. This is the true ground of that salutary and indispensable discretion, with which the courts are invested, of controlling and punishing all kinds of abuse, and lawless practice, in every officer belonging to their jurisdiction. If we were then to admit, as the counsel for the prisoner contended, that the prisoner was attached for violating the statute, I should be of opinion, that the attachment was proper, for the statute could not be violated, without involving in the breach of it, a contempt of the court, any more than a breach of the peace can be committed, in the presence of a court, without including in the commission of it, a contempt of such court.

But it is clear, from the facts stated in the order, that the court of chancery did not convict the prisoner of a contempt on the principal point, that being master, he had acted as solicitor. If that had been the ground of the contempt, much of the detail in the order would have been omitted, as superfluous. The averment, that while he was master he had acted as solicitor, by filing the bill, would have been sufficient. But an offence, certainly not within the statute, is set forth, and that is subscribing the name of Peter W. Yates to the bill, without his knowledge or consent, and carrying on the cause in the name of P. W. Yates. This is the strong and prominent gravamen set forth in the order, and it is a grievance and contempt, which the statute did not reach. It was essential to the dignity of the court, and to the purity and regularity of its practice, that such conduct should be noticed and punished. The animadversion was indispensable. ...

2. But admitting that the prisoner was committed for a contempt, his counsel have contended that the conviction was bad, because it was not founded upon sufficient evidence, as it is not stated in the order, that the prisoner was examined upon interrogatories.

It does not appear upon the return, whether the prisoner was, or was not examined upon interrogatories. The order is silent as to that fact, and it is by inference only that the counsel can draw such a conclusion from the return. Assuming that the prisoner was not examined, and that this court was authorized to review the proceeding, I am not prepared to say that such an examination was indispensable. This would depend upon the usage and practice of the court, and it must rest upon sound discretion, in each particular case; for it is a settled rule in chancery, that if the defendant be examined on oath, touching a contempt, his denial is not conclusive, and the court will examine witnesses on both sides, and decide according to the weight of testimony. There is then no reason that the party charged in chancery with a contempt, should be entitled to claim as a matter of right, to purge himself upon oath, because such purgation is no acquittal, as it is at law.[4]

---

4. See Curtis and Curtis, "The Story of a Notion in the Law of

(4 *Bl*. *Com*. 284. Doug. 516) But it is a decisive answer to this objection, that we have no authority to inquire upon this return into the proceedings in chancery, prior to the conviction. It is enough for us, that we see, on the face of the return, an adjudication or conviction for a contempt, and a commitment in pursuance of such conviction. By what means the court of chancery arrived to the adjudication, we are not to inquire, for this court is not intrusted by the constitution, with the power of sustaining appeals from chancery. We can only act judicially upon the facts appearing upon the return. We have not the proceedings and evidence before us; and to sit here in judgment upon them, with only *ex parte* suggestions and arguments to guide us, would be extravagant. I disclaim any such power. We are bound to presume, that the prosecution for the contempt down to the conviction, was duly conducted; and I entertain a persuasion, from the character of the court, that if all the facts were fairly before us, they would demonstrate the moderation and regularity of the proceedings. It is sufficient for us here, that we see by the return, a conviction for a contempt, and a commitment by a court of competent authority.

3. The last objection taken to the sufficiency of the return is, that the prisoner was committed until the further order of the court.

It was admitted that this is the usual form of the order of commitment for a contempt in chancery, as well as in the courts of common law. If we are all in an error, upon this point, it is time that the practice was revised; but it would ill become this court, to discharge the prisoner by reason of an exception which applies equally to the practice of this court, and which has been established in all the English courts, and in the two houses of parliament, from almost time immemorial.

The counsel for the prisoner traced the chancery practice, as laid down in the *Practical Register*, and in *West's Symbolography*, back to the period of the *Year Books*, to show that it had no foundation there. But it would be extremely unwise to overset an established practice, and course of precedents, because such a remote origin cannot be shown. Our most valuable institutions could not endure so severe a test. The forms of administering justice, in all their practical details, have undergone essential changes, and vast improvements. The time of the *Year Books* was even at Westminster Hall, a time of comparative ignorance, and barbarism; and if precedents from that infant period of our law, were admitted to control the cultivat-

---

Criminal Contempt", (1927) 41 *Harv*. *L*. *Rev*. 51.

ed jurisprudence of the present day, they would degrade, or at least tarnish the character which it now enjoys, in the maturity of its age, and the height of its prosperity.

The practice of commitments for contempts, during pleasure prevails in the house of assembly of this state, (Colony Journals, v. 2. 510. and State Journals for 1796) as well as in the house of commons in Great Britain. It has become too deep-rooted and inveterate a practice for us now to correct; and I am persuaded that there exist sound reasons for the universal adoption of it, and that it has not been found, upon experience, to be injurious to the liberty of the subject. The objection is at this time, new. It was taken in the Earl of Shaftsbury's case, and also in that of The Queen v. Paty and others; but in the latter case, though Ch. J. Holt objected to the sufficiency of the return, he took no notice of this objection; and Mr. Justice Powys said that a commitment during the pleasure of the house, was more favourable to the prisoner, and more for his benefit, than a commitment for a certain time, as it leaves to the house a power to discharge the prisoner upon his submission. He said that it was agreeable to the constant forms of commitment by the commons; and was conformable to the commitments by the K.B. which are implied to be during the pleasure of the court. (2 Ld. Raym. 1108) ...

The judicial is, from its very constitution, the feeblest department in government. "Des Trois puissances" says Montequieu, "dont nous avons parle, celle de juger est en quelque facon nulle." (L'Esprit des Lois, liv. 11. c. 6.) It is so checked, and so controlled, that it cannot essentially abuse its powers. The tendency of the times, is rather to induce the courts to relax, than increase in the severity of their ancient discipline, to exercise their power over contempts with extreme moderation, and never to resort to it, but when urged by the most commanding necessity. Sound discretion must use, and apply the power we have been considering, and sound discretion is and must be confided to the highest tribunals, on this subject. The trust is given to the courts, not for themselves, but for the public, who are deeply interested in the preservation of this power, in its accustomed vigour.

I am accordingly of opinion that the prisoner must be remanded.

Van Ness, J. and Thompson, J. were of the same opinion.[5]

The Court, thereupon, made the following order:

ORDERED, that the said John V. N. Yates be remitted to the custody of the sheriff, of the city and county of Albany, to remain in the same state in which he was, at the time of the

---

5. The dissenting opinions of Yates and Spencer, JJ. are omitted.

issuing of the said writ of habeas corpus.

Motion denied.

<u>Yates</u> v. <u>The People</u>
New York Court for the Trial of Impeachments
and the Correction of Errors, 1810
6 Johnson 337

[Following the above decision the case was taken to the highest court of the state on writ of error.[6] Thereupon a motion to quash the writ was filed and argued, the grounds of the motion being that the order of the Supreme Court denying the writ of habeas corpus was not reviewable. In the Court of Errors a doubt was expressed whether the judges of the Supreme Court, who were members of the Court of Errors, had a right to take part in the case or to express any opinion concerning the questions presented. The question was put to a vote and it was decided that the judges had a right to express their opinions. Thereupon Kent, C. J. delivered the following opinion on the motion to quash the writ of error.]

Kent, Ch. J. Before I enter upon consideration of the case, it will be proper to submit a few observations relative to the title under which I now claim the privilege of addressing the court. Doubts seem to have been entertained, by some of the members, whether the judges had authority to take any, and if any, what share in the important questions which have arisen in the course of this cause. Indeed it has been thought necessary, that a formal vote should be taken, allowing us to give an opinion, on the present occasion.

The 32d article of the constitution declares, that this court shall consist of the president of the senate, for the time being, and the senators, chancellor, and the judges of the supreme court, or the major part of them. These are the officers who are to constitute the court. This is its general description; its permanent and component organization. The remainder of the article qualifies and restricts the exercise of this judicial power by the chancellor and judges, in certain specified cases. In case of impeachment, the chancellor, or judge impeached, is suspended from exercising his office, until his acquittal. In this instance, the disqualification for the time being, becomes complete and absolute, and the officer cannot sit as a member. But in cases of appeals and writs of error, the language of the constitution is materially different.

---

6. The Chancellor after first issuing the writ had sought to prevent review by issuing a supersedeas. The Court of Errors held this effort was ineffective.

It imposes no other restriction upon the rights of the chancellor and judges, as full and perfect members of the court, than simply this: that on appeals, the chancellor shall not have a voice in the final sentence, and on writs of error, the judges shall not have a voice for the affirmance or reversal of the judgment. In every other respect, their rights, as members, remain in full force. Every exception to the general delegation of constitutional power is to be taken strictly. This is a settled rule of interpretation. The general grant is to them, as members; the exception is, that they shall not vote in the given case. The chancellor and judges are then regular constitutional members of this court, with powers and immunities equal to those of other members; and with an equal and perfect right to speak, act, and vote in all cases, and on all questions arising upon appeals and writs of error, subject only to the express and definite limitation which I have mentioned. There can be no just doubt of the correctness of this construction; and the rule of this court, made some years ago, (and before I was a member of the bench) declaring that the chancellor and judges should not have a voice in the decision of any question, arising on appeals, or writs of error, was a palpable denial of right, and is, of itself, null and void.[7] I could wish to be informed from whence this court derived the authority to make that rule. Every court may, undoubtedly, make rules to regulate its practice; but no court can limit or explain the powers of its coordinate members. The members are all equal and are not responsible to each other, and derive their authority from one common source. If majorities can vote down, or fritter away the rights of minorities, they might with equal facility, expel the chancellor and judges, and exercise, in this way, the most shameless tyranny. If doubts exist, as to the constitutional rights of the members, those doubts cannot be solved by any power short of the legislature, who have authority to establish regulations for this court. The act, organizing the court, was originally drawn with uncommon ability, and has not sanctioned any such invasion of right as that contained in the rule. It declares, generally, (1 <u>Rev. Laws</u>, 182.) that this court shall consist of

---

7. Thompson, J. summarized the provisions of this rule of court as follows: "It declares, that when a cause shall be brought into this court, by a writ of error, on the question of law in a judgment of the supreme court, the judges of such court may severally state their opinions, upon every matter, that may arise on such hearing, but shall not have a voice, in the decision of the court, on any question whatever, arising on the cause so brought into this court." 6 Johns. at 409.

the president of the senate, the senators, chancellor, and judges of the supreme court, or the major part of them; and that they shall hold such court during the sitting of the legislature. The statute is even silent, as to the restriction imposed upon the chancellor and judges, when the vote is to be taken on the final question in a cause; but leaves that restriction to rest upon the constitution, as being too clear to be mistaken, and too sacred to be invaded.

Having said this much in explanation of my rights, I shall not demand to go beyond the rule of the court, on the present occasion. It reserves to the judges the right to state their opinion, upon every matter which may arise upon the hearing of a cause brought up by writ of error. Though this leaves them in a mutilated condition, with rights half retained and half destroyed, I do not think that this is the proper moment to revise the rule. I mean only to be distinctly understood, that the opinion which I am not to deliver, I give, as a matter of right, not of license; that I stand here, not as a tenant at will, but on a constitutional freehold, from which I will not be driven, without a contest.

Upon the motion now before the court, two questions present themselves: 1. Whether a writ of error will lie, in any case, upon the award of the supreme court, remanding a prisoner, upon the return to a writ of habeas corpus.

2. Admitting that it will lie in any case, whether it ought to be sustained in the case before us.

So much has been said upon the argument respecting the powers and authority of this court, that it will be useful to endeavour, in the first place, to ascertain the true and legal limits of its jurisdiction.

This court is as much bound by law as any other court within the state. The idea, that it has an undefined discretion, in any case, is wholly unfounded. The members, when they enter upon the execution of their trust, take and subscribe the same oath that is taken by all other judicial officers. They are bound by the most solemn sanctions, legal, moral, and religious, to seek after, and to declare the law, without prejudice or partiality. Whether the law be in any case defective or unpalatable, is not to be made a question here. It is the business of the legislature to make, and amend the law, and the duty of every court, and equally so of this, to pronounce it, as they find it. This court cannot possibly approve of the suggestions of counsel, "to encourage an enlargement of its supervisory powers, to vindicate to itself the powers, that the best court of errors ought to have, and not to clip the rights of the subject, by English rules and technical standards." How can this court vindicate or assume to itself powers not given to it by law? This would be gross usurpation upon the legislative department. If such advice were to be followed, there would be an end of all law and security within these walls. We should have no certain measure or standard of justice. The citizen would never know when he was safe, or what were his rights. An uncertain rule of law, produces the most miserable servitude. The court would soon become the object of intrigue, the slave of prejudice, the organ of party, terrible to the suitor, and destructive of the established law of the land. In my opinion, no court should be more scrupulously cautious than this, of overleaping its constitutional and legal limits, because it is a court of final resort, and no other court can correct its abuses. Such an unchecked tribunal would soon become the public terror, or, perhaps, the public scorn, if it once dreams of discretion and usurpation. The court ought to turn a deaf ear to such dangerous flattery.

Nor can I believe that this court will relish the still more reprehensible invitation not to listen to the constitutional law members of the court, except on questions respecting private property. There, indeed, it is said they may be regarded; but in cases respecting the person or liberty of the subject, the senators are exhorted to disregard the legal opinions of those judicial characters, who have been intrusted, by their country, with the most exalted confidence, and are exclusively devoting their lives and talents to the administration of justice. And why not listen to the judges, who have equally the guardianship of the civil and criminal code, and whose efforts to hold up the law, as a protection to the innocent, and a punishment to the guilty, are in constant activity before the public eye? Is there to be no certain rule of decision, when personal rights are involved? In what volume do we read, that the liberty of the citizen is not as much under the protection, and defined by the rules of law, as his property? Will it be safe or becoming to follow our prejudices, our sympathies, or indignation in the one case more than in the other? And if the established judges are to be distrusted, from whom is the court to receive assistance, and on whom to bestow their reverence and confidence?

Such language cannot have been used with success. The constitution early taught me to cherish better hopes of this assembly. This venerable body is chosen from large districts, for long times, and by independent lords of the soil. It must be presumed to consist of gentlemen of intelligence, of integrity, and of extended reputation. They must feel all the pride and dignity of character, which their elevated station inspires. Whatever political divisions may agitate them in the exercise of their senatorial duties, they will lay them all aside when they assume the graver character, and high responsibility of judges. In this solemn temple, this last retreat of justice, they will assuredly discard every prejudice and follow firmly the law of the land. Neither the wishes nor the discipline of party will be discovered here. The public, we trust, will witness and admire the unrelaxing severity of their justice.

The constitution ordains, that this court shall be instituted, under the regulations which shall be established by the legislature. It further declares, that when a cause shall be brought up by a writ of error, on a question of law, on a judgment of the supreme court, the judges shall assign their reasons for their judgment, but shall not have a voice for its affirmance or reversal. It is, then, on a question of law on a judgment of the supreme court, that error lies. These are the words of the constitution; and the idea that it lies for any other errors, if any there be, than those involved in a judgment, is extremely incorrect. The statute was designed to institute and regulate the court; but it could not enlarge its jurisdiction, in the cases in which the constitution had already defined it. It could not authorize a writ of error, but upon a judgment rendered; nor does the statute admit of any other meaning. It is not good logic to reason from these preliminary expressions in the statute, that "all errors happening in the supreme court shall be corrected here"; unless we, at the same time, compare them with the context, and the other provisions in the act. Who ever heard of expounding a statute by reading one line only? The words all errors, mean all errors that are involved in a final judgment; and if we read and compare the whole section together, this meaning will be made manifest. The statute goes on and says, "that it shall be lawful, as well for the attorney-general, in behalf of the people, as for any party against whom any judgment shall be given, to sue out a writ of error, and to cause the transcript of such judgment, and all things concerning the same, to be brought into this court. The court is then to reverse or affirm such judgment, and to give such other judgment therein, as the law shall require, and to cause the transcript of the record, with the judgment thereon, to be remitted into the supreme court, where such further proceedings shall be had, as well for execution as otherwise, as may be agreeable to law and justice."

Here, then, we have, in one view, all the powers of this court, on the subject of a writ of error, as granted by the constitution, or declared by law. It is a wise and cautious provision. It gives this court no unusual appellate jurisdictions; no superintending discretion. It is a court with plain, precise, and intelligible barriers. No man could surmount them without being conscious of committing a crime. The power of review is simply confined to a judgment and final decree; and when the constitution spoke of a judgment of the supreme court, it used a technical term, perfectly familiar to the sages and patriots, who, enlightened and animated our first convention. They never intended any thing more than those ordinary writs of error, which, by the settled practice, lay to the exchequer-chamber, or the house of lords, upon the judgments of the court of King's Bench in England.

The convention of 1777 knew nothing of the revolutionary novelties, and madness of a subsequent period. They formed our constitution with all its legal and technical definitions, upon the approved wisdom, the sober sense of the English common law, which they most providentially ingrafted into our system. Nothing can be plainer than the path before us. Our constitution meant by a judgment of the supreme court, what was well understood under the colonial government, and was well understood in Westminster Hall, to be a final judgment of a court of law. It was not the design of the founders of this house, to bestow upon it a broader jurisdiction than that possessed by the house of lords. There was no motive occurring at that day which could have led to such an innovation.

The English system of jurisprudence, had fostered the soundest and most rational principles of civil liberty. Under it our fathers had lived and flourished, and from it they had imbibed, and I hope I may say, transmitted to us, that lively sense of order, of decency, of moderation, and of right, which is inculcated by its generous institutions. We must, therefore, constantly recur to the English common law, to explain the technical language, and the sound import of our laws, and constitution. If we depart from this plain standard of interpretation, we set everything afloat, and our constitution becomes a mass of unintelligible matter.

Assuming it, then, as a solid principle, that a writ of error lies here, only when it would lie on a judgment of the K.B. I proceed to show, by decisive authority that it will not lie in England, upon an award made on the return of a writ of habeas corpus. If I establish this point, as I most assuredly shall, the writ in the present case must be quashed; for this court will never violate the law which it is sworn to administer. ...

I now submit to the candour and judgment of this court, whether I have not sufficiently shown, that by the English law, a writ of error will not lie in this case. We have the unanimous opinion of the court of C.B. in the time of Lord Coke. We have the resolution of the house of commons, in the reign of Queen Anne. We have the unanimous opinion of the court of K.B. in the time of Geo. I., and, lastly, we have the sanction of Lord Ch. Baron Comyns; and all this, without a single case, or decision, or precedent, or opinion, to oppose to such a stream of authority. What intelligent person can then doubt of the law? "I speak as to wise men, judge ye what I say" I will not stoop to the criticism, that these were opinions of the courts, and not adjudications upon the point. The doctrine was laid down in Lord Coke's day, as of course, as being then the known and established law. The principle is of immemorial standing. It has become the uncontroverted maxim of ages. A great part of the magnificent structure of our jurisprudence is not built upon a sounder basis. The question is not whether the house has not a physical power to vote down this principle, but has it the legal and moral power?

This court, upon error brought, is not only to reverse the judgment of the supreme court, but to render such judgment as that court ought to have rendered. Let us pursue this idea to its practical consequences. Suppose the supreme court, upon habeas corpus, remands a prisoner, by refusing to bail him, or remands him, because the bail he offers is insufficient, and he brings a writ of error, what is this court to do in these cases? Are they to determine here, by vote, when a prisoner ought to be bailed, and in what sum, and with what sureties? Is this court created for such purposes? Have they any such discretion? Are they competent to exercise it? This would be assuming original criminal jurisdiction, without colour in law, or precedent upon record. Suppose, again, that the supreme court discharge a prisoner on bail, when he ought to have been remanded, or discharge him altogether, when he ought to have been delivered upon bail; are the people, by their attorney-general, to bring a writ of error, in order to reclaim the prisoner? If the prisoner can bring a writ of error, the right ought to be mutual, and exist equally on the side of the people. But how can this court cause a person to be retaken, who should, in their opinion, have been unduly set at large? Is the court to send back the transcript, with an order to the supreme court to issue a bench warrant to retake the party, and commit him? Can warrants issue but upon a charge supported by oath or indictment? Or suppose a grand jury shall, in the mean time, have passed upon the case, and rejected a bill of indictment, ought the party then to be harassed and recommitted? If a writ of error will lie in one case, it will lie in all these cases of habeas corpus; and this court would soon be obliged to abandon a new jurisdiction, which it is incompetent to execute.

2. But, laying all these general considerations aside, there are special reasons arising in this case, which render it impossible to sustain the writ of error. This I will now briefly, but conclusively, demonstrate.

The record shows us, that the prisoner brought into the supreme court, was detained by process from the court of chancery, founded upon a conviction in that court, of contempt and mal-practice. The legality or illegality of that conviction, never could have been considered in the supreme court, because the constitution does not give to that court any jurisdiction, by way of review or appeal, over a proceeding in chancery. The cognisance of such proceedings belongs exclusively to this court, which cannot, upon the writ of error, do anything, like final justice, in the case. It cannot do anything but what the supreme court ought to have done. The conviction in chancery is not before them. They cannot touch its merits. All that the supreme court had before it, and all that this court now has, is merely the process of execution, founded on that conviction. If the court could lawfully review the conviction in chancery, the review ought, at least, to come directly from that court, and bring up with it the proceedings at large. It is impossible to examine the merits of the conviction, from the very imperfect state of it which comes up circuitously, by means of the present return. If we attempt it, it would, in addition to the great injustice of the measure, by an inquiry to be governed by chance, and not by investigation. If the conviction is, in any shape, to be questioned here, the chancellor is entitled, by the constitution, to be heard, and to be called upon to assign his reasons for his order; and the judges of the supreme court are to sit, and not to give opinions merely, but to vote with the other members of the court. But by this strange proceeding, that privilege, that valuable right is done away.

Again, if this court, by means of some newly discovered power, could discharge the prisoner from the process of commitment, it would confer no honour, or lasting benefit, upon the prisoner, for the conviction would still remain in force. The party now complaining, would still be adjudged guilty, and might instantly be imprisoned on the same sentence. This would be an inevitable legal consequence; for to suppose a conviction can stand good, without satisfaction or reversal, and yet be without efficacy, or power of execution, would be to suppose an absurdity. ...

But it may be asked, if the writ of error will not lie, is this to be a case without redress? Can a solicitor be imprisoned, at the pleasure of the court of chancery, and no tribunal correct the abuse?[8] While I admit, that the court of chan-

---

8. In the course of a vigorous opinion arguing that the writ of error would lie, Senator Clinton made the following observations: "If the prisoner is brought up on a habeas corpus, the court is to remand him, the moment it is perceived to be for a contempt, and no writ of error will lie on this decision; and although this may be wicked and oppressive, and may operate as an imprisonment for life; yet the court so acting is not liable to punishment: for the commitment is a judicial act, and it is contended, that no judge can be questioned for his acts as such. Here then is a case ... where an unjust and tyrannical judge may, at pleasure, imprison an innocent man for life, and yet place punishment at defiance. A doctrine pregnant with such

cery is sufficiently amenable, in another way, I answer, that this is not the question before the court. It has nothing to do now with that inquiry. The court is called upon to say, whether a writ of error will lie upon a habeas corpus? If they find that it will not, they are bound by imperious duty to say so. I think I have sufficiently shown, that if the writ of error was to be pursued, it never could bring up the merits of the case. The wishes, then, of the most lively benevolence, could not be gratified by this course. The real merit of the case, as far as we can judge from the record, turns on this single point, was Yates justly convicted of malpractice committed, to the great injury of one Samuel Bacon, who exhibited charges against him? To this question, we are not to answer, because we have not the conviction, nor the proofs and proceedings which led to it. The intendment of law is, till the contrary be legally shown, that he was justly convicted. This court is bound to adopt, and to act upon that presumption. To act upon any other, would be indecorous; would be contrary to the benign maxim of the common law; and would be the highest injustice to the tribunal in question, which is not now brought here to meet or to answer that inquiry. I, therefore, lay all such extraneous considerations aside, as unbecoming the dignity, and as casting a shade over the purity, of this court. Not even the collateral point, how far the discharge, by Mr. Justice Spencer, was binding, could be examined and decided upon this return. The habeas corpus act says, that no such discharge is binding upon any court, having jurisdiction of the cause of the commitment; and how can

---

monstrous absurdities, and teeming with such horrible results, can never be in unison with the letter and spirit of a free and enlightened system of jurisprudence. And, although I trust we have nothing to apprehend from such practices, in the times in which we live, yet we ought to keep our eyes fixed on futurity. ... Why are we to expect an exemption from the common lot of nations? In the true course of events, we must, indeed, travel the round of human calamity. Pestilence and war, famine and oppression, will visit us; and we must anticipate that in some period, the Tresilians and the Jeffries of former times will live again in our tribunals, men who will imprison under the forms of justice, and murder with all the solemnities of law. And when such monsters arise, to scourge the human race, let me tell you, that they will be supported by the arm of power, and will be attended by their obsequious satellites, and smooth-faced parasites, who will deride the magna charta of your liberties, and laugh at the majesty of the people."
6 Johns. at 470-71.

this court determine whether the court of chancery had or had not jurisdiction of the cause, until we know, truly, what that cause was, by looking at the conviction itself, and the proofs and documents upon which it was founded?

Finally, if the Gordian knot is to be cut, we ought, at least, to call for the <u>dignus vindice nodus</u>. There ought to be an object befitting so bold a precedent. In this case, there is nothing which should disturb the tranquil course of the law. The party, say his counsel, might have appealed in the ordinary way. If he omitted to do so, within the time of limitation, it was his own fault, or his folly. He has no right, now, to complain, nor to call on this court, to break in upon principle, to help him. One of his counsel said, that if he could not be relieved now, it would be tantamount to an imprisonment for life. This was a very loose assertion. If he continues in prison, it must be imputed to his obstinacy. It is well understood, that, if an attorney be convicted of mal-practice, he can come out, upon paying costs, and making satisfaction to his injured client. Lord Chancellor Erskine lately ruled, (13 Vez. 69), that if an attorney was guilty of misconduct, he would make him pay costs, and bind him to make satisfaction.

For these reasons, I am of opinion, that the writ of error ought to be quashed.[9]

---

9. A majority of the court were of the opinion that the writ of error would lie and the motion to quash was denied. Thereupon the case was argued on its merits. A majority of the court voted to reverse the judgment of the Supreme Court. Chancellor Lansing wrote an opinion favoring affirmance; Senator Clinton wrote an opinion urging reversal. In the course of his opinion the Chancellor spoke as follows: "If the opinion, now under examination, is to govern, all those invaluable monuments of the wisdom of antiquity, the volumes that contain them, and the maxims preserved in them ... are to be consigned to indiscriminate, interminable destruction; and this solely by the uncontrollable power of this court. If this court can thus prostrate the common law, protected by what it is bound to deem the inviolable provisions of the constitution, it may, with as much ease, extend its irresistible arm, and by one tremendous blow, demolish the statute law with it. ... Bound to distribute justice according to the constitution and laws of the state, though this court might discover traits of excellence in other systems, dictated by the benevolent views of a despot, or by the sublimated theories of real or pretended patriots, who sometimes succeed in a free republic in identifying their opinion with that of the government of the country,

Yates v. Lansing[10]
Supreme Court of New York, 1810; 5 Johnson 282

Kent, Ch. J. The record before the court presents the case of a civil suit, brought against the chancellor of this state, for an act done by him in his judicial capacity, while sitting in the court of chancery. The pleadings admit that the defendant did, as chancellor, and not otherwise, at a court of chancery, held on the 15th day of September, 1808, order the plaintiff, after he had been discharged upon habeas corpus, by one of the judges of this court, to be recommitted for the contempt and mal-practice for which he had been originally imprisoned, and that the action is brought for such reimprisonment, and to recover the penalty mentioned in the 5th section of the habeas corpus act.

The counsel who appeared for the plaintiff at the last term (and who was the same counsel that argued the case upon the habeas corpus at the last February term) declined to argue this case, but would not consent that judgment should pass against the plaintiff by default, and pressed the court for a decision during the term, and accompanied his motion with an intimation that he intended to carry the cause, by writ of error, into the court for the correction of errors. This fact must be my apology for bestowing more time upon the case, than the doctrine which it involves, might seem to require. We have given it a deliberate attention, and in the opinion of the court, the action cannot be sustained upon any principle of law, justice or public policy.

The words of the statute upon which the suit is brought, are, "that no person who shall be set at large upon any habeas corpus, shall be again imprisoned for the same offence, unless by the legal order or process of the court wherein he is bound by recognisance to appear, or other court having jurisdiction of the cause; and if any person shall knowingly, contrary to this act, recommit or imprison, or cause to be recommitted or imprisoned for the same offence, any person so set at large, he shall forfeit to the party grieved, 1,250 dollars." There appears to be several strong reasons why this section in the statute cannot support the action.

---

it cannot adopt them in the cases on which it is required to decide. Decisions on the principles of abstract justice destroy the safety and liberty of the citizen, and strike at the most essential rights of property." 6 Johns. at 493-94.

10. This case came before the Supreme Court before the decision of the Court of Errors in Yates v. The People.

The order of the court of chancery was legal, inasmuch as the previous discharge of the plaintiff was not in a case authorized by the statute, and was null and void in law. This was the decision of the court at the last August term, and it will be unnecessary to review that point, or repeat what was then said. According to the judgment of the court, there cannot be a pretext for this suit, even if the defendant was otherwise liable for an undue exercise, or misapplication of the powers of his court.

But the point which I purpose now principally to consider is, whether there be any foundation in law for the suit, admitting that the defendant was mistaken in supposing that the discharge of the plaintiff under the habeas corpus, was unduly made. The statute allows the party so discharged, to be again imprisoned for the same offence, provided it be by the legal order or process of the court wherein he is bound by recognisance to appear, or other court having jurisdiction of the cause. Any court which has jurisdiction of the subject matter, may reimprison, notwithstanding the discharge. To state a plain case; if a person committed at a court of <u>oyer and terminer</u>, or sessions of the peace, of a felony, and imprisoned in the state prison, be discharged by a judge on habeas corpus, on the ground that the court had no authority to commit or that the order of commitment was invalid, would any one doubt that the court might cause the convict to be further reimprisoned either upon the same warrant, if it judged it sufficient, or by awarding a new and better one? The statute never intended such a destruction of principle, as to entrust to a judge in vacation, the power to control the judgment or to check the jurisdiction of a court of record.

Our system of appellate jurisprudence is built upon a sounder foundation, and instead of entrusting to the fiat of a single judge, to correct the errors of any court of justice, it has provided the constitutional process by appeal, or a writ of error. It is sufficient that the court which commits, has jurisdiction of the cause of commitment; and as the cause in the present case was an alleged malpractice and contempt, the court of chancery most undoubtedly had jurisdiction over the subject matter. It is decisive on the point, that the court considered the act of which it complained, to be a contempt and mal-practice, by being an unauthorized interference with the practice of the court. Every court judges exclusively for itself, of its own contempts; no other court, and much less a single judge out of court, can undertake to judge on the question. The plaintiff was recommitted, to use the language of the order, for "contempt and mal-practice"; and whether the court of chancery was right or wrong in considering that the plaintiff's conduct amounted to a contempt, and whether it took the proper steps to ascertain the contempt, is perfectly immaterial as to the point of jurisdiction. It had authority to punish contempts. It must judge what are contempts. Practising as solicitor, without leave, and practising in another's name, and practicing in another's name without his knowledge, are all misdemeanors, and contempts of the court. These are undeniable propositions.

On the ground which the court took, then, it certainly had jurisdiction of the subject matter. The case of Howell, the recorder of London, is to this purpose. He presided at a court of oyer and terminer, and fined and imprisoned a juror for bringing in a wrong verdict. In a suit against him for this act, the whole court of C.B. declared that the oyer and terminer had jurisdiction of the cause, because it had power to punish a misdemeanor in a juror; though in the case before the court, the recorder had made an erroneous judgment in considering the act of the juror as amounting to a misdemeanor, when in fact it was no misdemeanor. (Hammond v. Howell, 2 Mod. 218.)

To be prepared to give a sound construction to the statute giving the penalty in question, we ought to bear in mind the uniform and solemn language of the common law, as to the responsibility of judges, by private suit, for their judicial decisions. "We shall never know," says Lord Coke, "the true reason of the interpretation of the statutes, if we know not what the law was before the making of them." Where courts of special and limited jurisdiction exceed their powers, the whole proceeding is coram non judice, and all concerned in such void proceedings are held to be liable in trespass. (Case of the Marshalsea, 10 Co. 68 Terry v. Huntington, Hardres, 480) But I believe this doctrine has never been carried so far as to justify a suit against the members of the superior courts of general jurisdiction, for any act done by them in a judicial capacity. There is no such case or decision which I have met with, and I find the doctrine to be decidedly otherwise. In Miller v. Seeve, (2 Black. Rep. 1141) Lord Ch. J. De Grey said, that the judges of the king's superior courts of general jurisdiction were not liable to answer personally for their errors in judgment. The protection as to them was absolute and universal; with respect to the inferior courts, it was only while they act within their jurisdiction. The penalty sought for in the present suit, was, I think, very clearly imposed upon individuals only, acting ministerially or extrajudicially out of court. The words of the statute do not apply to the act of a court done of record; and we ought to require a positive application of the penalty to such a case, before we can in decency presume that the statute intended so far to humble and degrade the judicial department, as to render the judges responsible in a civil suit for their judicial acts.

The doctrine which holds a judge exempt from a civil suit or indictment, for any act done, or omitted to be done by him, sitting as judge, has a deep root in the common law. It is to be found in the earliest judicial records, and it has been steadily maintained by an undisturbed current of decisions, in the English courts, amidst every change of policy, and through every revolution of their government. A short view of the cases will teach us to admire the wisdom of our forefathers, and to revere a principle on which rests the independence of the administration of justice. Juvat accedere fontes atque haurire. [Discussion of authorities omitted.]

These cases, and many more opinions of the like effect, which could be gleaned from the Year Books, conclusively show, that judges of all courts of record, from the highest to the lowest, and even jurors, who are judges of fact, were always exempted from prosecution, by action or indictment, for what they did in their judicial character. It did not escape the discernment of the early sages of the law, that the principle requisite to secure a free, vigorous and independent administration of justice, applied to render jurors, as well as judges, inviolable; and I fully acquiesce in the opinion of Lord Ch. J. Wilmot, that trials by jury will be buried in the same grave with the authority of the courts who are to preside over them. But I proceed to show that in subsequent periods of the Englist law, the doctrine was equally asserted and enforced. ...

I shall close this review of the cases with noticing one arising in an American court. The case I allude to is that of Phelps v. Sill, lately decided in the supreme court of Connecticut. (1 Day's Cases in Error, 315) From the characters composing that court, I think the decision entitled to great consideration. That was a suit against a judge of probates for omitting to take security from a guardian, and the court held that the action would not lie. They said that "it was a settled principle, that a judge is not to be questioned in a civil suit for doing, or for neglecting or refusing to do a particular official act, in the exercise of judicial power. That a regard to this maxim was essential to the administration of justice. If by any mistake in the exercise of his office, a judge should injure an individual, hard would be his condition, if he were to be responsible for damages. The rules and principles, which govern the exercise of judicial power, are not, in all cases, obvious; they are often complex, and appear under different aspects to different persons. No man would accept the office of judge, if his estate were to answer for every error in judgment, or if his time and property were to be wasted in litigations with every man whom his decisions might offend."

After this recognition of the principle, I may confidently appeal to every sound and intelligent lawyer, whether it could possibly have been the meaning of the habeas corpus act, to make the chancellor, or any other judge of any other court of record, responsible in a civil suit, for a heavy penalty, for an action done of record by him, while sitting in his court of justice? Ought such a sacred principle of the common law, as the one we have been considering, to be subverted without an express declaration to that effect? Does such a construction appear ever to have been entertained in any book, or by any individual, from the time of the statute of Charles II, until the bringing of the present suit? Our act is but a transcript from the English statute, and Serjeant Hawkins (b.2.c.15 #23) expressly excludes every such construction. "The Habeas corpus act," he observes, "makes the judges liable to an action at the suit of the party, in one case only, viz. in refusing to award a habeas corpus, and seems to leave it to their discretion in all other cases, to pursue the directions of the act, in the same manner as they ought to execute all other laws, without making them subject to the action of the party, or to any other express penalty or forfeiture." The penalty to which the chancellor and judges are liable, is mentioned in the fourth section of the act; and that is given against them by name, and only for their refusal, in the vacation time, to allow a writ of habeas corpus, when duly applied for. The chancellor and judges may refuse such a writ, at their discretion, if applied for in term time, and the penalty will not attach. It is only when they refuse, in a more ministerial capacity, to allow a writ, that they are made responsible. The allowance of a writ in vacation, is not a judicial act. It is merely analogous to the case stated in Green v. The Hundred of B. (1 Loon. 323) where it was held, that an action on the case lay against a justice of the peace, for refusing to take the oath of the party robbed, because, in such case he did not act as a judge, but as a particular minister appointed by the statute of Eliz. to take examinations. The habeas corpus act does not, then, in any of its provisions, violate, or even touch the principle, that no suit lies for a judicial act. Though the judge is bound under a penalty to allow the writ, yet when the prisoner is brought before him he is to discharge, bail, or remand him, as he shall be advised; and no action or penalty is given for what he shall then do or refuse to do.

Judicial exercise of power is imposed upon the courts. They must decide and act according to their judgment, and therefore the law will protect them. The chancellor, in the case of the plaintiff, was bound in duty to imprison and re-imprison him, if he considered his conduct, as amounting to a contempt of his court. The obligations of his office left him no volition. He was as much bound to punish a contempt committed in his court, as he was bound in any other case to exercise his power. He may possibly have erred in judgment, in calling an act a contempt which did not amount to one, and in regarding a discharge as null, when it was binding. This court may have erred in the same way; still it was but error of judgment, for which neither the chancellor, nor the judges of this court, are or can be responsible in a civil suit. Such responsibility would be an anomaly in jurisprudence. No statute could have intended such atrocious oppression and injustice. The penalty is given only for the voluntary and wilful acts of individuals acting in a private or ministerial capacity. It is a mulct, and given by way of punishment. The person who forfeits it, must "knowingly, contrary to the act" reimprison, or cause the party to be reimprisoned. There must be the scienter or intentional violation of the statute; and this can never be imputed to the judicial proceedings of a court. It would be an impeachable offence, which can never be averred or shown, but under the process of impeachment.

No man can foresee the disastrous consequences of a precedent in favour of such a suit. Whenever we subject the established courts of the land to the degradation of private prosecution, we subdue their independence, and destroy their authority. Instead of being venerable before the public, they become contemptible; and we thereby embolden the licentious to trample upon everything sacred in society, and to overturn those institutions which have hitherto been deemed the best guardians of civil liberty.

I am, therefore, of opinion that judgment ought to be entered for the defendant.

Thompson, J. and Van Ness, J. concurred.

Yates, J. was absent.

Spencer, J. The decision of the court, at the last August term, in the matter of John V. N. Yates, entitles the defendant to judgment on the demurrer. A majority of this court held that the recommitment of the plaintiff, after he had been set at large on habeas corpus, was a legal and justifiable act.

I have not thought it necessary to examine the other point in the cause, with a view to deliver an opinion on it; but I have so far considered it, as to be unable to subscribe to several positions in the opinion just delivered; I must therefore, be considered as giving no opinion on that point.

Judgment for the defendant.

[After the decision in the Supreme Court the case was taken to the Court of Errors on writ of error where it was heard at the April term, 1811 (9 John. 395). Henry and Van Vechten were counsel for Lansing and Thomas Addis Emmet represented the appellant Yates.]

Henry and Van Vechten, contra.[11] It has been very justly observed that this cause is very important as regards the jurisprudence of the state. It involves the question as to the powers of courts to commit for contempts, and as to the jurisdiction of the court of chancery. It is to be regretted that the counsel for the plaintiff should consider these points as already adjudged by this court. We deem it our duty, however, with great respect, to examine them. It is not denied that the decisions of this court are immutable, as it regards inferior courts. But unless this court assumes to itself the attributes of perfection and infallibility, it will not consider itself bound by its own opinions, if, on further examination, they should be thought erroneous.

The greatest and most illustrious judges in England have changed their opinions and thereby changed the law. But we claim a right to examine these points; for a party is entitled to be heard before he is judged, and the defendant has not been heard on them.

A court of justice has a right to commit for a contempt, not only of its power, but against its purity. It has been said that a violence, or contempt, in the face of the court, may be punished; because the crime is merged in the atrocity of the contempt; but not acts done out of court, in contempt of the court. Contempts are either direct, or consequential. Any corrupt practices in the subordinate officers of a court are contempts. Attorneys, solicitors, sheriffs, bailiffs, parties, witnesses, jurors, &c. are all subject to the animadversion of courts, for contempts. There are various classes of constructive contempts, founded on the criminal conduct of the officers of courts, and involving also a criminality for which they are indictable. The power of a court to punish the offender in such cases is essential to the due administration of justice. The various contempts are stated by Hawkins. And contempts which do not strike directly at the power of the court, and which are indictable offences, may be proceeded against summarily by attachment; as in case of extortion of an officer, forging a writ &c. Signing a counsellor's name to a bill in equity, without his consent, has been punished as a contempt. Deceit is an offence punishable by statute, by fine and imprisonment; yet an attorney who is guilty of deceit, may be proceeded against by attachment for a contempt of court.

This law as to the powers of courts to punish for contempts, is the settled law of England, grounded upon immemorial usage, and recognized and confirmed by magna charta. By the 35th article of our constitution, it is also the common law of

---

11. Counsel's many citations of authority are omitted.

this state; for no statute has ever been passed to abrogate this law. Indeed, it seems to be admitted that courts have this power, and it is not denied that the court of chancery possesses it equally with the courts of common law.

If the conduct of the plaintiff amounted to a contempt, it was the duty of the chancellor to punish it, and protect the suitors in that court from the oppression of its officers. That the act of which the plaintiff was guilty was in violation of a statute, was an aggravation of the offence, but the suitor was not to be told to seek his remedy by indictment. Admitting it to have been an offence against the statute, the contempt was not merged in the crime. If that were the case, then extortion, bribery, and libels on courts, could not be punished as contempts. Will the power of either branch of the legislature to commit for a contempt be questioned? Whence is that power derived? Not from the constitution, but from the common law, the source from whence courts of justice derive their power.

The chancellor did not punish the plaintiff for a crime, but merely for a contempt. He describes the offence, it is true, as a crime, to show its aggravated nature; but though the offence may be double, there has been but one punishment by the chancellor, that for a contempt. How, then, has he assumed a criminal jurisdiction? A court is not to be presumed to act beyond its jurisdiction. That must be clearly and satisfactorily shown. But there is no evidence of it in this case; or that the plaintiff has been injured by the commitment for a contempt. Suppose a person should cut off the ear of a suitor in court; and the court, in its order of commitment for the contempt, should add that it was also against the statute; would this description be an assumption of criminal jurisdiction? The order of commitment, in this case, if fairly read, does not assume any such jurisdiction. Strictly speaking, the conduct of the plaintiff was not an offence against the statute; for, though a master is prohibited from acting as a solicitor yet he cannot be said to act as a solicitor, when the proceedings are carried on in the name of another person who is a solicitor. If he was, in fact, a solicitor of the court, while he held the office of master, his right to act as solicitor was suspended. But though not an offence within the words it is within the spirit of the act; and such an attempt to evade its provisions, was an aggravation of the contempt.

If, then, according to the fair construction of the order of commitment, the plaintiff was imprisoned for a contempt; the judge had no authority, under the habeas corpus act, to discharge him. ...

T. A. Emmet, in reply. It is said that Mr. Yates is a convict of record. It is true, that it is so stated in the pleadings. The court of chancery, as a court of equity, is not a court of record. The orders are of record, but not that the conviction was well founded. The plaintiff was not examined on interrogatories. The established mode of proceeding, in case of a contempt, is first to grant a rule to show cause why an attachment should not issue; and if no cause is shown, the attachment issues, and the party is brought into court; interrogatories are filed, and on the answers of the party, the master reports whether the party is in contempt. The party is not bound to speak, until called upon by interrogatories. We complain, then, that the plaintiff has been condemned unheard. Again, it is said that the commitment was for the nonpayment of the costs. Three things are recited in the order; the dismissal of the bill, the payment of costs, and the commitment for mal-practice and contempt. The last had no reference to the first and second. The costs were to be collected in the ordinary way, by an attachment for the nonpayment of them. Remuneration was not the object of the commitment. It was solely for the mal-practice and contempt. But we have supposed that this and the other points which could arise except the question of judicial inviolability, were definitely settled by this court, in the case of _The People_ v. _Yates_; and that the only point for discussion in this cause was, whether the defendant was liable for the penalty. But this court of _dernier resort_ has been called on to do, what no such court ever did, to overturn its former decisions. Inferior courts, it is true, have changed, and may change their decisions. But if the decisions of the court of the last resort are not to be permanent and unalterable, then there is no such thing as settled law. The decision in the case of _The People_ v. _Yates_, as soon as it was pronounced, was the established law. Is it to be changed because it is recent, and as yet in the gristle? Must it be ossified by time, before it can be fixed? The decisions of this court are and must be the law, until altered by the legislature. In England, in consequence of the decisions of their courts, the act of 10 and 11 Wm. III. c. 16 was passed to enable posthumous children to take in remainder, in the same manner as if they had been born in their fathers' lifetime. It is absurd, then to cite all the authorities and cases on points which this court has already settled. Why is this court called upon to change its decisions, and to subvert the maxim _stare decisis_? Is everything to be set afloat, and the character and consequence of the court to be lost? If it can thus change its decisions, the court itself ought to be changed. If its decisions are wrong, let them be set right by the legislature. But, if the court itself can alter its decisions, it is in vain to study the law. I protest, therefore, against going into an examination of the points already decided by this court, though I may be obliged incidentally to notice some of them. ...

Platt, Senator. In examining this interesting case, two cardinal points are presented:

1. Had the chancellor a right to recommit the plaintiff, after the discharge by Mr. Justice Spencer?

2. If he had no such right, is he liable for the penalty now claimed?

The consideration of the first question involves an inquiry:

1. Whether the original commitment by the chancellor was legal?

2. Whether Mr. Justice Spencer had a right to revise the adjudication of the chancellor, in the matter of complaint against John V. N. Yates; and discharge the prisoner on habeas corpus?

3. Whether the recommitment of Mr. Yates by the chancellor, after the actual discharge by Mr. Justice Spencer, was lawful?

Before I proceed to examine these questions, it is proper to notice a preliminary objection insisted on by the counsel for Mr. Yates. They contend that the door to these inquiries is now shut, by the decision of this court, at its last session, in the case of John V. N. Yates and The People.

I cannot admit the doctrine of immutability in the decisions of this court, to the unqualified extent claimed by the plaintiff's counsel:

The decisions of courts are not the law; they are only evidence of the law. And this evidence is stronger or weaker, according to the number and uniformity of adjudications, the unanimity or dissension of the judges, the solidity of the reasons on which the decisions are founded, and the perspicuity and precision with which those reasons are expressed. The weight and authority of judicial decisions depend also on the character and temper of the times in which they are pronounced. An adjudication at a moment when turbulent passions or revolutionary phrenzies prevail, deserves much less respect, than if it were made at a season propitious to impartial inquiry, and calm deliberation.

The peculiar organization and practice of this court, renders it difficult to establish a system of precedents. In the supreme court the judges confer together, compare opinions, weigh each other's reasons, and elicit light from each other. If they agree, one is usually delegated by the others, not only to pronounce judgment, but to assign reasons for the whole bench. But even in that court, and in the courts of Westminster hall, the judges who silently acquiesce in the result, do not consider themselves bound to recognize as law all the dicta of the judge who delivers the opinion of the court.

In this court, the members never hold any previous consultation together; we vote, for the most part, as in our legislative capacity. Few assign any reasons, and fewer still give written opinions which may be reported. For these reasons, I think it would be extravagant and dangerous, to consider the dicta and opinions of a single member, as settling definitely the law of the land, on all the points on which he chooses to give opinions, or to assign reasons.

In the Case of J. V. N. Yates at the last session, only one member (Mr. Clinton) gave a written opinion, or assigned reasons for reversing the judgment of the supreme court. (6 Johns. Rep. 496) A majority of the members voted for reversing that judgment; but whether upon the grounds taken, and the reasons assigned by Mr. Clinton, it is impossible to know. It is certain that a majority agreed in the result; but there is no certainty that any two of that majority, grounded their opinions on any one of the various points that were discussed and relied on by Mr. Clinton. ...

Clinton, Senator. Great pains and much argument have been employed by the counsel for the defendant, to overthrow a decision made by this court at the last session, and to demonstrate, not only that the conclusions, but the reasoning adopted on that occasion, were untenable and fallacious. Although this course is unprecedented and totally unwarranted, yet the patience of the court was yielded without reluctance to a protracted discussion, which terminated in establishing what was never questioned: that the court of chancery, as well as every other court, has a right to punish contempts, and to apply the rod of chastisement to the conduct of its officers. But that chancery has the power of punishing for crimes; that a violation of a statute is not a misdemeanor, and that judicial irresponsibility is to ride over the rights of the people, and the constitution of the land, are positions which yet remain totally unestablished. Although I am willing to yield every tribute of applause to the erudition and ingenuity of the counsel employed for the defendant, yet I cannot concede that they have succeeded in overturning the decision of this tribunal. If I could conceive it relevant to the discussion to enter into a defence of the judgment of the court, I should not consider it attended with any difficulty to present a complete vindication; but a measure of this kind would be an admission that a court might, at any time, and at all times, review its own decisions, or the decisions of its predecessors, and pronounce the law to be different, at different periods and on different occasions, thereby entirely destroying the authority of precedent, converting the judge into the legislator, and reducing us to a situation where we might truly say, "Misera est servitus ubi jus est aut vagum aut incognitum." In the case of Hartshorne and others v. Sleght, (3 Johns. Rep. 562) it was insinuated, with a view of obtaining the benefit of a second writ of error, that courts might and ought to review their decisions. On that occasion, I thought it my duty to resist a doctrine which I then considered, and still do consider, as of the most pernicious tendency; and I animadverted upon it in the following words: "This cause is now before us, and it does not avail the plaintiff in error to say that courts may and ought to review their own decisions. This court will hardly admit that doctrine. A motion for a rehearing after judgment has never been made or sustained, when a cause has been once settled. When a decision has been pronounced here, the law is established; and no power can change it but the legislature. The rule becomes binding, not only upon all subordinate tribunals, but upon this court."

A contrary determination would involve not only the greatest absurdities, but the greatest mischiefs. Inferior tribunals would be without chart or compass; the authority of decisions would be done away [with] and, one fourth of the senators of this court changing every year, adjudications would fluctuate with the mutations of members. What was law yesterday, would not be law to-day. It has never been known, at least in a court of *dernier resort*, that its decisions have been altered or revised in any other way than by the legislative power; and even in courts not of *dernier resort*, if a different course had been, at any time, pursued, it has been marked as a singularity. And when Lord Kenyon attempted to question the authority of an adjudication of his predecessor, it was considered as an anomaly, not as a rule in the conduct of judicial tribunals. *Stare decisis et non quieta movere*, is a maxim justly held in the highest veneration.

Admitting, then, the authority of the adjudication of last session, we have next to inquire into its bearing upon this cause. The present suit is brought to recover a penalty under the fifth section of the habeas corpus act, which is in the following words: "And be it further enacted, that no person, who shall be set at large upon any habeas corpus, shall be again imprisoned for the same offence, unless by the legal order or process of the court, or other court having jurisdiction of the cause. And if any person shall knowingly, contrary to this act, recommit or imprison, or cause to be recommitted or imprisoned, for the same offence or pretended offence, any person so set at large, or shall knowingly aid or assist therein, he shall forfeit to the party aggrieved 1,250 dollars, any colourable pretence or variation in the warrant of commitment notwithstanding." ...

It appears obvious to me, that the habeas corpus act was intended to invest the same power in a judge in vacation that the supreme court has in term. The same limitations of power that controlled their proceedings at common law were applied to the judge under the statute; and as he is, in this respect, a creature of the statute, it became necessary to define the power in the act communicating it. The common law restrictions upon the power of the court were imposed upon that of the judge; and if he cannot take cognisance of other commitments than for crimes, if he cannot meddle with convictions whether legal or illegal, they are equally restrained; and, perhaps, there is only one case in which the court will interfere in favour of a prisoner in which a judge will not, and that is in case of dangerous sickness, when the laws of humanity require their interposition; and in a situation like this, the common law, in a spirit of benevolence, has planted no check against judicial discretion.

If the power of the judge is only limited to commitments for crimes, as has been zealously contended for by the defendant, it would not bear him out in this case, because the conviction was for a crime, and therein principally consisted its illegality; but this construction is not only in the teeth of existing practice, but in the face of the statute. It cannot be denied that the power of the judge, or commissioner, is commensurate with all unjust imprisonment, except in treason and felony, and this has been the invariable understanding, and undisputed practice, until the agitation of this cause has elicited new and extraordinary doctrines. The object of the statute would be greatly frustrated, if a judge has no right to take notice of illegal convictions; if he is confined to crimes only, what remedy is there for all illegal imprisonments in other respects? Must the injured party wait until the sitting of the supreme court? And will damages to any extent in an action for a false imprisonment, atone for a violation of feeling, and personal liberty, and an infraction of the great rights which distinguish a free man from a slave? Suppose a child is torn from his parent, a wife from her husband, a citizen from his habitation, and placed in close confinement, is there no court of summary jurisdiction authorized to grant relief? Is he to be told that he must wait until the supreme court convenes, which may be in not less than three months? And are we to suppose that our law would be silent on a point of so great and of such obvious importance? But the law is not silent; it arms the judge with power over all persons imprisoned; whereas that of Great Britain is confined to crimes. Because the two statutes vary in that important respect, and because ours has not a preamble like that of the British statute, and because in the last edition of the revised laws, a preamble was struck out, it is maintained that they are similar or, in plain English, that they are alike, although they differ. ...

But it is maintained that admitting the illegality of the imprisonment, yet the chancellor, acting as a court, is irresponsible, particularly to private prosecutions or indictments;

and a variety of learning and not a little declamation, have been displayed in support of this position.

The Chief Justice, in his elaborate opinion, has exhausted all that can be said on this subject; and in noticing it, I shall certainly treat him with all the respect, so justly due to his high station and eminent talents. Whether he has travelled out of the usual routine of judicial conduct, to support a cause which was not then debated by the plaintiff, is not a material point for inquiry, because, in giving an opinion, he had undoubtedly a right to assign his reasons at large; and because, we have every reason to believe he considered it his duty to vindicate judicial irresponsibility to its full extent, from a sincere conviction that it is connected with the due administration of justice, and with the best interests of the country.

Where a judge acts within his jurisdiction, it would entirely destroy his independence and his usefulness, if he were liable to answer to individuals who might conceive themselves aggrieved by his decisions. It is the lot of humanity to err, and what man would take an office, which would expose him, in the execution of its duties, to the prosecutions of unfortunate or dissatisfied suitors? No judge would be able to stand up against the expense and vexation that would result from his position; and it is no less unjust than impolitic, to expose him to amenability for errors, to which we are more or less subject. This is the true principle and the true reason, why judges, acting as judges, that is, acting within the sphere of their delegated authority, are protected in England. It is true that a judge is held to be responsible to the king. The king being the fountain of honour and justice, and the judges being the delegated ministers of the judicial power, it is presumed that they ought to answer to him only, as their principal and constituent. But this can never be applicable here; and, in England, it cannot apply to cases where the judge has no jurisdiction. ...

The Chief Justice has triumphantly quoted Serjeant Hawkins on this subject, but he has inadvertently omitted a very material part. The whole section is as follows: "And as the law has exempted jurors from the danger of incurring any punishment in respect of their verdict in criminal causes, it hath also freed the judges of all courts of record from all prosecutions whatsoever, except in the parliament, for any thing done by them openly in such court as judges; for the authority of a government cannot be maintained, unless the greatest credit be given to those, who are so highly intrusted in the administration of public justice; and it would be impossible for them to keep up in the people that veneration of their persons, and submission to their judgments, without which it is impossible to execute the laws with vigour and success," (thus far the Chief Justice has quoted, but Hawkins proceeds) "if they should be continually exposed to the prosecutions of those whose partiality to their own causes would induce them to think themselves injured; yet if a judge will so far forget the honour and dignity of his post, as to turn solicitor in a cause which he is to judge, and privately and extrajudicially tamper with witnesses, or labour jurors, he hath no reason to complain, if he be dealt with according to the capacity to which he so basely degrades himself."

The last part of the sentence, which the Chief Justice omitted, is very material, because it contains a qualification of the general rule. It is admitted on all hands, with Hawkins, that for errors committed by a judge, quatenus a judge, he is not responsible, but it is equally contended, and Hawkins agrees in the doctrine, that if he acts extrajudicially, he is then responsible. Indeed, Hawkins carries it beyond the jurisdiction, for he intimates that if a judge acts out of character, "he will be dealt with according to the same capacity, to which he so basely degrades himself." Our constitution renders a judge liable to impeachment for male and corrupt conduct in office. And the punishment does not extend further than to removal from office, and disqualification to hold any place of honour, trust or profit; but the party so convicted is, nevertheless, liable and subject to indictment, trial, judgment and punishment according to the laws of the land. The male and corrupt conduct cannot be ascribed to any error of the understanding, or to any misconduct, however gross or oppressive, or however injurious to individuals unless it is attended by bad and corrupt motives. The malus animus is difficult at all times, to establish; and there is no cause, be it ever so desperate, no conduct, be it ever so abandoned, but it may find not only advocates, but advocates who can advance plausible arguments, and who can gild over high-handed acts of oppression, with declamatory appeals in favour of judicial independence and official dignity. It will, therefore, be a rare instance to bring proof sufficiently clear against a judge, in order to produce his removal. Impeachment is not only difficult to institute and hard to establish, but, when effected, what good does it do to the injured party? Does the removal of an unjust judge remunerate him for imprisonment, for multiplied vexations and accumulated expenses. The protection furnished to a court, is commensurate with its jurisdiction; for where jurisdiction ends, the judge also ceases to be a judge, and is not entitled to the immunities and rights of one. This is the recorded opinion of the defendant, delivered in the incipient stages of this affair. "Upon my judicially determining (says the chancellor) that the interference of a single judge, to obstruct the process, and impede the justice of this court, was unwarranted, that his proceedings were coram non judice, it followed, as a necessary consequence, that his reiterating his interference, might or might not, according to circumstances, be imputed to him as a contempt of this court; for though a judge acting in the sphere of his jurisdiction, cannot, unless actuated by corrupt motives, be impeached or questioned, it is otherwise, where such jurisdiction does not exist, he is then exposed to be treated as a contemner of the court, with whose process he interferes." (See printed case, Ex Parte Yates, p. 105) Here we have the authority of the chancellor himself, that when a judge of one of the highest tribunals exceeds his jurisdiction, and trespasses upon that of a coordinate tribunal, he may be punished for a contempt; and if liable in that way, he must surely be responsible in a civil suit, to the party aggrieved; and here let me add, that it comes with a very ill grace from superior tribunals, to say that whether they act within or without their jurisdiction, they are equally protected from accountability, but inferior courts must take care and keep within their jurisdiction, for although their knowledge of the law is not so extensive as that of the other courts, yet their ignorance shall be no excuse, and although they require a more extensive, yet they shall receive a more limited protection. And let me further add, that this doctrine is not only unreasonable in itself, repugnant to law and common sense, but it is contrary to the principles of our government. The principle of responsibility pervades every department of a free government; for wherever responsibility ends tyranny begins. That a judge may fine and imprison, and punish ad libitum; and whether he acts according to law or not, he cannot be reached by suit or indictment, is, in fact, saying that he may act the tyrant at pleasure. No man in the community is safe, if the judges who advocate such monstrous doctrines are, which I can never believe, prepared to exhibit their practical operation, unless they are effectually checked and controlled by this high tribunal. The institution of an impeachment, as I before stated is difficult. An accusation requires the sanction of two thirds of the assembly, and a conviction that of two thirds of this court, and the punishment neither furnishes any remedy to the injured party, nor does it extend to any personal penalties. How difficult must it be, then, to convict a tyrannical judge, especially under the aegis of mental error, and under the Telamonian shield of judicial irresponsibility? Our constitution contemplates an impeachment for male and corrupt conduct in office, for acts done as a judge; and whether considering the extraordinary evasions that have been practised, a party complained against, in a case like the present, might not say in his defence, that the facts alleged being extrajudicial, he is not liable as for official conduct, is a point which time alone can determine. I can, therefore, never subscribe to the doctrine of unaccountability in the higher courts. The true distinction has been very judiciously pointed out in the course of this discussion. An inferior court shall, when questioned, show that it acted within its jurisdiction. Whereas in courts of general jurisdiction, jurisdiction is presumed until the contrary is shown. ...

It is with not a little regret that I have seen the commencement and the progress of this controversy. Considering it as a dispute between two individuals, it dwindles into insignificance; but, in most of its stages, it has become a controversy between power and right, and between judicial tyranny and the liberty of the citizen. In this point of view, it has assumed an importance proportioned to the value of the objects which it embraces; and let not the unhallowed tongue of malignity insinuate, that the decision of this court, if against the judgment of the supreme court, will operate as a protection to malepractice, extortion and misdemeanors.

If the plaintiff is guilty, he is still liable to punishment; but whether guilty, or innocent, he ought to be legally proceeded against. This is a right which the most abandoned criminal has equally with the best citizen. But what is the true state of the case? The plaintiff, in common with many other masters in chancery, had filed bills and carried on equity suits, in the name of another solicitor. Complaint was made against him by a client. The solicitor, although he had received a fee for permitting another solicitor to be substituted, declared it was all done without his consent. The party was excluded from the benefit of a purgation on oath, according to the general, and, I may say, invariable course of chancery; and he was committed to prison, without limitation of time. If his oath had been received in explanation, it would have been at least equal to the panic-struck testimony of the principal witness against him. A commitment for the first offence, under these circumstances, was, to say the least, a very harsh, a very unnecessary, and a very unprecedented measure; and in this case it might be truly said, _jus summum saepe summa est malitia_. But the proceeding being on the very face of it for a crime, and consequently, illegal, he was discharged on a _habeas corpus_. Here, in all reason, and according to all law, the business ought to have been arrested. But Mr. Yates was recommitted in defiance of this great bulwark against tyranny, and then the transaction assumed a new, interesting and extraordinary aspect. It was no longer the case of an injured individual. It became the case of every member in the community; and among the novel and extraordinary doctrines which this controversy has elicited, we are at length told, with judicial solemnity, that a judge of the supreme court, or the chancellor, acting as such, are beyond the reach of prosecution or indictment, whether they act with or without jurisdiction, and be their conduct ever so illegal or oppressive. To these doctrines I can never subscribe. And

I consider the decision of this day as extending beyond the remuneration or punishment of individuals; that it will, in all its bearings and aspects, decide whether the ministers of justice may oppress with impunity! Whether the habeas corpus act shall any longer dispense its blessings, and whether the law shall bend to the judge, or the judge bend to the majesty of the law! ...

A majority of the court being of opinion that the judgment of the supreme court ought to be affirmed, it was thereupon,

Ordered and Adjudged, that the judgment given in the supreme court be affirmed, and the record remitted, &c. and that the plaintiff in error pay to the defendant his double costs, to be taxed, &c.

Judgment affirmed.[12]

2. The Common Law and Federalism

Trial of Gideon Henfield for Illegally Enlisting in a French Privateer

Circuit Court of the United States, District of Pennsylvania, 1793

Wharton - State Trials (1849) p. 49, 59

... Charge of Judge Wilson, as President of a Special Court of the United States, for the Middle Circuit and Pennsylvania district, holden at the Court House, in the city of Philadelphis, on the 22d day of July, 1793, to the Grand Jury of said Court.

Gentlemen of the Grand Jury: It is my duty to explain to you the very important occasion on which this Court is specially convened, and to state the points of law not less important

---

12. In the Revised Statutes of 1830, Vol. II, p. 571, Sec. 60, the earlier provision concerning the liability of the recommitting magistrate was strengthened and was given the following form: "If any person, either solely, or as a member of any court; or in the execution of any order, judgment or process; shall knowingly recommit, imprison or restrain of his liberty, or cause to be recommitted, imprisoned or restrained of his liberty, for the same cause ... any person so discharged ... he shall forfeit to the party aggrieved, one thousand two hundred and fifty dollars, and shall also be deemed guilty of a misdemeanor." For Kent's opinion of the provisions of the Revised Statutes on habeas corpus see 2 Kent's *Commentaries* (12th ed.) *28-31.

to the application of which that occasion gives rise.

To the Judge of the Pennsylvania district information was given on oath, that certain citizens of the United States had acted in several capacities as officers on board an armed schooner, said to be commissioned by France as a cruiser or private ship-of-war; and with others on board that schooner did capture and make prize of several ships or vessels belonging to his Britannic Majesty, and otherwise assist in an hostile manner in annoying the commerce of the subjects of his said Britannic Majesty, who is at peace with the United States, contrary to their duty as citizens of the United States.

On receiving this information the Judge issued his warrant for apprehending the persons against whom complaint was made, that they might answer for their doings in the premises, and be dealt with according to law.[1]

That legal proceedings in this and some other business might be had speedily, one of the Judges of the Supreme Court of the United States and the Judge of the Pennsylvania District issued their warrant, directing that on this day, and at this place a special session of the Circuit Court for this District should be held, and that Grand and Traverse Jurors should be summoned to attend it. As the Court however is authorized gen-

---

1. When Henfield was arrested, Citizen Genet, Minister Plenipotentiary from France, sent the following communication to Jefferson as Secretary of State: "I have this moment been informed that two officers in the service of the republic of France, citizens Gideon Henfield and John Singletary, have been arrested on board the privateer of the French republic, the Citizen Genet, and conducted to prison. The crime, laid to their charge - the crime which my kind cannot conceive, and which my pen almost refuses to state - is the serving of France, and defending with her children the common glorious cause of liberty.

"Being ignorant of any positive law which deprives Americans of this privilege ... I call upon your intervention, sir, and that of the President of the United States, in order to obtain the immediate releasement of the above mentioned officers, who have acquired by the sentiments animating them, and by the act of their engagement, anterior to every act to the contrary, the right of French citizens if they have lost that of American citizens." Wharton, _id_. 88.

Art. I, Section 8 of the Federal Constitution gives Congress the power "to define and punish ... offenses against the Law of Nations". Is that provision relevant to the problem of _Henfield's case_? See argument of counsel, _Talbot_ v. _Janson_, 3 Dallas 133, 144 (1795).

erally to try criminal causes, if any other crimes or offences cognizable in it be laid before you or are in your knowledge, it is your duty to present them. But to the business to which you have been particularly called, and to articles intimately connected with it, I shall confine the remarks that I have to give you in charge.

I introduce them by noticing, with pleasure, the near and endearing relation between the freedom and the dignity of man. In governments unfavourable to both, treaties and the construction of treaties are numbered among the arcana imperii, the secrets of empire, enclosed within the cabinets of princes and secluded from the judgment of the citizens, whose lives and fortunes however they chiefly affect; under our national Constitution, treaties compose a portion of the public and supreme law of the land, and for their construction and enforcement are brought openly before the tribunals of our country. Of those tribunals Juries form an essential part; under the construction given by those Juries, treaties will suffer neither in their importance nor in their sanctity.

Sapientissima res tempus - says the profound Bacon in one of his aphorisms, concerning the augmentation of the sciences - time is the wisest of things. If the qualities of the parent may be expected in the offspring, the common law, one of the noblest births of time, may be pronounced the wisest of laws.

This expression, says a great lawyer, Finch on Law, 74, 75, is not new and strange, or barbarous and peculiar to England. It is the proper term for other laws also. Euripides mentions the common laws of Greece; and Plato defines common law to be that, which being taken up by the common consent of a country, is called law. In another place the same illustrious philosopher names it the golden and sacred rule of reason which we call common law.

To the common law of England, however, the phrase is often peculiarly appropriated. Of this common law, the antiquity is unquestionably very high. But the precise era of its commencement, and the several springs from which it originally flowed, it is very difficult, if not altogether impracticable to trace. One reason for this may be drawn from the very nature of a system of common law. As it is accommodated to the situation and circumstances of the people; and as that situation and those circumstances insensibly change, a proportioned variation of laws insensibly takes place; and it becomes impossible to ascertain the period when this change began, or to mark the different steps of its progress.

It might be amusing and instructive, but at this time it would be improper, to sketch the general outlines of the system through the government of the Saxons down to the conquest of the Normans. Suffice it to observe, and the observation is important, that the common law, as now received in America, bears in its principles and in many of its more minute particulars, a stronger and a fairer resemblance to the common law as it was improved under the former, than to that law as it was disfigured under the latter.

The accommodating principle of a system of common law will adjust its improvement to every grade and species of improvement, Fort. 257, 264, in consequence of practice, commerce, observation, study or refinement. As the science of legislation is the most noble so it is the most slow and difficult of sciences. Willing to avail itself of experience, it receives additional improvement from every new situation to which it arrives; and in this manner attains, in the progress of time, higher and higher degrees of perfection, resulting from the accumulated wisdom of ages.

On some occasions the spirit of a system of common law is accommodating; but on others its temper is decided and firm. The means are varied according to times and circumstances, but its great ends are kept steadily and constantly in view.

How effectually has the spirit of liberty animated this system in all the vicissitudes, revolutions and dangers to which it has been exposed! In matters of a civil nature the common law works itself pure by rules drawn from the fountain of justice. In matters of a political nature it works itself pure by rules drawn from the fountain of freedom.

It was this spirit which dictated the frequent and formidable demands on the Norman princes, for the complete restoration of the Saxon jurisprudence. It was this spirit which, in Magna Charta, manifested a strict regard to the rights of the Commons as well as those of the Peers. It was this spirit which extracted sweetness from all the bitter contentions between the rival houses of York and Lancaster. It was this spirit which preserved England from the haughtiness of the Tudors and from the tyranny of the Stuarts. It was this spirit which rescued the States of America from the oppressive claims and from all the mighty efforts made to enforce the oppressive claims of a British Parliament.

The common law, says my Lord Coke, Calvin's case, 6 Rep. 88, is a social system of jurisprudence. She receives other laws and systems into a friendly correspondence; and associates to herself those who can give her information, or advice, or assistance.

Does a contract bear a peculiar reference to the local laws of any particular foreign country? By the local laws of that foreign country the common law will direct the contract to be interpreted and adjusted.

Does a mercantile question occur? She determines it by the law of merchants.

Does a question arise before her, which properly ought to be resolved by the law of nations? By that law she will decide the question. For that law in its full extent is adopted by her. The infractions of that law form a part of her code of criminal jurisprudence. 4 Blac. Com. 67.[2]

In our present business, gentlemen, this great subject deserves a full and a pointed illustration. Such as it is in my power, on a short notice, to give, I now proceed to lay before you.

The law of nature when applied to States or political societies, receives a new name, that of the law of nations. But though it receives a new appellation, it retains unimpaired its qualities and its powers. The law of nations as well as the law of nature, is of obligation indispensable. The law of nations as well as the law of nature is of "origin divine." ...

It seems to have been thought that the law of nations respects and regulates their conduct only in their intercourse with each other. A very important branch of this law containing the duties which a nation owes to itself, has in a great measure escaped attention.

Of a state, as well as of an individual, self-preservation is a primary duty.

To love and to deserve an honest fame is another duty of a state as well as of a man. To a state as well as to a man, reputation is a valuable and an agreeable possession. It represses hostility and secures esteem.

In transactions with other nations, the dignity of a state should never be permitted to suffer the smallest diminution.

Need it be mentioned here, that happiness is the centre to which states as well as men are universally attracted! To consult its own happiness, therefore, is the duty of a nation.

When men have formed themselves into a political society,

---

2. Two months earlier in the Federal Court at Richmond, Mr. Chief Justice Jay had charged a grand jury that the laws of the United States "admit of being classed under three heads of descriptions: 1st. All treaties made under the authority of the United States. 2d. The laws of nations. 3dly. The constitution and statutes of the United States." He had further called to the attention of the jury the Proclamation recently issued by the President in which American citizens were warned to remain impartial between the European belligerent powers, were advised that if they gave aid to the belligerents they would not receive the protection of the United States and were advised that the President had given instructions to the Federal officers "to cause prosecutions to be instituted against all persons who shall within the cognizance of the Courts of the United States, violate the law of Nations, with respect to the powers at war, or any of them." Wharton, id. 53.

they may reciprocally enter into particular engagements and contract new obligations in favour of the community or of its members. But they cannot, by this union, discharge themselves from any duties which they previously owned to those who form a part of the political association. Under all the obligations due to the universal society of the human race, the citizens of a state still continue. To this universal society it is a duty that each nation should contribute to the welfare, the perfection and the happiness of the others.

If so, the first degree of this duty is to do no injury. Among states as well as among men, justice is a sacred law. This sacred law prohibits one state from exciting disturbances in another, from depriving it of its natural advantages, from calumniating its reputation, from seducing its citizens, from debauching the attachment of its allies, from fomenting or encouraging the hatred of its enemies. Vat. 127.

But nations are not only prohibited from doing evil, they are also commanded to do good to one another. On states as well as individuals the duties of humanity are strictly incumbent; what each is obliged to perform for others, from others it is entitled to receive. Hence the advantage as well as the duty of humanity.

It may be uncommon, but it is unquestionably just to say, that nations ought to love one another. From the pure source of benevolence the offices of humanity ought to flow.

By a nation these enlarged and elevated virtues should be cultivated with peculiar assiduity and ardour; of an individual, however generous his disposition may be, the sphere of exertion is frequently narrow; but of a nation this sphere is comparatively boundless. By exhibiting a glorious example in her constitution, in her laws, and in the administration of her constitution and laws, she may diffuse instruction, she may diffuse reformation, she may diffuse happiness over the whole terrestrial globe.

These maxims of national law, though the sacred precepts of nature, and of nature's God, have been too often unknown and unacknowledged by nations. Even where they have been known and acknowledged, their calm still voice has been drowned by the clamours of ambition and by the thunder of war.

Is it then unnecessary or improper here to say, peace should be deemed the basis of the happiness of nations, "peace on earth"! This is a patriotic as well as an angelic wish.

But with war and rumours of war our ears in this imperfect state of things are still assailed.

Into this unnatural state ought a nation to suffer herself to be drawn without her own act, or the act of him or them, to whom for this purpose she has delegated her power?

Into this unnatural state should a nation suffer herself to be drawn by the unauthorized, nay by the unlicensed conduct of any of her citizens?

These, gentlemen, are questions to which you are now called to give the closest and deepest attention.

That a citizen, who in our state of neutrality, and without the authority of the nation, takes an hostile part with either of the belligerent powers, violates thereby his duty, and the laws of his country, is a position so plain as to require no proof, and to be scarcely susceptible of a denial. ...

In some instances citizens may be accountable for the conduct of their nation. In other instances the nation may be accountable for the conduct of its citizens.

It is impossible indeed that even in the best regulated state, the government should be able to superintend the whole behaviour of all the citizens and to restrain them within the precise limits of duty and obedience, Vat. 144; it would be unjust, therefore, immediately to impute to the nation the faults or offences which its members may commit. In every state, disorderly citizens are unhappily to be found. Let such be held responsible, when they can be rendered amenable for the consequences of their crimes and disorders.

If the offended nation have the criminal in its power, it may without difficulty punish him, and oblige him to make satisfaction. Vat. 145.

When the offending citizen escapes into his own country, his nation should oblige him to repair the damage, if reparation can be made, or should punish him according to the measure of his offence. Vat. 75. Bur. R. 1480, 4 Bl. 68, 69.

If the nation refuse to do either, it renders itself in some measure an accomplice in the guilt, and becomes responsible for the injury. Vat. 145.

To what does this responsibility lead? To reprisal certainly, Vat. 251, and if so, probably to war. Vat. 2. 4 Bl. Com. 68, 69.

And should the fortunes or the lives of millions be placed in either of those predicaments by the conduct of one citizen, or of a few citizens? Vat. 2, 89. Humanity and reason say no. The constitution of the United States says no. Vat. 2, 89.

By that constitution, many great powers are vested in the first executive magistrate: others are vested in him, "by and with the advice and consent of the senate." But neither he, nor he and they in conjunction, can lift up the sword of the United States. Congress alone have power to declare war, and to "grant letters of marque and reprisal".

Who indeed should have the power to declare war but these, as the immediate representatives of those who must furnish the blood and treasure upon which war depends?

With regard to this very interesting power, the constitution of the United States renews the principles known and practiced in England before the conquest.

This indeed may be reckoned one of the chief differences between the government of the Saxons and that of the Normans. In the former, the power of peace and war was invariably possessed by the Wittenagemote, Millar on Eng. Con. 305, and was regarded as inseparable from the allodial condition of its members. In the latter, it was transferred to the king; and this branch of the feudal system, which was accommodated perhaps to the depredations and internal commotions prevalent in that rude period, has remained in subsequent ages, when from a total change of manners, the circumstances by which it was recommended, have no longer any existence.

There is, by the way, a pleasure in reflecting on such important renovations of the venerable Saxon government; and in discovering that our national constitution is rendered illustrious by the antiquity, as well as by the excellence of some of its leading principles.

The principle now under our view was urged as one reason why this constitution should be adopted by Pennsylvania: if urged with propriety then, it may be urged with propriety now. For what was then adopted, ought now to be supported.

This system will not hurry us into war. It is calculated to guard against it. It will not be in the power of a single man or a single body of men to involve us in such distress. For the important power of declaring war is vested in the legislature at large - This declaration must be made with the concurrence of the House of Representatives.

From this circumstance we may draw a certain conclusion, that nothing but our national interest will draw us into a war. I cannot forbear on this occasion, the pleasure of mentioning to you the sentiments of the great and benevolent man, whose works I have already quoted (Mr. Neckar), who had addressed this country in language important and applicable, in the strictest manner, to its situation, and to the present subject. Speaking of war, and the great caution that all nations ought to use, in order to avoid its calamities - "And you, rising nation", says he, "whom generous efforts have freed from the yoke of Europe! Let the universe be struck with still greater reverence at the sight of the privileges you have acquired, by seeing you continually employed for the public felicity. Do not offer it as a sacrifice at the unsettled shrine of political ideas, and of the deceitful combinations of warlike ambition: avoid, or at least delay, participating in the passions of our hemisphere; make your own advantage of the knowledge which experience alone has given to our old age, and preserve for a long term, the simplicity of childhood; in short, honour human nature by showing, that when left to its own feelings, it is still capable of those virtues that maintain public order, and of that prudence which ensures public tranquillity." _Deb. of Conv. of Pennsylvania_, 434.

On this great subject of peace and war, the voice of all France is responsive to the language of our National Constitution. "When the interesting question was before her national assembly, its deliberations, we are told, were watched with anxiety by countless thousands. All Paris was in agitation, and when the decree was pronounced, that the lives and fortunes of twenty-five millions of men should not be at the disposal of a single individual, there was a shout of acclamation raised, which reached from the garden of the Tuileries to the extremest province of France."

Can we believe, for a moment, that this generous nation would wish to bereave us of a security, which they themselves so highly and so justly prize?

[After receiving this charge, the Grand Jury returned an indictment of Henfield in which he was charged with privateering against a friendly power and thus offending against a United States treaty, the laws and constitution of the United States, the laws of nations, "and against the peace and dignity of the said United States". Thereafter the case came on for trial before a jury in the United States Circuit Court in Philadelphia.]

It appeared in evidence that Gideon Henfield was a citizen of the United States and that his family resided in Salem, Massachusetts. Being a sea-faring man he had been absent from them some time, and about the 1st of May, 1793, being then at Charleston, South Carolina, and desirous of coming to Philadelphia, he applied to the master of a packet, who asked him more for his passage than he could afford to pay, whereupon he entered on board the Citizen Genet, a French privateer, commissioned by the French Republic and commanded by Pierre Johannen. Captain Johannen, it appeared, promised him the berth of prize-master on board the first prize they should capture, and the ship William, belonging to British subjects, having been captured about the 5th of May, he was put on board her as prize-master, with another person, and arrived in that capacity at Philadelphia. It appeared that on his examination before the magistrate, he protested himself an American, that as such he would die, and therefore could not be supposed likely to intend anything to her prejudice. He declared if he had known it to be contrary to the President's proclamation,[3] or even the wishes of the President, for whom he had the greatest respect, he would not have entered on board. About a month afterwards, being before

---

3. See, <u>supra</u>, note 2. The President's Proclamation had been issued on April 22, 1793. 1 Richardson, <u>Messages and Papers of the Presidents</u> (1896) 156.

the same magistrate, he declared he had espoused the cause of France, that he now considered himself as a Frenchman, and meant to move his family within their dominions.

[The summary of the arguments of the counsel is omitted.]

Judge Wilson, (with whom were Judge Iredell and Judge Peters) charged the jury as follows: - This is, gentlemen of the jury, a case of the first importance. Upon your verdict the interests of four millions of your fellow-citizens may be said to depend. But whatever be the consequence, it is your duty, it is our duty, to do only what is right.

(After stating the substance of the charges against the defendant, the learned Judge proceeded:)

It has not been contended, on the present occasion, that the defendant has any peculiar exclusive right to take a part in the present war between the European powers, in relation to all whom the United States are in a state of peace and tranquillity.

If he has no peculiar or exclusive right, it naturally follows, that what he may do every other citizen of the United States may also do. If one citizen of the United States may take part in the present war, ten thousand may. If they may take part on one side, they may take part on the other; and thus thousands of our fellow-citizens may associate themselves with different belligerent powers, destroying each other. In such a case, can we expect peace among their friends who stay behind? And will not a civil war, with all its lamentable train of evil, be the natural effect?

Yet what is right must be done, independent of the consequences, which I have only stated, in order to lay before you the necessity of seriously considering the case entrusted to you before you decide upon it.

Two principal questions of fact have arisen, and require your determination. The first is, that the defendant, Gideon Henfield, has committed an act of hostility against the subjects of a power with whom the United States are at peace: this has been clearly established by the testimony. The second object of inquiry is, whether Gideon Henfield was at that time a citizen of the United States. This he explicitly acknowledged to Mr. Baker; and, if he declared true, it was at that time the least of his thoughts to expatriate himself.

The questions of law coming into joint consideration with the facts, it is the duty of the Court to explain the law to the jury, and give it to them in direction.

It is the joint and unanimous opinion of the Court, that the United States, being in a state of neutrality relative to the present war, the acts of hostility committed by Gideon Henfield are an offence against this country, and punishable by its laws.

It has been asked by his counsel, in their address to you, against what law has he offended? The answer is, against many and binding laws. As a citizen of the United States, he was bound to act no part which could injure the nation; he was bound to keep the peace in regard to all nations with whom we are at peace. This is the law of nations; not an ex post facto law, but a law that was in existence long before Gideon Henfield existed. There are, also, positive laws, existing previous to the offence committed, and expressly declared to be part of the supreme law of the land. The Constitution of the United States has declared that all treaties made, or to be made, under the authority of the United States, shall be part of the supreme law of the land. I will state to you, gentlemen, so much of the several treaties in force between America and any of the powers at war with France, as applies to the present case. The first article of the treaty with the United Netherlands, declares that there shall be a firm, inviolable, and universal peace and sincere friendship between the States General of the United Netherlands and the United States of America, and between the subjects and inhabitants of the said parties.

The seventh article of the definitive treaty of peace between the United States and Great Britain, declares that there shall be a firm and perpetual peace between His Britannic Majesty and the United States, and between the subjects of the one and the citizens of the other. ...

These treaties were in the most public, the most notorious existence, before the act for which the prisoner is indicted was committed.

The notoriety may, indeed, be said to have been greater than that of the general Acts of Congress; since, besides the same mode of publication, they are expressly referred to in the Constitution.

Much has been said on this occasion, by the defendant's counsel, in support of the natural right of emigration; but little of it is truly applicable to the present question.

Emigration is, undoubtedly, one of the natural rights of man. Yet it does not follow from thence that every act inconsistent with the duty is inconsistent with the state of a citizen.

Nothing is more inconsistent with the duty of a citizen than treason; but it is because he still continues a citizen that he is liable to punishment.

After some other observations, explanatory of the legal principles which had been agitated in the course of the trial, the Judge concluded by remarking, that the jury, in a general verdict, must decide both law and fact, but that this did not authorize them to decide it as they pleased; they were as much bound to decide by law as the judges: the responsibility was equal upon both.

The jury retired about nine on Saturday evening, and came into court again about half-past eleven, when they informed the Court they had not agreed. They were desired to retire again, which they did, and returned on Monday morning, having delivered into the hands of Judge Wilson a privy verdict on Sunday morning, soon after the adjournment of the Court.

One of the jurymen now expressed some doubts, which occasioned the judges separately to deliver their sentiments on the points of law adverted to in the charge on Saturday evening, each of them assenting to the same, particularly as to the change of political relation in the defendant, from his having been some time absent from home previous to his entering on board the privateer.

The jury again retired, and the Court adjourned. At half-past four the Court was convened, and the jury presented a written verdict, which the Court refused to receive, as being neither general nor special. Another adjournment took place, and about seven o'clock a verdict of "Not Guilty" was delivered.[4]

---

4. Chief Justice Marshall (Life of Washington, p. 273-4 vol.2) thus notices the result:

"The administration received additional evidence of the difficulty that would attend an adherence to the system which had been commenced in the acquittal of Gideon Henfield.

"A prosecution had been instituted against this person, who had enlisted in Charleston on board a French privateer equipped in that port, which had brought her prizes into the port of Philadelphia. This prosecution had been directed under the advice of the attorney general, who was of opinion that persons of this description were punishable for having violated subsisting treaties, which by the constitution are the supreme law of the land, and that they were also indictable at common law, for disturbing the peace of the United States.

"It could not be expected that the Democratic party would be inattentive to an act so susceptible of misrepresentation. Their papers sounded the alarm, and it was universally asked, 'what law had been offended and under what statute was the indictment supported? Were the American people already prepared to give to a proclamation the force of a legislative act, and to subject themselves to the will of the Executive? But if they were already sunk to such a state of degradation, were they to be punished for violating a proclamation which had not been published when the offence was committed, if indeed it could be termed an offence to engage with France, combating for liberty against the combined despots of Europe.'

"As the trial approached, a great degree of sensibility

Trial of Isaac Williams for Accepting a Commission in a French Armed Vessel and Serving in Same Against Great Britain

Circuit Court of the United States
District of Connecticut, 1799
Wharton - State Trials (1849), p. 652

The indictment charged, that Isaac Williams, of Norwich, in the County of New London, in said district of Connecticut, a citizen of this United States, did, without the jurisdiction of any particular State, viz: at Guadaloupe, in the West Indies, on or about the twentieth day of February, A. D. 1797, he, the said Isaac Williams, then being a citizen of the United States, accept from the Republic of France, a foreign state, and then enemy to the King of Great Britain, and at open war with said king - said king then was, and ever since hath been, in amity with said United States - a commission and instructions to commit acts of hostility and violence against the said king and his subjects, all of which is contrary to the twenty-first article of the treaty of amity, commerce, and navigation then existing between Great Britain and the said United States, &c.

On the trial, it was admitted on the part of Williams, that he had committed the facts alleged against him in the indictment, but, in his defence, he offered to prove that, in the year 1792, he received from the Consul-General of the French Republic, a warrant, appointing him third-lieutenant on board the Jupiter, a French seventy-four gun ship; that, pursuant to this appointment,.he went on board the Jupiter, and took the command to which he was appointed; that the Jupiter soon after sailed for France, and arrived at Rochefort, in France, in the autumn of the same year; that at Rochefort he was duly naturalized in the various Bureaux in that place, the same autumn, renouncing his allegiance to all other countries, particularly to America, and taking an oath of allegiance to the Republic of France, all according to the laws of said Republic; that immediately after said naturalization he was duly commissioned by the Republic of France appointing him a second-lieutenant on board a French frigate called the Charont; and that before the

---

was displayed, and the verdict in favour of Henfield was celebrated with extravagant marks of joy and exultation. It bereaved the executive of the strength to be derived from an opinion, that punishment might be legally inflicted on those who should openly violate the rules prescribed for the preservation of neutrality; and exposed that department to the obloquy of having attempted a measure which the laws would not justify."

ratification of the treaty of amity and commerce between the United States and Great Britain, he was duly commissioned by the French Republic a second-lieutenant on board a seventy-four gun ship, in the service of said republic; and that he has ever continued under the government of the French Republic down to the present time, and the most of said time actually resident in the dominions of the French Republic; that during said period he was not resident in the United States more than six months, which was in the year 1796, when he came to this country for the purpose merely of visiting his relations and friends; that, for about three years past, he has been domiciliated in the island of Guadaloupe, within the dominions of the French Republic, and has made that place his fixed habitation, without any design of again returning to the United States for permanent residence. The Attorney for the District conceded the above mentioned statement to be true; but objected that it ought not to be admitted as evidence to the jury, because it could have no operation in law to justify the prisoner in committing the facts alleged against him in the indictment. This question was argued on both sides by Mr. Pierpont Edwards for the United States, and Mr. David Daggett for the prisoner.[1]

---

1. Daggett's argument has not been preserved. In Talbot v. Janson, 3 Dal. 131, 139 (1795) Ingersoll and DuPonceau, arguing for an alleged expatriate, had made an elaborate effort to show that expatriation was a right given by the law of nature. Does Mr. Chief Justice Elsworth in his charge to the jury in Williams' Case adequately meet the points which Ingersoll and DuPonceau had made? Their argument follows:

"...The right of expatriation is antecedent and superior to the law of society. It is implied, likewise, in the nature and object of the social compact, which was formed to shield the weakness, and to supply the wants of individuals - to protect the acquisitions of human industry, and to promote the means of human happiness. Whenever these purposes fail, either the whole society is dissolved, or the suffering individuals are permitted to withdraw from it. There are two memorable instances of the expatriation of entire nations (independent of the general course of the patriarchial, or pastoral life) the one in ancient, and the other in modern story. When the Persians approached Athens, the whole Athenian nation embarked in the fleet of Themistocles, and left Attica, for a time, in possession of the Persians. Plut. in vit. Themist. Trav. of Anachar. 1 vol. p. 268. In the year 1771, a whole nation of Tartars, called 'Tourgouths' making 50,000 families, or 300,000 souls, emigrated from the banks of the Wolga, in Russia, and, after a progress of inconceivable difficulty, settled in the dominions of the Emperor of China, who hospitably received them,

Judge Law (district judge) expressed doubts as to the legal operation of the evidence; and gave it as his opinion, that the evidence, and the operation of law thereon, be left to the consideration of the jury.

---

and erected a monument on the spot, to commemorate the event. Col. Mag. for Feb. 1788. But the abstract right of individuals to withdraw from the society of which they are members, is recognized by an uncommon coincidence of opinion; - by every writer, ancient and modern; by the civilian, as well as by the common-law lawyer; by the philosopher, as well as the poet; It is the law of nature, and of nature's god, pointing to 'the wide world before us, where to chuse our place of rest, and Providence our guide'. 2 Bynk. 125 Wickesort. b. I. c. 2. p. 116, Grot. b. 2. 5. s. 24. par. 2. 3. Dig. de cap. et post. Law. 12. s. 9. Wick. b. I. s. II. p. 244. Puff. b. 8. I. c. II. s. 3. p. 862. I Fred. Code. 34. 5. 2 vol. 10. I Gill, Hist. Greece. With this law, however, human institutions have often been at variance; and no institutions more than the feudal system, which made the tyranny of arms, the basis of society; chained men to the soil on which they were born; and converted the bulk of mankind into the villeins, or slaves of a lord, or superior. From the feudal system, sprung the law of allegiance; which pursuing the nature of its origin, rests on lands; for, when lands were all held of the Crown, then the oath of allegiance became appropriate: It was the tenure of the tenant, or vassal. Blac. Com. 366. The oath of fealty, and the ancient oath of allegiance, were, almost the same; both resting on lands; both designating the person to whom service should be rendered; though the one makes an exception as to the superior lord, while the other is an obligation of fidelity against all men. 2 Bl. Com. 53. Pal. 140. Service, therefore, was also an inseparable concomitant of fealty, as well as of allegiance. The oath of fealty could not be violated without loss of lands; and as all lands were held mediately, or immediately, of the sovereign, a violation of the oath of allegiance, was, in fact, a voluntary submission to a state of outlawry. Hence arose the doctrine of perpetual and universal allegiance. When, however, the light of reason was shed upon the human mind, the intercourse of man became more general and more liberal; the military was gradually changed for the commercial state; and the laws were found a better protection for persons and property, than arms. But even while the practical administration of government was thus reformed, some portion of the ancient theory was preserved; and, among other things, the doctrine of perpetual allegiance remained, with the fictitious tenure of all lands from the Crown to support it. Yet, it is to be remembered, that whether in its real origin,

Judge Ellsworth, the Chief Justice of the United States, stated his views nearly in the following language:

The common law of this country remains the same as it was before the Revolution. The present question is to be decided by two great principles; one is, that all the members of civil community are bound to each other by compact. The other is, that one of the parties to this compact cannot dissolve it by his own act. The compact between our community and its members is, that the community will protect its members; and on the part of the members, that they will at all times be obedient to the laws of the community, and faithful in its defence. This compact distinguishes our government from those which are founded in violence or fraud. It necessarily results, that the members cannot dissolve this compact, without the consent of default of the community.[2] There has been here no consent - no

---

or in its artificial state, allegiance, as well as fealty, rests upon lands, and it is due to persons. Not so, with respect to citizenship, which has arisen from the dissolution of the feudal system; and is a substitute for allegiance, corresponding with the new order of things. Allegiance and citizenship, differ, indeed, in almost every characteristic. Citizenship is the effect of compact; allegiance is the offspring of power and necessity. Citizenship is a political tie; allegiance is a territorial tenure. Citizenship is the charter of equality; allegiance is a badge of inferiority. Citizenship is constitutional; allegiance is personal. Citizenship is freedom; allegiance is servitude. Citizenship is communicable; allegiance is repulsive. Citizenship may be relinquished; allegiance is perpetual. With such essential differences, the doctrine of allegiance is inapplicable to a system of citizenship; which it can neither serve to control, nor to elucidate."

In general on the problem of expatriation see Tsiang, _The Question of Expatriation in America prior to 1907_ (1942).

2. In the effort to legalize the American Revolution, a gloss was added to the doctrine of _Calvin's Case_, 7 Rep. 1 (1607). Probably the most precise formulation of the American justification for abandoning allegiance to the King was in the preamble to the New Jersey Constitution of 1776: "Whereas, all the constitutional authority ever possessed by the kings of Great Britain over these Colonies or ther other dominions was by compact derived from the people, and held of them for the common interest of the whole society, allegiance and protection are, in the nature of things, reciprocal ties, each equally depending upon the other, and liable to be dissolved by the other's being refused or withdrawn: and whereas George the Third, King of Great

default. Default is not pretended. Express consent is not claimed; but it has been argued, that the consent of the community is implied by its policy - its conditions, and its acts.

In countries so crowded with inhabitants that the means of subsistence are difficult to be obtained, it is reason and policy to permit emigration. But our policy is different; for our country is but sparsely settled, and we have no inhabitants to spare.

Consent has been argued from the condition of the country; because we were in a state of peace. But though we were in peace the war had commenced in Europe. We wished to have nothing to do with the war; but the war would have something to do with us. It has been extremely difficult for us to keep out of this war; the progress of it has threatened to involve us. It has been necessary for our government to be vigilant in restraining our own citizens from those acts which would involve us in hostilities. The most visionary writers on this subject to not contend for the principle in the unlimited extent, that a citizen may at any and at all times, renounce his own, and join himself to a foreign country. Consent has been argued from the acts of our own government, permitting the naturalization of foreigners. When a foreigner presents himself here, and proves himself to be of a good moral character, well affected to the Constitution and government of the United States, and a friend to the good order and happiness of civil society; if he has resided here the time prescribed by law, we grant him the privilege of a citizen. We do not inquire what his relation is to his own country; we have not the means of knowing, and the inquiry would be indelicate; we leave him to judge of that. If he embarrasses himself by contracting contradictory obligations, the fault and the folly are his own. But this implies no consent of the government, that our own citizens should expatriate themselves. Therefore, it is my opinion that these facts which the prisoner offers to prove in his defence, are totally irrelevant; they can have no operation in law; and the jury ought not to be embarrassed or troubled with them; but by the constitution of the court the evidence must go to the jury.

The cause and the evidence were accordingly committed to

Britain, has refused protection to the good people of these Colonies; and by assenting to sundry acts of the British Parliament, attempted to subject them to the absolute dominion of that body; and has also made was upon them in the most cruel and unnatural manner, for no other cause than asserting their just rights - all civil authority under him is necessarily at an end, and a dissolution of government in each Colony has consequently taken place."

the jury. The jury soon agreed on a verdict, and found the prisoner guilty. The court sentenced him to pay a fine of one thousand dollars, and to suffer four months imprisonment.

The defendant was also indicted before the court, for having on the 23d of September, 1797, in a hostile manner, with a privateer commissioned by the French Republic, attacked and captured a British ship and crew on the high seas, contrary to the twenty-first article of the treaty between the United States and Great Britain, said Williams being then a citizen of the United States, the French Republic being then at war with the King of Great Britain, and said King being in amity with the United States. Williams' defence on the first indictment being of no avail, and having no other defence to this, he pleaded guilty. The court sentenced him to pay a fine of one thousand dollars, and to suffer a further imprisonment of four months.

In the Congressional debates concerning the enactment of the four statutes which came to be known as the Alien and Sedition Acts, not only did discussion concern itself with the constitutional power of Congress to adopt legislation concerning aliens and concerning seditious publications, but there was vigorous debate of the question whether the Courts of the United States had a common law jurisdiction over crimes. That issue was of much more than theoretical importance in view of the fact that the government had already sought to prosecute seditious utterances as common law offenses.[1] Though Mr. Justice Chase in 1798 at the April term of the Circuit Court in Philadelphia, had stated that an indictment in a United States Court could not be supported solely at common law, his associate, Judge Peters, had not agreed with him.[2] It is not surprising, therefore, that in Congressional debate attention was given to the question of the common law jurisdiction of the United States. In the House of Representatives the positions of the Federalists

---

1. See, Anderson, "Enforcement of Alien and Sedition Laws", Report of Am. Hist. Ass. 1912, (1914) 115, 118-19.

2. Worrall's Case, 2 Dal. 370: Wharton, State Trials 185 (1798). In 1792 the Federal Court in Massachusetts had held that it possessed a common law jurisdiction in criminal matters, and in the exercise of that jurisdiction could try a defendant for counterfeiting notes of the Bank of the United States. United States v. Smith, Fed. Cas. # 16323. That good Federalist, Theophilus Parsons, representing the defendant, had argued that no such jurisdiction could be exercised by a Federal Court.

and Republicans were set forth respectively by Harrison Gray Otis, of Massachusetts, and Albert Gallatin, of Pennsylvania, in debate concerning the Sedition Act.

Argument of Otis, 8 Annals of Congress 2145 et seq.

... Mr. Otis said the professions of attachment to the Constitution, made by the gentleman from Virginia [John Nicholas] are certainly honorable to him; and he could not believe that an attachment so deeply engrafted, as he states his to be, would be shaken by this bill. The gentleman had caught an alarm on the first suggestion of a sedition bill, which had not yet subsided; and though the present bill is perfectly harmless, and contains no provision which is not practised upon under the laws of the several States in which gentlemen had been educated and from which they had drawn most of their ideas of jurisprudence, yet the gentleman continues to be dissatisfied with it.

The objections of the gentleman from Virginia, he believed, might be reduced to two inquiries. In the first place, had the Constitution given Congress cognizance over the offences described in this bill prior to the adoption of the amendments to the Constitution? and, if Congress had that cognizance before that time, have those amendments taken it away? With respect to the first question, it must be allowed that every independent Government has a right to preserve and defend itself against injuries and outrages which endanger its existence; for, unless it has this power, it is unworthy the name of a free Government, and must either fall or be subordinate to some other protection. Now some of the offences delineated in the bill are of this description. Unlawful combinations to oppose the measures of Government, to intimidate its officers, and to excite insurrections, are acts which tend directly to the destruction of the Constitution, and there could be no doubt that the guardians of that Constitution are bound to provide against them. And if gentlemen would agree that these were acts of a criminal nature, it follows that all means calculated to produce these effects, whether by speaking, writing, or printing, were also criminal. From the nature of things, therefore, the National Government is invested with a power to protect itself against outrages of this kind, or it must be indebted to and dependent on an individual State for its protection, which is absurd. This essential right resulting from the spirit of the Constitution, was still more evident in the language of that instrument. The people of the individual States brought with them as a birthright into this country the common law of England, upon which all of them have founded their statute law. If it were not for this common law, many crimes which are committed in the United States would go unpunished. No State has enacted statutes for the punishment of all crimes which may be committed; yet in every State he presumed there was a Superior Court which claimed cognizance of all offences against good morals, and which restrained misdemeanors and opposition to the constituted authorities, under the sanction merely of the common law. When the people of the United States convened for the purpose of framing a federal compact, they were all habituated to this common law, to its usages, its maxims, and its definitions. It had been more or less explicitly recognised in the Constitution of every State, and in that of Maryland it was declared to be the law of the land. If, then, we find in an instrument digested by men who were all familiarized to the common law, not only that the distribution of power, and the great objects to be provided for, are congenial to that law, but that the terms and definitions by which those powers are described, have an evident allusion to it, and must otherwise be quite inexplicable, or at best of a very uncertain meaning, it will be natural to conclude that, in forming the Constitution, they kept in view the model of the common law, and that a safe recourse may be had to it in all cases that would otherwise be doubtful. Thus we shall find that one great end of this compact, as appears in the preamble, is the establishment of justice, and for this purpose a Judicial department is erected, whose powers are declared "to extend to all cases in law and equity, arising under the Constitution, the laws of the United States", &c. Justice, if the common law ideas of it are rejected, is susceptible of various constructions, but agreeably to the principles of that law, it affords redress for every injury, and provides a punishment for every crime that threatens to disturb the lawful operations of Government. Again what is intended by "cases at law and equity arising under the Constitution" as distinguished from cases "arising under the laws of the United States"? What other law can be contemplated but common law; what sort of equity but that legal discretion which has been exercised in England from time immemorial, and is to be learnt from the books and reports of that country? If it be answered that these words comprise civil controversies only, though no reason appears for this distinction, yet what is to be done with other terms, with trial, jury, impeachment, &c., for an explanation of all which, the common law alone can furnish a standard? It has been said by the gentleman that the Constitution has specified the only crimes that are cognizable under it; but other crimes had been made penal at an early period of the Government, by express statute, to which no exception had been taken. For example, stealing public records, perjury, obstructing the officers of justice, bribery in a Judge, and even a contract to give a bribe (which last was a restraint upon the liberty of writing and speaking) were all punishable, and why? Not because they are described in the Constitution, but because they are crimes against the United

States - because laws against them are necessary to carry other laws into effect; because they tend to subvert the Constitution. The same reasons applied to the offences mentioned in the bill.

Mr. Otis contended that this construction of the Constitution was abundantly supported by the act for establishing the Judicial Courts. That act, in describing certain powers of the District Court, contains this remarkable expression: "saving to suitors in all cases the right of a common law remedy, where the common law was competent to give it". He could not tell whence this competency was derived, unless from the Constitution; nor did he perceive how this competency applied to civil and not to criminal cases.

Argument of Gallatin, 8 Annals of Congress 2156 et seq.

Mr. Gallatin observed that ... the gentleman from Massachusetts (Mr. Otis) had attempted to prove the constitutionality of the bill by asserting, in the first place, that the power to punish libels was originally vested in Congress by the Constitution, and, in the next place, that the amendment to the Constitution, which declares that Congress shall not pass any law abridging the liberty of the press, had not deprived them of the power originally given. In order to establish his first position, the gentleman had thought it sufficient to insist that the jurisdiction of the Courts of the United States extended to the punishment of offences at common law, that is to say, of offences not arising under the statutes or laws of the Union - an assertion unfounded in itself, and which, if proven, would not support the point he endeavors to establish. That assertion was unfounded; for the judicial authority of those courts is, by the Constitution, declared to extend to cases of Admiralty, or affecting public Ministers; to suits between States, citizens of different States, or foreigners, and to cases arising under the Constitution, laws, and treaties, made under the authority of that Constitution; excluding, therefore, cases not arising under either - cases arising under the common law. It was preposterous to suppose, with the gentleman from Massachusetts, that, in cases arising under the Constitution, were included offences at common law; for the cases meant were only, either such as might arise from any doubtful construction of the Constitution for instance the constitutionality of a law - or those arising immediately under any specific power given or prohibition enjoined by the Constitution; such, for instance, as declaring a retrospective law of any State to be null and void. Nor was that gentleman more fortunate in his choice of arguments, when he thought he could derive any proofs in support of the supposed jurisdiction of the Federal Courts from the number of technical expressions in the Constitution - such as writ of habeas corpus, levying war, &c. which, as he supposed, recognized the common law. He had there confounded two very distinct ideas - the principles of the common law, and the jurisdiction over cases arising under it. That those principles were recognized in the cases where the courts had jurisdiction was not denied; but such a recognition could by no means extend the jurisdiction beyond the specific cases defined by the Constitution. But, had that gentleman succeeded in proving the existence of the jurisdiction of the Federal Courts over offences at common law, and more particularly over libels, he would thereby have adduced the strongest argument against the passing of this bill; for, if the jurisdiction did exist, where was the necessity of now giving it? If the judicial authority of the Federal Courts, by the Constitution, extended to the punishment of libels, it was unnecessary to pass this law, which modified as it is, was intended by its supporters for the sole purpose of enacting into a law of the United States the common law of libels. The gentleman from Massachusetts himself, by his efforts to obtain this law, had shown that he did not believe that the courts could act in the case of libels, without the assistance of a law; and every gentleman who had spoken in favor of this bill had explicitly declared, as his opinion, that the Federal Courts had no jurisdiction whatever over offences at common law. The fact was, that the gentleman from Massachusetts, although he had at first stated the question correctly, by saying that it was sufficient to prove that the power of passing this bill was given by the Constitution, had afterwards altogether forgotten his own position the position which it was incumbent upon him to prove - and had attempted to establish another point, unconnected with the first. The question was not whether the Courts of the United States had, without this law, the power to punish libels, but whether, supposing they had not the power, Congress had that of giving them this jurisdiction - whether Congress were vested by the Constitution with the authority of passing this bill?

The Alien and Sedition Acts, by their terms, expired in 1801. The question whether there was a common law of the United States, enforceable by the Federal Courts, had not, however, been settled either by the enactment or by the enforcement of those statutes. The issue once more came under vigorous Congressional debate when, in 1802, it was proposed to repeal the statute of the Adams administration establishing intermediate Circuit Courts. The Federalist position was presented in the House of Representatives by James A. Bayard of Delaware, and the Jeffersonian argument was developed by Joseph H. Nicholson of Maryland. (The most complete statement of the Jeffersonian position is in Tucker's edition of Blackstone (1803), Vol. 1. p. 378 _et seq._)

Argument of Bayard, 11 _Annals of Congress_ 613-14

The misconduct of the judges, however, on this subject, has been considered by the gentleman the more aggravated, by an attempt to extend the principles of the Sedition act, by an adoption of those of the common law. Connected with this subject, such an attempt was never made by the judges. They have held generally, that the Constitution of the United States was predicated upon an existing common law. Of the soundness of that opinion, I never had a doubt. I should scarcely go too far, were I to say, that, stripped of the common law, there would be neither Constitution nor Government. The Constitution is unintelligible without reference to the common law. And were we to go into our courts of justice with the mere statutes of the United States, not a step could be taken, not even a contempt could be punished. Those statutes prescribe no forms of pleadings; they contain no principles of evidence; they furnish no rule of property. If the common law does not exist in most cases, there is no law but the will of the judge.

I have never contended that the whole of the common law attached to the Constitution, but only such parts as were consonant to the nature and spirit of our Government. We have nothing to do with the law of the Ecclesiastical Establishment, nor with any principle of monarchical tendency. What belongs to us, and what is unsuitable, is a question for the sound discretion of the judges. The principle is analogous to one which is found in the writings of all jurists and commentators. When a Colony is planted, it is established subject to such parts of the law of the mother country as are applicable to its situation. When our forefathers colonized the wilderness of America, they brought with them the common law of England. They claimed it as their birthright, and they left it as the most valuable inheritance to their children. Let me say, that this same common law, now so much despised and villified, is the cradle of the rights and liberties which we now enjoy. It is to the common law we owe our distinction from the colonists of France, of Portugal, and of Spain. How long is it since we have discovered the malignant qualities which are now ascribed to this law? Is there a State in the Union which has not adopted it, and in which it is not in force? Why is it refused to the Federal Constitution? Upon the same principle that every power is denied which tends to invigorate the Government. Without this law the Constitution becomes, what perhaps many gentlemen wish to see it, a dead letter.

For ten years it has been the doctrine of our courts, that the common law was in force, and yet can gentlemen say, that there has been a victim who has suffered under it? Many have experienced its protection, none can complain of its oppression.

Argument of Nicholson, 11 Annals of Congress 805 et seq.

Was there a man who did not feel the highest astonishment at the honorable member's doctrine in relation to the common law? Is there any one who believes with him that "stripped of the common law, we have neither Constitution nor Government; that our Constitution would be unintelligible, and our statute useless?" Sir, the gentleman tells us "We must leave it to the discretion of the judges to declare what belongs to us, and what is unsuitable." He says we have nothing to do with anything of a monarchical tendency; yet even upon his own ground this is a question for the discretion of the judges. Have the people of this country ever consented to vest the judges with this extensive discretionary power? Have they ever sanctioned the principle that the judges should make laws for them instead of their Representatives? Is it not legislation to all intents and purposes, when your judges are authorized to introduce at pleasure the laws of a foreign country, to arm themselves with power? The American people never dreamed of such a principle in the Constitution, and never will submit to it. They never ought to submit to it. It is giving to the judges a power infinitely more transcendant than that vested in any other branch of the Government. The Legislature cannot recognise any principle of the common law having a monarchical tendency; yet this principle the judges may recognise, if you leave it to their discretion to introduce any part of the common law which they may think proper.

I have so often heard the gentleman from Delaware maintain upon this floor an opinion that the common law of England was the common law of the United States in their national capacity, and that therefore the Federal courts have a general common law jurisdiction, that I think proper to offer some remarks upon it lest silence on our part should be construed into acquiescence.

Let us then examine this subject, and inquire when and how the common law was introduced into this country. The gentleman from Delaware supposes it was brought here by our forefathers at the time of their emigration. To this opinion I might oppose that of the celebrated Judge Blackstone, who, in the first volume of his Commentaries on the laws of England declares, in the most positive terms, that the American plantations were either ceded by treaties, or conquered from the natives; and that therefore the common law of England, as such, had no force or authority there; but wherever it is in force, it arises from their having ingrafted it into their own municipal regulations. (Mr. Nicholson read sundry extracts from the 106th, 107th 108th and 109th pages of 1st vol. of Blackstone, to show that this was the opinion of the learned Judge.) For this opinion, however, sir, of Judge Blackstone, I do not contend. I have seen it very powerfully opposed by able writers, and I think the usage and practice of the colonies themselves furnish a sufficient argument against it. It may perhaps be correct in its application to New York, New Jersey, Pennsylvania, and Delaware, which, I believe, were originally settled by the Dutch and Swedes, and were ceded to the English by the Treaty of Breda, in the year 1667. These were therefore conquered countries, and the common law of England could not have been brought into them by the original emigrants. It may have been since practised under in these States, but is indebted for its introduction either to express statute, or to common usage. It goes however to establish the principle for which I contend, that our forefathers brought with them no law having a uniform operation over all the extent of country now contained within the limits of the United States; for when gentlemen speak of a common law of the United States, they must mean a law uniform throughout the whole extent, and equally obligatory upon the whole nation. I entertain no doubt myself that the common law of England, or so much of it as was applicable to their situation, was brought over by the original emigrants, to New England, to Maryland, to Virginia, and the other Southern States; and that it continued to be the law of the provinces until altered by their respective Legislatures. But it was the law of each province only, and not a general law operating upon the whole; for each was independent of the other, and the municipal regulations of the one could not bind the other. ... Permit me likewise to remark, that even if the common law had remained unaltered by the several Colonial Governments, yet it could not have been considered as a uniform rule of law operating upon them as a nation, because each was independent of the other and had emigrated at different periods, while the common law of England was undergoing the most material changes by act of Parliament. The colonization of Virginia took place in the reign of Queen Elizabeth, that of Maryland in the reign of Charles the First, and that of Georgia in the reign of George the Second. In the intervening spaces of time, the common law had been greatly ameliorated; and if it is now to be insisted on as constituting the law of the United States, in consequence of its introduction by our forefathers at the time of their emigration, we should be at a loss to determine which of these periods we should fix on as that which was to give the character to the common law; whether it is to be the common law in force in the reign of Elizabeth, or the common law as ameliorated by statute between that time and the reign of George the Second. I need not enter into a detail of these changes, for they will readily occur to most gentlemen who hear me; but as very material changes were made, I think it cannot be contended that the law as existing at one period or the other could have any uniform operation upon the several colonies, who were, as to each other, independent States governed by their own laws, and without any connexion, common government, or general law, prior to the declaration of independence. ...

We have been told by the member from Delaware, that without the common law the Constitution would be a dead letter. Every State in the Union, he says, has adopted it; and he asks why it is denied to the Federal Constitution? I could have wished that on this subject, as well as many others, the gentleman had offered us something like argument, instead of mere wild and arbitrary assertion. However highly we may estimate his talents, he must not expect that we are to yield to his political dogmas. We flatter ourselves that the Constitution may stand and flourish without those invigorating principles of the common law, which the gentleman is anxious to infuse into it. I agree that it has been adopted under various modifications by the respective States; but I do not admit that it has been adopted by the Federal Constitution. Where the States have adopted it, it has been by a solemn and positive act, expressly recognising it as a part of their code of laws. I might challenge the gentleman to put his finger on any part of the Federal Constitution containing any recognition of it whatever, as a law of the United States. Is it to be found in the enumeration of the powers vested in the Legislature? Is it to be found in the enumeration of the powers vested in the Executive, or in the enumeration of the powers vested in the Judiciary? It is to be found in neither. Is this adoption of the common law to be found in any article contained in the original instrument, or in any of the amendments afterwards ingrafted upon it? In one of the amendments, we find the words common law used, but I presume it will not be contended that the common law was adopted by this article; for it must be obvious to the plainest legal understanding, that the words "suits at common law" are only used in contradistinction to suits in equity. In the latter cases, the trial by jury is not used, but in the former the trial by jury is preserved by this amendment. And when the rules of the common law are mentioned in the latter part of the same article, they are merely referred to as rules of proceeding which are to govern in motions for new trials, and a few other cases, where facts decided by the verdict of a jury may be re-examined; but it can have no operation to confer jurisdiction. Might I not be permitted to ask why the common law of England was adopted by our Constitution more than the laws of any other nation; more than the laws of France, Spain, Sweden or Holland? When the Constitution was formed we were more intimately connected with those countries than with England, because with some of them we had treaties of alliance, with all we had treaties of commerce. Besides, if the common law of England was adopted by the Constitution, a very serious question might arise whether the common law did not thereby become a part of the Constitution; and, if a part of the Constitution, all laws since passed by Congress contrary to the principles of the common law would be null and void; such, for instance, as the act declaring the punishment of manslaughter and several others. That this would be a fair construction may be gathered from the opinions of those who formed the constitutions of New York, New Jersey, Delaware, Maryland and South Carolina, and likewise from the Convention of Virginia; who all retained the common law, but expressly declared it to be subject to the future alterations of their respective Legislatures. Now, if the common law was adopted by the Constitution without any provision that it should be subject to future alteration by Congress, a question might certainly arise whether Congress would have the power of passing any law varying the common law. However, if this difficulty is got over, another not very inferior in importance immediately presents itself. If the Constitution adopted the common law, or the common law attached itself to the Constitution, it immediately became a law of the United States, and is paramount to the laws and constitutions of the individual States. Wherever, therefore, the constitutions or laws of the States modified the common law, such modification was of no effect; for whenever a law of the United States clashes with the constitution or law of one of the States, the State Constitution or law must give way, as has been solemnly decided by the Federal courts in more instances than one; particularly in the case of Vanhorne's lessee against Dorrance, in the circuit court of Pennsylvania, and in the case of Ware and Hilton upon a writ of error in the Supreme Court of the United States. Whether the people of this country are inclined to submit to the train of evils which would follow the establishment of this principle, does not, I presume, admit of a doubt. ...

I think, sir, I have fully proved that the common law of England was not introduced by our ancestors at the time of their emigration, as a general and uniform law prevailing over all the extent of country comprised within the present limits of the United States; because the several colonies were planted at several periods, some of which were as remote from each other as one hundred and fifty years; because it was changed and modified at pleasure by the respective provinces, and because we were not at that time a nation, and therefore required no general uniform law to govern us. I think I have proved that it was not adopted by the Declaration of Independence, because we associated only for mutual defence against a common enemy, and there were no general questions among us which could possibly require the interference of common law, and Congress had no power to establish courts to carry the law into execution. And I think I have proved that it was not adopted by the Constitution, because there is no part of the Constitution declaring it to be the law of the land; because its implied adoption, without limitation or restraint, would either make it a part of the Constitution itself, and thereby prevent a most valuable exercise of Legislative authority, or by making it a law of the United States, would give it a controlling and repealing or nullifying power over the laws and constitutions of the individual States; and because almost every Congress, by enacting a variety of provisions already established by the common law, expressed an opinion, most unequivocally, that the common law was not the law of the United States in their national capacity.

The common law can have no possible existence in this country, but as it has been introduced by the different States. Some have engrossed it into their body of laws by their constitutions; others by express statute, and in one or two instances perhaps, the States have used and practised it from their original colonization: for it is not denied that the several colonies brought with them such both of the statute and common laws as were applicable to their situation. But the common law as introduced, used, and practised in any one State, can only be considered as a State law. After it was retained by Maryland, by an express article of her constitution, it was no longer the common law of England as such, but thereby became the law of the State of Maryland, under the various modifications which had been made by the provincial assemblies; and such it remains at this day. As a State law then, it cannot be construed to give jurisdiction to the Federal courts, any more than the numerous acts of Assembly which have passed both before and since the Revolution. By the common law of England, as it exists there, and as it likewise exists in Maryland, kidnapping, or the forcible abduction or stealing of man, or woman, or child, is an offence punishable with fine, imprisonment, and pillory: a statute of Maryland declares the stealing of a slave to be a capital offence. Now neither of these laws can give the Federal courts any jurisdiction over these offences, because they are both State laws, although one of them is likewise a part of the common law of England. ...

"Cursing or wishing ill to the King", is an offence punishable at common law by fine, imprisonment, and pillory; but this is not the law of any of the States, because after the Declaration of Independence we had no King, and therefore it was not applicable to our situation. To curse or wish ill to the Governor of a State, could not be punished, although he is the Chief Magistrate of the State; because cursing or wishing ill to the King of England is a contempt against his person and Government: but in America we do not regard the majesty of persons, nor do we admit that the Government belongs to any one man, but to the whole people. However, even if this part of the common law did form any part of the codes of the respective States, it could give no jurisdiction to the Federal courts, being a State law. It is with much regret, Mr. Chairman, I have heard that a man in New Jersey was indicted at common law and punished by a Federal court, for expressing a ludicrous wish in relation to a former President of the United States - a personage not known to the common law. Yet common law jurisdiction was assumed by the Federal court over this offence, and the sacred person of the President was substituted for the sacred person of the King.

In fine, sir, my opinion is, and I sincerely believe it to be correct and Constitutional opinion, that the common law of England, either as such or as it has been introduced into the several States, is not the common law of the United States in their national or federal capacity, and therefore cannot operate to give to the Federal courts any jurisdiction. On the present occasion, I wish to express my decided disapprobation of the doctrine contended for by the gentleman from Delaware, that the Federal judges have a discretionary power to introduce such parts of the common law as they please, and as they may think do or do not belong to us. This discretionary power in a judge is dangerous to liberty. It will sap the foundation of your Constitution itself. It will place the life and property of every man in the community in the most precarious situation. All security will be lost, all confidence will be destroyed. To vest a discretionary power of this kind in a judge, is to vest him with an arbitrary and unconstitutional power. That able and upright judge, the most excellent Lord Camden, who was an ornament not only to his profession, but to his country and to human nature, declares, that "The discretion of a judge is the law of tyrants; it is always unknown; it is casual, and depends upon constitution, temper and habit. In the best it is often caprice; in the worst it is every vice, folly, and passion, to which human nature is liable."

With the adoption of the Alien and Sedition Acts in the summer of 1798 the problem of their enforcement aroused in judges of Federalist inclinations an eager zeal for prosecutions. In Pennsylvania Alexander Addison, President of the Court of Common Pleas, showed particular energy in his efforts to persuade grand juries to return indictments against seditious persons and to assist the Federal government in the enforcement of the Alien Acts. Of this many vigorous charges to grand juries none were more forceful than those which he delivered in the summer and fall of 1798. They were printed by him in the appendix to Addison's Reports (1800).

Judge Addison's Charge to the Grand Jury, June Session, 1798
Addison's Reports, Appendix, 260, 268-70

A disgraceful and disorderly breach of the peace was committed in this town, in the dead of night, between the last day of April and the first day of this month of May. A number of persons assembled about midnight, and between that and two of the clock in the morning, with great noise and tumult, to the disturbance of the neighbourhood, erected, in the street, a pole, which they called a may-pole, hung to it colours, and to them the French flag. To erect a pole in a street or highway, at any time, is an offence, it is a public nuisance. To erect such pole, even on private ground, in a town, in the dead of night, with noise, and tumult disturbing the neighbourhood, is an offence, it is a public nuisance - And for citizens of America, at this time, to hang to such pole, the flag of a nation, which, contrary to all the rights of nature and nations and to solemn treaties, has long been carrying on a cruel, oppressive, and flagitious war against us, shows such a total want of all duty and allegiance to our country, and such an abandoned spirit of seditious and treasonable subjection to the will of a foreign and hostile government, as ought to excite the detestation of all good men, and lovers of their country.

On the same night, and at the hour of two of the clock in the morning, and from that to day light, some of the same party paraded through the streets of this town, beating a drum, and playing a fife, to the disturbance and alarm of the inhabitants. This is an offence, it is a public nuisance, as tending to excite alarm, and to deprive peaceable citizens of that seasonable repose, and quiet sleep, of which the laws engage to protect them in the enjoyment. To prevent great evils, you must prevent the least beginnings: for people naturally begin with little, and proceed from bad to worse.

Nothing is more certain, than that the greatest enemy to liberty is licentiousness, and that the surest way to destroy our privileges is to abuse them. Liberty of the press has always been considered as an important right; but, if it be abused, if it degenerate into licentiousness, the abuse must be corrected, if we would preserve the true liberty of the press. Printing is an useful art, and newspapers are important means of information. But if printers publish falsehood, indecency, or profaneness, they poison society, corrupt morals, and undermine religion. Nothing is more dangerous and detestable, than such printers and newspapers. They are public nuisances. Such newspapers ought to be rejected, and such printers punished.

In all calamity, the pious man looks up to God - And in all national calamity, pious rulers have constantly directed the minds of their people to God, and, for this end, have proclaimed days of fasting and humiliation. In the present alarming crisis, the president of the United States recommended a day of fasting and humiliation. In a newspaper published in this town, there was printed "A prayer for John Adams on the fast day". This paper, called a paper, represented the president of the United States as offering to the Almighty confessions and petitions of a ridiculous nature. When a man noted for piety and virtue is thus represented in a ridiculous light, as mocking God, the representation is an offence, a libel. When the man thus represented is a magistrate, and, much more, the chief magistrate, it becomes a seditious libel, dangerous to the just influence of public authority. When the object of this is to turn into ridicule a solemn act of religious duty; it becomes an impious libel. And, if it represent God as listening to mock confessions and petitions; it becomes a blasphemous libel. And, if those, whose duty it is to correct such enormities, do not discharge this duty, they give their countenance to scandal, sedition, impiety, and blasphemy.

Having discharged my duty, in the mention of these things, I leave them to your serious and conscientious consideration.

Judge Addison's Charge to the Grand Jury
September Session, 1798
Addison's Reports, Appendix, 270, 275-89

Congress, in its last session, has passed a law (14th July 1798) enacting, that, if any persons shall unlawfully combine together, with intent to oppose any measure of the government of the United States, or impede the operation of any law of the United States, or to prevent any person holding any office under the government of the United States from performing his duty; or shall, with such intent, advise, or attempt to procure, any insurrection, riot, unlawful assembly or combination; they shall be deemed guilty of a high misdemeanor, and be punished by a fine, not exceeding five thousand dollars, and by imprisonment, for not less than six months, nor more than five years; and may, further, be holden to sureties for good behaviour. And it further enacts, that if any person shall write, print, utter, or publish, or shall cause or procure to be written, printed, uttered, or published, or shall knowingly and willingly aid in writing, printing, uttering or publishing, any false, scandalous, and malicious writing, against the government of the United States, or either house of congress, or the president of the United States, with intent to defame the said government, or either house of congress, or the president; or to bring them, or either of them, into contempt or disrepute; or to excite against them, or either of them, the hatred of the people of the United States; or to excite unlawful combinations therein, for opposing or resisting any law of the United States, or any act of the president of the United States, done in pursuance of any such law, or of the powers vested in him by the constitution of the United States; or to oppose or defeat any such law or act; or to aid, encourage, or abet, any hostile designs of any foreign nation against the United States, their people or government; such person shall be punished by a fine, not exceeding two thousand dollars, and imprisonment, not exceeding two years.

This act, which seems to be best known by the name of the sedition act, provides, "that, if any person shall be prosecuted under it, for writing or publishing any libel, it shall be lawful for him, on the trial of the cause, to give in evidence, in his defence, the truth of the matter contained in the publication charged as a libel. And the jury who shall try the cause shall have a right to determine the law and the fact, under the direction of the court, as in other cases." This clause clearly borrowed from the section already quoted of the constitution of Pennsylvania, confirms, so far as concurrent expressions of different persons on the same subject can, the construction which I put on that section, that the time for giving in evidence the truth of the libellous matter is at the trial of the cause by the traverse jury.

No law seems to have been resisted in congress with more vehemence and passion, by those who opposed all the measures adopted, as measures of defence against the hostile spirit of France. And, out of doors, it has been attacked with sullen rancour, as a death wound to the progress of that detestable system of slander, which has been pursued with such malignant industry, and calamitous success, against every measure of the administration. And yet, strange as it may seem, this law does not create any new offence; for every thing forbidden by it appears to me to have been, before, an offence at common law. The combinations and attempts therein forbidden are misdemeanors. Any writing of an immoral or illegal tendency is a libel. And slanderous words spoken of the government, or its acts or authority, are punishable by indictment.

It may be said, then, why was this law made? Several reasons may be given for it.

1. It is no uncommon thing for a legislature to make an act declaratory of the common law. At this time, it was peculiarly proper to make such an act, as a solemn admonition to wicked or unthinking men, to abstain from practices, which spread slanders ans falsehood, foment divisions and seditions among the citizens, weaken the energy of the government, and thus rendering the nation defenceless, encourage France, by a prospect of impunity and success, to measures of aggression and hostility.

2. A doubt had been suggested whether the courts of the

United States had cognizance of any offences not expressly declared by the constitution, or some law or treaty of the United States. I do not think this doubt well founded. It has been supported by an assertion, that the judiciary of the United States has no common law jurisdiction: and this assertion has been triumphantly displayed in a variety of shapes, and propped up by a variety of illustrations. Yet, in my opinion, it is delusive, and founded on a misconception of ideas, and misconstruction and abuse of words. There is a common law jurisdiction incident to every man, to every state of society, and to every organization of civil government; a power necessary for self-preservation. A jurisdiction, to correct offences against individuals or society within it or against its own safety, is by common law, incident to the judiciary of each state. And a jurisdiction, to correct offences against the safety of the United States, is, by common law, incident to the judiciary of the United States. The judicial power of the United States extends to all cases arising under the constitution, the laws and treaties of the United States. Hence results a jurisdiction to try and punish, as misdemeanors, all acts tending to violate or weaken the authority of the constitution, or of any act or measure of the government of the United States. For it cannot be supposed, that such misdemeanors should pass unpunished, or that the government of the United States should be obliged to beg protection from the individual states. The doubt however existing, it might be thought proper to remove it.

3. It might be thought proper to pass this law, in order to limit the extent of punishment which might be inflicted on the offender; and to give him the advantage of proving the truth of the libel in his defence. ...

This law takes from no man any liberty, but a liberty of doing mischief. And, so far is it from being true, that this law is any violation of liberty, that, it may be safely averred without such laws, for punishing the abuse of the freedom of speech and of the press, liberty cannot be preserved: every man will be a slave to the malignant passions of every other; truth and justice will be banished, the authority of government destroyed, and malice, anarchy, confusion, and every evil work established.

Our constitution is excellent, our administration is wise and honest, and has no interest separate from that of the people. On the support of such an administration of such a government depends our liberty. But, let me repeat, no administration or government can stand against the corruption of public opinion and let me, therefore, solemnly admonish you, as you value the peace and liberty of yourselves and your posterity, seriously to reflect on the truth of this. We have seen an insurrection promoted by the corruption of public opinion - An invasion is invited by it. How many shocks of this kind our government is doomed to stand, only the Ruler of the world knows. Let us take warning from our own experience, and the fate of other nations. Let all friends to liberty and order unite in suppressing slander: for, where it prevails, there will be no happiness, no government. Of all slanders those of the press are most dangerous. Presses established to run down the government are the most destructive of all treasons. This ought to be well considered; for every one who encourages such presses, or contributes to their support, is a partner in their guilt. Every one, who reads their productions with approbation, sucks in disease upon his mind; and every one, who repeats them to others, spreads the infection. What would we think of a set of men, who should agree to hire a number of persons to run through the country, and report falsehoods and slanders? Precisely such, and more dangerous, is the guilt of those, who contribute to the support of a slanderous press. They are wounding their own and their country's peace, and undermining the government.

But you will say,"We desire to hear both sides, that we may know the truth." My friends, truth has but one side: and listening to error and falsehood is indeed a strange way to discover the truth. Take the representations which its friends have made of the conduct of government; have ye ever found falsehood in them? Take the contradictory statement made by its enemies; have ye ever found truth in them?

You may yet say,"We have not the means of knowing on which side the truth lies; and we, therefore, give no preference to any, but hear all." What would ye think of a Protestant who should say thus? "The Lutherans and Calvanists differ in opinion, the Catholics differ from both, and the Mohometans from them all; I know not on which side the truth is; I will therefore, pay a lutheran minister, a calvanist minister, a catholic priest, and a turkish iman; and then I shall be sure of knowing the truth." Would ye think, that this man had any regard to truth or religion? Instead of acquiring knowledge, would he not confuse his mind, and lose sight of both truth and duty? As in religion so in government, a sincere enquirer after truth will always find means of discovering it. And it is only their enemies, and hypocritical pretenders to sincerity, who, under pretence of searching for truth, wander through the endless varieties of error, and affect to think there is no certainty.

There is hardly any part of government, which, as of religion, has not been misrepresented by its enemies. Now, though of all its parts, the people generally have not had an opportunity of being fully satisfied, yet of some, they have had this opportunity. And, wherever they have had such opportunity, they must be satisfied, that the conduct of government has been right and the misrepresentations of it false and malicious. No part of the conduct of our government has been more misrepresented, than its conduct with respect to France. Yet, when fairly stated, in a way that the greatest slanderers dare not contradict, how honest, wise, and praise worthy does it seem! Ought we not, therefore, to believe, that, if we understood all the rest, as well as this part, the whole would appear as unexceptionable? This would be our duty between man and man; and it is also our duty, as between citizens and the government.

Another duty, and a mean of information, is to search at the best sources of information. You ought never to believe a slander on government, merely because it is stated in a newspaper, or a pamphlet, or reported by those, in whose judgment, veracity, and opportunity of knowing, you have not confidence. As if the thing concerned your own house or estate, or the character of your friend, go to those, in whose veracity and judgment, you would confide in matters of the greatest importance. For, be assured, no matter is of greater importance, than a just confidence in government. The men, who endeavour to rob you of this, are the worst enemies of your peace. If they can succeed in robbing your minds of this confidence, they rob you of your liberty; for they deprive government of its authority; and government without authority, is anarchy; and anarchy is the worst tyranny. No crime, therefore, is greater, than that slander, which diminishing the people's confidence in the government, diminishes their security, and destroys their liberty. And no crime more deserves the vigilant and severe animadversion of a grand jury.

Judge Addison's Charge to the Grand Jury
December Session, 1798
Addison's Reports, Appendix, 289, 304-310

Lest this law [the Alien Act], when tried by the words, and by the principles, of the constitution, should appear unexceptionable, and escape censure; it has been endeavoured to excite a clamour against it, by drawing a melting picture of the distress of aliens, who may thus be ordered to depart out of the country, at the will of one man.

This is all work of imagination. It cannot be denied, that there is a right in the United States, as in every other nation, to remove aliens; and that there may be cases, in which the safety of the nation will render it necessary to exert this right. And, I think, it cannot be denied, that, in the last session of congress, the United States were, if any nation ever was, in a condition that required it as a solemn duty, to exert this right. The rights and safety of individuals must never be put in competition with the rights and safety of a nation. Aliens have but an imperfect right, the right of hospitality and civility, to remain in any nation, to which they are not bound to permanent allegiance - And if the rulers of the nation, in which they have a temporary indulgence to reside, suspect any danger to the nation, from their residence, and order them to depart, they have no right to remain. The United States were threatened with danger from France, and by the same means which France has uniformly adopted, to bring danger and destruction on other countries, intestine divisions. Aliens having the least interest in the prosperity of this country, and owing the least duty, only a temporary duty, to it, were the most likely to yield themselves the readiest agents of France. And the little respect which, in this country, is paid to the rights of election, gives them, here, an opportunity of mischief, which they could in no other country enjoy. Though some of our own citizens may be base enough to yield themselves as instruments of a foreign power, the government of the United States has no authority to remove them. But it has, like every other government, in time of danger, authority to expel aliens; and the right and duty of common defence, and protection against invasion and domestic violence, required, that this right of expulsion should be exerted. Nor was the exertion of this right proper only against French aliens. The principles professed by the government of France, have excited through the world an enthusiasm, which nothing, but experience of their destructive consequences, can correct. There is, in all nations a number of warm speculative men, combined together, to promote the diffusion and prevalence of this theoretic liberty. Many of these, either expelled or flying from their own country, reside in the United States; and are, here, it seems, systematically united, not in support of the principles of our government, but, of an imaginary political millennium, a government which never existed, and, while man remains as he is, never can exist; in support of the fanciful principles, which, in the progress of its revolution to anarchy and despotism, have brought so much misery on France, and every country, where the arts and arms of France have prevailed. These dogmatists, invincible by reason or experience, united in principles, however dispersed in place, as a nation of themselves, are enemies to all governments; and, like the preachers of a new religion, think all other rights and duties ought to yield to the great duty of establishing their principles. To this duty they will sacrifice all other considerations; and nothing, however cruel or destructive, that can promote this, will, in their eyes, be a crime. Such men will be dangerous to any country, in which they reside. Instigated by the zeal of proselytism, the apparent benevolence in their principles will give them in irresistible influence on the young and inexperienced. And no country, in which such men prevail, can hope for safety against the arts of France. Nor can any Frenchman more earnestly promote the views and success of France, than any native of any country, who, by adopting her principles, has brought himself within the pale of this new political church. Become citizens of the world, they contemn all distinctions between nations, and cherish all people with equal affection; the love of country is lost in the love of mankind, and philanthropy extended beyond its natural limits, and exerted beyond its natural force is wasted in useless or self-destroying efforts. Insensible of error, and deaf to instruction, they are borne forward with the courage of conscience, the ardor of inspiration, and the obstinacy of impenitence, by an impetuous enthusiasm, to all the mischiefs, which guilt could effect. And, wherever there is no hope of conversion while we are in danger, the exertion of the right of expulsion becomes a duty, which the rulers owe to the safety of the nation.

If there may be cases of humanity, which may make this exertion, where not absolutely necessary, favour of severity; the question is, with whom the power of indulgence may be best lodged, so as best to accomplish the great object, public safety, and most to favour humanity.

As a measure of national defence, this discretion, of expulsion or indulgence, seems properly vested in the branch of the government peculiarly charged with the direction of the executive powers, and of our foreign relations. There is in it a mixture of external policy, and of the law of nations, that justifies this disposition.

It was never known, that a numerous and complex body of men had a more tender conscience, than an upright individual. Where many do wrong, each can cast the censure from himself upon others. But a responsible individual must take all the burden of the blame. Any man, with any claim to tenderness, would rather risk the success of that claim to an impartial and humane individual, than to a numerous body of men.

It remains, therefore, only to determine, whether the character of the president be such, as to render him a proper depositary of this power of indulgence. Has the president no feelings of humanity? Is a life of piety and justice no ground of confidence? The character of the president is well known. And no alien, who meddles not with politics and plots, who favours not the views of our enemies, and injures not the peace, safety or defence of the Country, has any thing to fear from this law. Even with respect to dangerous aliens, congress has provided, that the rights of humanity (so far as, consistently with the supreme law, the safety of the people, they can) shall be secured to them. For it is enacted, that it shall be lawful for any alien, who may be ordered to be removed from the United States, to take with him his property; or, if he leave any of it, that it remain subject to his order and disposal.

But is all our pity to be extended to strangers; and shall we extend no care to ourselves, our wives, and our children? The French have threatened us with pillage, plunder and massacre. Such threats they have carried into execution in other countries. They have threatened us with a party among ourselves, which will promote their views. Some of them, it is said, have told us, that we dare not resent their injuries; for there are Frenchmen enow among us, to burn our cities, and cut our throats. And, it seems, we dare not remove those gentle lambs! Gracious Heaven! Are we an independent nation, and dare we not do this? Shall our constitution, intended as a shield to defend, become a sword to wound us? Have we made a constitution, to restrain our administration from oppressing ourselves, and to retrain it, as to submit our cities to alien incendiaries, and our throats to alien assassins?

It is no unreasonable calculation, that there have been, at one time (and may be now) from twenty forty thousand French within the United States. There is also a great number of united Irish, and fugitives from other countries, notoriously disaffected to their own, to this, and every other government; and devoted to incessant revolution. If an invasion from France were projected, is any thing but arms, organization, and discipline wanting, to make all these as compleat a French army as if recruited in France, and transported under her banners to the United States? And will any one say, that the government of the United States, which is bound to protect each state against invasion, is not bound, on a reasonable fear of invasion to remove such internal enemies, before they are armed, organized, or disciplined?

Vain is all our defence against enemies without, if we guard not against enemies within. If we leave an Achan in the camp, can we hope for victory? If we leave a band of traitors in the fort, can we hope to defend it? If we suffer French spies to stroll through our cities, our harbours, our shores, and our country, and give information of all our strength and all our weakness; how can we be guarded against attack? If we suffer them to remain here, to give information of every ship that sails, that it may fall into the hands of some French privateer; how can we protect our trade? If we suffer French agents to remain here, to corrupt the minds of our citizens, our printers, and our officers, to pry into our councils, purchase our arms and ammunition, influence our opinions and elections, render our people careless, and our administration weak; what have we to expect, but all the horrors of a French invasion? What have we to expect, but to see our houses in flames, and our families in blood?

I trust in God, that this will not happen. I trust, the measures adopted by our administration, with cordial union among ourselves, will preserve us from this calamity. But, if it should come upon us, we will curse those, who have lulled us with a sweet song of security, and gentle fraternity of the French, who, professing motives of economy, have endeavoured to tie up the hands of the administration from effectual measures of defence; and, under the pretence of valuing and seeking peace, do, in the surest manner invite war.

We are, at present, in a perilous state, and it is to be feared, on the brink of some calamity. Menaced with the resentment of a foreign nation, we are distracted among ourselves. In proportion to our dissentions, will be our danger; and our safety lies in love to our constitution, and confidence in our administration. If the people will cordially unite in supporting active measures of the administration, France will change her tone, from resentment to complacency. But experience of her conduct towards all other nations must convince us, that it is her means only, and not her object, that she will change. Her object will remain the same, to reduce us to a subjection to her will. Let us beware, therefore, of supposing, that, when she speaks peace, she means peace. She will speak peace, while we support our administration; and again war, whenever she can persuade our people to oppose the administration of their government. Divide and subdue is her maxim.

With a view to lessen the grounds of distrust in our administration, so fatal to our own interest; and to increase that confidence in it, so essential to our safety; I have endeavoured, with candour and care, to examine the principles of a law, which has been made a pretext for vehement clamour. I have I think shewn that it is constitutional and necessary. I have said (what is well known) that there is such ground of confidence in the president, that there is no fear that he will suffer it to operate against any alien, who comes and remains honestly and innocently among us; and that he will exercise his authority only against aliens, who use the opportunity of their being here, for the purpose of disturbing our peace, alienating the minds of our citizens from our government, betraying our situation, corrupting our measures, or weakening our defence. And, I hope, it will appear, that, if our rulers had not exerted this authority, we should have had just reason to say, that they had betrayed their trust.

O! if the people would but love their constitution, and confide in its wise and honest administration, and turn away from those who harrass their minds with vain suspicions; how happy might we be! May the God of wisdom open our eyes to the excellence of our constitution, and the purity and prudence of our administration; and to the folly, madness, and wickedness of those demagogues, who mislead this people from their interests and duties, and glory in their guilt. May he wean us from all partialities and prejudices towards any foreign nation; unite our hearts in love, and support of our government; and preserve us from the machinations of a government, ambitious, desperate, faithless, and corrupt; which flatters, only to deceive; and caresses, only to destroy.

At length Judge Addison's vigor brought his career to an

end. His refusal to permit a Republican associate on the Court of Common Pleas to deliver charges to the grand and petit juries led to successful impeachment proceedings. Those proceedings were published in The Trial of Alexander Addison (1803).

United States v. Hodges[1]
Circuit Court of the United States,
District of Maryland - 1815 - Fed. Cas. #15374
2 Wheeler's Cr. C. 477

Elias Glenn, Esq. Counsel for the United States
U. S. Heath, J. E. Hall and Wm. Pinckney, Esqrs. Counsel for the Prisoner

The facts of the case were as follows: while the British army was on the retreat from the city of Washington, last summer, as they passed through George County, some of the people of the town of Upper Marlborough, took four stragglers, who were following the army. They were sent into the interior of the country together with a deserter. As soon as they were missed, they were demanded by the British commander, under a threat that the town should be destroyed if they were not obeyed. Communications passed between the two parties, the result of which was that the men were restored to the enemy.

It appeared by the testimony of John Randall and others, that on Saturday after the engagement at Bladensburgh, General Bowie brought three prisoners to Queen Anne, and asked Randall to stand guard over them, which he did. During the night Mr. William Lansdale brought another. Early in the morning the prisoner and his brother appeared and demanded them; they said that the British had threatened to destroy the town, unless this requisition was obeyed before 12 o'clock, &c. and that they would hold their wives and children as hostages.

The witness sent for General Bowie, who at first refused to suffer them to go; upon an explanation of the threat, he said it was hard, but he supposed they must be returned. They were delivered up to the prisoner, who surrendered them to the British.

Mr. Pinckney on behalf of the prisoner, read an address from the grand jury to the President of the United States in which the jurors expressed their respect for the motives of the

---

1. Although United States v. Hodges did not present questions under the Alien and Sedition Acts the trial procedure which was there followed should be kept in mind in considering what were the actual problems in securing enforcement of those statutes.

prisoner, and prayed a nolle prosequi.

Mr. Glenn prayed the court to direct the jury that the mere act of delivering up prisoners or deserters, is an overt act of high treason.

Pinckney. There is no law in this prayer, for it excludes that which is the essence of the offence, intention; and if it was otherwise, the court has no right to instruct the jury, as if this were a civil case. No instance has occurred in modern times of an attempt to bind the jury in such a case by the opinion of the court. What remedy is there for the party if you err? We may appeal to a higher tribunal, it is true, but what is the consequence? The man is hanged, and your judgment is reversed.

In England, did their courts interfere in this mode in the celebrated cases of Hardy, and Horne Tooke and others? No, it would not have been endured. The best security for the rights of individuals is to be found in the trial by jury. But the excellence of this institution consists in its exclusive power. The jury are here judges of law and fact, and are responsible only to God, to the prisoner, and to their own consciences. After the case is closed, you may indeed advise the jury, if they ask it, or if you think proper to do so; without being asked by them. But to interrupt the progress of the trial in the way proposed would be monstrous. Suppose the court to give the direction, I shall not submit to it as the prisoner's counsel. I will, on the contrary, tell the jury that it is not law. It is my right to do so, and in a case of blood, I dare not forego the exercise of it. I trust I shall not be placed in a predicament which will thus set my duty to a man whose life is in my charge, against my respect for this tribunal. I pray your honours to suffer this cause to go on in the customary and legal manner. ...

Mr. Glenn, in support of his prayer, read to the court the following authorities: 1 East, C. L. p. 70. If the joining with rebels be from fear of present death, and while the party is under actual force, such fear and compulsion will excuse him.

But an apprehension ever so well grounded, of having property wasted or destroyed, or suffering any other mischief, not endangering the person of the party, will be no excuse for joining or continuing with rebels. Ibid. p. 71. ...

The counsel then read Cranbourn's case from Salk. p. 633. He then admitted that he must prove a certain portion of the intention, and that in the present case there was but two inquiries to be made.

1st. Did he deliver up the prisoners?

2d. Did he intend to do so?

Both these questions must be answered affirmatively; and therefore the treason was proved, and he had no more to say upon the subject.

Pinckney. Nothing but an utter confusion of ideas could have introduced a doubt upon the subject. The gentleman's prayer excluded all idea of criminal intention; or it relied upon the influence of criminal motive, as a necessary corollary from the naked facts charged, as the overt acts in the indictment.

It might be affirmed as an universal proposition; that criminal intention is the essence of every species of crime. All indictments commence with an assertion of corrupt motives; and in indictments for treason, the overt acts laid are to show the manner in which the wicked intention is carried into execution. In the speeches Lord Erskine, to whom the world is so largely indebted for a correct knowledge of the principles of civil liberty and the law of treason, you will find him perpetually contending, and contending with effect, that although the crown had proved the facts charged, it had not shown the evil design, the corrupt purpose, without which the facts are nothing. ...

Duvall, C. J. The Court would have been better satisfied if the whole case had been gone through in the usual way; but as the District Attorney has prayed an opinion on the law, the Court will give their opinion.

1st. Hodges is accused of adhering to the enemy, and the overt act laid consists in the delivery of certain prisoners, and I am of opinion that the overt act laid in the indictment and proved by the witnesses, is high treason against the United States.

2d. When the act itself amounts to treason, it involves the intention, and such was the character of this act. No threat of destruction of property will excuse or justify such an act; nothing but a threat of life, and that likely to be put into execution.

3d. The jury are not bound to conform to this opinion, because they have a right, in all criminal cases, to decide on the law and the facts.

Houston J. said he did not entirely agree with the chief justice in any, except the last remark.

Pinckney then rose again, and addressed the jury.

The opinion which the chief justice has just delivered is not, and I thank God for it, the law of the land. If you have the slightest doubt on the subject, I will undertake to remove it, to show you that the cases have been misconceived, and that the conclusions drawn from them are erroneous.

No man can feel for the learned judge who has just given you his instruction, a reverence and affection more sincere than I do. But reverence and affection for him shall not stand in the way of the great duty which I owe to a fellow citizen who relies on me to shield his innocence from the charge of guilt, and his life from an attainder for treason. I had hoped that, since his motives were admitted, on all hands, to be entitled to praise, since the grand jury had associated with their indictment a certificate of the purity of his views, and a solemn recommendation that the prosecution should be abandoned, he would at least have been left by the District Attorney, and the Court, to obtain from you, as he could, a deliverance from the danger that encompassed him. In that hope I have been disappointed. As if the salvation of the state depended upon the conviction of this unfortunate man, whose situation, one would think, an inquisitor might deplore - the District Attorney has gone out of his way to bring down vengenance upon him; and one of the Court has told you that he is a traitor, and that you ought to find him so.

In a case where justice might be expected to be softened into clemency, and even to connive at acquittal, where every generous sentiment must take part with the accused, and law might be thought to fear the reproach of tyranny, if it should succeed in crushing him; in such a case the established order of trial is deserted, a pernicious novelty is introduced, the court is called upon to mix itself in your deliberations, to mutilate the defence of the prisoner's counsel, to harden your consciences against the solicitations of an enlightened mercy, and to sacrifice the prisoner to gloomy and exterminating principles, which would render the noble and beneficent system of law, for which we are distinguished, a hideous spectacle of cruelty and oppression. For the sake of the country to which I belong, as well as of my client, I will not only protest before you against these principles, but will examine and speak of them with freedom, restrained only by the decorum which this place requires. ...

This indictment charges Hodges with having done certain things, wickedly, maliciously, and traitorously. Must not the United States prove what they allege? When the law allows even words to be given in evidence, as explanatory of intention, to exculpate, it admits that exculpation may be made out by proof of innocent motives: - that overt acts alone do not furnish a criterion - that concomitant facts, illustrative of the state of the heart, must not be neglected.

A military force levies contributions - If you pay them, for the purpose of saving the country from farther mischief, although there be no fear or danger of death, the law says this is not treason. By the doctrine of the chief justice, however, it is treason, and consequently his doctrine is unsound.

On this occasion, the enemy were in complete power in the district where the transactions occurred, which are complained of in the indictment. They were unawed by the thing which we called an army, for it had fled in every direction. They were omnipotent. The law of war prevailed, and every other law was silent. The domestic code was suspended. They menaced pillage and conflagration; and after they had wantonly destroyed edifices which all civilized warfare had hitherto respected, was it to be believed that they would spare a petty village, which had renewed hostilities, before the seal of its capitulation was dry? There was menace - power to execute - probability - nay, certainty, that it would be executed.

How, then, can you find a wicked and traitorous motive in the breast of my client? ...

The conduct is in itself treasonable, says the chief justice, it necessarily imports the wicked intention charged by the indictment. The construction makes it treason, because it aids and comforts the enemy.

These are strong and comprehensive positions; but they have not been proved; and they cannot be proved until we relapse into the gulf of constructive treason, from which our ancestors in another country have long since escaped.

Gracious God! In the nineteenth century, to talk of constructive treason! Is it possible that in this favoured land - this last asylum of liberty - blest with all that can render a nation happy at home and respected abroad - this should be law? No. I stand up as a man to rescue my country from this reproach. I say there is no colour for this slander upon our jurisprudence. Had I thought otherwise I should have asked for mercy - not for law. I would have sent my client to the feet of the president, not have brought him, with bold defiance, to confront his accusers, and demand your verdict. He could have had a nolle prosequi. I confirmed him in his resolution not to ask it, by telling him that he was safe without it. Under these circumstances I may claim some respect for my opinion. My opportunities for forming a judgment upon this subject, I am compelled to say, by the strange turn which this cause has taken, are superior to those of the chief justice. I say nothing of the knowledge which long study and extensive practice enabled me to bring to the consideration of the case. I rely upon this; my opinion has not been hastily formed - since the commencement of the trial. It is the result of a deliberate examination of all the authorities, of a thorough investigation of the law of treason in all its forms, made at leisure, and under a deep sense of a fearful responsibility of my client. It depends upon me whether he should submit himself to your justice, or use with the chief magistrate the intercession of the grand jury, which could not have failed to have been successful. You are charged with his life and honour, because I assured him that the law was a pledge for the security of both. I declared to him that I would stake my own life upon the safety of his; and I declare to you now that you have as much power to shed the blood of the advocate as to harm the client whom he defends.

If the mere naked fact of delivery constitute the crime of treason, why not hang the man who goes under a flag of truce to return or exchange prisoners? According to the doctrine of the Chief Justice, this man is equally guilty with him who stands at the bar, if you are forbidden to examine his mind, but are commanded by the law to look only to his acts. I ask you to consider this, in the spirit of Stone's case: that doctrine, I pledge myself, goes through every nerve and artery of the law.

If the doctrine of the Chief Justice be the law of the land, every man concerned in the deeds of blood, that were acted during our recent war, was a murderer.

Our gallant soldiers who had repulsed the hostile step whenever it trod upon our shores; our gallant tars who unfurled our flag, acquired for us a name and rank upon the ocean which will not soon be obliterated - these are all liable to be arraigned at this bar. These men have carried dismay and death into the ranks of the foe; blood calls for blood. You dare not inquire into the causes which produced the circumstances; which attended the motives; which prompted the deeds of carnage. The act, you are told by the Chief Justice, and such is the reasoning of the attorney general, involves the intent.

Gentlemen! this desolating doctrine would sweep us from the face of the earth. Even when we deserved to be crowned with laurels, we should be stretched on a gibbet. I tremble for my children, for my country, when I reflect upon the consequences of these detestable tenets which reduces indiscretion and wickedness to the same level. Which of you is there that in some unguarded moment may not, with honest motives, be imprudent? Which of you can hope to pass through life without the imputation of crime, if your motives may be separated from your conduct, and guilt may be fastened upon your actions, although the heart be innocent?

Gentlemen! so solemnly, so deeply, so religiously do I feel impressed with this principle, that I know not how to leave the case with you, although at the present moment it strikes my mind in so clear a light that I know not how to make it more clear.

If this damnable prosecution should prevail, it would be the duty of the district attorney instantly to arraign Gen. Bowie, one of the witnesses in this case, than whom a purer patriot never lived. Nay, half Prince George's county would come within its baleful influence.

Yet such is the law the Chief Justice recommends to you - His associate does not concur with him. In this conflict of opinion I should be entitled to your verdict; but I rest the case upon more exalted grounds. I call upon you as honourable men, as you are just, as you value your liberties, as you prize your constitution, to say - and to say it promptly, that my client is not guilty.

The jury, without hesitating a moment, rendered a verdict of Not Guilty.

Perhaps the special circumstances in United States v. Hodges explain sufficiently the position which both court and counsel took with respect to the scope of the jury's responsibility. It is clear, however, that there was a considerable body of American authority supporting the doctrine that in criminal cases the jury has a right to decide questions of law as well as questions of fact.[1] It is not surprising, however, that the truculence of Mr. Justice Chase found that doctrine unacceptable in prosecutions under the Sedition Act.

Callender's Case
Circuit Court of the United States
District of Virginia, 1800
Wharton's State Trials 688, 709

[The defendant, James Callender, was indicted under the Sedition Act, for having published a seditious libel on President Adams in his pamphlet "The Prospect before US". In that publication he had stated that "the reign of Mr. Adams has been one continued tempest of malignant passions" and that Adams had labored "to extinguish the only gleam of happiness that glimmers through the dark and despicable farce of life". He had further characterized Adams as "this hoary headed incendiary". His position on the Presidential campaign was made quite clear in the closing plea: "Take your choice, then, between Adams, war and beggary, and Jefferson, peace and competency". Throughout the trial before Mr. Justice Chase and Judge Griffin there were constant altercations between the attorneys representing the defendant and Mr. Justice Chase. Only the last of those altercations is here reprinted.]

Mr. Wirt - Gentlemen of the jury, I am prevented from explaining to you the causes which have conspired to weaken our defence, and it is no doubt right that I should be prevented, as the court have so decided: permit me, then, gentlemen, to pass on abruptly to the law, under which we are indicted. You will find that a material part of your inquiry will relate to the powers of a jury over the subject committed to them, whether they have the right to determine the law, as well as the fact. In Virginia, an act of the assembly has adopted the common law of England; that common law, therefore, possesses in this state all the energy of a legislative act. By an act of Congress, the rules of proceedings in the federal courts, in the several states, are directed to conform to the rules of the states in which such court may be in session; by that act of

---

1. Howe, "Juries as Judges of Criminal Law" (1939) 52 Harv. Law Rev. 582.

Congress, it is therefore provided, that the practice of the courts of Virginia shall be observed in this court: to ascertain your power, therefore, as a jury, we have only to refer to the common law of England, which has been adopted in the laws of this state, and which defines the powers of juries in the state courts. By the common law of England, juries possess the power of considering and deciding the law as well as the fact, in every case which may come before them. I have no doubt but I shall receive the correction of the court, if I am wrong in these positions. If, then, a jury in a court of the state would have a right to decide the law and the fact, so have you. The federal Constitution is the supreme law of the land; and a right to consider the law, is a right to consider the Constitution: if the law of Congress under which we are indicted, be an infraction of the Constitution, it has not the force of a law, and if you were to find the traverser guilty, under such an act, you would violate your oaths.[1]

---

1. At the impeachment of Mr. Justice Chase, the following examination of George Hay, counsel for Callender in the above case, occurred:

"Mr. Harper. In your examination in chief you stated that you defended the cause and not the man. We are not capable of understanding your meaning, and beg you to explain it. Was it the cause of Callender, or was it some other cause?

"Mr. Hay. It was the cause of the constitution, and I did not mean to defend Callender farther than he was connected with that cause.

"Mr. Harper. Your object appears to have been to show that the law under which he was indicted was unconstitutional?

"Mr. Hay. That was one great cause.

"Mr. Harper. Not the sole one?

"Mr. Hay. I had previously made up my mind, that if a prosecution should take place in Virginia under that law, I for one should step forward and offer my services to the person who should be selected as its first victim."

1 <u>Trial of Samuel Chase</u> (Smith and Lloyd ed, 1805) 179.

In his summation on behalf of Mr. Justice Chase in the impeachment proceedings, Luther Martin made the following comment on this testimony of Hay's:

"One of the gentlemen who was counsel of Callender, has told us, that whenever a prosecution should be attempted under the sedition law, he had formed the determination to come forward to prove its unconstitutionality. That in consequence of

Here Judge Chase - Take your seat, sir, if you please. If I understand you rightly, you offer an argument to the petit jury, to convince them that the statute of Congress, entitled, "An act, &c.," commonly called the Sedition Law, is contrary to the Constitution of the United States, and, therefore, void. Now I tell you that this is irregular and inadmissible; it is not competent to the jury to decide on this point; but if you address yourselves, gentlemen, to the court, they will with pleasure hear any reasons you may offer, to show that the jury have the right contended for. Since I came into the commonwealth, I understood that this question would be stirred, and that the power of a jury to determine the validity or nullity of a law would be urged. I have, therefore, deliberately considered the subject, and I am ready to explain my reasons for concluding that the petit jury have not a right to decide on the constitutionality of a law, and that such a power would be extremely dangerous. Hear my words: I wish the world to know them, - my opinion is the result of mature reflection.

(Here the Judge then read part of a long opinion, to show that the jury had not the right contended for; after which, he told the counsel for the traverser, that he would hear with pleasure any arguments which could be urged to show that he was mistaken.)

Mr. Wirt - I shall state to the court, in a few words, the reasons which have induced me to ascribe this right to the jury. They are sworn to give their verdict according to the evidence, and the law is evidence; if the jury have no right to consider the law, how is it possible for them to render a general verdict? Suppose, for example, an indictment for murder - how can the jury pronounce a verdict of guilty, or not guilty, if they have not the right as well of ascertaining whether the facts have been committed, as whether they amount to a breach of law? This doctrine is too clearly established to require the aid of authorities.

Judge Chase - No man will deny your law - we all know that juries have the right to decide the law, as well as the fact - and the Constitution is the supreme law of the land, which controls all laws which are repugnant to it.

Mr. Wirt - Since, then, the jury have a right to consider

---

this determination in Callender's case, and only for that purpose he did appear in order to argue its unconstitutionality. He has told us further, that he had no hopes of convincing the court, and scarcely the faintest hope of inducing the jury to believe that the sedition law was unconstitutional; but yet that he wishes to argue the question, with a view of making a proper impression upon the public mind.... What barefaced, what unequalled hypocrisy doth he admit he practiced on that occasion! What egregious trifling with the court!" (2 id. 211-12)

the law, and since the constitution is law, the conclusion is certainly syllogistic, that the jury have a right to consider the Constitution.

Judge Chase - A _non sequitur_, sir.

Here Mr. Wirt sat down.

Mr. Nicholas then addressed the court. I am so much under the influence of duty that, though I am in the same situation with the gentleman who preceded me, and though the court seem to be impressed with the opinion, that the jury have no right to determine on the constitutionality of an act of Congress, yet, arduous as the task may be, I shall offer a few observations to show that they have this right. I intend to defend Mr. Callender by the establishment of two points.

First, that a law contrary to the Constitution is void; and, secondly, that the jury have a right to consider the law and the fact. First, it seems to be admitted on all hands, that when the legislature exercise a power not given them by the Constitution, the judiciary will disregard their acts. The second point, that the jury have a right to decide the law and the fact appears to me equally clear. In the exercise of the power of determining law and fact, a jury cannot be controlled by the court. The court have a right to instruct the jury, but the jury have a right to act as they think right; and if they find contrary to the directions of the court, and to the law of the case, the court may set aside their verdict and grant a new trial.

Judge Chase - Courts do not claim the right of setting aside the verdict in criminal cases.

Mr. Nicholas - From this right of the jury to consider law and fact in a general verdict, it seems to follow, that counsel ought to be permitted to address a jury on the constitutionality of the law in question; - this leads me back to my first position, that if an act of Congress contravene the Constitution of the United States, a jury have a right to say that it is null, and that they will not give the efficacy of a law to an act which is void in itself; believing it to be contrary to the Constitution, they will not convict any man of a violation of it: if this jury believed that the Sedition Act is not a law of the land, they cannot find the defendant guilty. The Constitution secures to every man a fair and impartial trial by jury, in the district where the fact shall have been committed: and to preserve this sacred right unimpaired, it should never be interfered with. If ever a precedent is established, that the court can control the jury so as to prevent them from finding a general verdict, their important right, without which every other right is of no value, will be impaired, if not absolutely destroyed. Juries are to decide according to the dictates of conscience and the laws of the country, and to control them would endanger the right of this most invaluable mode of trial.

I have understood that some reliance would be placed on

two decisions of the courts of this State, in which they determined two acts of our legislature to be unconstitutional; but when we come to analyze these decisions, they will not authorize the belief that the jury have not the right I contend for - they only prove that the judiciary can declare legislative acts to be unconstitutional; they do not prove that a jury may not have a similar power. In the case of Kamper v. Hawkins, they refused to carry into effect a law which gave the district courts a right to grant injunctions in certain cases, because they thought it unconstitutional, and that the courts had no power to act under the law: that case did not turn on a relative view of the power and connection of a court and jury; it was a question whether the courts would exercise a particular jurisdiction, and carry into effect that act as practiced by the judges in chancery; but they never decided that a jury had not a right to determine on the constitutionality of a law, nor could a question about this right have arisen in those two cases; the court said that the judiciary were not bound to carry into effect an unconstitutional law. I do not deny the right of the court to determine the law, but I deny the right of the court to control the jury; though I have not bestowed a very particular attention on this subject, I am perfectly convinced that the jury have the right I contend for; and, consequently, that counsel have a right to address them on that subject.

The act of Congress to which I have alluded, appears to have given to the jury the power of deciding on the law and the fact; and I trust, that when this whole question comes into consideration, the court will suffer the counsel for the traverser to go on to speak to the jury, subject to the direction of the court.

Mr. Hay rose, after Mr. Nicholas concluded, and observed that he was prepared to address the court on the extent of the powers of the jury in the case at bar. The arguments, said he, which I shall urge, I shall address to the court, not wishing to be heard by the jury, or to be attended to by the numerous auditory now present. A question of great importance depends on this decision; much of the public happiness, of the public peace, of the public liberty, depends on the final decision which shall be pronounced on this subject. I entertained doubts at first; but a calm and dispassionate inquiry, and the most temperate investigation and reflection, have led me to believe and to say, that the jury have a right to determine every question which is necessary to determine, before sentence can be pronounced upon the traverser. I contend that the jury have a right to determine whether the writing charged in the indictment to be false, scandalous and malicious, be a libel or not. If this question should be decided in the affirmative by the court, I shall endeavour to convince the jury that it is not a libel, because there is no law in force, under the government of the United States, which defines what a libel is, or prescribes its punishment. It is a universal principle of law, that questions of law belong to the court, and that the decision of facts belongs to the jury; but a jury have a right to determine both law and fact in all cases.

Here Judge Chase asked Mr. Hay whether he meant to extend his proposition to civil as well as criminal cases, and told him that if he did, the law was clearly otherwise.

Mr. Hay answered, that he thought the proposition universally true, but it was only necessary for him to prove it to be true in cases of a criminal nature.

Judge Chase again interrupted Mr. Hay, and briefly expressed his opinion of the law. And then Mr. Hay folded up and put away his papers, seeming to decline any further argument.

Judge Chase requested him to continue his argument, and added - "Please to proceed, and be assured that you will not be interrupted by me, say what you will."

Mr. Hay refused to proceed.

Judge Chase observed, that though he thought it his duty to stop the counsel when mistaking the law, yet he did not wish to interrupt them improperly; that there was no occasion to be captious; and concluded thus, "Act as you please, sir."

Judge Chase then proceeded. I will assign my reasons why I will not permit the counsel for the traverser to offer arguments to the jury, to urge them to do what the Constitution and law of this country will not permit; and which, if I should allow, I should, in my judgment, violate my duty, disregard the Constitution and law, and surrender up the judicial power of the United States, that is, the power intrusted by the Constitution to the Federal courts, to a petit jury, in direct breach of my oath of office.

The indictment charges that the traverser, on the 1st day of February, 1800, designing and intending to defame the President of the United States, and to bring him into contempt and disrepute, and to excite the hatred of the good people of the United States against him, did wickedly and maliciously write, print, utter, and publish (or did cause or procure to be printed and published) a false, scandalous, and malicious writing, against the said President of the United States, of the tenor and effect stated in the indictment. On examining the indictment, it appears, that twenty separate and distinct sets of words are set forth therein, as allegations or charges against the traverser. He has plead "not guilty" to all of them.

To support this indictment on behalf of the government of the United States, it must be proved to the jury; first, that the traverser did write, print, utter or publish, or did cause or procure to be printed or published, a false and scandalous writing against the President of the United States; secondly, that the said writing is false, scandalous, and malicious; and thirdly, that it was published with intent to defame the President, &c., as stated in the statute and charged in the indictment.

If these three facts shall be established to the satisfaction of the jury, they must find the traverser guilty, generally, unless he can prove to them the truth of the matter contained in the publication, in which case, the statute on which the traverser is indicted excuses him. If all the twenty sets of words, stated in the indictment as charges against the traverser, shall not be proved against him; or if he can prove that any of them are true, the jury will acquit him of such of them as shall not be established against him, and also of such of them as he can prove to be true; and they will find him guilty of the residue.

These inquiries, on behalf of the government of the United States, and on the part of the traverser, are proper for, and within the jurisdiction and the terms of the oath of the petit jury, who have been sworn "that they will well and truly try the issue joined between the United States and the traverser at the bar, and a true verdict give according to their evidence." The issue joined, therefore, is, whether the traverser is guilty of the several offences charged in the indictment; and to this issue no evidence is admissible (on the part of the government, or of the traverser) but what is pertinent or applicable to it. The petit jury, to discharge their duty, must first inquire, whether the traverser committed all or any of the facts alleged in the indictment to have been done by him, some time before the indictment. If they find that he did commit all or any of the said facts, their next inquiry is, whether the doing such facts have been made criminal and punishable by the statute of the United States, on which the traverser is indicted. For this purpose, they must peruse the statute, and carefully examine whether the facts charged and proved are within the provisions of it. If the words that create the offence are plain and intelligible, they must then determine whether the offence proved is of the species of criminality charged in the indictment; but if the words are ambiguous or doubtful, all construction should be rejected. The statute, on which the traverser is indicted, enacts "that the jury who shall try the cause shall have a right to determine the law and the fact, under the direction of the court, as in other cases." By this provision, I understand that a right is given to the jury to determine what the law is in the case before them; and not to decide whether a statute of the United States produced to them, is a law or not, or whether it is void, under an opinion that it is unconstitutional, that is, contrary to the Constitution of the United States. I admit that the jury are to compare the statute with the facts proved, and then to decide whether the acts done are prohibited by the law; and whether they amount to the offence described in the indictment. This power the jury necessarily possesses, in order to enable them to decide on the guilt or innocence of the person accused. It is one thing to decide what the law is, on the facts proved, and another and a very different thing, to determine that the statute produced is no law. To decide what the law is on the facts, is an admission that the law exists. If there be no law in the case, there can be no comparison between it and the facts; and it is unnecessary to establish facts before it is ascertained that there is a law to punish the commission of them.

The existence of the law is a previous inquiry, and the inquiry into facts is altogether unnecessary, if there is no law to which the facts can apply. By this right to decide what the law is in any case arising under the statute, I cannot conceive that a right is given to the petit jury to determine whether the statute (under which they claim this right) is constitutional or not. To determine the validity of the statute, the Constitution of the United States must necessarily be resorted to and considered, and its provisions inquired into. It must be determined whether the statute alleged to be void, because contrary to the Constitution, is prohibited by it expressly, or by necessary implication. Was it ever intended, by the framers of the Constitution, or by the people of America, that it should ever be submitted to the examination of a jury, to decide what restrictions are expressly or impliedly imposed by it on the national legislature? I cannot possibly believe that Congress intended, by the statute, to grant a right to a petit jury to declare a statute void. The man who maintains this position must have a most contemptible opinion of the understanding of that body; but I believe the defect lies with himself.

If any one can be so weak in intellect as to entertain this opinion of Congress, he must give up the exercise of the power, when he is informed that Congress had no authority to vest in any body whatsoever; because, by the Constitution, (as I will hereafter show) this right is expressly granted to the judicial power of the United States, and is recognized by Congress by a perpetual statute. If the statute should be held void by a jury, it would seem that they could not claim a right to such decision under an act that they themselves consider as mere waste paper. Their right must, therefore, be derived from some other source.

It appears to me that all the rights, powers, and duties of the petit jury, sworn in this cause, can only be derived from the Constitution, or statutes of the United States made agreeably to it; or from some statute of this commonwealth not contrary to the Federal Constitution or statutes of Congress; or from the common law, which was adopted by the Federal Constitution in the case of trials by jury in criminal cases.

It never was pretended, as I ever heard, before this time, that a petit jury in England (from whence our common law is derived) or in any part of the United States ever exercised such power. If a petit jury can rightfully exercise this power over one statute of Congress, they must have an equal right and power over any other statute, and indeed over all the statutes; for no line can be drawn, no restriction imposed on the exercise of such power; it must rest in discretion only.

If this power be once admitted, petit jurors will be superior to the national legislature, and its laws will be subject to their control. The power to abrogate or to make laws nugatory, is equal to the authority of making them. The evident consequences of this right in juries will be, that a law of Congress will be in operation in one state and not in another. A law to impose taxes will be obeyed in one state, and not in another, unless force be employed to compel submission.

The doing certain acts will be held criminal, and punished in one state, and similar acts may be held innocent, and even approved and applauded in another.

The effects of the exercise of this power by petit jurors may be readily conceived. It appears to me that the right now claimed has a direct tendency to dissolve the Union of the United States, on which, under Divine Providence, our political safety, happiness, and prosperity depend.

No citizen of knowledge and information, unless under the influence of passion or prejudice, will believe, without very strong and indubitable proof, that Congress will, intentionally, make any law in violation of the Federal Constitution, and their sacred trust. I admit that the Constitution contemplates that Congress may, from inattention or error in judgment, pass a law prohibited by the Constitution; and, therefore, it has provided a peaceable, safe, and adequate remedy. If such a case should happen, the mode of redress is pointed out in the Constitution and no other mode can be adopted without a manifest infraction of it.

Every man must admit that the power of deciding the constitutionality of any law of the United States, or of any particular state, is one of the greatest and most important powers that the people could grant.

Such power is restrictive of the legislative power of the Union, and also of the several states; not absolute and unlimited, but confined to such cases only where the law in question shall clearly appear to have been prohibited by the Federal Constitution, and not in any doubtful case. On referring to the ninth section of the first article of the Constitution, there may be seen many restrictions imposed on the powers of the national legislature, and also on the powers of the several state legislatures. Among the special exceptions to their authority, is the power to make ex post facto laws, to lay any capitation, or other direct tax, unless in proportion to the census; to lay any tax or duty on articles exported from any state, &c. &c.

It should be remembered that the judicial power of the United States is co-existent, co-extensive, and co-ordinate with, and altogether independent of, the Federal legislature, or the executive. By the sixth article of the Constitution, among other things, it is declared that the Constitution shall be the supreme law of the land. By the third article, it is established "that the judicial power of the United States shall be vested in one supreme court, and in such other inferior courts as Congress may from time to time ordain and establish; and that the judicial power shall extend to all cases in law and equity, arising under the Constitution and laws of the United States."

Among the cases which may arise under the Constitution, are all the restrictions on the authority of Congress, and of the state legislatures.

It is very clear, that the present case arises under the Constitution, and also under a law of the United States, and therefore it is the very case to which the Constitution declares the judicial powers of the United States shall extend.

It is incontrovertible that the Constitution is the supreme law, and therefore, it must be the rule by which the federal and state judges are bound to regulate their decisions. By the sixth article of the Constitution, it is provided (among other things) that all members of Congress, and of the several state legislatures, and all judicial officers of the United States, and of the several states, shall be bound by an oath or affirmation to support the Constitution. By this provision, I understand that every person, so sworn or affirmed promises that he will preserve the Constitution as established, and the distribution of powers thereby granted; and that he will not assent to any amendment or alteration thereof, but in the mode prescribed in the fifth article; and that he will not consent to any usurpation by any one branch of the legislature upon the other, or upon the Executive, or by the Executive upon either branch, or by any department or officer of government, of the power granted to another; or that the power granted to either shall be exercised by others.

I also understand by this engagement, that the person taking it, promises also that he will oppose by his example, argument, advice, and persuasion, and by all other means in his power, force only excepted, any design, advice or attempt to impair or destroy the Constitution.

If this exposition of this solemn obligation is substantially correct, I cannot believe that any person having the same understanding of it, will maintain that a petit jury can rightfully exercise the power granted by the Constitution to the federal judiciary.

From these considerations I draw this conclusion, that the judicial power of the United States is the only proper and competent authority to decide whether any statute made by Congress (or any of the state legislatures) is contrary to, or in violation of, the Federal Constitution.

That this was the opinion of the Senate and House of Representatives, and of General Washington, then President of the United States, fully appears by the statute, entitled "An Act to establish the judicial courts of the United States," made at the first session of the first Congress (on 24th September 1789 chap. xx § 8) which enacts, "that the justices of the Supreme Courts, and the district judges, shall take an oath or affirmation in the following words, to wit:

"I, A. B., do solemnly swear or affirm, that I will administer justice without respect to persons, and do equal right to the poor and to the rich, and that I will faithfully and impartially discharge and perform all the duties incumbent on me as   , according to the best of my abilities and understanding, agreeably to the Constitution and laws of the United States."

No position can be more clear than that all the federal judges are bound by the solemn obligation of religion, to regulate their decisions agreeably to the Constitution of the United States, and that it is the standard of their determination in all cases that come before them.

I believe that it has been the general and prevailing opinion in all the Union, that the power now wished to be exercised by a jury, properly belonged to the federal courts.

It was alleged that the tax on carriages was considered by the people of this commonwealth to be unconstitutional, and a case was made to submit the question to the Supreme Court of the United States, and they decided that the statute was not unconstitutional, and their decision was acquiesced in.

I have seen a report of a case (Kamper v. Hawkins) decided in 1793, in the general court of this commonwealth, respecting the constitutionality of a law which gave the district courts a power of granting injunctions in certain cases, in which case the judges of the general court (four to one) determined that the law was unconstitutional and void. On yesterday I saw the record of another case, the Court of Appeals of this commonwealth (in 1788), on which it appears, that the general assembly passed "An act to establish district courts," and the judges (ten being present), adjudged "that the Constitution and the said act were in opposition, and could not exist together, and that the court ought not to do anything officially in the execution of an act, which appeared to be contrary to the spirit of the Constitution." I also observed, that the then governor, Mr. Edmund Randolph, immediately on this decision, called the general assembly by proclamation; and I have been informed that they altered the law according to the opinion of the court.

From these two decisions, in the two highest courts of justice in this state, I may fairly conclude, that, at that period it was thought that the courts of justice were the proper judicature to determine the constitutionality of the laws of this commonwealth. It is now contended, that the constitutionality of the laws of Congress should be submitted to the decision of a petit jury. May I ask, whence this change of opinion? I declare that the doctrine is entirely novel to me, and that I never heard of it before my arrival in this city. It appears to me to be not only new, but very absurd and dangerous, in direct opposition to, and a breach of the Constitution: And I wish those who maintain this doctrine, and have sworn to support the Constitution, conscientiously to reconsider their opinions with a calm and deliberate temper, and with minds disposed to find the truth, and to alter their opinion if convinced of their error.

It must be evident, that decisions in the district or circuit courts of the United States will be uniform, or they will become so by the revision and correction of the Supreme Court; and thereby the same principles will pervade all the Union; but the opinions of petit juries will very probably be different in different states.

The decision of courts of justice will not be influenced by political and local principles, and prejudices. If inferior courts commit error, it may be rectified; but if juries make mistakes, there can be no revision or control over their verdicts, and therefore, there can be no mode to obtain uniformity in their decisions. Besides, petit juries are under no obligation by the terms of their oath, to decide the constitutionality of any law; their determination, therefore, will be extra judicial. I should also imagine, that no jury would wish to have a right to determine such great, important, and difficult questions; and I hope no jury can be found, who will exercise the power desired over the statutes of Congress, against the opinion of the federal courts.

I have consulted with my brother, Judge Griffin, and I now deliver the opinion of the court, "That the petit jury have no right to decide on the constitutionality of the statute on which the traverser is indicted; and that, if the jury should exercise that power, they would thereby usurp the authority entrusted by the Constitution of the United States to this court." Governed by this opinion, the court will not allow the counsel for the traverser to argue before the petit jury, that they have a right to decide on the constitutionality of the statute, on which the traverser stand indicted. If the counsel for the traverser had offered sufficient arguments to the court, to show that the petit jury had this right, the court, on being convinced that the opinion delivered was erroneous, would have changed it; for they hold it a much greater reproach for a judge to continue in his error, than to retract.

The gentlemen of the profession know, that questions have sometimes occurred in state courts, whether acts of assembly had expired, or had been repealed; but no one will say that such questions were ever submitted to a jury.

If the constitution of the United States had not given to the judiciary a right to decide on the constitutionality of federal laws - yet, if such power could be exercised, it could not be by a juror, from this consideration - it is a maxim of law in all the states, that the courts have the exclusive right to decide every question, as to the admissibility of evidence in every case, civil or criminal, whether the evidence be by act of assembly, or by deed, or other writing, or by witnesses.

Judge Chase concluded with observing, that, if he knew himself, the opinion he had delivered and the reasons offered in its support, flowed not from political motives, or reasons of state, with which he had no concern, and which he conceived never ought to enter courts of justice; but from a deliberate conviction of what the Constitution and the law of the land required. "I hold myself equally bound," said he, "to support the rights of the jury, as the rights of the court." I consider it of the greatest consequence to the administration of justice that the powers of the court, and the powers of the petit jury, should be kept distinct and separate. I have uniformly delivered the opinion, "that the petit jury have a right to decide the law as well as the fact, in criminal cases;" but it never entered into my mind that they, therefore, had a right to determine the constitutionality of any statute of the United States. It is my duty to execute the laws of the United States with justice and impartiality, with firmness and decision, and I will endeavour to discharge this duty with the assistance of the Fountain of wisdom, and the Giver of all human reason and understanding.

After two hours, the jury returned with a verdict of guilty ...[2]

---

2. The famous New York decision, People v. Croswell, 3 Johns Cas. 338 (1804), involved the same political controversies as those in which Callender was involved. Croswell was prosecuted under state law for libelling Jefferson in "The Wasp". Croswell was charged with stating that Jefferson had paid Callender for calling Washington a traitor, robber and perjurer and for calling Adams a hoary-headed incendiary. In Kent's famous opinion in the Croswell case he incorporated the substance of Alexander Hamilton's argument on behalf of the defendant. Kent's opinion in turn became the foundation of the statute adopted in New York in 1805 by which truth became a defense to a charge of criminal libel.

United States v. Coolidge et al.
Circuit Court of the United States
District of Massachusetts, 1813
1 Gallison 488

Story, J. The simple question is, whether the Circuit Court of the United States has jurisdiction to punish offences against the United States, which have not been previously defined, and a specific punishment affixed, by some statute of the United States.

I do not think it necessary, to consider the more broad question, whether the United States, as a sovereign power, have entirely adopted the common law. This might lead to very elaborate inquiries, and the present question may well be decided, without entering upon the discussion.

I admit in the most explicit terms, that the Courts of the United States are Courts of limited jurisdiction, and cannot exercise any authorities, which are not confided to them by the constitution and laws made in pursuance thereof. But I do contend, that when once an authority is lawfully given, the nature and extent of that authority, and the mode, in which it shall be exercised, must be regulated by the rules of the common law. In my judgment, the whole difficulty and obscurity of the subject has arisen from losing sight of this distinction.

Whether the common law of England, in its broadest sense, including equity and admiralty, as well as legal doctrines, be the common law of the United States or not, it can hardly be doubted, that the constitution and laws of the United States are predicated upon the existence of the common law. This has not, as I recollect, been denied by any person, who has maturely weighed the subject, and will abundantly appear upon the slightest examination. The constitution of the United States, for instance, provides that "the trial of all crimes, except in cases of impeachment, shall be by jury." I suppose that no person can doubt, that for the explanation of these terms, and for the mode of conducting trials by jury, recourse must be had to the common law. So the clause, that "the judicial power shall extent to all cases in law and equity arising under the constitution," &c. is inexplicable, without reference to the common law; and the extent of this power must be measured by the powers of Courts of law and equity, as exercised and established by that system. Innumerable instances of a like nature may be adduced. I will mention but one more, and that is in the clause providing, that the privilege of the writ of habeas corpus shall not be suspended, unless when in cases of rebellion or invasion the public safety may require it. What is the writ of habeas corpus? What is the privilege which it grants? The common law, and that alone, furnishes the true answer. The existence, therefore, of the common law is not only supposed by the constitution, but is appealed to for the construction and interpretation of its powers.

There can be no doubt, that congress may, under the constitution, confide to the Circuit Court jurisdiction of all offences against the United States. Has it so done? The judicial act of 24th of September, 1789, ch. 20, sect. 11, provides, that the Circuit Court "shall have exclusive cognizance of all crimes and offences cognizable under the authority of the United States, except where that act otherwise provides, or the laws of the United States shall otherwise direct, and concurrent jurisdiction with the District Courts of the crimes and offences cognizable therein." No subsequent act has narrowed the jurisdiction; it remains therefore in full operation. The jurisdiction is not, as has sometimes been supposed in argument, over all crimes and offences specially created and defined by statute. It is of all crimes and offences "cognizable under the authority of the United States", that is, of all crimes and offences, to which by the constitution of the United States, the judicial power extends. The jurisdiction could not, therefore, have been given in more broad and comprehensive terms.

The Court then having complete jurisdiction, the next point will be to ascertain, what are crimes and offences against the United States. And here I contend, that recourse must be had to the principles of the common law, taken in connexion with the constitution, in order to fix the definition, precisely as in other laws of Congress, we resort to the rules of the common law to give them an interpretation. For instance, Congress has provided for the punishment of murder, manslaughter and perjury, under certain circumstances; but it has no where defined these crimes. Yet no doubt is ever entertained on trials, that the explanation of them must be sought and exclusively governed by the common law; and upon any other supposition, the judicial power of the United States would be left, in its exercise, to the mere arbitrary pleasure of the judges, to an uncontrollable and undefined discretion. Whatever may be the dread of the common law, I presume, that such a despotic power could hardly be deemed more desirable.

The necessity and propriety of this principle will be rendered still more apparent upon a further consideration. There are a great variety of cases arising under the laws of the United States, and particularly those which regard the judicial power, in which the legislative will cannot be effectuated, unless by the adoption of the common law. Many cases may be governed by the laws of the respective States; but still whole classes remain, which cannot be thus disposed of. For example, in Massachusetts no Courts of equity exist, and consequently no recognition of the principles or practices of equity, as contradistinguished from law. How then shall a suit in equity pending in the Circuit Court for that district be managed or decided? There is no law of the United States, which provides for the process, the pleadings, or the principles of adjudication. By what rules then shall the Court proceed? Certainly all reasoning and all practice pronounce, by the rules of equity recognized and enforced in the Equity Courts of England. The illustration is yet more decisive, as to causes of admiralty and maritime jurisdiction; for these exclusively belong to the United States, and nothing in the laws or practice of the respective States can regulate the proceedings or the principles of decision. In my judgment, nothing is more clear, than that the interpretation and exercise of the vested jurisdiction of the Courts of the United States must, in the absence of positive law, be governed exclusively by the common law.

I would ask then, what are crimes and offences against the United States, under the construction of its limited sovereignty, by the rules of the common law? Without pretending to enumerate them in detail, I will venture to assert generally, that all offences against the sovereignty, the public rights, the public justice, the public peace, the public trade and the public police of the United States, are crimes and offences against the United States. From the nature of the sovereignty of the United States, which is limited and circumscribed, it is clear that many common law offences, under each of these heads, will still remain cognizable by the States; but whenever the offence is directed against the sovereignty or powers confided to the United States, it is cognizable under its authority. Upon these principles and independent of any statute, I presume that treasons, and conspiracies to commit treason, embezzlement of the public records, bribery and resistance of the judicial process, riots and misdemeanors on the high seas, frauds and obstructions of the public laws of trade, and robbery and embezzlement of the mail of the United States, would be offences against the United States. At common law, these are clearly public offences, and when directed against the United States, they must upon principle be deemed offences against the United States.

If then it be true, that these are offences against the United States, and the Circuit Court have cognizance thereof, does it not unavoidably follow, that the Court must have a right to punish them? In my judgment no proposition of law admits of more perfect demonstration. To suppose a power in a Court to try an offence, and not to award any punishment, is to suppose, that the Legislature is guilty of the folly of promoting litigation without object, and prohibiting acts, only for the purpose of their being scoffed at in the most solemn manner. If, therefore, it authorize a trial of an offence, it must be deemed to authorize the Court to render such a judgment, as the guilt or innocence of the party may require. As to civil actions, the application of the principle has never admitted a doubt; yet in no instance, that I recollect, is the form or the substance of the judgments prescribed by any law. These judgments, however, must unavoidably differ, not only in different actions, but in the same action, according to the nature of the claims and the pleadings of the parties. It is no answer, to say, that the laws of the States will govern in such cases; for these are not always applicable, as suits may be brought in the United States Courts, which are not cognizable by State Courts; as for instance, equity and admiralty causes. And further, no such general and universal adoption of the practice or laws of the States has been authorized by Congress, or sanctioned by the Courts of the United States. The invariable usage of these Courts has been, in all cases not governed by State laws, to regulate the pleadings and pronounce the judgment of the common law. When I speak here of the common law, I use the word in its largest sense, as including the whole system of English jurisprudence. For the same reason, therefore, that governs in civil causes, I hold that the cognizance of offences includes the power of rendering a judgment of punishment, when the guilt of the party is ascertained by a trial.

But it may be asked, what punishment shall be inflicted? The common law affords the proper answer. It is a settled principle, that where an offence exists, to which no specific punishment is affixed by statute, it is punishable by fine and imprisonment. This is so invariably true, that, in all cases, where the Legislature prohibit any act without annexing any punishment, the common law considers it an indictable offence, and attaches to the breach the penalty of fine and imprisonment. I have no difficulty in saying, that the same rule must be held to exist here, for the same reason that it is adopted there. If therefore treason had been left without punishment by the act of Congress, I have no doubt, that the punishment by fine and imprisonment must have attached to the offence.

Upon what ground the common law can be referred to, and made the rule of decision in criminal trials in the Courts of the United States, and not in the judgment or punishment, I am at a loss to conceive. In criminal cases, the right of trial by jury is preserved, but the proceedings are not specifically regulated. The forms of the indictment and pleadings, the definition and extent of the crime, in some cases the right of challenge, and in all the admission and rejection of evidence, are left unprovided for. Upon what ground then do the Courts apply in such cases the rules of the common law? I can perceive no correct ground, unless it be, that the Legislature have constantly had in view the rules of the common law, and deemed their application in casibus omissis peremptory upon the Courts.
...

I might enforce the view, which I have already taken of this subject, by an examination in detail of the organization and exercise of the judicial powers of the Courts of the United

States, with reference to their equity, admiralty, and legal jurisdiction; but it cannot be necessary. If I am right in the positions, which I have already assumed and explained, there is an end of the question, which has been submitted. If I am wrong the error is so fundamental that I cannot hope to reach its source by any merely illustrative process.

The result of my opinion is, 1. That the Circuit Court has cognizance of all offences against the United States. 2. That what those offences are, depends upon the common law applied to the sovereignty and authorities confided to the United States. 3. That the Circuit Court, having cognizance of all offences against the United States, may punish them by fine and imprisonment, where no punishment is specially provided by statute.

I have considered the point, as one open to be discussed, notwithstanding the decision in the United States v. Hudson & Goodwin, February term, 1812, which certainly is entitled to the most respectful consideration; but having been made without argument, and by a majority only of the Court, I hope that it is not an improper course to bring the subject again in review for a more solemn decision, as it is not a question of mere ordinary import, but vitally affects the jurisdiction of the Courts of the United States; a jurisdiction which they cannot lawfully enlarge or diminish. I shall submit, with the utmost cheerfulness, to the judgment of my brethren, and if I have hazarded a rash opinion, I have the consolation to know, that their superior learning and ability will save the public from an injury by my error.

That decision, however broad in its language, has not, as I conceive, settled the question now before the Court, so far as it respects offences of admiralty and maritime jurisdiction. The constitution has given to the judicial power of the United States the jurisdiction as "to all cases of admiralty and maritime jurisdiction," and this jurisdiction of course comprehends criminal, as well as civil suits. The admiralty is a Court of extensive criminal, as well as civil jurisdiction, and has immemorially exercised both. At least no legal doubt of its criminal authority has ever been successfully urged. By the law of the admiralty, offences, for which no punishment is specially prescribed, are punishable by fine and imprisonment ...; and as offences of admiralty jurisdiction are exclusively cognizable by the United States, it follows that all such offences are offences against the United States. We have adopted the law of the admiralty in all civil causes cognizable by the admiralty: must it not also be adopted in offences cognizable by the admiralty? It will perhaps be said, that express jurisdiction is given in civil cases of admiralty jurisdiction, but not in criminal cases. This is true in terms; but I contend, that criminal cases are necessarily included in the grant of cognizance of all "crimes and offences cognizable under the authority of the United States;" for crimes and offences within the admiralty jurisdiction are not only cognizable, but cognizable exclusively under the authority of the United States. And Congress, in punishing certain offences upon the high seas, which are neither piracies nor felonies, have undoubtedly acted upon the conviction, that such offences were of admiralty and maritime jurisdiction. Whatever room, therefore, there may be for doubt, as to what common law offences are offences against the United States, there can be none as to admiralty offences.

If this be true, then the reasoning, which I have before urged, applies in its full force, and I will not take up time in repeating it.

On the whole, my judgment is, that all offences within the admiralty jurisdiction are cognizable by the Circuit Court, and in the absence of positive law are punishable by fine and imprisonment.

See 4 Bl. Com. 5, 44, 268. - 2 Bro. Civ. and Adm. Law.

Davis, J. did not concur, with a view to bring the question solemnly before the Supreme Court; so it was certified to the Supreme Court, as upon a division of the judges.[1]

<u>Peele et al.</u> v. <u>Merchants Insurance Co.</u>
Circuit Court of the United States
District of Massachusetts, 1822
3 Mason 27

Story J. This cause has been here heard upon the merits, the respondents having appeared under a protest to the juris-

---

1. When the case reached the Supreme Court on certification the Attorney General, Richard Rush, considering that the issue had been settled by <u>United States</u> v. <u>Hudson and Goodwin</u>, 7 Cranch 32 (1812), declined to argue the case, and a majority of the Court was therefore unwilling to re-examine the decision in the Hudson case. <u>United States</u> v. <u>Coolidge</u>, 1 Wheat. 415 (1816). On the legislative history of relevant clauses in the Judiciary Act of 1789, see Warren, "New Light on the History of the Federal Judiciary Act of 1789" (1923), 37 <u>Harv. L. Rev.</u> 49, 73.

Commenting on Mr. Justice Story's opinion in the <u>Coolidge</u> case, Peter S. DuPonceau in his volume on <u>The Jurisdiction of the Courts of the United States</u> (1824) at p. 9-10, said: "This was an indictment for forcibly rescuing on the high seas, a prize which had been captured and taken possession of by two American vessels, and was on her way, under the direction of a prize master, to the port of Salem for adjudication. Whatever else it might be, it was clearly not a case of common law."

diction, and meaning to insist upon that objection, if there should be an appeal to the Supreme Court, they have filed a general denial, putting the material facts in issue, and thus brought the entire law as well as facts before the court for consideration. Upon the subject of jurisdiction I have no more to say, than that I have seen no reason to change the opinion which I expressed several years since, that originally and of right the jurisdiction did belong to the Admiralty.[1] Whether it is become obsolete by disuse, or by the preponderating authority of the common law courts, so that it cannot and ought not now to be exerted by our courts of admiralty, is a question upon which I have no right even to conjecture what will be the judgment of the appellate court. I have, indeed, hitherto supposed the point rather of theoretical than practical importance, presuming that from private convenience, the benefit of a trial by jury, and the confidence that is so justly placed in our state tribunals, the insured would almost universally elect a domestic forum. I shall most cheerfully acquiesce in any judgment which may be ultimately pronounced on the point of jurisdiction; but entertaining, as I do most sincerely, the opinion, that this Court is rightfully possessed of it, I feel myself compelled by a sense of duty to entertain the suit, and to give my deliberate judgment, however unavailing it may be, upon the great and interesting points which have been presented at the bar. I cannot, indeed, but express my deep regret, that the cause has come before this Court at all, and especially under circumstances of so much embarrassment and difficulty. My own situation in relation to it is somewhat delicate and perplexing. But every consideration of this sort becomes trivial, when put in comparison with the serious thought, that a very small sum only was originally in controversy; and that there is an almost moral certainty that the whole property will perish before the suit is finally terminated, so that a total loss, with all the expenses and charges of litigation, must be borne by the unsuccessful party. I may add too, that the case appears to be contested upon principle; that the conduct of the parties is perfectly fair; and that there is not the least reason to impute to either, any desire to avail them-

---

1. In DeLovio v. Boit, 2 Gall. 399 (1815). Mr. Justice Story there held that a policy of marine insurance was a maritime contract and that the Federal Court of Admiralty therefore had jurisdiction to hear a libel in personam for damages for the breach of such a contract. It was not until 1870 that the Supreme Court of the United States adopted the rule of DeLovio v. Boit. See New England Mutual Insurance Co. v. Dunham, 11 Wall. 1 (1870).

selves of any rule of law, which is not founded in general justice and equity, and which may not consist with the most liberal good faith in matters of insurance.

The policy on which the suit is brought, bears date on the 6th of December, 1820, and insures for the plaintiffs "thirty Thousand dollars on the ship Argonant, valued at $12,000, and on property on board - viz, $4000 on the vessel, $26,000 on the property on board, at and from Leghorn to her port of discharge in the United States." The loss is alleged to have been total, by reason of the perils of the sea, stranding and shipwreck.

The material facts, as disclosed in the testimony (for there is some contradiction upon collateral matters) appear to me to be these: The ship sailed from Leghorn on the 2d of February, 1821, in perfectly good order, on her voyage to the United States, having on board a cargo consisting of specie dollars, bags of rags, tile, &c. &c. Nothing material occurred until Saturday the 24th of March, when the vessel, about three o'clock in the morning, went ashore upon Gerrish's Island, near Portsmouth, in New Hampshire. The accident was not in the slightest degree attributable to any fault or negligence of the master or crew, but was occasioned entirely by mistaking the Light on the Isle of Shoals for Boston Light (both being revolving lights, and the former having been erected since the departure of the ship on her voyage) and also by mistaking Portsmouth Light for Baker's Island Light, and Boon Island Light for Cape Ann Light. The place where the ship went on shore was surrounded by breakers, and there being a heavy swell, and the ship having gone head upon the rocks, she strained very much, and thumped very hard, so that it was very difficult to stand upon deck. Every effort was made to get the vessel off, by the crew; and guns being fired for assistance, in the morning they procured it, and landed the specie. About noon the same day, the weather moderated, and lighters were got alongside, and they began to discharge the cargo. In the afternoon of the same day the vessel bilged, some of the planks of the bottom were broken, and large holes made in them, and the tide ebbed and flowed into her within four or five feet of the deck. During the night, on the ebb tide, they got out as much of the cargo as they could. On Sunday a storm commenced about 10 o'clock, A. M. and the impression of the master and other persons on board being that the ship would go to pieces, every effort was made to save as much as possible. There were at this time eighty or ninety people on board; and they cut away the running rigging without unreeving it, and cut the sails from the yards in any manner they could for the purpose of saving them, the ship being then considered in imminent danger. About one o'clock that day, the master and all the crew quitted the vessel, deeming it very hazardous to their lives to remain on board, and leaving there a part of the cargo. In the afternoon of the same day the weather moderated, but no attempt was made to get out any more of the cargo on that day. On Monday morning, the 26th of March, they went on board again, and continued to discharge the cargo. During all this period no hopes were entertained of saving the vessel, and her situation was generally deemed one of extreme hazard. The situation where she law was very much exposed to the sea, and if the wind had blown heavily from any quarter between southwest and northeast she must inevitably have gone to pieces. Different estimates were formed of her value at this time, but the opinion of the best judges was, that she was worth little more than her materials; and the chance of being gotten off was considered very small, so much so that the premium to insure it was by none valued at less than fifty per cent. and by many intelligent and skilful witnesses was valued at from seventy-five to ninety per cent. Capt. Ramage, of the U. S. schooner Porpoise, who went on board of the ship on Saturday, in a letter addressed to the owners on the 25th of March (Sunday) and which reached them the same evening, described her situation as follows: - "I left her about 7 o' clock last evening, bilged, with eight feet of water in her hold, about a mile and a half to the eastward of the Light, and lying on a ledge of rocks, thirty or forty yards from the shore. It is very doubtful whether she can be saved." The substance of this information was communicated to the underwriters the next day, soon after the abandonment. On Monday morning about 10 o'clock, with the knowledge of her previous situation, the plaintiffs, as owners, abandoned the ship to the various underwriters by whom she was insured, and among others, to the Respondents; to the Suffolk Insurance Company; and to the New England Marine Insurance Company. The cause assigned in the letter of abandonment was, that the ship was shipwrecked on Gerrish's Island. ...

The questions made and discussed at the Bar with great diligence, learning and ability, from which I have derived no small share of instruction, and have been taught the intrinsic difficulty of the subject, are first, whether the plaintiffs had a right of abandonment upon the 26th of March, under all the circumstances of the case; secondly, whether, assuming that there then existed no such right, there was an acceptance on the part of the underwriters, of the abandonment tendered by the plaintiffs, so that they are now bound to pay as for a total loss.

As preliminary to the first enquiry, I think it important to notice a difference between the courts of this country and those of England, in respect to the right of abandonment. With us, an abandonment once rightfully made, is conclusive between the parties, and the rights flowing from it are not divested by any subsequent events, which change the situation of the property, and make that, which was a total loss at the time of abandonment, a partial loss only. And the right of abandonment is to be decided by the actual facts at the time of the abandonment, and not merely by the information of the assured; and consequently, if the facts do not then warrant it, no prior or subsequent events will give it any greater efficacy. This is the established doctrine, as I take it, of all, or at least of the principal commercial States; and has been solemnly settled, upon the fullest deliberation, by the Supreme Court of the United States. Whether this decision has given entire satisfaction to the profession, is more than I can presume to say; and whether at a future time it may be fit to undergo a revision, as has been intimated at the bar, I pretend not to determine. I can only say, that the decision already made, is conclusive upon my present judgment; and so far as I have been able to comprehend the grounds on which it rests, it appears to be founded on sound reasoning, public convenience, and the great principles of equity, which regulate the contract of Insurance. The rule in the English Courts is, as we all know, very different. There it has been held, that if an abandonment be rightfully made, it is not absolute, but may be controlled by subsequent events; so that if the loss has ceased to be total at any time before action brought, the abandonment becomes inoperative. The cases in which this doctrine has been asserted, do not to my humble judgment, present any solid reasons to support it. They appear to me to trench very much upon the true principles of abandonment, and to be supported by analogies not very exact, or very cogent. And I find that they have struck the comprehensive and discriminating mind of Lord Chancellor Eldon in the same manner. The doubts which he has thrown out have not been as yet satisfactorily answered. And it is no slight recommendation of the American doctrine, that it stands approved by the cautious learning of Valin, the moral perspicacity of Pothier, and the practical and sagacious judgment of Emerigon.

It appears to me that this distinction has not at all times been sufficiently adverted to in our examinations of the later English cases. Some of the remarks to be found there have a tacit reference to this doctrine; and many things thus receive an easy explanation, which it would otherwise be found somewhat difficult to reconcile with our stricter notions on the subject of abandonment.

It has been said too at the argument, that abandonments are not to be favoured; that they have been liable to great abuses, and that Courts of Law are not disposed to enlarge the practice. I am very much inclined to believe, that of late years this consideration has had quite as much weight as it deserved; and it is by no means clear, if the spirit of the cases decided by that great man, Lord Mansfield, had been fairly followed, that much uncertainty as to the law would not have been done away, and many fruitful sources of litigation dried up. At present there is enough of doubt and obscurity as to the right of abandonment in cases of sea damage, stranding, shipwreck, and loss of the voyage by the ship, to encourage expensive suits, and to lead one to the conclusion, that it were far better for the question to be settled upon some general principle in any way, than to remain in its present condition. [The extensive review of English decisions is omitted.]

The cases which have been reviewed, do, as I think, authorize the conclusion, that the question of the right of abandonment of the ship is to be judged of by all the circumstances of each particular case; and that no such general rule has as yet been established, as that the injury to the ship by the perils insured against, must in all cases exceed one half her value, to justify an abandonment. At all events, I think I may say, that there is no English case, in which, under circumstances like the present, an abandonment of the ship has been adjudged void.

I do not think it necessary to comment at large on all the American cases cited at the bar; but shall content myself with a reference to a few, which have been supposed most strongly in point. The fair conclusion from Fontaine vs. The Phoenix Insurance Company, seems to me to be, that which the reporter has drawn, that if a vessel, after being stranded, should be deemed a wreck, or her situation desperate, it will justify an abandonment, though she should be got off by other persons, and repaired for a sum less than half her value. And the circumstances of that case bear a very strong resemblance to that now before the Court. The case of Goold vs. Shaw, turned upon the point, that the ship could have been repaired for less than half her value, and might have performed her voyage, which was broken up merely on account of the deterioration of the cargo. It stands therefore on the same ground as Alexander vs. Baltimore Insurance Company.

But the case which has been pressed with the most earnestness upon the Court, as decisive of the merits of this, is Wood vs. Lincoln and Kennebec Insurance Company. The opinion there delivered by the late learned Chief Justice, is certainly entitled to great weight and consideration, from the elaborate manner in which the subject is discussed. I have not the slightest inclination to doubt the authority of that case, upon its own particular circumstances. At the time of the abandonment there does not appear to have been any serious injury to the vessel; she was merely upset, and at high water was nearly covered; and it was not until after the abandonment, that she was disengaged from the rock and sunk in deep water. She was afterwards weighed and carried to her home port of destination which was only five miles distance. The learned judge himself, in commenting on the circumstances, observed, "that it was not stated, that she received any essential injury by this accident, or that an attempt to weigh her, and prepare for finishing her voyage, would have been hazardous, or very expensive." In the present case, on the contrary, the vessel was essentially injured, and in a very perilous situation; and the repairs must be very expensive, and of such a nature too, that they could not be completed under a long period of time, as long as the usual period of the whole voyage insured. The learned judge also laid stress upon the circumstance, that the vessel at the time of the abandonment was stranded, but not sunk in deep water. He added, that it did "not appear that the plaintiff made any attempt to weigh the vessel, or offered the defendants to make any, if assured of the reimbursement of his expenses." That also did not occur in the present case, because the vessel was thought in a desperate state, nor was it requested or offered on the other side. No objection was made to the abandonment, and so far from a desire being manifested at that time to have the insured undertake to get the vessel off, the underwriters declined the further agency of one of the owners, and appointed their own agent, under the supposition that the case, if not hopeless, at least was extremely hazardous. Agreeing then, as I do, to the authority of the decision in Wood v. The Lincoln and Kennebec Insurance Company, I may be permitted to say, that the material facts are unlike those of the present case; and that the Court in that case, rely in their judgment upon the non-existence of circumstances, which cogently press upon us in this. Having said thus much upon the merits of that decision, I hope it will not be deemed a want of due reverence and respect, to declare, that although in much of the reasoning (which is indeed drawn from obvious sources) I entirely concur, there are dicta in that opinion to which in the large sense in which I understood them, I cannot yield my assent, and to which I am sure, if the points had been directly in judgment, the learned judge would have given a more exact consideration.[2]

---

2. In Peele v. Suffolk Insurance Co., 7 Pick. 254 (1828) in an action brought in the Massachusetts court on another policy covering the Argonaut on the same voyage it was held that if the insurer does take the vessel into his possession and make repairs at an expense less than half the value of the vessel he may avoid paying for a total loss. Though cited in argument the Court made no reference to Story's decision in Peele v. Merchants Insurance Co. Subsequently, however, in Deblois v. Ocean Insurance Co. 16 Pick. 303 (1835) Mr. Justice Putnam, at p. 311, wrote of Story's opinion as follows: "Indeed I may now say, and with perfect respect to my very distinguished friend who pronounced that decree, that this Court has entertained

It it not however my intention now to comment on these dicta. ... [The discussion of other American cases is omitted.]

The American cases then may be dismissed without farther commentary, since they furnish no new rule on the subject of abandonment; at least, none which applies to circumstances like those of the case at bar. We are therefore driven back upon general principles, and must extract them, as we may, from the current of authorities, to aid us in the present inquiry. The right of abandonment has been admitted to exist, where there is a forcible dispossession or ouster of the owner of the ship, as in cases of capture; where there is a moral restraint or detention, which deprives the owner of the free use of the ship, as in case of embargoes, blockades, and arrests by sovereign authority; where there is a present total loss of the physical possession and use of the ship, as in case of submersion; where there is a total loss of the ship for the voyage, as in case of shipwreck, so that the ship cannot be repaired for the voyage in the port, where the disaster happens; and, lastly, where the injury is so extensive, that by reason of it the ship is useless and yet the necessary repairs would exceed her present value. None of these cases will, I imagine, be disputed. If there be any general principle, that pervades and governs them, it seems to be this, that the right to abandon exists, whenever, from the circumstances of the case, the ship, for all the useful purposes of a ship for the voyage, is, for the present, gone from the control of the owner, and the time when she will be restored to him in a state to resume the voyage is uncertain, or unreasonably distant, or the risk and expense are disproportioned to the expected benefit and objects of the voyage. In such a case, the law deems the ship, though having a physical existence, as ceasing to exist for purposes of utility, and therefore subjects her to be treated as lost. Try the Argonaut by the test of such a rule, and it is not difficult to come to the conclusion, that the plaintiffs had a good cause of abandonment. ... [Story's discussion of the problems of valuation is omitted.]

Vandenheuvel v. United Insurance Co.
Supreme Court of New York, 1801
2 Caines Cases in Error 217; 2 Johns. Cas. 127

... Radcliff, J. This was an insurance on the freight of the Astrea, from New York to Corunna in Spain. The policy was sub-

---

opinions in regard to the law of his case, essentially at variance with the opinions expressed in his elaborate argument. ... And in the cause at bar, we are obliged to declare the law applicable to this case as it was understood and declared in the case of the Argonaut."

scribed by the defendants on the 19th November, 1798, in consequence of a written representation from the plaintiff, stating the ship, freight and cargo to be his property.

The plaintiff was originally a subject of the United Netherlands and continued so till the 3d January, 1793, when he was naturalized as a citizen of the United States. He must, of course, have emigrated to America at least two years antecedent to that period and before the United Netherlands were involved in the late European war, and he is stated to have been personally known to the defendants.

The vessel during the voyage was captured by a British frigate as prize, carried to Gibraltar, and with her cargo, there condemned by the court of vice-admiralty, on the ground of her "belonging at the time of her capture to Spain, or to persons being subjects of the king of Spain, or inhabiting the territories of the king of Spain, enemies of Great Britain." From the situation of the plaintiffs, and the representation to the defendants, the insurance must be considered as made upon American or neutral property. The representation is to this purpose equivalent to a warranty of that fact, and liable to the same result. In my view of the subject two questions arise.

1st. Whether, upon the terms of the contract, the plaintiff is entitled to recover?

2d. Whether, in respect to the fact of neutrality, he is concluded by the foreign sentence?

If upon the contract he would be entitled to recover, and is not concluded by the sentence, it is conceded or offered to be proven that the property was in reality neutral, or such as was so represented to the defendants.

The second question has already been twice determined in this court; first, in the case of Ludlow and Dale, 1 Johns. Cas. 16, in which I gave no opinion, it being argued before I took my seat; and secondly, in the case of Goix and Low, 1 Johns.Cas. 341. In the last, although the subject in some respects presented itself to my mind in a different light, I was content to acquiesce in the opinion which had been previously delivered, considering the rule to have been definitely settled as far as depended on this court. The magnitude of the question has induced us to review it in this and other causes, but notwithstanding the able and zealous discussion it has received, I can perceive no new lights on which to change my opinion.

It may be premised that in the course of the argument much was said of the policy of the English courts in deciding this question in favour of the insurer, and the policy of our adopting a different rule. On a careful examination of the English decisions, I cannot discover any ground for this suggestion. They appear to rest on principles unconnected with any motive of policy, and are indiscriminately applied to their domestic as well as to foreign tribunals. If the consideration were proper in determining a rule for ourselves, I am unable to perceive its force or application.[1]

In every instance of a foreign condemnation a loss must necessarily happen. If the property be really American, and insured here, the burthen must fall on some of our citizens. It is then a question between them solely, and it can never be politic or just to seek to shift the loss from one description of citizens to another. If the property be not American, and insured in this country, an interested policy, if such could be justified, would dictate an opposite rule of decision, and lead to protect the American insurer against the foreign owner, and thus determine the question against the insured.

Again, if the property be American, and insured abroad, the remedy is placed beyond the reach of our laws, and it would be a vain presumption in the courts of this or any other country to attempt to prescribe a rule for foreign tribunals. But I dismiss this topic as unconnected with the merits of the question. Opinions founded on policy are necessarily various and fluctuating, and ought never to actuate a court of justice.[2] The ques-

---

1. Cf. Nott, J. in Bailey v. South Carolina Insurance Co., 3 Brev. (S.C.) 354, 363-4 (1813): "None of the reasons ... on which the decisions of the British courts have been bottomed, will support their opinions. ... The time was, when even England and France were, or at least, affected to be, governed by the rules of common honesty, and their courts of admiralty influenced by a sense of stern morality.... I have already shewn that even Sir William Scott, the great oracle of maritime law, and of the law of nations ... finding that he must give up his place, or his opinion, has had the weakness to surrender his principles, and an immortal fame, to sordid interest."

2. Cf. Sedgwick, Jr. in Baxter v. New England Marine Insurance Co., 6 Mass. 277, 282-83 (1810): "From these considerations, it is evident to me that it will be most beneficial to neutral commerce, and most for the interest of neutral nations, that the loss sustained by foreign sentences of condemnation ... should fall upon the insured. I think ... that condemnations will be more resolutely contended against, and that they will, in all probability, be less numerous. If the insurance be upon foreign neutral trade, it is manifest that the rule [of conclusiveness] will be most beneficial to us, because it will be a security to the assurers, who are our citizens. If both the insurer and insured belong here, it is then only a question of loss between them; and such a rule, consistent with justice, should be established as will reduce that loss as much as possible; and that, as I have suggested, is to throw it in all cases upon the assured."

tion in every instance must depend on its intrinsic merits arising from the nature of the contract and the general law of insurance, unless restrained by positive regulations.

In this view of the subject, the judicial determinations of courts in different countries, as well as the opinions of individuals, may differ, but that difference, I apprehend, can never, as has been imagined, become a matter of national concern. The regular administration of justice, when conducted with good faith, can never implicate the government with respect to foreign nations; and whatever rule may be established on this occasion, it can only be considered as affecting the rights of our own citizens; as existing between them solely. If foreigners should at all be interested, it must happen in consequence of their voluntary act to seek insurance here, and they cannot complain of the conduct of our courts, if they receive the same measure of justice which is administered to others. I therefore equally lay out of view every argument derived from this source. ...

1st. As between the insurer and insured, in case of a representation or warranty of neutral property, I think a condemnation in a foreign court of admiralty, when founded on the want of neutrality, operates definitely against the insured according to the terms and effect of the contract itself. During the existence of a maritime war, the state of commerce is necessarily more or less precarious. Neutrals are not exempt from this inconvenience, but neutrality, if respected, affords a great advantage. The neutral merchant, when he effects an insurance, may either retain the benefit of his neutrality, or, if diffident of its security, he may relinquish it, and specially insure his property against every possible loss. If he insure the property as neutral he thereby signifies his intention to avail himself of his neutrality, and of course will pay a less premium; but in doing this it must follow that he takes upon himself the risk of that neutrality. He thus far divides the risk, and is to be considered his own insurer. He cannot, by paying a less premium, enjoy the benefit of his neutrality and at the same time the benefit of an insurance for the want of it. ...

2d. The question in the English courts does not appear to have been examined in this light. They have been content to apply to the decisions of foreign courts of admiralty, a principle which has long been received and adopted in their domestic courts. They place them on the same footing, and consider the conclusiveness of their sentences as necessarily resulting from the right of jurisdiction. In relation to their own courts the rule has undoubtedly been long established, both before and since the revolution, and it is not confined to courts of peculiar or exclusive authority, but applies to all. Not only the sentences or judgments of their ecclesiastical and other courts, where they possess exclusive cognizance, but the decisions of all their courts in cases where they have concurrent jurisdiction are deemed to be equally conclusive. Indeed, a contrary position would involve the absurdity of a power competent to decide, and at the same time ineffectual in its decision.

They have also, in a variety of cases, extended the rule to foreign courts of a different description. Thus, a bill to be relieved against actions of trespass for seizing goods in an island of Denmark was dismissed in chancery, because sentence was given in the court of Denmark on the seizure (1 Ch. Cas.237). So in case of a bill of exchange, the acceptance of which was vacated in a court of Leghorn, Lord Chancellor King held not only that the cause was to be determined by the lex loci, but the acceptance having been vacated by a competent jurisdiction, he thought the sentence conclusive, and that it bound the court of chancery in England (12 Vin. 87). So by Lord Hardwicke if a marriage be declared valid by the sentence of a court in France having proper jurisdiction, it is conclusive, and he held "that this was so, although in a foreign court, by the law of nations; for otherwise the rights of mankind would be very precarious and uncertain" (1 Vez. 159, 1748)).

This doctrine applies, with peculiar force, to the sentences of courts of admiralty in relation to prize, and of every court proceeding on the general law of nations as the basis of its authority. While the capture of enemy-property is admitted to be the right of a belligerent party, the institution of courts to try the validity of such captures must also be admitted. They exist in every country, and are established in our own. The objects of their institution are every where the same. They are invested with similar powers, pursue the same principles, and profess to be governed by the same system of laws, unconnected with the municipal regulations of any country. In this manner they form a separate and independent branch of judicature, and although uncontrouled by a common superior, their determinations while they act with good faith will generally be uniform and consistent. Considering them in this light, acting on the same principles, and governed by the same law, they come within the reason of the rule which is applied to domestic tribunals of concurrent jurisdiction, and their decisions ought to possess equal force and authority.

But another principle of English and American jurisprudence arising from the nature of the subject and the system of our courts, appears to me strongly to enforce this doctrine - The question of neutrality is involved in the general question of prize - it is a necessary incident, and the want of neutrality forms the principal ground of capture and condemnation. It is a settled maxim, that the courts of common law have no jurisdiction on the question of prize; it may collaterally arise, but ex directo it is not within their cognizance - it belongs solely and exclusively to the courts of admiralty as courts of prize. This is established by a current of authorities both ancient and modern, and the reasons on which they are founded, are satisfactory and conclusive. If then the courts of admiralty have exclusive jurisdiction of the principal question of prize, which necessarily includes that of neutrality, and the courts of common law have no jurisdiction, it must follow that the decision of the former cannot be reviewed by the latter, and that whenever they occur directly or collaterally they must, like the judgment of other courts of peculiar jurisdiction, be considered as conclusive. If they were allowed to be reviewed, in what manner could we ascertain the merits of the former decision? Is the same evidence in our power, or in the power of the parties to obtain? The insurer is a stranger to the whole transaction; the circumstances are unknown to him; the proofs, if not detained abroad, are in the hands of his adversary; they are generally concealed, or may, with the greatest ease, be suppressed. How could he compel their production, or bring to light the merits of the case? To avoid these difficulties are we to be governed by the written depositions taken in the admiralty abroad, or could they be received as evidence? It is well known that the rules of evidence in those courts are different from our own. By what rules are we to be governed? If exclusively by our own, the result in our courts may differ, and yet both judgments as to the evidence on which they are founded be equally just. Allowing even that the insured engages merely to furnish the evidence of this neutrality in foreign courts, that evidence must surely be understood to be of a nature usually received and demanded in those courts; for it is there only that it can be material. The engagement, relating to such evidence of course excludes the idea of a decision upon any other, and the interference of a court of common law, requiring a different mode of proof, and acting on different principles, would contravene one of the direct objects of the stipulation. In every shape, therefore, in which this subject can be viewed, insuperable difficulties present themselves, and evince the propriety of considering the foreign sentences as final. ...

[The concurring opinions of Benson and Kent, JJ. in the Supreme Court are omitted. In the Court for the Trial of Impeachments and Correction of Errors, the decision of the Supreme Court was reversed. 2 Johns. Cas. 451 (1802). The following opinion of Senator Clinton represented the views of the majority. A concurring opinion of Senator Gold and a dissenting opinion of Senator Van Vechten are omitted.]

Clinton, Senator. The plaintiff having warranted a ship and cargo as American property, the question is, whether, in an action against the insurers, the sentence of a foreign court of admiralty, that such warranty was false, is conclusive evidence.

It is admitted by the plaintiff, that the sentence binds and changes the property, and that it is prima facie evidence of the fact set up against him; and on the other hand, it is conceded by the defendants, that in several cases, in an action of this kind, the judgment is not definitive in favour of the insurers; such as when on the face of it, it is founded on local ordinances, or contrary to the law of nations, or so ambiguous that the court cannot, from the reasons assigned, collect the grounds of it; and, that this case not coming within either of these descriptions, the contest between the parties still remains open, whether the foreign sentence be prima facie or conclusive evidence, against the insured, and whether it bind the property adjudicated only, or is conclusive to every extent, and in every modification of the subject.

Upon a question of such immense importance, either as it respects the interests of commerce, the honour of the nation, the rights of individuals, or the principles of justice, great and mature deliberation is requisite and essential. I know not any cause that has ever been discussed in this court, which embraces so many objects, to render the final result important. Attempts have been made, to establish the doctrine of conclusiveness; and, as far as I can comprehend them, they may be arranged under four general heads.

1st. Authorities, previous to the 19th April, 1775.

2d. Analogical reasoning from domestic courts.

3d. The nature and meaning of the contract of insurance; and

4th. National considerations of courtesy, comity, and the like.

The cases quoted, as existing anterior to the revolution, are not only few, but are either ambiguous or not in point. ...

In suits, brought in England, upon foreign judgments, between the same parties, the courts consider them only as prima facie evidence of the demand, and admit the defendant on a plea of nil debet, to contest the merits of the original cause of action. If a foreign judgment be not considered conclusive between the same parties, in cases of this nature, why of a foreign court of admiralty between third persons? The constitution of the United States provides, that "full faith and credit shall be given in each state, to the public acts, records, and judicial proceedings, of every other state". And the Congress may, by general laws, prescribe the manner in which such acts, records, and proceedings, shall be proved, and the effect thereof. Is it conceivable, that if the sentence of courts of disconnected nations are to be held in such high veneration, by each other, that the framers of the constitution could have thought it necessary to make this provision for sister states, in the closest bond of political connexion. The British have made the interests of commerce a primary object of their cares.

In the discovery and arrangement of wise plans, and the execution of efficacious measures, for the attainment of this important end, they stand unrivalled in the history of mankind. Their fleets now traverse every clime, and visit every sea, laden with the riches of the world; they bear in their hands the trident of the ocean. In the time of war, they enrich themselves with the plunder of neutrals; their courts appear every where, and condemnations are conducted, not according to the law of nations, or the rights of parties, but according to the instructions from the sovereign and the rapacity of the captors. "Much less" says Wooddeson, "ought any of our courts to slight a foreign sentence. Unless we give credit to their proceedings, we cannot expect the judgments here, should be thought to merit from them any reverence or attention". 2 Wooddeson 456. Here, then, is an explicit avowal that the doctrine is adopted with a view to a return. But France, having a different policy, has adopted a different system. Emerigon 457, 464. It is to be further considered, that Great-Britain is more than one-half her time at war; that she is an underwriting nation, and, therefore, highly interested in maintaining the rule laid down. Our policy is entirely different. Peace is no less our interest than our duty. Our courts are not liable to executive instructions, and, consequently, must go by the principles of justice; not according to the exigencies of the state. In establishing, therefore, a rule for our government, on this momentous subject, argumenta ab inconvenienti, ought to have great weight. France and England have set us the example; and, as the law of nations is, at least, doubtful, we are at liberty to adopt such a construction, as shall most subserve the solid interests of this growing country. We ought, also, to consider, that the object of insurance is indemnity; that instead of fixing the loss upon one, it divides it among many; that with a pacific nation like ours, an exposition that will release the insurer from war-risks, will be a deprivation of all the benefits that can arise from a neutral position, and will expose us to most of the calamities without any of the advantages derivable from a belligerent state.

Even Great-Britain, situated as she is, has found inconvenience, in many respects, from the generality of the rule she has adopted. Her courts have, by recent decisions, attempted to narrow it into a smaller compass. Several important exceptions have been sanctioned, and whenever a different course of policy shall be deemed advisable, the whole system will be destroyed. Our court has, unadvisedly, and in the first instance, without hearing argument, taken that direction, and with the best intentions, has perserved in a doctrine, which would inevitably lead to the spoliation of our citizens, and the destruction of our commerce.

There is nothing, either in the constitution of the admiralty courts of European nations, or the mode of proceeding in them, which entitle them to respect. They adopt the rules of the civil law. The Judges hold their offices during pleasure, and follow the instructions of the ministry. The captors, who are interested, are admitted as witnesses, and the Judges are paid in proportion to the condemnations. They are generally composed of needy adventurers; their great aim is plunder, and their primary incentive, avarice.

I have thus, in a cursory manner, glanced at the principal grounds of reasoning in the cause, and I must own, that I feel most deeply impressed with its importance. The effects of the decisions of this day, will be felt when we are no more; and I trust, that it will receive the approving voice of our consciences, and of our country. ...

Croudson v. Leonard
Supreme Court of the United States, 1808
4 Cranch 434

Johnson, J. The action below was instituted on a policy of insurance [in the Circuit Court of the District of Columbia].

On behalf of the insurers, it was contended that the policy was forfeited by committing a breach of blockade. It is not and cannot be made a question that this is one of those acts which will exonerate the underwriters from their liability. The only point below was relative to the evidence upon which the commission of the act may be substantiated. A sentence of a British prize court in Barbadoes was given in evidence, by which it appeared that the vessel was condemned for attempting to commit a breach of blockade. It is the English doctrine, and the correct doctrine on the law of nations, that an attempt to commit a breach of blockade is a violation of belligerent rights, and authorizes capture. This doctrine is not denied, but the plaintiff contends that he did not commit such an attempt, and the court below permitted evidence to go to the jury to disprove the fact on which the condemnation professes to proceed.

On this point, I am of opinion that the court below erred.

I do not think it necessary to go through the mass of learning on this subject, which has so often been brought to the notice of this court, and particularly in the case of Fitzsimmons, argued at this term. Nearly the whole of it will be found very well summed up in the 18th chapter of Mr. Park's Treatise. The doctrine appears to me to rest upon three very obvious considerations; the propriety of leaving the cognizance of prize questions exclusively to courts of prize jurisdiction; the very great inconvenience, amounting nearly to an impossibility, of fully investigating such cases in a court of common law, and the impropriety of revising the decisions of the maritime courts of other nations, whose jurisdiction is co-ordinate throughout the world.

It is sometimes contended that this doctrine is novel, and that it takes its origin in an incorrect extension of the principle in Hughes v. Cornelius. I am induced to believe that it is coeval with the species of contract to which it is applied. Policies of insurance are known to have been brought into England from a country that acknowledged the civil law. This must have been the law of policies at the time when they were considered as contracts proper for the admiralty jurisdiction, and were submitted to the court of policies established in the reign of Elizabeth. It is probable that, at the time when the common law assumed to itself exclusive jurisdiction of the contract of insurance, the rule was too much blended with the law of policies to have been dispensed with, had it even been inconsistent with common law principles. But, in fact, the common law had sufficient precedent for this rule, in its own received principles relative to sentences of the civil law courts of England. It may be true that there are no cases upon this subject prior to that of Hughes v. Cornelius, but this does not disprove the existence of the doctrine. There can be little necessity for reporting decisions upon questions that cannot be controverted. Since the case of Hughes v. Cornelius, the doctrine has frequently been brought to the notice of the courts of Great Britain in insurance cases, but always with a view to contest its applicability to particular cases, or to restrict the general doctrine by exceptions, but the existence of the rule, or its applicability to actions on policies, is nowhere controverted.

I am of opinion that the sentence of condemnation was conclusive evidence of the commission of the offense for which the vessel was condemned, and as that offense was one which vitiated the policy the defendants ought to have had a verdict.[1]

---

1. A concurring opinion of Washington, J. is omitted. Chase and Livingston, JJ. dissented without opinion.

Shortly after the decision in Croudson v. Leonard the same issue was presented to the Court of Errors and Appeals in Pennsylvania in Dempsey v. Insurance Co. of Pa. A majority of the Court, without published opinion, held that the decree of the British court of Vice-Admiralty was conclusive upon all interests. See note in 1 Binney 300. Judge Cooper, however, in pamphlet form, printed a long dissenting opinion in which he vigorously supported the position taken by the Court for the Trial of Impeachments and Correction of Errors in New York. The Pennsylvania legislature in the Act of March 29, 1809, which still appears in the statutes of Pennsylvania (Purdon's Pa. Stats. Ann., Title 12, Sec. 1031), provided that a foreign prize decree, though conclusive against the property condemned, should

Williams v. Suffolk Insurance Co.
United States Circuit Court
District of Massachusetts, 1838
3 Sumner 270

Assumpsit on a policy of insurance, dated the 19th of August, 1830, whereby the plaintiff caused to be insured by the defendant, for nine per cent. per annum, premium, warranting twelve per cent. "lost or not lost, forty-nine hundred and nineteen dollars, on fifteen sixteenths of Schooner Harriet, and eighteen hundred and seventy-five dollars on board said vessel, at, and from Stonington, (Connecticut), commencing the risk on the 12th day of August, instant, at noon, to the Southern Hemisphere, with liberty to stop for salt at the Cape de Verd Islands, and to go round Cape Horn, and to touch at all islands, ports, and places, for the purpose of taking seal, and for information and refreshments, with liberty to put his skins on board of any other vessel or vessels until she returns to her port of discharge in the United States. It being understood, that the value of the interest hereby insured, as it relates to this insurance, is not to be diminished thereby. It is understood and agreed, that if the Harriet shall not proceed southeasterly of Cape Horn on a voyage toward the South Shetland Islands, and there be no loss, then the premium is to be six per centum per annum, the assured warranting only nine per cent." Vessel valued at five thousand dollars, outfits valued at two thousand dollars.

There was a similar policy underwritten by the defendants for the plaintiff, on the same day for the like voyage in all respects, of thirty-five hundred dollars, on the Schooner Breakwater, and two thousand dollars on outfits on board, at the same premium; the vessel being valued at thirty-five hundred dollars, and the outfits at two thousand dollars; upon which also an action was brought.

---

only have prima facie effect as between the insured and the insurer. A similar statute was later enacted in Maryland. Chapter 164, Acts of 1813.

In New York efforts were made, after Croudson v. Leonard to secure a reversal of the decision in the Vandenheuvel case. Though Senator Redfield in the course of argument suggested that the decision of the Supreme Court of the United States "upon this commercial question, involving a point of national law" ought to be treated "with almost the same degree of deference as ... an Act of Congress", the Court in the end voted unanimously to stand by the earlier New York case. New York Firemen's Insurance Co. v. DeWolf, 2 Cow. 56, 67 (1823). See also Ocean Insurance Co. v. Francis, 2 Wend. 64 (1828).

The declaration upon each policy averred a total loss, by the seizure and detention of one Lewis Vernet and other persons, pretending to act by the authority of the Government of Buenos Ayres, with force and arms.

The causes came on to be heard together by the Court, upon certain facts and statements agreed by the parties. It appeared from these facts and statements, that both of the vessels insured were bound on a sealing voyage, and proceeded to the Falkland Islands in pursuance thereof, and were there both seized by one Lewis Vernet, acting as Governor of those islands, under the appointment and authority of the government of Buenos Ayres. The Harriet was seized on the 30th of July, 1831, and was subsequently carried by the captors to Buenos Ayres, where certain proceedings were had against her in the tribunals, and under the sanction of the government of Buenos Ayres. She has never been restored to the defendants; but has been condemned for being engaged in the seal trade at the Falkland Islands.

The Breakwater was seized at the Islands, on or about the 18th day of August, 1831, and was afterwards recaptured by the mate and crew who remained on board, and was by them brought home to the United States; and after her arrival, was libelled for salvage in the District Court of Connecticut District, and salvage was awarded of one third part of the proceeds of the vessel and property.

Copies of the orders and decrees of the Court of Buenos Ayres respecting the seal fisheries; of the appointment of Vernet as Governor of the Falkland Islands; of the proceedings against the Harriet; of the correspondence of the American government with the Buenos Ayrean government, respecting those seizures, and the claims of the Buenos Ayrean government to the jurisdiction of the Falkland Islands, were produced and read de bene esse in the case.

C. G. Loring for the plaintiff; and Theophilus Parsons for the defendant.

Story J. I do not think it necessary, in the present cases to examine many of the points made by the learned counsel on either side; because, in my judgment, the whole controversy turns upon a point, which, if decided in favor of the plaintiff, will render the examination of all others wholly unimportant. The government of Buenos Ayres insists, that the Falkland Islands constitute a part of the dominions within its sovereignty, and, consequently, that it has the sole jurisdiction to regulate and prohibit the seal fishery at those islands, and to punish any violation of its laws by a confiscation of the vessels and property engaged therein. On the other hand, the American government insists, that the Falkland Islands to not constitute any part of the dominions within the sovereignty of Buenos Ayres; and that the seal fishery at those islands is a trade free and lawful to the citizens of the United States, and beyond the competency of the Buenos Ayrean government to regulate, prohibit, or punish. The controversy is still undisposed of by the two governments, each maintaining its own claims and pretensions, and neither admitting the claims or pretensions of the other. In this state of the diplomacy between the two countries, while the whole matter is in contestation between them, or, as we may say, _flagrante lite_, the question is, whether it is competent for this Court to reexamine and decide, in its judicial capacity, upon the claims and pretensions of the two governments, and thus to interpose its positive umpirage to settle the matters in dispute, at least to the extent required for the proper adjudication of the cases now before it.

My judgment is, that this Court possesses no such authority; and that it is bound up by the doctrines and claims insisted on by its own government, and that it must take them to be rightful, until the contrary is established by some formal and authorized action of that government. It is very clear, that it belongs exclusively to the executive department of our government to recognize, from time to time, any new governments, which may arise in the political revolutions of the world; and until such new governments are so recognized, they cannot be admitted by our courts of justice to have, or to exercise the common rights and prerogatives of sovereignty. ...

Upon these grounds, this court must hold both of these seizures unlawful, and therefore the plaintiff is entitled to recover, as for a total loss, in the case of the _Harriet_. ...

I have not thought it necessary to discuss at large the points, suggested by the learned counsel for the defendants, that the loss was occasioned by the barratry or gross negligence of the master of the _Harriet_, in carrying on the seal fisheries at the Falkland Islands, after the alleged warning given to him by governor Vernet. Assuming that such a warning was given, I do not think, that it could, in the present case, change the rights of the defendant. There is no ground for deeming the master's conduct to be barratry; for it was not any fraudulent violation, or wilful abandonment of his duty to the owner. As to the point of gross negligence, not amounting to fraudulent conduct, if such a case were made out, it would not help the defence. It has been repeatedly settled by the Supreme Court of the United States, that if the immediate cause of a loss is a peril insured against, it is no ground of defence, that it was remotely caused by the negligence of the master or crew; the rule being, _Causa proxima, non remota spectatur_. This doctrine being founded, not upon local law, but upon the general principles of commercial law, would be obligatory upon this court, even if the decisions of the state court of Massachusetts were to the contrary; for upon commercial questions of a general nature, the courts of the United States possess the same general authority, which belongs to the state tribunals, and are not bound by the local decisions. They are at liberty to consult their own opinions, guided, indeed, by the greatest deference for the acknowledged learning and ability of the state tribunals, but still exercising their own judgment, as to the reasons, on which those decisions are founded. But I do not understand, that the supreme court of Massachusetts has adopted any positive doctrine inconsistent with the principles of the maxim above stated. On the contrary, in Delano v. The Bedford Ins. Co., (10 Mass. R. 347, 354) that learned court fully recognised the rule, that the immediate, and not the remote, cause of a loss was to be regarded in policies of insurance. I am aware of the decision of the same court, in Cleveland v. The Union Ins. Co. (8 Mass. R. 308;) but considering, that the ultimate decision was made by a minority of the court, (Mr. Chief Justice Parsons and Mr. Justice Thacher not sitting, and Mr. Justice Sewall dissenting) it can hardly be considered as a satisfactory authority.

But if the law were otherwise, nothing but very gross and criminal negligence of the master would bring the case within the category of the argument. Now, here is the case of a trade lawful, as I am bound to maintain, to American citizens, and rightfully carried on by them. Under such circumstances, and especially taking into consideration the past uninterrupted state of that trade, it seems too much to say, that a mere fear of molestation in the trade would have justified the master in breaking up the voyage. The underwriters were bound to know the ordinary perils of the trade, as much as the owner of the ship; and they took upon themselves the ordinary risks, arising from the known claims and decrees of the Buenos Ayrean government, known, I am to presume, as much to one party to the insurance, as to the other. I cannot say, that the master did not exercise a fair and reasonable discretion; or that his conduct was marked with such rashness, precipitation, and gross negligence, as to amount to a desertion of his proper duty, or to exonerate the underwriters from their liability. He appears to have acted with good faith, under a sense of duty, and in a lawful manner, in the maintenance of the rights of his country.

...

... If, upon every threat of illegal violence or seizure, he were bound to abandon his voyage, or the legal rights of the owner, there would be an end of all security to trade and commerce. It seems to me, therefore, that upon principle there is great reason to hold, if the loss is occasioned by the illegal act of a foreign government, it is a loss within the perils of the policy, even though it might have been avoided by the master by a different course of conduct, if his actual conduct was bona fide, in furtherance of the objects of the voyage, and in pursuance of his duty to his owners.

Upon these considerations my judgment is, that the plaintiff is entitled to recover for a total loss in the case of the Harriet, and for a partial loss (i. e. the salvage) in the case of the Breakwater.[1]

Swift v. Tyson
Supreme Court of the United States, 1842
16 Peters 1

This action was instituted in the Circuit Court upon a bill of exchange, dated at Portland, in the state of Maine, on the first day of May, 1836, for one thousand five hundred and thirty-six dollars and thirty cents, payable six months after date, drawn by Nathaniel Norton, and Jairus S. Keith, upon and accepted by the defendant, the bill having been drawn to the order of Nathaniel Norton, and by him endorsed to the plaintiff. The principal and interest on the bill, up to the time of trial, amounted to one thousand eight hundred and sixty-two dollars and six cents. The defence to the action rested on the answers to a bill of discovery filed by the defendant against the plaintiff; by which it appeared that the bill had been received by him from Nathaniel Norton, with another draft of the same amount in payment of a protested note drawn by Norton and Keith, and

---

1. In Fulton & Foster v. Lancaster Insurance Co., 7 Ohio (Part 2) 5 (1836) the Supreme Court of Ohio refused to follow those decisions of the Federal courts in which it was held that recovery against the marine insurance company was possible though negligence of the master was a remote cause of the loss. In Administrators of Perrin v. Protection Insurance Co., 11 Ohio 147 (1842) the Fulton case was overruled. In the course of his opinion, Lane, C. J. at p. 172, wrote as follows: "The present case distinctly lays before us the propriety of now adhering to our former decision. This is not a question of local law, springing from our own fountains of jurisprudence only, but a general commercial principle, resting on broader foundations, which ought to be uniform among all civilized nations. When the law of insurance has, in its fuller development, received an important modification, in the English and federal courts, and which, probably, will be the rule of the state courts, as fast as they act upon the question, it may be emphatically asked, whether the courts of Ohio should not conform to this change? It would be not a little inconvenient, as well as odd, if our citizens should receive one interpretation of the universal law merchant in our courts, while the stranger receives one different, by appealing to a different tribunal, which holds its seat by our side." Cf., Fletcher, J. in Nelson v. Suffolk Insurance Co., 8 Cush. 477, 496 (1851).

which had been paid by him to the Maine Bank. When the draft was received by the plaintiff, it had been accepted by the defendant, who resided in New York. The plaintiff had no knowledge of the consideration which had been received for the acceptance, and had no other transaction with the defendant. He had received the drafts and acceptances in payment of the protested note, with a full belief that the same were justly due, according to their tenor; and he had no other security for the payment of the protested note except the drafts nor had he any knowledge of any contract or dealing between the defendant and Norton, out of which the said draft arose.

The defendant then offered to prove that the bill of exchange was accepted by him as part consideration for the purchase of certain lands in the state of Maine, of which Keith and Norton, the drawers of the bill, represented themselves to be the owners, and represented them to be of great value, made certain estimates of them which were warranted by them to be correct, and also contracted to convey a good title to the land; all of which representations were in every respect fraudulent and false; and that said Keith and Norton have never been able to make a title to the lands: whereupon the plaintiff, by his counsel, objected to the admission of said testimony, or any testimony, as against the plaintiff, impeaching or showing the failure of the consideration on which said bill was accepted, under the facts aforesaid admitted by the defendant, and those proven by him, by reading said answers in equity of the plaintiff in evidence. And the judges of the Court divided in opinion on the point or question of law, whether, under the facts last mentioned, the defendant was entitled to the same defence to the action as if the suit was between the original parties to the bill, that is to say, the said Norton, or the said Norton and Keith, and the defendant. And whether the evidence so offered in defence and objected to was admissible as against the plaintiffs in this action.

And thereupon the said point or question of law was, at the request of the counsel for the said plaintiff, stated as above, under the direction of the judges of this Court to be certified under the seal of this Court to the Supreme Court of the United States, at the next session thereof to be held thereafter; to be finally decided by the said last mentioned Court.

The case was submitted to the Court on printed arguments by Mr. Fessenden, for the plaintiff; and by Mr. Dana, for the defendant.

Mr. Fessenden argued, that the defence offered and objected to is no defence as against the plaintiff in this action. The right of the plaintiff to recover, resting, in the first place, on admissions and proof, is established prima facie. The defendant, by his course of proceeding, has admitted: First, that the bill in suit was endorsed to the plaintiff during its course, as negotiable paper, about five months before it became due, according to its tenor.

Second, That when it was received by the plaintiff, he had no notice, or knowledge, or intimation of any fact to the dishonour of the bill; on the contrary, he was assured by his debtor it would be paid promptly at maturity, and that previous acceptances given in payment of the sale of land had been paid at maturity.

Third, That the acceptance was taken in payment of a preexistent debt, and that the plaintiff had no other security for the debt due to him by Norton and Keith but this acceptance,and an acceptance of the same character for the residue of his claim on Norton and Keith; and that on receiving the acceptance he had given up the note of Norton and Keith, which had been endorsed by one Child.

By the cases of Bank of Salina v. Babcock and others, 21 Wendell, 499, and Bank of Sandusky v. Scoville and others, 24 Wendell, 115, it distinctly appears, that the latest opinion of the Supreme Court of New York is - and seemingly as if that Court had never decided otherwise - that receiving negotiable paper in payment of an antecedent debt, is the same thing, in all respects, as regards the rights of the recipient endorsee of such paper, as if he had paid money, or any other valuable consideration for it, at the time, on the credit of the paper.

But if these cases cannot be reconciled with the plaintiff Swift's side of the present question, are they, unsustained as they are by like decisions in any other of the states in this Union; resting, as they do, on an obvious misinterpretation of the case of Coddington and Bay; and contradicting, as they do, the earlier decision of the same Court on the very point, in the case of Warren and Lynch, which has been referred to; and tending, as they do, to drive commercial negotiable paper out of one of the paths of its greatest utility - are they still to overthrow the decisions of this Court in the cases of Coolidge and Payson, and Townsley and Sumrall? It is contended, on the part of the defendant, that they are, and that this high Court is bound to follow them with unreasoning submission, because the bill in question was drawn on the city of New York, in the state of New York; and on account of the thirty-fourth section of the judiciary act of 1789, which provides, that "the laws of the several states, except where the Constitution, treaties, or statutes of the United States shall otherwise require or provide, shall be regarded as rules of decision, in trials at common law in cases where they apply."

In answer to this, it is urged that, in the first place after observing that it is not pretended that the decisions of the Supreme Court of New York referred to, are founded on, or are in exposition of, the constitution or any statute of that state, that the phrase "laws of the several states" in the thirty-fourth section of the judiciary act, means nothing else than the written constitutional system and statutes of such states; and that, if the framers of the act of Congress had not known that all the states had such written constitutions of government laws of paramount authority in those states; and had not wished to frame their enactments in language popular and comprehensive, as well as accurate, they would have used the word "statutes" the appropriate technical word for laws framed by the legislature, instead of the word "laws". If they had intended to embrace in the section the traditionary, or otherwise derived common law of such states, as expounded by the decisions of the state Courts; being, as they were, scholars as well as lawyers, they would have incorporated in the section, by way of substitute or addition, some such general phrase as "systems of law". In common parlance, the word "laws" in the plural, means, and did mean in 1789, legislative enactments. The same word also embraces, popularly and technically, when speaking of the regulations of the respective United States, their constitutions of government, as well as their legislative enactments; and the former, as well as the latter, were doubtless intended to be included in the thirty-fourth section. For these reasons the word "laws" instead of the word "statutes" makes part of the section.

It is admitted that if the bill had been delivered to the plaintiff by Norton for value delivered to him, Norton, at the time on the strength or credit of the bill, the defence should be rejected.

But it is contended on the part of the defendant, that inasmuch as the bill was received by the plaintiff in payment, though it were absolute payment of a pre-existing debt; and though he has no evidence of, or security for, such debt, except the new security in his hands, received in payment of the old; the bill in question was not endorsed to him in the usual course of trade, so as to give him any rights as the holder of it, different from those of the person who transferred it to him; however he may have received it fairly and in good faith, and without notice of any thing which would disenable the party transferring it to him, to recover it of the acceptor - and however the fact may be as to its original lawfulness. This is the question for the court to decide: and it is contended, that the bill being so transferred and received in payment of a pre-existing debt, gives the endorsee all the rights as against the acceptor which he would have had, if, at the time he received it, he had paid the amount of it, in money, to the endorser.

It certainly should be so. The use of negotiable paper has hardly been of greater service to civilized man, in facilitating the transmission of the equivalent of money, and thus in answering, in some respects, the purposes of money itself, than in preventing hostile proceedings in courts of law for the collection of money due. Indeed, one of the principal good effects of the former is, that it tends to prevent suits at law. In point of fact, thousands of suits have been prevented by receiving a bill of exchange or promissory note, with an additional name upon it, payable at a future day, in discharge of a debt, which, although due, the debtor at the moment could discharge in no other way. But if it comes to be settled by law, that the creditor upon such an occasion, must, at his peril, ascertain that the additional party, whose name is upon the paper, has no good defence to its payment as against the person proposing to transfer it to such creditor, it will deter him from receiving it, in lieu of the money he demands; and will, in many instances, lead to suits, which otherwise would not have been commenced.

This high Court has once and again decided the very question involved in this case, in the case of Coolidge et al v. Payson et al., 2 Wheaton, 66 to 73, and in Townsley v. Sumrall, 2 Peters 170 to 180.

The general rule as to negotiable paper is, that where it is not unlawful and void in its inception, he to whom it is transferred while current, in due form, and who receives it in good faith, and for a valuable consideration, without notice of any thing which would exonerate the maker or acceptor of it from paying it to the one from whom he receives it, can recover its amount from such maker or acceptor, although the party from whom he received it could not. Lord Raymond, 738; 1 Salkeld, 126; 3 Salkeld, 71; Grant v. Vaughan, 3 Burrows, 1516. But surely the discharge of a just debt is a valuable consideration. Comyn's Digest, New York ed. of 1824, vol. 1, page 300, title, "Action on the Case upon Assumpsit" B. 3, "Discharge of a debt a good consideration to raise an assumpsit." In Baker v. Arnold, 3 Caines' Rep. 279, it was decided by the Supreme Court of New York, that in an action by the endorsee of a note, not void in its creation, and endorsed before it became due, the consideration, as between the previous parties to the note, could not be inquired into. In Russell v. Ball, 2 Johns. Rep. 50, a decision upon similar principles will be found. Cited, also, Warren v. Lynch, 5 Johns. 339.

But it is contended on the part of the defendant, that later decisions by the Supreme Court of New York have established an opposite principle; and that receiving a note in payment of a pre-existing debt is not receiving it in the usual course of trade, nor on a consideration which gives the endorsee any rights on the paper beyond those of the endorser.

The phrase, "usual course of trade" is rather vague and indefinite. It was once the usual course of trade to pay debts and it should still be so. Most of the notes discounted at banks are given for the renewal of notes to fall due, or for the payment of pre-existing debts.

The later decisions of the Supreme Court of New York, referred to, are professedly founded on principles alleged to be decided in the case of Bay v. Coddington, 5 Johns. Chancery Rep. 54, and the same case under the name of Coddington v. Bay, decided in the Court for the Correction of Errors of that state, on appeal. 20 Johns. Rep. 637. This case does not sustain the position of the defendant. It was decided by Chancellor Kent expressly on the ground that "the defendant did not receive the notes in the course of business" nor in payment in part or in the whole of any then existing debt. In the Court for the Cor rection of Errors the decision of Chancellor Kent was affirmed. In the case of Ward et al. v. Howell, 9 Wend. 170, the note was not received in payment, but as a security. The other cases referred to, Rowsa v. Botherson, 10 Wend. 85; Ontario Bank v. Worthington, 12 Wend. 593; and Payne v. Cutler, 13 Wend. 605, are all founded on the principle laid down by Savage, Chief Justice, in the Ontario Bank v. Worthington, "If the plaintiff fails he loses nothing, he is in the same situation as before he took the paper, and it was his fault if he did not inquire into the value of the paper, and the defence against it; and all the cases assume that the case of Coddington v. Bay, decided what it did not decide."

Whensoever a person receives a note or bill in payment of a pre-existing debt, he does lose something if he cannot collect the substitute he receives. He loses the debt. He does not stand in the same situation as before he took the note or bill. The same parties holden on the old and extinguished evidence of debt, may be on the new which he receives, and they may not. If, then, these decisions of the Supreme Court of New York rest essentially on the principle stated by Chief Justice Savage, they are not at war with the law which is contended for in the present case.

For these reasons it is contended that the 34th section of the judiciary act does not render it obligatory upon this Court to disregard its own decisions, and follow those of any Court of the state of New York, upon a general question like the present, not affected by any statute of that state; although the bill of exchange in question was drawn on the city of New York.

But if law is otherwise, it is submitted that the decisions of the highest Court of the state is the Court for the Correction of Errors. Gelson v. Hoyt, 3 Wheaton, 248. In the Court of Errors of New York, the decision in Bay v. Coddington has been spoken of with disapprobation.

If there is any question of law, not local, but widely general in its nature and effects, it is the present question. It is one in which foreigners, the citizens of different states, in their contests with each other, nay, every nation of the civilized commercial world, are deeply interested. By all without the United States, this Court is looked to as the judiciary of the whole nation, known as the United States, whose commerce and transactions are as widely diffused as is the use of bills of exchange. The obvious and admitted wisdom of the thirty-fourth section of the judiciary act, in reference to our excellent, but delicate and complex system of government, if the section does not receive the construction contended for, and which it is believed the framers of that act designed, will lose its nature and become folly; and the section will, as it seems, be productive of mischiefs, in the experience and remembrance of which its benefits will be lost sight of, if the principle urged on the part of the defendant shall prevail. How can this Court preserve its control over the reason and affections of the people of the United States; that control in which its usefulness consists, and which its own untrammelled learning and judgment would enable it naturally to maintain; if its records show that it has decided - as it may be compelled to decide if the construction of the section referred to, advocated on the part of the defendant, is established - the same identical question, arising on a bill of exchange, first one way, and then the other, with vacillating inconsistency? In what light will the judicial character of the United States appear abroad, under such circumstances.

In cases in which the Courts of the United States have jurisdiction, by the Constitution and laws of the United States, the common mercantile law of the respective states applying to and governing those cases, is as much submitted to the actual consciences and judgments of the minds of the judges who constitute those Courts, to be considered and declared, without respect to the decision of any state Court, as binding authority, as the same law, in cases where the United States Courts have not jurisdiction, is to the best judgment of the state Courts, without respect to the decision of any Court of the United States, as binding authority. Congress, and Congress alone, has power to regulate commerce between the states. But it will be impossible for Congress to regulate commerce between the states, if it be left to state Courts to declare authoritatively in the absence of any statute upon the point, the force and meaning of, and the right of parties under that most important instrument of such commerce - the bill of exchange; when drawn and held in and by a citizen of one state, and accepted and payable in and by a citizen of another state.

Mr. Dana, for the defendant.

The first part of the argument of Mr. Dana was upon the question, whether the acceptance of the bill of exchange by the defendant having been given in New York, the contract was not to be regulated by the laws of that state. This question was not brought before the Court by the certificate of division, and the discussion of the point by the counsel of the defendant is therefore omitted.

Mr. Dana declined arguing the question whether, by the laws of the state of New York, the defence set up by the defendant would have been admissible, as he did not suppose it arose, properly, upon the certificate of division.

He thought the judges did not in fact divide upon that point; but, on the contrary, they gave judgment on a case made by the plaintiff, to set aside the verdict for defendant; and upon elaborate examination of all the decisions of the Courts of the state of New York, that the defence was good; and the verdict ought not to be set aside, if the laws of that state applied to the case.

Upon the question whether, by the thirty-fourth section of the judiciary act of 1789, the law of the state of New York must be the rule of decision of this case; he argued, that under the injunctions of the section that "the laws of the several states, except where the Constitution, treaties, or statutes shall otherwise provide or require, shall be regarded as rules of decision in trials at common law in the Courts of the United States, in cases where they apply," imposed on the Supreme Court an obligation, as well to apply the decisions of the Courts of this state, as the statutes, to cases which come before this Court.

It was necessary to adopt some system or code of law for the administration of justice, by the newly-erected Courts of the United States.

These Courts were anomalous in character, created by statute; under the general provision of the Constitution of the United States, limited in jurisdiction to certain subjects; and without rules of decision in the cases that would arise.

To have attempted to create a code of laws by legislative enactment, would have been without present avail to the Courts; and even with the aid of future experience and after years of labour, could not be expected to be perfect.

The alternative was to adopt an existing system of laws. The common law was sufficiently complete, and would have furnished rules of decision for all cases, as well as modes of judicial proceedings; but it would have then been one system of law in the Federal Courts, for the whole United States. It may be questioned whether the law of the place of the contract, although a principle recognised by the common law, would have had effect in reference to the several states. That principle has reference to a foreign contract. But the territorial limit of the jurisdiction of the Federal Courts would be one country and subject to one law. Wherever within that limit the cause of action might arise, it would be subject to the same administration of law by these Courts when resorted to for the purpose of enforcing the right.

This would have led to perpetual confliction between the state and Federal Courts.

Another objection would be, that the common law, however perfect in its structure, still had many peculiarities not adapted to the condition of things in this country, and requiring to be modified to meet the exigencies of an enterprising people. Such modification had in fact taken place in all the states, in all of which, at least those having an English origin, the common law had been adopted or rather inherited. Instead therefore of the entire body of the common law, with all its peculiarities, it could be adopted as modified by the states and by so doing, the Federal Courts would be made to harmonize with the state tribunals, and the law of the place of contract be preserved.

If the phraseology of the section in question be examined with reference to the whole subject that Congress was to provide for, it will be found substantially to express all that was necessary for the adoption of the state laws to the extent and for the purpose we have supposed to have been had in view. It is all the provision there is upon the subject; and in so far as it falls short of the adoption of laws for the direction of the Courts, the defect is still unprovided for. The common law has never been otherwise adopted, nor have the Courts power to create or adopt laws - they must administer the law as existing.

In support of this position it would be sufficient perhaps to refer to the cases of The United States v. Worrall, 2 Dallas 384; The United States v. Burr, (opinion delivered by the Chief Justice, Sept. 3d, 1807); The United States v. Hudson and Goodwin, 7 Cranch, 32; The United States v. Coolidge, 1 Wheaton, 415.

In these cases, it is true, the question was, whether the Courts of the United States had jurisdiction of crimes and offences at common law, which had not been provided for by the Constitution or laws of the United States; but they involved the general question, whether the common law had been adopted: for if it could be referred to at all, it was equally a source of jurisdiction as it would be the rule of decision. Accordingly, in the discussion of the question, it was thought necessary to assume, in the utmost latitude, that the common law was the basis of our federal jurisprudence, as it was of the several states; and the decision ought to be regarded as coextensive with the ground upon which the jurisdiction was asserted, and to have finally disposed of it.

Yet, as the Court were not unanimous, and the subject has been since debated with much learning and zeal by distinguished writers (see Duponceau on the Jurisdiction of the Courts of the United States; 1 Kent's Commentaries, 311, 322; North American Review, July No. 1825; 1 Story's Commentaries on the Constitution, 141;) it may not be supererogatory to examine it anew; as the question is now presented in a form that calls for a specific and final decision of the whole matter.

It would seem to be a self-evident proposition, that the adoption of the common law must have been by the Constitution or legislative enactment. Surely, the Courts could not of their own authority establish as the law of the land, a foreign code or system, no matter how consonant with our political character, or how familiar its principles. By the same authority they could as well have adopted the civil law as existing in France or Holland as the English law.

But, although it is conceded that there is no express recognition or adoption of the common law, either in the Constitution or laws of the United States; it is contended that the Constitution presupposes, and is predicated upon the existence of the common law. Justice Story, in The United States v. Coolidge, 1 Gal. 448; Bayard's Speech, Debates on the Judiciary in 1802, p. 372; North American Review, before cited.

Mr. Justice Story refers to the provisions in the Constitution and laws, in respect to trial by jury, the writ of habeas corpus, &c., as instances when recourse must be had to the common law for the interpretation of terms. 1 Gal. 488.

These observations are just - but what is the conclusion therefrom? Because we have used the terms, have we thereby appropriated the entire common law, and become subject to its authority? Do we not borrow terms in science and arts, without being pledged to the principles to which they may have been applied? The physician derives his nomenclature from the Greek language; but is his practice controlled by the false notions which those terms often indicate, or the theories of those who invented them? The common law itself has borrowed terms of pleadings and processes and familiar proverbs from the civil law, but do we look to the original for any supposed obligation? Our law idiom is essentially of common law origin, yet not foreign. It is the language familiar to us in the jurisprudence of the respective states. It is there assimilated and modified by our own circumstances and usages. In coming together from the respective states, the framers of the Constitution, and our representatives in Congress after them, must be regarded as having had in view the language, laws, and institutions of the states which they represented. If, therefore, in the organization of the federal judiciary, a system of laws is presupposed, it is the American law, which is now as distinct in its character as the English or French; yet, as it is not uniform in the states, the adoption of it in the Federal Courts would be necessarily subject to some legislative provision, as to the cases and circumstances to which the law should be applicable. The general language of the law would, however, obviously occur, and be used in any legislation upon the subject, without the necessity of definition as might be required, if some foreign code or any of its provisions were to be transferred and appropriated, like the Athenian law, which was transmuted in a mass by the Romans, into the twelve tables.

But it is said that some of the provisions of the Constitution can take effect only by recourse to the common law, as the clause in article 3, section 2, extending the judicial power to all cases in law and equity, arising under the Constitution, &c., and to admiralty and maritime jurisdiction. The laws and practices of the states, it is argued, cannot be referred to here, because in many of them no equity jurisprudence existed, and the maritime law of the states is supposed to have been too imperfect and unsettled to furnish any basis for that department of law. 1 Gal. 488.

To this it may be answered, that although in some of the states there were no equity tribunals distinct from the common law Courts, yet the principles of equity, as distinguished from those of common law, were perfectly understood in every state, and were in fact administered, although in some of them without the aid of a Court of Chancery. The present organization of the Federal Courts in fact conforms with the usage of those very states where this defect of equity power is supposed to exist there is an equity jurisprudence fully carried into effect, without separate Courts of Equity.

As to the maritime jurisdiction and course of proceeding, it was sufficiently settled; for the proceedings of our Courts in the exercise of that jurisdiction, are regulated now, not by the English admiralty law, but by the practice in our own country, engrafted on the English. 10 Wheaton, 473.

Mr. Dana cited the debates on the Constitution of the United States in the Convention of Virginia and in other states to show that without the aid of a statute the common law cannot be called in aid of the jurisdiction of the Courts, or for rules of decision as to the necessity of legislation for the authority and manner of proceeding in the Courts of the United States; he cited the opinion of Mr. Justice Iredell in Chisholm's Executors v. The State of Georgia, 2 Dallas, 432. That the provisions of the twenty-fourth section are not confined to "statutes" he cited, as decided in this Court, Jackson v. Chew, 12 Wheaton, 153; Henderson and wife v. Griffin, 5 Peters, 151; Green v. Neal, 6 Peters, 291; The United States v. Wanson, 1 Gallison, 5; Van Reimsdyke v. Kine et al., 1 Gallison, 371.

Mr. Justice Story delivered the opinion of the Court. ...

There is no doubt, that a bona fide holder of a negotiable instrument for a valuable consideration, without any notice of facts, which impeach its validity as between the antecedent parties, if he takes it under an endorsement made before the same becomes due, holds the title unaffected by these facts, and may recover thereon, although as between the antecedent parties the transaction may be without any legal validity. This is a doctrine so long and so well established, and so essential to the security of negotiable paper, that it is laid up among the fundamentals of the law, and requires no authority or reasoning to be now brought in its support. As little doubt is there, that the holder of any negotiable paper, before it is due, is not bound to prove that he is a bona fide holder for a valuable consideration, without notice; for the law will presume that, in the absence of all rebutting proofs, and therefore it is incumbent upon the defendant to establish by way of defence satisfactory proofs of the contrary, and thus to overcome the prima facie title of the plaintiff.

In the present case, the plaintiff is a bona fide holder without notice for what the law deems a good and valid consideration, that is, for a pre-existing debt; and the only real question in the cause is, whether, under the circumstances of the present case, such a pre-existing debt constitutes a valuable consideration in the sense of the general rule applicable to negotiable instruments. We say, under the circumstances of the present case, for the acceptance having been made in New York, the argument on behalf of the defendant is, that the contract is to be treated as a New York contract, and therefore to be governed by the laws of New York, as expounded by its Courts, as well upon general principles, as by the express provisions of the thirty-fourth section of the judiciary act of 1789, ch. 20. And then it is further contended, that by the law of New York, as thus expounded by its Courts, a pre-existing debt does not constitute, in the sense of the general rule, a valuable consideration applicable to negotiable instruments. [Discussion of New York decisions omitted.]

But, admitting the doctrine to be fully settled in New York, it remains to be considered, whether it is obligatory upon this Court, if it differs from the principles established in the general commercial law. It is observable that the Courts of New York do not found their decisions upon this point upon any local statute, or positive, fixed, or ancient local usage: but they deduce the doctrine from the general principles of commercial law. It is, however, contended, that the thirty-fourth section of the judiciary act of 1789, ch. 20, furnishes a rule obligatory upon this Court to follow the decisions of the state tribunals in all cases to which they apply. That section provides "that the laws of the several states, except where the Constitution, treaties, or statutes of the United States shall otherwise require or provide, shall be regarded as rules of decision in trials at common law in the Courts of the United States, in cases where they apply." In order to maintain the argument, it is essential, therefore, to hold, that the word "laws" in this section, includes within the scope of its meaning the decisions of the local tribunals. In the ordinary use of language it will hardly be contended that the decisions of Courts constitute laws. They are, at most, only evidence of what the laws are, and are not of themselves laws. They are often re-examined, reversed, and qualified by the Courts themselves, whenever they are found to be either defective, or ill-founded, or otherwise incorrect. The laws of a state are more usually understood to mean the rules and enactments promulgated by the legislative authority thereof, or long established local customs having the force of laws. In all the various cases, which have hitherto come before us for decision, this Court have uniformly supposed, that the true interpretation of the thirty-fourth section limited its application to state laws strictly local, that is to say, to the positive statutes of the state, and the construction thereof adopted by the local tribunals, and to rights and titles to things having a permanent locality, such as the rights and titles to real estate, and other matters immovable and intraterritorial in their nature and character. It never has been supposed by us, that the section did apply, or was designed to apply, to questions of a more general nature, not at all dependent upon local statutes or local usages of a fixed and permanent operation, as, for example, to the construction of ordinary contracts or other written instruments, and especially to questions of general commercial law, where the state tribunals are called upon to perform the like functions as ourselves, that is, to ascertain upon general reasoning and legal analogies, what is the true exposition of the contract or instrument, or what is the just rule furnished by the principles of commercial law to govern the case. And we have not now the slightest difficulty in holding, that this section, upon its true intendment and construction, is strictly limited to local statutes and local usages of the character before stated, and does not extend to contracts and other instruments of a commercial nature, the true interpretation and effect whereof are to be sought, not in the decisions of the local tribunals, but in the general principles and doctrines of commercial jurisprudence. Undoubtedly, the decisions of the local tribunals upon such subjects are entitled to, and will receive, the most deliberate attention and respect of this Court; but they cannot furnish positive rules, or conclusive authority, by which our own judgments are to be bound up and governed. The law respecting negotiable instruments may be truly declared in the language of Cicero, adopted by Lord Mansfield in Luke v. Lyde, 2 Burr. R. 883, 887, to be in a great measure, not the law of a single country only, but of the commercial world. Non erit alia lex Romae, alia Athenis alia nunc, alia posthac, sed et apud omnes gentes, et omni tempore, una eademque lex obtinebit.

It becomes necessary for us, therefore, upon the present occasion to express our own opinion of the true result of the commercial law upon the question now before us. And we have no hesitation in saying, that a pre-existing debt does constitute a valuable consideration in the sense of the general rule already stated, as applicable to negotiable instruments. Assuming it to be true (which, however, may well admit of some doubt from the generality of the language) that the holder of a negotiable instrument is unaffected with the equities between the antecedent parties, of which he has no notice, only where he receives it in the usual course of trade and business for a valuable consideration, before it becomes due; we are prepared to say, that receiving it in payment of, or as security for a pre-existing debt, is according to the known usual course of trade and business. Any why upon principle should not a pre-existing debt be deemed such a valuable consideration? It is for the benefit and convenience of the commercial world to give as wide an extent as practicable to the credit and circulation of negotiable paper, that it may pass not only as security for new purchases and advances, made upon the transfer thereof, but also in payment of and as security for pre-existing debts. The creditor is thereby enabled to realize or to secure his debt, and thus may safely give a prolonged credit, or forbear from taking any legal steps to enforce his rights. The debtor also has the advantage of making his negotiable securities of equivalent value to cash. But establish the opposite conclusion, that negotiable paper cannot be applied in payment of or as security for pre-existing debts, without letting in all the equities between the original and antecedent parties, and the value and circulation of such securities must be essentially diminished, and the debtor driven to the embarrassment of making a sale thereof, often at a ruinous discount, to some third person, and then by circuity to apply the proceeds to the payment of his debts. What, indeed, upon such a doctrine would become of that large class of cases, where new notes are given by the same or by other parties, by way of renewal or security to banks, in lieu of old securities discounted by them, which have arrived at maturity? Probably more than one-half of all bank transactions in our country, as well as those of other countries, are of this nature. The doctrine would strike a fatal blow at all discounts of negotiable securities for pre-existing debts.

This question has been several times before this Court, and it has been uniformly held, that it makes no difference whatsoever as to the rights of the holder, whether the debt, for which the negotiable instrument is transferred to him, is a pre-existing debt, or is contracted at the time of the transfer. In each case he equally gives credit to the instrument. The cases of Coolidge v. Payson, 2 Wheaton, R. 66, 70, 73, and Townsley v. Sumrall, 2 Peters, R. 170, 182, are directly in point.

In England the same doctrine has been uniformly acted upon. As long ago as the case of Pillans and Rose v. Van Meirop and Hopkins, 3 Burr. 1664, the very point was made and the objection was overruled. That, indeed, was a case of far more stringency than the one now before us; for the bill of exchange there drawn in discharge of a pre-existing debt, was held to bind the party as acceptor, upon a mere promise made by him to accept before the bill was actually drawn. Upon that occasion, Lord Mansfield, likening the case to that of a letter of credit said, that a letter of credit may be given for money already advanced, as well as for money to be advanced in future: and the whole Court held the plaintiff entitled to recover. From that period downward there is not a single case to be found in England in which it has ever been held by the Court, that a pre-existing debt was not a valuable consideration, sufficient to protect the holder, within the meaning of the general rule, although incidental dicta have been sometimes relied on to establish the contrary, such as the dictum of Lord Chief Justice Abbott in Smith v. De Witt, 6 Dowl. & Ryland, 120, and De la Chaumette v. The Bank of England, 9 Barn. & Cres. 209, where, however, the decision turned upon very different considerations.

Mr. Justice Bayley, in his valuable work on bills of exchange and promissory notes, lays down the rule in the most general terms. "The want of consideration" says he, "in toto or in part, cannot be insisted on, if the plaintiff or any intermediate party between him and the defendant took the bill or note bona fide and upon a valid consideration." Bayley on Bills, p. 499, 500, 5th London edition, 1830. It is observable that he here uses the words "valid consideration" obviously intending to make the distinction, that it is not intended to apply solely to cases, where a present consideration for advances of money on goods or otherwise takes place at the time of the transfer and upon the credit thereof. And in this he is fully borne out by the authorities. They go farther, and establish, that a transfer as security for past, and even for future responsibilities, will, for this purpose, be a sufficient, valid, and valuable consideration. Thus, in the case of Bosanquet v. Dudman, 1 Starkie, R. 1, it was held by Lord Ellenborough, that if a banker be under acceptances to an amount beyond the cash balance in his hands, every bill he holds of that customer's, bona fide, he is to be considered as holding for value; and it makes no difference, though he hold other collateral securities, more than sufficient to cover the excess of his acceptances. The same doctrine was affirmed by Lord Eldon in Ex parte Bloxham, 8 Ves. 531, as equally applicable to past and to future acceptances. The subsequent cases of Heywood v. Watson, 4 Bing R. 496, and Bramah v. Roberts, 1 Bing. New Ca. 469, and Percival v. Frampton, 2 Cromp. Mees. & Rose, 180, are to the same effect. They directly establish that a bona fide holder, taking a negotiable note in payment of or as security for a pre-existing debt, is a holder for a valuable consideration, entitled to protection against all the equities between the antecedent parties. And these are the latest decisions, which our researches have enabled us to ascertain to have been made in the English Courts upon this subject.

In the American Courts, so far as we have been able to trace the decisions, the same doctrine seems generally, but not universally to prevail. In Brush v. Scribner, 11 Conn. R. 388 the Supreme Court of Connecticut, after an elaborate review of the English and New York adjudications, held, upon general principles of commercial law, that a pre-existing debt was a valuable consideration, sufficient to convey a valid title to a bona fide holder against all the antecedent parties to a negotiable note. There is no reason to doubt, that the same rule has been adopted and constantly adhered to in Massachusetts; and certainly there is no trace to be found to the contrary. In truth, in the silence of any adjudications upon the subject in a case of such frequent and almost daily occurrence in the commercial states, it may fairly be presumed, that whatever constitutes a valid and valuable consideration, in other cases of contract, to support titles of the most solemn nature, is held a fortiori to be sufficient in cases of negotiable instruments, as indispensable to the security of holders, and the facility and safety of their circulation. Be this as it may, we entertain no doubt, that a bona fide holder, for a pre-existing debt, of a negotiable instrument, is not affected by any equities between the antecedent parties where he has received the same before it became due, without notice of any such equities. We are all, therefore, of opinion, that the question on this point, propounded by the Circuit Court for our consideration, ought to be answered in the negative; and we shall accordingly direct it so to be certified to the Circuit Court.

Mr. Justice Catron said:

Upon the point of difference between the judges below, I concur, that the extinguishment of a debt, and the giving a past consideration, such as the record presents, will protect the purchaser and assignee of a negotiable note from the infirmity affecting the instrument before it was negotiated. But I am unwilling to sanction the introduction into the opinion of this Court, a doctrine aside from the case made by the record, or argued by the counsel, assuming to maintain, that a negotiable note or bill pledged as collateral security for a previous debt, is taken by the creditor in the due course of trade; and that he stands on the foot of him who purchases in the market for money, or takes the instrument in extinguishment of a previous debt. State Courts of high authority on commercial questions have held otherwise; and that they will yield to a mere expression of opinion of this Court, or change their course of decision in conformity to the recent English cases referred to in the principal opinion, is improbable: whereas, if the question was permitted to rest until it fairly arose, the decision of it either way by this Court, probably, would, and I think ought to settle it. As such a result is not to be expected from the opinion in this cause, I am unwilling to embarrass myself with so much of it as treats of negotiable instruments taken as a pledge. I never heard this question spoken of as belonging to the case, until the principal opinion was presented last evening; and therefore I am not prepared to give any opinion, even was it called for by the record.

3. The Westward Transmission of Anglo-American Law

The thirteen original states at the close of the American Revolution each possessed a relatively settled legal system which was based on the combination of its English inheritance and its local tradition. Although the variations between the laws of the several states were considerable, those variations were from a common standard. That virtually no decisions of American courts had been published meant, of course, that the influence of one state's judge-made law upon that of another was almost non-existent. Yet the statutes of particular colonies and individual states had important influences elsewhere, and imitation of laws was nearly as striking a fact as conflict of laws.[1]

The preceding section of this Chapter has shown something of the problem of whether there was a national body of common law. This section is concerned with the contemporaneous problem of bringing law - both common and statutory - into the areas of American settlement beyond the borders of the original states.

In 1784 Jefferson submitted to the Continental Congress a plan for organizing government in the Western territory which had been and thereafter might be ceded to the United States. The plan proposed by Jefferson was never adopted, but a number of its elements were absorbed in the more elaborate and detailed provisions of the Northwest Ordinance of 1787. The Jeffersonian plan contemplated the creation of ten new states out of the territory between the Ohio and the Mississippi Rivers. With respect to the law which should be in force in such states before the establishment of their permanent constitutions and governments Jefferson's plan contained the following provision:

"That the settlers of any territory so purchased, and offered for sale, shall, either on their own petition, or on the

---

1. See, Riesenfeld, "Law-Making and Legislative Precedent in American Legal History", (1949) 33 Minn. L. Rev. 103.

order of Congress, receive authority from them with appointments of time and place for their free males of full ages, within the limits of their state to meet together for the purpose of establishing a temporary government, to adopt the constitution and laws of any one of the original states, so that such laws nevertheless shall be subject to alteration by their ordinary legislature: and to erect, subject to a like alteration, counties or townships for the election of members for their legislature." (26 Journals of the Continental Congress 275)

A provision, similar on its surface at least, was included in the Northwest Ordinance of July 13, 1787. That section defined the "legislative" power of the Governor and three judges during the first stage of territorial government, before the establishment of a territorial legislature. Its provisions follow:

"The governor and judges, or a majority of them, shall adopt and publish in the district such laws of the original states, criminal and civil, as may be necessary and best suited to the circumstances of the district,[2] and report them to Congress from time to time: which laws shall be in force in the district until the organization of the General Assembly therein, unless disapproved by Congress; but afterwards the Legislature shall have authority to alter them as they shall think fit." (2 Carter, Territorial Papers of the United States, 39, 42-43)

In another section of the Ordinance it was provided that in this first stage of government, there should be three judges "who shall have a common law jurisdiction". A supplemental article stated that "the inhabitants of the said territory shall always be entitled to the benefits ... of judicial proceedings according to the course of the common law". Later discussion of the issue whether the common law was to be considered as part of the basic law of the Northwest Territory and of the states subsequently carved out of that territory frequently turned upon the meaning and effect of these sections of the original ordinance.

During the first years of government in the Northwest Territory the Judges, over the largely ineffective opposition of Governor St. Clair, gave an expansive interpretation to their legislative powers. In considering legislation for the establishment of probate courts in 1788 the Governor expressed doubts which persistently bothered him. Writing to the judges

---

2. In an earlier form as drafted by a Congressional committee this clause read as follows: "That the judges shall agree on the criminal laws of some one state, in their opinion the most perfect ...." 1 Carter, id. 43, footnote 15.

he said, "I suspect we are overpassing the line of our duty in forming new laws in any case; and when we do the necessity of the case only can be our justification. The Ordinance of Congress empowers us to adopt and publish such laws of the original States, criminal and civil as may be necessary and best suited to the circumstances of the district. In departing from that rule, we certainly expose ourselves to censure from Congress, and besides there may be some doubt of the validity of such laws as we adopt and publish under any other; and it may not be unworthy your consideration whether, upon such an exception being taken before you in your judicial capacity, you would not be obliged to decide against the law and declare it a nullity."[3] Although the Governor thought it permissible for any particular provisions in the statutes of original states to be stricken from "adopted" statutes if those provisions did not seem suitable to the territory, he did not consider that he and the judges were empowered to "make a law (for here the word 'adopt' will not serve us) consisting of the different parts of laws of different states, and change the diction."[4] Judge Parsons and Varnum however felt differently: "The Ordinance of Congress empowers us to adopt such laws of the original States, civil and criminal, as may be necessary, and best suited to the circumstances of the district. Admitting a strict and literal construction should be given to this clause, the purposes of the Ordinance in general would be defeated. In the settlement of a new colony, and, indeed, we may add, of a new world a variety of prospects and objects arise, to which old countries must be strangers. Perhaps in their infancy their laws might have been suited to our situation, making allowance, however, for the progress of civil society; but the original States have revised their laws, and conformed their present codes to their present situation. Hence, it will be found that it would be out of our power to make the absolutely necessary regulations for protecting the persons and securing the property of the natives, and for preventing those unwarrantable intercourses, which might perpetuate their jealousies instead of conciliating their affections. ... We are sensible these observations rather tend to evince what the <u>powers should</u> have been than what they <u>are</u>. But we conclude they could not have escaped the notice of so wise a body of men as the framers of the Ordinance. If the clause in question admits of different constructions, we ought to adopt that which will best pro-

---

3. Letter of July 30, 1788; 2 <u>St. Clair Papers</u> (Smith, ed.) 67, 68.

4. Letter to Judges of August 7, 1788; <u>id</u>. 72, 75.

mote the purposes of the settlement. It was made *pro bono publico*, and therefore ought to be liberally expounded. We think it will admit of two constructions. One, that we can adopt entire laws of any of the old States *literatim et verbatim, mutatis et mutandis* for their State only. The other that we may admit such parts of any particular law as will be necessary, etc. If so, why will it not admit of another construction, that we may adopt a law, consisting of different parts of laws of any two or more States upon the same subject? And if this be granted, surely the diction ought to be rendered uniform. ... We presume, therefore, with great deference to your Excellency's opinion, that the following is the legal construction of the Ordinance: To adopt such laws as may be necessary and best suited to the circumstances of the district; provided, however, that such laws be not repugnant, but as conformable as may be to those of the original States, or of some one or more of them. This construction, it is true, admits the exercise of a legal discretion. But the exercise is checked by the tenure of our commissions, the necessity that the governor and two of the judges, or that all the judges,[5] must agree, and the final negative of Congress. If this construction be not admitted, we feel ourselves involved in difficulties that may prove insurmountable. For a time we must confine our legal operations to the principles of the Constitution, and the common law only. ...

"Were we to be confined for any length of time to the principles of the common law, we are fearful of very precarious consequences. The common law, as adopted in the States, while colonies, entered essentially into the principles of monarchical government, and therefore can not, with propriety, be applied here. But upon the present view of the subject, the common law must be applied, or the actions of men left to the direction of natural licentiousness. There are many cases of evident utility to which the common law doth not extend."[6]

In the quoted letter to Governor St. Clair, Judges Parsons and Varnum do not seem to have asserted that the legislative power extended to the enactment of original statutes, not based upon those of the original states. There is some reason to believe, however, that during the relatively brief time in which

---

5. There was considerable dispute between the Governor and the Judges as to whether the Ordinance required the Governor's concurrence in the legislation approved by all of the Judges for territorial adoption. See 1 *Transactions, Supreme Court of Michigan, 1805-1814* (Blume, ed.) xv-xvi.

6. 2 *St. Clair Papers* 69-71.

they held office, and during the first years of their successors' terms,[7] the Judges did in fact claim that authority and that the Governor, feeling that some statutory law was essential to order, concurred in its occasional exercise.[8] Until a close comparison between the statutes "adopted" during the term of Parsons's and Varnum's office and the statutes of the original states is made it will not be certain exactly how the legislative authority of the Governor and first Judges was exercised. Whatever research may ultimately establish to have been the fact in that matter, we do know that in 1795 the Judges then in office stated to St. Clair that they were willing to accept his theory that "the legislature ought to confine itself to the principle of adoption alone".[9] Thereafter all of the adopting legislation of the Governor and Judges specifically included in the enacting clause a designation of the state or states from which the provisions of the statute were drawn. It is noticeable, however, that individual statutes were modelled very frequently on the statutes of a number of different states. When this practice was later followed in the first stage of government in the Michigan Territory a critic of the Michigan judges described the process of adoption in the following way: "They parade the laws of the original states before them, on the table, and cull letters from the laws of Maryland, syllables from the laws of Virginia, words from the laws of New York, sentences from the laws of Pennsylvania, verses from the laws of Kentucky, and chapters from the laws of Connecticut - jumble the whole into such form as they conceive the most suitable to facilitate their scheme of peculation, and then call it a law, adopted from the laws of six of the original states...."[10]

The Ordinance of 1787, as we have seen, conferred upon the territorial judges, when acting in their judicial capacity "a common law jurisdiction". Although Judges Parsons and Varnum evidently considered that this provision, together with the clause of the Ordinance guaranteeing the territorial inhabitants the benefits of judicial proceedings "according to the course of the common law" served to extend the common law to

---

7. Parsons and Varnum died in 1789. The active Judges between 1790 and 1795 were John Cleves Symmes and George Turner.

8. See, 2 St. Clair Papers 356-57, 363-65, 450-53.

9. Id. 364.

10. 1 Transactions of the Supreme Court of Michigan, 1805-1814, xxiii.

the Northwest Territory, their successors in 1795 thought it advisable to take action which would more surely achieve this purpose. Accordingly, in that year the Virginia reception statute of 1776, by which the common law of England and the general acts of Parliament in aid of the common law prior to the fourth year of the reign of James I had been continued in force as Virginia law, was "adopted" by the Governor and Judges.[11] In later years doubts were frequently suggested as to the validity of this adoption. A technical basis for those doubts was the fact that when the act of adoption occurred in 1795 the Virginia statute had been repealed, having been superseded by a revised reception statute of 1792 which served to destroy the force, in Virginia, of the English statutes. Other less technical objections had, perhaps, more political vitality and legal validity. John Milton Goodenow, an early advocate of codification and energetic opponent of the common law expressed the political grounds for questioning the adoption of Virginia's reception statute, when he said, "This adoption by the governor and judges, was probably dictated by a kind of fashionable bigotry, peculiar to some men even of informed minds and classical erudition".[12] He denied validity to the act of adoption on more lawyer-like grounds when he said that the Northwest Ordinance required, as it specifically did, that the law adopted should be published in the Territory, and that the publication of the Virginia reception statute did not constitute an adequate publication of the innumerable rules of the common law incorporated in that statute by reference.[13] Salmon P. Chase, later Chief Justice of the United States, made the same objection when he said: "It was plainly the intention of congress ... that each law adopted should be published, that every citizen might know the extent and nature of his social obligations. Neither of these purposes could be answered by the adoption of the English law, written and unwritten, in the mass. Its adaptation to the circumstances of the district could not be ascertained, nor could the citizen be acquainted with its nature by publication."[14] Any significance which these objections to the reception statute of 1795 may originally have had, substantially disappeared as a prac-

---

11. Laws of the Northwest Territory, 1788-1800 (Pease, ed) 253.

12. Historical Sketches of the Principles and Maxims of American Jurisprudence (Steubenville, 1819) 384.

13. Id., 332.

14. I Statutes of Ohio, 1788-1833 (Chase, ed.) 190.

tical matter in 1799. In that year the first Territorial Legislature, which of course was not subject to the limitations by which the Governor and Judges had been restricted during the first grade of government, enacted a statute which by implication gave effect to the old Virginia reception statute of 1776.[15] When in 1800 and in 1805 the Territories of Indiana and Michigan were established, and began their governments upon the model of the Ordinance of 1787, it was assumed by the Governors and Judges in the two new territories that the Virginia act, adopted in the Northwest Territory in 1795 and recognized as effective by the Territorial legislature in 1799, was in force within their borders.[16] In Indiana the problem does not seem to have caused any special difficulties or stimulated any significant discussion.[17] The Governor and Judges in the Michigan Territory, however, were much troubled as to the confusion in the statutory law of that territory, which was made up of English statutes, acts adopted by the Governor and Judges in the Northwest Territory, statutes of the legislature of the Northwest Territory, Acts of Congress, perhaps the early legislation of the Indiana Territory and, in certain portions of the territory, an uncertain amount of French law. Accordingly, in 1810 the Governor and Judges of the Michigan Territory adopted a declaratory and repealing statute eliminating from the statutory law of the Territory all acts of Parliament, all French law, and all territorial legislation except that of Michigan itself.[18] It is noticeable, however, that the common law of England was not repudiated by this legislation.

In 1802 that portion of the old Northwest Territory which had survived as such after the establishment of the Indiana

---

15. Laws of the Northwest Territory, 1788-1800 (Pease, ed.) 353-54.

16. See 1 Transactions of Supreme Court of Michigan, 1805-1814, xxxviii. Though there was some uncertainty in the Michigan Territory, which had been carved out of the Indiana Territory, whether Indiana legislation of the years 1800-1805 was in effect in Michigan, it seems always to have been assumed that the statutes adopted and enacted in the Northwest Territory were in effect. Id., xxiv-xxvi.

17. See Laws of the Indiana Territory, 1801-1809 (Philbrick,ed.) c-cii. In 1807 the Indiand territorial legislature enacted a reception statute modelled upon the Virginia act of 1776. Id.,323.

18. I Laws of the Territory of Michigan, 900-902. See, 1 Transactions Supreme Court of Michigan, 1805-1814 xxxviii-xl.

Territory in 1800 became the State of Ohio. The first constitution of the state contained no more specific provision concerning the body of law which should continue in force than a section providing that "all laws, and parts of laws, now in force in this territory, not inconsistent with this constitution, shall continue and remain in full effect, until repealed by the legislature...". In 1805, however, the legislature enacted a reception statute identical to the Virginia act of 1776 and the territorial adopting statute of 1795.[19] In January, 1806, on grounds which still remain obscure, the Ohio legislature repealed its reception statute of the previous session, thus apparently eliminating from the law of the state not only all English statutes but the English common law as well.[20]

<u>Ohio</u> v. <u>Lafferty</u>
Court of Common Pleas, Ohio, 1817
Tappan's Reports 113

Lafferty was convicted, on three several indictments, for selling unwholesome provisions.

Wright, for the defendant, moved, in arrest of judgment, "for that there is no law of this state against selling unwholesome provisions." ...

President - The question raised on this motion, whether the common law is a rule of decision in this state? is one of very great interest and importance, and one upon which contradictory opinions have been holden both at the bar and upon the bench.

No just government ever did, nor probably ever can, exist, without an unwritten or common law. By the common law, is meant those maxims, principles, and forms of judicial proceeding, which have no written law to prescribe or warrant them, but which, founded on the laws of nature and the dictates of reason, have, by usage and custom, become interwoven with the written laws; and, by such incorporation, form a part of the municipal code of each state or nation, which has emerged from the loose and erratic habits of savage life, to civilization, order, and a government of law.

For the forms of process, indictment, and trial, we have no statute law directing us; and for almost the whole law of evidence, in criminal as well as in civil proceedings, we must

---

19. 1 <u>Statutes of Ohio</u> (Chase, ed.) 512. The act also specifically repealed the reception statute which the Governor and Judges of the Northwest Territory had adopted in 1795.

20. <u>Id</u>., 528.

look to the common law, for we have no other guide. Can it be said, then, that the common law is not in force, when, without its aid and sanction, justice cannot be administered; when even the written laws cannot be construed, explained, and enforced, without the common law, which furnishes the rules and principles of such construction?

We may go further and say, that not only is the common law necessarily in force here, but that its authority is superior to that of the written laws; for it not only furnishes the rules and principles by which the statute laws are construed, but it ascertains and determines the validity and authority of them. It is, therefore, that lord Hobart said, that a statute law against reason, as to make a man a judge in his own cause, was void.

As the laws of nature and reason are necessarily in force in every community of civilized men (because nature is the common parent, and reason the common guardian of man) so with communities as with individuals, the right of self-preservation is a right paramount to the institution of written law; and hence the maxim, the safety of the people is the supreme law, needs not the sanction of a constitution or statute to give it validity and force; but it cannot have validity and force, as law, unless the judicial tribunals have power to punish all such actions as directly tend to jeopardize that safety; unless, indeed, the judicial tribunals are the guardians of public morals and the conservators of the public peace and order. Whatever acts, then, are wicked and immoral in themselves, and directly tend to injure the community, are crimes against the community, which not only may but must be repressed and punished, or government and social order cannot be preserved. It is this salutary principle of the common law, which spreads its shield over society, to protect it from the incessant activity and novel inventions of the profligate and unprinciples, inventions which the most perfect legislation could not always see and guard against.

But although the common law, in all countries, has its foundation in reason and the laws of nature, and therefore is similar in its general principles, yet in its application it has been modified and adapted to various forms of government; as the different orders of architecture, having their foundation in utility and graceful proportion, rise in various forms of symmetry and beauty, in accordance with the taste and judgment of the builder. It is also a law of liberty; and hence we find, that when North America was colonized by emigrants who fled from the pressure of monarchy and priestcraft in the old world, to enjoy freedom in the new, they brought with them the common law of England (their mother country) claiming it as their birth-right and inheritance. In their charters from the crown they were careful to have it recognized as the foundation on which they were to erect their laws and governments: not more anxious was Aeneas to secure from the burning ruins of Troy his household gods, than were these first settlers of America to secure to themselves and their children the benefits of the common law of England. From thence, through every stage of the colonial governments, the common law was in force, so far as it was found necessary or useful. When the revolution commenced, and independent state governments were formed; in the midst of hostile collision with the mother country, when the passions of men were inflamed, and a deep and general abhorrence of the tyranny of the British government was felt; the sages and patriots who commenced that revolution, and founded those state governments, recognized in the common law a guardian of liberty and social order. The common law of England has thus always been the common law of the colonies and states of North America; not indeed in its full extent, supporting a monarchy, aristocracy, and hierarchy, but so far as it was applicable to our more free and happy habits of government.

Has society been formed and government instituted in Ohio, on different principles from the other states in this respect? The answer to this question will be found in our written laws.

The ordinance passed by the congress of the United States, on the 13th of July, 1787, "for the government of the territory of the United States North West of the river Ohio" is the earliest of our written laws. Possessing the North Western Territory in absolute sovereignty, the United States, by that instrument, provide for the temporary government of the people who may settle there; and, to use the language of that instrument, "for extending the fundamental principles of civil and religious liberty, which forms the basis whereon these republics, their laws and constitutions are erected; to fix and establish those principles as the basis of all laws, constitutions and governments, which forever hereafter shall be formed in the said territory; to provide also for the establishment of states and permanent government therein; and for their admission to a share in the federal councils, on an equal footing with the original states, at as early periods as may be consistent with the general interest," it was ordained and declared, "that the inhabitants of the said territory shall always be entitled to the benefits of the writ of habeas corpus, and of the trial by jury; of a proportionate representation of the people in the legislature, and of judicial proceedings according to the course of common law" - as one of the articles of compact between the original states, and the people and states in the said territory, to remain forever unalterable unless by common consent. Under this ordinance we purchased lands and made settlements, in this then N. Western Territory; we became voluntary parties to this contract, and made it, by our own act, what it was intended to be, "the basis of all our laws, constitutions and government" - and thus the common law became here, as it had become in the earliest colonies, the foundation of our whole system of jurisprudence.

That these articles of compact were of perpetual obligation upon the people and states to be formed in the territory, unless altered by the mutual consent of such states and of the original states, is a position which I have never heard controverted; yet it may not be useless to advert to express recognitions of it by both the contracting parties. First: the United States, by the act of congress entitled "an act to enable the people of the eastern division of the territory North West of the river Ohio, to form a constitution and state government, and for the admission of such state into the Union, on an equal footing with the original states, and for other purposes," under the authority of which Ohio became an independent state, authorised the people of said division to form a constitution and state government, "provided the same shall be republican, and not repugnant to the ordinance of the 13th of July, 1787, between the original states and the people and states of the territory North West of the river Ohio." Section 5th - Second: the people of Ohio by the preamble to their state consitution, declare, that they ordain and establish that constitution, "consistent with the constitution of the United States, the ordinances of congress of 1787, and the laws of congress."

The common law being a part of the existing system of jurisprudence at the time when the state government was formed, and its continuance being expressly provided for by the 4th section of the last article or schedule to this constitution, which declares that "all laws and parts of laws now in force in this territory, not inconsistent with this constitution, shall continue and remain in full effect until repealed by the legislature;" we will next examine the power of this court to enforce it.

The 1st section of the 3d article of the constitution declares, that "the judicial power of the state, both as to matters of law and equity, shall be vested in a supreme court, in courts of common pleas for each county", &c. The 2d section declares, that the supreme court "shall have original and appellate jurisdiction, both in common law and chancery, in such cases as shall be directed by law;" and the 3d section, that the "court of common pleas shall have common law and chancery jurisdiction in all such cases as shall be directed by law." These sections refer to future legislative provision to mark the boundaries of jurisdiction between the court of common pleas and the supreme court, and to fix their extent; but they do not refer to such provision, to point out the particular wrongs which may be redressed by petition in equity, by private suit, or by criminal prosecution. Such has been the uniform construction of these sections by the legislature, since the constitution was formed, as must be evident from the fact that no statute law has ever been made or projected, to detail those wrongs, private or public, which the judicial tribunals were to redress by virtue of their chancery powers, or "according to the course of the common law;" such a statute would indeed be a phenomenon, the result of a more perfect legislation than man has yet attained to.

But it has been urged, that the 4th section of the 3d article, is the only part of the constitution which gives this court jurisdiction in criminal cases, and that it expressly refers to future statutory provision, to point out the cases in which such jurisdiction may be exercised. The language of this section is: "The judges of the supreme court and courts of common pleas, shall have complete criminal jurisdiction, in such cases, and in such manner, as may be pointed out by law."

The laws in existence at the time when the constitution was formed, 29th Nov. 1802, and the state government commenced (beside those of the United States) where the common law, the statutes of other states adopted by the governor and judges of the territory, and the acts of the territorial legislatures; all which were continued in force by the constitution. This section of the constitution, by giving jurisdiction in matters of crime, "in such cases and in such manner as may be pointed out by law", must mean, in such cases and in such manner as may be now, or hereafter pointed out by law; for it must either intend to give the court jurisdiction according to the then existing laws, or to require of the legislature an immediate and perfect criminal code, and so operate as a repeal of the former; it could not intend the latter, because neither a convention or legislature can ever be construed to have exceeded their power, unless such intent is clearly and positively expressed; and so far is such intent from being expressed, by the section referred to, that the utmost latitude of construction leaves the intent that way ambiguous. It must intend the former; 1st. Because the convention who framed the constitution, were limited in their powers by the ordinance and law of congress; it had not power to deprive the people of Ohio of the benefit of judicial proceedings according to the course of the common law. 2d. Because the convention intended the constitution to be consistent with the ordinance and law. And 3d. Because the constitution expressly continues in force all existing laws.

Such seems ever to have been the opinion of the legislature of this state; for the first general assembly which sat under the constitution, passed an act to fix the extent of jurisdiction in the courts, and gave to the common pleas "cognizance of all crimes, offences and misdemeanors, the punishment whereof is not capital." 1st vol. stat. laws, 40. But neither the first or second general assembly deemed it necessary to make any material alteration in the criminal code they had received from the territorial government; nor had the state any other criminal laws, until the first of August, 1805. And when the state courts superceded the territorial, they were required "agreeable to their respective jurisdictions" to "take cognizance of all judgments, causes and matters whatsoever, whether civil or criminal, that are now pending, undetermined or unsatisfied" in the territorial courts; and they were "authorized and required to hear and decide upon the said matters." 1st vol. stat. laws, 50. In prosecutions at common law, then depending in the territorial courts, the state courts were thus directed to take cognizance, to hear and decide upon them, "according to the course of the common law."

But suppose that the position is a correct one, that the principles of the common law have no force or authority in this state, and what are the consequences? They are these: that there are no legal forms of process, of indictments, or trial; there is no law of evidence; and the statute laws cannot be enforced, but must remain inoperative from the uncertain signification of the terms used in defining criminal offences. Beside, the constitution gives jurisdiction to this court in criminal matters, "in such cases and in such manner as may be pointed out by law;" and as we have no statute pointing out the manner in which such jurisdiction shall be exercised, the consequence follows that it cannot be lawfully exercised in any manner whatever.

On the whole, therefore, it may be concluded, that were the written laws wholly silent on the subject, the principles and maxims of the common law must, of necessity, be the rule and guide of judicial decision, in criminal as well as in civil cases: to supply the defects of a necessarily imperfect legislation: and to prevent "the will of the judge, that law of tyrants" being substituted in the room of known and settled rules of law in the administration of justice.

And that by the ordinance of congress, the constitution and laws of the state, a common law jurisdiction in criminal cases is established and vested in this court. The motion in arrest is, therefore, overruled.

The defendant was fined 50 dollars in each case, with costs.

The decision in Ohio v. Lafferty impelled John Milton Goodenow, a somewhat stormy Ohio lawyer, to write his volume Historical Sketches of the Principles and Maxims of American Jurisprudence (1819). In that volume Goodenow had two objectives; first, to show that the English common law, as a whole, was not suited to American conditions, and, second, to establist that if it had ever been received in the Northwest Territory by legitimate processes (which he denied), it had been repudiated by the legislature of Ohio in 1806. More specifically, he attempted to show that the constitutional provision discussed by Judge Tappan in the Lafferty case abolished all common law crimes in Ohio. Although Goodenow's book had a very limited circulation outside of Ohio, there it seems to have had considerable influence in persuading the Supreme Court of the state that the Lafferty case should be repudiated. In 1828 Judge Burnet categorically stated that "the common law, in relation to the punishment of crimes and misdemeanors is not in force" in Ohio (Key v. Vattier, I Ohio 132, 144). By the end of the century this dictum had become well settled law, and credit for its adoption was given to Goodenow in Mitchell v. State, 42 Oh. St. 383, 386 (1884). Though Goodenow thus succeeded in persuading the judges that the whole of the criminal law of Ohio was to be found in the statutes of the State, his effort to persuade the bench and bar that the English common law in civil matters should be rejected was fruitless. In Carroll v. Olmsted, 16 Ohio 251, 259 (1847), the Supreme Court, in considering whether de donis was in force in Ohio, discussed the significance of the act of 1806 repealing the reception statute of the previous year. The effect of that repeal, said Judge Avery, "has not been to exclude the common law. That has always been in force, and it could not have been excluded without producing effects marked in character like those which follow in the train of a revolution. If that could have been actually excluded, we must from necessity, have been driven to adopt at once either the civil law, or some other code, to furnish a system of rules needed to act upon the countless and complicated interests of such a community as ours. No one can suppose, however, that there was ever a time when the common law of England was not in force here. It was indispensable to the action of our courts here."[1] The court then proceeded to find that de donis was not suited to the circumstances of Ohio and that an estate tail was therefore not to be recognized by the law of Ohio.

---

1. In Kerwhacker v. Railroad, 3 Oh. St. 172, 178 (1854) Bartley, J., suggests that between 1795 and 1806 that portion of the English common law which was suitable to Ohio had become the common law of Ohio, and that therefore the act of 1806 rejecting the English common law had virtually no effect.

Despite the legislative effort of 1806 to eliminate Englist statutes from the law of Ohio, it has been suggested that ancient English statutes which had become incorporated in the common law are still in force in Ohio. See, Birchard, C. J. in Crawford v. Chapman, 17 Ohio 449, 452-52 (1848). Cf. Lessee of Helfenstine v. Garrard, 7 Ohio 275 (1835).

CHAPTER FIVE

THE NINETEENTH CENTURY MOVEMENT FOR CODIFICATION

In considering the purposes which moved the American advocates of codification in the 19th century and in estimating the character of the proposals which were made, it should not be forgotten that, however intimately the cause which the reformers championed may have been related to contemporaneous American conditions, it was not new. As we have already seen, the same cause had enlisted the sympathy of Englishmen in the 17th century, and had borne fruit in the Massachusetts Bay Colony. Furthermore, the adoption of constitutions during and after the American Revolution may fairly be considered to have expressed a desire to have the unwritten traditions of public law given the relative precision of enacted law. The success of efforts to codify tradition in written constitutions quite naturally suggested to reformers the possibility of embodying the rules of private law in an enacted code.

The condition of American law in the first half of the 19th century doubtless gave special justification for its reform through codification. Yet it should be remembered that the movement for codification found its most articulate leader in the spirited person of Jeremy Bentham. His effusive, if not officious generosity led him to offer his codifying services to such dissimilar heads of state as James Madison and Alexander I, Emperor of all the Russians. Madison, apologizing for his five year delay in answering Bentham's letter of October, 1811, poured a little cold water on Bentham's enthusiasm, but expressed some interest in his proposal.[1] The Czar showed greater sympathy for Bentham's offer, and a somewhat more polished elegance of manners in his prompt reply, which was accompanied by a ring tendered to Bentham as a token of his particular esteem.[2] The ring, Bentham felt compelled to reject lest by accepting it the motive behind his offer to save the world from legal chaos by giving it refuge under his Pannomion might seem not to have been entirely disinterested. Though Bentham's appeal to the rulers was less effective than he had hoped that it might be, he did succeed in making his case known to their peoples, and thus in spreading the gospel of legal reform throughout the civilized world.

---

1. 4 Works of Bentham (Bowring, ed.) 467.

2. Id., 514-16.

In the United States the movement for codification from the first had the support of other than Benthamite radicals. One of its very earliest advocates, for instance, was Edmund Pendleton who, in 1777, sought to persuade Jefferson and the other revisors of Virginia's statutory law, that they should "abolish the whole existing system of laws, and prepare a new and complete Institute". This radicalism of the conservative was resisted by the conservatism of the radical. Jefferson opposed the suggestion, saying that "to abrogate our whole system would be a bold measure...; that to compose a new Institute like that of Justinian and Bracton, or that of Blackstone, which was the model proposed by Mr. Pendleton, would be an arduous undertaking, of vast research, of great consideration & judgment; and when reduced to a text every word of that text ... would become a subject of question and chicanery until settled by repeated adjudication; that this would involve us for ages in litigation, and render property uncertain until, like the statutes of old, every word had been tried, and settled by numerous decisions, and by new volumes of reports and commentaries...".[3]

Although Jefferson's argument prevailed with his associates, his Commission did bring about a reform of substantial value in persuading the legislature to enact such English statutes as were considered to be useful for Virginia in the form of Virginia statutes and to eliminate from Virginia's law all English statutes not thus adopted. Similar reforms were carried through, with varying success, in a number of states.[4] At the beginning of the 19th century, however, the demand for codification was pressed with renewed vitality. The movement, in differing forms and with varying justifications, continued throughout the whole of the 19th century. Though only occasionally meeting with the specific success which they sought, the advocates of codification nevertheless had an important influence on the growth of American law in the 19th century.

Trial of the Journeymen Cordwainers of the City of New York (1810)

[This case, published sub nom. People v. Melvin in Yates Select Cases 611, was the second important labor case to come

---

3. 1 Writings of Thomas Jefferson (Ford, ed.) 58-59.

4. See, e.g., Jones and Varick Revision (N. Y.), 1789; Kilty, A Report of English Statutes in Force in Maryland (1811); Report of the Judges (Pa., 1808), 3 Binney 595; Martin, Collection of Statutes in Force in North Carolina (1792).

before an American court. The first case, which is frequently referred to in Sampson's argument in the Melvin case, was the trial of the boot and shoemakers of Philadelphia in 1806 in which the members of a trade union were found guilty of a conspiracy to raise their wages. The pamphlet report of the trial is reprinted in 3 Documentary History of American Industrial Society (Commons, ed.) 59. The two cases are discussed in Nelles, "The First American Labor Case", 41 Yale L. J. 165 (1931) and in Morris, Government and Labor in Early America (1946) 162-63, 206-207. The only portion of the Melvin case here reprinted is the argument of William Sampson, one of the counsel representing the defendants./

Sampson opened the motion [to quash the indictment] as follows: - May it please this honourable court. The indictment we now move to have quashed contains nine distinct counts, each affecting to charge the defendants with a substantive crime of conspiracy; yet we maintain that, taken in the entire, it contains nothing to which we should be put to answer, either in law or fact. And we appeal to the discretionary power of the court, to save us from the hardship of pleading or demurring to facts, which, though proved, or admitted, could produce no legal result.

We understand, from the counsel for the prosecution, that they mean to support the indictment, without reference to any statute, but abstractedly upon the principles of the common law. On the other hand our positions are these:

That by the common law, in England, such combinations were never held to be conspiracies.

That even though they had been, they never were so in this country, either by statute or common law.

That in England such indictments lie only in virtue of the statutes regulating the wages and labour of the workmen, called Statutes of Labourers.

That such statutes were never in force in the United States of America, not when they were colonies, and certainly not since. ...

By too great familiarity with foreign law books, and too little attention to our own constitution and laws, we are often led into error, not considering how unsuitable these foreign laws may be to our condition. For instance: the English code and constitution are built upon the inequality of condition in the inhabitants. Here all are in one degree, that of citizens; and all equal in their rights. There are many laws in England which can only be executed upon those not favoured by fortune with certain privileges; some operating entirely against the poor. There one man is sovereign, and all others his subjects. Here no man is subject, and no man lord or master. Why should we, then, take lessons of prosperity or felicity from other countries. If they do not take them from us, let us at least remain contented with our own institutions, and wean out affections from such as are of no kin nor profit to us.

But how strangely are men the creatures of education and habit. At the same time that we have shaken off the supremacy of the English law, we imbibe its errors with our mother's milk. And the remarks of the profound and perspicacious Adam Smith, are realized here as in Great Britain. There, he observes, the master tradesmen are in permanent conspiracy against the workmen; so much so, that it passes unobserved as the natural course of things, which challenges no attention. Even so we see it here. These masters enter without fear into a sordid combination to oppress the journeymen; and if the workmen meet in opposition to them, they forthwith sound the alarm, and spread the cry of treason and conspiracy.

The difference, however, is, that in England there are statutes to warrant such prosecutions. Here there never were any such. There, there are precedents: here, there are none. But those precedents in England are not founded on the common law, but by statute, and in counteraction of it: and the proof is, that not one such case is to be found in any book of reports, treatise, abridgment or tables, till the passing of the statutes of labourers, which gave rise to them; and the first of which was in the reign of Edw. III. And I call upon my adversary, that great legal antiquarian, my learned countryman,[1] who lives amongst the old fathers of the law, who estranges himself from his friends, his wife, and lawfully begotten children to haunt with such musty companions. I call upon him who spends his mornings with Sir George Croke, and Sir Harbottle Grimstone and his evenings with the Mirror of Justice and Javaise of Tilbury, to tell me of any case of this nature prior to those statutes. If he cannot show when it was attempted, then it never was attempted. I challenge him now to do it, and I put the issue of this motion on the chance. ...

The substance of all the authorities in the English books, upon the head of transplanting the England law into new countries, is concisely stated in Peere Williams's Reports. There the master of the rolls is reported to have said, that the lords of the council had determined, upon appeal to the king and council from the plantations -

"1st. That if there be a new inhabited country found by English subjects, as the law is the birthright of every individual, so they carry their laws with them, and, therefore, such new found country is governed by the laws of England; though, after such country is inhabited by the English, acts of parliament made in England, without naming the foreign plan-

---

1. Thomas Addis Emmet.

tations, will not bind them; for which reason it has been determined, that the statutes of frauds and perjuries, requiring three witnesses to a devise of lands, does not bind Barbadoes.

"2dly. Where the king of England conquers a country it is a different consideration; for the conqueror, by saving the lives of the people conquered, gains a right and property in such people, in consequence of which he may impose upon them what he pleases." ...

A century ago, when the independence of this nation had never been imagined, when it was ruled as a colony by a despotic governor, two presbyterian clergymen were arrested by Lord Cornbury for preaching in an illegal conventicle. They were brought to trial, and the prosecution was founded upon the idea that the acts of conformity and uniformity were in force, and that the queen's church supremacy was to govern in the colony as in the mother country. The jury refused to find a special verdict at the desire of the prosecutor; but acquitted the defendants.[2] The matter was there dropped, and no such prosecution has ever since been attempted. But that which might have been before the revolution, _vexata questio_, is now surely past all doubt. Why was that prosecution then defeated? Because what was law in England was not then taken for law in the colony. Yet those statutes were law in England before the settling of this country; and the queen's supremacy was held part of the common law. But it required two things: first, that it was law in England; and, secondly, that it was useful or expedient to be adopted in the new country.

The more I reflect upon the advantages this nation has gained by independence, the more I regret that one thing should still be wanting to crown the noble arch - A NATIONAL CODE.

I lament that the authors of the revolution, wearied with toil and human waywardness, should, on the very threshold of perfect redemption, have failed, like the fabled poet of antiquity, by looking back, and suffered the object of their long and ardent cares to relapse again into the empire of Pluto; and themselves to sink at length breathless and spent under the burden of the common law.

Much, it is true, was done. A nation was rescued from colonial dependence; her citizens from prerogative, monopoly, and privilege; religion purged from intolerance; and a constitution was founded on the sacred rights of man. They might well exclaim, _sat patria_, who have done so much, and having done so much, perhaps, having thought it beneath their high achievements

---

2. See, "A Narrative of a New and Unusual American Imprisonment of Two Presbyterian Ministers" (1707), 4 Force, _Tracts_, No. 4.

to stay and strip the dead. They might think it wiser to trust to peaceful posterity and tranquil times to perfect their great work. Why, then, do not those who live beneath the shade which they have planted, generously answer to their intentions, and fulfill their great designs?[3]

I have said that there was no American precedent for this indictment, unless it were imported from Great Britain in this present year, and I hold in my hand a minute report of a similar case in Philadelphia, where the law was fully and ably discussed at the bar, and where it appeared, ex concessis, that no such precedent existed in America. The only opinion as yet to sanction it is that of a single judge, Mr. Levy, the recorder of Philadelphia. Before that becomes precedent and law, I shall, without personal disrespect, canvass, with due freedom, the doctrines he lays down to the jury as law. He first warns the jury against the arguments of counsel, as being but appeals to their passions, and then reminds them that such combinations will enhance the price of their own boots, touching, I think, himself upon a very sordid passion. Boots, he says, are arti-

---

3. Emmet, answering Sampson's argument, spoke as follows: "I shall briefly dismiss a considerable part of the argument offered on the other side; not for any deficiency of respect to the counsel from whom it has proceeded, or to the learning and research which he has displayed; but because I do not consider it entirely relevant to this cause, nor properly addressed to this court. To the legislature, or a convention, the observations we have heard upon the absurdities of the common law, and the impropriety of its being received as part of our legal code, might be correctly made if they were in truth well founded; but they appear to me extremely misplaced when offered to a court, the judges of which are bound and sworn to administer justice according to that common law, and who certainly have no authority to shake the foundations of the system under which they themselves are constituted. Lest, however, I should be thought by my silence to acquiesce in the justice of these observations, let me ask the learned counsel how he proposes to fill the void which would be created in our jurisprudence by the entire and indiscriminate abrogation of the common law? Has he digested a better code, and is he prepared to submit it to the world? If he has, I shall for one willingly take it into consideration; but most assuredly I shall not, without the most obvious and certain benefits, be induced to part with that to which our habits of thinking, reasoning, and acting are peculiarly formed, to which our institutions are all adapted, and upon the improvement of which and the application and the fitting of it to the constitution and wants of society, the wisdom, industry and talents of the ablest, most judicious and upright men have been laboriously, unceasingly and immemorially employed." p. 94-5.

cles of first necessity. I cannot there agree with him. When I think how many patriarchs have reached the blessed abode of their fathers, and never worn boots, how many serjeants have trod the thorny mazes of the common law, and worn no boots, and how many poor poets have bestrode the fiery courser of the muses and had no boots, I cannot think them things of such necessity. But equal justice is of first necessity, and when that is given for the sake of boots, boots are too dear. ...

The eulogium of the learned judge upon the common law is, to my judgment, something exaggerated, when he likens it to the divine system of providence.[4] "It is in the volume of the common law" he says, "that we are to seek for the far greater number, as well as the most important, of the cases that come before our tribunals. That valuable code has ascertained and distinguished with critical precision, and with a consistency that no fluctuating political body could or can attain, not only the civil rights of property, but the nature of all crimes from treason to trespass."

When such arguments are used to induce a conviction of a great portion of the American citizens, it is the duty of their advocate to speak out honestly. At the time when the common law had its origin, no part of which time could be since the beginning of the reign of Rich. I. called in law time of memory and that is about six or seven hundred years ago, no property existed under any of the modifications which now regulate it. There was no commerce, few arts, and little circulation; so that if we were to look into "that volume" alone, we should not find a rule to square with any transaction of our lives. If, therefore, it be like divine providence, divine providence has long abandoned us. And were we now to adopt the usages of those times, we should be like masqueraders upon the present stage of society. Touching shoemakers certainly we should find no laws, for lord and lady, knight and esquire, all went barefooted; and, possibly, whoever lived in the days of the Druids, might have counted the ten toes of her majesty the queen. Therefore, if we can find no usages touching the matter nearer at hand, it is useless to look for them so far. ...

The enemies of the common law, says the recorder of Philadelphia, when they attack the common law, single out some detached branch of it, and declare it absurd and unintelligible, without understanding it. If this be so, I think it is not the worst generalship; all enemies attack each other in the weakest

---

4. "In the profound system of law, (if we may compare small things with great) as in the profound systems of Providence, there is often great reason for an institution, though a superficial observer may not be able to discover it. Obedience alone is required in the present case...." Pamphlet Report of Trial, p. 147.

part of their lines. I do not profess to attack the common law, though I have no superstitious reverence for it, and think there are other systems as good. But since it is the common law which is set on to trample down my clients, I have resolved to take the bull by the horns. It is said that no man who does not understand the whole of it is fit to judge of any part of it. If that be so, I think it will have its privilege of clergy, for there lives not a judge upon earth who is entitled to cognisance of it. Lord Coke, who inked more paper with it, and bestowed more time and study upon it, than perhaps any other, exclaims, that ever with increase of knowledge cometh increase of doubt. He also says, that in its fictions consist all its equity. He that is to judge of it then must not increase his learning, for that would increase his doubts, and render him as it were, a Doctor Dubitantium. And he must addict himself to fiction to comprehend its equity. When he has done this he will have the qualifications that belong to knave and fool. ...

Why did our constitution repeal the English statutes, and declare that nothing of the common law, repugnant to that constitution, should remain, if antiquated barbarities were still to be revived and visited upon us; and if we are not to be allowed even to inquire whether they are attacks upon our rights or not? We should then be worse off than the English people are; for many of the old common law doctrines are abrogated by English statutes, but in which the colonies were never named, and with which the colonial legislators never meddled, not supposing them to have had force of law on this side the Atlantic. Our case would be singular on the earth. Our judges might then unlearn all they had studied of national or congenial institutions, to make themselves proficients in Mercian lage and Dane lage. They might study more majorum in hollow trees and caverns, till they forgot to read or write, and become Druids at common law. ...

Those who framed the constitution under which we live did not abolish all the common law, and they did right, because in that, as in other systems, there is always something to approve and use had sanctioned it. They did not pursue it through all its complex details, for that would have been endless and impossible: but they abolished all the English statutes, and by a general clause, abrogated all of the common law that should prove in contrariety with the constitution they established. In Philadelphia, the recorder says, you shall not even inquire whether the act in judgment is or is not an attack upon the rights of man.[5] But the constitution of this state is founded

5. In his charge to the jury, Recorder Levy had spoken as follows: "An attempt has been made to shew that the spirit of the

on the equal rights of men, and whatever is an attack upon those rights is contrary to the constitution. Whether it is or is not an attack upon the rights of man, is, therefore, more fitting to be inquired into, than whether or not it is conformable to the usages of Picts, Romans, Britons, Danes, Jutes, Angles, Saxons, Normans, or other barbarians, who lived in the night of human intelligence. - Away with all such notions.

Shall all others, except only the industrious mechanic, be allowed to meet and plot; merchants to determine their prices current, or settle the markets, politicians to electioneer, sportsmen for horseracing and games, ladies and gentlemen for balls, parties and bouquets; and yet these poor men be indicted for combining against starvation? I ask again, is this repugnant to the rights of man? If it be, is it not repugnant to our constitution? If it be repugnant to our constitution, is it law? And if it is not law, shall we be put to answer to it? ...

The liberty I take in protesting against this undiscriminating adoption of the common law, will appear less adventurous if it be considered, that a great portion of the British empire though governed by one monarch, and represented in one parliament, has not thought proper to adopt any part of it. The Scotch, less favoured than the English in soil and climate, and other physical advantages, yet, as moral beings, are surely not inferior, and out of their mountains and their moors come men able to assume and maintain stations in the intellectual world before unoccupied or unclaimed. If the common law were like the divine system how could this be? Would not those who were formed under its luminous auspices as far transcend all others as truth excels error? for laws and religion are the fountains of education, from which national character is derived. But the Scotch, when broken by unsuccessful rebellion, and the disastrous chances of war, were brought to surrender their independent monarchy, their philly-beg and kilt, but never would consent to the laws or religious establishments of England. If then, so important a portion of the British island can do so well without any part of the common law, can it be necessary for us superstitiously to adopt every part of it?

---

revolution and the principle of the common law, are opposite in this case. That the common law, if applied in this case, would operate an attack upon the rights of man. The enquiry upon that point, was unnecessary and improper. Nothing more was required than to ascertain what the law is. ... After that is discovered, whatever may be its spirit or tendency, it must be executed, and the most imperious duty demands our submission to it." Pamphlet report, p. 141.

The Irish had the common law forced on them. Their melancholy history is now well understood. And from the scintillations of exalted genius which emanate from the ruins of Ireland it may be imagined what a mass of excellence lies brutalized and benumbed by vitious institutions.

The Irish had an ancient code which they revered. It was called the law of the judges, or the Brehon law. What it was it is difficult to say; for with the other interesting monuments of that nation's antiquity, it was trodden under the hoof of the satyr that invaded her.

Sir William Blackstone in treating of the subjection of the Irish to the English laws, has had need of all his flexibility, and the authors he refers to are chiefly interested or official calumniators. After slightly touching upon the conquest and planting (by which planting is meant, settling new adventurers upon the tombs of the slaughtered) he says, the inhabitants are, for the most part, descended from the English, which is a mistake, for one half of them do not use the English language, even at this day. "King John" he says, "went over, carrying with him many able sages of the law, and there, by his letters patent, in right of dominion of conquest, ordained, that Ireland should be governed by the laws of England." King John was a vile king. He murdered his brother's first born, and made a footstool of his neck for the servant of a pope; and if we judge of his sages by himself, we can believe nothing good of them. It is curious, that the same author, in the same page, says, that the same laws which king John and his sages then ordained, had before been sworn to under Henry II at the council of Lismore; yet so much were they detested, that afterwards Henry III and Edward I were obliged to renew the injunction. "And" adds the author, "at length, in a parliament holden at Kilkenny, 40 Edw. III under Lionel, Duke of Clarence, then lord lieutenant of Ireland, the Brehon law was formally abolished, it being declared to be indeed no law, but a lewd custom, crept in of later times." What they meant by a lewd custom, crept in of later times, I know not; but the statutes of Kilkenny, which came after it, are, of all laws that ever were enacted, the most atrocious; and lewd, indeed, must the custom be, that was not ill exchanged for them.

No wonder that the "wild natives" even in the days of Elizabeth, still kept and preserved their Brehon law, of which its enemies are constrained to say, "that it was a rule of right, unwritten, but declared by tradition from one to another, (like the common law) in which, oftentimes, there appeared a great show of equity, though it was repugnant both to God's laws and man's."

What happened in Ireland must happen here, if we acknowledge ourselves subject to the common law of England. Whatever statutes have modified the common law in England to the exigencies of the times, not having force in this country, we should have the laws of the Tudors, and the Stewarts, unless we adopt something like Poyning's law, acknowledging our inferiority to the English, and making their laws our laws. The Irish, at one time, could make no laws in their parliament, that were not first certified under the great seal of England; so that the laws were made first, and the parliament held afterwards, to enact them. Is not this verifying the saying of Marquis Beccaria, that the judicial system of every country is two or three hundred years behind its progress in civilization. Are we bound to this by any, and what necessity? ...

If it be clear, from all these authorities, that such indictments are not conformable to our laws or constitution; that none such were ever known in England till the time of the statutes of labourers; and that none such were ever prosecuted to judgment in America, because there never were any such statutes then I shall conclude with the words of Judge Tucker, an author worthy of confidence, "that neither the law of England, nor that of any other country, can have any obligation in this state; and that no offence created by statute in England can, for that reason, be deemed an offence against the United States and that all statutory offences against the laws of England, are therefore only to be regarded as offences in that kingdom, and not as having any existence either in the state of Virginia, or in the United States." The same may surely be said of New York, where the whole body of the English statutes has been at once repealed, and where the statutes which created the offence here indicted, never were in force at any time.

I have only now to apologize to the court, for the unavoidable length of my argument, to return my thanks for its patient indulgence, and to commit my clients to its protection; leaving to my learned associate to complete the argument which I have left so imperfect.[6]

---

6. The motion to quash the indictment was denied. After trial of the merits the case was sent to the jury after it had received the instructions of DeWitt Clinton, Mayor, sitting as Justice of the Sessions. In the course of his charge, Mayor Clinton addressed the jury as follows: "Much has been said as to the application of the common law of England to the case. ... It was well know, that many of the ancient rules of the common law on this and other subjects had been exploded or become obsolete, and that little of the mass of absurdities complained of by defendant's counsel, remained in force even in England. In this state the court could not be at a loss in deciding how far the common law of England was applicable. Our immediate ancestors claimed it as their birthright. ... The constitution

Thomas S. Grimke - An Oration on the Practicability and Expediency of Reducing the Whole Body of the Law to the Simplicity and Order of a Code
Delivered to the South Carolina Bar Association
17 March 1827

Law, in the appropriate and comprehensive meaning of the term, includes, as essential ingredients, the ideas of simplicity and order. For, whether we contemplate the self-obedient agency of intelligent beings, or the involuntary action of material existence, order and simplicity are still involved in our conceptions of Law. If we lift our eyes to the heavens above, or look abroad over the surface of our globe; if we penetrate the hidden recesses of our earth, or the still more curious and wonderful depths of the ocean; simplicity and order appear in all, that we behold, whatever may be its magnitude, or minuteness. Although, to the gaze of ignorance, Creation is naught, but complexity and chaos; yet, to the eye of Science, the works of God are equally admirable for the simplicity of their elements, and the completeness of their system. The Barbarian, who beholds the wilderness of greater and lesser lights which crowd the firmament, never suspects that they are obedient to a government, perfect in wisdom and benevolence. The Savage, who traverses the forest, or stands in amazement on the shore of the mysterious ocean; or launches his frail bark on the river, or the lake, imagines not, that all are pervaded by the silent, secret influence of Laws, at once surprising for their simplicity and order. But Science has discovered, by the profound and unwearied studies of genius, that all the endless

---

of this state had also expressly adopted it, and declared, that such parts of the common law of England, and the statute law of England and Great Britain, and of the acts of the legislature of the colony of New York, as together did form the law of said colony on the 19th April, 1775, and not repugnant to the constitution, should be and continue the law of this state.... No alteration having been made by our constitution or laws, the common law of England, as it existed at the period last mentioned, must be deemed to be applicable, and by that law the principles already stated appeared to be well established. No precedents, it was true, of convictions or judgments upon them had been produced from our own courts, but no strong inference could be drawn from that, as until lately such precedents had not been preserved, and no printed reports of adjudged cases had been published." Trial, p. 166. The jury returned a verdict of guilty and the defendants were fined one dollar.

variety and seeming perplexity of Nature, are reducible to systems, equally simple and harmonious in their principles.

To the eye of the Poet and the Painter, the natural world appears invested with a sublimity, characterized by the awful and majestic; with a beauty, distinguished for delicacy or richness. But the harmonizing magic of Philosophy gives a new elevation to the sublime, and a fresh interest to the loveliness of Nature. All, that man can know of physical existence, above, around, beneath him, has been systematized. The birds of the air, and the tribes of insects; the beasts of the forest and the fishes of the sea, have been subjected to the luminous arrangements of Science. The flowers, which adorn our gardens; the herb and the grass of the plain, the valley and the hill; the fruit-tree, yielding fruit after its kind; and the forest-tree of every clime, have been classed by the master hand of Philosophy. The fountains of living waters, the brook and the river, the tides of the deep, the mineral kingdom, clouds and lightening, wind and rain; and all the phenomena of the earth, the ocean, and the air, have become obedient to the wand of the enchanter - Science. Nor have the heavenly bodies escaped the observation of man; for the labours of Copernicus and Kepler, of Newton, Herschel, and La Place, have demonstrated, that the Laws of their being are pre-eminent in simplicity and order.

Such is the natural world, in the eye of the Savage and the Sage; chaos to the one, because he is ignorant of principles - system to the other, because he has discovered them. The study of the natural world is obviously a result of the inborn curiosity, of the human mind; and of man's dependence on the objects around him, for the necessities and comforts, the conveniences, pleasures, and elegancies of life. But the moral world, so much more important to the best interests of man has been comparatively neglected. If the minuteness of research, the profound investigation, the variety of talent, and the inexhaustible stores of learning, which have been lavished on the natural world, had been dedicated to the improvement of man, in all the diversified relations of his moral being, we had now beheld him centuries in advance of his actual condition. Then, the code of international Law, political and civil rights; the structure and administration of government; political economy, in all its relations to finance, commerce, agriculture, manufactures, and the whole circle of arts and trades; religion, morals, and manners; in a word, all that concerns the public and private duties, the domestic and social happiness of man, would have been profoundly and comprehensively examined; would have been developed with the simplicity, beauty, and harmony of system. Then, the world had not been amused and imposed upon by the dreams of political Philosophy. The Atlantis of Plato, the Utopia of Moore, the Republic of the Sun, and the Oceana of Harrington had never appeared: nor had the Fundamental Constitutions of Locke and the speculations of the spirit of Laws called aside the attention of man, from the practical operation and matter of fact character of government, legislation, political economy, and the administration of justice.

Even in our day, though much has been done to educe order out of chaos in these and other particulars, how imperfect is the condition of the moral, in comparison of the natural sciences! But the day of neglect has passed away; for the practical science and philosophical common sense, now at work, in the civilized world, will never rest; till the moral relations of man, religious, political and civil, social and domestic, are brought to the test of principles, to the standard of experimental wisdom.[1] The Reformation shut for ever the dark book of despotism, in religion, politics, and science; and, in the fear of God and good will to man, opened, (we trust never to be closed) the volume of free, practical inquiry - This spirit is ruling the world. This spirit will remodel the world. The constitutional principles of English liberty are its noblest achievement, in the old world; the Revolution of '76, a still more glorious triumph in the new. "Its sound has gone out into all lands, and its words into the ends of the world." The essential character of this spirit is, that it never rests satisfied; till it reduces all things to the simplicity and order of system, and tries all things by the power and responsibility of principles. It indulges in speculation, only so far, as a knowledge of theory is indispensible, to the experimental nature of its means, and the practical character of its ends. Those ends are the education of mankind, as capable of self-government, of regulated freedom, of intellectual culture, of progressive improvement in their moral condition. All that belongs to art and science, to experiment and speculation, to rights and duties, have been called into the service of this master spirit of the age. We behold it every where, in our own delightful and happy land, meliorating the condition of the young, the poor, the ignorant; improving the present, and preparing still more abundant blessings, for the succeeding generation: and acting universally on the fundamental principle of true wisdom and benevolence; the children of yesterday are the men to-day - the children of to-day will be the men to-morrow. ...

All are deeply sensible of the exceedingly confused and imperfect state of our laws: and none can be more thoroughly convinced of these truths, than the Judges and the members of

---

1. Cf. Blackstone's conception of Law as Science and Mystery as described in Boorstin, _The Mysterious Science of Law_ (1941), Chapter I.

our profession. Hence has arisen the question, so much and so anxiously considered of late, "Is it practicable and expedient to reduce the whole body of our Law, to the simplicity and order of a code?" That it is expedient, will be denied by none. That it is practicable, has been doubted by many, perhaps by most, at the Bar and in the Legislature. If practicable, it is not only expedient, but a duty of the highest order - It is a duty which the rulers owe to the people, the people to themselves, and both to their posterity. It is an example, which is due to the sister States of our own Union: to our sister Republics of South-America: to our English ancestors: and to other civilized nations of Europe. It is a practical commentary on the great principle of the political creed of our day, that the welfare of the people is the chief end of government. The laws are made by the Delegates of the People: and can have no legitimate object, but to protect, improve, and bless that people. So far as they attain not this end, the Legislature and the Courts of Justice do not answer the purposes of their institution. ...

It is not uncommon for the champions of reform, in replying to the arguments drawn from the character and state of the Common Law, to pronounce that Law a chaos of absurdity and injustice; of antiquated rules, inapplicable to modern society, and even hostile to its progressive improvement. In a word, with them, the Common Law is, "*Monstrum horrendum, informe, ingens, cui lumen ademptum*."

But for myself, as one of the advocates of reformation, I do protest emphatically and anxiously against such views. So far from regarding the Common Law as a monster, whose extermination would be a glorious achievement of patriot chivalry, it is my admiration of the Common Law, and the singular excellence of its standard rules and maxims, which creates the strong desire, to see it redeemed from the bondage of a barbarous state of society, and accommodated to the enlightened, benevolent, practical spirit of our own times. That it ought to be done, I dare not question. That it can be done, I doubt not. That it will be done, I believe. ...

I now proceed to take a nearer and more practical view of the work to be done, and of the method of performing it. Let us exclude from the legal literature of England, all the elementary works, and especially the digests and abridgments, and let us then propose the duty of mastering and arranging the scattered, heterogeneous, and discordant materials of English law. Such an undertaking would, indeed, be Herculean, whether, as Legislators, we had to cleanse the Augean stable, or as Lawyers, to reduce this chaos into order. The former has never been done, the latter often. That could never have been advantageously undertaken, without this; for it cannot be denied, that our elementary books, when written with learning and talent, are eminently serviceable, not only to the Judge and the Lawyer, but to the wise and discreet Legislator. If this be true, with regard to particular portions of the Law, how much more just is the observation, when we contemplate a reform of the entire Law! Such a reform is comparatively easy in England, with the aid of all the best elementary treatises of her distinguished Jurists. In this State, it is incomparably easier, with the same assistance. Indeed, I shrink not from the declaration, that the work has already been executed in England, though very imperfectly and ineffectually; because it has been the fruit of professional research, not of legislative labour: and is designed for the Bench and the Bar, and not for the people. What, indeed, are Viner's abridgment and Comyn's Digest, but codes of English Law? without authority, it is true, like those of Gregory and Hermogenes; but still, like them, destined to render essential service to those, who shall engage in the compilation of a Theodosian or Justinian code of English Law. If such a work were undertaken, will it not be conceded, that, with very few exceptions, the principles and rules of the whole Common Law, now of force in Great Britain, may be found in Comyn, sufficiently clear, definite, and full, to form the basis of a code? My own deliberate judgment is in the affirmative, with regard to the Law of this State; though I venture not to pronounce a decisive opinion, as to English Law. If our Legislature were simply to declare, that no part of the Common Law should be considered of force, except it were contained in Comyn's Digest, I believe it might be safely asserted, that, in the Chief Baron's work, would be found all the principles and rules, which are and ought to be obligatory. Now, if the Legislature, after so determining our standard of the Common Law, were to raise a commission, merely to extract so much of the Common Law contained in Comyn, as is now of force in Carolina, would any well read lawyer of talent and experience, find it a very arduous task, to make such a selection? And would he not feel a strong assurance, that with, perhaps, a few rare exceptions, all that he should adopt or reject would be approved by a vast majority of the educated members of his profession? Again, if the Legislature, having appointed commissioners, were to require them to reduce the whole of our Law to the form of a Code, following Blackstone's plan, with all its divisions and subdivisions, so far as might be advisable and practicable, will not all admit, that such a code, faithfully and skilfully executed, would be a noble monument in the history of Carolina jurisprudence? And do we discover any remarkable difficulties in its accomplishment, other than such, as attend every great undertaking, complex in its scheme, multifarious in its parts, durable in its character, and extensive in its operations? It hath been said by an Englist writer, that whatever is worth doing, is worth doing well:

and a Poet of the Augustan age has written -

"__________ Nil sine magno
"Vita labore dedit mortalibus ___"

A work, such as that proposed, is worthy of the most cultivated judgment, the best talents, and the soundest learning, which adorn our State. Executed by them, it would exemplify the moral beauty of the English author's sentiment, and the philosophical justness of the Roman's. ...

Let us now examine some of those considerations of expediency, which recommend a code to our adoption, and which are sufficient, in my judgment, to justify the attempt. And here again, I must record my dissent from such arguments of my fellow-labourers in the cause of reformation, as presuppose two results - first, that the people at large will become better acquainted with the laws: and secondly, that litigation will disappear, to a very great extent. These are desirable effects but no code will ever accomplish them.

As to the first, if a code were printed and placed in the house of every man, how few would have either time or inclination to peruse the book! how few could understand or remember it! how few would know, where to find what they wanted, or how to apply it! Such a book would be too uninteresting to invite, much less engage the serious study of all, even of educated persons. The pious, among the poor and ignorant, would be contented with their Bible: and all others accustomed to read, would prefer the Novel and the Poem, Travels, Biography, and History, or even Political Economy, and the abstract Sciences. A few, and a very few men of peculiar habits, tastes, and views would be exceptions to these remarks, and would doubtless be devoted students of the new code. But the people at large would have neither time nor leisure, inclination nor improvement, sufficient for the task of perusing, understanding, and applying the code to the business of life. A scheme of laws for the regulation of the various and complex affairs of a changeable state of society, can never be reduced within the compass of the decalogue, neither is it susceptible of the plain, matter of fact, compendious simplicity of Christian morals.

Nor can I assent to the second supposed operation of a code, viz: to diminish in a great ratio, the number of law suits. Such, certainly, must be the effect, in some degree; for every Lawyer of talent and experience knows, that if the composition of any statute had been entrusted to him, he could have prevented, by a due consideration of the subject some at least of the questions, which have sprung from their language. No human foresight could have anticipated all: and doubtless no mortal skill can so construct every single clause of a general law, as to obviate all the doubts and difficulties, which may afterwards arise. Such is the testimony of experience;

although reasoning, a priori simply, may have led to a different conclusion. Let our laws be as particular, or as general; as concise, or as voluminous, as we please. Let them shrink into one little volume, like those of San Marino; or swell to twenty ample quartos, like the British statutes, and still cases and distinctions, without number, must crowd on each other, like wave on wave, in endless succession. Until it shall be possible for all men to think and speak, and write alike; to adopt the same unvarying forms of contracts; and to stand in the same relation to kindred, neighbours, and strangers; to debtors and creditors; to the great community of the public, and to the countless private associations of individuals: until society shall become as uniform and unchangeable, as the castes of Hindostan; as servile in the transmission of arts and trades, as the East-Indian; and as imitative, to the very letter, as the Chinese, we cannot expect to see the end of litigation. A multitude and a variety of suits, must ever spring up spontaneously and prodigally, in the soil of free institutions, free thoughts, and free actions: where rights are valued on principle, as the noblest property, and this is counted as worthless, except as the fruits of those.

Discarding then, such considerations as these, I proceed to state the reasons of expediency, which are to me, decisive recommendations of a code.

1. The first, which I shall mention, will assuredly meet the cordial approbation of all improved understandings. In every department of human affairs, and in every branch of human knowledge, it is considered, that a most important object has been accomplished, when method is substituted for confusion. A state of order, as contrasted with a state of chaos, is justly esteemed, whether we regard theory or practice, as a prize of inestimable value. In matters of little moment, regularity is held to be a merit; but in those of great magnitude, all acknowledge it, as a duty and a virtue. In all the concerns of man, whether they affect an individual or a family; the social circle or a society; the community of a village or city, of a district or State; it is a truth, equally attested by Philosophy and common sense, that the introduction of order improves, far beyond any previous estimate, the condition of mankind, in happiness, usefulness, and virtue. Relying on such evidences, we might securely challenge even a disciple of Pyrrho, to deny that a code must be eminently a public blessing.

2. My second argument is drawn from a consideration, somewhat similar. The value of principles, as compared with a heterogeneous mass of facts and details, of unconnected rules and observations, will be questioned by no one. In this state of things, principles are shorn of their light, and stripped of a large portion of their power. But when they assume the

organized forms of a system, they exercise a legitimate influence, at once salutary, commanding, and permanent. Our laws, in their present condition, may be called the grave, rather than the cradle of principles.

3. My third reflection, is, that a code will have the happiest effect in several important particulars on legislation itself.

(1) And first - the existence of a code will be the most efficient barrier against careless and hasty, superfluous or merely convenient legislation. At present, if we judge from matter of fact, it is considered of very little consequence, how much and how often the Law is altered. Little or no respect is felt for the Law, in its actual condition; and the opinion seems practically to be, that, as it is a chaos, the accumulations of every session will make no difference, in its essential character and value. But give us a code, and the justice or expediency of a new Law, additional to, or amendatory of, that code, must be clear beyond question, before the Legislature will agree to its adoption. Let that code be the result of time and mature deliberation; the harvest gathered by talents and learning, in the fields of wisdom and experience. Let it have been for some time, before the People and the Legislature, the Bench and the Bar, ere it shall have been consecrated by popular affection, and ordained by public authority, as the standard of civil jurisprudence. In such case, we may predict, that legislation will no longer be precipitate and thoughtless, superfluous or merely convenient. Something of sanctity, which has invested the Constitution, and has protected it, I may almost say, from annual innovation, will then become the property of the code.

(2) The second advantage is, that, after the establishment of a system, Legislation will be conducted on principles, and with a direct reference to an existing body of laws, in their state of clear and simple arrangement. At present, Legislation is and can be nothing but patchwork: and the Law, while the existing order of things endures, must continue to be a fit parallel for the cabinet of Chatham, delineated by Burke, with so much felicity and pleasantry. There is no division or even subdivision of our Law, which does not admit of many, and does not require, at least some considerable improvements. Is there an act of any importance, whether ancient or modern, which may not be amended? Unless the whole body of our Law shall assume the form of a code, it is obvious, that Legislation will consist, for an indefinite period, of additions and amendments. Is it not a reflection upon our sense of justice and duty - and upon our estimate of the value of wise and stable laws, that we should submit to such a necessity for perpetual alterations? Hitherto, our acts having been suggested by particular circumstances or cases, are generally

limited to them. But, under the influence of a code, cases and circumstances would be regarded only as guides to principles; and Legislation would consist, almost if not altogether, in expanding or recasting the principles of a known, fixed system.

(3) The third effect on the Legislative department relates to the forms of laws; the space, which they would occupy; the facility of reference; and the complete separation of public and private acts. The clearness and simplicity of a code require the divisions and subdivisions of books, titles, chapters, sections, and numbers. Our acts would thereafter assume an analogous character, and nothing would be easier than to connect them with the code itself, by the proper use of similar designations. It is well known, that the titles and preambles of our acts, the awkward and circuitous mode of referring to former statutes, the mass of superfluous words, the endless repetition of the same things(witness the appropriation, tax and incorporation bills) require at least twice as many pages, every year, as are necessary. Add to these considerations, that subjects totally different, are frequently mixed together; while public and private acts are confounded, instead of being kept as much apart, as the acts and resolutions. It will be likewise a great improvement, that, instead of a table of contents, classed only by pages, we should have a proper index, referring to each separate topic, under the numerical arrangement of the code system, and fashioned after the plan of the index to the code. It would be an obvious advantage of the new system, in connexion with the same department, that our Legislature could then act understandingly, as to the existing Law. But now, it is often next to impossible, on account of the actual condition of our laws, to ascertain what the Law is; what statutes are of force; how far they are contradicted, modified, or explained by subsequent acts; and what will be the effect of amendatory or additional clauses.

4. A fourth recommendation of a code is, that it must exercise a happy influence on the character and usefulness of the Law. The former will be elevated and dignified; because the Law will then exhibit the elements, forms, and arrangements of science. The latter will be extended and strengthened; for the law will then be more easy of comprehension, more consistent in itself, and more in accordance with common sense and natural justice. We all know, how much the respectability of the Law has been impaired by the received opinions, as to its confused and uncertain state, as to the difficulty of determining exactly what the Law is, and as to its vain repetitions, awkward circumlocutions, uncouth phraseology, and obsolete provisions. No one will deny, that the Law has been exposed to much odium, contempt, and ridicule, from the causes just enumerated: nor do I believe that any intelligent man, who comprehends the causes, will question but that a code must exercise

a salutary influence in moderating their effects, though it may not altogether remove them. Assuredly, I need not say, that such results will be accounted eminent blessings.

5. I cannot but mention, as a fifth argument, in favour of a code, a consequence flowing from the preceding remarks. If the Law itself shall become more respectable, in the opinion of the community at large, it seems a very fair conclusion, that the Legislator and the Judge, as well as the Professors of the Law, will rise, in a correspondent ratio, in public estimation. Let Philosophy be again degraded by the Logic and Metaphysics of the schools, and it must again be contemptible and ridiculous. Whatever, then, can have a decisive and permanent effect on the standing of the Legislature, the Bench, and the Bar, must be regarded as invaluable, especially in a free country, where a constant action and reaction exist between those institutions and the people. It is impossible to deny, if we judge correctly of human nature, that the estimation, in which an employment is held, has, generally speaking, a decisive influence over the standing of those, who occupy that station. We may admire the sentiment of Epaminondas; but must we not acknowledge, that few have the strength of mind and the good fortune, to win the prize of true honour? We behold the same principles remarkably illustrated in the judgment of Pepin, who felt the absolute necessity of redeeming himself, by some gallant deed, from that secret contempt, which he knew would otherwise be his destiny, on account of his diminutive stature. - Human nature, in this view of it, has been ever the same - Let us, therefore, dignify the Law, and we shall dignify the Legislature, the Bench, and the Bar.

6. Connected with the preceding, so far as the Judge, and the Profession are concerned, I may here advert to a sixth reason, in favour of a code: viz. the control, which Science invariably exercises over those, who are engaged in a pursuit, to which it applies. Is there any man, who beholds with more delight and approbation, than the members of the Bench and Bar, the admirable results, which are flowing from the application of the principles of science, to the various arts and trades, under the influence of mechanic institutions, in Europe and America? And shall not the very men, who rejoice so much, at the accelerated march of mind, in other departments of business, challenge also for themselves, similar improvements, from the correspondent operation of similar causes? Shall we rest satisfied, in a state of comparative chaos, when we behold the creative power or order and principles, scattering abroad light and beauty and harmony over the works of man, in the moral and physical world?

7. A seventh argument in favour of a code, may, with propriety, have preceded the sixth, when we reflect, that the succession on the Bench and at the Bar, can only be preserved

by those, who shall, at a future day, share the dignity of the one, and the reputation of the other. They are now the boys in our schools, the youths in our colleges, and the young men in our offices. We may expect at no distant period, the establishment of a Professorship of Law, in the South Carolina College, and the institution of Lectures, in emulation of those so honorable to Reeves and Gould, to Kent and Dorsey. Assuredly, I need not pause a moment to point out to my superiors of the Bench, and to my brethren of the Bar, the eminent advantages of a code, not only to the professor and lecturer, but to the private instructor. Who is insensible to the superior advantages enjoyed by the students of the Civil Law, over those of the Common Law! Who will deny, that system and principles, no less than the ornaments of style, have distinguished pre-eminently the professors of the Civil, from those of the Common Law? The illustrious exceptions of Mansfield and Hardwicke, of Blackstone and Jones, are to be ascribed, rather to Justinian, and his master commentators, than to Bracton, Lyttleton, and Coke.

8. The last reason, to be now assigned in favour of a code, is found in a fact, which is becoming every day more obvious and more important. Let us look abroad through our land, and see how vast an influence, educated men are every where exercising, under every possible variety of form and circumstance, over life, liberty, and property: over character and education over public and private improvement and happiness. This is preeminently true, as to education and politics. And must not the same influence exist in relation to Law, so far as it gives form and being to the social business of life? Let us consider the various capacities, in which intelligent men are continually serving, and it must be cheerfully conceded, that they would find in a code, the best preparative for their duties. I speak not now of Judges and Lawyers, but of other educated men in our community. Such persons are constantly acting as jurymen, arbitrators, and commissioners; as legislators and public officers; as guardians, executors, administrators and agents. They are continually appealed to, by friends and neighbours, and even by strangers: and, in numerous instances, advise and prepare their contracts and their wills. Law, indeed, it is obvious, pervades in its operations, all society. There is no circle, however small, which is exempt from its influence: none however extended, which does not acknowledge its power. - Hence it is the only science and the only art, of which it is the interest and duty of every man, as far as his education and opportunities permit, to know, at least, the elements. To know them, is to enable him, with comparative ease and success, to discharge the various duties, above mentioned. I have already said, that the people at large will not have time, patience, or opportunity, for the study of the code: and beyond question,

the aera never can arrive, when every man will be his own Lawyer; until society can subsist with a mere decalogue of civil jurisprudence. But very many of the educated men of our State (and the number must increase and never can diminish) will find it their duty, their interest, and their pleasure, to bestow much time on the study of the code. Its influence on their capacity, and fitness for public and private usefulness, needs neither comment nor illustration. ...

Frederick Robinson - on Reform of Law and the Judiciary
in an oration delivered before the Trades' Union of
Boston and Vicinity, July 4, 1834
Blau, Social Theories of Jacksonian Democracy
(1947), p. 320, 327

In the savage state each individual produces for himself whatever he consumes, and of course no union with others is required to protect his labor. But in a state of society where no one labors for his own consumption alone, but each receives the labor of others in exchange for his own, the price of labor in each division of labor, to prevent fraud, ought to be fixed by agreement among the laborers themselves. The right of the producer to fix the price of his own labor is unquestionable; for its denial admits the right of slavery. But every effort which the producing classes have ever made for the enjoyment of this most obvious right has always met with the most determined opposition of the aristocracy. Wherever they have held all political power, laws have been enacted inflicting fines, imprisonment, and transportation on those that attempt by unions among themselves to fix the price of their labor. Where they have not all political power, they have recourse to everything within their reach, to every argument, to every quibble, every sophistry in order to flatter the people to relinquish, or drive them to renounce this right. Those that have not the unblushing confidence to deny this right altogether contend that it is an individual and not a social right. For although each individual may fix the price of his own labor, yet no two or more individuals have a right to agree among themselves to fix the price. But when men enter into a state of society all those rights which it is impossible to enjoy without the aid of others become social rights and must be enjoyed, if at all, by concert with others. It is unreasonable to suppose that we are possessed of rights which we have not the power to enjoy. But if we have not the social right to fix the price of our own labor, it is perfectly useless to allow us the right at all. For how can an unaided individual without wealth, without education, ignorant of the world, and even of the value of his own labor, who must command immediate employment or starve, enjoy this right as an individual right? If he enjoys it at all, the interests of others engaged in the same or other employments must secure it to him. No law has ever been enacted in this country in relation to this subject. But the aristocracy have notwithstanding attempted to frighten the people with the semblance of law. The judiciary in this State, and in every State where judges hold their office during life, is the headquarters of the aristocracy. And every plan to humble and subdue the people originates there. One of the most enormous usurpations of the judiciary is the claim and possession of common law jurisdiction. Common law, although contained in ten thousand different books, is said to be unwritten law, deposited only in the head of the judge, so that whatever he says is common law, must be common law, and it is impossible to know, before the judge decides, what the law is. But still in order to justify the judge in all iniquitous decisions, they have recourse to precedents, or previous decisions. And however unjust and wicked any decision may be, if a previous decision of the same kind can be found, either in ancient or modern times, in Great Britain or in any of the States in this Union, the judge justifies himself before the public and escapes with impunity.

Now, common law is said to consist of all the precedents or practices of the courts of Great Britain and of all acts of Parliament up to the time of the formation of our government. Previously to the Revolution, acts of Parliament had been passed to prevent unions of the people to fix the price of labor. Although these laws have since been repealed in Great Britain, and since the year 1824 there has been no law in England in relation to this subject,[1] the aristocracy contend that these laws, which we have never enacted, have not been repealed by our legislature, although the power that made them has since destroyed them, are, notwithstanding, in full force among us. We ought not therefore to be surprised if we soon hear of indictments on these old and repealed English laws, if juries can be found ignorant and servile enough to follow the dictation of lawyers and judges. Indeed attempts have already been made for this purpose. One of the judges in this city, not long since, charged the grand jury to indict the working men who attempt by unions to fix the price or regulate the hours of labor; although this judge, and indeed all the judges, are members of a secret trades union of lawyers, called the bar, that has always regulated the price of their own labor and by the strictest concert contrived to limit competition by denying to everyone the right of working in their trade, who will not in every respect comply with the rules of the bar.

---

1. This is something of an oversimplification. Cf. Dicey, <u>Law and Public Opinion in England during the Nineteenth Century</u> (1905) 190-200.

All prices fixed by bar rules are in the minimum, allowing no one to take less than a fixed sum for each service; but everyone may take as much more as he can. What then ought we to think of the man who, being a member of the secret trades union of the bar, calls upon the jury to indict the members of the open Trades Union of the people, who join not for the purpose of injuring others, but for the enjoyment of their most inestimable right, to be deprived of which must always keep them in want, ignorance, and slavery? Does it not become us, fellow citizens, when we see the enemies of the equal rights of man everywhere combined to maintain their ascendency, to unite and employ our power of numbers against the power of their wealth and learning, for the recovery and protection of our rights?

Who are they who complain of trades unions? Are they not those whose combinations cover the land and who have even contrived to invest some of their combinations with the sanctity of law? Are they not those who are the owners of all kinds of monopolies, who pass their lives in perpetual caucuses, on 'change, in halls connected with banks, composing insurance companies, manufacturing companies, turnpike, bridge, canal, railroad, and all other legalized combinations? Do not each of the learned professions constitute unions among themselves to control their own business? And have they not fortified their unions by alliance with each other and with the rich, and thus established a proud, haughty, overbearing, fourfold aristocracy in our country? Well may the capitalists, monopolists, judges, lawyers, doctors, and priests complain of trades unions. They know that the secret of their own power and wealth consists in the strictest concert of action; and they know that when the great mass of the people become equally wise with themselves and unite their power of numbers for the possession and enjoyment of equal rights, they will be shorn of their consequence, be humbled of their pride, and brought to personal labor for their own subsistence. They know from experience that unions among themselves have always enabled the few to rule and ride the people; and that, when the people shall discover the secret of their power and learn to use it for their own good, the scepter will fall from their hands and they themselves will become merged in the great "vulgar" mass of the people.

The judge knows this. He knows that he is a member of a combination of lawyers, better organized, and more strict and tyrannical in the enforcement of their rules than even masonry itself. He knows that when the dispositions in the community to investigate and destroy secret societies turns itself upon the bar, abuses will be discovered so enormous as completely to eclipse those of every other combination. We shall then discover that we have been "fishing for minnows and let slip the leviathan." We shall discover that by means of this regularly organized combination of lawyers throughout the land the whole government of the nation has always been in their hands, that the laws have always been molded to suit their purposes, and what are called Courts of Justice are only engines to promote their interests and secure their ascendency in the community. The judges know that this combination has enabled them to usurp one entire branch of our government and to turn all the rest of the citizens out of doors. For who dares to go into our public courts and attend to his own concerns or to perform the business of his neighbor? We all know that this preposterous state of things could only have been brought about by union among lawyers and by their combination to involve the laws and the practice of the law in inexplicable obscurity and formality, by the adoption of all the cumbrous learning of British courts.

It is for the interest of this trades union of lawyers to have the laws as unintelligible as possible, since no one would pay them for advice concerning laws which he himself could understand. Can we believe that our laws would be the dark chaos they now are if our legislators had been disinterested men, of only common education and good understanding? Instead of living under British laws after we had thrown off the government which produced those laws, we should have adopted republican laws, enacted in codes, written with the greatest simplicity and conciseness, alphabetically arranged in a single book, so that every one could read and understand them for himself. "Ignorance of the law" it is said, "excuseth no man." Can we then who call ourselves freemen, any longer live under laws which it is impossible to understand? Without a knowledge of the laws under which we live, are we not deceiving ourselves if we suppose ourselves to be freemen? The people of Rome in the most corrupt ages justly considered it the most intolerable tyranny when one of their despots had the laws written in a small hand and posted up so high that the people could not conveniently read them. But shall we, who claim to be free and equal, voluntarily continue in a state of almost total ignorance, with laws so multiplied, so obscure, and so contradictory, as to render the general knowledge of them impossible?

But we can easily conceive how this state of things is perpetuated, by means of the quarterly meetings of bar unions in every county throughout the nation. After having consulted together on the best way of fortifying themselves in their illegal and unconstitutional monopoly, they very naturally enter into social conversations and agreements as to what individuals among them would be most likely to succeed in any election for the principal officers of the government; for President, members of Congress, governors, and state legislators. Having agreed on what course to be pursued, they dissolve and distribute themselves in the different cities, towns, and villages, throughout the nation. Each performs his individual part; and, by acting in concert, by secret confidential communications, by speaking publicly and privately in favor of their candidates, they have generally succeeded in electing the men predestined to office by the bar. Having in this way succeeded in electing the appointing officers, where will the appointments be most likely to fall? In what way besides this can we account for the fact that almost every office of honor and profit remains in the hands of members of the bar? But the evil of the secret trades union of the bar does not stop here. When the legislature assembles, every senator and every representative of the bar is prepared. They are all acquainted with each other; they feel that it is for their interest to act in concert. United efforts are always made by this fraternity to choose the president of the Senate and the speaker of the House of Representatives from the bar. This effected, the whole business of legislation is completely in their hands. The president of the Senate and the speaker of the House have the appointing of all committees, and, being lawyers, they are always careful to put a majority of their brethren on every committee which has anything to do with the laws; and in this way laws are drafted, introduced, and talked through the legislature by members of the bar. While the people submit to these abuses, it is easy to account for the continued existence of the dark and intricate labyrinth of our laws.[2]

Of all the reforms which we have pledged ourselves to accomplish the reform of the judiciary and of the laws is the most important. Let us then go about the work with never ceasing efforts, until the great mass of our fellow laborers, who always constitute an overwhelming majority, shall see the necessity of a thorough law reform. In the first place judges should be made responsible to the people by periodical elections. The boast of an independent judiciary is always made to deceive you. We want no part of our government independent of the people. Those who are responsible to nobody ought to be entrusted

---

2. Until 1836 the rules of the Suffolk County Bar fixed minimum fees which its members might charge and forbade those members "to advise or consult, or be in any manner associated" with any non-member in the profession who should not have subscribed to its rules. In 1836, evidently fearing that the association of lawyers might be considered an illegal or criminal conspiracy, it was voluntarily dissolved and a new organization more loosely constituted was formed. See, Nelles, "Commonwealth v. Hunt", (1932), 32 Columbia L. Rev. 1128, 1138. For the scale of fees of the Suffolk Bar, see 4 Law Reporter 283 (1841).

by nobody. But to whom are the judges responsible? The aristocracy always center around power placed beyond the reach of the people; and until we can fill the bench with men of learning, good sense, and sound judgment who do not belong to the secret fraternity of the bar, all attempts to simplify the laws and the practice of the law will be in vain. For why need we attempt to legislate, while the judges hold legislative power and can nullify our laws at their pleasure?

Joseph Story - "Law, Legislation, Codes"
Appendix to VII Encyclopedia Americana
(Lieber editor, new edition, 1835), p. 476, 589

...The question is often discussed in our day, how far it is practicable to give a complete system of positive law, or a complete code of direct legislation. And, if practicable, the farther question arises, how far it is desirable, or founded in sound policy. These questions have been the subject of ardent controversy among the civilians and jurists of the continent of Europe, living under the civil law; and, as may well be supposed, different sides have been taken by men of distinguished ability and learning; and the controversy is, and probably for a long period will be, pursued with great animation and powers of reasoning. In the countries governed by the common law, and especially in England and the United States, the same questions have of late been matter of wide discussion among the legal profession, as well as among statesmen, and a great diversity of opinion has been exhibited on the subject. It will be our object, in the sequel of these remarks, to put the reader in possession of some of the main grounds of the controversy.

The legislation of no country, probably, ever gave origin to its whole body of laws. In the very formation of society, the principles of natural justice, and the obligations of good faith, must have been recognised before any common legislature was acknowledged. Debts were contracted, obligations created, property, especially personal property, acquired, and lands cultivated, before any positive rules were fixed, as to the rights of possession and enjoyment growing out of them. The first rudiments of jurisprudence resulted from general consent or acquiescence; and when legislation began to act upon it, it was rather to confirm, alter, or add to, than to supersede, the primitive principles adopted into it. We, in fact, know of no nation, or, at least, of no civilized nation, whose history has reached us, in which a positive system of laws for the exigencies of the whole society was coeval with its origin; and it would be astonishing if such a nation could be found. Nations, in their origin, are usually barbarous or rude in their habits, customs and occupations. They are scanty in population and resources, and have neither the leisure, nor the inclination, nor the knowledge, to provide systems for future use, suited to the growing wants of society, or to their own future advancement in the arts. A few positive rules suffice, for the present, to govern them in their most pressing concerns, and the rest are left to be disposed of according to the habits and manners of the people. Habits soon become customs; customs soon become rules; and rules soon fasten themselves as firmly upon the existing institutions, as if they were positive ordinances. Wherever we trace positive laws, in the early stages of society, they are few, and not of any wide extent; directions for special concerns, rather than comprehensive regulations for the universal adjustment of rights. No man can pretend that, in Asia, any such universal rules were established by positive legislation, at the origin of the great nations by which it is peopled. The instructions of Moses, as promulgated by divine authority, for the government of the Jews, are not (as every one perceives) designed for every possible exigency of contract, or right, or injury, or duty, arising in the course of the business and history of that wonderful people. They are rather positive precepts, adapted to great occasions, and to govern those concerns which respected their wants, their spiritual advancement, and their duties as the chosen people of God. The Greeks are not known to us, in their early or later history, as having had a code of universal extent. The Romans, in their early history, had few positive laws; and those seem to have been borrowed from other sources. We often, indeed, see it stated, that the common law of England was originally formed from statutes now obsolete and unknown. But this assertion is wholly gratuitous. There is no reason to suppose that, in the early history of its jurisprudence, more was done than is usual in other nations, at the same period of their progress, such as the promulgating of some leading regulations, or the forming of some great institutions for the security of the public. In fact, a great portion of the English common law is of modern growth, and can be traced distinctly to sources independent of legislation. The commercial law of England is not two centuries old, and scarcely owes any thing important to positive legislation.

In truth, the formation of codes, or systems of general law, for the government of a people, and adapted to their wants is a business which takes place only in advanced stages of society, when knowledge is considerably diffused, and legislators have the means of ascertaining the best principles of policy and the best rules for justice, not by mere speculation and theory, but by the results of experience, and the reasoning of the learned and the wise. Those codes with which we are best acquainted, are manifestly of this sort. The institutes, and pandects, and code of Justinian, were made in the latter ages of Roman grandeur - nay, when it was far on the decline - not by instituting a new system, but by embodying the maxims, and rules, and principles, which the ablest jurists had collected in different ages, and from all the various lights of reason, and juridical decision, and general experience. No man imagines that Rome, in her early history, was capable of promulgating, or of acting upon, such a system. And this system, large as it was, has no pretension to be deemed complete, even for Rome itself. It left an infinite number of human concerns undecided by its text, which were, of course, to be submitted to judicial decision, and to receive the judgment of the wise men, who should be called, from time to time, to declare the law _ex aequo et bono_. It may indeed be assumed, as a general truth, that the body of every system of law which has hitherto governed human society, had its origin as customary law; and if it has ever assumed the form of positive legislation, it has been to give it greater sanctity and extent, as well as greater uniformity of operation. This is certainly true in respect to the common law. That system, as administered in England and the United States, is, as compared with the positive code, or statutes, of an immeasurably wider extent, both in its principles and its practical operation. A man may live a century, and feel (comparatively speaking) but in few instances the operation of statutes, either as to his rights or duties; but the common law surrounds him, on every side, like the atmosphere which he breathes.

Returning, then, to the question before stated, it may be inquired, whether it be practicable, in a refined and civilized state of society, to introduce a positive code, which shall regulate all its concerns. That such a code could be formed in a refined age, when learning, and large experience, and enlightened views, and a sagacious forecast might guide the judgments of the legislature, is the point before us. In the first place, it has never yet been done by any people, in any age. The two most illustrious instances of codification are that of Justinian and that of Napoleon. Neither of these purports to be a complete system of laws and principles, superseding all others, and abolishing all others. As far as they go, they purport to lay down positive rules to guide the judgment of all tribunals, in cases within them. But other cases are left to be decided as they may arise, upon such principles as are applicable from analogy, from reasoning, from justice, from the customary law, or from judicial discretion. A positive prohibition to decide in cases not provided for by these codes, is not contained in either. But is it possible to foresee, or to provide beforehand for all such cases? Society is ever varying in its occupations and concerns, in its objects and pursuits, in its institutions, its pleasures, its inventions, its intelligence, and, in short, in innumerable relations and diversities of measures and means. How is it possible to foresee or to limit, these relations or diversities? How is it possible, especially in free governments, to reduce all human acts to the same positive elements? to prevent contracts, and obligations, and rights, and equities, and injuries, and duties, from becoming mixed up in an infinite series of permutations and combinations? Until it has been ascertained what are the utmost limits of human relations, and those limits, with all their intermediate details, can be clearly defined, in every shade of difference, how can any system of laws be adequate to provide for, or to guard them, or to fix the rights growing out of them? To suppose that man is capable of all this, is to suppose that he is omniscient, all-wise, and all-powerful; that he is perfect, or that he can attain perfection; that he can see all the future in the past, and that the past is present to him in all its relations. The statement of such a proposition carries with it its own refutation. While man remains as he is, his powers, and capacities, and acts, must forever be imperfect. But it may be said, that a positive code may be framed, and a declaration made that it shall be deemed the sole guide and rule, and that all other rules shall be prohibited. Certainly this may be done. But the effect of this would be, not to form a perfect code for all the future exigencies of society; but to declare that whatever was left unprovided for in the code, should be neither matter of right nor wrong. It would be to declare, that, as to all other transactions, now and hereafter, society should be utterly lawless; and, of course, it would be to declare, that a system confessedly imperfect, and not meeting the wants or exigencies, the rights or the wishes of society, should still govern it. What would this be, but to provide a bad code for human concerns which it could not measure or manage?

From these considerations, we may assume it as a concession granted on all sides, that a perfect code, to regulate all present, and a fortiori, all future concerns of any civilized society, by positive rules, applicable to them, is morally impossible. The only real question is, whether a positive code can be provided, adequate, in a general sense, to the present known wants of society. That codes may be formed, more or less comprehensive, to regulate many or few concerns, to supply defects, or to give symmetry and order to the law on particular subjects, cannot be doubted. It has been often done. Perhaps no civilized nation has ever existed, in which there was not, at the same time, a written and unwritten law, or, in other words, a rule of positive institution and a rule of customary law. All special decrees and ordinances of the sovereign power are of the former kind. Many subjects are of such a nature as to require some positive rule, seeing that natural law cannot fix them upon any invariable basis. For example, there is nothing in the nature of things by which we can say, that land shall, in all possible states of society, descend to the possessor's heirs, or who those heirs shall be; that he shall have a right to dispose of them by testament or deed, and how that testament or deed shall be evidenced; whether bills of exchange and promissory notes shall be negotiable or not, and to what extent binding upon the parties. These subjects, in the origin of a society, must either be positively provided for, or no rights can exist (strictly speaking) until they have become, by usage, fixed in a particular form. But most nations, with whose history we are acquainted, have had many positive laws. And to suit their institutions to the exigencies of society, in all its changes, there must be ordinances to change the old and to frame new rules. In ancient Rome, in the modern governments of continental Europe, and especially in France and in England, great alterations have, from time to time, been made in the existing system of laws. Fundamental laws have been abrogated; amendatory provisions have been established; existing rules have been methodized, confirmed, explained, and limited; and new rules prescribed for new cases. The ordinances of Louis XIV, of 1673 and 1681, on the subject of maritime and commercial affairs, are striking instances of this sort. The abolition of feudal tenures; the regulation of uses and charities; the allowance of last wills and testaments, made in a prescribed mode; the provisions to suppress frauds, in the statute of frauds; the registration of conveyances of lands; the negotiability of promissory notes; and, above all, the positive enactments, various and almost innumerable, in the criminal code, are illustrations of the same fact, in the history of English legislation. All these statutes furnished, to a limited extent, a code on the particular subject. And we have recently seen, in the consolidation of the criminal laws of England into a few statutes, under the auspices of sir Robert Peel, a striking instance of substantive codification of the criminal law of England, in many of its most important provisions. But the objections often urged against codes, are not meant to be applied to legislation of this sort, but to systems, which are promulgated for the government of the great concerns of nations, in all their various departments and interests. How far this can be done, has been a matter of considerable theoretical discussion. But the question has been practically answered by the celebrity of several positive codes. And among those whose success and wisdom have been most generally acknowledged, are the code of Justinian and the code of Napoleon. That either of them furnishes complete rules for all the concerns of society, or excludes the necessity of judicial interpretation, or positive legislation, cannot be affirmed. That each of them covers a vast mass of the ordinary concerns of society, and fixes, positively and clearly, a great many wrongs and rights, and points out the proper redress, in cases where rights are to be vindicated and wrongs repressed cannot well be denied.

The question, then, is fairly presented, how far codes of this sort (the only ones which, in the actual state of society are morally possible) are desirable, and founded in sound policy. It is here, that the advocates and the opponents of codes, under the jurisprudence of the common law, meet on debatable ground. The lovers of ancient institutions, of existing laws, of customary principles, oppose codes as inconvenient and unnecessary. They hold them to be inconvenient, because they fix a stubborn rule, which shall govern future cases, instead of leaving them open to the free operations of the common law, which adapts itself to all the circumstances of the age. They maintain, also, that codes are unnecessary; for, so far as there is any rule, it is already known in the common law; and positive legislation cannot make it more so. It is added (and it is true) that law is gradually formed, and must differ in different ages, according to the different circumstances of society; that it must be varied according to the progress or regress of a nation; that it can rarely settle comprehensive principles; and must, by degrees, thread its way through the intricacies of human actions; and that an inflexible rule might work quite as much mischief as none at all; that no legislature can make a system half so just, or perfect, or harmonious, both from want of time, and experience, and opportunity of knowledge as judges, who are successively called to administer justice, and gather light from the wisdom of their predecessors. Most, if not all of these suggestions may be admitted to be correct, and yet they do not settle the controversy.

In the first place, the objectors must admit, that, under the common law, there are positive statutes, which regulate many great concerns and rights of the countries governed by it. The descent and distribution of real estates, the making of last wills and testaments, the forms and ceremonies attendant upon conveyances of real estate, to say nothing of other important subjects, are, in every one of the United States, provided for by positive statutes. Here we have a rule, which is absolute and inflexible. To say that, if found inconvenient, it may be altered, so as to suit the future interests of the particular state, is, in effect, no argument at all; for the same may be said as to any provision of a systematic code. No code is supposed to be unalterable. Again, if it be said, that the legislature may, and often does, in an early stage of society, fix great principles and institutions, and then leaves the rest to judicial decisions, and thereby shows its wisdom, the true answer is, that the same reasoning applies to all codes, however extensive, if they leave the judicial tribunals at liberty to decide upon new cases, not governed by, or necessarily included in, the terms of the code. So far as the legislature has laid down principles (whether more or less extensive is of no consequence) these govern; beyond them, all is left as before. Again, the common law is itself, as far as it goes, a system of rules. These rules are fixed, certain, and invariable, as to all cases falling within them. They are quite as unyielding as any code can be. When the common law has declared that the eldest son shall be the sole heir, and that the half-blood shall not inherit, a court has no more liberty to depart from these rules, or to refuse to apply them to any case falling within them, upon any notion of hardship, or inconvenience, or ill adaptation to the exigencies of society, than it has a right to say, that a last will and testament shall be good, though not executed according to the requirements of a statute. In each case, it is bound, and bound to the same extent. If the question were, whether a positive code should contain a clause prohibiting courts of justice from deciding upon cases not within the purview of the code, there might be much to urge against the policy and reasonableness of such a clause; but it would furnish no objection to other parts of the code. The only point, with reference to a code, which, under this aspect, would deserve consideration, is, how far it would be desirable to provide for cases which may be foreseen, but have not, as yet, actually been subjected to legislative decision. On one side, it may be said, that it would be best to leave all such cases to be decided, as they arise, upon the result of human experience and human judgment, then acting upon all the circumstances. On the other hand, it may be said, that it is better to have a fixed, present rule, to avoid litigation, and to alter it in future, if unexpected inconveniences should arise. The reasoning on each side is sound, when applied to particular cases. On each side, it admits of question, when applied to all cases. It may be best, in many cases, to leave the rule to be made, when the case arises in judicial controversy. In others, it may be far better to establish a present rule, to clear a present doubt, or fix a limit to what is now uncertain. Take the case of a bill of exchange, or promissory note; and suppose the question were, at what time demand of payment should be made, when it was payable on time, and no rule existed, and yet there was an immense amount of property dependent upon having a fixed, uniform rule; and, until so fixed, there must be endless litigation. Can any one doubt of the benefit of a rule, such as is now fixed in the commercial law of our country, for the purpose of securing certainty, viz, that payment must be demanded on the day on which it becomes due. On the other hand, suppose it were now proposed to make a law, fixing what should be the rate of wages in all future times, in all private employments; would it not, at once, occur to be impolitic to act upon a rule, the effects of which might immediately, or in future, press unequally and injuriously upon different interests in society? Again, it is said to be unnecessary to reduce the rules of the common law to a code, for they are as certain now as they would be in a positive code. They are even more so, because the legislature cannot be presumed able to lay down a positive rule, with all the limitations and qualifications of the common law. Now, both of these suggestions admit of a satisfactory answer. If the rule exists and has certainty in the common law, it can be stated. If there are any known exceptions, limitations and qualifications, upon a rule, those also can be stated. If nothing beyond a particular limit is known, then legislation can, at least, go to that limit. And as to all other cases, the same uncertainty exists, both at common law and in legislation.

The difficulty of the argument consists in assuming, that, because the legislature has prescribed the same rule as the common law, the courts are thereby prohibited from doing what they possessed the power to do before, in the absence of any rule, viz. to find out what is the rule that ought to govern. Now, the legislature may as well leave this power in the courts, after a code, as the common law; and it will be best, unless there is a positive prohibition to the contrary. The other part of the suggestion applies only to the point, whether the code is well or ill formed by the legislature. If badly formed, it will, of course, be proportionally bad; but that furnishes no objection to a code, but to the mode in which it is executed. Then, again, as to the suggestion that it is unnecessary, because the rule already exists in the common law, and has certainty: to this several answers may be given. In the first place, if it be conceded, that there is entire certainty in the rule, at common law, there can be no harm in making the rule positive. It may do good; for it will instruct many, in and out of the profession, in respect to their rights and duty, who are now sadly ignorant of both, or are liable to be misled by their imperfect inquiries, or their limited sources of information. Every man may be able to peruse a concise text; but every man may not have leisure or ability to study a voluminous commentary. Besides, even in relation to the doctrines of the common law, many of them lie scattered in different cases, and many of them are not so clear as not to admit of different interpretations, by minds of different learning and ability. Even lawyers of great research and accuracy, especially where the doctrine, though on the whole clear, is matter of deduction and inference, may not, at once, come to the correct conclusion; and others of less learning and ability may plunge into serious errors. Now it would be no small gain to have a positive text, which should give, in such cases, the true rule, instead of leaving it open to conjecture and inference by feeble minds. Again, there are many subjects of great intricacy and complexity, which can be fully mastered only by very able minds, resting, as they do, upon nice, and, sometimes, upon technical reasonings, not seen by the common reader. In such cases, the text may admit of very exact statement, but the commentaries necessary to deduce it, may be exceedingly elaborate. The demonstration, or last result, may be clear, but the steps in arriving at it, exceedingly perplexed and embarrassing. It may require an analysis by the greatest minds to demonstrate; but, when once announced, it may be understood by the most common minds. For instance, the subject of contingent remainders and executory devises is of uncommon complexity in the common law, and many a lawyer may read Mr. Fearne's admirable treatise on the subject, without feeling competent to expound all its doctrines. And yet, put every principle into a positive text, with all its limitations and restrictions (not to be made out by argument and inference, but given in a direct form) and his labors and his reasoning would be materially abridged, and certainty exist where darkness before overshadowed his mind. Again, the common law has now become an exceedingly voluminous system; and as its expositions rest, not on a positive text, but upon arguments, analogies and commentaries, every person, who desires to know much, must engage in a very extensive system of reading. He may employ half his life in mastering treatises, the substance of which, in a positive code, might occupy but a few hundred pages. The codes of Justinian, for instance, superseded the camel-loads of commentaries, which were antecedently in use, and are all now buried in oblivion. The Napoleon codes have rendered thousands of volumes only works of occasional consultation, which were before required to be studied very diligently, and sometimes in repeated perusals. Again, what is to be done in the common law, where there are conflicting decisions on the same point, or converging series of opposite doctrines, approaching towards a conflict? The rule is here confessedly uncertain. Why should not the legislature interfere, in such a case, and fix a rule, such as, on the whole, stands upon the better reasoning, and the general analogies of the law? In point of fact, this is often done. Declaratory laws, in form, are unusual among us; but laws to clear doubts and difficulties are very common. Such interferences ought, doubtless, to be made with caution and prudence, and great deliberation. But this furnishes no just objection to a reasonable exercise of the power.

But in the practice under the common law, there is a still stronger ground for interference. In the first place, what the common law is, is always open to question; and if authorities are suggested on either side, it is common enough to find the rule deduced from them, doubted, denied, or explained away, by parties in an opposite interest. Courts are bound to hear as well as to decide; and although a court may think the rule of the common law clear, from their own prior researches and reasoning, it will rarely feel at liberty to stop eminent counsel, when they deny the rule, or seek to overthrow the authorities and reasonings by which it is supported. The spirit of our tribunals, and the anxious desire, not only to do, but to appear to do justice, lead to a vast consumption of time in these discussions. If the legislature had once recognised the rule in a positive code, there would be an end of all such reasoning. The only question which could remain, would be whether the rule were applicable to the case. In the next place, there are, upon some doctrines of the common law, a vast multitude of authorities to examine, compare and understand, which requires not only great diligence, but great skill. In some cases, there are shades of difference fit for comment; in others, obiter dicta, which are to be qualified; in others, doubts thrown out upon collateral heads; in others, reasoning not altogether satisfactory. Under such circumstances, what is to be done? The advocate on the one side comments on every case, and the language of every judge, which furnishes any color of support for his client. His arguments must be met and answered on the other side, not only because no advocate can know what the judges will decide, but what will be the influence upon their minds of a dictum, or doubt, or incidental remark or reason. It is indispensable, therefore, to examine the whole, although, perhaps, neither party doubts what the amount of authority, on the whole, supports. On one point (we believe) a learned English judge said, many years ago, that there were then more than 170 authorities. It is most probable that the number is now doubled; and yet, upon this very point, a legislative enactment of three lines might put controversy at rest for ever. Perhaps no man in or out of the legal profession would now doubt what the rule ought to be. The difficulty is, that a rule has either been adopted which works inconveniently in particular cases, or a rule has grown out of a hasty adjudication, which subsequent judicial subtilty has been desirous of escaping from; but it is not easy to do so, without breaking in upon the acknowledged force of the rule. Hence distinctions, nice, and, perhaps, not very satisfactory, are found, as blemishes in some parts of the law, which need the legislative hand to extirpate or correct them.

But it has been urged, as has been already incidentally noticed, that it is a great advantage to have law a flexible system, which will yield to the changing circumstances of society; and that a written code gives a permanence to doctrines, which would otherwise be subject to modification, so as to adapt them to the particular character of the times. This objection has been already in part answered. In respect to the common law doctrines, they cannot now be changed, whatever may be the changes of society, without some legislative enactment.

They furnish a guide to all cases governed by them, until the legislature shall promulgate a new rule. Courts cannot disturb or vary them; and the question of their application to new cases is equally open, whether there be, or be not a code. The legislature can, with the same ease, vary its code as its common law. It can repeal, amend or modify either. But another principal objection is often suggested, and that is, that all the parts of the common law are not in a state susceptible of codification; and that, as we cannot form a complete system of it, one great object of a code must fail. It may be admitted, that some parts of the common law are too imperfectly settled in principles, and too little understood in practice, to allow of any exact codification. But these parts are principally obsolete, or of rare occurrence and application in the common business of life; so that, if they admitted of being reduced to a text, it may be well doubted if they were important enough to deserve it. There are other parts, again, which have grown up in modern times, which may be admitted to be yet in an immature and forming state, in respect to which, perhaps, it were better to wait the results of experience, than to anticipate them by positive law.

Conceding all this, it falls far short of establishing the inutility of a code in other departments of the common law, not open to the like objections. Because we cannot form a perfect system, does it follow that we are to do nothing? Because we cannot, without rashness, give certainty to all possible or probable details of jurisprudence, shall we leave every thing uncertain and open to controversy? There is not a single state of the Union that has not repeatedly revised, changed, and fixed, in a positive code, many of its laws. The criminal code has almost every where received, in some of its principal branches, a methodical form. Virginia, long ago, reduced some important portions of her law to a positive text. New York has recently gone much farther, and, in the form of a revised code, made very extensive alterations in this common law, as well as in her statutable law. England, in our own time, has consolidated the most important heads of her criminal jurisprudence, in a new and methodized text. No man can doubt, that revisions of this sort may be useful, and, indeed, indispensable for the wants and improvements of society, in its progress from one stage to another. The question of more or less is a mere matter of expediency and policy. It is not a little remarkable, that, in England, almost every change in the general structure of her laws, by positive legislation, has, in all ages, met with a similar objection and resistance, and, when once adopted, has been generally, if not universally satisfactory. But there are many branches of the common law which can, without difficulty, be reduced to a positive text. Their main principles are embodied in treatises, accurate and full, and there can be no want of learned men ready to form an outline of them for the consideration of the legislature. Our commercial law is generally in this state. The law of bills of exchange and promissory notes, of insurance, of shipping and navigation, of partnership, of agency and factorage, of sales, of bailments, and many kindred titles, admits of codification to a very high degree of certainty; and yet, in these branches, there is still room enough to controvert particular decisions and authorities, to make it desirable to give a positive sanction to the better doctrine, and thus to save the profession from laborious researches, and the public from expensive litigation. The ordinance of Louis XIV, on commercial law, dried up a thousand sources of disputation; and the present code of commerce of France has settled, in a positive manner, most of the questionable points, which had been found unprovided for by that ordinance, and were resigned to judicial decision in the intermediate period. Besides, a code furnishes the only safe means of incorporating qualifications upon a general principle, which experience has demonstrated to be proper and politic. Courts often lament that a principle is established in too broad terms for the public good, and yet do not feel themselves at liberty to interpose exceptions which the principle does not sanction. This article has already spread out into a great length, and must now be closed. The result of the whole view, as to codes, is, that neither the friends nor the opponents of them are wholly right in their doctrines or their projects; that, in every civilized country, much may be done to simplify the principles and practice of the law by judicious codification, and to give it uniformity and certainty; that How much ought to be done? is a question not admitting of any universal response, but is, or may be, different as to different countries, or, in different ages, as to the same country; that every code, to be useful, must act upon the existing institutions and jurisprudence, and not, generally, supersede them; that what, with reference to the customs, habits, manners, pursuits, interests, and institutions of one country, may be fit and expedient, may be wholly unfit and inexpedient for another; and that the part of true wisdom is, not so much to search out any abstract theory of universal jurisprudence, as to examine what, for each country in particular, may best promote its substantial interests, preserve its rights, protect its morals, and give permanence to its liberties.

Two years after the publication of the above article on "Law, Legislation, Codes" Story, with four other commissioners, made a report to the Governor of Massachusetts on the practicability and expediency of reducing the common law of Massachusetts to a systematic code. The general attitude of the report was very similar to that of Story's article. The affirmative recommendations of the commissioners were that "the labors of codification should be strenuously and sedulously directed" to that portion of the law "which is of daily occurrence in the common business of life ... in civil cases" and to that portion "which defines and punishes crimes, and ascertains the rules of proceeding in criminal cases". The commissioners also earnestly recommended the codification of the law of evidence. The only action which the legislature took on the basis of these recommendations was the appointment of a commission to codify the criminal law. The Code recommended by the commissioners in 1844 was, however, rejected by the legislature.

Robert Rantoul, Jr., Oration at Scituate, Massachusetts 4 July, 1836, Memoirs, Speeches and Writings of Robert Rantoul, Jr. (1854) p. 251, 277.

... Our legislation, also, should be of indigenous growth. The laws should be intelligible to all, equal in their operation; and should provide prompt and cheap remedies for their violation. The revision of the Statutes of this Commonwealth, just completed, has done something towards this great end, - how much, the public are hardly yet aware. It would have been worth all the time, expense, and labor spent upon it, even though they had been ten times greater than they were. It is the most important act of our legislation since the revolution. Not only is the whole mass systematized, condensed, simplified, modernized, and made consistent with itself, but improvements, almost innumerable, have been introduced into every part, more in number and greater in value, than our general court would have elaborated, in their ordinary mode of legislation, for many years.[1]

---

1. The Revised Statutes of 1836 were based upon recommendations of a commission constituted of Charles Jackson, Asahel Stearns, and John Pickering. The Commissioners in preparing the revision had been moved by the persuasion that "it was highly desirable in a national point of view that this Commonwealth should cooperate in gradually effecting, so far as should be practicable, a general conformity among the codes of the several States of the Union." (Commissioners' Report, vi.) In preparing their suggested revision of the statutes they had, therefore, sought to follow the form and substance of the Revised Statutes of New York. That revision, which had considerable importance throughout the nation, had gone farther in the direction of putting the rules of common law in a statutory form than the Massachusetts commissioners considered desirable. Mr. Justice Jackson and his Massachusetts associates described

But the Revised Statutes, excellent as they are, contrasted with the chaos for which they are substituted, still cover but a small part of the ground. We are governed principally, by the common law; and this ought to be reduced, forthwith, to a uniform written code.

It is said by writers on the subject, that there are numerous principles of the common law, which are definitely settled and well known, and that the questionable utility of putting these into the form of a positive and unbending text, is not sufficient to outweigh the advantages of leaving them to be applied by the courts, as principles of common law, whenever the occurrence of cases should require it.

---

their attitude towards codification in the following way: "It may, perhaps, be a subject of observation ... that the Commissioners have not attempted to embody in the present revision the principles of the common law, any further than has heretofore been gradually done at different periods of our legislation. This has not been the result of inattention or accident; but the Commissioners, on consideration, came to the conclusion that the questionable utility of putting into the form of a positive and unbending text, numerous principles of the common law, which are definitely settled and well known, was not sufficient to outweigh the advantages of leaving them to be applied by the Courts, as principles of common law, whenever the occurrence of cases should require it.

"It has been remarked by distinguished American jurists, that the common law is peculiarly well fitted to the rapidly advancing state of our country, because it possesses in an eminent degree the capacity of adapting itself to the gradual progress of improvement among us; and that this accommodating principle, which pervades it, will adjust itself to every degree and species of improvement that may be suggested by practice, commerce, observation, study, or refinement." Id., p. x.

In the Preface to the New York Revised Statutes of 1830, the Commissioners, John Duer, Benjamin F. Butler, and John C. Spencer had described their effort to make some portions of the common law, statutory law. "In numerous instances", they said "the rules of the common law have been reduced to a written text, and inserted in their proper place in connexion with the statutory provisions on the subject to which they relate; whilst in other instances those rules have been enlarged, modified or varied, the more fully to conform them to the nature of our government, and the habits and exigencies of the people." 1 Revised Statutes (1829) iii-iv. On the New York Revised Statutes in general see, Butler, Revision of the Statutes of New York and the Revisers (1889).

How can that which is definitely settled and well known, be applied otherwise than as a positive and unbending text? It is because judge-made-law is indefinitely and vaguely settled, and its exact limits unknown, that it possesses the capacity of adapting itself to new cases, or, in other words, admits of judicial legislation.

Imperfect statutes are, therefore, commended because they leave the law, in the omitted cases, to be enacted by the judges. Why not carry the argument a little further, and repeal the existing statutes, so that the judges may make all the laws? Is it because the Constitution forbids judges to legislate? Why, then, commend the legislation of judges?

The law should be a positive and unbending text, otherwise the judge has an arbitrary power, or discretion; and the discretion of a good man is often nothing better than caprice, as Lord Camden has very justly remarked, while the discretion of a bad man is an odious and irresponsible tyranny.

Why is an ex post facto law, passed by the legislature, unjust, unconstitutional, and void, while judge-made law, which, from its nature, must always be ex post facto, is not only to be obeyed, but applauded? Is it because judge-made law is essentially aristocratical? It is said, the judge only applies to the case the principles of common law which exist already; but the legislature applies to a whole class of cases the principles of common sense and justice, which exist already, and which have existed from a much more remote antiquity.

The common law sprung from the dark ages; the fountain of justice is the throne of the Deity. The common law is but the glimmering taper by which men groped their way through the palpable midnight in which learning, wit, and reason were almost extinguished; justice shines with the splendor of that fulness of light which beams from the Ineffable Presence. The common law had its beginning in time, and in the time of ignorance; justice is eternal, even with the eternity of the all-wise and just Lawgiver and Judge. The common law had its origin in folly, barbarism, and feudality; justice is the irradiance of divine wisdom, divine truth, and the government of infinite benevolence. While the common law sheds no light, but rather darkness visible, that serves but to discover sights of woe - justice rises, like the Sun of Righteousness, with healing on his wings, scatters the doubts that torture without end, dispels the mists of scholastic subtilty, and illuminates with the light that lighteth every man that cometh into the world. Older, nobler, clearer, and more glorious, then, is everlasting justice, than ambiguous, base-born, purblind, perishable common law. That which is older than the creation may indeed be extolled for its venerable age; but among created things, the argument from antiquity is a false criterion of worth. Sin and death are older than the common law; are they, therefore, to be preferred to it? The mortal transgression of Cain was anterior to the common law: does it therefore furnish a better precedent?

Judge-made law is ex post facto law, and therefore unjust. An act is not forbidden by the statute law, but it becomes by judicial decision a crime. A contract is intended and supposed to be valid, but it becomes void by judicial construction. The legislature could not effect this, for the Constitution forbids it. The judiciary shall not usurp legislative power, says the Bill of Rights: yet it not only usurps, but runs riot beyond the confines of legislative power.

Judge-made law is special legislation. The judge is human, and feels the bias which the coloring of the particular case gives. If he wishes to decide the next case differently, he has only to distinguish, and thereby make a new law. The legislature must act on general views, and prescribe at once for a whole class of cases.

No man can tell what the common law is; therefore it is not law; for a law is a rule of action, but a rule which is unknown can govern no man's conduct. Notwithstanding this, it has been called the perfection of human reason.

The common law is the perfection of human reason - just as alcohol is the perfection of sugar. The subtle spirit of the common law is reason double distilled, till what was wholesome and nutritive becomes rank poison. Reason is sweet and pleasant to the unsophisticated intellect; but this sublimated perversion of reason bewilders, and perplexes, and plunges its victims into mazes of error.

The judge makes law, by extorting from precedents something which they do not contain. He extends his precedents, which were themselves the extension of others, till, by this accommodating principle, a whole system of law is built up without the authority or interference of the legislator.

The judge labors to reconcile conflicting analogies, and to derive from them a rule to decide future cases. No one knows what the law is, before he lays it down; for it does not exist even in the breast of the judge. All the cases carried up to the tribunal of the last resort, are capable of being argued, or they would not be carried there. Those which are not carried up are not law, for the Supreme Court might decide them differently. Those which are carried up, argued, and decided, might have been decided differently, as will appear from the arguments. It is, therefore, often optional with the judge to incline the balance as he pleases. In forty per cent of the cases carried up to a higher court, for a considerable term of years, terminating not long ago, the judgment was reversed. Almost any case, where there is any difference of opinion, may be decided either way, and plausible analogies found in the great storehouse of precedent to justify the decision. The law, then, is the final will or whim of the judge, after counsel for both parties have done their utmost to sway it to the one side or the other.

No man knows what the law is after the judge has decided it. Because, as the judge is careful not to decide any point which is not brought before him, he restricts his decision within the narrowest possible limits; and though the very next case that may arise may seem, to a superficial observer, and even upon a close inspection by an ordinary mind, to be precisely similar to the last, yet the ingenuity of a thoroughbred lawyer may detect some unsuspected shade of difference, upon which an opposite decision may be founded. Great part of the skill of a judge consists in avoiding the direct consequences of a rule, by ingenious expedients and distinctions, whenever the rule would operate absurdly: and as an ancient maxim may be evaded, but must not be annulled, the whole system has been gradually rendered a labyrinth of apparent contradictions, reconciled by legal adroitness.

Statutes, enacted by the legislature, speak the public voice. Legislators, with us, are not only chosen because they possess the public confidence, but after their election, they are strongly influenced by public feeling. They must sympathize with the public, and express its will: should they fail to do so, the next year witnesses their removal from office, and others are selected to be the organs of the popular sentiment. The older portions of the common law are the work of judges, who held their places during the good pleasure of the king, and of course decided the law so as to suit the pleasure of the king. In feudal times, it was made up of feudal principles, warped, to be sure, according to the king's necessities. Judges now are appointed by the executive, and hold their offices during good behavior - that is, for life, and are consequently out of the reach of popular influence. They are sworn to administer common law as it came down from the dark ages, excepting what has been repealed by the Constitution and the statutes, which exception they are always careful to reduce to the narrowest possible limits. With them, wrong is right, if wrong has existed from time immemorial: precedents are every thing: the spirit of the age is nothing. And suppose the judge prefers the common law to the Constitutions of the State and of the Union; or decides in defiance of a statute; what is the remedy? An astute argument is always at hand to reconcile the open violation of that instrument with the express letter of the Constitution, as in the case of the United States Bank - or to prove an obnoxious statute unconstitutional, as would have happened in the case of the Warren Bridge, but for the firmness of Judge Morton.[2] Impeachment is a bugbear, which has lost its

---

2. In Charles River Bridge v. Warren Bridge, 7 Pick. 344 (1829)

terrors. We must have democratic governors, who will appoint democratic judges, and the whole body of the law must be codified.

It is said, that where a chain of precedents is found running back to a remote antiquity, it may be presumed that they originated in a statute which, through lapse of time, has perished. Unparalleled presumption this! To suppose the legislation of a barbarous age richer and more comprehensive than our own. It was without doubt a thousand times more barren. But what if there were such statutes? The specimens which have survived do not impress us with a favorable opinion of those that may have been lost. Crudely conceived, savage in their spirit, vague, indeterminate, and unlimited in their terms, and incoherent when regarded as parts of a system, the remains of ancient legislation are of little use at present, and what is lost was probably still more worthless. If such laws were now to be found in our statute book, they would be repealed at once; the innumerable judicial constructions which they might have received would not save them. Why then should supposed statutes, which probably never had any but an imaginary existence, which if they ever existed were the rude work of barbarians, which cannot now be ascertained, and if they could be, would be despised and rejected as bad in themselves, and worse for our situation and circumstances - why should such supposed statutes govern, in the nineteenth century, the civilized and intelligent freemen of Massachusetts?

These objections to the common law have a peculiar force in America, because the rapidly advancing state of our country is continually presenting new cases for the decision of the judges; and by determining these as they arise, the bench takes for its share more than half of our legislation, notwithstanding the express provisions of the Constitution that the judiciary shall not usurp the functions of the legislature. If a

---

Mr. Justice Morton, Wilde, J. concurring, wrote an opinion sustaining the constitutional validity of the much debated act of the state legislature permitting the establishment of a free bridge between Boston and Charlestown despite an earlier charter of incorporation issued to a company charging tolls for use of its bridge over the same waters. Wilde, J. and Parker, C.J. considered that the statute was unconstitutional. The Court being equally divided the bill for equitable relief was dismissed. The dismissal was affirmed on its merits in the Supreme Court of the United States, Story J. dissenting. 11 Peters 420 (1837). Justice Morton, who was on the Supreme Judicial Court from 1825 to 1840, was leader of the Democratic party in the state and its candidate for Governor in every election between 1828 and 1843.

common law system could be tolerable anywhere, it is only where every thing is stationary. With us, it is subversive of the fundamental principles of a free government, because it deposits in the same hands the power of first making the general laws, and then applying them to individual cases; powers distinct in their nature, and which ought to be jealously separated.

But even in England, common law is only a part of a system, which, as a whole, would be incomplete without equity. We strive to make the part supply the place of the whole. Equity is the correction of that wherein the law by reason of its generality is deficient; yet we have taken the law, deficient as it confessedly is, without the correction, except in certain cases, where by degrees, and almost without the knowledge of the people, equity powers have been given to the courts. A court of chancery would not be tolerated here, for reasons which I have not time to enter upon; and without that adjunct, the common law system would not be tolerated in England. The remedy is to fuse both into one mass, adopting such principles of equity as are really necessary, simplifying the whole, enacting the result in the form of statutes, and, from time to time, supplying defects and omissions, as they are discovered. It is hardly necessary to observe, that in doing this, opportunity should be taken to reform and remodel the great body of the law, which stands in need of such a revision more than any other science. Some immense advances, it is true, have been made within the last two years, of which the total abolition of special pleading is not the least remarkable. But instead of being satisfied with what has been gained, it should only encourage us to step forward more boldly in what remains to do. All American law must be statute law. ...

<u>Commonwealth</u> v. <u>Hunt</u> <u>&</u> <u>Others</u>
Supreme Judicial Court of Massachusetts, 1842
4 Metcalf 111

Shaw, C. J. Considerable time has elapsed since the argument of this case.[1] It has been retained long under advisement, partly because we were desirous of examining, with some attention, the great number of cases cited at the argument, and others which have presented themselves in course, and partly because we considered it a question of great importance to the Commonwealth, and one which had been much examined and considered by the learned judge of the municipal court.

---

1. Robert Rantoul, Jr. was counsel for the defendants. Concerning Rantoul's argument in the case, see Nelles, "Commonwealth v. Hunt" (1932) 32 <u>Columbia</u> <u>L</u>. <u>Rev</u>. 1128.

We have no doubt, that by the operation of the constitution of this Commonwealth, the general rules of the common law, making conspiracy an indictable offense, are in force here, and that this is included in the description of laws which had, before the adoption of the constitution, been used and approved in the Province, Colony, or State of Massachusetts Bay, and usually practised in the courts of law. Const. of Mass. c. VI § 6. It was so held in Commonwealth v. Boynton, and Commonwealth v. Pierpont, cases decided before reports of cases were regularly published, and in many cases since. Commonwealth v. Ward, 1 Mass. 473, Commonwealth v. Judd, and Commonwealth v. Tibbetts, 2 Mass. 329, 536. Commonwealth v. Warren, 6 Mass. 74. Still, it is proper in this connexion to remark, that although the common law in regard to conspiracy in this Commonwealth is in force, yet it will not necessarily follow that every indictment at common law for this offence is a precedent for a similar indictment in this State. The general rule of the common law is, that it is a criminal and indictable offence, for two or more to confederate and combine together, by concerted means, to do that which is unlawful or criminal, to the injury of the public, or portions or classes of the community, or even to the rights of an individual. This rule of law may be equally in force as a rule of the common law, in England and in this Commonwealth; and yet it must depend upon the local laws of each country to determine, whether the purpose to be accomplished by the combination, or the concerted means of accomplishing it, be unlawful or criminal in the respective countries. All those laws of the parent country, whether rules of the common law, or early English statutes, which were made for the purpose of regulating the wages of laborers, the settlement of paupers, and making it penal for any one to use a trade or handicraft to which he had not served a full apprenticeship - not being adapted to the circumstances of our colonial condition - were not adopted, used or approved, and therefore do not come within the description of the laws adopted and confirmed by the provision of the constitution already cited. This consideration will do something towards reconciling the English and American cases, and may indicate how far the principles of the English cases will apply in this Commonwealth, and show why a conviction in England, in many cases, would not be a precedent for a like conviction here. The King v. Journeymen Tailors of Cambridge, 8 Mod. 10, for instance, is commonly cited as an authority for an indictment at common law, and a conviction of journeymen mechanics of a conspiracy to raise their wages. It was there held, that the indictment need not conclude contra forman statuti, because the gist of the offence was the conspiracy, which was an offence at common law. At the same time it was conceded, that the unlawful object to be accomplished was the raising of wages above the rate fixed by a general act of parliament. It was therefore a conspiracy to violate a general statute law, made for the regulation of a large branch of trade, affecting the comfort and interest of the public; and thus the object to be accomplished by the conspiracy was unlawful, if not criminal.

But the rule of law, that an illegal conspiracy, whatever may be the facts which constitute it, is an offence punishable by the laws of this Commonwealth, is established as well by legislative as by judicial authority. Like many other cases, that of murder, for instance, it leaves the definition or description of the offence to the common law, and provides modes for its prosecution and punishment. The Revised Statutes, c. 82, §28, and c. 86, §10, allowed an appeal from the court of common pleas and the municipal court, respectively, in cases of a conviction for conspiracy, and thereby recognized it as one of the class of offences, so difficult of investigation, or so aggravated in their nature and punishment, as to render it fit that the party accused should have the benefit of a trial before the highest court of the Commonwealth. And though this right of appeal is since taken away, by St. of 1839, c. 161, this does not diminish the force of the evidence tending to show that the offence is known and recognized by the legislature as a high indictable offence.

But the great difficulty is, in framing any definition or description, to be drawn from the decided cases, which shall specifically identify this offence - a description broad enough to include all cases punishable under this description, without including acts which are not punishable. Without attempting to review and reconcile all the cases, we are of opinion, that as a general description, though perhaps not a precise and accurate definition, a conspiracy must be a combination of two or more persons, by some concerted action, to accomplish some criminal or unlawful purpose, or to accomplish some purpose, not in itself criminal or unlawful, by criminal or unlawful means. We use the terms criminal or unlawful, because it is manifest that many acts are unlawful, which are not punishable by indictment or other public prosecution; and yet there is no doubt, we think, that a combination by numbers to do them would be an unlawful conspiracy, and punishable by indictment. Of this character was a conspiracy to cheat by false pretences, without false tokens, when a cheat by false pretences only, by a single person, was not a punishable offence. Commonwealth v. Boynton, before referred to. So a combination to destroy the reputation of an individual, by verbal calumny which is not indictable. So a conspiracy to induce and persuade a young female, by false representations, to leave the protection of her parent's house, with a view to facilitate her prostitution. Rex v. Lord Grey; 3 Hargrave's State Trials, 519. ...

From this view of the law respecting conspiracy, we think it an offence which especially demands the application of that wise and humane rule of the common law, that an indictment shall state, with as much certainty as the nature of the case will admit, the facts which constitute the crime intended to be charged. This is required, to enable the defendant to meet the charge and prepare for his defence, and, in case of acquittal or conviction, to show by the record the identity of the charge, so that he may not be indicted a second time for the same offence. It is also necessary, in order that a person, charged by the grand jury for one offence, may not substantially be convicted, on his trial, of another. This fundamental rule is confirmed by the Declaration of Rights, which declares that no subject shall be held to answer for any crime or offence, until the same is fully and plainly, substantially and formally described to him.

From these views of the rules of criminal pleading, it appears to us to follow, as a necessary legal conclusion, that when the criminality of a conspiracy consists in an unlawful agreement of two or more persons to compass or promote some criminal or illegal purpose, that purpose must be fully and clearly stated in the indictment; and if the criminality of the offence, which is intended to be charged, consists in the agreement to compass or promote some purpose, not of itself criminal or unlawful, by the use of fraud, force, falsehood, or other criminal or unlawful means, such intended use of fraud force, falsehood, or other criminal or unlawful means, must be set out in the indictment. Such, we think, is, on the whole, the result of the English authorities, although they are not quite uniform. 1 East P. C. 461. 1 Stark. Crim. Pl. (2d ed.) 156. Opinion of Spencer, Senator, 9 Cow. 586, &seq. ...

With these general views of the law, it becomes necessary to consider the circumstances of the present case, as they appear from the indictment itself, and from the bill of exceptions filed and allowed.

One of the exceptions, though not the first in the order of time, yet by far the most important, was this:

The counsel for the defendants contended, and requested the court to instruct the jury, that the indictment did not set forth any agreement to do a criminal act, or to do any lawful act by any specified criminal means, and that the agreements therein set forth did not constitute a conspiracy indictable by any law of this Commonwealth. But the judge refused so to do, and instructed the jury, that the indictment did, in his opinion, describe a confederacy among the defendants to do an unlawful act, and to effect the same by unlawful means; that the society, organized and associated for the purposes described in the indictment, was an unlawful conspiracy, against the laws of this Commonwealth; and that if the jury believed, from the evidence in the case, that the defendants, or any of them, had engaged in such a confederacy, they were bound to find such of them guilty.

We are here carefully to distinguish between the confederacy set forth in the indictment, and the confederacy or association contained in the constitution of the Boston Journeymen Bootmakers' Society, as stated in the little printed book, which was admitted as evidence on the trial. Because, though it was thus admitted as evidence, it would not warrant a conviction for any thing not stated in the indictment. It was proof, as far as it went to support the averments in the indictment. If it contained any criminal matter not set forth in the indictment, it is of no avail. The question then presents itself in the same form as on a motion in arrest of judgment.

The first count set forth, that the defendants, with divers others unknown, on the day and at the place named, being workmen, and journeymen, in the art and occupation of bootmakers, unlawfully, perniciously and deceitfully designing and intending to continue, keep up, form, and unite themselves, into an unlawful club, society and combination, and make unlawful by-laws, rules and orders among themselves, and thereby govern themselves and other workmen, in the said art, and unlawfully and unjustly to extort great sums of money by means thereof, did unlawfully assemble and meet together, and being so assembled, did unjustly and corruptly conspire, combine, confederate and agree together, that none of them should thereafter, and that none of them would, work for any master or person whatsoever, in the said art, mystery and occupation, who should employ any workman or journeyman, or other person, in the said art, who was not a member of said club, society or combination, after notice given him to discharge such workman, from the employ of such master; to the great damage and oppression, &c.

...

The manifest intent of the association is, to induce all those engaged in the same occupation to become members of it. Such a purpose is not unlawful. It would give them a power which might be exerted for useful and honorable purposes, or for dangerous and pernicious ones. If the latter were the real and actual object, and susceptible of proof, it should have been specially charged. Such an association might be used to afford each other assistance in times of poverty, sickness and distress; or to raise their intellectual, moral and social condition; or to make improvement in their art; or for other proper purposes. Or the association might be designed for purposes of oppression and injustice. But in order to charge all those, who become members of an association, with the guilt of a criminal conspiracy, it must be averred and proved that the actual, if not the avowed object of the association, was criminal. An association may be formed, the declared objects of which are innocent and laudable, and yet they may have secret articles, or an agreement communicated only to the members, by which they are banded together for purposes injurious to the peace of society or the rights of its members. Such would undoubtedly be a criminal conspiracy, on proof of the fact, however meritorious and praiseworthy the declared objects might be. The law is not to be hoodwinked by colorable pretences. It looks at truth and reality, through whatever disguise it may assume. But to make such an association, ostensibly innocent, the subject of prosecution as a criminal conspiracy, the secret agreement, which makes it so, is to be averred and proved as the gist of the offence. But when an association is formed for purposes actually innocent, and afterwards its powers are abused, by those who have the control and management of it, to purposes of oppression and injustice, it will be criminal in those who thus misuse it, or give consent thereto, but not in the other members of the association. In this case, no such secret agreement, varying the objects of the association from those avowed, is set forth in this count of the indictment.

Nor can we perceive that the objects of this association, whatever they may have been, were to be attained by criminal means. The means which they proposed to employ, as averred in this count, and which, as we are now to presume, were established by the proof, were, that they would not work for a person, who, after due notice, should employ a journeyman not a member of their society. Supposing the object of the association to be laudable and lawful, or at least not unlawful, are these means criminal? The case supposes that these persons are not bound by contract, but free to work for whom they please or not to work, if they so prefer. In this state of things, we cannot perceive, that it is criminal for men to agree together to exercise their own acknowledged rights, in such a manner as best to subserve their own interests. One way to test this is, to consider the effect of such an agreement, where the object of the association is acknowledged on all hands to be a laudable one. Suppose a class of workmen, impressed with the manifold evils of intemperance, should agree with each other not to work in a shop in which ardent spirit was furnished, or not to work in a shop with any one who used it, or not to work for an employer, who should, after notice, employ a journeyman who habitually used it. The consequences might be the same. A workman, who should still persist in the use of ardent spirit, would find it more difficult to get employment; a master employing such an one might, at times, experience inconvenience in his work, in losing the services of a skilful but intemperate workman. Still it seems to us, that as the object would be lawful, and the means not unlawful, such an agreement could not be pronounced a criminal conspiracy. ...

The second count, omitting the recital of unlawful intent

and evil disposition, and omitting the direct averment of an unlawful club or society, alleges that the defendants, with others unknown, did assemble, conspire, confederate and agree together, not to work for any master or person who should employ any workman not being a member of a certain club, society or combination, called the Boston Journeymen Bootmaker's Society, or who should break any of their by-laws, unless such workmen should pay to said club, such sum as should be agreed upon as a penalty for the breach of such unlawful rules, &c; and that by means of said conspiracy they did compel one Isaac B. Wait, a master cordwainer, to turn out of his employ one Jeremiah Horne, a journeyman boot-maker, &c. in evil example, &c. So far as the averment of a conspiracy is concerned, all the remarks made in reference to the first count are equally applicable to this. It is simply an averment of an agreement amongst themselves not to work for a person, who should employ any person not a member of a certain association. It sets forth no illegal or criminal purpose to be accomplished, nor any illegal or criminal means to be adopted for the accomplishment of any purpose. It was an agreement, as to the manner in which they would exercise an acknowledged right to contract with others for their labor. It does not aver a conspiracy or even an intention to raise their wages; and it appears by the bill of exceptions, that the case was not put upon the footing of a conspiracy to raise their wages. Such an agreement, as set forth in this count, would be perfectly justifiable under the recent English statute, by which this subject is regulated. St. 6 Geo. IV. c. 129. See Roscoe Crim. Ev. (2d Amer. ed.) 368, 369. ...

The third count, reciting a wicked and unlawful intent to impoverish one Jeremiah Horne, and hinder him from following his trade as a boot-maker, charges the defendants, with others unknown, with an unlawful conspiracy, by wrongful and indirect means, to impoverish said Horne and to deprive and hinder him, from his said art and trade and getting his support thereby, and that, in pursuance of said unlawful combination, they did unlawfully and indirectly hinder and prevent, &c. and greatly impoverish him.

If the fact of depriving Jeremiah Horne of the profits of his business, by whatever means it might be done, would be unlawful and criminal, a combination to compass that object would be an unlawful conspiracy, and it would be unnecessary to state the means. Such seems to have been the view of the court in <u>The King</u> v. <u>Eccles</u>, 3 Doug. 337, though the case is so briefly reported, that the reasons, on which it rests, are not very obvious. The case seems to have gone on the ground, that the means were matter of evidence, and not of averment; and that after verdict, it was to be presumed, that the means contemplated and used were such as to render the combination unlawful and constitute a conspiracy.

Suppose a baker in a small village had the exclusive custom of his neighborhood, and was making large profits by the sale of his bread. Supposing a number of those neighbors, believing the price of his bread too high, should propose to him to reduce his prices, or if he did not, that they would introduce another baker; and on his refusal, such other baker should, under their encouragement, set up a rival establishment, and sell his bread at lower prices; the effect would be to diminish the profit of the former baker, and to the same extent to impoverish him. And it might be said and proved, that the purpose of the associates was to diminish his profits, and thus impoverish him, though the ultimate and laudable object of the combination was to reduce the cost of bread to themselves and their neighbors. The same thing may be said of all competition in every branch of trade and industry; and yet it is through that competition, that the best interests of trade and industry are promoted. It is scarcely necessary to allude to the familiar instances of opposition lines of conveyance, rival hotels, and the thousand other instances, where each strives to gain custom to himself, by ingenious improvements, by increased industry, and by all the means by which he may lessen the price of commodities, and thereby diminish the profits of others.

We think, therefore, that associations may be entered into, the object of which is to adopt measures that may have a tendency to impoverish another, that is, to diminish his gains and profits, and yet so far from being criminal or unlawful, the object may be highly meritorious and public spirited. The legality of such an association will therefore depend upon the means to be used for its accomplishment. If it is to be carried into effect by fair or honorable and lawful means, it is, to say the least, innocent; if by falsehood or force, it may be stamped with the character of conspiracy. It follows as a necessary consequence, that if criminal and indictable, it is so by reason of the criminal means intended to be employed for its accomplishment; and as a further legal consequence, that as the criminality will depend on the means, those means must be stated in the indictment. If the same rule were to prevail in criminal, which holds in civil proceedings - that a case defectively stated may be aided by a verdict - then a court might presume, after verdict, that the indictment was supported by proof of criminal or unlawful means to effect the object. But it is an established rule in criminal cases, that the indictment must state a complete indictable offence, and cannot be aided by the proof offered at the trial. ...

It appears by the bill of exceptions, that it was contended on the part of the defendants, that this indictment did not set forth any agreement to do a criminal act, or to do any lawful act by criminal means, and that the agreement therein set forth did not constitute a conspiracy indictable by the law of this State, and that the court was requested so to instruct the jury. This the court declined doing, but instructed the jury that the indictment did describe a confederacy among the defendants to do an unlawful act, and to effect the same by unlawful means - that the society, organized and associated for the purposes described in the indictment, was an unlawful conspiracy against the laws of this State, and that if the jury believed, from the evidence, that the defendants or any of them had engaged in such confederacy, they were bound to find such of them guilty.

In this opinion of the learned judge, this court, for the reasons stated, cannot concur. Whatever illegal purpose can be found in the constitution of the Bootmakers' Society, it not being clearly set forth in the indictment, cannot be relied upon to support this conviction. So if any facts were disclosed at the trial, which, if properly averred, would have given a different character to the indictment, they do not appear in the bill of exceptions, nor could they, after verdict, aid the indictment. But looking solely at the indictment, disregarding the qualifying epitets, recitals and immaterial allegations, and confining ourselves to facts so averred as to be capable of being traversed and put in issue, we cannot perceive that it charges a criminal conspiracy punishable by law. The exceptions must therefore, be sustained, and the judgment arrested.

Several other exceptions were taken and have been argued; but this decision on the main question has rendered it unnecessary to consider them.[2]

Rufus Choate, The Position and Functions of the American Bar, as an Element of Conservatism in the State An Address to the Law School in Cambridge, July 3,1845 (1 Works of Rufus Choate (1862), 414, 417 et seq.)

Let me premise, ... that instead of diffusing myself in a display of all the modes by which the profession of the law may claim to serve the State, I shall consider but a single one, and that is its agency as an element of conservation. The position and functions of the American Bar, then, as an element of conservation in the State - this precisely and singly is the topic to which I invite your attention.

And is not the profession such an element of conservation? Is not this its characteristical office and its appropriate

---

2. For conflicting views of the grounds of this decision see Nelles, supra, Note 1, and Pound, The Formative Era of American Law (1938) p. 86-88.

praise? Is it not so that in its nature, in its functions, in the intellectual and practical habits which it forms, in the opinions to which it conducts, in all its tendencies and influences of speculation and action, it is and ought to be professionally and peculiarly such an element and such an agent - that it contributes, or ought to be held to contribute, more than all things else, or as much as anything else, to preserve our organic forms, our civil and social order, our public and private justice, our constitutions of government, - even the Union itself? In these crises through which our liberty is to pass, may not, must not, this function of conservatism become more and more developed, and more and more operative? May it not one day be written, for the praise of the American Bar, that it helped to keep the true idea of the State alive and germinant in the American mind; that it helped to keep alive the sacred sentiments of obedience and reverence and justice, of the supremacy of the calm and grand reason of the law over the fitful will of the individual and the crowd; that it helped to withstand the pernicious sophism that the successive generations, as they come to life, are but as so many sucessive flights of summer flies, without relations to the past or duties to the future, and taught instead that all - all the dead, the living, the unborn - were one moral person - one for action, one for suffering, one for responsibility, - that the engagements of one may bind the conscience of another; the glory or the shame of a day may brighten or stain the current of a thousand years of continuous national being? Consider the profession of the law, then, as an element of conservation in the American State. I think it is naturally such, so to speak; but I am sure it is our duty to make and to keep it such. ...

... I think I may take for granted that conservatism is, in the actual circumstances of this country, the one grand and comprehensive duty of a thoughtful patriotism. I speak in the general, of course, not pausing upon little or inevitable qualifications here and there, - not meaning anything so absurd as to say that this law, or that usage, or that judgment, or that custom or condition, might not be corrected or expunged, - not meaning still less to invade the domains of moral and philanthropic reform, true or false. I speak of our general political system; our organic forms; our written constitutions; the great body and the general administration of our jurisprudence; the general way in which liberty is blended with order, and the principle of progression with the securities of permanence; the relation of the States and the functions of the Union, - and I say of it in a mass, that conservation is the chief end, the largest duty, and the truest glory of American statesmanship.

There are nations, I make no question, whose history, condition, and dangers, call them to a different work. There are those whom everything in their history, condition, and dangers admonishes to reform fundamentally, if they would be saved. With them the whole political and social order is to be rearranged. The stern claim of labor is to be provided for. Its long antagonism with capital is to be reconciled. Property is all to be parcelled out in some nearer conformity to a parental law of nature. Conventional discriminations of precedence and right are to be swept away. Old forms from which the life is gone are to drop as leaves in autumn. Frowning towers nodding to their fall are to be taken down. Small freeholds must dot over and cut up imperial parks. A large infusion of liberty must be poured along these emptied veins and throb in that great heart. With those, the past must be resigned; the present must be convulsed, that "an immeasurable future" as Carlyle has said, "may be filled with fruitfulness and a verdant shade."

But with us the age of this mode and this degree of reform is over; its work is done. The passage of the sea, the occupation and culture of a new world, the conquest of independence - these were our eras, these our agency, of reform. In our jurisprudence of liberty, which guards our person from violence and our goods from plunder, and which forbids the whole power of the State itself to take the ewe lamb, or to trample on a blade of the grass of the humblest citizen without adequate remuneration; which makes every dwelling large enough to shelter a human life its owner's castle which winds and rain may enter but which the government cannot - in our written constitutions, whereby the people, exercising an act of sublime self-restraint have intended to put it out of their own power forever, to be passionate, tumultuous, unwise, unjust; whereby they have intended, by means of a system of representation; by means of the distribution of government into departments, independent, coordinate for checks and balances; by a double chamber of legislation; by the establishment of a fundamental and paramount organic law; by the organization of a judiciary whose function, whose loftiest function it is to test the legislation of the day by this standard for all time, - constitutions, whereby by all these means they have intended to secure a government of laws, not of men; of reason, not of will; of justice, not of fraud, - in that grand dogma of equality, - equality of right, of burthens, of duty, of privileges, and of chances, which is the very mystery of our social being - to the Jews, a stumbling block; to the Greeks, foolishness - our strength, our glory, - in that liberty which we value not solely because it is a natural right of man; not solely because it is a principle of individual energy and a guaranty of national renown; not at all because it attracts a procession and lights a bonfire, but because when blended with order, attended by law, tempered by virtue, graced by culture, it is a great practical good; because in her right hand are riches, and honor, and peace; because she has come down from her golden and purple cloud to walk in brightness by the weary ploughman's side, and whisper in his ear as he casts the seed with tears, that the harvest which frost and mildew and canker-worm shall spare, the government shall spare also; in our distribution into separate and kindred States, not wholly independent, not quite identical, in "the wide arch of the ranged empire" above - these are they in which the fruits of our age and our agency of reform are embodied; and these are they by which, if we are wise - if we understand the things that belong to our peace, - they may be perpetuated. It is for this that I say the fields of reform, the aims of reform, the uses of reform here, therefore, are wholly unlike the fields, uses, and aims of reform elsewhere. Foreign examples, foreign counsel - well or ill meant - the advice of the first foreign understandings, the example of the wisest foreign nations, are worse than useless for us. Even the teachings of history are to be cautiously consulted, or the guide of human life will lead us astray. We need reform enough, Heaven knows; but it is the reformation of our individual selves the bettering of our personal natures; it is a more intellectual industry; it is a more diffused, profound, and graceful, popular, and higher culture; it is a wider development of the love and discernment of the beautiful in form, in color, in speech, and in the soul of man, - this is what we need - personal, moral mental reform - not civil - not political! No, no! Government substantially as it is; jurisprudence, substantially as it is; the general arrangements of liberty, substantially as they are; the Constitution and the Union, exactly as they are - this is to be wise, according to the wisdom of America. ...

I do not know that in all the elaborate policy by which free States have sought to preserve themselves, there is one device so sure, so simple, so indispensable, as justice - justice to all; justice to foreign nations of whatever class of greatness or weakness; justice to public creditors, alien or native; justice to every individual citizen, down to the feeblest and the least beloved; justice in the assignment of political and civil right, and place, and opportunity; justice between man and man, every man and every other, - to observe and to administer this virtue steadily, uniformly, and at whatever cost - this, the best policy and the final course of all governments, is preeminently the policy of free governments. Much the most specious objection to free systems is, that they have been observed in the long run to develop a tendency to some mode of injustice. Resting on a truer theory of natural right in their constitutional construction than any other policy, founded in the absolute and universal equality of man, and permeated and tinged and all astir with this principle through all their frame, and, so far, more nobly just than any other, the doubt which history is supposed to suggest is, whether they do not reveal a tendency towards injustice in other ways. Whether they have been as uniformly true to their engagements. Whether property and good name and life have been quite as safe. Whether the great body of the jus privatum has been as skilfully composed and rigorously administered as under the less reasonable and attractive systems of absolute rule. You remember that Aristotle, looking back on a historical experience of all sorts of governments extending over many years - Aristotle who went to the court of Philip a republican, and came back a republican - records, in his Politics, injustice as the grand and comprehensive cause of the downfall of democracies. The historian of the Italian democracies extends the remark to them. That all States should be stable in proportion as they are just, and in proportion as they administer justly, is what might be asserted.

If this end is answered; if every man has his own exactly and uniformly, absolutism itself is found tolerable. If it is not, liberty - slavery, are but dreary and transient things. Placida quies sub libertate, in the words of Algernon Sydney and of the seal of Massachusetts - that is the union of felicities which should make the State immortal. Whether Republics have usually perished from injustice, need not be debated. One there was, the most renowned of all, that certainly did so. The injustice practised by the Athens of the age of Demosthenes upon its citizens, and suffered to be practised by one another, was as marvellous as the capacities of its dialect, as the eloquence by which its masses were regaled, and swayed this way and that as clouds, as waves - marvellous as the long banquet of beauty in which they revelled - as their love of Athens, and their passion of glory. There was not one day in the whole public life of Demosthenes when the fortune, the good name, the civil existence of any considerable man was safer there than it would have been at Constantinople or Cairo under the very worst forms of Turkish rule. There was a sycophant to accuse, a demagogue to prosecute, a fickle, selfish, necessitous court - no court at all, only a commission of some hundreds or thousands from the public assembly sitting in the sunshine, directly interested in the cause - to pronounce judgment. And he who rose rich and honored, might be flying at night for his life to some Persian or Macedonian outpost, to die by poison on his way in the temple of Neptune.

Is there not somewhat in sharing in that administration, observing and enjoying it, which tends to substitute in the professional and in the popular mind, in place of the wild consciousness of possessing summary power, ultimate power, the wild desire to exert it, and to grasp and subject all things to its rule - to substitute for this the more conservative sentiments of reverence for a law independent of, and distinct from, and antagonistical to, the humor of the hour? Is there not something in the study and administrative enjoyment of an elaborate, rational, and ancient jurisprudence, which tends to raise the law itself, in the professional and in the general idea, almost up to the nature of an independent, superior reason, in one sense out of the people, in one sense above them - out of and above, and independent of, and collateral to, the people of any given day? In all its vast volumes of provisions, very little of it is seen to be produced by the actual will of the existing generation. The first thing we know about it is, that we are actually being governed by it. The next thing we know is, we are rightfully and beneficially governed by it. We did not help to make it. No man now living helped to make much of it. The judge does not make it. Like the structure of the State itself, we found it around us at the earliest dawn of reason, it guarded the helplessness of our infancy, it restrained the passions of our youth, it protects the acquisitions of our manhood, it shields the sanctity of the grave, it executes the will of the departed. Invisible, omnipresent, a real yet impalpable existence, it seems more a spirit, an abstraction, the whispered yet authoritative voice of all the past and all the good - than like the transient contrivance of altogether such as ourselves. We come to think of it, not so much as a set of provisions and rules which we can unmake, amend, and annul, as of a guide whom it is wiser to follow, an authority whom it is better to obey, a wisdom which it is not unbecoming to revere, a power - a superior - whose service is perfect freedom. Thus at last the spirit of the law descends into the great heart of the people for healing and for conservation. Hear the striking platonisms of Coleridge: "Strength may be met with strength: the power of inflicting pain may be baffled by the pride of endurance: the eye of rage may be answered by the stare of defiance, or the downcast look of dark and revengeful resolve: and with all this there is an outward and determined object to which the mind can attach its passions and purposes, and bury its own disquietudes in the full occupation of the senses. But who dares struggle with an invisible combatant, with an enemy which exists and makes us know its existence, but where it is we ask in vain? No space contains it, time promises no control over it, it has no ear for my threats, it has no substance that my hands can grasp or my weapons find vulnerable; it commands and cannot be commanded, it acts and is insusceptible of my reaction, the more I strive to subdue it, the more am I compelled to think of it, and the more I think of it, the more do I find it to possess a reality out of myself, and not to be a phantom of my own imagination; - that all but the most abandoned men acknowledge its authority, and that the whole strength and majesty of my country are pledged to support it; and yet that for me its power is the same with that of my own permanent self, and that all the choice which is permitted to me consists in having it for my guardian angel or my avenging fiend. This is the spirit of Law - the lute of Amphion - the harp of Orpheus. This is the true necessity which compels man into the social state, now and always, by a still beginning, never ceasing, force of moral cohesion."

In supposing that conservation is the grand and prominent public function of the American Bar in the State, I have not felt that I assigned to a profession, to which I count it so high a privilege to belong, a part and a duty at all beneath its loftiest claims. I shall not deny that to found a State which grows to be a nation, on the ruins of an older, or on a waste of earth where was none before, is, intrinsically and in the judgment of the world, of the largest order of human achievements. Of the chief of men are the conditores imperiorum. But to keep the city is only not less difficult and glorious than to build it. Both rise, in the estimate of the most eloquent and most wise of Romans, to the rank of divine achievement. I appreciate the uses and the glory of a great and timely reform. Thrice happy and honored who leaves the Constitution better than he found it. But to find it good and keep it so, this, too, is virtue and praise.

It was the boast of Augustus - as Lord Brougham remembers in the close of his speech on the improvement of the law, - that he found Rome of brick and left it of marble. Ay. But he found Rome free, and left her a slave. He found her a republic, and left her an empire! He found the large soul of Cicero unfolding the nature, speaking the high praise, and recording the maxims of regulated liberty, with that eloquence which so many millions of hearts have owned - and he left poets and artists! We find our city of marble, and we will leave it marble. Yes, all, all, up to the grand, central, and eternal dome; we will leave it marble, as we find it. To that office, to that praise, let even the claims of your profession be subordinated. Pro clientibus saepe; pro lege, pro republica semper.

The Field Codes in New York

1. First Report of the Commissioners of the Code (1858) by David Dudley Field, William Curtis Noyes, and Alexander W. Bradford

The Commissioners of the Code, appointed by the Act of April 6, 1857,[1] beg leave to make this their first Report:

---

1. In Section 24 of Article VI of the New York Constitution of 1846 it had been provided that the Legislature at its first session should appoint a commission "whose duty it shall be to re-

Immediately upon their appointment, they entered upon the performance of the duties committed to them, impressed with the magnitude of the undertaking, the difficulty of its accomplishment, and the necessity of caution and deliberation in every step they should take, but with a determination to recoil from no obstacle, possible to be overcome by their efforts, and to submit to any amount of labor and sacrifice necessary for the preparation of a Code of the whole body of the law.

It is known to the Legislature, that the duty which the Commissioners are performing is one of the greatest, most difficult, and most responsible.

Nothing within the range of government can exceed in magnitude the task of collecting, condensing and arranging the jurisprudence of a people. The structure of government and society, and all their complex relations, are comprehended within it. Public order, sound morals, all advancement in the arts of civilization, and all growth in true prosperity, are dependent, in a great degree, upon those rules of action, which the state prescribes for the conduct of its citizens.

The difficulty and responsibility, in this instance, are increased by two considerations; the present state of the law, and the necessity of some modification to make a harmonious system. The condition of our law at the present time, is not unlike that of the Roman law in the time of Justinian, or of the French law in the time of Napoleon. From the date of the Twelve

---

vise, reform, simplify and abridge the rules and practice, pleadings, forms and proceedings of the courts of record of this state". Prompt action by the legislature and the commissioners, of whom the dominant member was David Dudley Field, resulted in the adoption of a Code of Procedure in 1848.

Section 17 of Article I of the Constitution of 1846 directed that the legislature at the first session after the adoption of the constitution should appoint three commissioners "whose duty it shall be to reduce into a written and systematic code the whole body of the law of this state, or so much and such parts thereof as to the said commissioners shall seem practicable and expedient". The commissioners first appointed under this section showed considerable reluctance to undertake the task assigned them. At length, in 1857, the legislature took effective action when it named Field, William Curtis Noyes and Alexander W. Bradford commissioners, and specifically directed them to prepare for submission to the legislature a code which should be divided into three parts, the Political Code, the Civil Code, and the Penal Code. The Commissioners in 1860 reported the text of a proposed Political Code; in 1865 they submitted texts of the Civil and the Penal Codes.

Tables to the age of Justinian, the polity and institutions of the Romans had so largely changed, so many new and various laws had been added, and the numerous decisions consequent upon the extension of commerce, the enlargement of the Republic and Empire, the modifications of social relations, and the conflict of laws of different provinces and nations, had become so complicated, that a Code, which is a condensed and reformed Digest, was a matter of necessity. Something of the same kind is observable now.[2]

Our law is the product of ten centuries, most of them filled with tumult and disorder; it is compounded of many incongruous elements, Saxon and Norman customs, Feudal and Roman law, provincial usages, and the decisions of various and disagreeing tribunals. We have Equity law, Admiralty law, Canon law, as the law of marriage and succession, and two kinds of Common law, one contradistinguished from Statute, and the other from Equity. Society has undergone an entire transformation. The feudal system has fallen to pieces; monarchial institutions have given place to republican; land from being almost inalienable has become an article of daily and hourly traffic; and commerce, once so narrow and timid, embraces the world. Personal rights, and personal property have assumed an importance never before known; the numberless questions arising from modern enterprise, travel, emigration, and the expansion of industry and commerce, have developed new departments of jurisprudence; while the multiplication of courts required by the necessities of an increased population, and a traffic constantly augmenting, has produced a mass of adjudications, painful for the student to contemplate, and often difficult if not impossible to reconcile. Thus we have arrived at the period of which the Roman historian complained so justly, when "the infinite variety of laws and legal opinions had filled many thousand volumes, which no fortune could purchase, and no capacity could digest".

How far, in the preparation of a Code, changes should be recommended, is a question of much delicacy. They should, without doubt, be cautiously admitted. Law is the growth of time and circumstance. An original system of jurisprudence, founded upon mere theory, without reference to national characteristics, habits, traditions and usages, would be a failure. The science of government and law is progressive; new regulations spring from necessity, or are suggested by experience, and the application of the rules of justice to human affairs is constantly modified by the changing circumstances of society. The process is easily understood. In the earlier stages of civilization, when communities are small and isolated, local customs are more dis-

---

2. Cf. Mr. Justice Story, <u>supra</u>, p. 469-70.

tinct, in conformity with local character; but as cultivation and intercourse gradually break down provincial peculiarities, and eradicate partial customs, the tendency to assimilation enables the legislator to disregard inconvenient rules, venerable only from age and habit, and gradually to introduce changes which have the experience of other communities to recommend them, and which seem better adapted to an advanced civilization. We thus reach a stage, in which valuable improvements may be borrowed from other systems and engrafted into our own, without impairing the harmony of our laws, by the introduction of unsuitable elements. For example, the law of special or limited partnerships, the off-spring of the commerce of the middle ages, unknown to the common law, has within a recent period been adopted into our own legislation, with manifest advantage.[3] So we have also seen the influence of our jurisprudence reflected back upon the country from which we derived our language and our laws; and reforms, readily admitted by our plastic legislation, slowly adopted there, after having been tested by our experience; though the settled constitution and the fixed habits of England might have prevented their origination in that country.[4]

Thus two great purposes are to be subserved in revising the jurisprudence of a nation; one, the reduction of existing laws into a more accessible form, resolving doubts, removing vexed questions, and abolishing useless distinctions; the other the introduction of such modifications as are plainly indicated by our own judgment or the experience of others. We are satisfied that this work should be performed with delicacy, caution and discrimination, that nothing should be touched, from the mere desire of change, or without great probability of solid advantage.

A Code of all the law of a commercial and opulent people can only be made after the most patient study and incessant toil. A superficial observer might, perhaps, suppose a year or two of labor sufficient for it, but he who reflects upon the infinite variety of human affairs, and that the law aims to furnish a rule for every known relation and every foreseen transaction, knows how idle it is to expect it to be hastily, if it

---

3. In 1822 the New York legislature adopted a statute concerning Limited Partnerships which, in its essentials, was based upon the provisions of the French Code of Commerce. The New York statute was subsequently closely followed in the legislation of other states. See, Troubat, <u>The Law of Commandatary and Limited Partnership</u> (1853) 45 <u>et seq</u>.

4. No American had greater influence on the movement for law reform in England during the first half of the 19th century than Edward Livingston. See, 1 Radzinowicz, <u>History of English Criminal Law</u> (1948) 577.

be faithfully performed. The task should seem, indeed, to be hopeless, if it were designed to provide an express rule for every case which can possibly present itself for judicial decision. It is of course impossible to foresee all the questions which will arise in the future, or to collect and arrange all those which have arisen and been solved, so as to meet every contingency in human affairs, by a definite legal rule. That which in the judgment of the Commissioners can reasonably be attempted is to collect, condense and arrange those general and comprehensive rules of action, resting upon fundamental principles, recognized by the law or by reasòn, which will afford, as far as possible, a guide in regard to the rights of person and of property. There should be neither a generalization too vague nor a particularity too minute, in the Code of an enlightened and free people, whose intelligence demands that the law should be written, and brought within the knowledge of all, and whose liberty requires that no greater restraints be imposed upon their action than policy and necessity dictate. ...

2. Introduction to the Completed Civil Code (1865)
by David Dudley Field and Alexander W. Bradford

... Whether a general Code of the law be possible, should seem, from the nature of the subject, hardly to be doubtful. The common law of New York, like the common law of England, from which it is in great part derived, consists of a vast number of rules of property and of conduct, which have been applied by the judicial tribunals, and which had their origin either in legislative enactments, now forgotten, or in traditions from ancient times, or in the consciences of the judges, as the cases came before them. The decisions of the tribunals have been for ages preserved in writing. If there was ever a time when they were held in the memory alone, that time has long passed. All that we now know of the law, we know from written records. To make a Code of the known law is therefore but to make a complete, analytical, and authoritative compilation from these records. The records of the common law are in the reports of the decisions of the tribunals; the records of the statute law are in the volumes of legislative acts. That these records are susceptible of collation, analysis, and arrangement, might have been assumed beforehand, even if we had not the proof in our libraries, in digest upon digest, more or less perfect, to which we daily resort for convenience and instruction. The more perfect a digest becomes, the more nearly it approaches the Code contemplated by the Constitution. In other words, a complete digest of our existing law, common and statute, dissected and analyzed, avoiding repetitions and rejecting contradictions, moulded into distinct propositions, and arranged in scientific order, with proper amendments, and in this form sanctioned by the Legislature, is the Code which the organic law commanded to be made for the people of this State. That this was possible, was all but proven by what had been already done among ourselves.

It was fully proven by what had been done in respect to the law of other countries. The law of Rome in the time of Justinian was, to say the least, as difficult of reduction into a Code as is our own law at the present day. Yet it was thus reduced, though, no doubt, to the disgust and dismay of many a lawyer of that period. The concurring judgment of thirteen centuries since, has, however, pronounced the Code of Justinian one of the noblest benefactions to the human race, as it was one of the greatest achievements of human genius.

France, at the beginning of her revolution, was governed partly by Roman and partly by customary law. The French Codes made one uniform system for the whole country, supplanting the former laws, and forming a model by which half of Europe has since fashioned its legislation. It should seem, therefore, to be quite beyond dispute, that a general Code of the law is possible.

Whether it is also expedient, is a different question. One of the objections made is, that it is not possible to provide for all future cases. You may, it is said, stretch your foresight to its utmost limit; you may exhaust all the sagacity and ingenuity of the humand mind; the future, nevertheless, is a sealed book: you cannot look into its unopened leaves; and, therefore, attempting to provide for what they contain, is spending your strength in a vain and fruitless effort. This does not appear to be an objection of any weight whatever. Because we cannot provide for all cases, should be thought a poor reason for not providing for as many as possible. To render the existing law as accessible, and as intelligible as we can, is a rational object, through we cannot foresee what ought to be the law in cases yet unknown. To cast aside known rules which are obsolete, to correct those which are burdensome, or unsuitable to present circumstances, to reject anomalous or ill-considered cases, to bring the different branches into a more perfect order and agreement, may be of immense value, though we cannot look beyond the present, to make provision for what has never yet appeared. ...

If a case unprovided for could not arise under the code of Civil Procedure, much less could it arise under the Code of Criminal Procedure. It may, therefore, be safely affirmed, that there is but one of the five Codes, that is to say, the Civil Code, to which, with any semblance of justice, it may be made an objection that it cannot provide for all future cases. This Code is, undoubtedly, the most important and difficult of all; and of this it is true, that it cannot provide for all possible cases which the future may disclose. It does not profess to provide for them. All that it professes is, to give the general rules upon the subjects to which it relates, which are now known and recognized, so far as they ought to be retained, with such amendments as seemed best to be made, and saving always such of the rules as may have been overlooked. In cases where the law is not declared by the Code, it is to be hoped that analogies may nevertheless be discovered which will enable the courts to decide. If, in any such case, an analogy cannot be found, nor any rule which has been overlooked and omitted, then the courts will have either to decide, as at present, without reference to any settled rule of law, or to leave the case undecided, as was done by Lord Mansfield, in King v. Hay, 1 W. Bl. 640, trusting to future legislation for future cases.

The language of the Code in this respect should seem to be sufficiently guarded, thus:

"Sec.2. Law is a rule of property and of conduct, prescribed by the sovereign power of the State.

Sec.3. The will of the sovereign power is expressed:

1. By the Constitution, which is the organic act of the people;
2. By statutes, which are the acts of the Legislature, or by the ordinances of other and subordinate legislative bodies;
3. By the judgments of the tribunals enforcing those rules, which, though not enacted, form what is known as customary or common law.[1]

Sec.4. The common law is divided into:

1. Public law, or the law of nations;
2. Domestic, or municipal law.

Sec.5. The evidence of the common law is found in the decisions of the tribunals.

Sec.6. In this State there is no common law, in any case, where the law is declared by the five Codes.

Sec. 2032. The rule that statutes in derogation of the common law are to be strictly construed, has no application to this Code.

Sec. 2033. All statutes, laws and rules heretofore in force in this State, inconsistent with the provisions of this Code, are hereby repealed or abrogated; but such repeal or abrogation does not revive any former law heretofore repealed, nor does it affect any right already existing or accrued, or any proceeding already taken, except as in this Code provided."

Therefore, if there be an existing rule of law omitted from this Code, and not inconsistent with it, that rule will continue

---

1. In the first draft of the Code (1862) there was no reference to "common law"; the unenacted rules were all embraced by the description "customary law".

to exist in the same form in which it now exists; while if any new rule, now for the first time introduced, should not answer the good ends for which it is intended, which can be known only from experience, it can be amended or abrogated by the same law-giving department which made it; and if new cases arise, as they will, which have not been foreseen, they may be decided, if decided at all, precisely as they would now be decided, that is to say, by analogy to some rule in the Code, or to some rule omitted from the Code and therefore still existing, or by the dictates of natural justice. ...

Having thus considered the principal objections to the codification of the law, it should next be considered whether there are advantages in it. Assuming that it is possible to have a body of written law in a convenient form, and in scientific order, containing the materials and framed in the manner already described, what benefits will it confer? In the first place, it will enable the lawyer to dispense with a great number of the books which now incumber the shelves of his library. In the next place, it will thus save a vast amount of labor, now forced upon lawyers and judges, in searching through the reports, examing and collecting cases, and drawing inferences from the decisions, and so far facilitate the dispatch of business in the courts. In the third place, it will afford an opportunity for settling, by legislative enactment, many disputed questions, which the courts have never been able to settle. In the fourth place, it will enable the Legislature to effect reforms in different branches of the law, which can only be effected by simultaneous and comprehensive legislation. Thus, for example, the closer assimilation of the law of real and personal property, and the changes in the relation of husband and wife, as to property, cannot be effected by any other means so wisely and safely, as by a General Code. The making of a Code involves a general revision of the law. It is indeed in this way alone that such a revision seems practicable. The occasion is thereby afforded to look at the law of the land, as a whole, to lop off its excrescences, reconcile its contradictions and make it uniform and harmonious. In the fifth place, the publication of a Code will diffuse among the people a more general and accurate knowledge of their rights and duties, than can be obtained in any other manner. This is an object of great importance in all countries, but more especially in ours. If every person can have before him, in an authentic form, the laws which are to affect his property, and govern his conduct, he can have an additional guaranty of his rights, and a better acquaintance with his duties. Here, more than anywhere else, all classes of citizens interfere in all the affairs of the State. They elect, directly, nearly all the officers who make, administer, or execute the laws. If in Holland, or in Germany, or France, a Civil Code has been found beneficial, much more is it likely to be beneficial to us.

So far as the choice lies between law, to be made by the legislature, and law to be made by the judiciary, there cannot be a doubt that whatever may be the determination elsewhere, the people of this State prefer that theirs shall be made by those whom they elect as legislators, rather than by those whose function it is, according to the theory of the Constitution, to administer the laws as they find them. Hence, the idea of a Code has taken such hold of our people that they have made provision for it by their organic law.

3. The Civil Code as Drafted

During the first half of the 19th century discussion of reform through codification was largely concerned with theory. In the consolidation and revision of statutes, of course, the effectiveness of systematically inclusive legislation had been tested. Yet the successes of revision had not established the practicability of the wholesale translation of common law into statutory law. When the Field Codes were submitted to the New York legislature theory met the test of actuality. An example of the result of Field's labors will indicate the general character of his effort and give some basis for judgment as to the value of his labor. The following excerpt from the draft Civil Code of 1861 gives the first title of Part II of the Third Division of the Code which concerned "Obligations". Citations which followed each of the sections in the draft submitted to the legislature have been omitted.

Title I

Nature of a Contract

Chapter I

Definition

Sec. 744. A contract is an agreement to do or not to do a certain thing.

Sec. 745. It is essential to the existence of a contract that there should be:
1. Parties capable of contracting;
2. Their consent;
3. A lawful object; and,
4. A sufficient cause or consideration.[1]

---

1. An anonymous critic of Field's Code of Procedure had ridi-

Chapter II

Parties

Sec. 746. All persons are capable of contracting, except minors, persons of unsound mind, and persons deprived of civil rights.

Sec. 747. Minors, and persons of unsound mind, have only such capacity as is defined by Part I of the First Division of this Code.

Sec. 748. It is essential to the validity of a contract, not only that the parties should exist, but that it should be possible to identify them.

Sec. 749. A contract, made expressly for the benefit of a third person, may be enforced by him at any time before the parties thereto rescind it.

Chapter III

Consent

Sec. 750. The consent of the parties to a contract must be:

1. Free;
2. Mutual; and,
3. Communicated by each to the other.

Sec. 751. A consent which is not free is nevertheless not absolutely void, but may be rescinded by the parties, in the manner prescribed by the chapter on Rescission.

Sec. 752. An apparent consent is not real or free when obtained through:

1. Duress;
2. Menace;
3. Fraud;
4. Undue influence; or,
5. Mistake.

Sec. 753. Consent is deemed to have been obtained through one of the causes mentioned in the last section, only when it would not have been given had such cause not existed.

---

culed the form of the draft submitted to the legislature in the following passage:

"To imitate the admired diction of the Bode, I fear that I am getting to be

1. Tired;
2. Tiresome; and
3. Tedious.

And therefore, I hasten to a close." Juvenus Alumnus, Crudities of the Code and Codifiers (1850); 25.

Sec. 754. Duress consists in:

1. Unlawful confinement of the person of the party, or of the husband or wife of such party, or of an ancestor, descendent, or adopted child of such party, husband or wife;
2. Unlawful detention of the property of any such person; or,
3. Confinement of such person, lawful in form, but fraudulently obtained, or fraudulently made unjustly harassing or oppressive.

Sec. 755. Menace consists in a threat:

1. Of such duress as is specified in the first and third subdivisions of the last section;
2. Of unlawful and violent injury to the person or property of any such person as is specified in the last section; or,
3. Of injury to the character of any such person.

Sec. 756. Fraud is either actual or constructive.

Sec. 757. Actual fraud, within the meaning of this chapter, consists in any of the following acts, committed by a party to the contract, or with his connivance, with intent to deceive another party thereto, or to induce him to enter into the contract.

1. The suggestion, as a fact, of that which is not true, by one who does not believe it to be true;
2. The positive assertion, in a manner not warranted by the information of the person making it, of that which is not true, though he believes it to be true;
3. The suppression of that which is true, by one having knowledge or belief of the fact;
4. A promise, made without any intention of performing it; or,
5. Any other act fitted to deceive.

Sec. 758. Constructive fraud consists:

1. In any breach of duty which, without an actually fraudulent intent, gains an advantage to the person in fault, or any one claiming under him, by misleading another to his prejudice, or to the prejudice of any one claiming under him; or,
2. In any such act or omission as the law specially declares to be fraudulent, without respect to actual fraud.

Sec. 759. Actual fraud is always a question of fact.

Sec. 760. Undue influence consists:

1. In the use, by one in whom a confidence is reposed by another, or who holds a real or

apparent authority over him, of such confidence or authority for the purpose of obtaining an unfair advantage over him;

2. In taking an unfair advantage of another's weakness of mind; or,
3. In taking a grossly oppressive and unfair advantage of another's necessities or distress.

Sec. 761. Mistake may be either of fact or of law.

Sec. 762. Mistake of fact is a mistake, not caused by the neglect of a legal duty on the part of the person making the mistake, and consisting in:

1. An unconscious ignorance or forgetfulness of a fact past or present, material to the contract; or
2. Belief in the present existence of a thing material to the contract, which does not exist, or in the past existence of such a thing, which has not existed.

Sec. 763. Mistake of law constitutes a mistake, within the meaning of this article, only when it arises from:

1. A misapprehension of the law by all parties, all supposing that they knew and understood it, and all making substantially the same mistake as to the law; or,
2. A misapprehension of the law by one party, of which the others are aware at the time of contracting, but which they do not rectify.

Sec. 764. Mistake of foreign laws is a mistake of fact.

Sec. 765. Consent is not mutual, unless the parties all agree upon the same thing in the same sense. But in certain cases defined by the chapter on Interpretation, they are to be deemed so to agree without regard to the fact.

Sec. 766. Consent can be communicated with effect, only by some act or omission of the party contracting, by which he intends to communicate it, or which necessarily tends to such communication.

Sec. 767. If a proposal prescribes any conditions concerning the communication of its acceptance, the proposer is not bound unless they are conformed to; but in other cases any reasonable and usual mode may be adopted.

Sec. 768. Consent is deemed to be fully communicated between the parties as soon as the party accepting a proposal has put his acceptance in the course of transmission to the proposer, in conformity to the last section.

Sec. 769. Performance of the conditions of a proposal, or the acceptance of the consideration offered with a proposal, is an acceptance of the proposal.

Sec. 770. An acceptance must be absolute and unqualified, or must include in itself an acceptance of that character, which the proposer can separate from the rest, and which will conclude the person accepting. A qualified acceptance is a new proposal.

Sec. 771. A proposal may be revoked at any time before its acceptance is communicated to the proposer, but not afterwards.

Sec. 772. A proposal is revoked:

1. By the communication of notice or revocation by the proposer to the other party, in the manner prescribed by sections 766 and 768, before his acceptance has been communicated to the former;
2. By the lapse of the time prescribed in such proposal for its acceptance, or if no time is so prescribed, the lapse of a reasonable time without communication of the acceptance;
3. By the failure of the acceptor to fulfill a condition precedent to acceptance; or,
4. By the death or insanity of the proposer.

Sec. 773. A contract which is voidable solely for want of due consent, may be ratified by a subsequent consent.

Sec. 774. A voluntary acceptance of the benefit of a transaction is equivalent to a consent to all the obligations arising from it, so far as the facts are known, or ought to be known, to the person accepting.

Chapter IV

Object of a Contract

Sec. 775. The object of a contract is the thing which it is agreed, on the part of the party receiving the consideration, to do or not to do.

Sec. 776. The object of a contract must be lawful when the contract is made, and possible and ascertainable by the time the contract is to be performed.

Sec. 777. Everything is deemed possible, except that which is impossible in the nature of things.

Sec. 778. Where a contract has but a single object, and such object is unlawful, whether in whole or in part, or wholly impossible of performance, or so vaguely expressed as to be wholly unascertainable, the entire contract is void.

Sec. 779. Where a contract has several distinct objects, of which one at least is lawful, and one at least is unlawful in whole or in part, the contract is void as to the latter, and valid as to the rest.

Chapter V

Consideration[2]

Sec. 780. Any benefit conferred, or agreed to be conferred, upon the promiser, by any other person, to which the promiser is not lawfully entitled, or any prejudice suffered, or agreed to be suffered, by such person, other than such as he is at the time of consent lawfully bound to suffer, as an inducement to the promiser, is a good consideration for a promise.

---

2. In the Code of Georgia, adopted in 1861, the intended to "embody the great fundamental principles of our jurisprudence from whatever source derived" (Preface, p. iii), Chapter III, Title 7, of Part 2 dealt with Consideration in the following sections:
Sec. 2703. A consideration is essential to a contract, which the law will enforce. An executory contract, without such consideration, is called nudum pactum, or a naked promise. In some cases, a consideration is presumed, and an averment to the contrary, will not be received; such are generally contracts under seal, and negotiable instruments alleging a consideration upon their face, in the hands of innocent holders without notice who have received the same, before dishonored.
Sec. 2704. A consideration is valid, if any benefit accrues to him who makes the promise, or any injury to him who receives the promise.
Sec. 2705. Considerations are distinguished into good and valuable. A good consideration, is such as is founded on natural duty and affection, or on a strong moral obligation. A valuable consideration, is founded on money or something convertible to money, or having a value in money, except marriage, which is a valuable consideration.
Sec. 2706. Mere inadequacy of consideration, alone, will not void a contract. If the inadequacy be great, it is a strong circumstance to evidence fraud. And on a suit for damages for breach of the contract, the inadequacy of consideration will always enter as an element in estimating the damages.
Sec. 2707. If the consideration be founded in a mistake of fact or of law, the promise founded thereon cannot be enforced.
Sec. 2708. A promise of another, is a good consideration for a promise. So in mutual subscriptions for a common object, the promise of the others is a good consideration for the promise of each.
Sec. 2709. If the consideration be good in part and void in part, the promise will be sustained or not according as it is

Sec. 781. An existing legal obligation resting upon the promiser, or a moral obligation, originating in some benefit conferred upon the promiser, or prejudice suffered by the promisee, is also a good consideration for a promise, to an extent corresponding with the extent of the obligation, but no further or otherwise.

Sec. 782. The consideration of a contract must be lawful, within the meaning of section 827.

Sec. 783. If any part of a single consideration for one or more objects, or of several considerations for a single object, is unlawful, the entire contract is void.

Sec. 784. A consideration may be executed or executory, in whole or in part. In so far as it is executory, it is subject to the provisions of chapter IV of this Title.

Sec. 785. When a consideration is executory, it is not indispensable that the contract should specify its amount or the means of ascertaining it. It may be left to the decision of a third person, or regulated by any specified standard.

Sec. 786. When a contract does not determine the amount of the consideration, nor the method by which it is to be ascertained, or when it leaves the amount thereof to the discretion of an interested party, the consideration must be so much money as the object of the contract is reasonably worth.

Sec. 787. Where a contract provides an exclusive method by which its consideration is to be ascertained, which method is on its face impossible of execution, the entire contract is void.

Sec. 788. Where a contract provides an exclusive method by which its consideration is to be ascertained, which method appears possible on its face, but in fact, is, or becomes, impossible of execution, such provision only is void.

---

entire or severable as hereinafter prescribed. But if the consideration be illegal in whole or in part, the whole promise fails.

Sec. 2710. An impossible consideration, is insufficient to sustain any promise, otherwise if the consideration be possible but improbable.

Sec. 2711. If there be a valid consideration for the promise, it matters not from whom it moved. The promisee may sustain his action, though a stranger to the consideration.

Sec. 2712. If the consideration ... fails either wholly or in part before the promise is executed, such failure may be pleaded in defence to the promise. If it be partial an apportionment must be made according to the facts of each case.

4. The Field Codes in the 1880's

Although the Field Commissioners had submitted the Penal and Civil Codes to the Legislature in 1865 no action was taken on them for many years. In 1879 the Penal Code was passed by the legislature but was vetoed by the Governor. In 1881, however, both the Penal Code and the Code of Criminal Procedure were enacted into law. Efforts were made at the same time to have the Civil Code at length adopted, but the opposition of the bar, led by the Association of the Bar of the City of New York and James C. Carter, prevented its adoption. In the first years of the 80's there was extensive discussion of the issues raised by this final New York effort to have the common law codified. The following selections are from the writing of that time.

Argument of Professor Munroe Smith in opposition to the Bill "To Establish a Civil Code" before the Joint Meeting of Judiciary Committees of the Senate and Assembly, Feb. 25, 1886. (Abstract of Stenographic Report)

Prof. Smith believed, in common with many other lawyers, that it was inexpedient to codify that part of the law which was rather theoretical than practical. He thought that legislation should confine itself to positive and concrete rules of conduct (what it was customary to call laws) and that vague general maxims, definitions and rules of interpretation should be excluded from a code. This was the opinion held by the majority of European jurists, as the result of centuries of experience. All the rest of Justinian's codes put together were not responsible for a tithe of the confusions and uncertainties which had been produced by the one title of "rules" or maxims. These maxims had obtained so evil a repute that no such title was to be found in any modern code except the proposed code of New York.[1] But there were other things besides maxims which it had been found inadvisable to put into statutory form, viz., definitions and rules of interpretation. There were a great

---

1. Part IV of the Civil Code as drafted by the Field Commission was made up of a long series of familiar maxims, largely derived from the Roman law but frequently reiterated in the decisions of the courts of common law and equity. Among the maxims proposed for adoption were the following: "No one should suffer by the act of another"; "For every wrong there is a remedy"; "The law respects form less than substance"; "The law disregards trifles"; "The greater contains the less"; "Superfluity does not vitiate"; and "Interpretation must be reasonable".

many of these in the Code Napoleon. How had they worked? As badly as the maxims of Justinian's Digest. M. Theophile Huc, Professor of the Code Napoleon at Toulouse, had declared, in a recent book, that all these portions of the code had proved either useless or dangerous. Count Kaunitz had admirably indicated, more than a century ago, what things belonged in a code, and what things did not belong there. In his instructions to the commissioners appointed to draft a vode for Austria, Kaunitz directed them to omit everything which belonged in the mouth of a professor lecturing to students rather than in the mouth of the legislator. These were utterances of persons friendly to codification. Another such utterance, and a very recent one, was that of Mr. Grey, a London barrister. Mr. Field had apparently sent Mr. Grey a copy of the code, and Mr. Grey had written in answer a courteous letter containing some rather carefully worded praise of the code. But on one point Mr. Grey expressed his opinion frankly. He did not think it was wise to codify the maxims. If European jurists agreed upon any question, it was upon this. And the reason was obvious. These maxims, definitions and rules of interpretation represented the scientific side of the development of law. The formulation of the positive rules might properly be taken from the courts and intrusted to a legislature. But the science of the law could not be developed by legislative enactment. But this was exactly what the code proposed to do. The code borrowed and combined the worst features of the codes of Justinian and of Napoleon; it borrowed the maxims of the one, the definitions and rules of interpretation of the other.

Another ground upon which the speaker objected to the proposed code was that it had been deemed expedient to codify the common law. What did that mean? Simply the substitution of statutory for judge-made law? That was generally assumed to be the only question involved; and the constant reference made by the supporters of this code to the great codes of modern Europe seemed to indicate that they imagined that this was the question which had been settled in France and Italy, and which was being settled in Germany and Switzerland. They seemed to think that those countries had codified or were codifying in order to get rid of judge-made law. Nothing could be more untrue. Why did France codify? Not to turn judge-made law into statute law, but to get a common, i. e., a national law. They had some eighty principal systems of provincial law and some two hundred odd minor systems; and the only means of establishing common or national law was by statute. Why did Italy codify? For the same reason. Italy was not united until 1859-1860, and in the new kingdom there were half-a-dozen distinct systems of local law. A common law could be created only by statute. Why had Switzerland codified a great part of its law? Because of the multiplicity of different laws in the different cantons. Why was

Germany codifying? Because in the new empire there were five principal systems of written law, and the Germans wanted a national law. Not in any of these cases was it the declared object to replace judge-made law by statute law. The declared object was to get a common, a national law. In most of these cases the local law which the great national codes superseded was written law; in many of these cases the local law had already assumed the form of a code. All these great codes of the nineteenth century were adopted to make the law national.

Was this what the bill now before the legislature proposed to do? It proposed the direct opposite. It proposed to substitute local law - New York law - for the common law, which was a national law. The interpretation and development of the common law rested, it was true, in the hands of State judges. But the local courts were in the habit of regarding the decisions rendered by judges in other States. There was a constant and conscious effort to keep the law common, to make its development harmonious all over the United States. This common, national law was to be superseded in New York by a local statute. It was true that the code assumed merely to declare the common law. But even if that was true, what would be the effect of its adoption? Mr. Birdseye had shown that all legislation begot legislation. How much common law would be left in the New York code after twenty years of revision, repeal and amendment? Suppose all the thirty-eight States of the Union in possession of codes originally identical - how much resemblance would there be in twenty years?

There was no analogy between the proposed local codification of law in New York and the great national codification of Europe. To find a true analogy it was necessary to go back of this century. The legal history of Germany from the sixteenth to the nineteenth century offered a true and most instructive parallel. In the sixteenth century Germany had a common law. It was the Roman law. That law was only in part statutory law. The most important part, the Digest of Justinian, was, as Mr. Rives had said, case-law, and that law the courts developed by interpretation. They regarded each other's decisions and strove to keep the development of the common law uniform. In the seventeenth century some of the single States of the Empire began to codify. Their codes were only declaratory of the common law. But as soon as they had codes they began to amend them, and the law of the different states began to diverge. In the eighteenth and nineteenth centuries the volume of legislation in the several States increased constantly; new codes appeared that were not declaratory of the common law, but superseded it. In this century the laws of the different German States had become so different that commerce was handicapped and family relations became complicated. The demand for the re-establishment of a common law became more and more imperious. But there was no central legislative power until 1867 - none for all Germany until 1871. As soon as that legislative power was created, national codification began. The Federal legislative power was at first limited, like ours. But the people were determined to have common law, and in 1873 a constitutional amendment was adopted bringing the entire civil law within the sphere of the Federal legislation, and a commission was immediately appointed to codify it.

If the analogies of history meant anything, the destruction of national law by local codification meant the eventual overthrow of local codes by national codification. If the members of the New York legislature desired to hasten the time when, by constitutional amendment, the States should be stripped of this power of civil legislation and this power transferred to the national government, they could take a long step in that direction by passing this code.

Defense of the Civil Code by Robert Ludlow Fowler
in his Codification in the State of New York (1884)

... Having now completed a hurried survey of the States which have had recourse to codification as a means of bettering the condition of their organic law, we may next glance at the theories of codification prevailing in England and America. The nature of the dispute as to the merits or demerits of expressing laws in formulae, is not new. Students of philosophy will recognize a phase of this very discussion in the distinction which they draw between Plato and Aristotle. Aristotle's aim was to reduce philosophy to science. Plato thought truth too many sided to be shackled by mere verbal expressions. The result is well known, it was by the inexorable logic of Aristotle that men were first enabled to detect with accuracy the true from the false. The party opposed to codification simply adhere to the old position that truth is too many sided to be shackled; the party of codification to the old position, that certain fundamental propositions of law may be so formulated as to afford great aid to the arrangement and discussion of the propositions not formulated. It is not strange that Mr. Field is unwilling to repeat in detail the answers long ago conceded to meet the very objections now put forward by the adherents of the historical school of law. It must also be remembered, in this connection, that these answers are already existent in the literature of codification which is extremely complete.

In England the question of codification has for some reason become confused with the discussion concerning the merits of consolidation, revision or other substitutional escape from complications in which their wide-spread empire helps to involve them. The scientific faction of the English bar would, in the main, seem to adhere to a very highly scientific plan of codification. Recognizing that positive laws are concerned either with rights or with duties they are engaged in a discussion as to whether rights or duties afford the best basis for a successful codification - a question about which the practical codifiers of the world have wasted very little breath. Prof. Holland of Oxford, in some respects the most distinguished scientific jurist now living, has but lately succeeded in squaring the circle of the jurisprudents by a distribution of the entire subject-matter of jurisprudence on the basis of rights, a problem Austin notably failed to solve.[1] It ought at this juncture, to be noted that Professor Holland has disclaimed that his system of jurisprudence was ever intended as a basis of English codification. Other persons, however, less discriminating than Professor Holland, and imbued with the classifications of Austin, Mill or some other founder of a system, would make these classifications the basis of English codification without regard to the needs of those lawyers who must always practice their profession as an art rather than as a science. The supreme motive in codification - to subject a body of law to a form which best fits it to the concrete purposes of technical law - is thus lost sight of at the outset.

The practical work of codification has always been performed by practical lawyers, those familiar with the needs of practical lawyers. They have generally been men with a scientific bent, but above all possessed of some knowledge of the science of legislation upon which successful codification most depends. By this assertion it is not intended to ignore the great contributions which the scientific and speculative writers have rendered to the cause of codification. It is for example easy to misconceive Bentham's position in this connection and to describe him as an impracticable theorist or enthusiast, for in some respects his convictions induced him to overlook the elements of stability in human affairs. Bentham was great, not as a constructor of codes, but as a scientific legislator. He was the greatest master of the science of legislation who has yet lived; a _fons philosophiae_ from which all men derive something: "Pillaged by all the world yet always rich," Talleyrand is reported to have said of him. He was barely a lawyer, except nominally or by profession, and yet nearly every legislative reform which he projected has been adopted by the State and its wisdom ultimately acquiesced in by all practical lawyers. An enemy of feudalism and of formalism of all kinds, Bentham is today justly regarded as one of the benefactors of the human race. It is not strange that some common lawyers are found to complain of Bentham for he did much to break up the power of the sect which

1. Holland, _Elements of Jurisprudence_ (1880).

for some centuries claimed to be the exclusive repository of the common law. ...

The truth of Mr. Carter's most sweeping proposition, now urged against the Civil Code of New York, that all codification is unscientific in theory, depends much on what is meant by scientific. Science is most commonly referable to a body of knowledge arranged in an orderly manner. To be at all relevant to the pending measure, then, this proposition can only mean that in its present state the common law is better arranged than in any code, or else, that any statutory arrangement is unphilosophic. In order to discuss even so plain a proposition, it is necessary to be rid of ambiguous terms and, therefore, to decide in which of its conflicting meanings the term "common law", as it is of extended significance, is intended to be used. It has been said that the best way to define "common law" is by the things to which it is opposed: (1) as contrasted with statute law; (2) with equity; (3) with the law founded on the civil law, with the exclusively local, or military, law. As contrasted with all these things, it is the residuum of a nation's law. There is still another definition quite opposed to the former, or rather inclusive of the very things contrasted in the first definition. In this latter or secondary meaning, the common law becomes the designation of the entire jurisprudence of England, or of any one of its colonial offshoots. Mr. Carter uses this term indifferently, and it is therefore necessary to observe closely in which sense he means it, for the common law of England, in the larger sense of the term, is in a faint degree only identical with the common law of New York.

In the original colonies of England, the common law contains, independently of its mere arrangement, an element of great uncertainty, which it is thought codification will entirely obliterate. The common law of New York, for example, owing to the colonial conditions under which English law was introduced here, is based upon an illogical hypothesis, most damaging to its certainty and to legal administration. The hypothesis in question is that the common law of New York is fundamentally identical with the common law of England in the last century, in so far only as this latter is suited to colonial conditions. Now, how far the English law of the eighteenth century is suited to colonial conditions is one of the most perplexing problems with which the American judicatories have to deal. It is not strange that such should be the fact, if we consider the embarrassment of introducing a body of law made exclusively for one country into another, far distant and originally not intended to be included within its operation. Every one knows of the interest which originally attached to Buckle's attempt to demonstrate that civilization was the product of climate and locality, and realizes now that the failure of the demonstration was inevitable from the vast scope of the proposition. Yet few will deny that jurisprudence, a component of civilization, is to some extent a local product, and that its introduction elsewhere, than in the land of its origin, is full of embarrassment. In order to make more apparent what is meant by the assertion, that the common law of New York is founded upon an illogical hypothesis, some further digression must be condoned. About the time that law of English original was being first introduced by the English government in countries out of England, the English institutional writers and, for that matter, many English judges, frequently resorted to figurative explanations of legal phenomena. The common law, like the Roman ius civile, was made for men in a certain status only and the embarrassment of accounting for the application of the common law in the English dependencies, taxed greatly the English judges' ingenuity. With one accord they finally agreed that the English common law was in force in the crown possessions "extra 4 (quatuor) mare", as the possessions in question were quaintly described, because it was the "birth-right of English subjects everywhere". Now it needs no examination to detect that this assertion is purely figurative. Sometimes the institutional writers went farther into detail when the English common law was described as introduced into uninhabited countries, discovered and planted by English subjects, upon the "birth-right" theory, but into countries conquered by Englishmen by express legislation only. The fact is this contrast is unsound; law of English original could be introduced into any countries out of England only by express legislation of some sort, and the distinction denoted by Blackstone is pure fiction. Until new countries are subjected to constituted authority, the inhabitants are subject to the law of nature only, and that was the doctrine of the earlier English cases. After a government is once established the constituted authority promulgates laws; and in the case of the English colonies, laws of English original. Sometimes the legislative machinery has been and, doubtless, now is concealed in the crown-governor's commission, or in his instructions, but it is always present somewhere. The institutional writers in order to account for the unfamiliar limitation usually contained in the colonial constitutions - that the law of English original should be in force in the new countries only in so far as suited to the new conditions - proceeded to amplify their theory accordingly. They chose to regard the common law as "carried" by the colonists, but only so much of it as was needed. Yet no one will now pretend that any particular colonist carried any particular law, so that a little reflection enables us to detect that the commonly received account of the mode in which English laws were introduced here is figurative. ...

That a considerable body of lawyers should persistently

adhere to the traditional form of the law, or to the law as they know it, is not strange when we have reference to the bias created by educational methods and by force of habit. Every avenue to legal preferment has so long been through the ancient methods that any change in the venerable system by one in our midst is in some quarters inclined to be resented as an affront; it is fairly regarded as an encroachment upon personal environment. No property is so personal as his law in the abstract is to the lawyer and its would-be-invader is not regarded with favor by those who, consciously or unconsciously, have this feeling to a marked extent. It may be unfair to regard this as an element of the late discussion and yet we must concede that if there is an opposition without sound reason, it is occasioned by bias and by bias only. Another mode of accounting for unreasonable opposition to a change in the form of the law, relates to the state of our juristic literature. This also is inextricably confused with the traditional form of the law. When we reflect how entirely the contributions of most American legal writers are posed upon the antique models, it is not extraordinary that many of their readers' preference should be for the older arrangement of the law. Yet this feeling cannot be admitted to be universal: Americans appreciate original contributions to literature. The Revised Statutes of New York, though impugned by Chancellor Kent, have been extensively followed; the Field Codes, though derided by a few, have been widely adopted and loudly praised for literary and legislative excellence. The discussion which has succeeded to all these measures only demonstrates, that there is a limitation to the soundness of the criticism of those who have grown up under the purely traditional methods of legal development. ...

Several other propositions, uttered by the opponents of codification, require notice in any account of the discussion, notably the mystical one - for mysticism is most dangerous to codification - that law is best fostered or developed by leaving it wholly to a class of experts who, in imperceptible modes, voice "the national standard of justice". This idea of Mr. Carter's is not entirely new; it is not very far from the theory which underlies many of Savigny's arguments and at first glance it must be confessed to be captivating, but in reality it is a plea for the lawyers and that law be relegated exclusively to them. It is distinctly opposed to any legislative interference with law. Carried to its legitimate consequence, this mode of legal development means a dominant legal class, such as the jurisconsults of Rome, or the barrister-class in England. In a country where there is practically free-trade at the bar and where the safer tendency is toward that primitive condition when almost any man might be constituted court-agent to suitors, there can be no very consistent development of law outside of the legislature. The theory of democratic States is that an exclusive class of lawyers shaping the destinies of the State by means of a ius prudentibus compositum, is not desirable. The opposite theory demands a highly trained, exclusive class, divided into factions whose controversy is the substitute for legislative debate and whose best work demands the mystery and seclusion of counsel's chambers. But we should not forget that the genius of this country, notwithstanding many debased exceptions, has exhibited itself in legislation. Nearly every single distinctively American institution, either in the region of public or of private law, is due to legislation, not to the action of the judicature. Is not then the true American policy to perfect that which is natural rather than to return to the methods of either Roman or Anglican legal development? - the more especially as our native policy is consistent with a more widely spread knowledge of the law, the foreign, with a narrow learning, inevitably tending to sophistries and to over-refinements.

The Civil Code, reported as a legislative bill by Mr. Field has unfairly, as some persons venture to think, been the subject of adverse criticism - criticism, it must be confessed, occasionally uttered by gentlemen eminent in the practice of the law. But eminence in the practice of the law, it should not be forgotten, does not alone entitle a criticism of codification to be regarded as final, or even as oracular. Codification is a science, a science of the form of the law, possessing a literature of its own, quite apart from ordinary juristic literature. An eminent legislator, Sir James Stephen, expressed surprise that a lawyer of undoubted ability as a practitioner was able, in a considerable space of time, to even understand the details of the Criminal Code, his attention never before having been directed to the science of legislation. This surprise indicates, at least, the value Sir James Stephen would place upon the off-hand opinions of eminent practising lawyers. The retort of the so-called practical men to any such suggestion as this is of course that the exponents and disciples of codification "undervalue the teachings of experience". This retort may be true in some instances; it is in no degree true of Mr. Field, and is true sub modo in any instance. The theoretical codifiers undervalue the teachings of experience, no doubt, but to the same extent only that the empirical practitioners undervalue the teachings of science and philosophy. If the purely legal scientist is too much engrossed with his abstractions to be a wise legislator for the wants of law-men, certainly the purely practical lawyer is too much engrossed with his docket, too apt to gaze at public questions from his office window, to be a safe criterion of the true legislative policy of a State. But the natural opposition between these widely opposed schools of lawyers is not new. We see it fully delineated in Cicero's De Legibus; in his sneers at the quibbling trifles of the practical lawyers; in his patronizing query to Atticus, "Would you have me put forth little treatises on Servitudes and Party Walls?" In view of Cicero's defined position, it is not strange that those who pride themselves on being practical lawyers, are induced to join in the modern censure of Cicero, and to forget that Cicero's weaknesses - weaknesses never impairing the majesty of his splendid intellect - were external. When Mr. Carter takes his turn at Cicero's technical deficiencies, it only exemplifies how much human nature is alike at different epochs, for if Mr. Carter thinks lightly of Cicero's legal attainments, it is equally true that Cicero thought lightly of the attainments of the practical men who, Mr. Carter intimates, are not now consulted by the "apostles of codification".

This digression permits one to further emphasize that the dispute between the historical school of law and the philosophical school of law is the creature of no age or clime. As German discussion relative to codification shows, the true standard of legal progress is midway between practice and theory; a little of both, not too much of either. The mental make-up of many of the practical men who instinctively resist all change in the form of the law and in legal evolution, would have induced them, had they lived at an earlier day, to have resisted every change in the common law which the past two centuries have effected; they would have delighted in the barbarous law-jingle prevailing in England down to the reign of George II. and in that bewitching conceit, that the seizin to feed contingent uses by a _scintilla juris_ was in _mare_, in _terra_, in _custodia legis_, or anywhere a disordered fancy could imagine it. They would, in short, have maintained the old court of chancery, even though its curious proceedings often absorbed the entire estate protected, for the law to them is the one thing which must not be subjected to change; it is the one old thing never to be improved. History shows, in short, that in no country in the world has codification been greatly promoted by lawyers as a class. There seems to be an indescribable charm in the modes to which they are accustomed, and an abhorrence of change of all kinds. While this conservatism, doubtless, has the merit of adding an element of stability to American institutions, it is sometimes fatal to progress in the right direction. Without intending to even intimate that Mr. Carter's personal objections to codifications are open to any such coarse criticism as that just here made, the criticism itself is not without force when applied abstractly to class-bias and tendencies. ...

The finality of Mr. Carter's admiration of the common law as it is, even conceding to the judiciary establishment a greater power of change than he would think consistent with its functions, is that no statutory change whatever can be for the better. The difficulty with the present state of the law - and Mr. Carter admits that there is a difficulty - is, he thinks, only with the judiciary, and with the decline in the character of legislation. There may be room for improvement in both the directions thus indicated, but far too much is laid at the door of the judiciary which should be placed elsewhere. The judiciary of the State of New York very fairly represents the bar. Both bench and bar are the result of traditional methods of legal education, if education that may be called which has been picked up anywhere and anyhow. It is said, for instance, by those competent to judge, that there is not a single institutional treatise on the common law which is adapted to the purposes of sound legal education. Certain is it that the antique mode of legal training in vogue with us, while it is not wholly unsuited to mere practical success at the bar, is not unlikely to be at the root of that which Mr. Carter would lay at the door of the judiciary and the legislature. We should all take our just share of the blame which attaches to the present condition of things. Few of us can deny that we would not have profited by having approached jurisprudence in a more scientific fashion.

The school to which Mr. Field belongs and certainly leads, in this country, thinks that it perceives the remedy for the acknowledged legal ills, in the reform of the form of the law, in simpler and more direct legal methods, and in a higher, though still voluntary, type of legal education. Is not the plan worth trying?

This is an era of legislation, in Europe, in South America and elsewhere. Not a civilized nation, England not excepted, but addresses itself seriously to the work of codification, and to the simplification of traditional legal methods. Here, as elsewhere, codification of the substantive law must come. If it does not come in the shape of Mr. Field's legislative draft, as there is no adequate preparation for a better it will come in a less meritorious form, but it will come. When it does come, the merits of Mr. Field's Civil Code will not be denied, for, legal literature has its own Nemesis who both punishes the ungenerous critic and ignores unjust censure of honest effort.

Francis Wharton, Commentaries on Law (1881)

Sec. 28. It may be objected that the position that laws are on the long run operative only when in harmony with national conscience and national need, assumes an unchecked democracy changing law from moment to moment to suit its will. But so far from the two positions being interdependent, they are contradictory opposites. It is, of course, possible to conceive of a nation voting, as was the case sometimes in republican Rome, particular laws by a plebiscite. But even were continuous government by plebiscite practicable, it could not be established without destroying that gradual and tentative evolution of law which in its beginnings is unconscious, and which depends for its applicability and efficiency on the slow instinctive processes of generations. It is as impossible, in fact, to create a system of law in a day by a decree as it would be to create an oak forest in a day by machinery. It is part, as we have seen, of the theory before us that laws, unless declaratory of that which exists, are inoperative; and so far from legislation by plebiscite being declaratory in this sense, it would be likely from its haste, and from the temporary passions to whose influence it is open, to be subversive of the underlying law of the nation rather than declaratory of that law. The fact is, the processes of national juridical evolution and of national momentary will are far from being coincident. Just as a man in a passion may in a moment ruin himself, so a nation in a passion may in a moment ruin itself. Men may be prevented from thus ruining themselves by the checks of conscience, of family affection, and by the inability to put the impulse to self-ruin into operation until cooling time has arrived. Nations, also, which, from the sympathetic force of public excitement are as likely as individuals to ruin themselves, are kept, in constitutional systems, from such catastrophes by the checks which prevent sudden popular passions from taking effect; and in no country are these checks so numerous as in the United States. The imposition of such checks preventing, as a rule, any legislation which is not merely declaratory of the settled policy and permanent conscientious conviction and sense of need of the nation, is the best means not merely of producing law in its right sense, but of promoting the economical growth of the country. The doctrine, in fact, of law being the outgrowth in long processes of gestation of national conscience and national sense of need, so far from being promotive of unchecked democracy, is irreconcilable either with unchecked democracy or unchecked despotism. Had the question been put to the English people by a pelbiscite during the reign of George III., the Church of England would have had assigned to it perpetual and exclusive religious control in England and Ireland; the laws disfranchising Papists would have been made more stringent and would have been pronounced irrepealable; slavery in the West Indies and slave-trade on the high seas would have been solemnly ratified; the limitations imposed by the five acts on free speech would have been worked into the constitution as a finality; the landed interest, whose dependents formed then a majority of the people, would have placed a perpetual embargo on the introduction of foreign corn; and the old system of capital punishment for crimes, pretty as well as great, would have remained unmodified. The constitution that gives play to the growth of a liberal and sound jurisprudence is the constitution that imposes the most effective checks on precipitate law making, whether by plebiscite, or parliamentary action, or sovereign decree. And such, in fact, is the position taken by those who have led in the advocacy of the system here vindicated. Burke, by whom the position that laws in the right sense are only declaratory was maintained with such luminous rhetoric during the whole of his career, went so far in his dread of paper legislation as to maintain that even an unreformed house of commons would be better than a house of commons which, elected by universal suffrage at some popular panic, chosen as the period for a dissolution, might override the system which national conscience and national wants had in the growth of centuries been generating. Although he argued, in his tract on the Popery Laws, religious toleration was demanded by national conscience and national need, he admitted that it might at any time be refused by a popular vote, as it certainly would then have been refused by parliament and king, and that the system of toleration gradually growing up would be exposed to destruction, especially in its incipient stage, if interfered with by speculative legislation. But such processes should not be interfered with by speculative legislation. The law should be allowed to grow by itself; the reason being that the unconscious tendencies of a Christian nation, itself an aggregation of families with the unselfishness and tenderness and industry that family life produces, are more wise and healthy than the conscious policy of its legislators or rulers, or even of its own component members meeting for popular deliberation. And so insisted Savigny: "In the common consciousness of the people", he declared, "exists positive law", positive law being used by him in the sense of law which is from the return of things imposed. Yet Savigny, in his dread of speculative legislation interfering with this spontaneous growth, was a conservative of the conservaties. It was this, in fact, that distinguished him and his disciples from the "theorists" as he called them, who were for establishing everywhere a system of cosmopolitan law based on what they regarded as speculative right. They, who called themselves liberals, were, he argued, the absolutists; he, who was called by them the absolutist, was, he maintained, the true liberal. His absolutism consisted in non-interference with national growth. Their liberalism, he urged, consisted in capricious and absolutist interference with such growth.

Sec. 29. On another point in this connection the conclusions of Blackstone are to be questioned: "How" asks that eminent jurist, "are these general customs or maxims to be known, and by whom is their validity to be determined? The answer is," so he replies, "by the judges of the land. They are the depositaries of the laws; the living oracles who must decide in all cases of doubt, and who are bound by an oath to decide according to the law of the land. ... It has been uniformly considered to be the duty of those who administer the law to conform to the precedents thus (by decisions) established." If exact conformity to a precedent be required as a prerequisite to a decision, then no case could be decided, since no case is precisely the same as any prior case that has been adjudicated. If all that is meant is that no point of law that arises shall be decided in any other way than in accordance with precedent, to this the replies are: (1) there are innumerable new social and economical conditions which require rulings for which there are no precedents; (2) as a matter of fact, of the rulings now made in the courts of England and of the United States, by far the greater number are, as elsewhere stated, more or less departures from the common law rule; since there can be no judicial affirmation of an old precedent "without putting something more into it, and fixing, as it were, a new starting-point". Common law precedents, in fact, are only binding on superior courts, so far as they are consistent with the conscience of the community and the need of the times. When they are in permanent conflict with either, they cease to bind.

Sec. 30. As has been well said, judge-made law is superior to statutory law in the skill and persistent caution and circumspection with which it is prepared. It seems almost impossible to prevent bills amending the law from being tinkered, on their progress through the legislature, in a way that sometimes impairs, sometimes perverts, sometimes destroys their effect. An amendment, apparently plausible, is sprung on a bill at a late hour, and is accepted without due consideration; and the consequence is that the act, as has been the case with several important English statutes, does not work, or works even mischievously. Undoubtedly from the legislature must come revolutionary changes in the law, such as make a catastrophic transition from one era to another. But, when the change is one of logical evolution, it is likely to be done far more accurately by the judiciary than by the legislature. The principal difficulty in the way of the acceptance of this position is that the nature of the duty is not always fully recognized. Courts are too apt, even when they are tearing up the common law by the roots, to declare that they are simply restoring it. But applications of germinal principles of justice to an advanced civilization are no more revivals of such principles in their rudimentary conditions than is the horse, that, by the gradually cultivated instincts of a long line of descent, has acquired docility and dexterity in answering the wants of man, the revival of the wild horse of the desert. As with animal, so with juridical growth, that which is inconsistent with surrounding conditions is set aside, that which is adapted to surrounding conditions survives. The peculiarity of juridical evolution, however, is this, that while animal evolution works itself out without human agency, juridical evolution is worked by the agency in part of jurists and text writers, in part of legislatures, in part of courts. It is by the courts, however, as we have seen, that the work is mainly effected; and, perhaps, the chief difficulty in the way of the work being thoroughly done is that those doing it are not always aware of the important mission in which they are the necessary co-workers. Too often we still hear, even from judges of the highest courts, that judges cannot be legislators; and too often this is the reason given for the pushing, even to consequences to which it does not legitimately extend, some rule which should be thrown overboard as obsolete. Judges are not legislators for the purpose of revolutionizing the law, but they are legislators for the purpose of evolving from it rules which should properly govern present issues, and winnowing from it limitations which are withered and dead. And when this duty - a duty which is a necessary incident of judicial office - is frankly recognized by the judiciary, the process of legal development and of supersession will be carried on much more effectively and wisely than it can be done by those who shut their eyes to the duty. For no disclaimer can relieve the judiciary from the function of gradually modifying the law, both by adaptation and rejection. So absolute is the necessity that the very statutes which are passed to correct the action of the courts require the action of the courts not only for their execution, but for their construction.

Sec. 33. It may be objected, also, to the doctrine of juridical evolution, as above stated, that it is part of a system of philosophy which asserts the inexorable and unvarying process of physical law, and which ignores the existence of a superior being by whom human events are controlled. What may be the opinion on these points of the eminent men who are the chief exponents of evolution in England, it is not necessary to inquire; though it may be incidentally remarked, that among them are some who are among the stoutest vindicators of theism, and that evolution no more by itself weakens the proof of a divine creator and organizer, than does a clock that goes for a year disprove the existence of a watchmaker which a clock that goes for a day might be admitted to establish. It is enough to say that the doctrine of juridical evolution was taught long before that of physical evolution came prominently before the public eye; and that the truth that the "fit" must from the nature of things survive the "unfit" was, as we have seen, announced and defended by Burke, Savigny, and Puchta, long before these terms were made familiar to us by the great English scientists who are supposed to have inaugurated a new school. What Burke and Savigny argued was that a law of which people have no need, and of which the national conscience does not dictate the continuance, will die out, and be displaced by a growth more congenial to the soil and more needed by the people by whom the soil is cultivated. What may be needful, in other words, in one community, may not be needful in another; the custom which the peculiarities of one country may foster, in another country will be intolerable; in this way distinct nationalities will have their own jurisprudences, in each nationality that which is unfit dying out, and that which is fit surviving. But by these eminent thinkers it was also declared that there is no inexorable law, physical or spiritual, binding either men or nations to specific destinies, but that with nations, as well as with individuals, spontaneity is the basis of growth. There is development: the goal of yesterday in jurisprudence is the starting point of to-day; but it is development which, whether individual or national, is self-elective. Nor is the objection that this system is antagonistic to theism entitled to greater weight. It is remarkable that by no one is the doctrine that law emanates from the people taught with greater emphasis than by a great English teacher, who is as much distinguished for his devotion to the Christian faith as for his lofty and catholic philosophy. Reason and revelation, so declares Hooker, are coordinate factors, and all law relating to mutual objects is mutable in accordance with the requirements of reason. And among the materials reason invokes in determining how far law is to be affirmed or modified, are national conscience, national aptitudes, and national customs adopted either consciously or unconsciously. That a nation evolves its laws in subordination to its own sense of right, is, he holds, in entire consistency with a scheme which assumes that this sense of right is divinely implanted, either directly or through a written revelation; and which, after such laws have thus been produced, assumes that they are open to be affirmed or modified by formal legislation. Nor is such a process any more inconsistent with a comprehensive and wise scheme of divine government than is the leaving local affairs to local option inconsistent with a comprehensive and wise scheme of human government. "When a thing ceases to be available unto the end which gave it being" so declares Hooker, "the continuance of it must then of necessity appear superfluous". Thus, under the influence of "environments" such is the drift of his exposition, laws which affect society in its mutable relation can grow up when of use, and when useless vanish. And he proceeds boldly to declare, in opposition to the Puritans, that it is part of the divine economy that there should be a gradual growth of law governing man. Change, in adaptation to the growth of society, is one of the features that even the divine law in this relation incorporates in itself. It is a law "requiring" as Hooker expresses it, "itself to be changed". It is, therefore, a law, in its human aspect, not of immobility, but of evolution.

5. Codification in Action

Although the successes of the movement for codification in New York were distinctly limited, the efforts of Field and his supporters bore fruit elsewhere. Of the many states which adopted the Field codes, none was more important than California. In the debates of the 1880's concerning the final enactment of the codes in New York, the experience of California in enforcing them was frequently cited. One of the opponents of codification spoke, for instance, of the fact that in California "the enormous growth of the power of corporations under the Code, drove the people to Kearneyism and a half communistic Constitution". (Miller, Destruction of our Natural Law by Codification (1882) p. 8.) Professor Pomeroy in 1884 wrote a series of papers in the West Coast Reporter criticizing in great detail the provisions of the California codes, and his essays were made much of by the New York bar in its successful efforts to defeat complete codification in New York.

The serious and philosophical aspects of the issue were not always predominant. It was, however, with a serious purpose that the editors of the American Law Review in 1886 (Vol. 20, p. 764) reprinted the following story from the Los Angeles Weekly Express of December 18, 1873.

A Strange Story

We surrender a large portion of our columns today to the report of a case which has attracted and absorbed the attention of the whole community, and created a greater excitement than any which has heretofore occurred in this section of the State. The indignation of the public generally at this disgraceful result of the careless manner in which the new codes have been gotten up is excessive; and as there is a painful suspicion that other defects as yet undeveloped may exist, the feeling is universal that the Civil Code should be at once repealed and the other codes referred to a competent commission to revise them.

The case referred to is that of the People v. Oades, just decided in the County Court of San Bernardino. Oades is an Englishman of good education, who came to that county about two years ago, and purchased and settled upon a farm in Temescal township. In January last he married Mrs. Nancy Foreland, a young widow lady of great beauty, residing in that neighborhood by whom he has since had a child, now about one month old. Both parties have always been regarded in the neighborhood as eminently respectable.

About two months ago a woman, accompanied by three children - two boys and a girl - arrived at the city of San Bernardino, and after inquiring of Oades' whereabouts proceeded to his residence, where she has since continued to reside. It afterwards transpired that this woman and Oades comported themselves towards each other as man and wife, and the neighbors, indignant at such open profligacy, laid a criminal complaint against them before Justice Billings, under the act of March 15th, 1872, for "open and notorious cohabitation and adultery". When the parties were brought up for trial, however, they produced a certificate of marriage, and proved by it and other authentic documents that the woman was Oades' wife - having been married to him in England about twenty years ago and moved with him to New Zealand, where their children had been born. The accused were therefore acquitted and returned to their home, where Oades continued to live with the two women as before.

Thereupon another complaint was laid before the same justice against Oades and Mrs. Oades No. 2, charging them with the same offense. On this trial it was proved that about eight years ago Oades was living in Wellington County, New Zealand, on the frontiers; when, without warning, the Maoris - a tribe with whom the English were at peace - made an inroad into the settlements. Oades was at the time temporarily absent in Victoria, and returned only to find his homestead burnt and his family disappeared. Some human remains were found in the ruins; and from this and from such information as he could gain during the ensuing two years he was gradually forced to the conviction that his wife and children were dead; and being loth to remain amid the scenes of his distress he left New Zealand and came to California. Upon this state of facts Oades claimed that his marriage with Mrs. Oades No. 2 was valid under the second subdivision of the sixty-first section of the Civil Code, which provides that the marriage of a person having a former husband or wife living is void, "unless such former husband or wife was absent and not known to such person to be living for the space of five successive years immediately preceding such subsequent marriage, in which case the subsequent marriage is void only from the time its nullity is adjudged by a proper tribunal." Upon an examination of the law this proposition was found too clear to be disputed, as there was no doubt that when Oades married his second wife he had been ignorant of the existence of his first wife for more than five years. The complaint was therefore dismissed.

Oades still continuing in open cohabitation with the two women, a deputation was sent by the neighbors to lay the matter before Mr. Cokeman, the district attorney, who, after examining the case, referred it to the grand jury, who found a true bill against Oades for bigamy. The trial, which took place last Monday, attracted a large crowd of eager spectators, among whom, the observed of all observers, appeared the two Mrs. Oades. The same state of facts was proven, and after the close of the evidence Mr. Cokeman, the district attorney, opened the case for the prosecution in an able and eloquent argument, of which we can only give a brief abstract: -

"The law," he urged, "was to be construed according to its spirit and intent, and the language where contrary thereto was to be disregarded. These time-honored principles have been expressly adopted in the new code: 'Where the reason of a rule ceases, so should the rule itself. Cessante ratione legis, cessat ipsa lex.' And again, 'where the reason is the same, the rule should be the same. Ubi eadem ratio ibi eadem jus.' And again, 'he who considers merely the letter goes but skin deep into the meaning. Qui haeret in litera haeret in cortice.' Now, in this case," he continued, "the evident intention of the law was simply to provide against the illegitimacy of the children of the second marriage, and it certainly never could have been intended to make bigamy lawful. It is true, that at the date of the second marriage, Oades was ignorant of the existence of his first wife, but his voluntary cohabitation with both women, after learning the facts, was to be taken as conclusive proof of a guilty intention, ab initio. And, in support of this view, the counsel cited 'The Six Carpenters' Case." That case was very similar in principle to this, and it was adjudged that "the law judges by the subsequent act the quo animo or intent, for acta exteriora indicant interiora secreta."

On the other hand, the counsel for the accused relied upon the provision of the Penal Code in relation to bigamy, which expressly provides that no person shall be held guilty of bigamy "whose husband or wife has been absent for five successive years" (prior to the second marriage), without being known to such person within that time to be living; and in reply to the argument of the district attorney, he urged upon the court that in criminal matters it would be a dangerous precedent to adopt so liberal a principle of construction as that contended for by Mr. Cokeman; and he cited in support of his position the following maxims: "A verbis legis non est recedendum," "Index animi sermo," and "Maledicta est expositio quae corrumpet textum," the meaning of which, as he explained for the benefit of the court, was that in the interpretation of statutes "we must stick to the letter." That it is true that the intention must govern, but "the language is the evidence of the intention," and that "it is wrongly called interpretation when we alter the text."

The learned judge said that however desirable it might be to convict the prisoner, the position taken by his counsel was clearly the right one, and accordingly he instructed the jury to acquit, which was done, and Oades returned home triumphantly with his two wives.

Thereupon all the most eminent counsel of San Bernardino were retained by citizens interested in the virtue of the community, with a view of ascertaining some means of removing this terrible scandal of Oades and his two wives; and after an exhaustive examination of the case they came to the conclusion that the only method of annulling the marriage was to proceed under the second sub-division of the eighty-second section of the Civil Code, which provides that a marriage may be annulled where the "former husband or wife is living" at the time of the second marriage. But, as under the second subdivision of the eighty-third section of the Civil Code, an action for the annulment of such a marriage can be brought only by one of the parties to the second marriage, or by the husband or wife of the first marriage, it was evident that as neither Oades nor either of his wives were willing to bring the suit, the difficulty remained as great as ever.

What further steps will be taken is at present unsettled. But the people are very much excited and determined not to let the matter drop. Eminent counsel in San Francisco and Sacramento, including one of the Code Commissioners, have been written to, but as yet no answer had been received. We will keep the public informed of further developments.

This case still continues the all-absorbing subject of interest to the community. We give the latest, information upon the subject as furnished by a special correspondent, dispatched by us several days since to San Bernardino. Our correspondent interviewed Mr. Cokeman last night, from whom he learned some details not hitherto divulged. It seems that last Wednesday, Mr. John Howlett, of San Bernardino, was by advice of counsel dispatched to seek an interview with Mrs. Oades No. 1, with a view of offering her inducements to bring a suit to annul the marriage of Oades with Mrs. Oades No. 2. It was thought that she, being the party principally injured by the second marriage, might easily be persuaded to do so. After considerable difficulty and some danger - having on one occasion been run off by Oades with a shotgun - Howlett on Thursday morning managed to secure a private interview with Mrs. Oades No. 1, while Oades was out riding with his second wife. She appeared to be a mild, timid woman, but it was impossible to induce her to move in the matter - although Mr. Howlett offered her large inducements to do so. Oades, she said, had sworn that if she attempted to annul his second marriage he would not only beat her half to death, but also would never live with her any more; that she wouldn't mind the beating so much, but that she preferred to submit to the present state of circumstances rather than lose Oades altogether, especially as being married to him she couldn't marry any one else. Howlett therefore returned without affecting anything; and after consultation of counsel, was again dispatched to make the same proposition to Mrs. Oades No. 2. But neither would she accept the offer. "If there was any way," she said, "of annulling Oades' first marriage she might be induced to move in the matter, although she really didn't mind Mrs. Oades No. 1 much; as she was getting too old to be a very formidable rival; and, besides, she found her a considerable help about the house; but as to her bringing suit to annul her own marriage there was no use talking about it, as she was perfectly well satisfied with Oades even with the incumbrance of his first wife and children.

Upon the receipt of this information the Rev. Mr. Kiggett, a minister of great and deserved influence in the community, was dispatched to expostulate with Oades himself. Oades received him courteously and discussed the matter with great frankness. Theoretically, he said, he was a monogamist, and believed that the law should not allow a man to have more than one wife. He therefore joined with his reverend friend in saying that the action of the Code Commission in allowing bigamy could not be too severely condemned. "But such matters," he continued, "after all, are to be settled in each State as the legislators in their wisdom should deem best, it being now a settled principle in jurisprudence that all rights and obligations have their cources solely in legislative enactment; that all the most eminent jurisprudents, including the New York and California Code Commissioners, are agreed that right is what the legislature wills, this being the fundamental idea upon which the Civil Code is based. As to the old notion of natural right, that is entirely exploded. Nous avons change tout cela," said Oades (who appears to be somewhat of a literary turn). "If there were such a thing," he continued, "the appointment of the Code Commission to reduce all law or right into a code would have been as absurd as to have appointed them to codify chemistry or mathematics - it would, in short, have been to repeal principles established by the Almighty, and to substitute in their place the shallow notions of ignorant and fallible men. For his part he didn't pretend to be wiser or more virtuous than the laws; and as the laws allowed him two wives his conscience didn't disturb him for having them; neither of his wives were willing to give him up and to tell the truth he couldn't get along very well without both of them. He loved them both so well (he added facetiously) that he was like the ass between two bundles of hay, and didn't know how to choose between them. Besides, if either marriage was annulled it would have to be the last one; and while he might possibly stand the loss of the old woman (that is, his first wife), nothing on earth would induce him to part with the last."

The reverend gentleman thereupon left in great and just indignation; which was greatly increased on Sunday at seeing Oades who had always been regular in his attendance at church - seated in his pew with his two wives, listening complacently to the sermon.

As we stated yesterday the San Bernardino lawyers had written to one of the code commissioners. Our correspondent was shown the answer but did not have the opportunity of taking a copy. He was able, however, to send us a very full abstract of its contents.

The codifier - who appears from his letter to be a much

more sensible man than one would think (judging only from the codes) wrote that it was a bad thing and that he didn't see what was to be done about it; but that the commission was not responsible for it; that all they had done was to copy the code of that eminent codifier Mr. David Dudley Field; that it was evidently the intention of the legislature that the commission should pursue this course; for it they had wanted a new code made they certainly should have known better than to refer the matter to them; that it couldn't be expected that a commission of three men, without any special training or experience for the purpose, could complete in two years a work for which Justinian had found it necessary to employ the great Tribonian and seventeen other of the most eminent lawyers in the Empire during many years; a work of such transcendent difficulty that the greatest of English jurisprudents, Austin, had thought it necessary to recommend that a large number of the ablest men should be especially educated for it and should devote their whole lives to it; a work, finally, so extensive that it had taken even Mr. David Dudley Field some time to accomplish it. As for himself, he said he never had pretended to be much of a codifier, but the position was offered to him with a good salary and he didn't feel called upon to decline it; that he made it a rule never to decline anything that was offered on account of his own incompetency - that being a matter that concerned only those who employed him; that if any one were to offer to employ him to make a piano or a steam engine - which was as much out of his line as codifying itself, he would accept the offer provided always that it was on a salary, and that he was not to be paid by the job; that in his opinion the other commissioners were no better than himself, and finally that the whole commission reminded him very forcibly of Pantagruel's opinion of the French lawyers, which he quoted as follows: "Seeing that the law is excerpted out of the very middle of moral and natural philosophy, how should these fools have understood it, who, par Dieu, have studied less in philosophy than my mule."

All other means failing, yesterday a mass meeting was called to deliberate about the matter, which was largely attended by the citizens of San Bernardino, and also of Los Angeles and San Diego. After much discussion it was finally proposed, as the only remedy, to petition the legislature to pass a special act dissolving Oades' last marriage. But Oades, who was present, immediately rose to address the meeting, and told them that that was no go; for by the twentieth section of the fourth article of the constitution of California it is expressly provided that "no divorce shall be granted by the legislature." As Oades produced the book itself, this argument was unanswerable. It was then proposed that the legislature should be petitioned to call a constitutional convention for the purpose of annulling one or the other of Oades' marriages; but Oades produced the constitution of the United States, and read the tenth section of the first article, which expressly provides that "no State * * * shall pass any law * * * impairing the obligation of contracts," "and marriage," he said, "was well settled to be a contract, and therefore no earthly power could deprive him of his vested right in his two wives." This brought the assembly to a stand still; for it was very evident that nothing short of an amendment of the constitution of the United States could reach his case. At length, however, the silence was relieved by a prominent citizen of Los Angeles, who proposed - as a simple and effectual means of meeting the difficulty - to hang Oades. "This," he said, "was a very common way of arranging such affairs in Los Angeles, and it had always met the public approbation except on one occasion; when, indeed, they had perhaps gone a little too far in hanging seventeen Chinamen." This suggestion took so well with the meeting that Oades took the hint and left while the Los Angeles man was explaining his views. The meeting at once broke up in pursuit, but Oades, after a close race, reached his house, where he barricaded himself and drove off the crowd with a shotgun.

After the crowd had dispersed our correspondent interviewed Oades at his house. He found him just sitting down to supper with his two wives, all in high spirits, and was cheerfully invited to join them. He had a long and interesting conversation with Oades, but this morning it had entirely escaped his memory, and our correspondent is too truthful to invent an account of what passed. He says, however, that he found Oades a very genial companion, and that they only separated at three o'clock in the morning, after the consumption of two flasks of whisky between them. The latter part of his letter is indeed a little incoherent, and were it not for the well known steadiness of his character, might give rise to a suspicion that he has himself been converted by the sight of Oades' connubial felicity - for he says that Oades is a good fellow, and that in his opinion, the whole affair has grown out of the jealousy of the people of San Bernardino; which is an old Mormon settlement; and that they are mad with envy at seeing Oades in the enjoyment of a privilege of which the laws have deprived them.

Genthiner Straße 13
10785 Berlin
productsafety@degruyterbrill.com

Bei Fragen zur Produktsicherheit wenden Sie sich bitte an:
If you have any questions regarding product safety,
please contact:

Walter de Gruyter GmbH
Genthiner Straße 13
10785 Berlin
productsafety@degruyterbrill.com